Distributional Semantics

Distributional semantics develops theories and methods to represent the meaning of natural language expressions, with vectors encoding their statistical distribution in linguistic contexts. It is at once a theoretical model to express meaning, a practical methodology to construct semantic representations, a computational framework for acquiring meaning from language data, and a cognitive hypothesis about the role of language usage in shaping meaning. This book aims to build a common understanding of the theoretical and methodological foundations of distributional semantics. Beginning with its historical origins, the text exemplifies how the distributional approach is implemented in distributional semantic models. The main types of computational models, including modern deep neural language models, are described and evaluated, demonstrating how they address various types of semantic issues. Open problems and challenges are also analyzed. Students and researchers in natural language processing, artificial intelligence, and cognitive science will appreciate this book.

ALESSANDRO LENCI, Ph.D., is Professor of Linguistics and Director of the Computational Linguistics Laboratory at the University of Pisa. His research interests include distributional semantics, computational linguistics, and natural language processing. The recipient of the "10-year Test-of-Time-Award" from the Association for Computational Linguistics in 2020, he has published extensively and coordinated many projects on natural language processing and cognitive science.

MAGNUS SAHLGREN, Ph.D., is Head of Research for Natural Language Understanding at AI Sweden. Known primarily for research on computational models of meaning, Sahlgren's work lies at the intersection of computational linguistics, machine learning, and artificial intelligence. His doctoral dissertation, entitled "The Word-Space Model," was awarded the prize for the "Most Prominent Scholarly Achievement of 2006" by the Stockholm University Faculty of Humanities.

STUDIES IN NATURAL LANGUAGE PROCESSING

Volumes in the SNLP series provide comprehensive surveys of current research topics and applications in the field of natural language processing (NLP) that shed light on language technology, language cognition, language and society, and linguistics. The increased availability of language corpora and digital media, as well as advances in computer technology and data sciences, has led to important new findings in the field. Widespread applications include voice-activated interfaces, translation, search engine optimization, and affective computing. NLP also has applications in areas such as knowledge engineering, language learning, digital humanities, corpus linguistics, and textual analysis. These volumes will be of interest to researchers and graduate students working in NLP and other fields related to the processing of language and knowledge.

Also in the Series

Douglas E. Appelt, *Planning English Sentences*

Madeleine Bates and Ralph M Weischedel (eds.), *Challenges in Natural Language Processing*

Steven Bird, *Computational Phonology*

Peter Bosch and Rob van der Sandt, *Focus*

Pierette Bouillon and Federica Busa (eds.), *Inheritance, Defaults and the Lexicon*

Ronald Cole, Joseph Mariani, Hans Uszkoreit, Giovanni Varile, Annie Zaenen, Antonio Zampolli, and Victor Zue (eds.), *Survey of the State of the Art in Human Language Technology*

David R. Dowty, Lauri Karttunen, and Arnold M Zwicky (eds.), *Natural Language Parsing*

Ralph Grishman, *Computational Linguistics*

Graeme Hirst, *Semantic Interpretation and the Resolution of Ambiguity*

András Kornai, *Extended Finite State Models of Language*

Kathleen R McKeown, *Text Generation*

Martha Stone Palmer, *Semantic Processing for Finite Domains*

Terry Patten, *Systemic Text Generation as Problem Solving*

Ehud Reiter and Robert Dale, *Building Natural Language Generation Systems*

Manny Rayner, David Carter, Pierette Bouillon, Vassilis Digalakis, and Matis Wiren (eds.), *The Spoken Language Translator*

Michael Rosner and Roderick Johnson (eds.), *Computational Lexical Semantics*

Richard Sproat, *A Computational Theory of Writing Systems*

George Anton Kiraz, *Computational Nonlinear Morphology*

Nicholas Asher and Alex Lascarides, *Logics of Conversation*

Margaret Masterman (edited by Yorick Wilks), *Language, Cohesion and Form*

Walter Daelemans and Antal van den Bosch, *Memory-based Language Processing*

Laurent Prévot (eds.), *Ontology and the Lexicon: A Natural Language Processing Perspective*

Thierry Poibeau and Aline Villavicencio (eds.), *Language, Cognition, and Computational Models*

Bind Liu, *Sentiment Analysis: Mining Opinions, Sentiments, and Emotions, Second Edition*

Marcos Zampieri and Preslav Nakov, *Similar Languages, Varieties, and Dialects: A Computational Perspective*

Tommaso Caselli, Eduard Hovy, Martha Palmer, Piek Vossen, *Computational Analysis of Storylines: Making Sense of Events*

Piek Vossen and Antske Fokkens (eds.), *Creating a More Transparent Internet*

Chu-Ren Huang, Nicoletta Calzolari, Aldo Gangemi, Alessandro Lenci, Alessandro Oltramari,

Kiyong Lee, *Annotation-based Semantics for Space and Time in Language*

"Lenci and Sahlgren's textbook is a landmark contribution to the fast-growing and increasingly important discipline of distributional semantics. They have managed to distill 60 years of diverse research on distributional semantics, from its beginning in structural and corpus linguistics and psychology, through the application of techniques from information retrieval and linear algebra, to the most recent developments driven by deep neural networks and large language models in NLP. The authors synthesize the major findings from different fields and integrate these diverse traditions into a comprehensive and coherent framework of distributional meaning. Lenci and Sahlgren's text promises to be the new standard for reference and teaching in this area."

– James Pustejovsky, Brandeis University

Distributional Semantics

ALESSANDRO LENCI
University of Pisa

MAGNUS SAHLGREN
AI Sweden

CAMBRIDGE
UNIVERSITY PRESS

Shaftesbury Road, Cambridge CB2 8EA, United Kingdom

One Liberty Plaza, 20th Floor, New York, NY 10006, USA

477 Williamstown Road, Port Melbourne, VIC 3207, Australia

314–321, 3rd Floor, Plot 3, Splendor Forum, Jasola District Centre,
New Delhi – 110025, India

103 Penang Road, #05–06/07, Visioncrest Commercial, Singapore 238467

Cambridge University Press is part of Cambridge University Press & Assessment,
a department of the University of Cambridge.

We share the University's mission to contribute to society through the pursuit of
education, learning and research at the highest international levels of excellence.

www.cambridge.org
Information on this title: www.cambridge.org/9781107004290

DOI: 10.1017/9780511783692

First published 2023

A catalogue record for this publication is available from the British Library

*A Cataloging-in-Publication data record for this book is available from the Library of
Congress*

ISBN 978-1-107-00429-0 Hardback

Contents

Preface

What Is Distributional Semantics?

Language is used to convey *meaning*, and meaning is the quintessence of language. In fact, meaning is the "holy grail" (Jackendoff, 2002) of linguistics, philosophy, psychology, and neuroscience, as well as of Natural Language Processing (NLP) and Artificial Intelligence (AI). No research field that has at its center language and its use in communication by human or artificial agents can avoid inquiring into issues such as: What is the meaning of linguistic expressions at different levels of complexity (e.g., words, phrases, sentences, etc.)? How can meaning be represented? How is meaning structured and organized in language(s) and in the human mind? How does meaning represent the world? What meaning relations exist between words and sentences? How are word meanings combined to form the interpretation of sentences and discourses? How is meaning acquired? How does meaning interface with aspects of human cognition such as concepts, reasoning, perception, and action?

These and other similar questions are the object of study of *semantics*. This book is concerned with *distributional semantics*, an approach to meaning that develops theories and methods for quantifying and categorizing semantic properties of linguistic items based on their distributional properties in text corpora, as samples of language data. Grounded in the *Distributional Hypothesis*, according to which words with similar linguistic contexts tend to have similar meanings, the essence of distributional semantics can be described as follows:

> The meaning of a linguistic expression is represented with a real-valued *vector* (nowadays commonly called *embedding*) that encodes its statistical distribution in contexts.

The continuous nature of its representations distinguishes distributional semantics from other theoretical frameworks that instead represent meaning with symbolic structures. Moreover, there is a large array of computational methods to learn semantic representations from corpus data, which are then used in NLP and AI applications, as well as for cognitive and linguistic analyses. We refer to such methods as *distributional semantic models* (DSMs).

Distributional semantics lies at the crossroad of computational linguistics, AI, and cognitive science. Therefore, it is the combination of various characters: (i) it is a theoretical model to represent meaning, (ii) a computational framework to acquire it from language data, (iii) a practical methodology to construct semantic representations, and (iv) a cognitive hypothesis about the role of language usage in shaping meaning. This makes distributional semantics a fascinating research area and a privileged vantage point to combine theoretical, cognitive, and computational perspectives on language.

The Need for a Common Ground

Distributional semantics is a relatively novel approach to the study of meaning, but it has undergone deep transformations since its outset. Three main generations of models have followed one another: (i) *count DSMs* that build distributional vectors by recording co-occurrence frequencies; (ii) *predict DSMs* that learn vectors with shallow neural networks trained to predict surrounding words; (iii) *contextual DSMs* that use deep neural language models to generate inherently contextualized vectors for each word token, and therefore radically depart from previous *static DSMs* that instead learn a single vector per word type. Across its history, the changes in distributional semantics involve the way to characterize linguistic contexts, the methods to generate word vectors, the nature of such vectors, and the model complexity itself, which has exponentially grown especially with the last generation of deep neural DSMs.

Though it has been extensively practiced since the 1990s, the popularity of distributional semantics has exploded only recently, thereby becoming the leading approach to meaning representation in computational linguistics and cognitive science. This has coincided with the advent of neural network methods as the dominant computational paradigm for AI and NLP, which has produced a proliferation of models to learn semantic vectors and has fostered their use in downstream applications. Several "off-the-shelf" pretrained vectors are nowadays available, and provide ready-to-use resources for experimentation and system development. The fast and unprecedented expansion of distributional semantics is surely a positive fact that has boosted research in this area, but it also has its drawbacks. Like many novel scientific fields, distributional semantics lacks a common understanding of its theoretical and methodological foundations. This often prompts a rather opportunistic attitude, which not only fosters rapid development but also risks hindering progress by constantly "reinventing the wheel," and encourages a strong tendency to focus on the last "trendy" model, without considering whether and to what extent it brings significant advances over the previous ones, whether it can address qualitatively different issues or simply provides some quantitative improvement on old problems. Moreover, pretrained distributional vectors are often used in a kind of "black box" fashion, with little awareness of the effects of the different training settings and of the general properties and limits of distributional representations. This leads to a dangerous polarization between enthusiastic and skeptical attitudes toward distributional approaches to meaning, which prevents a rational and critical analysis of their actual potentialities.

Our goal with this book is to contribute to establishing distributional semantics as a *unitary and general framework to represent and study meaning*, which is implemented in various computational models and applied to address different semantic issues. We aim at building a common understanding of the theoretical and methodological foundations of distributional semantics by:

- tracing its historical origins;
- discussing and clarifying what is meant by *distributional* and *semantic* in this discipline;
- exemplifying how the distributional approach is implemented in DSMs;
- identifying, distinguishing, and evaluating the main types of DSMs;
- presenting how various types of semantic issues are addressed with DSMs;
- analyzing the open problems and challenges.

Distributional semantics is a fast and continuously moving field. It would be as impossible as it is useless to provide an exhaustive account of all its variations. Therefore, some of them have been left out by necessity. Up-to-date details may be easily obtained by browsing online resources such as the *ACL Anthology* or *arXiv*. This book has a different and more ambitious aim: Abstracting from the wealth of works in this area a general view that may help the reader to understand and master the common methodological paradigm that lies behind the increasingly large number of studies in distributional semantics.

Outline of the Book

The book consists of three main parts. *Part I – Theory* presents the major methodological aspects of distributional semantics as a framework for meaning investigation. Chapter 1 deals with the epistemological principles of distributional semantics, in particular the Distributional Hypothesis, its historical foundations, and its place in theoretical and computational linguistics. Chapter 2 introduces the basic notions to construct distributional semantic representations from corpora: various types of linguistic contexts, vectors, co-occurrence matrices and their dimensionality reduction to extract latent dimensions, vector similarity measures, and so on.

Part II – Models presents the most important families of static DSMs. Chapter 3 contains a synoptic view of the different types and generations of models. We then focus on static DSMs, since they are still the best-known and most widely studied family of models, and they learn context-independent distributional representations that are useful for several linguistic and cognitive tasks. Chapter 4 illustrates matrix models, which organize distributional information into co-occurrence matrices, Chapter 5 discusses models based on the use of random patterns to accumulate low-dimensional vectors in an incremental way, and Chapter 6 reviews predict DSMs that use shallow neural language models.

Part III – Practice explores how distributional semantics addresses different aspects of meaning. Chapter 7 focuses on the main methods and benchmarks to evaluate DSMs and analyzes the results of a comparative evaluation of the models described in Part II on a large range of tasks and datasets. Chapter 8 illustrates the most important applications of distributional semantics to the study of lexical meaning (e.g., word senses, paradigmatic relations, etc.). Chapter 9 discusses the main distributional approaches to the compositional interpretation of complex linguistic expressions and the last generation of deep neural language models that learn contextual embeddings and provide new tools to explore the context-sensitive nature of meaning.

Chapter 10 concludes the book with a general summary of the current state of distributional semantics, its future prospects, and challenges.

Distributional semantics is a multidisciplinary field. This book is intended for NLP and AI scholars and practitioners, linguists, and cognitive scientists. The background and interests of this potential audience are extremely heterogeneous, like the toolbox of distributional semantics, which includes notions from theoretical and computational linguistics, linear algebra, statistics, neural networks, and so on. We have tried to make this book as self-contained as possible, and we have added mathematical notes that introduce the key concepts. We expect the book to be accessible to a large number of readers from different fields, but of course it has been impossible to present all the mathematical and computational methods used by DSMs and their applications. However, gaps will be easily filled by consulting general handbooks or introductory texts, some of which have been listed in the further reading section at the end of each chapter.

Terminological Issues

Distributional semantics is mainly concerned with the *lexicon*, which includes *words* as well as complex *set phrases* and *constructions*, such as idioms and multiword expressions. In computational linguistics and information retrieval, words and set phrases are also referred to as *terms*. In this book, we use *lexeme*, *lexical item*, *term*, and *word* interchangeably, unless differently specified, because the concept of term has a strong overlap with the concept of lexeme, and words are the most typical targets of DSMs.

We distinguish between meaning and sense. We use *meaning* to refer to the general semantic content of a lexeme and *sense* to refer to a particular use of a lexeme in a context (or class of contexts). Theories of lexical meaning typically assume the notion of sense as their starting point. On the other hand, distributional semantics dispenses with senses as a primitive theoretical notion. In fact, distributional representations are primarily representations of the content (i.e., meaning) of a lexeme, rather than of its senses. Chapter 8 discusses how the notion of sense can be represented in DSMs.

The widespread adoption of neural networks in distributional semantics has popularized the term "embedding," which is, however, used in different ways, sometimes to mean a vector learnt by neural models, sometimes as a generic equivalent of distributional representation. In this book, we use *distributional vector* to refer to any vector that encodes distributional information. Instead, we reserve *embedding* for all kinds of low-dimensional, dense vectors, independently of the method that creates them.

Acknowledgments

Writing this book took much longer than we expected. However, this delay has also had positive effects because we have been able to witness the rapid and dramatic changes that distributional semantics has undergone in the last years.

We are very grateful to everyone at Cambridge University Press who helped us throughout this work, in particular Becca Grainger, Lauren Cawles, Johnathan Fuentes, and Kaitlin Leach. We would like to thank Chu-Ren Huang for having believed in this project since its outset and for having patiently, but trustfully, waited for its completion. The first stages of this work were carried out with Marco Baroni. Though life and work lead us along different roads, we cannot forget the inspiring discussions we had on these themes.

Our gratitude goes to Patrick Jeuniaux, Amaru Cuba Gyllensten, and Martina Miliani for their precious work on the experiments included in Chapter 7; Giovanna Marotta for insightful comments on Chapter 1; and Alessandro Bondielli, Lucia Passaro, and Paolo Pedinotti for having read and commented on the manuscript. We thank all our past and present students and collaborators, who have always been our compass in writing the book.

We deeply thank our beloved ones for the constant support they gave us throughout this long journey. Without their help, patience, and understanding, none of this would have been possible.

Part I

Theory

1

From Usage to Meaning
The Foundations of Distributional Semantics

Distributional semantics is the study of how distributional information can be used to model semantic facts. Its theoretical foundation has become known as the **Distributional Hypothesis**:

> Lexemes with similar linguistic contexts have similar meanings.

This chapter presents the epistemological principles of distributional semantics. In Section 1.1, we explore the historical roots of the Distributional Hypothesis, tracing them in several different theoretical traditions, including European and American structuralism, the later philosophy of Ludwig Wittgenstein, corpus linguistics, and psychology. Section 1.2 discusses the place of distributional semantics in theoretical and computational linguistics.

1.1 The Distributional Hypothesis

Distributional semantics was born in the early 1960s within the emerging field of computational linguistics. One of the first explicit mentions of this term is in Garvin (1962), who defines it as follows:

Distributional semantics is predicated on the assumption that linguistic units with certain semantic similarities also share certain similarities in the relevant environments. [...] it may be possible to group automatically all those linguistic units which occur in similarly definable environments, and it is assumed that these automatically produced groupings will be of semantic interest. (Garvin, 1962, p. 388)

This definition already contains all the essential ingredients of distributional semantics, in particular its grounding assumption:

> **Distributional Hypothesis**
> The semantic similarity between two lexemes is a function of the similarity of their linguistic contexts.

DISTRIBUTIONAL HYPOTHESIS

The Distributional Hypothesis is a tree with many branches and multifarious roots. There are at least three different theoretical soils from which the Distributional Hypothesis has sprung: American structuralism (Section 1.1.1), the writings of later Wittgenstein (Section 1.1.2), and corpus linguistics (Section 1.1.3). These are very different theoretical traditions, but they share a descriptive perspective on language, and they all emphasize the importance of language use as the primary datum in linguistic theory. In Section 1.1.4, we illustrate the influence of distributionalism in psychology and the interpretation of the Distributional Hypothesis as a cognitive principle.

1.1.1 The Distributional Methodology in Structural Linguistics

The history of the Distributional Hypothesis predates computational linguistics, and originates outside the realm of traditional semantics. Its main root lies in the **distributionalism** advocated by American structuralists as the central method for making linguistics an empirical science. Prominent figures in this tradition include Bernard Bloch, Archibald Hill, Charles Hockett, Martin Joos, and George Trager, in addition to ZELLIG S. HARRIS (1909–1992), who is widely recognized as one of the fathers of mathematical approaches to linguistics, and the most influential theoretician of distributionalism. Harris' distributional program is delineated in his *Methods in Structural Linguistics* (1951), and is a consistent topic throughout works such as *Distributional Structure* (1954), *Mathematical Structures of Language* (1968), and *A Theory of Language and Information: A Mathematical Approach* (1991).

DISTRIBU-
TIONALISM

According to Harris, the basic elements of language can be identified in terms of their relative distributions:

To be relevant these elements must be set up on a distributional basis: x and y are included in the same element A if the distribution of x relative to the other elements B, C, etc. is in some sense the same as the distribution of y. (Harris, 1951, p. 7)

The essence of the distributional methodology, as defined by Harris in the quote above, is thus quite clear and simple: The basic building blocks of language can be identified by their relative distributions in (samples of) language. This means that if we have two elements x and y with identical distributions, then they are functionally equivalent and should be regarded as the same distributional element. Of course, everything depends on what we mean by "distribution." Harris clarifies his use of the term in the following words:

The ENVIRONMENT or position of an element consists of the neighborhood, within an utterance, of elements which have been set up on the basis of the same fundamental procedures which were used in setting up the element in question. [...] The DISTRIBUTION of an element is the total of all environments in which it occurs, i.e. the sum of the (different) positions (or occurrences) of an element relative to the occurrence of other elements. (Harris, 1951, pp. 15–16)

The term "environment" refers here to the **linguistic context** of an element and is formed by its neighboring elements. Harris' statement above thus constitutes a very clear and concise formulation of the distributional methodology:

LINGUISTIC CONTEXT

DISTRIBUTION

> Linguistic elements are identified by their **distributions**, defined as the sum of the contexts in which they occur.

In the same way, categories of elements can be identified by the distributional similarity of their constituent elements. For Harris (and other proponents of the distributional methodology), the entirety of language – phonology, morphology, grammar – could be described according to distributional criteria.

As explicitly acknowledged by Harris, distributionalism originates in the pioneering works of **EDWARD SAPIR**[1] (1884 – 1939) and **LEONARD BLOOMFIELD** (1887 – 1949), whose program for a **structural** and **descriptive** linguistics is founded on three main tenets:

STRUCTURAL LINGUISTICS

1. every language has a structure of its own, and there are no universal linguistic categories;
2. the study of language must be primarily synchronic;
3. linguistics must be autonomous with respect to other disciplines, especially psychology.

The distributional method is considered instrumental in achieving these goals, in particular to provide linguistics with an independent and methodologically sound foundation: The only data that are scientifically valid for Bloomfield are observable linguistic phenomena in the form of distributional patterns.

---

[1] Quoting a letter by Morris Swadesh, Nevin (1993) suggests that the origin of the use of the term distribution in linguistics was Sapir, who employed it as a geographical metaphor: "It was an application of the usage represented by 'geographic distribution', an expression which was much used by Sapir as by other anthropologists and linguists."

Distributionalism and Meaning

It is a common conception that semantics is in the periphery, if not completely ignored, in the structural linguistic tradition in general, and in the works of Zellig Harris in particular.[2] It is certainly true that Harris himself does not offer a distributional semantics and that his distributional project is primarily occupied with phonology and morphology, but the reason for this seemingly agnostic stance toward semantics is less commonly understood.

In order to fully appreciate Harris' perspective of the relationship between distributional properties and meaning, it is useful to first flesh out the ultimate conclusion of Harris' concerns about the scientific status of linguistic methodology. At the core of these concerns is the realization of the peculiar position of linguistics as a science, since it does not have recourse to a metalanguage that is external to its object of study. On the contrary, *language contains its own metalanguage*. We cannot describe language in something other than language, and any use of symbols needs to be defined ultimately in language:

There is no way to define or describe the language and its occurrences except in such statements said in that same language or in another natural language. Even if the grammar of a language is stated largely in symbols, those symbols will have to be defined ultimately in a natural language. (Harris, 1991, p. 274)

This quandary has an important consequence: If the information in language can only be described in language, then it follows that this information cannot be an encoding of some prior representation of the information (e.g., a mental representation). This is a strong argument against mentalism, and for the scientific viability of the distributional approach. For Harris, this means that the science of language cannot deal with anything other than the elements of language, and their relationships to one another, that is, their distribution.

Following this line of reasoning, Harris argues – just like Bloomfield – that the form of a lexeme is not something different from the meaning conveyed by it. In the words of Bloomfield (1943): "in language, forms cannot be separated from their meanings." This is a point in the descriptive tradition that is often misconstrued. The insistence on the unity of form and meaning should not be understood as a denial of the existence of extralinguistic meaning. On the contrary, Harris – and even more explicitly Bloomfield – vigorously argues that meaning in all its social manifestations is most decidedly outside the scope of linguistic theory. As Bloomfield states: "the statement of meanings is therefore the weak point in language study, and will remain so until human knowledge advances far beyond its present state" (Bloomfield, 1933, p. 140). The best we

---

[2] Some commentators even label the whole American structuralist tradition "anti-semantic" (e.g., Murphy, 2003).

can do within the descriptive linguistic project is to describe the observable manifestations of meaning, and indeed, *any* meaning (regardless of what it is and where it comes from) that can be conveyed in language *must* have a formal manifestation, since otherwise it would not be expressible in language: "a language can convey only such meanings as are attached to some formal feature: the speakers can signal only by means of signals" (Bloomfield, 1933, p. 168). Therefore, Bloomfield concludes, "in all study of language we must start off from forms and not from meanings" (Bloomfield, 1943, p. 402). The proper interpretation of this claim is that semantic considerations cannot enter into the definition of linguistic elements (e.g., "nouns denote things"), which must instead be defined in distributional terms (Goldsmith and Huck, 1991).[3]

Likewise, according to Harris, linguistic analysis cannot be founded on "some independently discoverable structure of meaning" (Harris, 1954, p. 152). It is meaning that must be studied as a function of linguistic distributions:

MEANING AND DISTRIBUTION

if we consider words or morphemes A and B to be more different in meaning than A and C, then we will often find that the distributions of A and B are more different than the distributions of A and C. In other words, difference of meaning correlates with difference of distribution. (Harris, 1954, p. 156)

Harris' words echo those of another structuralist, Martin Joos, who claims that "the linguist's meaning of a morpheme [...] is by definition the set of conditional probabilities of its occurrence in context with all other morphemes" (Joos, 1950, p. 708). The point is that a difference in meaning between two lexemes will be reflected by a difference in distribution, and this difference in distribution will be observable through distributional analysis:

If A and B have almost identical environments except chiefly for sentences which contain both, we say they are synonyms: *oculist* and *eye-doctor*. If A and B have some environments in common and some not (e.g. *oculist* and *lawyer*) we say that they have different meanings, the amount of meaning difference corresponding roughly to the amount of difference in their environments. (Harris, 1954, p. 157)

In his later works, Harris characterizes linguistic environments in terms of syntactic dependencies involving relations between a word acting as **operator** and a word acting as its **argument**. The "selection" (i.e., the distribution) of a word

OPERATOR AND ARGUMENT

---

[3] Bloomfield's semantic skepticism concerns any approach to meaning, including the behaviorist and physicalist ones that he favored, since statements about meaning lie well beyond the limits of linguistic science: "There is nothing in the structure of morphemes like *wolf, fox,* and *dog* to tell us the relation between their meanings. This is problem for the zoölogist. The zoölogist's definition of these meanings is welcome to us as a practical help, but it cannot be confirmed or rejected on the basis of our science" (Bloomfield, 1933, p. 162).

is the set of operators and arguments with which it co-occurs with a statistically significant frequency, and is strongly correlated with its meaning:

It is thus that selection can be considered an indicator, and indeed a measure, of meaning. Its approximate conformity to meaning is seen in that we can expect that for any three words, if two of them are closer in meaning to each other than they are to the third, they will also be closer in their selection of operators and arguments. (Harris, 1991, p. 329)

Meaning "is a concept of no clear definition" (Harris, 1991, p. 321), but distributional analysis can turn it into a measurable and scientific notion:

Selection is objectively investigable and explicitly statable and subdividable in a way that is not possible for meanings – whether as extension and referents or as sense and definition. (Harris, 1991, p. 329)

The goal of Harris' distributional program is therefore not to exclude meaning from the study of language (Harris, 1991, pp. 42–43), but rather to provide a scientific foundation for its investigation. Even if Harris has never explicitly formulated the Distributional Hypothesis, he argues that if we are to deal with meaning in language, *we can only do so through distributional analysis*. It is this idea of a correlation between meaning differences and distributional properties that lies at the heart of distributional semantics.

Syntagms and Paradigms: Distributionalism in Europe

Distributionalism is a direct product of American structuralism but is also strongly indebted to European structuralists like Ferdinand de Saussure, Louis Hjelmslev, and the Prague School, most notably represented by Nikolai Trubetzkoy and Roman Jakobson. According to Harris, the (semantic) relation between two words or morphemes is defined differentially, based on their distributional behavior within the language system, without recourse to an external world. This view recalls the words of the father of structuralism, FERDINAND DE SAUSSURE (1857–1913): "dans la langue il n'y a que des differences" ("in language there are only differences"; Saussure, 1916, p. 166).

VALUE AND SYSTEM

In structuralist theory, as it emanates from Saussure's posthumously published seminal work *Cours de linguistique générale* (1916), the term **valeur** "value" is used to define the function of a lexeme within the **language system**. A lexeme has a value only by virtue of being *different* with respect to the other lexemes. Such a differential view on the functional distinctiveness of linguistic elements highlights the importance of the system as a whole, since differences cannot exist in isolation from the system itself. A single isolated lexeme cannot enter into difference relations, since there are no other lexemes to differ from (and no system to define it functionally). In this view, the language system

Table 1.1 Syntagmatic and paradigmatic relations

	Paradigmatic relations Selections: "x or y"			
Syntagmatic relations	she	adores	green	paint
Combinations:	he	likes	blue	dye
"x and y"	they	love	red	colour

becomes an interplay of functional differences, which can be divided into two   SYNTAGMATIC
kinds: **syntagmatic** and **paradigmatic relations**.[4]   RELATIONS

> Syntagmatic relations hold between lexemes that co-occur in sequential combinations. A **syntagm** is such an ordered combination of lexemes.

PARADIGMATIC
RELATIONS

> Paradigmatic relations hold between lexemes that do *not* themselves co-occur, but that co-occur with the same *other* lexemes. Paradigmatically related lexemes can be substituted for one another in the same context. Such a set of substitutable lexemes constitutes a **paradigm**.

The term "syntagm" corresponds to what we have called "context." The only difference is that the former term implies an ordered set of neighboring lexemes, while the latter term does not. Syntagmatic and paradigmatic relations can be depicted as orthogonal axes in a two-dimensional grid. In the example in Table 1.1, the paradigms correspond to morphosyntactic classes, like adjectives and verbs, but they also define semantic categories, such as color terms.

In his essay *On linguistic aspects of translation*, **ROMAN JAKOBSON** (1896–1982) argues that meaning is a linguistic phenomenon:

The meaning of the words "cheese," "apple," "nectar," "acquaintance," "but," "mere," and of any word or phrase whatsoever is definitely a linguistic – or to be more precise and less narrow – a semiotic fact [...]. There is no *signatum* without *signum*. The meaning of the word "cheese" cannot be inferred from a nonlinguistic acquaintance with cheddar or with camembert without the assistance of the verbal code. (Jakobson, 1959, p. 232)

Like for De Saussure, words have meaning only within a linguistic system, in which they are used and entertain various relations with other expressions. It is

---

[4] Saussure uses the term *associative* relation rather than paradigmatic relation. It was Hjelmslev who introduced the term "paradigmatic" relation.

LINGUISTIC
AND DIRECT
ACQUAINTANCE
the knowledge of such relations that Jakobson calls **linguistic acquaintance**, whose importance supersedes the role of the **direct acquaintance** with the entities words refer to. The latter may lack (e.g., we can use *ambrosia* correctly even without direct experience of its referent), while linguistic acquaintance is essential to understand the meaning of any lexeme (cf. Sections 8.7–8.8).

Compared to its American counterpart, European structuralism attributes considerable importance to word meaning analysis. **Structural seman-**
STRUCTURAL
SEMANTICS
tics, represented by Jost Trier, Adrienne Lerher, Eugenio Coseriu, Algirdas Greimas, John Lyons, Alan Cruse, among many others, is a family of theories focusing on the paradigmatic organization of the lexicon (Murphy, 2003; Geeraerts, 2010). The theoretical apparatus of structural semantics includes:

SEMANTIC
FIELDS
1. **lexical** or **semantic fields**, sets of mutually related lexemes defining the conceptual structure of a certain domain, such as the color domain;

SEMANTIC
FEATURES
2. **semantic components** or **features**, inspired by structuralist phonology and used to describe meaning in terms of basic oppositions (e.g., $+/-$ ANIMATE); and

SEMANTIC
RELATIONS
3. **paradigmatic semantic relations** between lexemes, such as **synonymy** (sameness in meaning; *sofa – couch*), **antonymy** (opposition in meaning, *good – bad*), **hypernymy** (a taxonomic relation where a **hypernym** is a more general term than its **hyponym**, *animal – dog*), and **co-hyponymy** (lexemes that share the same hypernym; *dog – cat*).

Structural semantics is autonomous from distributionalism, but the latter is often adopted as a method to define semantic paradigms in terms of syntagmatic relations. The Distributional Hypothesis can indeed be reformulated in structuralist terms (Sahlgren, 2006):

> Words sharing syntagmatic contexts have similar paradigmatic properties.

For instance, Apresjan (1966) refers to Harris' distributional methodology as a way to provide more objectivity to the investigation of semantic fields by grounding it on linguistic evidence. Apresjan carries out a distributional analysis of adjectives in terms of their frequency of co-occurrence with various syntactic contexts. The interplay between syntagmatic and paradigmatic dimensions is also central for Cruse (1986): The greater the paradigmatic "affinity" of lexical items, the more congruent their patterns of syntagmatic relations.

1.1.2 Meaning as Use: The Echoes of Wittgenstein

The central principle of structuralism and the distributional methodology – that we should let data decide what our models of language encompass – echoes in

Wittgenstein's insistence that we should "look and see" (Wittgenstein, 1953, §66) rather than presume. The intellectual work of **LUDWIG WITTGENSTEIN** (1889–1951) can be divided into two distinct periods: the early period of the *Tractatus Logico-Philosophicus* (1922), where he professes a logic-centered view on language, and the later period of *Philosophical Investigations* (1953), in which he explicitly rejects his earlier ideas about the nature of language. In this work, Wittgenstein is openly polemic against the view that we need a logical representation to obliterate the vagueness and incompleteness of natural language. Wittgenstein urges us not to *assume* a general and fixed meaning of words. Instead, we should look at *how* the words are being used:

> For a large class of cases – though not for all – in which we employ the word "meaning" it can be defined thus: the meaning of a word is its use in the language. (Wittgenstein, 1953, §43)

This has sometimes been called a **usage-based theory** of meaning, but Wittgenstein is not so much offering a theory of meaning in his later works as pointing out a misconception regarding the nature of meaning. The misconception, according to him, consists in construing meaning as primarily a naming relation, in such a way that meaning is something (like a mental or physical object) that a word (or phrase or sentence) names. Such a *nomenclaturist* view on meaning has been both widespread and withstanding in the history of linguistics and the philosophy of language (although Wittgenstein's aim was primarily to attack his own earlier views), and the *anti-nomenclaturist* stance is a position the later Wittgenstein shares with the structuralist movement, and in particular with the contemporary Saussure (Harris, 1988).

MEANING AS USE

This is not the only point of contact between the ideas of Wittgenstein and structuralist linguistics, and more specifically with the ideas of Saussure.[5] The former's view on meaning as founded in the use of language has striking similarities to the latter's concept of *valeur*: It is the *role* of the lexeme in language that constitutes its meaning. Wittgenstein even expresses himself in terms that could as well have been Saussure's: "the sign (the sentence) gets its significance from the system of signs, from the language to which it belongs" (Wittgenstein, 1958, p. 5). For both Wittgenstein and Saussure, meaning can be likened with the role or function of a word within language; indeed, they make heavy use of the game-metaphor – and in particular chess – for describing the holistic functional character of the language system.

Wittgenstein also stresses the importance of the social aspect of meaning and language use, just as the prominent figures of the structuralist tradition

---

[5] Despite the similarities between the ideas of Wittgenstein and Saussure, there is no evidence that they were influenced by (or even aware of) each other's works (Harris, 1988).

had done. Wittgenstein even argues that language cannot exist in isolation from a language community. This is the essence of the so-called "private language argument," in which we are invited to imagine someone inventing a private language for naming a private sensation. One of the problems with such a private language is that there would be no criterion of correctness for using the private name: How could the private language user tell whether she uses the name in the correct way or not? Wittgenstein's point is that in order for there to be a criterion of correctness of use, there must be other language users that agree on this criterion, since correctness in language is established by convention. Wittgenstein coined the term **language game** to emphasize that language use is a *social activity* that requires other users, and for which there are *rules* that are established by convention between the language users, and which determine correctness of usage. The point is that the rules of the language game define the language system, and so are a prerequisite for meaning: Lexemes simply cannot have a meaning if there is no language game to be played. Therefore, the meaning of lexemes can be understood only by observing how they are used in language games.

LANGUAGE
GAMES

In summary, although there is no concrete evidence that Wittgenstein had any direct influence on the development of distributionalism as formulated by the American structuralist tradition, there are some striking similarities between his usage-based view of meaning and the Distributional Hypothesis. Both adopt a descriptive perspective on language and emphasize the importance of usage data as the primary source of information for semantic analysis. Of course the term "use" in Wittgenstein does not refer only to linguistic distributions but to the more general usage in communicative situations, which include but are not limited to linguistic contexts. However, Wittgenstein's view of meaning strongly resonates with the one grounding distributional semantics.

1.1.3 Distributionalism and Corpus Linguistics

If Wittgenstein's influence on structuralism, and in particular the American distributionalists, remains obscure, it is much more explicit when it comes to European corpus linguistics. The idea that language use and distributional analysis is the key to understanding word meaning has flourished within the linguistic tradition stemming from the British linguist JOHN R. FIRTH (1890–1960). In fact, **corpus linguistics** represents another important root of distributional semantics. Firth laments the lack of interest in meaning by American structuralists, but he shares with them the idea that linguistics should address meaning in its own terms, the question being "not how much meaning can be *excluded*, but how much meaning can legitimately be included" (Firth,

CORPUS
LINGUISTICS

1955, p. 102). Differently from structural semanticists, Firth privileges the analysis of syntagmatic relations between lexical items over the paradigmatic ones.

Firth's **contextual view of meaning** is based on the assumption that mean- CONTEXTUAL ing is a very complex and multifaceted reality, inherently related to language VIEW OF use in contexts (e.g., social setting, discourse, etc.). One of the key "modes" MEANING of meaning of a word is what he calls "meaning by collocation" (Firth, 1951), determined by the context of surrounding words:

As Wittgenstein says, "the meaning of words lies in their use." The day to day practice of playing language games recognizes customs and rules. It follows that a text in such established usage may contain sentences such as "Don't be such an ass!," "you silly ass!," "What an ass he is!" In these examples, the word *ass* is in familiar and habitual company, commonly collocated with *you silly –*, *he is a silly –*, *don't be such an –*. You shall know a word by the company it keeps! (Firth, 1957, p. 11)

Collocations are lexical items that tend to co-occur in the same linguistic COLLOCATIONS context: "Collocations of a given word are statements of the habitual or customary places of that word in collocational order [. . .] it is an order of *mutual expectancy*. The words are mutually expectant and mutually prehended" (Firth, 1957, p. 12). The meaning of a lexeme is thus defined by its **collocates**, other COLLOCATE lexemes that have a syntagmatic relation with it: "One of the meanings of *night* is its collocability with *dark*, and of *dark*, of course, collocation with *night*" (Firth, 1951, p. 196). The analogy with Harris' claim on the relationship between meaning and linguistic distributions is patently very strong.

JOHN M. SINCLAIR (1933–2007), one of the fathers of corpus linguistics and of modern computational lexicography, deeply elaborates Firth's idea of the centrality of collocations to describe lexical meaning:

the formal meaning of an item A is that it has a strong tendency to occur nearby items B, C, D, less strong with items E, F, slight with G, H, I, and none at all with any other item. (Sinclair, 1966, p. 417)

Like Harris, Sinclair uses the term "environments" to refer to the linguistic contexts of lexemes. Semantic analysis must start from the collection of the "environments" of a lexeme in a corpus. Since not all of them are equally important to characterize word meanings, significant collocations are distinguished from "casual" ones with statistical tests applied to the frequency distributions of collocates (Jones and Sinclair, 1974). Sinclair thus pioneered the use of computational techniques to extract collocations from corpora. The theoretical concept of collocation was introduced by Firth, but it is Sinclair who turned it into a quantitative method for semantic analysis. The study of collocations has grown as an independent line of research, but its theoretical assumptions and methods are deeply intertwined with distributional semantics (cf. Chapter 2).

1.1.4 The Distributional Hypothesis in Psychology

As argued by Goldsmith (2005), Harris' structuralist program is perfectly compatible with the interpretation of distributional analysis as a cognitive process:

Harris was interested in determining what procedures IN PRINCIPLE could lead to a deep understanding of a natural language system, so it shouldn't be surprising that the one existing system that actually acquires a natural language should display a set of behaviors that resemble in interesting ways a Harrisian system. (Goldsmith, 2005, p. 729)

Indeed, Harris' distributional methodology had a significant impact on psychology. At the beginning, it was mainly regarded as a way to explain the strength of **word associations** produced by subjects. The word association technique is a common method in psychology, and consists in asking a subject to respond to a stimulus word (e.g., *dog*) with the first word that occurs to him or her (e.g., *cat*). Association strength is then measured by counting the number of subjects that have produced a given word in response to a stimulus.

The analysis of word associations plays a central role in **behaviorist psychology**, which pursues an associationist view of meaning, based on the idea that simple association or co-occurrence of stimuli is the primary basis of thought and learning. Jenkins (1954) suggests that word associations can be interpreted as a result of the statistical distribution of stimuli and responses in language. In particular, the association strength would depend both on **paradigmatic** and **syntagmatic similarity** between stimulus and response. Jenkins defines these notions in structuralist terms, explicitly referring to Harris:

The similarity between any two words can be conceived linguistically as the degree of similarity in distribution. [...] this similarity may be profitably divided into two classes, *paradigmatic* and *syntagmatic*. Two words are considered paradigmatically similar to the extent that they are substitutable in the identical frame (this corresponds rather closely to Zellig Harris' use of the term "selection") and syntagmatic to the extent that they follow one another in utterances. (Jenkins, 1954, p. 11)

Analogously, Deese claims that the **associative meaning** of a word, defined in terms of the responses it evokes on a word association test, depends on its distributional properties: "the extent to which words share associative

Margin notes: WORD ASSOCIATIONS · BEHAVIORISM · ASSOCIATIVE MEANING

distributions is determined by the extent to which they share contexts in ordinary discourse" (Deese, 1965, p. 128).

Vector-based representations of meaning, like those later adopted in distributional semantics, were pioneered in psychology by Charles Osgood, who is one of the first to refer to the semantic system as a **semantic space**. Osgood (1952) and Osgood et al. (1957) represent concepts in terms of n-dimensional feature vectors. However, the dimensions of Osgood's semantic spaces are not distributional,[6] but are built with the **semantic differential** method: Subjects are asked to locate the meaning of a word along different scales between two polar adjectives (e.g., *happy – sad, slow – fast, hard – soft*, etc.), and their ratings determine its position in the semantic space, which mainly captures connotative aspects of meaning. Such feature vectors are then used to measure the psychological distance between words.

The interest of psychologists in distributionalism survives the crisis of the behaviorist paradigm, and the consequent downfall of associationism. A strenuous supporter of the importance of linguistic distributions in shaping semantic representations is **GEORGE A. MILLER** (1920–2012), one of the fathers of **cognitive psychology**. Miller is deeply acquainted with contemporary structuralist linguistic theories (Miller, 1954) and considers Harris' distributional analysis as a method to provide an empirical foundation to the notion of **semantic similarity** (Miller, 1967). Judgments of semantic similarity between words (e.g., *dog* is semantically more similar to *cat* than to *car*) play a key role in the exploration of the mental lexicon, and they are routinely used as an explanatory factor in psychological experiments.

Rubenstein and Goodenough (1965) carry out computational experiments showing that semantic similarity judgments on 65 noun pairs strongly correlate with the overlap of the linguistic contexts of the two words. The contexts are collected from sentences produced by a different group of subjects for each noun in the test pairs. Miller (1967) also distinguishes syntagmatic distributional similarity from paradigmatic one, and mentions the ongoing research in computational linguistics to measure semantic similarity with distributional data automatically extracted from corpora (cf. Section 1.2.1).

A distributional definition of semantic similarity is theorized by Miller and Charles (1991), who conceive it as a "function of the contexts in which words are used" (p. 3). Like Firth, they advocate a contextual view of meaning:

What people know when they know a word is not how to recite its dictionary definition – they know how to use it (when to produce it and how to understand it) in

SEMANTIC SPACE

SEMANTIC DIFFERENTIAL

COGNITIVE PSYCHOLOGY

SEMANTIC SIMILARITY

---

[6] Osgood et al. (1957) are actually quite critical of Harris' distributional methodology for semantic analysis.

everyday discourse [...] And because words are used together in phrases and sentences, this starting assumption directs attention immediately to the importance of context. (Miller and Charles, 1991, p. 4)

Even if context in a broad sense must also include the extra-linguistic information about the communicative and social setting, Miller and Charles claim that speakers are able to acquire many new words only using distributional information (cf. Section 8.8). The repeated observations of a word in linguistic contexts lead to the formation of its **contextual representation**:

CONTEXTUAL
REPRESENTA-
TION

> The *contextual representation* of a word is knowledge of how that word is used. [...] That is to say, a word's contextual representation [...] is an abstract cognitive structure that accumulates from encounters with the word in various (linguistic) contexts. (Miller and Charles, 1991, p. 5)

Contextual representations correspond to the distributional representations we introduce in Chapter 2. Judging the semantic similarity of two words thus consists in comparing the similarity of their contextual representations. This is what Miller and Charles (1991) call **contextual hypothesis**, stating that "two words are semantically similar to the extent that their contextual representations are similar" (p. 5). The contextual hypothesis is related to Harris' distributional methodology, a debt that Miller and Charles explicitly acknowledge.

CONTEXTUAL
HYPOTHESIS

1.2 Distributional Semantics in Language Research

Because of its different roots, distributional semantics is a manifold program for semantic analysis, which is pursued in different disciplines, like computational linguistics and cognitive science. This contributes to its being a framework with multiple souls and goals, which, however, share common methods. In fact, we can identify two major views of distributional semantics that also correspond to alternative ways to interpret the Distributional Hypothesis.

First of all, distributional semantics is an empirical methodology for semantic analysis. This view is based on a **Weak Distributional Hypothesis** (Lenci, 2008) that postulates a correlation between semantic content and linguistic distributions, and exploits such correlation as an "observable" of meaning. The distribution of words in contexts is determined by their meaning (*whatever this might be*) and the semantic properties of lexical items act as constraints governing their syntagmatic behavior. Consequently, by inspecting a relevant number of distributional contexts, we can identify those aspects of meaning

WEAK DISTRI-
BUTIONAL
HYPOTHESIS

that are shared by lexemes with similar linguistic distributions. The Weak Distributional Hypothesis does not entail that word distributions are themselves constitutive of the semantic properties of lexical items at a cognitive level, but rather that meaning is a kind of "latent variable" responsible for the distributions we observe, which we try to uncover by analyzing such distributions.

> Distributional semantics is a theoretical and computational framework to **learn and study the semantic properties of lexemes from their distribution in linguistic contexts** collected from text corpora.

The investigation of lexical meaning typically relies on two kinds of evidence: (i) native speakers' intuitions about the semantic properties of linguistic expressions and (ii) the description of meanings in lexical resources, like dictionaries. Distributional semantics adds a third type of empirical evidence: *The computational analysis of lexeme distributions in linguistic contexts.*

Datasets with human semantic judgments (e.g., similarity ratings) are commonly used in cognitive science, but collecting them is a complex and time-consuming task (e.g., rating 100 words for their pairwise semantic similarity amounts to collecting 4,950 judgments per participant, which raise to 19,900 for 200 words). Although crowdsourcing methods facilitate the elicitation process, collecting speakers' semantic intuitions can hardly scale up to cover large lexical samples. Computational lexicons like WordNet (Fellbaum, 1998) provide important information about word senses and their organization. A major limit of such resources is that they contain "second-hand" evidence, as the organization of the semantic space heavily depends on the lexicographers' choice. Moreover, they have a limited coverage, are hand-built, and therefore hard to maintain and extend to new domains. In fact, the lexicon is a dynamic entity, with new items and new senses constantly appearing. Lexical meanings are highly context sensitive and undergo continuous modification and modulation in contexts (cf. Section 9.1.1).

Given the ever-increasing availability of digital texts, distributional semantics can rely on huge amounts of empirical evidence to characterize the semantic properties of lexemes. Building distributional models for large samples of the lexicon is fast and cheap, at least comparatively to other methods of collecting semantic information, and can be performed for any language or domain, as long as we have enough textual data. From a computational linguistic perspective, distributional semantics is an efficient and effective method to build corpus-based lexical resources, and to learn semantic representations for NLP and AI systems. Moreover, since distributional models are grounded in language usage, they are more suitable to capture its variability and dynamicity, thereby offering new perspectives to analyze the complex interplay between meaning and context. Obviously, distributional data do not replace other types of semantic evidence but rather complement them. For instance, speakers' judgments provide benchmarks for the evaluation of distributional models (cf. Chapter 7), which can in turn be employed to expand lexical resources.

According to a second view, distributional semantics is a methodology to investigate and model how meanings are acquired and represented in the mental lexicon. This conception directly stems from the psychological research we have reviewed in Section 1.1.4 and is grounded on the assumption that the linguistic contexts of a word have a causal role in creating and shaping STRONG DISTRI- its neurocognitive representation (cf. the Contextual Hypothesis by Miller and BUTIONAL Charles, 1991). We call this the **Strong Distributional Hypothesis** (Lenci, HYPOTHESIS 2008), since it regards the distributional behavior of a lexeme as an explanatory factor of its cognitive properties.

> Distributional semantics is a theoretical and computational framework to **build models of semantic memory** based on the hypothesis that the distribution of words in the linguistic input contributes to determine their **conceptual representations**.

Semantic memory stores concepts and general world knowledge as mental representations that allow us to recognize entities in the world, interact with them, and interpret language (McRae and Jones, 2013). Semantic memory is shaped by our *experience*, which includes both **sensory-motor experiences** of perceiving and acting in the world, and **linguistic experiences** of using and being exposed to language. Distributional models of semantic memory "hypothesize a formal cognitive mechanism to learn semantics from repeated episodic experience in the linguistic environment (typically a text corpus)" (Jones et al., 2015, p. 239). The contribution and role of linguistic experience vis-à-vis other kinds of extralinguistic inputs in building concepts is an empirical question that is widely debated in cognitive science (Vigliocco et al., 2009; Dove, 2014). Distributional semantics is a scientific framework to investigate the structure and origin of semantic representations in mind and brain (cf. Section 8.8).

Distributional semantics is both a method to represent meaning, and a family of computational models to learn such representations from linguistic data. Therefore, it allows us to explore a wide range of issues related to meaning dynamics, including its acquisition, change, and use. The actual descriptive and explanatory adequacy of distributional semantics is of course an empirical matter. It is one of the main purposes of this book to investigate this issue. In the following sections, we briefly review the past and present of distributional semantics in computational linguistics and semantic theory.

1.2.1 Computational Linguistics

Today, distributional semantics is a mainstream research paradigm in computational linguistics. However, this is just the last step of a long process whose beginnings date back to the early 1960s and were influenced by the cultural and scientific environment we have analyzed in Section 1.1. The first experiments in the distributional analysis of meaning were aimed at building thesauri for machine translation and information retrieval (Sparck Jones, 2005). A **thesaurus** is a lexical resource in which words are grouped together accord- THESAURUS ing to paradigmatic relations, like synonymy and hypernymy, or because they belong to the same semantic field. Thesauri were considered extremely useful to provide machine translation systems with semantic information about lexical items, but the experiments with existing resources like *Roget's Thesaurus* did not prove wholly satisfactory. Hand-made thesauri turned out to be extremely laborious to produce and suffered from limited coverage. Hence the idea of exploiting distributional information for the automatic identification of synonyms and the semantic classification of lexical items.

Hays (1960) and Garvin (1962) use the term distributional semantics to refer to a research program in machine translation inspired by Harris' idea that similarity of meaning depends on similarity of linguistic contexts (cf. the quotation at the beginning of Section 1.1). Harper (1961, 1965) provides experimental tests of such program, by measuring the similarity between 40 Russian nouns in terms of their syntactic dependencies extracted from a small corpus. Parallelly, Sparck Jones (1961, 1964) carries out experiments to identify synonyms with distributional information extracted from a machine-readable dictionary.

An essential contribution to the development of distributional semantics has come from the **Vector Space Model** in information retrieval (Salton et al., VECTOR SPACE 1975), which was pioneered in the SMART system (Salton, 1964, 1971a). The MODEL AND INFORMATION core idea of the vector space model is to represent a collection of documents RETRIEVAL (i.e., texts to be retrieved) with a **term-document matrix**: The row vectors correspond to terms (i.e., lexical items), the column vectors correspond to documents, and each matrix entry records the occurrences of a term in a document (cf. Chapter 2). Similarity between documents is computed by measuring the similarity between their column vectors. Queries are treated as "pseudo-documents" and represented with column vectors in the same matrix, thus the relevance of a document to a query is computed by measuring the similarity of the document vector to the query vector.

Since its outset, the Vector Space Model was also applied to automatic thesaurus construction. In fact, one major problem that retrieval systems face is that the same information can be described with different terms.[7] This negatively impacts on the system recall (i.e., its ability to retrieve documents relevant with respect to the user's query), because the term in the query (e.g., *production of automobiles*) may not be the same one used to index a document (e.g., *manufacture of motor vehicles*). Various experiments were carried out to exploit co-occurrence statistics extracted from document collections to identify semantically associated words (Stiles, 1961; Stevens et al., 1964). Jones (1964) explicitly relates this research line to Harris' distributionalism on the one hand, and associationist psychology on the other (cf. Section 1.1.4). Giuliano and Jones (1962), Salton (1964), Dattola and Murray (1967), and Sparck Jones (1971) use the term-document matrices to compute term similarity with row vector similarity. Lewis et al. (1967) discriminate synonyms and antonyms from other kinds of related terms with distributional statistics. Instead of term frequency in a document, Hirschman et al. (1975) represent words with vectors recording their co-occurrences with particular grammatical relations in texts, and cluster the vectors to obtain semantic classes.

LINEAR
ALGEBRA

The Vector Space Model in information retrieval has introduced **linear algebra** as the core mathematical framework for distributional semantics. Notions that have become standard in distributional models of meaning, like co-occurrence matrices and vector representations of lexical items, were already in place in the first researches in the 1960s. Unfortunately, the quality of the resulting thesauri and their effectiveness in applications were greatly hampered by the technological limitations of the time, in particular the small size of the corpora, and the computational cost required to build co-occurrence matrices and measure distributional similarity (Salton and Lesk, 1966; Salton, 1971b).

While distributional semantics continued to be pursued in information retrieval, it was virtually ignored in computational linguistics throughout this early period. Except for works on collocation analysis (Church and Hanks, 1989) and on the acquisition of lexical information from machine-readable dictionaries (Wilks et al., 1990), formal and logic methods dominated mainstream computational semantics, as proved by the fact that distributional semantic themes were practically absent from any major conference or journal. In the early 1990s, the new empiricist turn in computational linguistics

---

[7] According to Furnas et al. (1983), two people choose the same word to refer to the same object less than 20% of the time.

and the emergence of statistical natural language processing, together with the availability of larger corpora and more powerful computers, favored a fast-growing interest in distributional semantics. Hindle (1990) is one of the first works of this new trend to explicitly mention Harris's distributional hypothesis. Hindle derives a distributional classification of words in English from their co-occurrences with syntactic relations automatically extracted from a parsed corpus.

A major innovation was represented by **Latent Semantic Analysis** (LSA), also known as **Latent Semantic Indexing** (LSI), proposed by Deerwester et al. (1990). LSA extends the Vector Space Model of information retrieval by applying Singular Value Decomposition (SVD) to the term-document matrix. This linear-algebraic method allows a more sophisticated analysis of distributional data by projecting the co-occurrence matrix onto a new reduced one, with the purpose of finding higher-order associations between terms and documents and uncovering the "latent semantic structure" in the original matrix (cf. Section 2.5.1). Schütze (1992, 1997, 1998) and Schütze and Pedersen (1993) apply SVD to matrices recording co-occurrences between lexical items appearing within the same text window. While previous models almost exclusively aimed at the identification of similar terms for thesaurus construction, Schütze was one of the first to apply distributional methods to more advanced semantic problems, like word sense induction and disambiguation. Schütze's works, together with those by Gallant (1991), Ruge (1992), Pereira et al. (1993), Dagan et al. (1993), Grefenstette (1994), and Niwa and Nitta (1994) among many others, contributed to spreading distributional methods in computational semantics.

Research in distributional semantics has kept on growing steadily in the 1990s and the first decade of the new millennium. Most of the distributional models presented in Chapters 4 and 5 were created in this period, and the range of semantic tasks addressed with distributional methods has been increasing since then, and now includes topics like compositionality, inference, multi-modality, semantic change, and several others (cf. Part III). Lately, a most significant breakthrough has occurred with the emergence and fast success of **deep learning** methods, which have dramatically changed computational linguistics and distributional semantics by developing a new generation of models based on **artificial neural networks** (cf. Chapter 6). Deep learning has also spread the use of the term **(word) embedding** for distributional vectors. The last years have witnessed a further significant novelty, with the appearance of so-called **contextual embeddings** generated by a new kind of deep neural models that represent each word token with a distinct, context-sensitive vector (cf. Chapter 3 and Section 9.6.3).

LATENT
SEMANTIC
ANALYSIS

DEEP LEARNING

NEURAL
NETWORKS

EMBEDDINGS

CONTEXTUAL
EMBEDDINGS

Deep learning has also radically modified the scope of distributional semantics itself, boosting an exponential growth of interest in this field. Neural networks represent words with vectors, and embeddings trained on larger corpora are nowadays routinely used in deep learning architectures to initialize their word representations. These **pretrained embeddings** allow neural networks to capture lexical semantic properties that are beneficial to carry out downstream supervised tasks. Pretrained vectors can be directly used as **features** in classification algorithms or **fine-tuned** to address specific tasks. The main novelty is that distributional semantics is no longer just a computational method to measure semantic similarity or to build lexical resources from corpora, but a general approach to provide NLP and AI applications with knowledge about the meaning of linguistic expressions.

PRETRAINED
EMBEDDINGS

1.2.2 Semantic Theory

The research landscape in linguistics is characterized by two major semantic approaches that are not based on the distributional hypothesis: cognitive semantics and formal semantics. These theories present prima facie striking differences with distributional semantics, which, however, turn into important similarities or at least potential synergies at a closer and deeper look.

Cognitive linguistics is based on the work by Ronald Langacker, George Lakoff, Charles Fillmore, William Croft, Adele Goldberg, and many others, who argue for a **conceptualist** view of meaning. In **cognitive semantics**, the meaning of a lexical expression is a particular conceptualization of an entity or situation. Conceptual representations are conceived as inherently grounded in our physical embodiment: "The meaning of words in languages and how they can be used in combination depends on our perception and categorization of the world around us" (Ellis et al., 2016, p. 25). The central role of **grounding** and **embodiment** in cognitive semantics apparently contrasts with the main tenets of distributional semantics and its program of constructing meaning from linguistic co-occurrences. However, as we show in Sections 8.7 and 8.8, distributional semantics is not incompatible with grounded models of meaning.

COGNITIVE
SEMANTICS

GROUNDING

An important commonality between distributional and cognitive semantics is the **usage-based** perspective. Many cognitive linguists advocate a **usage-based model** of language acquisition and change (Goldberg, 1995; Tomasello, 2003; Croft and Cruse, 2004; Goldberg, 2006; Bybee, 2010; Hoffman and Trousdale, 2013), according to which "use of language figures critically in determining the nature of cognitive representations of language, or put another way, usage events create linguistic structure" (Bybee, 2013, p. 68). Language is

USAGE-BASED
MODELS

viewed as a complex adaptive system whose structure is *emergent* from underlying, domain-general processes that operate in areas of human cognition other than language itself (Elman, 1998; MacWhinney, 1999; Beckner et al., 2009; MacWhinney and O'Grady, 2015). In distributional approaches, lexical representations emerge from co-occurrences with linguistic contexts (Ellis, 1998), and semantic spaces are built with domain-independent learning algorithms that record the distributional statistics in the linguistic input.

Moreover, cognitive linguists regard neural networks and connectionism as a computational paradigm implementing emergent and usage-based representations (Elman et al., 1996; Ellis, 1998; Bybee and McClelland, 2005; McClelland et al., 2010). The goal of **connectionism** and the **Parallel Distributed Processing** (PDP) approach (Rumelhart and McClelland, 1986) is to explain cognition with artificial neural networks (Jones et al., 2015), as domain-independent algorithms that learn representations from co-occurrence statistics across stimulus events in the environment (cf. Section 6.1). Connectionism is consistent with the distributional hypothesis, since linguistic co-occurrences are just a particular type of stimuli that can be used by neural networks. Landauer and Dumais (1997) and Schütze (1993) already give a connectionist interpretation of their models, and neural networks today are widely used in distributional semantics. A further element of convergence with cognitive semantics is its emphasis on linguistic categories characterized by gradience and prototype effects (Taylor, 1995), which can be modeled with continuous representations like distributional vectors (Acquaviva et al., 2020). In fact, distributional semantics nowadays has a growing number of applications in linguistics, to study polysemy, semantic change, productivity, selectional preferences, and so on (cf. Chapters 8 and 9). CONNECTIONISM

If important "family resemblances" characterize distributional and cognitive semantics, the relationship with formal semantics is more complex and controversial. Stemming from the work by Gottlob Frege, Rudolf Carnap, Alfred Tarsky, Richard Montague, David Lewis, Hans Kamp, Barbara Partee, among many others, **formal (model-theoretic) semantics** is a rich family of models that share a **referential (denotational)** view of meaning (cf. Section 9.1). Its main assumption is that meaning is a relation between linguistic symbols and entities external to language, and that the goal of semantics is to characterize the **truth-conditions** of sentences as a function of the reference (denotation) of their parts. Lewis (1970) claims that "semantics with no treatment of truth conditions is not semantics" (p. 18), and Heim and Kratzer (1998) that "to know the meaning of a sentence is to know its truth conditions" (p. 1). FORMAL SEMANTICS MEANING AND TRUTH

The core notions of Frege's program for formal semantics – *truth*, *reference*, and *logical form* – are as different as possible from those of Harris' program for distributional semantics – *linguistic contexts, use*, and *co-occurrence statistics*. Formal and distributional semantics have indeed proceeded virtually ignoring each other, focusing on totally different semantic phenomena. As a matter of fact, a whole range of issues in the agenda of formal semantics, such as compositionality, quantification, inference, anaphora, modality, tense, and so on, have usually remained beyond the main horizon of distributional semantics, which has instead mostly concentrated on lexical meaning. Recently, the relationship between formal and distributional semantics has changed, and the barriers between these paradigms are now reducing. Distributional research has begun to explore the potential synergies with formal models of meaning and to address problems like compositionality, inference, and reference (Erk, 2013; Baroni et al., 2014b; McNally and Boleda, 2016; Chersoni et al., 2019; Boleda, 2020). The aim is to combine the effectiveness of distributional semantics in learning and representing word meaning with the capacity of formal models to account for compositional semantics and logical inference (cf. Chapter 9).

1.3 Summary

In this chapter, we have identified the origins of distributional semantics in structural linguistics, and in particular in the distributional methodology pioneered by Bloomfield and refined by Harris. We have also noted its close kinship with the philosophy of the later Wittgenstein and with Firthian corpus linguistics, and its impact on psychology. We have charted the course of distributional semantics in computational linguistics and cognitive science, and we have tried to articulate the position of distributional semantics in relation to current research in linguistics.

Our main findings from this journey through the history of distributional semantics can be summarized in the following way:

- its theoretical foundation is the **distributional hypothesis**;
- the distributional hypothesis is primarily a conjecture about **semantic similarity**, which is modeled as a function of **distributional similarity**. Semantic similarity is therefore the core notion of distributional semantics;
- the distributional hypothesis is primarily a conjecture about **lexical meaning**, so that the main focus of distributional semantics is on the **lexicon**; and
- distributional semantics is based on a **contextual** and **usage-based** view of meaning: The meaning of a lexeme is determined by the way it is used in linguistic contexts.

1.4 Further Reading

- Distributional semantics and structural linguistics: Sahlgren (2006, 2008); Gastaldi (2021)
- Information retrieval and the Vector Space Model: Manning et al. (2008)
- General introductions to distributional semantics: Lenci (2008, 2018); Turney and Pantel (2010); Erk (2012); Clark (2015)
- Distributional and linguistic semantics: Geeraerts (2010); Acquaviva et al. (2020); Boleda (2020)

2

Distributional Representations

DISTRIBUTIONAL REPRESENTATION Distributional semantics is founded on the relation between meaning and linguistic distributions, stated in the Distributional Hypothesis. **Distributional representations** encode the distributional properties of lexemes.

> The **distributional representation** of a lexical item is a **vector** representing its co-occurrences with linguistic contexts.

DISTRIBUTIONAL VECTORS This chapter introduces the basic method to collect **distributional vectors**, which consists in the following procedure:

1. co-occurrences between lexical items and linguistic contexts are extracted from a corpus (Sections 2.1 and 2.2);
2. the distribution of lexical items is represented with a co-occurrence matrix, whose rows are labeled with lexical items, columns with contexts, and the entries are frequency-based weights that estimate the importance of the contexts to characterize the lexemes (Section 2.3);
3. lexical items are represented with high-dimensional, explicit distributional vectors corresponding to the rows of the co-occurrence matrix (Section 2.4);
4. the co-occurrence matrix is optionally mapped onto a reduced matrix, whose columns correspond to latent dimensions, and rows to low-dimensional, implicit distributional vectors called **word embeddings** (Section 2.5); and
5. the semantic similarity between lexemes is measured with the similarity of their explicit or implicit distributional vectors (Section 2.6).

WORD EMBEDDINGS

It is worth remarking that there are also other methods to learn distributional vectors that do not require the construction of a co-occurrence matrix. We will cover such approaches in Part II, Chapters 5 and 6.

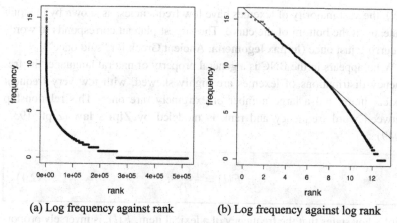

(a) Log frequency against rank   (b) Log frequency against log rank

Figure 2.1 Rank–frequency distribution and Zipf's law in the BNC obtained by counting the tokens of lemmatized word types

2.1 Corpus Selection and Processing

Distributional representations are generated from co-occurrence data extracted from a **training corpus**, as a sample of linguistic input. The **content** of the corpus (i.e., the type of language data it contains) obviously has great effects on the resulting distributional representations. If the corpus consists of texts sampled from the law domain, it is very likely that most of the distributional data about *suit* will concern the legal sense of this term, rather than its clothing interpretation. At the same time, the **size** of the training corpus is also a key factor because of the properties of word frequency distributions in language.

TRAINING CORPUS

2.1.1 Word Frequency Distributions

The most common way to explore word distributions consists in analyzing the relationship between the **frequency** (i.e., the number of tokens) of a word type and its **rank**. Each word type is assigned a rank depending on its position in a frequency-ordered list, so that the most frequent word has rank one, the second most frequent word has rank two, and so on (words with the same frequency can be ranked in any order). Figure 2.1a shows the rank–frequency distribution of lemmatized word types in the British National Corpus (BNC) (Burnard, 1995). The striking feature of this plot is the steep decrease of word frequencies on the y axis, which are plotted on a logarithmic scale (otherwise, the curve would fall almost vertically). Besides a small number of words with very high frequency (including articles, prepositions, pronouns, conjunctions,

WORD FREQUENCY AND RANK

etc.), the vast majority of lexemes have low frequencies, as shown by the long plateaus at the bottom of the curve. The largest plateau corresponds to words occurring just once (**hapax legomena**, Ancient Greek for "said once").

What appears in the BNC is a general property of natural language: the frequency distributions of lexemes are highly skewed, with few very frequent lexical items and a large number of extremely rare ones. This relationship

between word frequency and rank is modeled by **Zipf's law** (Zipf, 1935, 1949):

$$F(l) = \frac{C}{r(l)^a}. \tag{2.1}$$

Zipf's law states that the frequency of a lexical item, $F(l)$, is inversely proportional to its rank, $r(l)$, given the constants C and a that depend on the text (the value of a is usually very close to 1). The model predicts a very fast decrease of frequency among the first ranks, similar to what happens in Figure 2.1a. If we assume $a = 1$, the most frequent lexeme has rank one and therefore its frequency is equal to C, which corresponds to the highest frequency value in the corpus. The word with rank two is then expected to have half of the top frequency, the word with rank three one-third of the top frequency, and so on. Frequency decrease then slows down as ranks become bigger. The logarithm of a fraction is equal to the difference of the logarithms of its numerator and denominator and $\log x^k$ equals $k \log x$. If we take the logarithm of both sides of Equation 2.1, we thus obtain the equation of a straight line:

$$\log F(l) = \log C - a \log r(l). \tag{2.2}$$

Zipf's law predicts that the logarithm of the frequency of a lexeme decreases linearly as a function of the logarithm of its rank, with intercept $\log C$ and slope $-a$. In Figure 2.1b, the rank–frequency distribution in the BNC is plotted on logarithmic scales on both axes and closely approximates the Zipf's fitting line (the parameters have been estimated using the least squares method: $\log C = 16.19$, $a = 1.01$). The fitting is less perfect for the most frequent words (i.e., frequency decreases slower than expected) and for the least frequent words (i.e., frequency decreases faster than expected). The law was originally proposed by **GEORGE K. ZIPF** (1902–50) and later modified by Benoît Mandelbrot to achieve a better fit with empirical data.

Since frequency is proportional to a negative power ($-a$) of rank, Zipf's law belongs to the family of **power laws**. One crucial property of such distributions

is **scale invariance**, that is, they remain the same whatever scale we look at it on. Figure 2.2 compares the rank–frequency distribution in the BNC with the

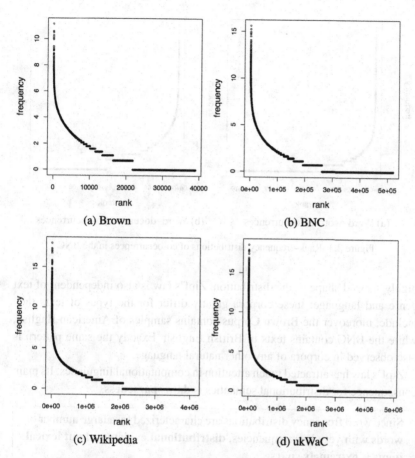

Figure 2.2 Rank–frequency distributions in four lemmatized corpora

same distributions derived from three other English corpora. The Brown Corpus (Francis and Kučera, 1964) contains about a million tokens of American English that was put together at Brown University in the 1960s and 1970s, and is therefore much smaller than BNC, which includes about 100 million tokens. The Wikipedia and the ukWaC (Baroni et al., 2009) corpora are instead much bigger than the BNC: the former consists of a mid-2009 dump of the English Wikipedia of about 820 million tokens and the latter about 1.9 billion tokens of Web texts. Despite their different size, the rank–frequency distribution is the same in the four corpora, and the top frequent words are also very similar (e.g., they include *a*, *and*, *be*, *of*, *the*, and *to*). Bigger corpora have higher word frequencies, but also a proportionally larger number of word types. Therefore, the increase of corpus size only acts as a scaling factor, without changing the

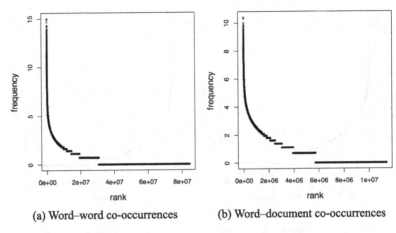

(a) Word–word co-occurrences (b) Word–document co-occurrences

Figure 2.3 Rank–frequency distributions of co-occurrences in the BNC

highly skewed shape of the distribution. Zipf's law is also independent of text genre and language: these corpora greatly differ for the types of texts they include, moreover the Brown Corpus contains samples of American English, while the BNC contains texts of British English. Exactly the same pattern is also observed in corpora of any other natural language.

Zipf's law has attracted much attention in computational linguistics. Its main consequence for distributional semantics is **data sparseness**.

DATA
SPARSENESS

> Since word frequency distributions are characterized by a large number of words with very low frequencies, **distributional evidence about lexical items is extremely sparse**.

In the BNC, almost 260,000 lemmas occur just once, about 50% of all the attested lemmas. The number of lemmas occurring at least ten times is about 91,000, corresponding to just 17% of all lemmas. In ukWaC, the number of lemmas with frequency at least equal to ten is obviously higher than in the BNC (almost 700,000), but it is again a tiny fraction of the corpus vocabulary, around 14%. This is a direct effect of the scale invariance of Zipf's law.

Co-occurrence data also have highly skewed frequencies. A small amount of lexical items are distributionally promiscuous, while most of them only occur in a very limited number of contexts. Figure 2.3 shows the rank–frequency distribution of word–context pairs extracted from the BNC: the contexts in the left plot are the words that co-occur within a distance of five tokens to the left or to the right of the target lexeme (cf. Section 2.2.1), while the contexts in the right plot are documents corresponding to the text samples in the BNC (cf.

Section 2.2.2). In both cases, the large number of low-frequency distributional data is evident. The hapax lexical co-occurrences are about 63% of the whole pairs extracted from the BNC, those occurring at least ten times are just 7% of the total. Complex linguistic constructions have similarly skewed frequencies. Korhonen (2002), Ellis and O'Donnell (2012), and Ellis et al. (2014) show that argument constructions in the BNC have a Zipfian distribution, with few high-frequency constructions and a long tail of low-frequency ones. The distribution of verb types co-occurring with each construction is also Zipfian.

The skewed distribution of language data is a "pain in the neck" for distributional semantics, like for any type of statistical approach to linguistic modeling. Various solutions are adopted to mitigate the negative effects of Zipf's law, such as removing high-frequency words and applying minimum frequency thresholds (cf. Section 2.2), using weighting functions to identify the most informative linguistic contexts (cf. Section 2.3.1), and reducing the dimensionality of distributional data (cf. Section 2.5). As a consequence of data sparseness, for the vast majority of lexical items attested in the training corpus there is not enough evidence about their co-occurrence properties. Therefore, we can build reliable distributional representations only for a tiny fraction of the corpus vocabulary. This has a significant impact on the choice of the training corpus.

2.1.2 Choosing the Training Corpus

The selection of the training corpus is arguably the most important decision, since distributional representations encode the statistical regularities therein. Table 2.1 lists the nearest neighbors (cf. Section 2.6) of *meaning* derived from three English corpora. Clearly, different corpora lead to very different semantic neighborhoods for the same target. This is confirmed by the systematic evaluation carried out by Antoniak and Mimno (2018), which reveals the high degree of variability in distributional representations determined by the composition and size of the training corpus. Moreover, Bolukbasi et al. (2016) and Caliskan et al. (2017) show that distributional representations contain all sorts of stereotypes, including gender biases and negative ethnic and religious prejudices (cf. Section 8.5.2). In fact, this is hardly surprising, since distributional semantic spaces only reflect what is in the linguistic data. Distributional representations encode negative or potentially dangerous stereotypes because these associations are contained in the texts used to train them.

Corpora of many different types are nowadays commonly available for almost every language, domain, and variety. Even if we cannot find an off-the-shelf training corpus that fits our needs, we can assemble one in a reasonably

Table 2.1 Nearest neighbors of *meaning*
computed with the SGNS model (cf. Section
6.3) respectively trained on the BNC, the
Reuters Corpus Volume 1 (RCV1) (Lewis
et al., 2004), and the ukWaC corpus

BNC	RCV1	ukWaC
particularity	significance	denotative
indexical	mean	connotative
referent	terminology	language-game
lexis	ambiguity	truth-conditions
historicity	interpret	signification
existent	jargon	truth-conditional
actualize	phrasing	connotation
predicate	ebonics	signatum
literal	presumption	significance
implicature	confine	givenness

small amount of time by sampling from the huge amounts of digital texts that are available online. This can be performed automatically using a Web crawling program that browses the Web and fetches pages satisfying particular requirements (e.g., language, topic, etc.). Text digitalization programs also allow us to use texts that are not available in electronic format yet, and the latest generation of automatic speech recognizers can be applied to perform fast and reliable transcriptions of large quantities of recorded speech.

How to choose the right training corpus to learn distributional representations? Ideally, we should try to optimize both **qualitative** and **quantitative** criteria by selecting a corpus compiled in such a way to be as **representative** as possible of the language variety we want to model, and at the same time large enough to provide reasonable amounts of distributional evidence about the target lexical items. For example, **balanced corpora** like the BNC and the Corpus of Contemporary American English (COCA) (Davies, 2009) aim at improving representativeness by granting texts of various types a share of the sample composition that is proportional to their supposed relevance in the whole population. In practice, the negative consequences of data sparseness motivate the trend toward larger and larger training corpora, independently of any concern for representativeness. This is consistent with the common assumption in contemporary computational linguistics that "having more training text is normally more useful than any concerns of balance, and one should simply use all the text that is available" (Manning and Schütze, 1999, p. 120).

REPRESENTATIVE
CORPUS

BALANCED
CORPORA

State-of-the-art distributional models are nowadays trained on corpora of several billion words, typically consisting of Web texts. Given the growing availability of digital texts and the increasing power of computational devices, this trend can be expected to continue (cf. Chapter 10). Enlarging the size of the training corpus augments the coverage of the model and smooths the negative impact of data sparseness, thereby improving the quality of distributional representations. For instance, Bullinaria and Levy (2007) show that a model performance always decreases if the corpus size is reduced. Recchia and Jones (2009) also report that a simple distributional measure estimated on large amounts of data correlates better with human similarity judgments than a more sophisticated model trained on a smaller corpus. In fact, the interaction between corpus size and text quality is quite complex. Huge Web corpora can be very noisy and this may negatively affect distributional representations. Sridharan and Murphy (2012) and Lapesa and Evert (2014) show that a smaller corpus of high quality outperforms a much larger corpus of poor quality. However, the method used to learn representations is an important factor as well. Artificial neural networks (cf. Chapter 6) are extremely "text greedy" and achieve suboptimal performances when trained on small corpora (Sahlgren and Lenci, 2016).

On the other hand, there are several research scenarios in which the use of huge training corpora is neither possible nor desirable. In digital humanities, distributional models are applied to ancient languages, used to analyze the lexical space of a literary author, or to study semantic change (cf. Section 8.6). In these cases, training corpora are typically very small, at least in comparison with Web corpora, because of the intrinsically limited number of texts for the target language variety, or of their scarce availability in digital form. Similar problems exist for low-resource languages (e.g., minority, regional, endangered, or heritage languages). Another example is the use of distributional semantics to model language acquisition. Billion-sized Web corpora do not provide the ideal training data for this type of investigation because they are far bigger than and different from the input received by small children in the early phases of language acquisition. For instance, Cristia et al. (2019) report that an average US child is exposed to 25 million words in three years of life. This is the reason why smaller corpora of transcribed child-directed speech, like those in the CHILDES database (MacWhinney, 2000), are a better option to train distributional models to study semantic acquisition (Asr et al., 2016). In such cases, the goal of enhancing the cognitive plausibility of the distributional models downgrades the importance of the corpus size in favor of a closer attention to its representativeness.

Distributional semantic methods can be extremely promising even when applied to limited amounts of textual data, as in these cases, but we must not forget that their results can be heavily affected by data sparseness. Antoniak and Mimno (2018) show that the intrinsic input-dependent variability of semantic spaces drastically increases with small corpora. This means that extreme caution must be exercised when we analyze distributional representations learnt from small amounts of linguistic data.

2.1.3 Corpus Annotation

The type of corpus processing is an important choice to make before training distributional models. Alternatives range from using no preprocessing at all (i.e., training the model on raw data) to using elaborate linguistic annotation, like part-of-speech tagging or dependency parsing. In this section, we summarize some general issues regarding corpus preprocessing and annotation. More information can be found in general NLP textbooks like Manning and Schütze (1999) and Jurafsky and Martin (2008).

Tokenization and Normalization

TOKENIZATION The training corpus must be at least tokenized. **Tokenization** is the process of chopping texts into **tokens**, instances of character strings regarded as basic units for automatic processing. Tokens include words, punctuation, acronyms, numbers, dates, and so on. Tokenization is a preliminary, albeit essential, step to identify lexical items and the elements that can contribute to the specification of their contexts (e.g., punctuation marking sentence boundaries). If the corpus consists of texts crawled from the Web, tokenization is typically preceded by the removal of the markup codes that do not provide useful information for distributional analysis and may hinder the following levels of text processing. The exception is represented by tags that encode the document structure and can be exploited to identify textual units, such as paragraphs and document sections, to be used as contexts (cf. Section 2.2.2). A by-product of tokeniza-

SENTENCE SPLITTING tion is **sentence splitting**, to segment texts into sentences. This is a key aspect of corpus processing because various levels of linguistic analysis, like syntactic parsing, presuppose the correct recognition of sentence boundaries, which are also employed to select linguistic contexts (cf. Section 2.2.1).

Tokenizers mainly rely on the whitespace characters (space or tab) used as orthographic delimiters, and on other shallow textual cues (e.g., punctuation, acronym lists, etc.). In languages that do not separate words with spaces (e.g., Chinese), tokenization is instead a much less trivial task and is typically

WORD SEGMENTATION referred to as **word segmentation** because words must be segmented out of the continuous stream of characters. Word segmentation requires the combined use of lexical analysis, grammatical heuristics, and statistical information.

However, even whitespace is not always a reliable criterion to determine the boundaries of lexical units. In fact, languages contain a wide array of **multiword expressions** (MWEs), combinations of multiple orthographic MULTIWORD EXPRESSIONS words that together form a single lexical item (Sinclair, 1991; Jackendoff, 1997). Examples of MWEs are phrasal verbs (*get up, carry out, call back,* etc.), support (light) verb constructions (*make a decision, take a walk,* etc.), noun compounds (*web page, credit card, information retrieval,* etc.), idioms (*kick the bucket, spill the beans,* etc.), and many other cases (Sag et al., 2002). As lexical items, MWEs can play the role of targets and contexts in distributional models. Tokenizers easily tackle basic MWEs like fixed expressions (e.g., *ad hoc*) and proper names (e.g., *New York*), but most other cases need to be identified with dedicated modules. On the other hand, in languages like German and Finnish most compound terms are written without intervening spaces (e.g., in Finnish the single word *iihmisoikeussopimukseen* corresponds to the complex English expression *convention for human rights*). These are kinds of word sequences "without space" that need to be split into their component lexical units.

Token segmentation is also accompanied by various processes of **text nor-** NORMALIZATION **malization** to deal with capitalized words and spelling variation (e.g., *database* also appears in texts as *data-base* or *data base*). Letter case can provide useful information. Capitalization is often the only distinguishing feature of lexemes that are used both as proper and common nouns. Normalizing case conflates these two distinct usages of the lexeme, and thus introduces ambiguity. However, since capitalization is also used for other purposes (most notably to signal the start of a sentence), there are a large number of lexemes that occur both as capitalized and noncapitalized versions. Therefore, a common strategy is to do **case-folding** by down-casing all tokens. This way, from the sentence *Dogs* CASE-FOLDING *chase dogs* we can extract two occurrences of the same word type *dogs*.

Stemming, Lemmatization, and Part-of-Speech Tagging

Lexemes can be morphologically inflected. Both sentences in (1) contain instances of the lexical items *dog* and *like*, despite the fact that they appear with different inflectional endings:

(1)   a.   The little spotty dog likes cookies.
        b.   The dogs liked to play with the ball.

Moreover, many lexemes are morphosyntactically ambiguous and belong to multiple parts of speech:

(2)   My dog eats like a wolf.

The word *like* in (1) is not the same lexeme as the one appearing in (2): the former is the verb *like*, while the latter is the preposition *like*.

Table 2.2 Tokenized, lemmatized, and
POS-tagged sentences

id	token	lemma	POS
1	The	the	DT
2	little	little	JJ
3	spotty	spotty	JJ
4	dog	dog	NN
5	likes	like	VBZ
6	cookies	cookie	NNS
7	.	.	.
1	The	the	DT
2	dogs	dog	NNS
3	liked	like	VBD
4	to	to	TO
5	play	play	VB
6	with	with	IN
7	the	the	DT
8	ball	ball	NN
9	.	.	.
1	My	my	PRP$
2	dog	dog	NN
3	eats	eat	VBZ
4	like	like	IN
5	a	a	DT
6	wolf	wolf	NN
7	.	.	.

To address these issues, the training corpus can undergo various types of lex-
STEMMING ical analysis. The simplest form is **stemming**, a heuristic process that removes
the ends of words using a simple list of morphological affixes. Stemming
is fast and simple, but produces very approximate normalizations (e.g., by
stripping the suffix *-ed*, *reduced* is normalized as *reduc*, instead of *reduce*),
LEMMATIZATION especially for highly inflected languages. **Lemmatization** usually refers to
a more linguistically informed normalization involving the use of a lexicon
and morphological analysis of words, normally aiming to remove inflectional
endings only and to return the base or dictionary form of a word, which is
POS TAGGING known as the lemma. **Part-of-speech (POS) tagging** instead is a process of
morphosyntactic disambiguation that assigns to each token its part of speech.

Table 2.2 reports the sentences in (1) and (2) tokenized, lemmatized, and
POS-tagged with *Stanza*, a suite of integrated natural language analysis tools
(Qi et al., 2020). The numbers in the first column uniquely identify each token
in a sentence. Full stops are correctly treated as distinct tokens marking sen-

tence boundaries, even if there is no whitespace between them and the previous word. The second column contains the output of the lemmatizer, and the tokens *likes*, *liked*, and *like* have been associated with the lemma *like*. The third column specifies the POS codes, according to the Penn Treebank tag set, assigned to each token by the tagger. The tokens *like* in (1a) and (1b) are identified as verbs (VBZ and VBD, respectively, correspond to the third singular present and the past verb forms), while in (2) the same string is identified as a preposition (corresponding to the IN tag). Given the text in Table 2.2, we identify three instances of the lemma *dog*, two co-occurring with the verb *like* and one with the preposition *like*.

Lemmatization and POS tagging are the most common and basic levels of corpus analysis in distributional semantics. By generalizing over inflected forms, lemmatization reduces the effect of sparse data, as the frequencies of the individual lexemes increase. The POS tagging can help cope with morphosyntactic ambiguities, though it aggravates data sparseness by distinguishing co-occurrences with different POS. On the negative side, both processes are not error-free and therefore generate further noise in the distributional analysis.

Parsing

Syntactic parsing (or simply **parsing**) refers to the identification of the syntactic analysis (**parse**) of a sentence. **Shallow parsing** (or **chunking**) con- CHUNKING sists in a flat segmentation into syntagmatic units to obtain an underspecified representation of the sentence structure. This is the output of chunking (1a):

(3)   [NP The little spotty dog] [VP likes] [NP cookies].

Full (or **deep**) **parsing** aims at reconstructing the full-fledged syntactic structure of sentences. **Phrase-structure parsing** represents syntactic analyses in PHRASE-terms of recursive phrase structure trees. The following is the phrase structure STRUCTURE analysis of (1a) by the *Stanza* parser: PARSING

(4)   (ROOT (S (NP (DT The) (JJ little) (JJ spotty) (NN dog)) (VP (VBZ likes) (NP (NNS cookies))) (. .)))

Dependency parsing instead represents the syntactic structure in terms of a DEPENDENCY directed graph whose nodes correspond to lexical items and edges are labeled PARSING with **dependency relations** (Tesnière, 1959). The example in (5) shows the syntactic analysis of (1a) according to the Universal Dependencies[1] annotation scheme (de Marneffe et al., 2014) produced by the *Stanza* parser:

---

[1] https://universaldependencies.org/.

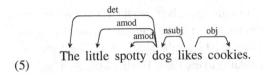

(5)   The little spotty dog likes cookies.

The contrast between shallow and full parsing is evident in the examples discussed. While chunking does not distinguish between the subject and direct object of the input sentence, this information is implicitly represented by their different position in the phrase-structure tree in (4), and explicitly encoded by the dependencies in (5). Despite the prima facie differences, dependency and phrase-structure representations are instead almost interchangeable (Manning and Schütze, 1999). Dependency parsing has become increasingly popular in NLP, and is surely the preferred approach to syntactic analysis in distributional semantics. The main reason is that labeled dependencies provide an easy and straightforward way to identify syntactic co-occurrences.

Parsing is a time-consuming process and still produces several errors, depending on the type of language and text. Moreover, the added cost of parsing training corpora does not always determine a significant improvement of the distributional representation quality (cf. Section 2.2.1 and Chapter 7).

2.2 Extracting Co-occurrences

Given a set of **target lexemes**, the first step in building distributional representations is to extract their **co-occurrences** with **linguistic contexts** from the training corpus.[2] We represent co-occurrences as target–context pairs.

CO-
OCCURRENCES

> Let $T = \{t_1, \ldots, t_m\}$ be a set of target lexemes and $C = \{c_1, \ldots, c_n\}$ a set of contexts. The **distribution** of T with C, $D_{T,C}$, is a list of pairs $\langle t, c \rangle$, each recording an individual **co-occurrence** of the target $t \in T$ with the context $c \in C$ in a training corpus.

TARGET
LEXEMES

The target lexemes T are a subset of the **vocabulary** V that contains all the lexical **types** in the corpus.[3] Targets are selected according to different criteria such as **frequency**, **POS**, and so on. Importantly, target frequency in the training corpus must be high enough to collect a reasonable amount of distributional evidence. Bullinaria and Levy (2007) show that the quality of distributional representations is lower for rare words. Therefore, T usually includes lexical

---

[2] Unless differently specified, in this chapter we assume that the training corpus is at least lemmatized and POS-tagged.

[3] See Sections 8.2 and 9.6.3 for distributional models whose targets are instead lexical tokens.

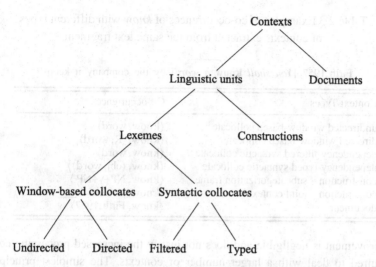

Figure 2.4 Main types of linguistic contexts in distributional semantics

types whose frequency is above a certain threshold. The **frequency threshold** FREQUENCY
is determined heuristically and obviously depends on the corpus size, but it THRESHOLD
is advisable to exclude at least the words that occur less than 50 times. Since
the vast majority of lexical items in V have very low frequency (cf. Section
2.1.1), T covers only a small fraction of the corpus vocabulary. Targets can be
morphologically inflected lexemes (e.g., *runs* and *ran* count as distinct targets),
lemmas (e.g., the distribution of the target *run* includes the co-occurrences of
its inflected forms), or POS-disambiguated lemmas (e.g., the noun *run* and the
verb *run* are treated as distinct targets).

Distributional representations differ for the type of linguistic context (cf.
Figure 2.4 and Table 2.3). The main distinction is between modeling contexts
with *co-occurring linguistic units* or with *documents*.

2.2.1 Contexts as Co-occurring Linguistic Units

The most common type of linguistic context in distributional semantics is the
"company" of lexemes co-occurring with the target. These context lexemes are COLLOCATES
also called **collocates** (Firth, 1957; Sinclair, 1991; cf. Section 1.1.3).

The **context lexemes** $C_l = \{l_1, \ldots, l_n\}$ are a subset of the corpus vocabulary V, possibly coinciding with the targets T. The number of contexts CONTEXT
greatly varies in the literature and depends on the corpus size, but a typi- LEXEMES
cal value is between 10,000 and 50,000. Kiela and Clark (2014) and Lapesa
and Evert (2014) show that, beyond these numbers, the model's performance

Table 2.3 Examples of co-occurrences of *know* with different types
of contexts extracted from the same text fragment

Firth_1957. [*You shall* **know** *a word*] by the company it keeps!

Context Types	Co-occurrences
undirected window-based collocate	$\langle$know, word$\rangle$
directed window-based collocate	$\langle$know, $\langle$R, word$\rangle\rangle$
dependency-filtered syntactic collocate	$\langle$know, word$\rangle$
dependency-typed syntactic collocate	$\langle$know, $\langle$obj, word$\rangle\rangle$
construction – subcategorization frame	$\langle$know, NP+v+NP $\rangle$
construction – joint context	$\langle$know, you shall ___ a word $\rangle$
document	$\langle$know, Firth_1957$\rangle$

improvement is negligible and does not justify the increased processing cost required to deal with a larger number of contexts. The simplest principle for context selection is **frequency** (for other criteria, cf. Section 2.3.2): V is ordered by decreasing frequency and the top n lexemes are selected as contexts. It is also customary to filter out some words that are not informative from the semantic point of view. These are called **stop words** and include the most frequent lexemes in any corpus (cf. Section 2.1.1), such as grammatical function words (prepositions, conjunctions, articles, etc.) and "semantically light" lexemes (e.g., *have*, *man*, etc.). Knowing that a word co-occurs with *the* is relevant to characterize its morphosyntactic properties as a noun, but not to discriminate its semantic content because articles tend to co-occur with any noun. Like for target selection, it is important to set a lower **frequency threshold** for context lexemes because rare words are unreliable to build distributional representations (Bullinaria and Levy, 2007). Frequency thresholding can be done as a preprocessing step either by removing the words from the corpus data or by ignoring the words during co-occurrence extraction. Depending on corpus processing, C_l includes morphologically inflected lexemes (e.g., *runs* and *ran* are distinct contexts), lemmas (e.g., the inflected forms of *run* are the same context), or POS-disambiguated lemmas (e.g., the noun *run* and the verb *run* are treated as distinct contexts).

STOP WORDS

FREQUENCY
THRESHOLD

The type of co-occurrence relation between target and context lexemes determines different kinds of collocates and consequently different kinds of distributional representations.

Window-based Collocates

The **window-based collocates** of a target t are context lexemes that occur within a certain linear distance from t specified by a **context window**. This

CONTEXT
WINDOW

is the most common way to characterize lexical collocates, directly derived from the Firthian tradition of collocation analysis.

> A context lexeme $l \in C_l$ is a **window-based collocate** of a target t if and only if l occurs inside a **context window** surrounding t.
> **Window-based co-occurrences** are co-occurrences in which the context is a window-based collocate of the target.

Given the context window in (6), we derive the co-occurrences $\langle dog, little \rangle$, $\langle dog, spotty \rangle$, $\langle dog, enjoy \rangle$, and $\langle dog, run \rangle$, each containing a window-based collocate of *dog*: WINDOW-BASED CO-OCCURRENCES

(6)   The [*little spotty* **dog** *enjoys running*] and jumping.

In this case, *jump* is not a collocate of *dog*, because it occurs outside the window. The context window is normally advanced one target at a time until all the co-occurrences are extracted – hence the name of **sliding window**. Context windows are defined by the following parameters:

Unit – The default units to measure the window size are word tokens (a WINDOW UNIT less common option is characters, see Schütze, 1992). A further parameter is whether all tokens (with the possible exception of punctuation, numbers, etc.) or instead some subset of lexemes are used to compute the window span. For instance, it is possible to determine the window size by counting the context lexemes in C_l only. In (7b), the extension of a $[3, 3]$ window is computed by considering only verbs, nouns, and adjectives, while in (7a) the span of same window is determined using all word tokens:

(7)   a.   The cat and [*the little spotty* **dog** *jumped into the*] big red car.
       b.   The [*cat and the little spotty* **dog** *jumped into the big red*] car.

Size – The size of a context window is defined by pairs of integers $[m, n]$ WINDOW SIZE that fix the number of units to the left of the target (its left span m), and the number of units to the right of the target (its right span n). The total size k of a window $[m, n]$ is given by $m + n + 1$. If $m = n$, the window is said to be **symmetric** with respect to the target, otherwise the window is **asymmetric**. Example (8) contains an asymmetric window $[2, 5]$:

(8)   The cat and the [*little spotty* **dog** *jumped into the big red*] car.

If $m = 0$, the window extends only to the right of the target, which marks its left border (9a); if $n = 0$, the window instead extends only to the left of the target, which marks its right border (9b):

(9)   a.   The cat and the little spotty [**dog** *jumped into the big red*] car.

         b.   The [*cat and the little spotty* **dog**] jumped into the big red car.

The context window size can also be determined by the length of the text units (typically sentences) in which the target occurs, instead of being fixed a priori. In this case, the window span is variable because it depends on the text unit size, and a context lexeme is a collocate of the target if and only if they co-occur in the same text unit.

WINDOW
BOUNDARY

Boundary – The context window can cross or not sentence and/or paragraph boundaries. The same $[5, 5]$ window extends beyond the sentence boundary in (10a), but not in (10b):

(10)   a.   The car stopped in front of [*the house. The little spotty* **dog** *ran and jumped into the*] car.

         b.   The car stopped in front of the house. [*The little spotty* **dog** *ran and jumped into the*] car.

WINDOW
DIRECTION

UNDIRECTED
COLLOCATES

Direction – Context windows can be **undirected** or **directed**. The former do not distinguish between context lexemes appearing to the left and to the right of the target. We refer to these contexts as **undirected collocates**. Given an undirected window, we extract from (11) two tokens of the same window-based co-occurrence $\langle chase, dog \rangle$:

(11)   Yesterday, [*the black dog* **chased** *the white dog*] in the garden.

DIRECTED
COLLOCATES

On the other hand, directed windows treat context lexemes appearing to the left and to the right of the target as different collocates. We refer to them as **directed collocates**, which we represent as pairs $\langle p, l \rangle$, such that $p \in \{$L(EFT), R(IGHT)$\}$ and $l \in C_l$. Given a directed window, we extract from (11) two distinct co-occurrence pairs, $\langle chase, \langle$L$, dog \rangle \rangle$ and $\langle chase, \langle$R$, dog \rangle \rangle$. Directed collocates encode syntactic information related to word order (e.g., subjects tend to occur to the left of the verb in English declarative sentences). On the other hand, the number of contexts doubles (if $|C_l| = n$, we obtain $2n$ directed collocates), and data sparseness increases, because collocates occurring to the left and to the right of the target are treated as distinct co-occurrence counts.

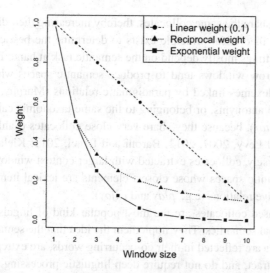

Figure 2.5 Collocate weighting as a function of the window size

Shape – In **rectangular windows**, all collocates are treated alike inde- <small>WINDOW SHAPE</small>
pendently of their distance from the target. Alternatively, collocates may
be weighted as a function of their distance from the target. In **triangu-
lar windows**, closer collocates are assigned higher weights than more
distant ones, consistently with the hypothesis that context lexemes near
to the target are more relevant to characterize its meaning (Bullinaria
and Levy, 2007). Figure 2.5 shows some weighting schemes for trian-
gular windows. The linear distance weighting decreases the weight of
some constant (in this case 0.1) for every step away from the target lexeme. The reciprocal and exponential weightings assign to a collocate the
weight respectively according to the formulas $\frac{1}{n}$ and 2^{1-n}, where n is
the collocate distance from the target. These latter weighting schemes
determine a faster decrease in the salience of farther context lexemes.

The choice of the context window, in particular its size, deeply affects the
type of collocates that are extracted for a given target:

(12)   The man played the violin, the woman played the guitar, and the
        audience enjoyed their music.

If we select a very narrow window (e.g., [2,2]), *play* and *enjoy* have different
collocates (e.g., *man* and *audience*, respectively), and therefore different distributional properties. Using a context window spanning the whole sentence

the two verbs share the same collocates, thereby increasing their distributional similarity. No theoretical principle exists to determine the best context window and its settings mostly depend on the semantic task at hand. Experiments show that narrow windows tend to produce semantic spaces whose nearest elements are lexemes linked by paradigmatic relations (Murphy, 2003), like synonyms and antonyms, or belonging to the same taxonomic category (e.g., *violin* and *guitar*), because they share very close collocates (Sahlgren, 2006; Bullinaria and Levy, 2007, 2012; Baroni and Lenci, 2011; Kiela and Clark, 2014). Conversely, collocates extracted with larger context windows typically generate semantic spaces whose closest elements are lexical items linked by more associative relations (e.g., *play* and *enjoy*).

Window-based collocates are the most popular kind of linguistic contexts in distributional semantics. They implement the idea that the semantic properties of lexemes are reflected in their co-occurring words, are extremely simple and fast to extract, and do not require deep linguistic processing of the training corpus (even a simply tokenized text may suffice). On the other hand, window-based collocates do not take into account linguistic structures. Context windows are in fact treated as sums of independent words ignoring any sort of syntactic information. This view of linguistic contexts, known in the lit-

BAG-OF-WORDS
MODEL

erature as **bag-of-words model** (Manning et al., 2008), provides a very shallow and impoverished representation of their structure. As Harris correctly claims, "language is not merely a bag of words" (Harris, 1954, p. 17).

Syntactic Collocates

The **syntactic collocates** of a target t are lexemes that have a syntactic relation with t. The standard way to identify syntactic collocates is in terms of

DEPENDENCY
RELATIONS

dependency relations (cf. Section 2.1.3).

> A context lexeme $l \in C_l$ is a **syntactic collocate** of a target t if and only if there is a syntactic dependency relation between t and l.
> **Syntactic co-occurrences** are co-occurrences in which the context is a syntactic collocate of the target.

SYNTACTIC CO-
OCCURRENCES

The co-occurrences of *dog* derived from (13) are $\langle dog, little \rangle$, $\langle dog, spotty \rangle$, $\langle dog, garden \rangle$, and $\langle dog, chase \rangle$, each containing a syntactic collocate:

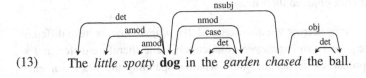

(13)   The *little spotty* **dog** in the *garden chased* the ball.

Syntactic collocates have the following parameters:

Relation type – the set of dependencies we select to identify the collo- RELATION TYPE
cates. For example, we can use only the dependencies that refer to the
core arguments in a sentence (e.g., subject, direct object, etc.), or instead
include inter-clausal relations too.

Path length – the number of dependency edges separating the target and PATH LENGTH
the collocate. In (13) *dog* and *chase* have a path of length one, because
there is just one dependency relation between them. Conversely, *dog* and
ball have a dependency path of length two. The most common choice
is to restrict contexts to syntactic collocates with dependency path of
length one, that is **direct syntactic relations**, but longer dependency
paths are also used to select collocates linked by **indirect syntactic
relations** (Padó and Lapata, 2007).

Filtering versus typing – Syntactic dependencies can be used to iden- FILTERING
tify the syntactic collocates, without entering into the specification of VERSUS TYPING
the contexts themselves. We refer to them as **dependency-filtered col-** DEPENDENCY-
locates. In this case, identical lexemes linked to the target by different FILTERED
dependency relations as in (14) are mapped onto the same context: COLLOCATES

(14)   Yesterday, the black dog chased the white dog in the garden.

Therefore, two tokens of the same co-occurrence type $\langle chase, dog \rangle$
are extracted from (14). Alternatively, syntactic dependencies can type
the collocates by being encoded in the contexts. We refer to them as
dependency-typed collocates, which we represent as pairs $\langle r, l \rangle$, such DEPENDENCY-
that r is a dependency relation and $l \in C_l$. Two distinct co-occurrences TYPED
with typed collocates are extracted from (14), $\langle chase, \langle nsubj, dog \rangle \rangle$ and COLLOCATES
$\langle chase, \langle obj, dog \rangle \rangle$. Typing collocates with dependency relations captures more fine-grained syntactic distinctions, but on the other hand
produces a much larger number of distinct contexts and increases data
sparseness.

Syntactic co-occurrences are attractive because they take into account the
linguistic structure of contexts, which cannot be reduced to the linear relations recorded by sliding windows. On the negative side, identifying syntactic
collocates is more complex, because they need to be extracted from parsed corpora (cf. Section 2.1.3). Parsing is a time-consuming process and errors, which
are still quite frequent in current systems, introduce a large amount of noise.

An empirical issue is estimating the actual contribution of syntactic information to distributional representations. Some experiments suggest that syntactic collocates tend to generate semantic spaces whose nearest elements are taxonomically related lexemes, mainly co-hyponyms (Peirsman et al., 2007; Van de Cruys, 2008; Levy and Goldberg, 2014a). However, these semantic relations are also captured with narrow context windows, showing that there is a strong overlap between window-based and syntactic collocates under certain parameter settings. In general, the question whether syntactic information provides a real advantage over bag-of-words representations of contexts is still open and highly dependent on the semantic task (Kiela and Clark, 2014; Lapesa and Evert, 2017; Lenci et al., 2022).

Constructional Contexts

Collocate-based distributional representations record co-occurrences of lexemes one independently from the other, and treat each co-occurring lexeme as a distinct context. However, the meaning of lexical items is also related to more structurally complex aspects of their linguistic contexts. Two verbs may share independent collocates despite being very dissimilar from the semantic point of view. In (15), *kill* and *heal* have the same direct objects but are highly different if we consider the subject-object combination as a single context:

(15)   a.   The doctor healed the patient.
        b.   The poison killed the patient.

The meaning of a lexeme is also strongly correlated with its syntactic environments (Levin, 1993; Levin and Rappaport Hovav, 2005). For instance, verbs like *give* and *send* can occur with the prepositional construction NP+v+NP+PP-*to* (e.g., *The man gave a bone to the dog*) and the ditransitive NP+v+NP$_1$+NP$_2$ one (e.g., *The man gave the dog a bone*), such that the argument realized as PP-*to* in the former is realized as NP$_1$ in the latter. Instead, verbs like *donate* and *contribute* only admit the prepositional construction.

In addition to lexical collocates, complex linguistic structures can be employed as contexts to learn distributional representations. We use the term CONSTRUCTION **construction** to refer to patterns of linguistic items.

> A **construction** is any kind of complex lexico-syntactic structure.

Constructions differ in their level of complexity and schematicity (Hoffman and Trousdale, 2013). They span from fully specified structures (e.g., *The player kicked the ball*), to abstract structures such as argument patterns (e.g., the transitive construction), passing through partially lexicalized constructions with various degrees of abstractness and idiomaticity (e.g., *take* NP *for granted*).

Schulte im Walde (2006, 2009) and Sun and Korhonen (2009) use schematic constructions representing **subcategorization frames** to identify verbs belonging to the same semantic classes. Consider the following sentences:

(16)   a.   The little spotty dog wants to **eat**.
       b.   The little spotty dog **ate** the bone.
       c.   The man **knows** that the little spotty dog enjoys running.
       d.   The man **knows** the story about the little spotty dog.

If the contexts are the constructions NP+v+NP (transitive construction), NP+v (intransitive construction), and NP+v+S-*that* (*that*-complement construction), we extract from (16) the co-occurrences $\langle eat,$ NP+$v\rangle$, $\langle eat,$ NP+v+NP$\rangle$, $\langle know,$ NP+v+S-*that*$\rangle$, and $\langle know,$ NP+v+NP$\rangle$.

Melamud et al. (2014) represent the distributional properties of verbs with lexicalized constructions called **joint contexts**, which consist of window-based lexical patterns surrounding a target word. For instance, the joint context of *eat* in (16b) is the lexical pattern *the little spotty __ the bone*. Chersoni et al. (2016) use a structured variant of joint contexts, formed by the syntactic dependencies headed by the target lexeme. In this case, the context of *eat* in (16b) is the syntactic construction *dog*-nsubj __ *bone*-obj. joint contexts

2.2.2 Contexts as Documents

Documents can be used as contexts for the lexemes occurring therein.

> **Documents** are uniquely identifiable text samples (e.g., books, web pages, newspaper articles, chapters, paragraphs, sentences, dialogue turns, etc.).
> **Document co-occurrences** are co-occurrences such that the context is a document in which the target appears.

In the following example, Harris' article *Distributional Structure* and Wittgenstein's book *Philosophical Investigations* are assumed as the contexts of the target lexemes *meaning* and *use*: document co-occurrences

(17)   Harris (1954): "[...] difference of **meaning** correlates with difference of distribution."
        Wittgenstein (1953): "[...] the **meaning** of a word is its **use** in the language."

We thus extract from (17) the document co-occurrences ⟨*meaning*, Harris (1954)⟩, ⟨*use*, (Wittgenstein, 1953)⟩, and ⟨*meaning*, (Wittgenstein, 1953)⟩.

The use of document as contexts derives from the vector space model in information retrieval (cf. Section 1.2.1), whose basic ingredients are lexemes (or **terms** in information retrieval terminology) and documents, and the primary semantic relation is that of **topicality**, or **aboutness**. In order for a document to be relevant to a query it must match the topic of the query: It must be *about* the topic being queried for. Topicality is normally operationalized as term overlap. If the query asks for *distributional semantics*, the documents should minimally contain this term (or, in more sophisticated models, some other term with the same topicality). Documents, or texts, are thus represented with their lexeme distribution, and, symmetrically, lexical items with their distribution in texts, where these can be regarded as "episodes" (Landauer and Dumais, 1997) that become associated with the words therein encountered. Therefore, lexemes are similar to the extent that they appear in the same episodes.

TOPICALITY

A document is a somewhat imprecise notion of a linguistic context, since it contains a large number of items that may not be related to the target lexeme. Furthermore, documents are represented according to the bag-of-words model, and are simply viewed as a sum of independent words. On the other hand, there are several advantages to using documents as contexts which also explain their widespread use in distributional semantics. Modeling contexts as documents is in fact an easy and straightforward way to represent lexeme distributions, since it requires a very limited amount of text processing. Given the bag-of-words assumption, collecting distributional evidence about a target lexeme amounts to recording its occurrences in each document in the training corpus.

2.3 The Co-occurrence Matrix

The standard way to represent distributional data extracted from a training corpus is to arrange them in a **co-occurrence matrix**. Given the distribution $D_{T,C}$ of the targets $T = \{t_1, \ldots, t_m\}$ with the contexts $C = \{c_1, \ldots, c_n\}$:

CO-OCCURRENCE FREQUENCY

1. The tokens of all co-occurrence pair types in $D_{T,C}$ are counted to obtain the **co-occurrence frequency** of the targets with the linguistic contexts:

> The **co-occurrence frequency** of $t \in T$ with $c \in C$, $F(t, c)$, is the number of pairs $\langle t, c \rangle$ in $D_{T,C}$.

WEIGHTING FUNCTION

2. A **weighting function** uses co-occurrence frequency to estimate the informativeness of contexts to characterize the target lexemes:

Mathematical note 1 – matrices and vectors

A **matrix** is a two-dimensional array of numbers:

$$\mathbf{A} = \begin{pmatrix} a_{11} & a_{12} & \dots & a_{1n} \\ a_{21} & a_{22} & \dots & a_{2n} \\ \vdots & \vdots & \ddots & \vdots \\ a_{m1} & a_{m2} & \dots & a_{mn} \end{pmatrix}$$

The **size** of a matrix is given by the numbers of its rows and columns. The size of a matrix with m rows and n columns is $m \times n$; $n \times n$ matrices are called **square matrices**. We use upper case letters to refer to matrices and we indicate size with subscripts ($\mathbf{A}_{m \times n}$). The scalar values in a matrix are called **entries** and are represented with subscripts referring to their row and column: $a_{i,j}$ is the entry in the ith row and jth column of matrix $\mathbf{A}$.

The rows and columns of a matrix are vectors. A real-valued **vector** is an ordered list of real numbers $(v_1, ..., v_n)$, where each number v_i is the ith component of the vector. Vectors can be treated as matrices with only one row (**row vectors** of size $1 \times n$) or only one column (**column vectors** of size $m \times 1$). We use lowercase boldface letters ($\mathbf{u}$, $\mathbf{v}$, $\mathbf{w}$, etc.) to denote vectors, and subscripts to refer to the component values from 1 to n (e.g., if $\mathbf{a} = (3, 1, 3)$, $a_2 = 1$). We refer to entire rows (or columns) in a matrix by replacing the second (or first) index with an asterisk and using a bold lower-case symbol to emphasize that we are referring to vectors: $\mathbf{m}_{i,*}$ is the ith row vector, and $\mathbf{m}_{*,j}$ is the jth column vector.

The **weighting function** $W : T \times C \to \mathbb{R}$ assigns to each co-occurrence pair $\langle t, c \rangle$ a real-valued **weight** $w_{t,c}$ that depends on $F(t, c)$.

3. The weighted co-occurrences are arranged in a **co-occurrence matrix** with size $|T| \times |C|$:

CO-OCCURRENCE MATRIX

The **co-occurrence matrix** $\mathbf{M}$ is a $|T| \times |C|$ matrix such that rows are labeled with $t_i \in T$, columns are labeled with $c_j \in C$, and each entry m_{t_i, c_j} corresponds to w_{t_i, c_j}:

$$\begin{array}{c} \\ t_1 \\ t_2 \\ \vdots \\ t_m \end{array} \begin{array}{cccc} c_1 & c_2 & \dots & c_n \end{array} \\ \begin{pmatrix} w_{t_1,c_1} & w_{t_1,c_2} & \vdots & w_{t_1,c_n} \\ w_{t_2,c_1} & w_{t_2,c_2} & \vdots & w_{t_2,c_n} \\ \vdots & \vdots & \ddots & \vdots \\ w_{t_m,c_1} & w_{t_m,c_2} & \vdots & w_{t_m,c_n} \end{pmatrix}$$

Suppose we have extracted and counted the co-occurrences of the targets $T = \{bike, car, dog, lion\}$ with the context lexemes $C = \{bite, buy, drive, eat, get, live, park, ride, tell\}$ in a corpus, obtaining this frequency distribution:

(18)

t	c	$F(t,c)$	t	c	$F(t,c)$
bike	buy	9	dog	eat	9
bike	get	12	dog	get	10
bike	park	8	dog	live	7
bike	ride	6	dog	tell	1
car	buy	13	lion	bite	6
car	drive	8	lion	eat	1
car	get	15	lion	get	8
car	park	5	lion	live	3

RAW
FREQUENCY
The simplest kind of co-occurrence weighting function uses **raw frequency**. The distribution in (18) is represented with the co-occurrence matrix $\mathbf{M}_{|T| \times |C|}$, where $m_{t,c} = F(t,c)$, and $m_{t,c} = 0$, if t never co-occurs with c:

(19)

$$
\begin{array}{c}
 \\
bike \\
car \\
dog \\
lion
\end{array}
\begin{array}{ccccccccc}
bite & buy & drive & eat & get & live & park & ride & tell \\
\left(\begin{array}{ccccccccc}
0 & 9 & 0 & 0 & 12 & 0 & 8 & 6 & 0 \\
0 & 13 & 8 & 0 & 15 & 0 & 5 & 0 & 0 \\
0 & 0 & 0 & 9 & 10 & 7 & 0 & 0 & 1 \\
6 & 0 & 0 & 1 & 8 & 3 & 0 & 0 & 0
\end{array} \right)
\end{array}
$$

WORD-BY-
WORD
MATRIX
A matrix like (19), with rows labeled with target lexemes and columns with context lexemes, is called **word-by-word** matrix. Analogously, a matrix whose columns are labeled with documents is called **word-by-document** matrix.

2.3.1 Co-occurrence Weighting Functions

One of the main tenets of distributional semantics is that co-occurrence frequency is a crucial clue to estimating the importance of distributional data in characterizing a target lexeme. Co-occurrences can also be weighted with a **binary function**, such that $w_{t,c} = 1$, if t co-occurs with c, regardless of its
BINARY
WEIGHTING
FUNCTION
frequency, otherwise $w_{t,c} = 0$ (Manning and Schütze, 1999). The limit of the binary function is that it is not able to discriminate casual co-occurrences from significant ones. The mere fact that t co-occurs with c does not suffice to qualify c as a relevant context for t. However, weighting co-occurrences with their raw frequency, like in (19), turns out not to be the optimal solution because of the skewed distribution of language data, with few very frequent lexical

log freq. $\quad 1 + \log F(t, c)$ cond. prob. $\quad p(c|t) = \dfrac{F(t, c)}{F(t, *)}$

PMI $\quad \log_2 \dfrac{p(t, c)}{p(t)p(c)}$ t-test $\quad \dfrac{p(t, c) - p(t)p(c)}{\sqrt{p(t)p(c)}}$

idf $\quad \log \dfrac{|C|}{|t, *|}$ entropy $\quad 1 + \displaystyle\sum_{j=1}^{n} \dfrac{p(t, d_j) \log_2 p(t, d_j)}{\log_2 |C|}$

Figure 2.6 Most common weighting functions in distributional semantics

items and a large number of extremely rare ones (cf. Section 2.1.1). Frequent lexemes tend to co-occur with many different words. Such co-occurrences are uninformative, even if they are very frequent, since they lack semantic discriminative power. Because of these artifacts introduced by the frequency distribution of co-occurrence counts, distributional representations use various forms of **weighting functions** aiming to overcome the problems of raw WEIGHTING frequencies and to assign higher weights to co-occurrences that are more FUNCTION important to characterize the content of the target lexemes. In this section, we present some popular weighting functions in distributional semantics (see Figure 2.6), using the following notation (see Lin, 1998a; Curran and Moens, 2002; Curran, 2003):

$F(t, *)$ - total frequency of the co-occurrence pairs with target $t \in T$:

$$F(t, *) = \sum_{j=1}^{n} F(t, c_j). \qquad (2.3)$$

$F(*, c)$ - total frequency of the co-occurrence pairs with context $c \in C$:

$$F(*, c) = \sum_{i=1}^{m} F(t_i, c). \qquad (2.4)$$

$F(*, *)$ - total frequency of co-occurrence pairs:

$$F(*, *) = \sum_{i=1}^{m} \sum_{j=1}^{n} F(t_i, c_j). \qquad (2.5)$$

Frequency Transformations

The skewed word frequencies in corpora can misrepresent their distributional similarities, so that words with (dis)similar frequency end up having more (dis)similar representations than they actually are (Lowe, 2000, 2001; Padó and Lapata, 2007). Consider the third column in Table 2.4, reporting co-occurrence data extracted from ukWaC: $F(truck, drive)$ is closer to $F(dog, drive)$ and $F(lion, drive)$, than to $F(car, drive)$; symmetrically, $F(lion, eat)$ is closer to $F(car, eat)$ and $F(truck, eat)$ than to $F(dog, eat)$. This distorted picture follows from the large disparity in frequency between the targets. In ukWaC, *car* is much more frequent than *truck* (about 600,000 vs. 30,000), and *dog* is much more frequent than *lion* (about 180,000 vs. 17,000). Obviously, their co-occurrence counts are also proportionally very different. Therefore, if the distributional representations of *car* and *truck* contained raw co-occurrence frequencies, they would eventually look more different than they should be, and analogously for the representations of *dog* and *lion*.

LOGARITHMIC
TRANSFORMA-
TION

Some of the negative effects of frequency distributions in corpora can be addressed with simple mathematical transformations of raw co-occurrence counts, such as the **logarithmic transformation**:

$$1 + \log F(t, c). \tag{2.6}$$

Because $\log 1 = 0$, we add one to the log frequency to ensure that pairs occurring once are not zeroed. The logarithm dampens big numbers and shrinks large differences: $100,000 - 10,000$ is much bigger than $100 - 10$, but after their logarithmic transformation, they become identical (i.e., 2.30). The general effect of the logarithmic transformation is to smooth frequency distributions, giving less weight to high-frequency co-occurrences. As shown in Table 2.4, $F(car, drive) = 17,217$ and $F(truck, drive) = 1,108$, but $1 + \log F(car, drive) = 10.75$ and $1 + \log F(truck, drive) = 8.01$. The log transformation thus shrinks the gap between the linguistic distribution of *truck*

SQUARE ROOT
TRANSFORMA-
TION

and *car*, thereby enhancing the similarity of their distributions. An analogous effect is achieved with the **square root transformation**, $\sqrt{F(t, c)}$. The square root reduces the skewness of the frequency distribution, albeit more moderately than the logarithm.

From the co-occurrence counts in Table 2.4, we would also erroneously infer that the verb *eat* is a more important context for *car* than for *lion*, simply because $F(car, eat)$ is larger than $F(lion, eat)$. This again follows from ignoring the frequency difference between the two targets and can be avoided

CONDITIONAL
PROBABILITY

by normalizing $F(t, c)$ with respect to $F(t, *)$. This corresponds to computing the **conditional probability** of the context given the target:

$$p(c|t) = \frac{F(t, c)}{F(t, *)}. \tag{2.7}$$

Table 2.4 Co-occurrence frequencies from ukWaC within a [5, 5] context window, together with their logarithmic and conditional probability transformations. In this example,
$$F(t, *) = F(t, drive) + F(t, eat)$$

t	c	$F(t, c)$	$1 + \log F(t, c)$	$F(t, *)$	$p(c|t)$
car	drive	17, 217	10.75	17, 524	0.98
dog	drive	263	6.57	1, 669	0.16
lion	drive	33	4.50	270	0.12
truck	drive	1, 108	8.01	1, 136	0.97
car	eat	307	6.73	17, 524	0.02
dog	eat	1, 406	8.25	1, 669	0.84
lion	eat	237	6.47	270	0.88
truck	eat	28	4.33	1, 136	0.02

After normalization, $p(eat|car) = 0.02$ and $p(eat|lion) = 0.88$, and therefore *eat* receives a much higher weight when it co-occurs with *lion*, despite the low value of $F(lion, eat)$. Vice versa, *drive* and *eat* have the same conditional probability with respect to *car* and *truck*, thereby canceling the bias due to the frequency gap between these two targets.

Association Measures

Co-occurrence frequency is not always indicative of the information provided by distributional data about the content of target lexemes. For instance, in ukWaC *dog* co-occurs with *get* more than twice it co-occurs with *bark*, but *bark* is surely a more informative context about the meaning of *dog* than *get*. Frequency transformations can help in smoothing skewed frequencies, but they are not able to address this issue. In fact, even if we turned frequencies into probabilities, the co-occurrence pair ⟨*dog, get*⟩ would still receive a higher weight than ⟨*dog, bark*⟩. In order to obtain a better estimation of the informativeness of distributional data, co-occurrences are weighted with **association scores** ASSOCIATION that measure the strength of association between the target and the context as a SCORES function not only of their joint frequency, but also of their general distribution in the training corpus. The verb *get* is less informative about *dog* than *bark*, because *get* co-occurs with many distinct targets, while *bark* co-occurs with *dog* and a much smaller number of other items (e.g., *seal*).

Co-occurrences with context lexemes are typically weighted with association scores derived from the computational analysis of collocations (Firth, 1957; Sinclair, 1991; Manning and Schütze, 1999; Evert, 2008). The most POINTWISE common association score of this kind is the **pointwise mutual information** MUTUAL (PMI) (Church and Hanks, 1989, 1990): INFORMATION

$$\mathrm{PMI}_{\langle t,c \rangle} = \log_2 \frac{p(t,c)}{p(t)p(c)}. \qquad (2.8)$$

The probabilities in Equation 2.8 are estimated as follows:

$$p(t,c) = \frac{F(t,c)}{F(*,*)} \qquad p(t) = \frac{F(t,*)}{F(*,*)} \qquad p(c) = \frac{F(*,c)}{F(*,*)}. \qquad (2.9)$$

Therefore, PMI is computed as:

$$\mathrm{PMI}_{\langle t,c \rangle} = \log_2 \frac{F(t,c)F(*,*)}{F(t,*)F(*,c)}. \qquad (2.10)$$

PMI measures how much the probability of a co-occurrence pair $\langle t, c \rangle$ estimated in the training corpus is higher than the probability we should "expect" if t and c occurred independently of one another. In such a case, $p(t, c)$ would be equal to $p(t)p(c)$, and PMI would be zero. The higher the ratio in Equation 2.8, the less t and c are statistically independent, and therefore the stronger their association. PMI thus assigns higher weight to co-occurrences whose context is more strongly associated with the target. For instance, given the frequency distribution in (18), we obtain the following values of PMI for the co-occurrences $\langle dog, bite \rangle$ and $\langle dog, get \rangle$, with $F(dog, eat) = 9$, $F(dog, *) = 27$, $F(*, eat) = 10$, $F(dog, get) = 10$, $F(*, get) = 45$, $F(*, *) = 121$:

$$\mathrm{PMI}_{\langle dog,eat \rangle} = \log_2 \frac{F(dog, eat)F(*,*)}{F(dog,*)F(*,eat)} = \log_2 \frac{9 \times 121}{27 \times 10} = 2.01.$$

$$\mathrm{PMI}_{\langle dog,get \rangle} = \log_2 \frac{F(dog, get)F(*,*)}{F(dog,*)F(*,get)} = \log_2 \frac{10 \times 121}{27 \times 45} = -0.01.$$

Despite *get* being the most frequent context for *dog*, $\mathrm{PMI}_{\langle dog,eat \rangle}$ is higher than $\mathrm{PMI}_{\langle dog,get \rangle}$, because *dog* and *get* occur one independently of the other more often than they occur together.

PMI has negative values when $p(t)p(c)$ is larger than $p(t, c)$, meaning that the frequency of $\langle t, c \rangle$ is lower than we would expect by chance. However, negative values of PMI tend to be unreliable unless they are estimated with huge amounts of data (Church and Hanks, 1989). Therefore, only positive values of PMI are normally used as weighting scores in distributional representations, obtaining the **positive pointwise mutual information** (PPMI) weighting scheme (Dagan et al., 1993; Niwa and Nitta, 1994; Bullinaria and Levy, 2007; Turney and Pantel, 2010):

POSITIVE PMI

$$\mathrm{PPMI}_{\langle t,c \rangle} = \begin{cases} \mathrm{PMI}_{\langle t,c \rangle} & \text{if } \mathrm{PMI}_{\langle t,c \rangle} > 0 \\ 0 & \text{otherwise} \end{cases}. \qquad (2.11)$$

The following matrix contains the PPMI weights computed from the raw co-occurrence frequencies in (19):

(20)

	bite	buy	drive	eat	get	live	park	ride	tell
bike	0	0.50	0	0	0	0	1.09	1.79	0
car	0	0.80	1.56	0	0	0	0.18	0	0
dog	0	0	0	2.01	0	1.65	0	0	2.16
lion	2.75	0	0	0	0.26	1.01	0	0	0

One notorious limit of PMI is its bias toward low-frequency events. For instance, *tell* co-occurs with *dog* just once in (18) and $\mathrm{PMI}_{\langle dog,tell \rangle} = 2.16$, with the rather odd result that *tell* becomes a more salient context for *dog* than *eat*, because $\mathrm{PMI}_{\langle dog,tell \rangle} > \mathrm{PMI}_{\langle dog,eat \rangle}$. PMI tends to promote rare co-occurrences containing idiosyncratic contexts of the target, which might not occur even with highly similar lexemes. This bias can be reduced with smoothing techniques (e.g., Laplace smoothing) to raise the probability of sampling rare contexts (Turney and Littman, 2003; Jurafsky and Martin, 2008). Levy et al. (2015b) compute the PPMI using a smoothed probability $p_\alpha(c)$ estimated by raising the context frequency to the power of α:

$$p_\alpha(c) = \frac{F(*,c)^\alpha}{\sum_c F(*,c)^\alpha}. \qquad (2.12)$$

The exponent increases the probability of rare contexts, lowering their PPMI. Levy et al. (2015b) report that $\alpha = 0.75$ improves the quality of representations over unsmoothed PPMI. A simple variant of PPMI is the **positive local** <small>POSITIVE LMI</small> **mutual information** (PLMI) (Evert, 2008; Baroni and Lenci, 2010):

$$\mathrm{PLMI}_{\langle t,c \rangle} = F(t,c) * \mathrm{PPMI}_{\langle t,c \rangle}. \qquad (2.13)$$

PLMI increases the weight of more frequent contexts, because it multiplies PPMI by the target-context co-occurrence frequency.

Another popular association score used for co-occurrence weighting in <small>T-TEST</small> distributional semantics is the **t-test** (Curran, 2003):

$$\text{t-test}_{\langle t,c \rangle} = \frac{p(t,c) - p(t)p(c)}{\sqrt{p(t)p(c)}}. \qquad (2.14)$$

Table 2.5 Top 15 collocates for *dog* weighted with PPMI, PLMI, and t-test, and their co-occurrence frequencies with the target

c	$F(t,c)$	PPMI	c	$F(t,c)$	PLMI	c	$F(t,c)$	t-test
bark	2047	8.60	cat	10972	77001.83	cat	10972	1183.31
kennel	1044	7.66	owner	5660	27032.71	bark	2047	889.63
puppy	1635	7.09	bark	2047	17608.83	puppy	1635	466.37
cat	10972	7.02	breed	2337	15125.18	kennel	1044	457.71
agility	601	6.69	hunting	2348	14543.48	breed	2337	450.35
handler	1038	6.50	guide	3261	11952.14	hunting	2348	408.94
breed	2337	6.47	puppy	1635	11570.95	owner	5660	379.43
collar	1180	6.41	walk	3105	11362.01	collar	1180	313.28
pet	1748	6.24	pet	1907	10080.56	handler	1038	302.96
warden	848	6.22	animal	2604	8989.97	pet	1907	265.79
hunting	2348	6.19	train	2099	8622.51	warden	848	248.32
stray	291	6.06	hearing	1950	8487.37	agility	601	246.39
flea	406	6.01	collar	1180	7566.27	fox	838	195.93
groom	401	5.89	horse	1867	7507.55	hearing	1950	189.82
breeder	520	5.75	keep	3405	7287.29	guide	3261	187.36

The t-test also compares the probability of the co-occurrence pair $\langle t, c \rangle$ with its expected probability $p(t)p(c)$ computed under the assumption that the target and the context are statistically independent. Like PLMI, the t-test assigns higher weights to frequent co-occurrences over rare ones.

In order to evaluate the different effects of these associations scores, we have selected as targets T and contexts C the 10,000 most frequent nouns, verbs, and adjectives in ukWaC (the minimum frequency is 5,421) and we have extracted their co-occurrences using a $[5, 5]$ context window, for a total amount of about 2.8 billion target-context pairs. Table 2.5 reports the top 15 collocates or the target *dog* according to PPMI, PLMI, and t-test. Looking at the co-occurrence frequencies $F(t, c)$, we notice that PLMI and t-test tend to promote more frequent contexts than PPMI. This trend is confirmed by the global distribution of the association scores for all the extracted co-occurrences. The positive PLMI and t-test scores have a much higher correlation with raw frequencies (respectively, Pearson $r = 0.79$, $R^2 = 0.63$, and $r = 0.34$, $R^2 = 0.12$), than PPMI (Pearson $r = 0.04$, $R^2 = 0.002$). In turn, there is a large difference between the PPMI and PLMI weights, which are very weakly correlated (Pearson $r = 0.12$, $R^2 = 0.01$).

Relevance Measures

Measures like PMI can be applied to estimate the association between a target and any type of context, including constructions (Stefanowitsch and Gries,

2003; Gries and Ellis, 2015) and documents (Pantel and Lin, 2002b). However, distributional representations built from textual contexts typically employ a different family of relevance measures derived from information retrieval. Lexical items used as terms to index documents within a collection are weighted to estimate their relevance for characterizing the document content (Witten et al., 1999; Manning et al., 2008). Term weighting schemes in information retrieval typically consist of two components: a **local weight**, corresponding to the term frequency in a specific document (Luhn, 1957, 1958) or some function thereof, and a **global weight**, measuring the overall informativeness of the term to index the documents in the collection. The global weight reduces the importance of terms that occur in many documents, because they are expected to be less informative about the topic of a specific text, and increases the weight of terms that are more associated to specific documents. Analogously, document co-occurrences are weighted taking into account the informativeness of the target lexeme, measured with its distribution over the documents in the training corpus. The more distributed a target t is among documents, the less informative are its occurrences in a specific context document d (Landauer and Dumais, 1997). Conversely, if t appears in few distinct documents, its observations in d are very informative to characterize its content. LOCAL WEIGHT GLOBAL WEIGHT

A common global weight is the **inverse document frequency** (**idf**) (Sparck Jones, 1972; Manning et al., 2008), where $|C|$ is the total number of documents in the corpus and $|t, *|$ is the number of distinct documents t occurs in: INVERSE DOCUMENT FREQUENCY

$$\text{idf}_t = \log \frac{|C|}{|t, *|}. \tag{2.15}$$

The fewer the documents the target occurs in, the higher its idf. The **tf-idf** weighting scheme combines the idf global weight with the term frequency or its log transformation: TF-IDF

$$\text{tf-idf}_{\langle t,d \rangle} = (1 + \log F(t, d)) \times \text{idf}_t. \tag{2.16}$$

Tf-idf is actually a family of weighting schemes with many different variants (Salton and Buckley, 1988; Witten et al., 1999; Manning et al., 2008). A co-occurrence pair with target t and context document d receives a tf-idf weight that is higher when t occurs many times within a small number of documents in the training corpus, and lower when the term occurs fewer times in d or occurs in many documents.

Another global weight is the **entropy** of the target (Dumais, 1991; Landauer and Dumais, 1997; Martin and Berry, 2007): ENTROPY

Table 2.6 Weighting document distributions with tf-idf and
entropy

t	$F(t,d)$	$|t,*|$	idf_t	$tf\text{-}idf_{\langle t,d\rangle}$	H_t	$\log H_{\langle t,d\rangle}$
car	3	3,018	1.20	2.52	0.20	0.42
truck	1	262	3.64	3.64	0.44	0.44
way	3	8,114	0.21	0.44	0.06	0.12

$$\mathbf{H}_t = 1 + \sum_{j=1}^{n} \frac{p(t,d_j)\log_2 p(t,d_j)}{\log_2 |C|}. \qquad (2.17)$$

H_t is based on the definition of entropy in information theory (Shannon, 1948), which is measured in bits (hence the log to the base 2). The probability $p(t,d)$ is estimated with $F(t,d)$ divided by the total number of times t appears in the documents of the training corpus, $F(t,*)$. The denominator $\log_2 |C|$ is a normalization factor making H_t range between 0 and 1. Differently from idf, entropy also takes into account the distribution of the target in the documents. Lower entropy values correspond to targets that are more evenly distributed across context documents. Dumais (1991) multiplies H_t by the log frequency of $\langle t,d\rangle$, obtaining the **log entropy** weighting scheme:

LOG ENTROPY

$$\log \mathbf{H}_{\langle t,d\rangle} = (1 + \log F(t,d)) \times \mathbf{H}_t. \qquad (2.18)$$

Table 2.6 reports the idf and entropy for the targets *car*, *truck*, and *way*, computed on ukWaC taking as contexts 10,000 randomly selected documents: *truck* has a larger idf than *car* and *way*, because it occurs in fewer documents in the corpus. As expected, since *way* is a very general and frequent lexeme, it appears in many documents and therefore has the lowest idf. The fifth column shows the tf-idf weighting of the co-occurrence pairs $\langle t,d\rangle$, such that d is a document in which the targets appear with the frequencies reported in the second column. Even if $F(truck,d) = 1$, this co-occurrence has a higher weight than the others. Observing *truck* just once in a document is more important than observing *car* and *way* three times, because the former target is more informative than the latter ones. Analogously, since *way* is more evenly distributed across the context documents, it has a very low entropy, which therefore decreases the weight of its co-occurrences. According to Dumais (1991), log entropy outperforms tf-idf in some specific settings, but these weighting schemes are indeed highly similar, as proven by the fact that the Pearson correlation coefficient r between idf and entropy of the 10,000 most frequent noun, verb, and adjective targets extracted form ukWaC is 0.98 ($R^2 = 0.96$).

Tf-idf and entropy are also used to weight lexical co-occurrences. In this case, the co-occurrence frequency is combined with a global weight measuring the informativeness of a context lexeme l as inversely related to the co-occurrence of l with all the targets in the corpus. This is a rather different approach from PPMI and other association functions that instead compare the observed co-occurrence frequency with the independent distribution of target and context. The following is a variation of the tf-idf weighting scheme that reduces the weight of co-occurrences pairs whose context lexemes also co-occur with many different targets (Curran, 2003; Ciobanu and Dinu, 2013):

$$\text{tf-idf}_{\langle t,l \rangle} = (1 + \log F(t,l)) \times \log \frac{|T|}{|*,l|}. \tag{2.19}$$

where $|*,l|$ is the number of co-occurrence pairs containing the lexeme l as context. For instance, given the frequency distribution in (18), the idf of *get* is $log\ 1 = 0$, because it co-occurs with every target, while the idf of *eat* is $log\ 2 = 0.69$, as it co-occurs only with *dog* and *lion*. Grefenstette (1994) adopts a variation of the log entropy scheme measuring the informativeness of a context lexeme with its entropy in the corpus (see also Dagan, 2003):

$$\log \mathbf{H}_{\langle t,l \rangle} = (1 + \log F(t,l)) \times 1 + \sum_{i=1}^{n} \frac{p(t_i|l) \log_2 p(t_i|l)}{\log_2 F(*,*)}. \tag{2.20}$$

The probability $p(t|l)$ is estimated with $F(t,l)$ divided by the number of times l appears in training corpus, $F(*,l)$. The entropy is then normalized with respect to the total number of co-occurrences extracted from the corpus. The contexts that are more evenly distributed with the targets receive lower entropic scores and are thus less important to characterize the target lexemes: The entropy of *get* in (18) is 0.71, while the entropy of *eat* is 0.93.

2.3.2 Context Selection

Contexts are not equally important to characterize the semantic properties of target lexemes. The process of identifying the subset of linguistic contexts that are most informative about the targets is referred to as **context selection**. There CONTEXT SELECTION are two types of context selection strategies, respectively applying before and after collecting co-occurrence data.

As we have seen in Section 2.2.1, we can utilize the frequency distribution of lexemes in the corpus to define an admissible frequency range for the context items to be used for co-occurrence extraction. In effect, this usually entails ignoring very high-frequent and low-frequent items. The idea is that the former are assumed to be mainly function words devoid of meaning, and the latter are subject to data sparseness and thus contribute inferior statistical evidence. Besides frequency, other "top-down" criteria can be adopted to select contexts, such as lexical items belonging to a given POS (e.g., only nouns and verbs) or chosen according to a priori assumptions about their relevance to capture particular semantic dimensions (e.g., Osgood et al., 1957; Gallant, 1991).

Once we have collected the co-occurrence matrix, we can perform a further process of context selection. Co-occurrence weights quantify the importance of distributional data, and we can thus use such measures to decide which contexts to include in the distributional representations. PPMI in fact carries out an implicit form of context selection, because it zeros all the contexts having a negative association score with the target. This corresponds to representing targets only with the subset of contexts having a positive PMI. Gamallo and Bordag (2011) and Polajnar and Clark (2014) propose a similar method for context selection in which the top n highest weighted contexts per targets are selected, and the rest of the values are discarded (by setting to zero). Polajnar and Clark (2014) show that, given a co-occurrence matrix with 10,000 context lexemes, distributional representations with $n = 240$ significantly improve their performance in various semantic tasks.

Other approaches to context selection **rank** the columns in the co-occurrence matrix $\mathbf{M}_{|T| \times |C|}$ according to some criterion, and then select the k top ones. Ranking criteria for the matrix columns include the number of non-zero counts, the sum of their components, and their variance (Burgess, 1998). The variance of the column corresponding to the context c_j is computed as:

$$\sigma_j^2 = \frac{\sum_{i=1}^{m} (w_{t_i, c_j} - \mu)^2}{m}, \tag{2.21}$$

where w_{t_i, c_j} is the weighted co-occurrence count of the target t_i and context c_j, μ is the mean of the weight of c_j over the m lexemes. Contexts with very low variance have similar distributional counts over the lexemes, which indicates that they are not very useful for discriminating between the targets and can thus be discarded without loss of information.

Mathematical note 2 – vector length and vector space

Given a system of perpendicular Cartesian axes, **vectors** with n components define **points** in n-dimensional spaces, each component corresponding to the coordinate of the points on an axis. The same vectors also define **arrows** from one point, the origin, to another point, the endpoint (see Figure 2.7). The vector components correspond to the **displacement** from the origin to the endpoint. Vectors with n components are n-dimensional, and the component v_i is the vector value of dimension i. Vector components determine the **direction** and the **length** of the displacement arrow. The **length** or **(Euclidean) norm** $||\mathbf{v}||$ of a vector $\mathbf{v}$ is the length of the arrow representing it, and is computed as follows:

$$||\mathbf{v}|| = \sqrt{v_1^2 + \cdots + v_n^2} = \sqrt{\sum_{i=1}^{i=n} v_i^2}.$$

The vectors $\mathbf{a}$ and $\mathbf{b}$ below have the same length 3.6 but point in different directions, while $\mathbf{a}$ and $\mathbf{c}$ have the same direction, but $||\mathbf{c}|| = 10.8$:

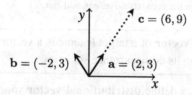

A **vector space** is a set of vectors with the following rules:

> **vector addition** of two n-dimensional vectors $\mathbf{x}$ and $\mathbf{y}$ is defined as a vector $\mathbf{z} = \mathbf{x} + \mathbf{y}$, such that $z_i = x_i + y_i$, for each $1 \leq i \leq n$;
> **scalar multiplication** of a n-dimensional vector $\mathbf{x}$ by a scalar k is defined as a vector $\mathbf{z} = k\mathbf{x}$, such that $z_i = kx_i$, for each $1 \leq i \leq n$.

Scalar multiplication changes the length but not the direction of $\mathbf{x}$ (if k is negative, the orientation is inverted). The vector $\mathbf{c}$ above is a scalar multiple of $\mathbf{a}$, as $\mathbf{c} = 3\mathbf{a}$. The vector space of all n-dimensional vectors is indicated with $\mathbb{R}^n$.

2.4 Distributional Vectors

The co-occurrence matrix represents lexemes as **distributional vectors**. Vectors are used to represent objects with quantitative **features** (e.g., images with vectors of pixels, texts with vectors of features corresponding to the frequency of their words). Distributional vectors encode **distributional features**:

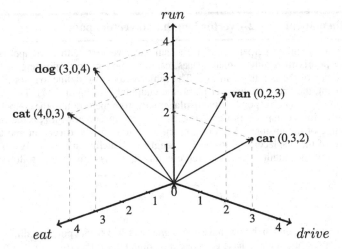

Figure 2.7 Distributional vectors of *car*, *cat*, *dog*, and *van*, represented in a space whose dimensions are the contexts *drive*, *eat*, and *run*

> The **distributional vector** of a target lexeme is a vector of distributional features representing its co-occurrence statistics.

Co-occurrence matrices define **distributional vector spaces** and each row is the distributional vector of a target lexeme. Therefore, they provide a **geometrical representation** of the lexicon as a **semantic space**, in which the position of any lexeme depends on its co-occurrences with linguistic contexts. In Figure 2.7, the targets *car*, *cat*, *dog*, and *van* are represented in a three-dimensional vector space (we indicate the vector of a lexeme with the lexeme in boldface).

> The co-occurrence matrix $\mathbf{M}_{|T| \times |C|}$ defines an n-dimensional **distributional vector space** such that:
>
> (i) the dimensions of the vector space are the linguistic contexts C;
> (ii) the **distributional representation** of a target lexeme $t_i \in T$ is the **distributional vector** $\mathbf{t_i} = \mathbf{m}_{t_i,*} = (w_{t_i,c_1}, w_{t_i,c_2}, \ldots, w_{t_i,c_n})$.

In linear algebra, vectors are typically treated as column vectors (i.e., equivalent to $m \times 1$ matrices). As it is customary in distributional semantics, we instead treat distributional representations as **row vectors** (i.e., equivalent to $1 \times n$ matrices), unless differently specified.

Importantly, each lexical type is assigned a single distributional vector. This is the standard approach in distributional semantics, which is shared by all the models in Part II, including those that do not employ co-occurrence matrices (cf. Chapters 5 and 6). Therefore, when we use the term distributional vector, we mean a **type vector**, unless otherwise indicated. In Sections 9.6.2 and 9.6.3, we discuss models that represent each word token with a distinct vector.

2.4.1 Explicit Distributional Vectors

The distributional representations produced by co-occurrence matrices have three main properties:

1. each vector dimension represents a (weighted) co-occurrence count with a specific context. Following Levy and Goldberg (2014b), we call this type of distributional representation **explicit vector**;
2. the number of contexts in language data tends to be very large. Therefore, explicit vectors are **high-dimensional**;
3. because of the Zipfian distribution of co-occurrence data, explicit vectors are **sparse**, which means most of their dimensions are zero. For instance, given a distributional representation such that T and C correspond to the 10,000 most frequent nouns, verbs, and adjectives in ukWaC, and distributional pairs are collected using a $[5, 5]$ context window and weighted with PPMI, the average density (i.e., the percentage of non-zero components) of the row vectors in $\mathbf{M}_{|T| \times |C|}$ is 24.2%.

> An **explicit distributional vector** is a n-dimensional feature vector $\mathbf{u}$, such that each component u_i corresponds to a distinct context $c_i \in C = \{c_1, \ldots, c_n\}$. Explicit vectors are **high-dimensional** and **sparse**.

Explicit vectors have a number of potential disadvantages. First of all, their high-dimensionality may raise concerns about memory consumption and computational complexity. The bigger the data, the more storage space the distributional vectors will require, and the operations we perform using the distributional vectors (e.g., similarity calculation) have a computational cost proportional to the number of co-occurrence events recorded in the vector. However, these problems can be addressed by exploiting the fact that explicit vectors are sparse. If a **sparse format** is used to store the distributional vectors, only non-zero elements are represented. In fact, it is the density rather than the dimensionality that contributes to the computational complexity. This suggests that one way of approaching the problem of building distributional models from big data is to concentrate on sparsifying the distributional vectors by carefully selecting which co-occurrence events to record (cf. Section 2.3.2). If we can drastically reduce the number of co-occurrence events, we do not have to worry about the dimensionality of the distributional space.

Note the difference between the *data sparseness* discussed in Section 2.3.1 and *sparsifying a distributional vector*. While the former term refers to the problem of insufficient statistical data for the distributional models, the latter term concerns the benefit of selecting which of the observed co-occurrence events to retain in the vectors. Data sparseness is negative because it means lack of observation, but vector sparsity is positive because it means efficient computation. As long as we reach the vector sparsity in a principled manner that does not aggravate the data sparseness problem, our model will benefit.

Besides concerns of computational efficiency, the huge number of vector components may impact negatively on the quality of distributional representations. The term **curse of dimensionality** refers to a bundle of problems related to high-dimensional vectors (Assent, 2012; Zimek, 2014). Two aspects of the curse of dimensionality are particularly relevant for distributional similarity: (i) **distance concentration**, which refers to the tendency of objects in high-dimensional vector spaces to be almost equidistant, thereby becoming increasingly difficult to discriminate similar from dissimilar ones (Beyer et al., 1999); and (ii) **hubness**, which denotes the emergence of *hubs*, that is, vectors close to a large number of other vectors (Radovanović et al. 2010a, 2010b). Therefore, adding dimensions does not only mean more information but also means more noise in the resulting distributional vector space.

High-dimensional explicit vectors indeed miss important generalizations in distributional data. Since they regard each context as a distinct feature, they do not take into account the fact that contexts may in turn be very similar and strongly correlated one to another. For instance, *buy* and *purchase* are close synonyms, and treating them as separate contexts may fail to capture the similarity between a word co-occurring with the former and a lexeme instead co-occurring with the latter. Moreover, many of the zero dimensions of sparse explicit vectors might indeed correspond to relevant distributional features of the target that simply do not occur in the corpus. In ukWaC, *croissant* co-occurs with *buy*, but not with *purchase*, despite they are both plausible collocates of *croissant*. Therefore, explicit vectors suffer from the fact that many possible co-occurrences remain unobserved in corpora regardless of its size, just because of data sparseness.

2.4.2 Implicit Distributional Vectors (Word Embeddings)

As an alternative to explicit vectors, lexemes can be represented with a different kind of distributional vector such that:

CURSE OF
DIMENSIONAL-
ITY

DISTANCE CON-
CENTRATION

HUBNESS

1. dimensions correspond to k **latent features** extracted from co-occurrences;
2. the number of latent features, typically in the order of a few hundreds, is much smaller than the n linguistic contexts in C;
3. most of the components are non-zero.

WORD EMBEDDING

We call this representation **implicit distributional vector**, as there is no direct correspondence between its components and contexts, or **word embedding**.

> An **embedding** is a k-dimensional implicit distributional vector **u**, such that each component u_i corresponds to a latent feature extracted from co-occurrences. Embeddings are **low-dimensional** ($k \ll n$) and **dense**.

A word embedding is therefore an embedding that represents a lexical item. This term has been popularized by the advent of neural models (cf. Chapter 6), but we use it here to refer to any kind of low-dimensional, dense, implicit vector, independently of the computational method to build it.

DIMENSIONALITY REDUCTION

Embeddings are created with **dimensionality reduction** techniques that map the data in the high-dimensional space of linguistic contexts to a space of fewer latent dimensions. An alternative name for dimensionality reduction is **feature extraction**, because the dimensions of the reduced space are new features extracted from the original data. Turney and Pantel (2010) report at least four main goals of feature extraction: (i) discovering latent semantic structures in distributional data, (ii) reducing the noise, (iii) capturing high-order co-occurrences, and (iv) smoothing data sparseness.

FEATURE EXTRACTION

LATENT FEATURES

The main assumption is that co-occurrences collected from corpora are noisy data that hide more abstract semantic structures. Feature extraction aims to uncover such a latent structure and to get rid of the surface noise (Deerwester et al., 1990). Instead of representing lexemes using the linguistic contexts they co-occur with, we represent them in a **latent semantic space** of implicit vectors with a much smaller set of abstract features discovered in data.

The notion of latent feature can be understood by comparing the vector spaces in Figure 2.8, whose points correspond to two-dimensional explicit vectors, as shown by the contexts labeling their axes. The vectors in the left plot are scattered throughout the space, as *buy* and *think* are very different contexts and lexemes that co-occur with the former might not co-occur with the latter, and vice versa. The space in the right plot instead shows some kind of underlying structure. Since *buy* and *purchase* are close synonyms, they share a lot of co-occurrences. Therefore, the two dimensions are strongly correlated and the points tend to cluster along the dashed line d. If we project each original vector **u** onto a point **û** on d, such that **u** and **û** are connected by a straight line orthogonal to d, **u** is represented in a reduced space with d as a new latent feature, which better captures the structure hidden in distributional data (i.e., the correlation between *buy* and *purchase*). The data variation with respect to d can be regarded as noise that is removed with little loss of information by exploiting the generalizations and redundancies in the data and projecting the vectors onto d. While the original vector $\mathbf{u}$ is an explicit representation, its projection $\hat{\mathbf{u}}$ on d is an implicit vector. In fact, the new dimension d does not correspond to any context. It can rather be taken to represent an abstract semantic feature shared by both *buy* and *purchase*, such as the fact of denoting events of commercial transaction.

    It is generally claimed that dimensionality reduction discovers high-order co-occurrence relations in distributional data. **First-order co-occurrences** are lexical items that directly co-occur with the same contexts. **High-order co-occurrences** (or **indirect co-occurrences**) are lexemes co-occurring with contexts that are similar because they in turn share first-order co-occurrences (Landauer and Dumais, 1997; Lemaire and Denhière, 2006; Turney and Pantel, 2010). To see why feature extraction captures high-order co-occurrences, consider again the vectors $\mathbf{u}$ and $\mathbf{v}$ in Figure 2.8. Despite being quite far in the explicit two-dimensional space, when projected onto the latent dimension d they eventually become quite near. Suppose that the lexeme l_1 co-occurs with *buy* but not with *purchase*, and the target l_2 vice versa. In this case, l_1 and l_2 are not first-order co-occurrences and can be distant in the two-dimensional space. However, l_1 and l_2 are high-order co-occurrences, as they co-occur with contexts that are in turn very similar, because they share many other targets. Therefore, by projecting l_1 and l_2 on the latent dimension d, we can enhance the similarity between l_1 and l_2, despite the fact that they never co-occur with the same contexts. This example also shows the smoothing effects of dimensionality reduction, which decreases the negative bias of unobserved co-occurrences. The fact that l_1 and l_2, respectively, never co-occur with *purchase* and *buy* is treated as noise removed by their projection on the new latent dimension.

    Both explicit vectors and embeddings are distributional representations, because they represent linguistic co-occurrences. However, they do this in two very different fashions. Explicit vectors *directly* encode co-occurrences into their components, while embeddings represent co-occurrences *indirectly*, as their components encode latent features extracted from distributional data. Dimensionality reduction is usually regarded to be an important factor to enhance the quality of semantic spaces, but such improvements are not always constant and depend on many factors (i.e., the method for feature extraction, the semantic task, etc.). From the practical point of view, low-dimensional dense vectors are easier to use in applications: Machine learning methods, like

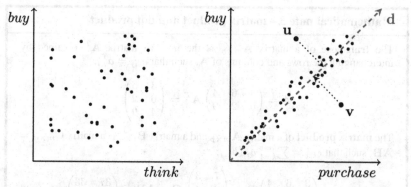

Figure 2.8 Left plot: The contexts *buy* and *think* are independent features. Right plot: The contexts *buy* and *purchase* are strongly correlated and data could fit onto the line *d*, which represents a new latent feature

neural networks, need to learn a much lower number of parameters if they represent lexemes with embeddings rather than with high-dimensional explicit vectors.

2.5 Reducing Vector Dimensionality

Feature extraction in distributional representations is typically performed by mapping the co-occurrence matrix onto a reduced latent semantic space with a **matrix reduction function**. Other methods to generate embeddings without a co-occurrence matrix are analyzed in Chapters 5 and 6.

MATRIX FACTORIZATION

> The **matrix reduction function** $R : \mathbf{M}_{|T| \times |C|} \to \mathbf{M}'_{|T| \times |D|}$ transforms the sparse co-occurrence matrix $\mathbf{M}_{|T| \times |C|}$ into the embedding matrix $\mathbf{M}'_{|T| \times |D|}$ such that $D = \{d_1, \ldots, d_k\}$ are latent features and $|D| \ll |C|$.

R typically consists in a **factorization** (or **decomposition**) of the co-occurrence matrix into the product of other matrices.

2.5.1 Singular Value Decomposition (SVD)

The most popular matrix reduction algorithm in distributional semantics is **Singular Value Decomposition** (SVD) (Deerwester et al., 1990; Schütze, 1992; Landauer and Dumais, 1997), which factorizes an $m \times n$ co-occurrence matrix M into the product of three other matrices, where $z = min(m, n)$:

SVD

$$\mathbf{M}_{m \times n} = \mathbf{U}_{m \times z} \mathbf{\Sigma}_{z \times z} (\mathbf{V}_{n \times z})^T. \qquad (2.22)$$

Mathematical note 3 – matrix product and dot product

The **transpose** of a matrix $\mathbf{A}_{m\times n}$ is the $n \times m$ matrix $\mathbf{A}^T$ obtained by interchanging the rows and columns of $\mathbf{A}$, such that $a_{i,j} = a_{j,i}^T$:

$$\mathbf{A} = \begin{pmatrix} 3 & 6 & 4 \\ 5 & 2 & 9 \end{pmatrix} \quad \mathbf{A}^T = \begin{pmatrix} 3 & 5 \\ 6 & 2 \\ 4 & 9 \end{pmatrix}$$

The **matrix product** of a matrix $\mathbf{A}_{m\times p}$ and a matrix $\mathbf{B}_{p\times n}$ is a matrix $\mathbf{C}_{m\times n} = \mathbf{AB}$, such that $c_{i,j} = \sum_{k=1}^{k=p} a_{i,k}b_{k,j}$:

$$\mathbf{A} = \begin{pmatrix} 3 & 6 & 4 \\ 5 & 2 & 9 \end{pmatrix} \quad \mathbf{B} = \begin{pmatrix} 7 & 3 \\ 2 & 4 \\ 1 & 0 \end{pmatrix} \quad \mathbf{C} = \mathbf{AB} = \begin{pmatrix} 37 & 33 \\ 48 & 23 \end{pmatrix}$$

If the number of columns of $\mathbf{A}$ does not match the number of rows of $\mathbf{B}$, then $\mathbf{AB}$ is undefined. Matrix product is not commutative: $\mathbf{AB} \neq \mathbf{BA}$. Since n-dimensional row vectors correspond to $1 \times n$ matrices, a special case of matrix product is the **inner** or **dot product** of two vectors. Given the n-dimensional vectors $\mathbf{u}$ and $\mathbf{v}$ their dot product is defined as follows:

$$\mathbf{u} \cdot \mathbf{v} = \mathbf{u}\mathbf{v}^T = u_1v_1 + \cdots + u_nv_n = \sum_{i=1}^{i=n} u_iv_i$$

The dot product is thus a scalar obtained by multiplying two vectors componentwise and summing across components. Therefore, each entry $c_{i,j}$ of the matrix product $\mathbf{C} = \mathbf{AB}$ can be expressed as $\mathbf{a}_{i,*} \cdot \mathbf{b}_{*,j}$, where $\mathbf{a}_{i,*}$ is the ith row vector of $\mathbf{A}$ and $\mathbf{b}_{*,j}$ is the jth column vector of $\mathbf{B}$. The dot product is related to the angle θ between the two vectors:

$$\mathbf{u} \cdot \mathbf{v} = ||\mathbf{u}||\,||\mathbf{v}||\cos(\theta)$$

As $\cos(90°) = 0$, two vectors whose dot product is zero are **orthogonal**.

LEFT AND RIGHT SINGULAR VECTORS

The columns of $\mathbf{U}_{m\times z}$ are called **left singular vectors**, and those of $\mathbf{V}_{n\times z}$ **right singular vectors**. The matrices $\mathbf{U}$ and $\mathbf{V}$ have orthonormal columns: They have unit length (cf. Section 2.6.1) and they are all orthogonal to each other, so that each dimension is uncorrelated to the others. $\mathbf{\Sigma}_{z\times z}$ is a square diagonal matrix (i.e., a square matrix with non-zero entries only along the diagonal) containing **singular values**, sorted in descending order. The factorization is illustrated in Figure 2.9a, with $z = n$.

SINGULAR VALUES

The columns of the matrices $\mathbf{U}$ and $\mathbf{V}$ represent latent dimensions in the original data, ordered by the amount of variance they account for. We can view SVD as a method for rotating the axes of the n-dimensional space into a new latent semantic space, such that the first axis runs along the direction of largest variation among the contexts, the second dimension runs along the direction

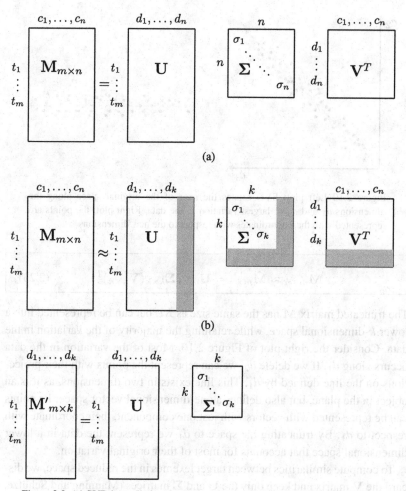

Figure 2.9 (a) SVD is applied to the co-occurrence matrix $\mathbf{M}_{m \times n}$; (b) $\mathbf{M}$ is truncated to its top k singular values; (c) $\mathbf{M}'_{m \times k}$ is the reduced matrix of embeddings with latent features $D = \{d_1, \ldots, d_k\}$

with the second largest variation, and so forth (see Figure 2.10, left plot). The matrices $\mathbf{U}$ and $\mathbf{V}$, respectively, contain the coordinate of the target lexemes and contexts in the new latent space (see Figure 2.10, right plot). The singular values in $\boldsymbol{\Sigma}$ express the importance of each new dimension: σ_i indicates the amount of variation of the data along the latent dimension d_i.

By deleting all but the first k singular values and singular vectors, we obtain a new matrix $\hat{\mathbf{M}}$ that is the best approximation of $\mathbf{M}$ in a reduced k-dimensional space, such that the distance between the two matrices $||\mathbf{M} - \hat{\mathbf{M}}||_F$ is minimized. The $|| \ldots ||_F$ is the **Frobenius norm** and corresponds to the Euclidean norm and distance for matrices (cf. Section 2.6.1). This reduction is known as **truncated SVD** (see Figure 2.9b):

FROBENIUS
NORM

TRUNCATED
SVD

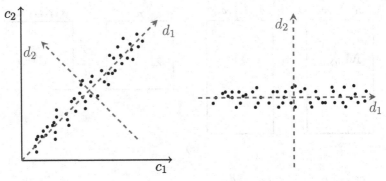

Figure 2.10 Left plot: SVD rotates the axes of the original space along the dimensions d_1 and d_2 of largest variation in the data. Right plot: the points are represented with their coordinates with respect to the new dimensions

$$\mathbf{M}_{m \times n} \approx \hat{\mathbf{M}}_{m \times n} = \mathbf{U}_{m \times k} \mathbf{\Sigma}_{k \times k} (\mathbf{V}_{n \times k})^T. \qquad (2.23)$$

The truncated matrix $\hat{\mathbf{M}}$ has the same size as $\mathbf{M}$, but can be represented into a lower k-dimensional space, while retaining the majority of the variation in the data. Consider the right plot of Figure 2.10. Most of the variation in the data occurs along d_1. If we delete d_2, we can represent the points with their projections on the line defined by d_1. This line exists in two dimensions, as it is an object in the plane, but also defines a one-dimensional vector space: Its points can be represented with vectors with just one component, their coordinate with respect to d_1. By truncating the space to d_1 we represent the data in a lower dimensional space that accounts for most of their original variation.

To compute similarities between target lexemes in the reduced space, we discard the $\mathbf{V}$ matrix and keep only the $\mathbf{U}$ and $\mathbf{\Sigma}$ matrices (Manning and Schütze, 1999). Their product gives a new reduced matrix $\mathbf{M}'_{m \times k}$ (see Figure 2.9c):

$$\mathbf{M}'_{m \times k} = \mathbf{U}_{m \times k} \mathbf{\Sigma}_{k \times k}. \qquad (2.24)$$

The row vectors of the reduced matrix $\mathbf{M}'$ are embeddings of the targets in a latent semantic space with dimensions $D = \{d_1, \ldots, d_k\}$. Alternatively, the singular value matrix can be dismissed and the row vectors of $\mathbf{U}$ directly used as embeddings of the targets:

$$\mathbf{M}'_{m \times k} = \mathbf{U}_{m \times k}. \qquad (2.25)$$

The relation between Equations 2.24 and 2.25 is straightforward, because Σ is simply a scaling factor of $\mathbf{U}$: The positions of the targets in the vector space are the same except that each of the axes has been stretched or shrunk in proportion to the corresponding singular value. Levy et al. (2015b) show that Equation 2.25 indeed improves the quality of semantic representations.

The steps leading from explicit vectors to word embeddings through SVD are exemplified below. The sparse, explicit co-occurrence matrix (19), reported here as (21), is factorized into the matrices (22) – (24):

$$
(21) \quad \mathbf{M} =
\begin{array}{c}
\\
bike \\
car \\
dog \\
lion
\end{array}
\begin{array}{cccccccccc}
bite & buy & drive & eat & get & live & park & ride & tell \\
\left(\begin{array}{ccccccccc}
0 & 9 & 0 & 0 & 12 & 0 & 8 & 6 & 0 \\
0 & 13 & 8 & 0 & 15 & 0 & 5 & 0 & 0 \\
0 & 0 & 0 & 9 & 10 & 7 & 0 & 0 & 1 \\
6 & 0 & 0 & 1 & 8 & 3 & 0 & 0 & 0
\end{array}\right)
\end{array}
$$

$$
(22) \quad \mathbf{U} =
\begin{array}{c}
\\
bike \\
car \\
dog \\
lion
\end{array}
\begin{array}{cccc}
d_1 & d_2 & d_3 & d_4 \\
\left(\begin{array}{cccc}
-0.57 & 0.24 & -0.78 & -0.06 \\
-0.72 & 0.31 & 0.62 & -0.05 \\
-0.32 & -0.83 & 0.01 & -0.45 \\
-0.23 & -0.39 & -0.01 & 0.89
\end{array}\right)
\end{array}
$$

$$
(23) \quad \Sigma =
\begin{pmatrix}
29.28 & 0 & 0 & 0 \\
0 & 13.83 & 0 & 0 \\
0 & 0 & 7.61 & 0 \\
0 & 0 & 0 & 6.51
\end{pmatrix}
$$

(24)

$$
\mathbf{V}^T =
\begin{array}{c}
\\
d_1 \\
d_2 \\
d_3 \\
d_4
\end{array}
\begin{array}{ccccccccc}
bite & buy & drive & eat & get & live & park & ride & tell \\
\left(\begin{array}{ccccccccc}
-0.05 & -0.49 & -0.20 & -0.11 & -0.78 & -0.10 & -0.28 & -0.12 & -0.01 \\
-0.17 & 0.45 & 0.18 & -0.57 & -0.28 & -0.50 & 0.25 & 0.10 & -0.06 \\
-0.01 & 0.13 & 0.65 & 0.01 & -0.01 & 0.01 & -0.41 & -0.62 & 0.00 \\
0.82 & -0.17 & -0.06 & -0.48 & 0.20 & -0.07 & -0.11 & -0.05 & -0.07
\end{array}\right)
\end{array}
$$

The new matrices are then truncated to their first two dimensions (i.e., $k = 2$):

$$
(25) \quad \mathbf{U} =
\begin{array}{c}
\\
bike \\
car \\
dog \\
lion
\end{array}
\begin{array}{cc}
d_1 & d_2 \\
\left(\begin{array}{cc}
-0.57 & 0.24 \\
-0.72 & 0.31 \\
-0.32 & -0.83 \\
-0.23 & -0.39
\end{array}\right)
\end{array}
$$

$$
(26) \quad \Sigma =
\begin{pmatrix}
29.28 & 0 \\
0 & 13.83
\end{pmatrix}
$$

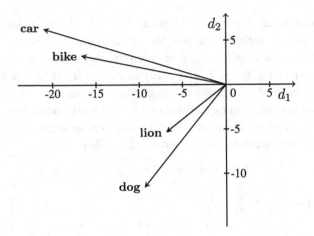

Figure 2.11 The targets in $\mathbf{M}'$ represented in latent semantic space

$$(27) \quad \mathbf{V}^T = \begin{array}{c} d_1 \\ d_2 \end{array} \begin{pmatrix} \overset{bite}{-0.05} & \overset{buy}{-0.49} & \overset{drive}{-0.20} & \overset{eat}{-0.11} & \overset{get}{-0.78} & \overset{live}{-0.10} & \overset{park}{-0.28} & \overset{ride}{-0.12} & \overset{tell}{-0.01} \\ -0.17 & 0.45 & 0.18 & -0.57 & -0.28 & -0.50 & 0.25 & 0.10 & -0.06 \end{pmatrix}$$

Finally, the embeddings of the targets are the row vectors in the matrix $\mathbf{M}'$:

$$(28) \quad \mathbf{M}' = \begin{array}{c} bike \\ car \\ dog \\ lion \end{array} \begin{array}{cc} d_1 & d_2 \\ \begin{pmatrix} -16.68 & 3.30 \\ -21.02 & 4.32 \\ -9.44 & -11.55 \\ -6.91 & -5.34 \end{pmatrix} \end{array}$$

The distributional representations in $\mathbf{M}'$ are embeddings whose components are the latent features d_1 and d_2. Such implicit vectors capture important aspects of the similarity among the target lexemes, as shown in Figure 2.11. We can also observe the effect of SVD in smoothing the original data and discovering high-order generalizations. For instance, in (21) *bite* co-occurs with *lion* but not with *dog*. The latent features in the reduced space enhance the similarity between *bike* and *car* on the one hand, and *dog* and *lion* on the other, which, respectively, have positive and negative values along d_2. This new dimension can be taken to correspond to the semantic contrast between animate and inanimate entities. Therefore, SVD is able to transform a noisy, sparse, high-dimensional co-occurrence matrix into a new, much smaller embedding matrix that describes the data in terms of its most important orthogonal dimensions, filtering out redundancy and reducing data sparseness.

The choice of the reduced latent dimensions k is normally a trade-off between performance and efficiency. The smaller the k the more computationally efficient the resulting distributional representation, but the larger the k the more closely the reduced vector will resemble the original one. Landauer and Dumais (1997) argue that optimal performance is achieved using around 300 latent dimensions, which has become a sort of "magic number" and de facto standard for dense vector dimensionality. However, later work has revealed a much more variable behavior. The extensive comparative experiments performed by Bullinaria and Levy (2012) show that model performance peaks at a much higher number of dimensions, and Lapesa and Evert (2014) argue that the optimal dimension of reduced vectors depends on the semantic task and dataset, with a general recommended setting of 500 latent features.

The standard practice is to use the latent dimensions in the reduced matrix with the highest singular values. However, further research has proved that this is not the optimal solution. Caron (2001) finds that improved results with SVD applied to information retrieval and question-answering tasks can be obtained by weighting the latent features through an exponent factor $p \in \mathbb{R}$:

CARON
P-TRANSFORM

$$\mathbf{M}'_{m \times k} = \mathbf{U}_{m \times k} \boldsymbol{\Sigma}_{k \times k} \rightarrow \mathbf{U}_{m \times k} \boldsymbol{\Sigma}^p_{k \times k}. \qquad (2.26)$$

We refer to this weighting as the **Caron p-transform**. If $p = 0$, Equation 2.26 reduces to Equation 2.25. Bullinaria and Levy (2012) show that the optimum exponent parameter for DSMs is $p < 1$, which corresponds to giving more emphasis to the dimensions with smaller singular values while decreasing the importance of the top latent features. Overall, Bullinaria and Levy (2012) report a perfect score of 100% on the TOEFL synonym test (cf. Chapter 7) with $k = 5,000$ and $p = 0.25$. Bullinaria and Levy (2012) achieve equally high improvements by removing the first singular values, with best results obtained when skipping the top 100 latent features. We refer to this method as **top-dimensions removal** or **inverse truncated SVD**. The benefit brought by downgrading (or removing) top latent dimensions has found several empirical confirmations (Levy et al., 2015b; Österlund et al., 2015). The explanation is that the top latent features represent the dimensions with the highest variance and tend to contain a large amount of "noisy" information that hides important patterns in the semantic space. For instance, the dimension d_1 in Figure 2.11 has no discriminative power, since all the targets have negative values. The relevant dimension is d_2, which separates *dog* and *lion* from *bike* and *car*.

INVERSE
TRUNCATED
SVD

Mathematical note 4 – linear transformations

When a n-dimensional row vector $\mathbf{u}$ is multiplied by a $n \times m$ matrix $\mathbf{A}$, the matrix is a **function** that transforms $\mathbf{u}$ into an m-dimensional vector $\mathbf{v} = \mathbf{u}\mathbf{A}$ (if $\mathbf{u}$ and $\mathbf{v}$ are column vectors, $\mathbf{v} = \mathbf{A}\mathbf{u}$). This directly follows from the definition of matrix product (cf. Mathematical note 3 in Section 2.5.1): $\mathbf{u}$ corresponds to a $1 \times n$ matrix, and its product by $\mathbf{A}_{n \times m}$ generates the $1 \times m$ matrix corresponding to $\mathbf{v}$, such that $v_j = \sum_{i=1}^{n} a_{i,j} u_i$. The components of the output vector are a linear combination (i.e., a weighted sum) of the input components. The matrix entry $a_{i,j}$ contains the weight determining how much the ith component of $\mathbf{u}$ contributes to the jth component of $\mathbf{v}$.

The matrix $\mathbf{A}_{n \times m}$ is called a **linear transformation** (or **linear map**) $f : \mathbb{R}^n \to \mathbb{R}^m$, a function that turns n-dimensional input vectors into m-dimensional output vectors. For instance, the following matrix $\mathbf{A}_{2 \times 2}$ is a function that rotates each 2-dimensional vector through $90°$:

$$\mathbf{u} = \begin{pmatrix} 2 & 0 \end{pmatrix} \quad \mathbf{A} = \begin{pmatrix} 0 & 1 \\ -1 & 0 \end{pmatrix} \quad \mathbf{v} = \mathbf{u}\mathbf{A} = \begin{pmatrix} 0 & 2 \end{pmatrix}$$

Let $A_{n \times n}$ be a square matrix and $\mathbf{u}$ a n-dimensional column vector. The vector $\mathbf{u}$ is an **eigenvector** of $\mathbf{A}$ if and only if $\mathbf{A}\mathbf{u} = \lambda\mathbf{u}$ for some scalar λ, which is called the **eigenvalue** of $\mathbf{u}$. Vectors are transformed by matrix product: The eigenvectors of a matrix are those vectors that are stretched or shrunk by $\mathbf{A}$ of a value λ, but do not change their direction. Therefore, if $\mathbf{u}$ is an eigenvector of $\mathbf{A}$, then $\mathbf{A}\mathbf{u}$ is a scalar multiple of $\mathbf{u}$. Eigenvectors can be regarded as the axes along which linear maps act, elongating or compressing the input vectors. They are the main directions of the transformation produced by a matrix.

2.5.2 Principle Component Analysis (PCA)

PCA

Another dimensionality reduction technique closely related to SVD is **Principle Component Analysis** (PCA), which is applied to the mean-centered covariance matrix derived from $\mathbf{M}_{|T| \times |C|}$. Mean-centering the data corresponds to move them so that their center corresponds to the origin of the vector space. To mean-center a matrix, we subtract the mean of a column vector from each of its components. Therefore, the mean of every column vector becomes zero.

COVARIANCE
MATRIX

The **covariance matrix** $\mathbf{C}_{n \times n}$ is computed from the mean-centered co-occurrence matrix:

$$\text{cov}(\mathbf{M}_{m \times n}) = \mathbf{C}_{n \times n} = \frac{1}{m-1}\mathbf{M}^T\mathbf{M}. \quad (2.27)$$

This is the covariance matrix derived from the matrix (21):

$$(29) \quad \begin{array}{c} \\ bite \\ buy \\ drive \\ eat \\ get \\ live \\ park \\ ride \\ tell \end{array} \begin{array}{ccccccccc} bite & buy & drive & eat & get & live & park & ride & tell \\ 9 & -11 & -4 & -3 & -6.5 & 1 & -6.5 & -3.0 & -0.5 \\ -11 & 43 & 20 & -18.3 & 18.5 & -18.3 & 21.8 & 7.0 & -1.8 \\ -4 & 20 & 16 & -6.7 & 10 & -6.7 & 4.7 & -4 & -0.7 \\ -3 & -18.3 & -6.7 & 19 & -4.8 & 13.7 & -10.8 & -5 & 2.2 \\ -6.5 & 18.5 & 10 & -4.8 & 8.9 & -6.2 & 8.3 & 1.5 & -0.4 \\ 1 & -18.3 & -6.7 & 13.7 & -6.2 & 11 & -10.8 & -5 & 1.5 \\ -6.5 & 21.8 & 4.7 & -10.8 & 8.2 & -10.8 & 15.6 & 9.5 & -1.1 \\ -3 & 7 & -4 & -5 & 1.5 & -5 & 9.5 & 9 & -0.5 \\ -0.5 & -1.8 & -0.7 & 2.2 & -0.5 & 1.5 & -1.1 & -0.5 & 0.2 \end{array}$$

The covariance matrix is a square matrix whose rows and columns correspond to the columns of the co-occurrence matrix $M_{|T| \times |C|}$ and each entry c_{ij} contains the covariance between the vectors $\mathbf{m}_{*i}$ and $\mathbf{m}_{*j}$. The covariance between two n-dimensional vectors $\mathbf{u}$ and $\mathbf{v}$ is defined as follows: <small>VECTOR COVARIANCE</small>

$$\text{cov}(\mathbf{u}, \mathbf{v}) = \frac{\sum_{i=1}^{n}(\mathbf{u}_i - \bar{\mathbf{u}})(\mathbf{v}_i - \bar{\mathbf{v}})}{n - 1}. \quad (2.28)$$

where $\bar{\mathbf{u}}$ is the mean of the components of $\mathbf{u}$. The covariance between two vectors is a measure of their correlation: positive (negative) values correspond to positive (negative) correlations, and zero to independence.[4] Therefore, the covariance matrix reports the correlations between the features in the original co-occurrence matrix. For instance, in (29) *buy* is positively correlated with *park*, because these contexts co-occur with the same targets.

The PCA of the co-occurrence matrix $M_{|T| \times |C|}$ is carried out by the following factorization of its covariance matrix $\mathbf{C}$:

$$\mathbf{C}_{n \times n} = \mathbf{W}_{n \times n} \mathbf{\Lambda}_{n \times n} (\mathbf{W}_{n \times n})^T. \quad (2.29)$$

This factorization is known as **eigenvalue decomposition**: $\mathbf{W}_{n \times n}$ is an <small>EIGENVALUE DECOMPOSITION</small> orthogonal matrix containing the eigenvectors of $\mathbf{C}_{n \times n}$, and $\mathbf{\Lambda}_{n \times n}$ is a diagonal matrix containing their eigenvalues, sorted in decreasing order. If we only retain the k first eigenvectors, we can reduce the dimensionality of the data in $\mathbf{M}$ by multiplying it with the truncated eigenvector matrix $\mathbf{W}$, obtaining the reduced matrix $\mathbf{M}'_{|T| \times |D|}$ with size $m \times k$:

$$\mathbf{M}'_{|T| \times |D|} = \mathbf{M}_{m \times n} \mathbf{W}_{n \times k}. \quad (2.30)$$

---

[4] The covariance divided by the product of the standard deviations of the two vectors is the Pearson product-moment correlation r.

PRINCIPAL
COMPONENTS

PCA is essentially equivalent to the SVD of the covariance matrix. The singular values of $\mathbf{C}_{n \times n}$ are in fact related to its eigenvalues, as $\sigma_i^2 = (n-1)\lambda_i$. Like singular vectors, the eigenvectors ordered by their decreasing eigenvalues represent the directions of maximal variation in the data and are called **principal components**. The principal components are latent features in the distributional data. Therefore, PCA projects the original co-occurrence matrix onto a reduced matrix $\mathbf{M}'$ whose row vectors are embeddings of the targets in a latent semantic space with mutually independent dimensions $D = \{d_1, \ldots, d_k\}$. Lebret and Collobert (2014, 2015) show that better results can be obtained by applying PCA to the square root of the word co-occurrence probability matrix. They call this method **Hellinger PCA**, because it amounts to minimizing the difference between the original and reduced matrix according to the Hellinger distance, which measures the similarity between two probability distributions.

HELLINGER
PCA

2.5.3 Nonnegative Matrix Factorization (NMF)

NMF

SVD and PCA are especially suitable for normally distributed data. Therefore, they might be suboptimal when applied to the skewed distributional data (Manning and Schütze, 1999). **Non-negative Matrix Factorization** (NMF) (Lee and Seung, 2001) is a more recent dimensionality reduction algorithm that has been proposed to address this limit. NMF approximately factorizes an $m \times n$ co-occurrence matrix $\mathbf{M}$ into two other **non-negative matrices** (i.e., all the entries are equal to or greater than zero):

$$\mathbf{M}_{m \times n} \approx \mathbf{W}_{m \times k} \mathbf{H}_{k \times n}. \qquad (2.31)$$

NON-NEGATIVE
MATRICES

where $\mathbf{W}_{m \times k}$ is a matrix describing the original rows in a k-dimensional space of latent features, and $\mathbf{H}_{k \times n}$ is a matrix describing the original columns in the reduced space. In contrast to SVD and PCA, the decomposition does not have to be truncated in order to reduce the dimensionality, since k is chosen from the start. Furthermore, NMF tries to minimize the "divergence" of $\mathbf{M}$ from $\mathbf{WH}$:

$$D(\mathbf{M}\|\mathbf{WH}) = \sum_i \sum_j (m_{ij} \log \frac{m_{ij}}{(wh)_{ij}} - m_{ij} + (wh)_{ij}). \qquad (2.32)$$

If $\mathbf{M}$ and $\mathbf{WH}$ are normalized so that $\sum_{ij} m_{ij} = \sum_{ij} (wh)_{ij} = 1$, they can be regarded as probability distributions and $D(\mathbf{M}\|\mathbf{WH})$ corresponds to the Kullback-Leibler divergence (cf. Section 2.6). This has been argued to provide a better fit to language data than the normality assumption underlying SVD and PCA (Van de Cruys, 2010b).

The matrices $\mathbf{W}$ and $\mathbf{H}$ are formed by iteratively alternating between the following update rules to the initially random matrices (Lee and Seung, 2001):

$$h_{a\mu} \leftarrow h_{a\mu} \frac{\sum_i w_{ia} \frac{m_{i\mu}}{(wh)_{i\mu}}}{\sum_k w_{ka}} \tag{2.33}$$

$$w_{ia} \leftarrow w_{ia} \frac{\sum_\mu h_{a\mu} \frac{m_{i\mu}}{(wh)_{i\mu}}}{\sum_v w_{av}}. \tag{2.34}$$

The algorithm halts after a fixed number of iterations, or according to some stopping criterion, such as $D(\mathbf{M}\|\mathbf{WH})$ dropping below a certain threshold.

The following matrices are the product of the NMF of the co-occurrence matrix $\mathbf{M}_{|T|\times|C|}$ in (21), with $k = 2$:

$$
(30) \quad \mathbf{W}_{m \times k} = \begin{array}{c} \\ bike \\ car \\ dog \\ lion \end{array} \begin{array}{c} d_1 \quad d_2 \\ \begin{pmatrix} 1 & 0 \\ 1 & 0 \\ 0 & 1 \\ 0 & 1 \end{pmatrix} \end{array}
$$

$$
(31) \quad \mathbf{H}_{k \times m} = \begin{array}{c} d_1 \\ d_2 \end{array} \begin{pmatrix} bite & buy & drive & eat & get & live & park & ride & tell \\ 0 & 1 & 1 & 0 & 0.41 & 0 & 1 & 1 & 0 \\ 1 & 0 & 0 & 1 & 0.59 & 1 & 0 & 0 & 1 \end{pmatrix}
$$

$\mathbf{W}_{m \times k}$ is then used as the reduced matrix $\mathbf{M}'_{|T|\times|D|}$:

$$\mathbf{M}'_{|T|\times|D|} = \mathbf{W}_{m \times k}. \tag{2.35}$$

$\mathbf{W}_{m \times k}$ contains the embeddings of the target lexemes. The non-negativity constraint also implies a probabilistic interpretation of the NMF: If the column vectors of $\mathbf{W}$ and the row vectors of $\mathbf{H}$ are normalized so that they sum to one, $\mathbf{W}$ represents the probability of a target given a particular latent feature, and $\mathbf{H}$ gives the probability of a feature given a context. In this case, NMF is equivalent to probabilistic latent variable models (cf. Chapter 4.4).

2.6 Vector Similarity

The Distributional Hypothesis states that the semantic similarity between lexemes is a function of their **distributional similarity**.

DISTRIBUTIONAL
SIMILARITY

> The **distributional similarity** between two lexemes u and v is measured
> with the similarity between their distributional vectors **u** and **v**.

On the basis of the Distributional Hypothesis, measures of distributional
similarity are taken as measures of semantic similarity (cf. Chapter 7 for
a discussion on the complex relation between distributional and semantic
similarity).

VECTOR
SIMILARITY
MEASURE

Let **T** be a distributional vector space representing the targets T. The elements of **T** can be either explicit vectors or embeddings. In order to quantify
the distributional similarity of two lexemes, we apply a **vector similarity
measure** to their distributional representations.

> A **vector similarity measure** is a function $S : \mathbf{T} \times \mathbf{T} \to \mathbb{R}$ such that,
> for every pair of vectors **u** and **v**, $S(\mathbf{u}, \mathbf{v})$ is proportional to the degree of
> similarity between **u** and **v**. S obeys the following conditions:
>
> S1. $S(\mathbf{u}, \mathbf{v}) \leq 1$;
> S2. $S(\mathbf{u}, \mathbf{v}) = 1$ if and only if **u** and **v** are identical;
> S3. $S(\mathbf{u}, \mathbf{v}) = S(\mathbf{v}, \mathbf{u})$ (*symmetry*).

NEAREST
NEIGHBORS

Once we have computed the pairwise distributional similarity between the
targets, we can search for the k **nearest neighbors** of each lexeme.

> The k **nearest neighbors** of a target lexeme t are the k targets with the
> highest similarity score with t.

VECTOR
DISSIMILARITY
MEASURE

It is also possible to measure how much two vectors are different. A **vector
dissimilarity measure** is a function $DS : \mathbf{T} \times \mathbf{T} \to \mathbb{R}$ such that:

D1. $DS(\mathbf{u}, \mathbf{v}) \geq 0$;
D2. $DS(\mathbf{u}, \mathbf{v}) = 0$ if and only if **u** and **v** are identical;
D3. $DS(\mathbf{u}, \mathbf{v}) = DS(\mathbf{v}, \mathbf{u})$ (*symmetry*).

Dissimilarity is therefore the converse of similarity: The higher $DS(\mathbf{u}, \mathbf{v})$,
the smaller the similarity between **u** and **v**. We can transform a dissimilarity
measure into a similarity one in the following way:

$$S(\mathbf{u}, \mathbf{v}) = \frac{1}{1 + DS(\mathbf{u}, \mathbf{v})}. \tag{2.36}$$

Euclidean distance	$\mathrm{dsim}_{L2}(\mathbf{u}, \mathbf{v}) = \sqrt{\sum_{i=1}^{n} |u_i - v_i|^2}$
Manhattan distance	$\mathrm{dsim}_{L1}(\mathbf{u}, \mathbf{v}) = \sum_{i=1}^{n} |u_i - v_i|$
Cosine	$\mathrm{sim}_{\cos}(\mathbf{u}, \mathbf{v}) = \dfrac{\mathbf{u} \cdot \mathbf{v}}{||\mathbf{u}||\,||\mathbf{v}||} = \dfrac{\sum_{i=1}^{n} u_i v_i}{\sqrt{\sum_{i=1}^{n} u_i^2} \sqrt{\sum_{i=1}^{n} v_i^2}}$
Jaccard	$\mathrm{sim}_{\mathrm{Jaccard}}(\mathbf{u}, \mathbf{v}) = \dfrac{\sum_{i=1}^{n} min(w_{u,c_i}, w_{v,c_i})}{\sum_{i=1}^{n} max(w_{u,c_i}, w_{v,c_i})}$
Dice	$\mathrm{sim}_{\mathrm{Dice}}(\mathbf{u}, \mathbf{v}) = \dfrac{2 * \sum_{i=1}^{n} min(w_{u,c_i}, w_{v,c_i})}{\sum_{i=1}^{n} (w_{u,c_i} + w_{v,c_i})}$
Lin	$\mathrm{sim}_{\mathrm{Lin}}(\mathbf{u}, \mathbf{v}) = \dfrac{\sum_{i \in C_u^+ \cap C_v^+} (w_{u,c_i} + w_{v,c_i})}{\sum_{i \in C_u^+} w_{u,c_i} + \sum_{i \in C_v^+} w_{v,c_i}}$
KL divergence	$\mathrm{dsim}_{KL}(\mathbf{u}, \mathbf{v}) = D(p||q) = \sum_f p(f|u) log \dfrac{p(f|u)}{q(f|v)}$
JS divergence	$\mathrm{dsim}_{JS}(\mathbf{u}, \mathbf{v}) = \dfrac{1}{2} \left[D\left(p||\dfrac{p+q}{2}\right) + D\left(q||\dfrac{p+q}{2}\right) \right]$

Figure 2.12 Vector similarity (sim) and dissimilarity (dsim) measures

The denominator in Equation 2.36 ensures that the similarity of identical objects is one, because their dissimilarity is zero.

In the sections below, we present the main vector (dis)similarity measures used in distributional semantics, most of them derived from information retrieval and information theory (see Figure 2.12). There is actually a large variation in the nearest neighbors selected by different measures. Weeds et al. (2004) compare a large group of (dis)similarity measures and report that for many pairs of target lexemes the nearest neighbor sets identified by each measure do not have even half their members in common. Determining the most appropriate vector similarity measure strongly depends on the semantic task as well as on the parameters of the distributional representations, such as the type of contexts, weighting scheme, and dimensionality reduction.

2.6.1 Geometric Measures

The **geometric** approach defines similarity in spatial terms (Markman, 1999). According to this view, the semantic similarity between lexemes depends on the *proximity* of their distributional vectors: *Similar n-dimensional vectors are closer in n-dimensional space than dissimilar ones.*

The **Euclidean distance** or **L2 norm** between two vectors measures how far apart they are in the vector space:

$$\text{dsim}_{L2}(\mathbf{u}, \mathbf{v}) = \sqrt{\sum_{i=1}^{n} |u_i - v_i|^2}. \qquad (2.37)$$

The $L2$ norm is a dissimilarity measure obeying the conditions D1-D3 above and the *triangle inequality*, which states that the distance between two points is always shorter than taking any detour passing through a third point:

D4. $L2(\mathbf{u}, \mathbf{v}) \leq L2(\mathbf{u}, \mathbf{w}) + L2(\mathbf{w}, \mathbf{v})$

A function that satisfies the axioms D1-D4 is called a **distance** or **metric**. The $L2$ norm is a special case of the **Minkowski metric**, with $m = 2$:

$$\text{Lm}(\mathbf{u}, \mathbf{v}) = (\sum_{i=1}^{n} |u_i - v_i|^m)^{\frac{1}{m}}. \qquad (2.38)$$

If we set $m = 1$ we obtain another common metric, the **Manhattan distance**, also known as **L1 norm** or **City-block distance**:

$$\text{dsim}_{L1}(\mathbf{u}, \mathbf{v}) = \sum_{i=1}^{n} |u_i - v_i|. \qquad (2.39)$$

The $L2$ norm is a generalization of Pythagora's theorem to n-dimensional spaces: the Euclidean distance between the points $\mathbf{u}$ and $\mathbf{v}$ in the left panel of Figure 2.13 is the hypothenuse of the right triangle whose legs are segments in the direction of the perpendicular axes, with lengths equivalent to the absolute differences between the vector dimensions (i.e., $|u_i - v_i|$). The $L1$ norm instead measures the distance between $\mathbf{u}$ and $\mathbf{v}$ following a grid-like path (similar to the street layout in Manhattan, hence the name of the measure), and is the sum of the legs of the same right triangle (see Figure 2.13, right panel).

The Euclidean and Manhattan distances are sensitive to vector length, which in turn depends on the magnitude of the vector components (cf. Mathematical note 2 in Section 2.4). Consider the vectors $\mathbf{a} = (0, 3)$, $\mathbf{b} = (3, 0)$, and $\mathbf{c} = (0, 9)$. The vector $\mathbf{c}$ is a scalar multiple of $\mathbf{a}$: It points in the same direction as $\mathbf{a}$ but it is three times longer ($\|\mathbf{a}\| = 3$ and $\|\mathbf{c}\| = 9$). The vectors $\mathbf{a}$ and $\mathbf{b}$ have the same length, but are very different, because they do not share any component. The vector $\mathbf{c}$ is similar to $\mathbf{a}$, since the former is just a stretched version

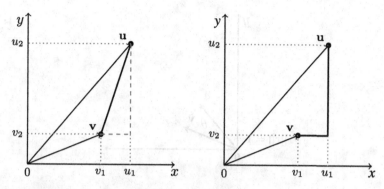

Figure 2.13 Left: Euclidean distance ($L2$). Right: Manhattan distance ($L1$)

of the latter, but the Euclidean distance between **a** and **b** turns out to be smaller than the one between **a** and **c**: $dsim_{L2}(\mathbf{a}, \mathbf{c}) = 6$ and $dsim_{L2}(\mathbf{a}, \mathbf{b}) = 4.2$ (the same happens with the L_1 norm). This example shows one important property of the Euclidean and Manhattan distances as measures of vector similarity: Words might eventually appear less similar than they actually are, just because of differences in the magnitude of vector components.

In order to abstract from the effects of vector length, we can **normalize** the VECTOR NORMALIZATION vectors before measuring their distance. We normalize a vector **v** by stretching or contracting it to a vector $\hat{\mathbf{v}}$ of length one in the same direction and orientation. Vectors are normalized by dividing each component by the vector length:

$$\hat{\mathbf{v}} = \frac{\mathbf{v}}{||\mathbf{v}||}. \qquad (2.40)$$

As illustrated in Figure 2.14, normalized vectors correspond to the points of the unit circle with radius one and centered at the origin. After normalization, COSINE the distance between vectors depends only on their direction. SIMILARITY

The most popular vector similarity measure is the **cosine similarity**:

$$\text{sim}_{\cos}(\mathbf{u}, \mathbf{v}) = \cos(\theta) = \frac{\mathbf{u} \cdot \mathbf{v}}{||\mathbf{u}|| ||\mathbf{v}||} = \frac{\sum_{i=1}^{n} u_i v_i}{\sqrt{\sum_{i=1}^{n} u_i^2} \sqrt{\sum_{i=1}^{n} v_i^2}}, \qquad (2.41)$$

where θ is the angle between the vectors and $\mathbf{u} \cdot \mathbf{v}$ is the vector dot or inner product (cf. Mathematical note 3 in Section 2.5.1). The latter also measures vector similarity, because it computes the correlation between the vector components: $\mathbf{u} \cdot \mathbf{v}$ is high, if **u** tends to be high where **v** is also high, and low where **v** is low. The problem is that the dot product is sensitive to vector length and

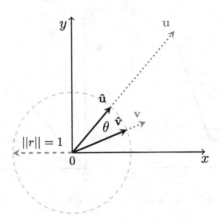

Figure 2.14 Vector normalization

unbounded (e.g., identical longer vectors have higher dot product than identical shorter vectors). The denominator in Equation 2.41 is the product of the vector lengths and normalizes the dot product, so that the cosine ranges from 1 for identical vectors to -1 (0, if the vectors do not contain negative values): The lower the cosine, the lower the vector similarity. Cosine similarity can thus be interpreted as the normalized correlation coefficient between vectors.

Equation 2.41 derives from the equivalence $\mathbf{u} \cdot \mathbf{v} = ||\mathbf{u}|| \, ||\mathbf{v}|| cos(\theta)$ (cf. Mathematical note 3 in Section 2.5.1). The cosine of θ in turn relates to the width of θ and therefore to the direction of the vectors. Consider the figure in Mathematical note 5. The vectors $\hat{\mathbf{p}}$, $\hat{\mathbf{h}}$ and $\hat{\mathbf{u}}$ form a right triangle with the first two sides as legs, the third as hypotenuse. The **cosine** of the angle θ is the ratio of the length of the leg adjacent to θ (i.e., $\hat{\mathbf{p}}$) to the length of the hypotenuse (i.e., $\hat{\mathbf{u}}$). Since $\hat{\mathbf{u}}$ is a unit vector, the cosine of θ is the length of $\hat{\mathbf{p}}$. If the angle between the vectors widens, $\hat{\mathbf{p}}$ shrinks and the cosine as well. We can imagine the endpoint of $\hat{\mathbf{u}}$ moving along the dashed unit circle, from where it overlaps with $\hat{\mathbf{v}}$ so that $\theta = 0°$ and $cos(\theta) = 1$, to a point perpendicular to $\hat{\mathbf{v}}$, where the vectors form a $90°$ angle, $\hat{\mathbf{p}}$ has vanished, and therefore $cos(\theta) = 0$. When θ is wider than $90°$, $\hat{\mathbf{p}}$ points in the opposite direction of $\hat{\mathbf{u}}$ and the cosine has negative sign, with $cos(180°) = -1$. Cosine similarity captures the intuitive notion that vectors pointing in similar directions are similar, because they have similar values across dimensions. Moreover, it is not affected by length: No matter how we stretch or contract two vectors, the angle θ remains the same.

Table 2.7 reports the ten nearest neighbors for *bike*, *car*, *dog*, and *lion*, according to cosine similarity. The distributional vectors were learnt from ukWaC, using as targets T and contexts C the $10,000$ most frequent nouns, verbs, and adjectives in this corpus. Co-occurrences were collected with a $[5, 5]$

COSINE AND
VECTORS

Mathematical note 5 – vector projections and cosine

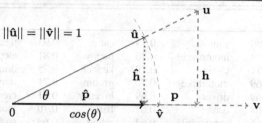

$$\|\hat{\mathbf{u}}\| = \|\hat{\mathbf{v}}\| = 1$$

Let $\mathbf{h}$ be a vector from the endpoint of $\mathbf{u}$ to $\mathbf{v}$, and perpendicular to the latter. The **projection** of $\mathbf{u}$ onto $\mathbf{v}$ is the vector $\mathbf{p}$ parallel to $\mathbf{v}$ that ends where $\mathbf{h}$ intersects $\mathbf{v}$, defined as $\mathbf{p} = c\mathbf{v}$. The projection $\mathbf{p}$ is a scalar multiple of $\mathbf{v}$. The scalar c is defined as follows:

$$c = \frac{\mathbf{u} \cdot \mathbf{v}}{\mathbf{v} \cdot \mathbf{v}}$$

Since $\mathbf{u} \cdot \mathbf{v} = \|\mathbf{u}\|\|\mathbf{v}\|cos(\theta)$ (cf. Mathematical note 3 in Section 2.5.1) and $\mathbf{v} \cdot \mathbf{v} = \|\mathbf{v}\|^2$, the length of the projection $\mathbf{p}$ is:

$$\|\mathbf{p}\| = \frac{\mathbf{u} \cdot \mathbf{v}}{\mathbf{v} \cdot \mathbf{v}}\|\mathbf{v}\| = \frac{\|\mathbf{u}\|\|\mathbf{v}\|cos(\theta)}{\|\mathbf{v}\|^2}\|\mathbf{v}\| = \|\mathbf{u}\|cos(\theta)$$

If $\hat{\mathbf{u}}$ and $\hat{\mathbf{v}}$ are unit vectors, the projection of $\hat{\mathbf{u}}$ onto $\hat{\mathbf{v}}$ is $\hat{\mathbf{p}} = c\hat{\mathbf{v}}$ and $c = \hat{\mathbf{u}} \cdot \hat{\mathbf{v}}$. In this case, $\|\hat{\mathbf{p}}\| = cos(\theta)$. The vector $\mathbf{h}$ is the projection of $\mathbf{u}$ orthogonal to $\mathbf{v}$, and $\mathbf{h} = \mathbf{u} - \mathbf{p}$. The theorem of **orthogonal decomposition** states that, given a vector $\mathbf{v}$, every vector $\mathbf{u}$ can be written in the form:

$$\mathbf{u} = \mathbf{w} + \mathbf{k}$$

such that $\mathbf{w}$ is parallel to $\mathbf{v}$ and $\mathbf{k}$ is orthogonal to $\mathbf{v}$.

---

context window and weighted with raw frequency. The targets are thus represented with explicit vectors whose components contain the raw co-occurrence frequency of targets and contexts. This is a very basic distributional representation, but we can notice that the distributional neighbors show a strong semantic similarity with the targets. The *car* and *bike* neighbors all pertain to the domain of vehicles, while those of *dog* and *lion* to the animal domain.

The left column of Table 2.8 contains the neighbors of *dog* obtained by measuring the L2 norm of unnnormalized vectors. Distances have been turned into similarities with Equation 2.36. Since *dog* is very frequent, the magnitude of its components is very high, thereby resulting in a very long vector. Therefore, it is far away in semantic space from any other word, as shown by the very small similarity values with its nearest neighbors, which are very different from the ones identified by the cosine and include high-frequent words such as *suppose* or *prefer*. This is a direct consequence of the sensitivity of

Table 2.7 Nearest neighbors according to the cosine similarity measure with
raw frequency weighting and no dimensionality reduction

bike		car		dog		lion	
bicycle	0.80	van	0.73	cat	0.93	tiger	0.71
ride_V	0.74	motorcycle	0.70	puppy	0.81	elephant	0.68
motorbike	0.71	cheap	0.70	kennel	0.75	dragon	0.56
biker	0.69	motorbike	0.70	groom	0.71	monkey	0.55
ride_N	0.69	driver	0.69	breeder	0.71	creature	0.55
rider	0.68	drive	0.67	bark	0.70	monster	0.55
try	0.66	automobile	0.64	rabbit	0.69	snake	0.53
one	0.66	hire	0.64	chase	0.69	turtle	0.53
ready	0.65	vehicle	0.64	kitten	0.67	hunt	0.52
horse	0.65	motorist	0.62	vet	0.67	beast	0.52

Table 2.8 Nearest neighbors of *dog* according to the L2
norm with raw frequency weighting and no
dimensionality reduction. Left: unnormalized vectors.
Right: normalized vectors

unnormalized vectors		*normalized vectors*	
cat	$5.941 * 10^{-5}$	cat	0.723
horse	$3.879 * 10^{-5}$	puppy	0.618
feed	$3.847 * 10^{-5}$	kennel	0.588
pick	$3.793 * 10^{-5}$	groom	0.570
tend	$3.782 * 10^{-5}$	breeder	0.569
kid	$3.778 * 10^{-5}$	bark	0.562
pet	$3.704 * 10^{-5}$	rabbit	0.558
suppose	$3.702 * 10^{-5}$	chase	0.557
prefer	$3.679 * 10^{-5}$	kitten	0.551
wonder	$3.678 * 10^{-5}$	vet	0.550

the Euclidean distance to vector length: Frequent words appear far away from
the other words and their neighbors tend to be other frequent words, regardless of their actual semantic similarity, while low-frequent ones tend to cluster
together close to the origin of the space (Widdows, 2004). The right column of
Table 2.8 shows the neighbors according to the Euclidean distance of normalized vectors. The frequency bias has disappeared, and the neighbors are like
those in Table 2.7. In fact, the cosine gives the same ranking of similarities as
the L2 norm, when the latter is applied to normalized vectors (Manning and
Schütze, 1999).

2.6.2 Nongeometric Measures

According to **feature-theoretic** approaches, the similarity between two objects does not depend on their geometric distance in a representation space, but rather on the number of features they share (Tversky, 1977). Non-geometric measures are typically used only with explicit vectors, whose similarity is computed by comparing their distributional features.

The **Jaccard** similarity measure (also called **Tanimoto** or **min/max**) computes the (weighted) number of features shared by the two vectors (Curran, 2003; Dagan, 2003):

JACCARD SIMILARITY

$$\mathrm{sim}_{\mathrm{Jaccard}}(\mathbf{u}, \mathbf{v}) = \frac{\sum_{i=1}^{n} min(w_{u,c_i}, w_{v,c_i})}{\sum_{i=1}^{n} max(w_{u,c_i}, w_{v,c_i})}. \tag{2.42}$$

w_{u,c_i} and w_{v,c_i} are, respectively, the weights of the ith feature of the vectors $\mathbf{u}$ and $\mathbf{v}$. This measure was originally designed for binary vectors but was extended to vectors of weighted features by Grefenstette (1994). The denominator in Equation 2.42 is a normalizing factor: The Jaccard ranges from 0, if the vectors do not have any overlapping feature (because in this case the non-zero component in one vector are zero in the other, and vice versa), to 1 for identical vectors. A variation of the Jaccard is the **Dice** measure, which uses as normalization factor the total value of non-zero features (Curran, 2003):

DICE SIMILARITY

$$\mathrm{sim}_{\mathrm{Dice}}(\mathbf{u}, \mathbf{v}) = \frac{2 * \sum_{i=1}^{n} min(w_{u,c_i}, w_{v,c_i})}{\sum_{i=1}^{n} (w_{u,c_i} + w_{v,c_i})}. \tag{2.43}$$

The Jaccard and Dice measures are derived from information retrieval. The **Lin** measure is very close to Dice but is introduced by Lin (1998b) specifically as a measure for lexical similarity, where C_u^+ and C_v^+ are the sets of positive components of $\mathbf{u}$ and $\mathbf{v}$:

LIN SIMILARITY

$$\mathrm{sim}_{\mathrm{Lin}}(\mathbf{u}, \mathbf{v}) = \frac{\sum_{i \in C_u^+ \cap C_v^+} (w_{u,c_i} + w_{v,c_i})}{\sum_{i \in C_u^+} w_{u,c_i} + \sum_{i \in C_v^+} w_{v,c_i}}. \tag{2.44}$$

This is the variant of a more general measure proposed by Lin (1998a), which defines the similarity between two objects as the ratio between the amount of information contained in the commonality between the objects (i.e., the overlapping features of $\mathbf{u}$ and $\mathbf{v}$) and the amount of information in the total description of the objects (i.e., the sum of the features representing either vector). In its original version, the Lin measure is applied to vectors whose

Table 2.9 Nearest neighbors of *bike*, *car*, *dog*, and *lion*
according to the Lin measure applied to vectors weighted with
PPMI

bike		car		dog		lion	
car	0.74	bike	0.74	cat	0.79	elephant	0.67
bicycle	0.71	vehicle	0.72	rabbit	0.71	beast	0.66
ride_V	0.70	van	0.71	horse	0.70	creature	0.66
ride_N	0.67	park	0.67	puppy	0.69	dragon	0.66
gear	0.67	truck	0.66	pet	0.69	snake	0.65
scooter	0.66	motorcycle	0.65	pig	0.65	bear	0.64
wheel	0.66	bus	0.64	kitten	0.65	tiger	0.64
motorcycle	0.66	bicycle	0.63	animal	0.64	wolf	0.63
rider	0.65	scooter	0.62	bite	0.62	man	0.63
boat	0.63	taxi	0.62	cow	0.62	sword	0.62

components are PMI scores between targets and contexts. Table 2.9 reports the ten nearest neighbors of *bike*, *car*, *dog*, and *lion* according to the Lin measure.

Some types of distributional representations use distributional vectors whose components represent the conditional probability of a feature f given the target (cf. Chapter 4.4). Suppose that $\mathbf{u}$ and $\mathbf{v}$, respectively, correspond to the probability distributions $p(f|u)$ and $q(f|v)$. The issue of the (dis)similarity between $\mathbf{u}$ and $\mathbf{v}$ can thus be recast as the question about the (dis)similarity of p and q (Dagan et al., 1997, 1999). The **Kullback-Leibler (KL) divergence** or **relative entropy** is a standard information-theoretic measure of the dissimilarity between two probability distributions (Cover and Thomas, 2006):

KULLBACK-
LEIBLER
DIVERGENCE

$$\text{dsim}_{\text{KL}}(\mathbf{u}, \mathbf{v}) = D(p||q) = \sum_f p(f|u) log \frac{p(f|u)}{q(f|v)}. \qquad (2.45)$$

The KL divergence measures how well q approximates distribution p, or how much information is lost if we assume distribution q when the true distribution is p. However, the KL divergence has two shortcomings as a distributional (dis)similarity measure: It is not symmetric (i.e., generally $D(p||q) \neq D(q||p)$),[5] and is undefined if there is a dimension i such as $q(v_i) = 0$ and $p(u_i) > 0$, which is problematic if applied to sparse distributional vectors, unless we preliminarily smooth them to remove the zeros.[6] One alternative is to use the **Jensen-Shannon (JS) divergence** or **total divergence to the aver-**

JENSEN-
SHANNON
DIVERGENCE

---

[5] Since it is not symmetric and does not satisfy the triangle inequality, the KL divergence is not a metric. However, it is usually claimed to express the "distance" between distributions (Cover and Thomas, 2006).

[6] Like Cover and Thomas (2006), we instead assume that $0 \log \frac{0}{0} = 0$ and $0 \log \frac{0}{q} = 0$.

age (Dagan et al., 1997) or **information radius** (Manning and Schütze, 1999), which represents the divergence of each distribution from the mean of the two, and does not have problems with zero dimensions (Lee, 1999):

$$\text{dsim}_{JS}(\mathbf{u}, \mathbf{v}) = JS(p, q) = \frac{1}{2}\left[D\left(p\middle\|\frac{p+q}{2}\right) + D\left(q\middle\|\frac{p+q}{2}\right)\right]$$

$$(2.46)$$

The JS divergence is a symmetric dissimilarity measure ranging between 0 for identical distributions to 1, for maximally different distributions.[7]

2.7 Summary

In this chapter, we have introduced the notion of **distributional representation** and its mathematical formalization in terms of **distributional vectors**. We have presented the basic method to build distributional representations, which consists in collecting distributional statistics extracted from a corpus in a **co-occurrence matrix** with the following **parameters**:

- the set of **targets lexemes** representing the elements of the vector space;
- the set of **contexts** characterizing the linguistic distribution of the target lexemes. The main types of contexts are lexical collocates and documents;
- the **weighting function**, to assign higher weights to the linguistic contexts that are more informative about the content of target lexemes;
- the optional **matrix reduction function**, which maps the co-occurrence matrix onto a new matrix whose columns correspond to latent dimensions in the original distributional data; and
- the **vector similarity measure**, which measures the distributional similarity of the target lexemes by computing the similarity of their vectors.

We have further distinguished between **explicit distributional vectors** – if lexemes are represented with the high-dimensional, sparse row vectors in the co-occurrence matrix – and **embeddings** – if lexemes are represented with low-dimensional, dense, implicit distributional vectors of latent features.

The parameters of distributional representations – targets, contexts, weighting function, dimensionality reduction function, and vector similarity measure – can be combined in several ways, giving rise to a large variety of **distributional semantic models**. We cover some of the most common models in Part II, and we compare the effect of various parameter settings in Chapter 7.

---

[7] The JS divergence is a measure of vector dissimilarity, but it not a metric because it is does not satisfy the triangle inequality (while its squared version does).

2.8 Further Reading

- Word frequency distributions: Baayen (2001); Baroni (2008)
- Corpus processing: Manning and Schütze (1999); Jurafsky and Martin (2008)
- Collocations and association measures: Evert (2008)
- Vector space model in information retrieval: Witten et al. (1999); Manning and Schütze (1999); Manning et al. (2008)
- Geometrical models of meaning: Widdows (2004)
- Linear algebra, SVD, and PCA: Strang (2016)
- Distributional similarity measures: Curran (2003); Weeds et al. (2004)

Part II

Models

3

Distributional Semantic Models

The preceding chapter introduced the basic components of distributional representations. We saw that there are a number of parameters that have to be decided upon when learning them: the selection of target lexemes, the definition of context type, the choice of weighting scheme, the application of dimensionality reduction, and the choice of vector similarity metric. Each configuration of these parameters gives rise to a different type of representation. In Part II, we introduce the most common types of **distributional semantic models** (DSMs). DISTRIBUTIONAL SEMANTIC MODELS

> A **distributional semantic model** is a computational model that learns distributional representations of target lexemes encoding their co-occurrence statistics with linguistic contexts.

There are many different ways to typologize DSMs. However, the two major dimensions of separation between the various existing (and possible) models are: (i) the **type of linguistic context** (see Figure 3.1) and (ii) the **method to learn distributional vectors** (see Figure 3.2).

The context choice is an important parameter of DSMs, which is likely CONTEXT TYPE to affect the similarity relations they identify. As the philosopher Nelson Goodman points out, there is no absolute notion of similarity:

[. . .] similarity is much like motion. Where a frame of reference is tacitly or explicitly established, all is well; but apart from a frame of reference, to say that something moves is as incomplete as to say that something is to the left of. We have to say what a thing is to the left of, what it moves in relation to, and in what respects two things are similar. (Goodman, 1972, p. 444)

In fact, any two things can be said to be similar or dissimilar depending on the respects in which similarity is described: A horse is more similar to a lion than to a car with respect to animacy, but this similarity relation is reversed if

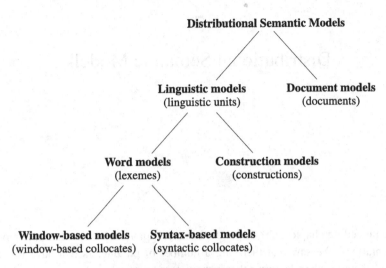

Figure 3.1 A classification of DSMs based on context types

we instead focus on their function as means of transportation. Therefore, similarity statements are by themselves empty unless we specify the dimensions along which two things are compared. Analogously, linguistic contexts provide the frame of reference to measure distributional similarity. Concerning context type, a major contrast divides **linguistic models** and **document models**, since they represent two radically different approaches to semantic similarity. In fact, linguistic models assume that two lexemes are similar if they tend to co-occur with the same *other* linguistic units (e.g., lexical collocates). In turn, various kinds of linguistic units may be chosen as contexts (cf. Section 2.2.1), giving rise to several types of DSMs. On the other hand, document models assume that two lexemes are similar if they tend to co-occur in the *same* texts. These two definitions of distributional similarity sometimes coincide, but in many cases the differences in the resulting semantic space can be dramatic.

LINGUISTIC
AND
DOCUMENT
MODELS

METHOD TYPE

The second dimension of variation among DSMs is the method to learn distributional representations (see Figure 3.2 and Table 3.1). The first generation of DSMs dates back to the 1990s and is characterized by so-called **count models**, which learn the distributional vector of a target lexical item by recording and *counting* its co-occurrences with linguistic contexts. The classic and most popular type of count DSMs are **matrix models**, directly stemming from the Vector Space Model in information retrieval (Salton et al., 1975), whose components are described in Chapter 2. Matrix models arrange distributional data into co-occurrence matrices (or similar, albeit more complex geometric objects, like tensors). The matrix is a mathematical representation of the *global*

COUNT MODELS

MATRIX
MODELS

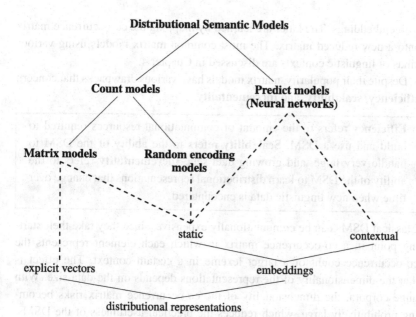

Figure 3.2 A classification of DSMs based on the computational method and the type of distributional representation they learn

Table 3.1 Some of the most influential DSMs

Model name	References
Hyperspace Analogue of Language (HAL)	Lund and Burgess (1996)
Latent Semantic Analysis (LSA)	Landauer and Dumais (1997)
Random Indexing (RI)	Kanerva et al. (2000)
Dependency Vectors (DV)	Padó and Lapata (2007)
Topic Models (LDA)	Griffiths et al. (2007)
Bound Encoding of the Aggregate Language Environment (BEAGLE)	Jones and Mewhort (2007)
Random Indexing with permutations	Sahlgren et al. (2008)
Distributional Memory (DM)	Baroni and Lenci (2010)
word2vec (CBOW, Skip-Gram)	Mikolov et al. (2013a, 2013b)
Global Vectors (GloVe)	Pennington et al. (2014)
FastText	Bojanowski et al. (2017)
Embeddings from Language Models (ELMo)	Peters et al. (2018)
Bidirectional Encoder Representations from Transformers (BERT)	Devlin et al. (2019)

distributional statistics extracted from the corpus. The weighting functions use such global statistics to estimate the importance of co-occurrences to character-ize target lexemes. Matrix DSMs can represent lexemes with explicit vectors or with embeddings. The latter are learned by mapping the co-occurrence matrix onto a new reduced matrix. The most common matrix models using various kinds of linguistic contexts are discussed in Chapter 4.

Despite their popularity, matrix models have various drawbacks that concern **efficiency**, **scalability**, and **incrementality**.

> **Efficiency** refers to the amount of computational resources required to build and use a DSM. **Scalability** refers to the ability of the DSM to handle very large, and growing data sets. **Incrementality** refers to the ability of the DSM to learn distributional representations that change over time when new linguistic data is encountered.

EFFICIENCY AND SCALABILITY

Classical DSMs can be computationally expensive, since they take their starting point in a co-occurrence matrix in which each element represents the co-occurrence count of a target lexeme in a certain context. The effect is that the dimensionality of the representations depends on the data size. With huge corpora, the dimensionality of the co-occurrence matrix risks becoming prohibitively large, which reduces the practical usefulness of the DSMs. One way to alleviate the problem of high dimensionality is to use some kind of dimensionality reduction technique (cf. Section 2.5). However, dimensionality reduction can be computationally extremely onerous when applied to large co-occurrence matrices. Furthermore, they reduce the cost of the similarity computation phase by producing low-dimensional vectors, but they do not reduce the cost of constructing the semantic spaces, since they require the co-occurrence matrix to be accumulated as a starting point.

INCREMENT-ALITY

Incrementality is a central aspect of human learning, which takes place sequentially and over time. Humans continuously learn new words and new uses of known words that they integrate into their existing semantic space. When new linguistic facts become available, semantic representations are updated locally, without systematically revising everything known. Matrix DSMs instead lack incrementality because they are *batch learners*, as they rely on the global statistics collected in the co-occurrence matrix. If new distributional data are added, the whole semantic space must be built again from scratch. This reduces the cognitive plausibility of matrix DSMs, and hamper

RANDOM ENCODING MODELS

their use to model dynamic aspects of lexical acquisition and change. In Chapter 5, we present *incremental* count DSMs, **random encoding models**. Rather than first collecting global co-occurrence statistics into a geometric object and then reducing them to dense vector, random encoding models directly learn low-dimensional embeddings by assigning each lexeme a random vector that is incrementally updated depending on the co-occurring contexts.

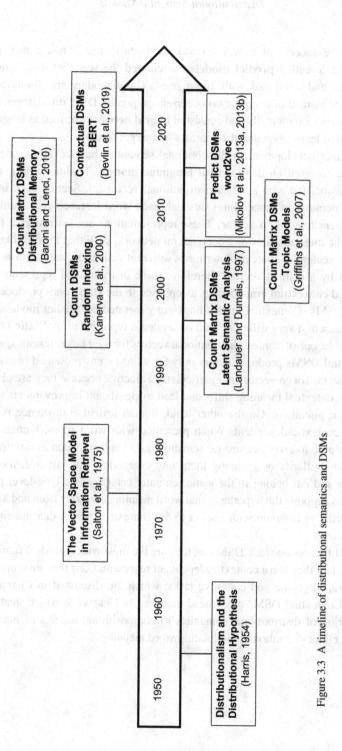

Figure 3.3 A timeline of distributional semantics and DSMs

With the success of neural network methods in the 2010s, a new generation of so-called **predict models** has entered the scene of distributional semantics and competed with count ones. These models are discussed in Chapter 6. Instead of counting co-occurrences, predict DSM directly generate embeddings incrementally and consist of **neural networks** trained as language models that learn to *predict* the contexts of a target lexeme.

A further development in distributional semantics has recently come out from the research on deep **neural language models**. Traditionally, a word type is associated with a single distributional vector (cf. Section 2.4). In the latest generation of embeddings, instead, each word instance gets a unique, context-sensitive **token vector**. These representations are learned as a function of the internal states of a deep neural network, such that a word token in different sentential contexts determines different activation states and is represented by a distinct vector. Therefore, these distributional representations are called **contextual embeddings** as opposed to the **static** ones produced by earlier DSMs. Contextual embeddings are generated by predict models, but they represent a very different kind of semantic representation. **Static DSMs** learn stable, out-of-context distributional vectors for their target lexemes, while **contextual DSMs** produce vectors only for word tokens presented in sentential contexts. Token vectors are particularly attractive because they are able to capture contextual meaning shifts and lead to significant improvements when used in applications. On the other hand, human lexical competence is also largely context-independent. When presented with word types, human subjects are able to carry out several semantic tasks on them, such as rating their semantic similarity or grouping them into categories. For instance, the fact that *dog* and *cat* belong to the same semantic category is a type-level property. This supports the hypothesis that word meanings abstract from and are (at least partially) invariant with respect to the contexts in which their tokens are observed.

Part II focuses on static DSMs, as they are the most widely studied family of models, and they learn context-independent representations that are employed in several linguistic and cognitive tasks, which are discussed in Chapters 7 and 8. Contextual DSMs are instead analyzed in Chapter 9, which treats the application of distributional semantics to compositional aspects of meaning and the effect of context in modulating word meaning.

4
Matrix Models

This chapter is devoted to discussing the major types of **matrix models**, a rich and multifarious family of DSMs that extend and generalize the Vector Space Model in information retrieval (cf. Section 1.2.1), from which they derive the use of **co-occurrence matrices** to represent distributional information.

Section 4.1 focuses on a group of matrix DSMs that we refer to as **classical models**, since they directly implement the basic procedure to build distributional representations introduced in Part I. The next sections then present DSMs that propose extensions and variants to classical ones: **Latent Relational Analysis** uses pairs of lexemes as targets to measure the semantic similarity of the relations between them (Section 4.2); **Distributional Memory** represents distributional data with a higher-order tensor, from which different types of matrices are derived to address various semantic tasks (Section 4.3); **Topic Models** (Section 4.4) and **GloVe** (Section 4.5) introduce new approaches to reduce the dimensionality of the co-occurrence matrix, respectively based on probabilistic inference and a method inspired by neural DSMs.

4.1 Classical Matrix Models

A **classical DSM** is a matrix model defined by the following components (cf. also Lowe, 2001; Padó and Lapata, 2007):

A **classical DSM** is a tuple $< T, C, W, \mathbf{M}, R, S >$ such that:

T is a set of **target lexemes**, $\{t_1, \ldots, t_m\}$;
C is a set of **linguistic contexts**, $\{c_1, \ldots, c_n\}$;
W is a **weighting function**, $W : T \times C \to \mathbb{R}$;

> **M** is a **co-occurrence matrix** with size $|T| \times |C|$;
> R is an optional **matrix reduction function**, $R : \mathbf{M}_{|T| \times |C|} \rightarrow \mathbf{M}'_{|T| \times |D|}$, such that $D = \{d_1, \dots, d_k\}$ are **latent features** and $|D| \ll |C|$;
> S is a **vector similarity measure**, $S : \mathbf{T} \times \mathbf{T} \rightarrow \mathbb{R}$, with $\mathbf{T}$ a **distributional vector space** representing the targets T such that the elements of $\mathbf{T}$ are the row vectors of $\mathbf{M}$ or $\mathbf{M}'$.

The arguably most common setting of these parameters is as follows:

1. $T = C$ and correspond to a **subset of the corpus vocabulary** V, typically selected by fixing a frequency threshold;
2. the co-occurrence matrix $\mathbf{M}_{|T| \times |C|}$ is a square matrix containing **window-based undirected collocates** identified using a narrow rectangular context window spanning two or three items on each side of the target lexeme;
3. the co-occurrence matrix is weighted with **PPMI**; and
4. vector similarity is computed with the **cosine**.

STANDARD
MODEL

WINDOW-BASED
DSM

We refer to such a DSM as the **standard model**, because it represents a kind of de facto standard in distributional semantics and its settings have been shown to produce good results in a number of semantic tasks, although there is no universally optimal parameter configuration. The standard model is a **window-based DSM**. In fact, models using lexical collocates rather than documents produce representations that better adhere to the original formulation of the distributional hypothesis (Sahlgren, 2008). The size of the context window is also an important parameter that affects the type of information represented by the model (cf. Section 2.2.1). It has been demonstrated that narrow context windows lead to representations that better capture synonymy than wider windows, which instead produce representations that are more associative in nature (Sahlgren, 2006; Bullinaria and Levy, 2007, 2012).

The output of the standard model is explicit distributional vectors. There are two common variants of this model that instead produce embeddings:

PPMI-SVD – it applies SVD to the PPMI-weighted co-occurrence matrix, reducing the dimensionality to the first k dimensions, with k typically ranging between 100 and 300;

PPMI-iSVD – it applies Caron-p transformed SVD (or simply discards the first 100 dimensions of the SVD (iSVD for inversely-truncated SVD) to the PPMI-weighted co-occurrence matrix.

Experimental evidence shows that iSVD outperforms the other variants (Bullinaria and Levy, 2012; Österlund et al., 2015; Sahlgren and Lenci, 2016).

In the next sections, we present some popular classical DSMs which contain significant variations with respect to the standard model, most notably with respect to the type of contexts and weighting schemes.

4.1.1 Hyperspace Analogue to Language (HAL)

The **Hyperspace Analogue to Language** (HAL) is a DSM developed in HAL cognitive science to model semantic memory (Lund et al., 1995; Lund and Burgess, 1996; Burgess, 1998; Burgess and Lund, 2000). HAL is one of the earliest DSMs, and one of the most influential ones. It is a window-based model directly inspired by Schütze (1992), but differently from the latter it uses directed collocates and does not reduce the co-occurrence matrix with SVD. In its original formulation, HAL employs a $[10, 10]$ context window with distance weights to populate a **directional matrix**, whose row and column vectors DIRECTIONAL encode raw co-occurrence counts to the left and right of the target lexeme. The MATRIX window weighting function, called **linear ramp**, assigns to a context lexeme LINEAR RAMP c the weight $w - p + 1$, such that w is the window size and p is the position WEIGHTING of c with respect to the target t. For instance, words immediately adjacent to the target are assigned a weight of ten, words appearing at a distance of two words from the target are assigned a weight of nine, and so on. The following is an example of the HAL co-occurrence matrix that Lund and Burgess (1996) derive from the sentence *The horse past the barn fell* using a $[5, 5]$ window:

$$
(1) \quad \mathbf{M} = \begin{array}{c} \\ barn \\ fell \\ horse \\ past \\ raced \\ the \end{array} \begin{array}{c} \begin{array}{cccccc} barn & fell & horse & past & raced & the \end{array} \\ \left(\begin{array}{cccccc} 0 & 0 & 2 & 4 & 3 & 6 \\ 5 & 0 & 1 & 3 & 2 & 4 \\ 0 & 0 & 0 & 0 & 0 & 5 \\ 0 & 0 & 4 & 0 & 5 & 3 \\ 0 & 0 & 5 & 0 & 0 & 4 \\ 0 & 0 & 3 & 5 & 4 & 2 \end{array} \right) \end{array}
$$

The row and column vectors of the HAL model represent co-occurrences with preceding and succeeding items, respectively. Each target lexeme is then represented with the concatenation of its row and column vectors. This leads to very high-dimensional explicit vectors containing directed collocates (with $2n$ dimensions, where n is the size of the vocabulary, in the extreme case). In order to reduce the dimensionality of the resulting vectors, HAL simply discards dimensions with low variance (cf. Section 2.3.2). Distributional similarity is measured with the Euclidean distance applied to normalized vectors.

HIDEX

There are several variations of the basic HAL model. The **High Dimensional Explorer** (HiDEx) is a direct generalization of HAL, with a larger range of settings for its parameters (Shaoul and Westbury, 2006, 2010). The

COALS

Correlated Occurrence Analogue to Lexical Semantics (COALS) (Rohde et al., 2006) uses a co-occurrence matrix with undirected collocates extracted with a smaller context window (e.g., with size $[4, 4]$). Instead of variance, COALS selects contexts according to their frequency. Co-occurrences are then

PEARSON CORRELATION

weighted with the **Pearson correlation** (cf. the notation in Equations 2.3–2.5):

$$w_{t,c} = \frac{TF(t,c) - F(t,*) \cdot F(*,c)}{(F(t,*) \cdot (T - F(t,*)) \cdot F(*,c) \cdot (T - F(*,c)))^{\frac{1}{2}}}, \quad (4.1)$$

where $T = F(*,*)$. The weights w derived from the co-occurrence frequencies in the matrix range between -1 for negative correlations and $+1$ for positive correlations. Since negative correlations both make less sense and are less reliable for co-occurrence data, negative values are normally discarded, like with PPMI. The remaining positive correlations are then square rooted to magnify the many small values with respect to the few large ones, and correlation is again used to compute vector similarities.[1] COALS also optionally employs SVD to reduce the representations before computing similarities.

4.1.2 Latent Semantic Analysis (LSA)

LSA

As discussed in Section 1.2.1, **Latent Semantic Analysis** (LSA) was originally developed as a refinement of the Vector Space Model with primary application in information retrieval (Furnas et al., 1988; Deerwester et al., 1990).[2] The development of LSA was motivated by the inability of the Vector Space Model to handle synonymy. Documents are ranked as relevant to a query only to the extent that they share terminology with the query. Thus, a query on *computational models of meaning* will not match documents about *distributional semantics* unless they explicitly contain the words *computational*, *models*, and *meaning*. It would be advantageous if the model could utilize the distributional similarity between *meaning* and *semantics* when matching the

---

[1] Rohde et al. (2006) note that correlation is identical to cosine similarity except that the mean value is subtracted from each vector component in the correlation measure.

[2] The method is also known as **Latent Semantic Indexing (LSI)**, a name mainly used in the context of information retrieval.

query to the documents. LSA was first introduced as an elegant solution to the synonymy problem in information retrieval and other document processing tasks by computing similarity between document and query vectors in a latent semantic space. Later on, Landauer and Dumais (1997) proposed LSA as a general psychological theory of knowledge acquisition from co-occurrence statistics. LSA has in fact become one of the most popular DSMs in cognitive science to estimate word semantic similarity.

LSA is a **document DSM** and represents the distributional properties of target lexemes with a **word-by-document** co-occurrence matrix like the following one, which contains the imaginary frequency distribution of target lexemes in four texts corresponding to Frege's *On Sense and Denotation*, Russell's *On Denoting*, and Wittgenstein's *Tractatus* and *Philosophical Investigations*:

WORD-BY-DOCUMENT MATRIX

$$
(2) \quad
\begin{array}{l}
 \\
game \\
meaning \\
truth \\
use
\end{array}
\begin{array}{cccc}
Sense\_and\_Den & On\_Den & Tractatus & Phil\_Inv \\
0 & 0 & 0 & 19 \\
4 & 5 & 9 & 13 \\
6 & 2 & 15 & 7 \\
0 & 1 & 0 & 25
\end{array}
$$

The co-occurrence matrix is typically weighted with log entropy (Dumais, 1991, 1993) or tf-idf (Nakov et al., 2001) (cf. Section 2.3.1), and then reduced to k latent dimensions with SVD, which represents the hallmark of LSA. Obviously, the number of retained dimensions in the reduced matrix determines the granularity of the latent representation: Increasing the number of dimensions in the latent space enables more fine-grained distinctions to be made. Finding the optimal value of the reduced space is therefore a trade-off between generality and specificity. The optimal value of k depends on the task and the size of the data. Typical choices of k are on the order of hundreds: Furnas et al. (1988) and Deerwester et al. (1990) use 100 dimensions, Landauer and Dumais (1997) 300 dimensions, and Bradford (2008) 400 dimensions.

The role of SVD is crucial for computing word semantic similarity in document DSMs. In a word-by-document matrix, the distributional similarity between two words depends on the extent they co-occur together in the same documents. In fact, the nearest neighbors computed without SVD are typically lexemes that are syntagmatically related to the target, as shown in the top row of Table 4.1. For example, the proximal space of *lion* is populated by neighbors such as *come* and *see*, presumably because these are high-frequency words that appear in the same documents as the target. In the bottom row of Table 4.1, we can notice the drastic change in the semantic space brought by SVD: Several neighbors are now words that are paradigmatically related to the target (e.g., *van* for *car* and *tiger* for *lion*). Dimensionality reduction extracts high-order

Table 4.1 LSA nearest neighbors of *bike*, *car*, *dog*, and *lion* ranked by cosine similarity before (top part) and after (bottom part) SVD with the top 300 latent dimensions

bike		car		dog		lion	
ride_V	0.41	take	0.52	puppy	0.33	elephant	0.15
rider	0.35	do	0.51	pet	0.30	come	0.14
ride_N	0.30	get	0.51	do	0.30	see	0.14
cycling	0.29	make	0.51	go	0.30	go	0.14
motorcycle	0.28	time	0.51	take	0.30	great	0.14
cyclist	0.26	good	0.51	get	0.30	know	0.14
road	0.24	go	0.51	time	0.30	man	0.14
get	0.23	more	0.50	make	0.30	do	0.14
cycle	0.23	see	0.50	see	0.30	take	0.14
bicycle	0.23	year	0.50	come	0.30	say	0.14
biker	0.93	park_V	0.81	kennel	0.93	beast	0.81
off-road	0.87	drive	0.79	puppy	0.93	snake	0.80
ride_V	0.84	van	0.74	bark	0.90	tiger	0.79
bicycle	0.83	motor	0.72	pet_A	0.79	eagle	0.78
ride_N	0.83	park_N	0.71	breed	0.77	elephant	0.74
motorcycle	0.83	mileage	0.71	pup	0.77	dragon	0.73
motorbike	0.83	vehicle	0.71	greyhound	0.75	bear	0.72
rider	0.82	bumper	0.70	pet_N	0.74	desert	0.72
biking	0.77	driver	0.69	flea	0.74	wolf	0.71
riding	0.76	parking	0.68	groom	0.72	donkey	0.71

The targets are the 10, 000 most frequent nouns, verbs, and adjectives in ukWaC. The contexts are 554, 931 documents

co-occurrences from distributional data (cf. Section 2.4.2). In this case, SVD induces similarities between lexemes that do not themselves co-occur, but that co-occur with the same *other* lexemes. This entails that paradigmatically similar words can become very close neighbors even if they do not themselves co-occur, provided they appear in documents that are in turn highly similar because they share many words.

Table 4.1 also shows how SVD mitigates the negative effects of the curse of dimensionality. Neighbors in the unreduced space have very low and highly close values. This is an example of the phenomenon of distance concentration affecting high-dimensional vectors, with neighbors tending to be all equidistant from the target. In the reduced space, nearest neighbors have instead higher cosines and a much larger range of values. This means that SVD can bring about a more fine-grained discrimination of similarity relations.

ESA   A variation of LSA is **Explicit Semantic Analysis** (ESA), a document DSM trained on Wikipedia (Gabrilovich and Markovitch, 2007). ESA represents lexemes with distributional vectors whose dimensions are Wikipedia articles, and the values are tf-idf scores of the lexeme in each respective article. Differently from LSA, ESA does not use dimensionality reduction, and the term "explicit" is meant to highlight the fact that it is built from a knowledge source explicitly defined by humans, instead of using latent dimensions. Gabrilovich and Markovitch (2007) argue that ESA can represent world knowledge in a way that is not available to other DSMs. The idea is that since each Wikipedia article (in theory) discusses a specific topic or concept (e.g., distributional semantics), using such articles as contexts will produce DSMs that take advantage of the knowledge encoded in the construction of the Wikipedia taxonomy. However, *all* text corpora are produced by humans, and in that sense encode world knowledge. The only difference between Wikipedia and other training data is that the topic being discussed in an article is explicitly available in Wikipedia as the title of the article, whereas in other corpora the topic is not normally explicitly defined. However, that difference has no effect on the information coded in ESA, which uses only document co-occurrences.

4.1.3 Dependency Vectors (DV)

We use the name **Dependency Vectors** (DV) to refer to the general framework to build **syntax-based DSMs** proposed by Padó and Lapata (2007). Syntactic information extracted from shallow or fully parsed corpora are extensively employed in distributional semantics (Hindle, 1990; Grefenstette, 1994; Lin, 1998a; Lee, 1999; Curran and Moens, 2002; Baroni and Lenci, 2010; Kiela and Clark, 2014; Lapesa and Evert, 2017). DV is the first systematic attempt to formalize the use of syntactic contexts in matrix DSMs. DV SYNTAX-BASED DSM

DV represents the distributional properties of lexemes with syntactic collocates defined over dependency-based representations, such as the following one from Padó and Lapata (2007):

(3)
$$\overset{\text{subj}}{\overset{\text{det}}{\overbrace{\text{A lorry}}}} \overset{\text{aux}}{\overbrace{\text{might}}} \overset{\text{obj}}{\overbrace{\text{carry}}} \overset{\text{mod}}{\overbrace{\text{sweet apples.}}}$$

DV extends the definition of classical DSM at the outset of Section 4.1 with the following functions applied to dependency graphs:

Context selection function $(cont)$ – selects the dependency paths that provide the syntactic contexts representing a target lexeme. In particular, it is possible to set the path length (e.g., $\langle lorry, carry \rangle$ has length one, while $\langle lorry, carry, apples \rangle$ has length two), to define syntactic CONTEXT SELECTION FUNCTION contexts with collocates at various distances from the target (cf. Section 2.2.1);

PATH VALUE
FUNCTION **Path value function** (v) – assigns weights to dependency paths. Padó and Lapata (2007) propose a **length weight**, in which paths receive a weight inversely proportional to their length (giving higher weights to more direct syntactic relations), and a linguistically informed **gram-rel weight** that takes into account the Accessibility Hierarchy by Keenan and Comrie (1977). In the latter case, subjects receive a weight of five, direct objects of four, and so on, accounting for the different salience of grammatical relations;

BASIS MAPPING
FUNCTION **Basis mapping function** (μ) – maps the selected paths onto the matrix columns. In the **word-based basis mapping**, all paths ending at lexeme l are mapped onto the matrix column labeled with l. This mapping produces dependency-filtered collocates as contexts (cf. Section 2.2.1). Alternatively, paths can be mapped onto dependency-typed collocates.

The following is a co-occurrence matrix derived from (3) using paths of length one, gram-rel weighting, and word-based mapping:

$$(4) \quad \begin{array}{c} \\ lorry \\ apple \end{array} \begin{array}{cccc} lorry & carry & sweet & apple \\ \left(\begin{array}{cccc} 0 & 5 & 0 & 0 \\ 0 & 4 & 1 & 0 \end{array} \right) \end{array}$$

The columns of this matrix are instead dependency-typed collocates selected with paths of length ≤ 2 and weighted according to $1/length$:

$$(5) \quad \begin{array}{c} \\ lorry \\ apple \end{array} \begin{array}{cccc} \langle subj, carry \rangle & \langle obj, carry \rangle & \langle mod, sweet \rangle & \langle obj, apple \rangle \\ \left(\begin{array}{cccc} 1 & 0 & 0 & 0.5 \\ 0 & 1 & 1 & 0 \end{array} \right) \end{array}$$

DV is a meta-model that subsumes all kinds of syntax-based DSMs. For their experiments, Padó and Lapata (2007) employ dependency-filtered collocates LOG-
LIKELIHOOD
RATIOS weighted with **log-likelihood ratios** (Dunning, 1993), an association measure that emphasizes high-frequency collocates, like LMI. Vector similarity is then computed with the Lin measure applied to the unreduced co-occurrence matrix.

4.2 Latent Relational Analysis (LRA)

Classical DSMs measure the semantic similarity of lexical items, which appear LRA as targets in the co-occurrence matrix. **Latent Relational Analysis** (LRA) is instead a distributional method to measure the similarity of relations between word pairs (Turney, 2005; Turney and Littman, 2005; Turney, 2006a, 2006b,

2008a, 2008b). The **relational similarity** between two pairs of lexemes $\langle a, b \rangle$ RELATIONAL
and $\langle c, d \rangle$ depends on the degree of correspondence between the relation link- SIMILARITY
ing a to b and the relation linking c to d (cf. Section 7.1). For instance,
$\langle wheel, car \rangle$ is relationally similar to $\langle finger, hand \rangle$, because the former
item of each pair is a meronym (i.e., denotes a part) of the latter. LRA measures
relational similarity by representing lexeme pairs $\langle l_i, l_j \rangle$ with vectors encoding
the statistical distribution of **lexico-syntactic patterns** connecting l_i and l_j in LEXICO-
a corpus. SYNTACTIC
PATTERNS

The use of lexico-syntactic patterns to mine semantic relations from texts
was pioneered by Hearst (1992), who selects patterns, henceforth known as
Hearst patterns, deemed to be indicative of the hyponymy relation. For exam- HEARST
ple, the identification in a text of the string (6b) as an instance of the pattern in PATTERNS
(6a) is taken as evidence that *kangaroo* is a hyponym of *animal*.

(6) a. *such* NP$_1$ *as* NP$_2$
     b. ...such animals as the kangaroo...

By searching for pairs of words that occur with the selected patterns,
Hearst aims at automatically acquiring hyponyms from large corpora to
populate hand-built thesauri. Hearst's pattern-based approach has become
extremely popular in computational linguistics and has been applied to identify meronymy (Berland and Charniak, 1999), concept properties (Almuhareb
and Poesio, 2004), Pustejovsky's qualia roles (Cimiano and Wenderoth, 2007;
cf. Section 8.1), verb semantic relations (Chklovski and Pantel, 2004), and so
forth (cf. Section 8.3.1).

Hearst patterns are typically small in number and hand-selected. This
requires the linguist to decide a priori which patterns are associated with which
semantic relations. The goal is to find patterns that are able to produce a relation instance using an exact match of a single co-occurrence. This strategy
has various shortcomings. First of all, it runs into data sparseness problems,
since the relevant patterns are generally very rare, even in the largest corpora.
Secondly, and most crucially, this approach works well only provided that we
are able to choose patterns *univocally* associated with the target relation. Most
patterns are instead polysemous and encode very different types of semantic
relations. For instance, the pattern *X has Y* can be used to express meronymy
(e.g., *a car has four wheels*), but also possession (e.g., *this man has a car*).
Instead of using hand-selected patterns, Snow et al. (2004) introduce an automatic method (already hinted by Hearst) to harvest patterns associated with a
certain semantic relation from a set of seed instances of that relation: Given a
seed pair $\langle l_1, l_2 \rangle$ for the relation R, the syntactic patterns linking l_1 and l_2 in a

dependency-parsed corpus are used as features to identify new instances of R. Variations of this methodology have extensively been applied to semantic relation identification and classification (Pantel and Pennacchiotti, 2006; Carlson et al., 2010; Riedel et al., 2013; Shwartz et al., 2016, among several others).

Pattern-based approaches share many methodological assumptions with distributional semantics, above all the idea that relational similarity between lexeme pairs is a function of their co-occurrence with similar linguistic contexts. The main novelty of LRA is to make explicit such a connection by incorporating aspects of pattern-based methods within the general framework of classical DSMs. LRA is grounded on an extension of the Distributional Hypothesis called **Latent Relation Hypothesis** (Turney, 2005, 2006b, 2008a):

LATENT
RELATION
HYPOTHESIS

> Two pairs of lexemes that co-occur with similar patterns tend to have similar semantic relations.

EXTENDED
DISTRIBU
TIONAL
HYPOTHESIS

This is the reverse of the **Extended Distributional Hypothesis** proposed by Lin and Pantel (2001) to identify inference rules for question-answering by measuring the semantic similarity between syntactic patterns. According to Lin and Pantel (2001), patterns that occur with similar lexeme pairs tend to have similar meanings: for instance, the pattern X *wrote* Y is semantically similar to the pattern X *is the author of* Y because they share a large number of noun pairs co-occurring with them. Pattern similarity is computed by applying the Lin measure to distributional vectors representing the patterns.

LRA is a matrix DSM such that:

1. the targets T are a set of **lexeme pairs**, $\{\langle l_1, l_2 \rangle, \ldots, \langle l_m, l_r \rangle\}$;
2. the contexts C are a set of **patterns**, $\{p_1, \ldots, p_n\}$; and

PAIR-BY-
PATTERN
MATRIX

3. the co-occurrence matrix $\mathbf{M}_{|T| \times |C|}$ is a **pair-by-pattern** matrix, in which each entry represents the number of times the corresponding target pair appears in the training corpus with the corresponding pattern:

$$(7) \quad \begin{array}{c} \\ \langle wheel, car \rangle \\ \langle car, vehicle \rangle \end{array} \begin{array}{ccc} NP_1\_is\_a\_NP_2 & such\_NP_1\_as\_NP_2 & NP_1\_of\_NP_2 \\ \left(\begin{array}{ccc} 0 & 0 & 10 \\ 3 & 6 & 0 \end{array} \right) \end{array}$$

The pair-by-pattern matrix may contain either hand-selected Hearst patterns (Turney and Littman, 2005) or automatically harvested ones. Patterns differ in the level of abstraction and range from simple n-grams to dependency paths extracted from parsed corpora (Lin and Pantel, 2001; Snow et al., 2004). Turney (2006b) searches in the corpus for short phrases that begin with one member of the target pairs and end with the other, and then creates several patterns out of these phrases by replacing words with wild cards. For example, if the target pair ⟨*wheel, car*⟩ appears in the phrase *the wheel of the car*, the following patterns are generated: *of the*, *of **, ** the*, and ** **. The resulting high-dimensional sparse matrix is weighted with log entropy and reduced with SVD. Relational similarity between two target pairs is computed by measuring the cosine between their corresponding row vectors in the reduced matrix.

Turney (2006b) tests LRA on the SAT word analogy questions (cf. Section 7.2.4). The SAT pairs are represented with LRA distributional vectors and the pair with the highest cosine similarity to the stem pair of each analogy is selected as answer. LRA is also used to classify the semantic relation of 600 noun-modifier pairs from Nastase and Szpakowicz (2003), manually labeled with 30 classes of semantic relations (e.g., *student protest* is classified as AGENT, because the students are the agents of the protest).

4.3 Distributional Memory (DM)

Distributional Memory (DM) is a framework for distributional semantics pro-   DM
posed by Baroni and Lenci (2010) which extends classical DSMs by providing a general-purpose format to represent distributional information and address a wide range of semantic tasks. The aim of DM is to overcome the traditional *"one semantic task, one distributional model"* approach in distributional semantics, in which each task (or set of closely related tasks) is treated as a separate problem addressed with task-specific representations and models. For example, LRA measures relational similarity using an ad hoc pair-by-pattern matrix, which has nothing in common with the word-by-word matrix used to target word similarity. This contrasts with the common view in cognitive science that humans resort to a general-purpose semantic memory, a relatively stable long-term knowledge database, adapting the information stored there to the various tasks at hand (Murphy, 2002; Rogers and McClelland, 2004; McRae and Jones, 2013). From a practical perspective, going back to the corpus to train a different model for each application is inefficient, and it runs the risk of overfitting the model to a specific task, while losing sight of its adaptivity – a highly desirable feature for any intelligent system.

According to Baroni and Lenci (2010), the lack of generalization in distributional semantics stems from the choice to represent co-occurrence statistics directly as matrices, thereby losing sight of the fact that different semantic spaces actually rely on the same kind of underlying distributional information. The DM framework instead consists of two major components: (i) a **distributional memory** of corpus-extracted lexeme-relation-lexeme tuples represented

Table 4.2 Weighted distributional tuples (Baroni and Lenci, 2010)

lexeme	*relation*	*lexeme*	*weight*	*lexeme*	*relation*	*lexeme*	*weight*
marine	own	bomb	40.0	sergeant	use	gun	51.9
marine	use	bomb	82.1	sergeant	own	book	8.0
marine	own	gun	85.3	sergeant	use	book	10.1
marine	use	gun	44.8	teacher	own	bomb	5.2

as a **third-order tensor**, and (ii) a set of **matrices** generated from the tensor in order to perform semantic tasks in the vector spaces they define.

4.3.1 Distributional Tuples and Tensors

DISTRIBUT-
IONAL MEMORY DM consists of a **distributional memory** formed by **weighted tuples** extracted from the corpus.

> Let L_1 and L_2 be sets of lexemes, and R a set of strings representing syntagmatic co-occurrence relations (e.g., syntactic dependencies, shallow lexico-syntactic patterns, etc.). A **DM weighted tuple** $\langle\langle l_1, r, l_2\rangle, v\rangle$ consists of (i) a tuple $\langle l_1, r, l_2\rangle \in L_1 \times R \times L_2$ such that L_1 co-occurs with L_2 and R is the type of this co-occurrence relation; (ii) a real-value weight v assigned to the tuple by a scoring function $\sigma : L_1 \times R \times L_2 \to \mathbb{R}$.

WEIGHTED
TUPLE For instance, the tuple $\langle$*marine, use, bomb*$\rangle$ in Table 4.2 encodes the piece of distributional information that *marine* co-occurs with *bomb* in the corpus, and *use* specifies the type of the syntagmatic relation between these lexemes. The scoring function σ can be any of the weighting schemes in Section 2.3.1.

Baroni and Lenci (2010) formalize the DM tuples as a **third-order tensor** (see Figure 4.1, top), from which semantic spaces are then derived through the operation of matricization (cf. Section 4.3.2). A **tensor** is a multi-way array, TENSOR conventionally denoted by a boldface Euler script letter: $\mathcal{X}$ (Kolda and Bader, 2009; Turney, 2007). The order (or n-way) of a tensor is the number of indices needed to identify its elements. We indicate the tensor order with a superscript number (e.g., $\mathcal{X}^3$ is a third-order tensor). Tensors are a generalization of vectors and matrices. The entries in a vector can be denoted by a single index. Vectors are thus first-order tensors. Matrices are second-order tensors, since their elements are identified with two indices. An array with three indices is a third-order (or three-way) tensor. The element (i, j, k) of a third-order tensor $\mathcal{X}^3$ is denoted by $x_{i,j,k}$. The dimensionality of a third-order tensor is the product of the dimensionalities of its indices $I \times J \times K$.

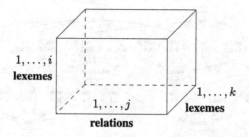

	j=1:own	j=2:use	j=1:own	j=2:use	j=1:own	j=2:use
	k=1:bomb		k=2:gun		k=3:book	
i=1:marine	40.0	82.1	85.3	44.8	3.2	3.3
i=2:sergeant	16.7	69.5	73.4	51.9	8.0	10.1
i=3:teacher	5.2	7.0	9.3	4.7	48.4	53.6

Figure 4.1 Top: A third-order tensor. Bottom: A tensor of dimensionality $3 \times 2 \times 3$ representing weighted distributional tuples (Baroni and Lenci, 2010)

> A set of DM weighted tuples built from L_1, R and L_2 is represented as a **third-order tensor** $\mathcal{X}^3_{DM}$ with its three indices labeled by L_1, R and L_2, respectively, and such that for each weighted tuple $\langle\langle l_1, r, l_2\rangle, v\rangle$ there is a tensor entry $x_{l_1, r, l_2} = v$.

In other terms, a DM tuple structure corresponds to a tensor whose indices are labeled with the string sets forming the triples, and whose entries are the tuple weights. A convenient way to display third-order tensors is via nested tables such as the one at the bottom of Figure 4.1, which contains the weighted tuples in Table 4.2. The first index is in the header column, the second index in the first header row, and the third index in the second header row. The entry $x_{3,2,1}$ of the tensor in the table is 7.0 and the entry $x_{1,1,2}$ is 85.3.

Baroni and Lenci (2010) produce three instances of the DM tensor differing for the set of relations R (e.g., syntactic dependencies, lexico-syntactic shallow patterns, etc.). These tensors belong to the family of syntax-based DSMs, but the definition of DM tuple is actually able to subsume all kinds of co-occurrences. For example, L_2 could be a larger set of relata including not only lexemes, but also documents. Similarly, R could comprise generic relations expressing the occurrence of a term in a document, or window-based co-occurrence relations. Therefore, DM tuples provide a general representation format for any type of distributional data.

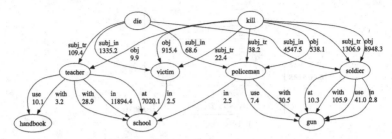

Figure 4.2 A graph-based representation of a fragment of distributional memory
(Baroni and Lenci, 2009)

TUCKER
DECOMPOSI-
TION

NON-NEGATIVE
TENSOR
FACTORIZATION

Tensor dimensionality can be reduced with decomposition algorithms, such as those described by Kolda and Bader (2009). For example, the **Tucker decomposition** of a tensor is a higher-order generalization of SVD which transforms the sparse tensor $\mathcal{X}$ into a dense tensor $\tilde{\mathcal{X}}$ with a lower number of latent dimensions. Turney (2007) compares the performance of four algorithms to decompose a third-order tensor on a synonym detection task. Van de Cruys (2010a) applies the **non-negative tensor factorization**, a generalization of NMF to multi-way data, to model the selectional preferences of predicates with a tensor representing subject-verb-object tuples. Tensor decomposition is indeed useful to smooth the original data, which are even sparser than in standard matrices, and to capture patterns of higher-order co-occurrences, but, at the same time, it is in general computationally very intensive.

WEIGHTED
GRAPH

An alternative representation of DM tuples is with **weighted graphs**, like in Figure 4.2: L_1 and L_2 are the nodes and the relations R label the weighted edges (Baroni and Lenci, 2009). A graph-based representation of distributional data is also used in the JoBimText framework (Biemann and Riedl, 2013; Biemann, 2016). However, in this case, differently from DM, the graph edges do not represent syntagmatic co-occurrences, but the similarity between two lexical nodes, computed as the overlap count of their respective contexts.

4.3.2 From Tensors to Matrices

MATRICIZATION

FIBER

Instead of modeling semantic tasks directly with the tensor, Baroni and Lenci (2010) generate different vector spaces with **matricization**, which rearranges a higher-order tensor into a matrix (Kolda, 2006; Kolda and Bader, 2009). The simplest case is mode-n matricization, which arranges the mode-n fibers to be the columns of the resulting $d_n \times d_j$ matrix (where d_n is the dimensionality of the nth index, d_j is the product of the dimensionalities of the other indices). A **fiber** is equivalent to matrix rows and columns in higher-order tensors, and is obtained by fixing the values of all indices but one. A mode-n fiber is a fiber where only the nth index has not been fixed: In the tensor at the bottom of Figure 4.1, $\mathbf{x}_{*,1,1} = (40.0, 16.7, 5.2)$ is a mode-1 fiber, $\mathbf{x}_{2,*,3} = (8.0, 10.1)$ is a mode-2 fiber and $\mathbf{x}_{3,2,*} = (7.0, 4.7, 53.6)$ is a mode-3 fiber. Each mode-n fiber of a tensor is labeled with the binary tuple whose elements are the labels of the corresponding fixed index elements. In Figure 4.1, the mode-1 fiber $\mathbf{x}_{*,1,1} = (40, 16.7, 5.2)$ is labeled with the pair ⟨*own, bomb*⟩, the mode-2 fiber $\mathbf{x}_{2,*,1} = (16.7, 69.5)$ is labeled with the pair ⟨*sergeant, bomb*⟩, and the mode-3 fiber $\mathbf{x}_{3,2,*} = (7.0, 4.7, 53.6)$ is labeled with the pair ⟨*teacher, use*⟩.

Mode-n matricization of a third-order tensor corresponds to the process of making vertical, horizontal, or depth-wise slices of a three-way object, and arranging these slices sequentially to obtain a matrix. Matricization unfolds the tensor into a matrix with the nth index indexing the rows of the matrix and a column for each pair of elements from the other two tensor indices.

MODE-n MATRICIZATION

> **Mode-n matricization** maps each tensor entry $(i_1, i_2, ..., i_N)$ to matrix entry (i_n, j), where j is computed as follows (Kolda and Bader, 2009):
>
> $$j = 1 + \sum_{\substack{k=1 \\ k \neq n}}^{N} \left((i_k - 1) \prod_{\substack{m=1 \\ m \neq n}}^{k-1} d_m\right) \qquad (4.2)$$

Figure 4.3 reports the matrices $\mathbf{A}$, $\mathbf{B}$, and $\mathbf{C}$, respectively, obtained by applying mode-1, mode-2, and mode-3 matricization to the tensor in Figure 4.1. For example, mode-1 matricization results in the matrix $\mathbf{A}$ with the entries vertically arranged as they are in the table, but replacing the second and third indices with a single index ranging from 1 to 6. The tensor entry $x_{3,1,1}$ is mapped to the matrix cell $a_{3,1}$; $x_{3,2,3}$ is mapped to $a_{3,6}$; and $x_{1,2,2}$ is mapped to $a_{1,4}$. The rows (columns) of the three matrices resulting from n-mode matricization of a third-order tensor are vectors in spaces whose dimensions are the corresponding column (row) elements. Such vector spaces can be used to perform all standard linear algebra operations applied in distributional semantics: measuring vector similarity, reducing matrix dimensionality, and so on.

In their own implementation of the DM framework, Baroni and Lenci (2010) obtain four distinct vector spaces from $\mathcal{X}_{DM}$, with which they address a large battery of experiments. For instance, the "lexeme by relation-lexeme" matrix contains vectors labeled with lexemes l_1, whose dimensions are labeled with tuples of type ⟨r, l_2⟩. This is the standard word-by-word matrix with dependency-typed collocates as contexts, and is employed to measure the

A_{mode-1}	1:⟨own, bomb⟩	2:⟨use, bomb⟩	3:⟨own, gun⟩	4:⟨use, gun⟩	5:⟨own, book⟩	6:⟨use, book⟩
1:marine	40.0	82.1	85.3	44.8	3.2	3.3
2:sergeant	16.7	69.5	73.4	51.9	8.0	10.1
3:teacher	5.2	7.0	9.3	4.7	48.4	53.6

B_{mode-2}	1:⟨marine, bomb⟩	2:⟨serg., bomb⟩	3:⟨teacher, bomb⟩	...	7:⟨marine, book⟩	8:⟨serg., book⟩	9:⟨teacher, book⟩
1:own	40.0	16.7	5.2	...	3.2	8.0	48.4
2:use	82.1	69.5	7.0	...	3.3	10.1	53.6

C_{mode-3}	1:⟨marine, own⟩	2:⟨marine, use⟩	3:⟨sergeant, own⟩	4:⟨sergeant, use⟩	5:⟨teacher, own⟩	6:⟨teacher, use⟩
1:bomb	40.0	82.1	16.7	69.5	5.2	7.0
2:gun	85.3	44.8	73.4	51.9	9.3	4.7
3:book	3.2	3.3	8.0	10.1	48.4	53.6

Figure 4.3 Mode-1, mode-2, and mode-3 matricization of the tensor at the bottom of Figure 4.1 (Baroni and Lenci, 2010)

semantic similarity between lexical items. On the other hand, the vectors of the "lexeme-lexeme by relation" matrix represent lexeme pairs $⟨l_1, l_2⟩$ in a semantic space whose dimensions are relations r. This matrix corresponds to the pair-by-pattern one used by LRA to measure relational similarity and to identify semantic relations. The main novelty of DM is that the different semantic spaces are now alternative views of the same underlying distributional object. Apparently unrelated semantic tasks can thus be addressed in terms of a general distributional memory, harvested only once from the source corpus.

It is worth noticing that the DM approach is consistent with the current mainstream paradigm in NLP and AI based on general models that learn linguistic knowledge from corpus data and are then tuned to specific applications and tasks (cf. Section 9.6.3). Moreover, the third-order tensor formalization of corpus-based tuples in DM allows distributional information to be represented in a similar way to other types of knowledge. In linguistics and cognitive science, semantic and conceptual knowledge is modeled with symbolic structures built around typed relations between elements, such as synsets, concepts, properties, and so forth (cf. Section 8.1). Therefore, DM provides a bridge between vector and symbolic models of semantic representation (cf. Section 9.8).

4.4 Topic Models (TMs)

The term **Topic Models** (TMs) refers to a family of **document DSMs** that TOPIC MODELS
use probabilistic frameworks for quantifying the importance of co-occurrence
events. While LSA can be seen as a refinement of the Vector Space Model,
TMs can be regarded as a refinement of LSA. TMs explicitly assume the existence of small number of **latent topics** that constitute the underlying thematic TOPICS
structure of the data. Each topic is represented by a probability distribution
over a set of lexemes. For example, a text on semantics will likely contain lexemes like *meaning*, *word*, and *language*, while a text on computer science will
likely contain words like *computer*, *algorithm*, and *program*. TMs assume that
a document usually contains a mixture of different topics. A text that contains
the lexemes *meaning* and *computer* can be said to discuss computer science
and semantics and consists of a (quantifiable) mixture of these two topics.

> Topic Models assume that a document is a **mixture of topics**, where
> topics are **probabilistic distributions over lexemes**.

The starting point of TMs is a word-by-document co-occurrence matrix.
However, while LSA uses linear algebra (i.e., SVD) to infer the latent factors, TMs use **Bayesian inference** to estimate the topic mixtures and lexeme BAYESIAN
distributions from the observed co-occurrences. INFERENCE

> **Bayesian inference** models the **posterior** (or **conditional**) probability of
> an event with **Bayes' rule**:
>
> $$p(a|b) = \frac{p(b|a)p(a)}{p(b)}, \qquad (4.3)$$
>
> where $p(a|b)$ is the posterior probability of a given b, $p(a)$ is the **prior**
> **probability** of a, $p(b|a)$ is the **likelihood** of b given a, and $p(b)$ is a
> normalizing constant sometimes referred to as the **marginal likelihood**.

TMs differ with respect to how the inference of topics mixtures and lexeme
distributions is computed, but they all share the assumption that the **observed**
linguistic data has been produced by a **generative process** containing some GENERATIVE
latent (hidden) topic structure. For each document, the generative process PROCESS
first selects a mixture of topics, and then generates lexemes from the topics

Table 4.3 The ten most probable lexemes for three topics derived from ukWaC using LDA applied to a matrix containing 10, 000 most frequent nouns, verbs, and adjectives as target lexemes, and 554, 931 documents as contexts

lexemes	$p(l|z)$	lexemes	$p(l|z)$	lexemes	$p(l|z)$
car	0.090	school	0.175	book	0.140
road	0.052	teacher	0.058	read	0.077
vehicle	0.034	education	0.046	write	0.069
bus	0.030	pupil	0.042	story	0.024
station	0.027	class	0.025	reading	0.024
train	0.024	teach	0.015	author	0.024
driver	0.023	primary	0.014	reader	0.021
drive	0.023	lesson	0.014	writer	0.017
route	0.022	educational	0.013	publish	0.016
traffic	0.022	secondary	0.013	writing	0.014

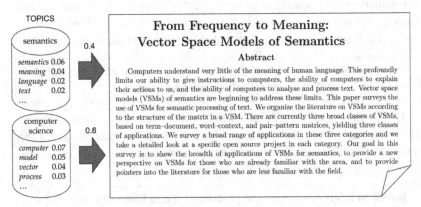

Figure 4.4 Topic models assume that a document like Turney and Pantel (2010) is generated from a mixture of topics, such as those on the left

to populate the document (see Figure 4.4). The generative story is that we first decide what we want to talk about (e.g., computer science and semantics), then, for each word token in the document, we select a topic from the mixture (e.g., computer science) and generate a lexeme from that topic (e.g., *computer*). The inference problem is to infer the underlying hidden topics (i.e., one collection of lexemes related to computer science and another collection of lexemes related to semantics) based on the observed data (e.g., a sentence like *Computers understand very little of the meaning of human language*).

Formally, each topic z is a probability distribution over the lexemes l in the training corpus, $p(l|z)$, and the content of the topic is reflected in the words to which it assigns high probability. Table 4.3 shows three topics derived from ukWaC. The lexeme probability characterizes the semantic dimension captured by each topic, respectively, from left to right, transportation, education, and publishing. In the following section, we discuss **Latent Dirichlet Allocation**, which is by far the most popular TM and has spawned a large number of variants and applications in distributional semantics.

4.4.1 Latent Dirichlet Allocation (LDA)

Latent Dirichlet Allocation (LDA) (Blei et al., 2003; Blei, 2012) is a gen- LDA
erative **mixture model**, which represents each document as a mixture of MIXTURE MODEL
probabilistic distributions over latent topics, and each topic is a distribution over lexemes. LDA uses **mixture decomposition** to arrive at a latent MIXTURE
representation of the observed data, corresponding to the lexical items in DECOMPOSITION
documents.

> A **mixture model** assumes the data has been generated by a mixture
> of probability distributions. **Mixture decomposition** is the problem of
> inferring the component distributions and their parameters.

LDA is a refinement of **probabilistic Latent Semantic Analysis** (pLSA) (Hof- PLSA
mann, 1999), which is in turn an extension of LSA. Similarly to LSA, LDA was
originally developed for information retrieval and document classification, but
then it has been proposed as a model for human semantic memory by Steyvers
et al. (2006), Griffiths et al. (2007), and Steyvers and Griffiths (2007).

Given a set of lexemes $L = \{l_1, \ldots, l_m\}$, a set of documents $D = \{d_1, \ldots, d_n\}$ (represented according to the bag-of-words model), and k latent topics
$Z = \{z_1, \ldots, z_k\}$, LDA assumes that each token of l in d is generated by:

$$p(l|d) = \sum_{i=1}^{k} p(l|z_i)p(z_i|d), \qquad (4.4)$$

where $p(z|d) = \theta^{(d)}$ is the probability of a topic z given document d – that is
the topic mixture over documents – and $p(l|z) = \phi^{(z)}$ is the probability of l
given topic z.[3] The parameters ϕ and θ indicate which lexemes are important
for which topic and which topics are important for a particular document.

---

[3] Blei et al. (2003) use β as notation for the per-topic lexeme distribution, but here we use the ϕ
  notation by Steyvers and Griffiths (2007).

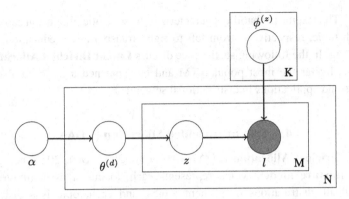

Figure 4.5 Graphical model of the LDA generative process

The distinctive feature of LDA is the use of a Dirichlet prior for the per-document topic mixtures (and in some versions also for the per-topic word distributions).[4] LDA assumes the following generative story a document d:

1. generate a per-document topic distribution (mixture) $\theta^{(d)}$ from a Dirichlet prior $\text{Dir}(\alpha)$;
2. for each lexeme slot in the document:
   a. generate a topic z from $\theta^{(d)}$;
   b. generate a lexeme l from the per-topic lexeme distribution $\phi^{(z)}$.

DIRICHLET
DISTRIBUTION The **Dirichlet distribution** $\text{Dir}(\alpha)$ models the variability of a set of distributions, and can be seen as a distribution over distributions. The hyperparameter α is a k-dimensional vector with elements $\alpha_i > 0$. Each hyperparameter α_i can be interpreted as a prior observation count for the number of times topic z_i is sampled in a document, before having observed the words from that document. $\text{Dir}(\alpha)$ is used because it is a conjugate prior (i.e., it has the same functional form) for $\theta^{(d)}$, thereby simplifying the process of statistical inference.

The graphical model of the LDA generative process is shown in Figure 4.5. Gray and white circles respectively represent observed and hidden variables.

---

[4] This is the main novelty with respect to pLSA, which instead assumes uniform distributions. Moreover, pLSA has been criticized for not providing a well-defined generative model of documents, since it cannot assign likelihoods to unseen documents (Blei et al., 2003; Aggarwal and Reddy, 2013). In fact, in pLSA d is a random variable whose values are the documents in the training corpus. Therefore, the model learns the topic mixtures $p(z|d)$ only for those documents on which it is trained. Another problem is that the number of parameters for a model with k topics, m lexemes, and n documents is $kn + km$, which grows linearly with the size of the data. Not only will this become computationally intractable with large data, but it also makes the model prone to overfitting. On the other hand, LDA is able to assign probabilities to documents outside the training set, and its parameters do not grow linearly.

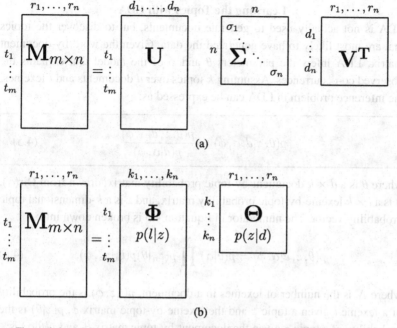

Figure 4.6 (a) LSA: SVD factorizes the word-by-document matrix $M_{m \times n}$ using $\{d_1, \ldots, d_n\}$ latent dimensions; (b) Topic Models: LDA factorizes the word-by-document matrix $M_{m \times n}$ using $\{k_1, \ldots, k_n\}$ topics

Arrows mark conditional dependencies between variables, and the rectangles, called *plates*, represent replication. The M plate denotes the lexemes within a document, and the N plate denotes the documents within the corpus. As a very simplified example, imagine we only have two topics – computer science and semantics – and that our document contains four word tokens. We first generate the topic distribution for our document. We then generate a topic and a word from that topic for each token: for instance, *meaning* from the semantics topic for the first token, *computer* from the computer science topic for the second token, *vector* from the computer science topic for the third token slot, and lastly the lexeme *sense* from the semantics topic for the fourth token.

LDA can also be interpreted as factorizing the word-by-document matrix, with a striking parallelism with LSA, as illustrated in Figure 4.6. The word-by-document matrix is split into two parts: a word-by-topic matrix Φ, corresponding to the U matrix in LSA, and a topic-by document matrix Θ, corresponding to the V^T matrix in LSA. However, differently from LSA, the Φ and Θ matrices are probability distributions, and therefore are non-negative and sum up to one, with a close resemblance to NMF (Ding et al., 2008).

Learning the Topics with LDA

LDA is not actually used to generate documents, but to discover the topics that are most likely to have generated the data. Given the word-by-document matrix, LDA infers the parameters θ and ϕ of the model that explains the observed co-occurrences. Assuming k topics over d documents and l lexemes, the inference problem in LDA can be expressed as:

$$p(\theta, z | d, \alpha, \phi) = \frac{p(\theta, z, d | \alpha, \phi)}{p(d | \alpha, \phi)}, \quad\quad (4.5)$$

where θ is a $d \times k$ document-by-topic probability matrix, drawn from $\mathrm{Dir}(\alpha)$, ϕ is a $l \times k$ lexeme-by-topic probability matrix, and z is a k-dimensional topic probability vector. The numerator in Equation 4.5 is broken down into:

$$p(\theta, z, d | \alpha, \phi) = p(\theta | \alpha) \prod_{n=1}^{N} p(z_n | \theta) p(l_n | z_n, \phi), \quad\quad (4.6)$$

where N is the number of lexemes in a document, $p(l | z, \phi)$ is the probability of a lexeme l given a topic z and the lexeme-by-topic matrix ϕ, $p(z | \theta)$ is the probability of a topic z given the document-by-topic matrix θ, and $p(\theta | \alpha)$ is:

$$p(\theta | \alpha) = \frac{\Gamma(\sum_{i=1}^{k} \alpha_i)}{\prod_{i=1}^{k} \Gamma \alpha_i} \prod_{i=1}^{k} \theta_i^{\alpha_i - 1}, \quad\quad (4.7)$$

which is the Dirichlet density function, where $\Gamma(x)$ is the Gamma function.

The main difficulty in LDA is to compute the denominator in Equation 4.5, which describes the marginal probability of the observations (i.e., the probability of observing the current data under any instance of the topic model), and works out as follows, integrating over θ:

$$p(d | \alpha, \phi) = \frac{\Gamma(\sum_{i=1}^{k} \alpha_i)}{\prod_{i=1}^{k} \Gamma \alpha_i} \int \left(\prod_{i=1}^{k} \theta_i^{\alpha_i - 1} \right) \left(\prod_{n=1}^{N} \sum_{i=1}^{k} \prod_{j=1}^{V} (\theta_i \phi_{i,j})^{l_n^j} \right) d\theta. \quad (4.8)$$

Unfortunately, this expression is not tractable to compute, because of the coupling between θ and ϕ in the summation over topics (Dickey, 1983; Blei et al., 2003). In order to compute exact inference, we would need to sum the joint distribution over all possible topic structures, which is a prohibitively large computation. Various approximation techniques have been proposed since exact inference of the LDA model is not possible. To generalize, there are two main approaches for approximating the posterior distribution: sampling-based and variational methods (Blei, 2012).

The general idea of **sampling-based algorithms** is to draw samples from the <small>SAMPLING-</small>
distribution in order to approximate it. If we view the probability distribution <small>BASED</small>
<small>ALGORITHMS</small>
we wish to sample from as a state space (i.e., the set of possible values) with
more and less probable documents, it is desirable that a sampling algorithm
is designed so that it spends more time in high-probability documents than
in low-probability documents to draw samples. **Gibbs sampling**, which is an <small>GIBBS</small>
instance of **Markov Chain Monte Carlo** (MCMC) sampling, is one particular <small>SAMPLING</small>
way to select such states. The general idea of a Gibbs sampler is to draw a large
number of samples at random (which is what makes it a Monte Carlo method),
but to do so in such a way that the probability of selecting a sample depends
on the previously selected sample (which makes it a Markov Chain). The idea
is that MCMC will sample from a probability distribution in such a way that
the samples are drawn more often from the high-probability documents.

Gibbs sampling, more specifically, samples each of the variables in the joint
distribution one at a time, conditioned on the current estimates of the other
variables in the distribution. Thus, at each step of the sampling, a variable is
selected, and a value is sampled from the conditional distribution. The new
value is used in the next step of the iteration, where the value of another variable is calculated. Steyvers and Griffiths (2007) and Griffiths et al. (2007)
describe Gibbs sampling for a document collection that estimates topic assignments for each lexeme token in turn, conditioned on the topic assignments of
all other word tokens. The topic assignments are dependent on both the probability of a lexeme token given a topic (how likely is the word for a topic),
and the probability of a topic given a document (how dominant is the topic in
the document). A single pass through the document collection (i.e., generating topic assignments for all word tokens in the data) constitutes one Gibbs
sample. The first samples are generally discarded (this is called the *burn-in*
period), since the estimates tend to be very poor approximations of the posterior at the beginning of sampling. After the burn-in period, samples begin
to approximate the posterior, and are thus saved at regular intervals to prevent
correlations between samples.

Gibbs, and other types of MCMC sampling, lead to good approximations
of the posterior distribution if they are allowed to run for a sufficient amount
of time. The potential drawback is that this amount of time can be quite considerable in some cases, which makes the approximation slow and inefficient.
Variational algorithms – such as mean-field variational inference – present a <small>VARIATIONAL</small>
deterministic, and potentially faster alternative to sampling, which can be very <small>ALGORITHMS</small>
useful in cases where efficiency is a factor. Variational methods formulate the
inference problem as an optimization problem, where the posterior distribution is approximated by optimizing a set of *variational parameters* of a much

simpler distribution. In this simpler distribution, any dependencies between variables – which is what makes the denominator in Equation 4.8 difficult if not impossible to compute – are removed, so that the variables are assumed to be independent of each other. Each of the variables (the topics, the per-document topic proportions, and the per-word topic assignments) has its own variational parameter, which is normally an independent Dirichlet or multinomial distribution. These parameters are fit to the posterior using the KL divergence (cf. Section 2.6.2). Hoffman et al. (2010) describe an online version of variational inference that does not require a full pass through the data at each iteration, which makes it possible to scale the variational inference to very large document collections, by operating on single documents (*mini-batches*).

4.4.2 Representing Lexemes with Topic Models

Given a word-by-document co-occurrence matrix and k topics, TMs learn the word distribution for each topic, ϕ, and the topic distribution for each document, θ. TMs were primarily developed for document processing scenarios, where we are interested in computing document-document similarities, using the per-document topic distributions θ. However, TMs are also used to create vectors of lexical items and compute their similarities. We call these embeddings **topic vectors**. A first type of topic vector contains the per-topic word distribution ϕ (Mitchell and Lapata, 2010):

TOPIC VECTORS

> Given a set of k topics $\{z_1, \ldots, z_k\}$, the **topic vector** of a target lexeme t is the vector $\mathbf{t} = (\phi_1, \ldots, \phi_k)$, such that $\phi_i = p(t|z_i)$, for $1 \leq i \leq k$.

Alternatively, a target lexeme t can be represented with its probability distribution over the topics (Steyvers and Griffiths, 2007):

> Given a set of k topics $\{z_1, \ldots, z_k\}$, the **topic vector** of a target lexeme t is the vector $\mathbf{t} = (p(z_1|t), \ldots, p(z_k|t))$.

Each $p(z|t)$ is the conditional probability of the topic z given the target, and can be obtained from the ϕ distribution with Bayes' rule (cf. Equation 4.3):

$$p(z|t) = \frac{p(t|z)p(z)}{p(t)}. \qquad (4.9)$$

Griffiths et al. (2007) compute $p(t)$ as follows:

$$p(z|t) = \frac{p(t|z)p(z)}{\sum_{j=1}^{k} p(t|z_j)p(z_j)}. \qquad (4.10)$$

Table 4.4 TM nearest neighbors ranked by cosine similarity, using 100 topics learned with LDA

bike		*car*		*dog*		*lion*	
ride	0.98	park	0.99	cat	0.99	rear_V	0.97
biker	0.98	pedestrian	0.99	angling	0.99	hunt	0.96
rider	0.97	motorist	0.99	tortoise	0.99	perch	0.96
racing	0.97	congestion	0.99	kitten	0.99	hunter	0.95
podium	0.97	bus	0.99	carp	0.99	primate	0.95
lap	0.97	vehicle	0.99	bait	0.99	hare	0.95
racer	0.97	cyclist	0.99	angler	0.99	monkey	0.95
race	0.97	livery	0.99	veterinary	0.99	hunting	0.95
marathon	0.97	van	0.99	pup	0.99	guinea	0.95
runner	0.97	freight	0.99	puppy	0.99	fly_N	0.95

The targets are the $10,000$ most frequent nouns, verbs, and adjectives in ukWaC. The contexts are $554,931$ documents

Assuming a uniform distribution over topics (i.e., $p(z) = \frac{1}{k}$), we obtain:

$$p(z|t) = \frac{p(t|z)}{\sum_{j=1}^{k} p(t|z_j)}. \tag{4.11}$$

Therefore, the topic vector $\mathbf{t} = (p(z_1|t), \dots, p(z_k|t))$ corresponds to the ϕ distribution of t, normalized by the sum of the ϕ values across the topics.

Topic vectors constitute distributional representations, since they are created using latent dimensions extracted from the co-occurrence matrix. Table 4.4 shows LDA nearest neighbors computed with cosine similarity applied to distributional vectors made of 100 topic dimensions extracted from a sample of ukWaC. Several neighbors are broadly related to the target (e.g., *pedestrian* and *car*), consistently with the character of topics, which typically correspond to large semantic fields. Thus, TMs tend to identify lexemes that are topically similar, as they belong to the same domains (cf. Section 7.1), rather than taxonomically related neighbors.

The distributional representations produced by TMs are embeddings, because topics are latent dimensions. One often-mentioned advantage of TMs is that topics are more interpretable than the latent dimensions produced by SVD or other dimensionality reduction methods (Griffiths et al., 2007; Steyvers and Griffiths, 2007). The fact that topics are probability distributions over lexemes typically makes it easier to identify the semantic dimensions they capture, as in Table 4.3. This feature of topics is also useful to investigate polysemy, by assuming that the senses of a lexeme are its most likely topics

Table 4.5 Topics corresponding to two senses of *play*
(left) and *plant* (right).

play		plant	
music	team	plant	energy
band	club	tree	waste
song	play	grow	gas
play	sport	garden	climate
album	player	flower	fuel
track	season	crop	use
sound	football	soil	oil
dance	game	seed	power
cd	match	use	water
musical	fan	farmer	air

Lexemes are ordered by decreasing probability given a topic

(cf. Section 8.2.1). For example, the topics in Table 4.5 can be regarded to correspond to the musical and sportive senses of *play*, and to the botanic and industrial senses of *plant*. However, the semantic interpretation of topics is not always straightforward, and there is no one-to-one relation between topic and semantic dimensions, since several topics may cover the same domain. Like for SVD, choosing the number of topics is an empirical parameter whose optimal value depends on the corpus size or on the task at hand.

TMs were originally developed to work on word-by-document matrices, but they can be applied to any context type. In fact, LDA is a general method to extract latent semantic dimensions from a co-occurrence matrix, similar to SVD or NMF. In Chapters 8 and 9, we review DSMs that use topic vectors derived from window-based and syntactic collocates.

4.5 Global Vectors (GloVe)

Finding a suitable transformation of the co-occurrence counts (e.g., discovering latent dimensions with SVD or TMs) is an important component of DSMs, since it enables generalization, dimensionality reduction of observed data, and

GLOVE exploitation of redundancies in observed data. **Global Vectors** (GloVe) (Pennington et al., 2014) is a matrix model that learns word embeddings with a method strongly inspired by neural DSMs.

GloVe is based on two assumptions. First of all, embeddings should represent not only similarity relations but also structural regularities in the semantic space. For instance, the meaning of *man* resides both in its high similarity with *woman*, and in the gender dimension that distinguishes these targets and makes them similar to several other lexeme pairs, like *father* and *mother*, or

Table 4.6 Probability ratios discriminate the meaning of target
lexemes *ice* and *steam* better than co-occurrence probabilities
(Pennington et al., 2014)

Probability and ratio	$c = solid$	$c = gas$	$c = water$	$c = fashion$
$p(c|ice)$	high	low	high	low
$p(c|steam)$	low	high	high	low
$p(c|ice)/p(c|steam)$	high	low	≈ 1	≈ 1

king and *queen* (cf. relational similarity in Sections 4.2 and 7.1). Following
Mikolov et al. (2013d), GloVe assumes that these regularities are encoded LINEAR
in **linear substructures** of the vector spaces and are represented by **vector** SUBSTRUCTURES
differences (e.g., the relation between *woman* and *man* is represented by the
vector **woman** − **man**; cf. Section 7.2.4). Secondly, **probability ratios** cap- PROBABILITY
ture meaning differences better than co-occurrence probabilities. As shown RATIOS
in Table 4.6, adapted from Pennington et al. (2014), $p(solid|ice)$ is expected
to be high and $p(solid|steam)$ low, because *solid* co-occurs more frequently
with *ice* than with *steam*. However, $p(water|ice)$ and $p(water|steam)$ are
both expected to be high, because *water* is a common context of the two lex-
emes. The probability ratio $p(c|ice)/p(c|steam)$ is instead likely to be high
for a context c (*solid*) associated with *ice* but not *steam*, low for a context (*gas*)
associated with *steam* but not with *ice*, and to approximate one for contexts
that are either unrelated (*fashion*) or associated (*water*) with both targets.

The goal of GloVe is to generate word vectors that encode the information brought by probability ratios into their differences. Given a word-by-word
matrix **M** where each entry $m_{i,j}$ corresponds to the co-occurrence frequency
$F(t_i, c_j)$ of a target lexeme t_i and a context lexeme c_j, GloVe learns two separate sets of embeddings for a vocabulary V, the **target embeddings** (**t**) and TARGET AND
the **context embeddings** (**c**), by optimizing the following training objective: CONTEXT
EMBEDDINGS

$$\mathbf{t} \cdot \mathbf{c} = \log p(c|t), \qquad (4.12)$$

where $p(c|t)$ is the probability that the lexeme c appears as context of the tar-
get t. Since the logarithm of a ratio equals the difference of logarithms, the
logarithm of probabilities ratios corresponds to vector differences:

$$(\mathbf{t_i} - \mathbf{t_j}) \cdot \mathbf{c} = \log \frac{p(c|t_i)}{p(c|t_j)}, \qquad (4.13)$$

Equation 4.12 is then rewritten as follows:

$$\mathbf{t} \cdot \mathbf{c} = \log p(c|t) = \log(\frac{F(t,c)}{F(t,*)}) = \log F(t,c) - \log F(t,*), \qquad (4.14)$$

where $F(t, *) = \sum_{j=1}^{n} F(t, c_j)$ (cf. Equation 2.3). The final function used by GloVe to learn the embeddings is a slight variation of Equation 4.14, and

is cast as the **weighted least squares regression** objective of minimizing, for each training pair $\langle t, c \rangle$, the distance between $\mathbf{t} \cdot \mathbf{c}$ and the overall log frequency of t and c in the co-occurrence matrix $\mathbf{M}$ derived from the corpus:

$$J_{GloVe} = \sum_{i,j=1}^{|V|} f(m_{i,j})(\mathbf{t_i} \cdot \mathbf{c_j} + \beta_i + \beta_j - \log m_{i,j})^2, \qquad (4.15)$$

where $|V|$ is the size of the vocabulary, β_i and β_j are scalar bias terms for the target and the context vectors, and $f(m_{i,j})$ is the weighting function:

$$f(m_{i,j}) = \begin{cases} \left(\frac{m_{i,j}}{x_{\max}}\right)^{\alpha} & \text{if } m_{i,j} < x_{\max} \\ 1 & otherwise \end{cases}, \qquad (4.16)$$

where $x_{\max} = 100$, and $\alpha = 3/4$, which is defined empirically. This function reduces the weight of rare and high-frequency co-occurrences. The model is trained with AdaGrad, a variant of stochastic gradient descent (cf. Section 6.1).

When using a symmetric co-occurrence matrix, which is the standard case, the targets and context embeddings will be more or less equivalent (modulo differences due to random initialization). One may thus use only one of the vectors when computing similarity. However, in the original GloVe formulation, the two types of vectors are combined (by summation) to produce the final distributional vectors. Pennington et al. (2014) use window-based co-occurrences, but Li et al. (2017) apply the GloVe model to syntax-based contexts.

Because of Equation 4.12, GloVe is a **log-bilinear model**, a type of neural language model (cf. Section 6.2.2). In fact, its objective function makes GloVe very similar to neural DSMs, in particular to the Skip-Gram model (cf. Section 6.4). However, Skip-Gram is a predict DSM that directly learns embeddings without building a co-occurrence matrix. GloVe instead operates on a matrix that collects the global distributional statistics extracted from the corpus, and then aims to find a useful transformation of the data. In fact, GloVe is a regression model to reduce the dimensionality of the co-occurrence matrix, but it represents an interesting bridge between matrix and predict DSMs.

4.6 Summary

In this chapter, we have presented DSMs that share the feature of collecting corpus data into a **co-occurrence matrix** providing a representation of global distributional statistics. Matrix models stem from the Vector Space

Model in information retrieval. The DSMs we have called **classical models** use word-by-word (contexts are window-based collocates in the **Hyperspace Analogue of Language** and syntactic collocates in **Dependency Vectors**) or word-by-document (**Latent Semantic Analysis**) matrices. The standard matrix reduction algorithm is SVD, which is an essential component of LSA.

The other matrix models we have reviewed consist in extensions and variations of this basic schema. The aim of **Latent Relational Analysis** is measuring relational similarity, and for this purpose it uses a different type of co-occurrence matrix with rows corresponding to lexeme pairs and columns to lexico-syntagmatic patterns linking them. Instead of collecting distributional data directly into a matrix, **Distributional Memory** provides a generalized representation of co-occurrences as ternary tuples that are formalized as a third-order tensor. Semantic tasks are then addressed using different matrices generated from the same underlying distributional tensor. Finally, **Topic Models** and **GloVe** introduce new methods (respectively, Bayesian inference and weighted regression) to reduce the matrix dimensionality and generate dense implicit distributional representations.

4.7 Further Reading

- Matrix models: Turney and Pantel (2010); Clark (2015)
- Latent Semantic Analysis: Landauer et al. (2007)
- Topic Models and their variations: Griffiths et al. (2005, 2007); Gruber et al. (2007); Boyd-Graber and Blei (2009); Andrews and Vigliocco (2010)

5

Random Encoding Models

Dimensionality reduction to embed high-dimensional data into dense vectors is an important aspect of distributional semantics. In matrix models, it is performed with various methods applied to the co-occurrence matrix. In this chapter, we look at a different approach based on the use of random patterns to accumulate implicit embeddings where the co-occurrence information is spread across vector dimensions. These **random encoding models** directly reduce the dimensionality of distributional data without first building a co-occurrence matrix. While matrix DSMs output either explicit or implicit distributional vectors, random encoding models only produce low-dimensional word embeddings, and emphasize efficiency, scalability, and incrementality in building distributional representations. In fact, random encoding DSMs are particularly suitable to process very large corpora or continuous streams of data.

In Section 5.1, we discuss the mathematical foundation for models based on random encoding, the **Johnson–Lindenstrauss lemma**. We then introduce **Random Projection** (Section 5.2), before turning to **Random Indexing** (Section 5.3). Section 5.4 presents the **Bound Encoding of the Aggregate Language Environment** (BEAGLE), a random encoding model that encodes sequential information in distributional vectors. Section 5.5 introduces a variant of Random Indexing that uses **random permutations** to represent the position of the context lexemes with respect to the target, similar to BEAGLE. In Section 5.6, we discuss **Self-Organizing Maps**, an unsupervised neural network that shares important similarities with random encoding models.

5.1 The Johnson–Lindenstrauss Lemma

Dimensionality reduction methods like SVD embed high-dimensional vectors into lower dimensional spaces. One shortcoming of SVD is that it does not

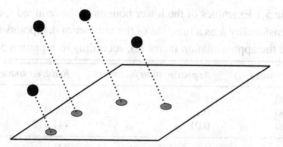

Figure 5.1 Projection of points in a 3-dimensional space onto a 2-dimensional plane

guarantee the local properties of the reduced space, which means that distances between points might not be preserved by the dimensionality reduction. The **Johnson–Lindenstrauss lemma** (Johnson and Lindenstrauss, 1984) provides such constraint by stating that a set of points in a high-dimensional space can be embedded into a much lower-dimensional space without distorting the distances between the points by more than a predictable factor ϵ:

JOHNSON–
LINDENSTRAUSS
LEMMA

> Given $\epsilon > 0$ and a set P of m points in $\mathbb{R}^n$, there exists a mapping $f : \mathbb{R}^n \to \mathbb{R}^k$ where $k = O(\epsilon^{-2} \log m)$, such that for all $u, v \in P$,
> $$(1 - \epsilon) \parallel u - v \parallel^2 \, \leq \parallel f(u) - f(v) \parallel^2 \, \leq (1 + \epsilon) \parallel u - v \parallel^2, \quad (5.1)$$

where $f(u)$ and $f(v)$ are projections of u and v, n is the **representational dimensionality** (i.e., the dimensionality of the original space), and k is the dimensionality of the reduced space. The Johnson–Lindenstrauss lemma guarantees that the resulting embedding does not distort the distances by more than the approximation factor. Figure 5.1 demonstrates the general idea of projecting a set of points into a lower-dimensional space while retaining the (approximate) pair-wise similarities between the points.

Given the Johnson–Lindenstrauss lemma, if the original space contains m number of points in n dimensions, then it can be mapped to a space of dimensionality $O(\epsilon^{-2} \log m)$,[1] so that the distances between the points are preserved by a factor of $(1 \pm \epsilon)$. Subsequent proofs of the lemma improved on the lower bounds of the dimensionality of the reduced space (Frankl and Maehara, 1987; Indyk and Motwani, 1998). Dasgupta and Gupta (2003) show that we can compute the (theoretical) lower bounds of the dimensionality of the reduced space k given the number of data points m and a certain approximation factor ϵ:

---

[1] This notation means that $\epsilon^{-2} \log m$ is the asymptotic upper bound of the dimensionality of the reduced space.

Table 5.1 Examples of the lower bounds of the reduced space
dimensionality k as a function of the number of datapoints (m)
and the approximation factor (ϵ), according to Equation 5.2

Datapoints (m)	Approximation factor (ϵ)	Reduced space (k)
10,000	1	221
10,000	0.1	7,894
10,000	0.01	741,772
100,000	1	276
100,000	0.1	9,868
100,000	0.01	927,215
1,000,000	1	331
1,000,000	0.1	11,841
1,000,000	0.01	1,112,658

$$k = 4(\frac{\epsilon^2}{2} - \frac{\epsilon^3}{3})^{-1} \log m. \tag{5.2}$$

Table 5.1 reports some examples for various numbers of data points and
various numbers of different approximation factors.

Note that the dimensionality n of the original space does not feature in the
equation of the bounds. It is only the number of data points in the original space
that is a factor in the equation. As we see in the following sections, these lower
bounds are very conservative,[2] and it is often possible to reach viable performance with a much lower dimensionality of the reduced spaces. The ability
to use a very compact approximation instead of the full representation is very
useful in applications where the computational cost is a function of the dimensionality of the data. One example of such an application is DSMs, where data
dimensionality can be very high, affecting both the cost of constructing the
semantic spaces, and the cost of performing nearest neighbor search.

5.2 Random Projection

Random Projection is a dimensionality reduction technique that applies the
Johnson–Lindenstrauss lemma to reduce the dimensionality of a given matrix
$\mathbf{A}_{m \times n}$ to a matrix $\mathbf{A}'_{m \times k}$ by multiplying $\mathbf{A}$ with (or projecting it through) a
random projection matrix $\mathbf{R}_{n \times k}$, where $k \ll n$:

---

[2] As Li et al. (2006) point out, one reason for the conservativeness of the Johnson–Lindenstrauss
lemma is its use of Bonferroni correction, which controls for the number of comparisons (i.e.,
hypotheses being tested) in statistical models.

$$\mathbf{A}'_{m \times k} = \mathbf{A}_{m \times n} \mathbf{R}_{n \times k}. \tag{5.3}$$

The first formulations of the Johnson–Lindenstrauss lemma relied on projection matrices with orthonormal column vectors (Johnson and Lindenstrauss, 1984; Frankl and Maehara, 1987). If the random column vectors in $\mathbf{R}$ are orthogonal (i.e., their dot product is zero; cf. Mathematical 3 in Section 2.5.1), then $\mathbf{A} = \mathbf{A}'$. However, it was realized that strict orthogonality is not necessary in order to achieve a viable projection matrix. All that is needed is **randomness** (Indyk and Motwani, 1998).[3] If the entries of the projection matrix $\mathbf{R}_{n \times k}$ are independent random variables with zero mean and unit variance, then the resulting column vectors will point in uniformly random directions. Random vectors in high-dimensional spaces are *nearly orthogonal* to each other with high probability (Achlioptas, 2003). Therefore, simply choosing random directions will suffice to reach approximate orthogonality of the projection matrix. If the random vectors are nearly orthogonal, then $\mathbf{A} \approx \mathbf{A}'$ in terms of the similarity of their rows. RANDOMNESS

A common choice for the projection matrix is to use a random matrix with a Gaussian distribution. However, basically any distribution with zero mean and unit variance will give a mapping that satisfies the Johnson–Lindenstrauss lemma (Bingham and Mannila, 2001). Achlioptas (2003) introduces a **sparse projection matrix R** with distribution:

$$r_{i,j} = \sqrt{3} \times \begin{cases} +1 & \text{with probability } 1/6 \\ 0 & \text{with probability } 2/3 \\ -1 & \text{with probability } 1/6 \end{cases} \tag{5.4}$$

SPARSE PROJECTION MATRIX

Li et al. (2006) improve on this sparse model even further, suggesting a **very sparse projection matrix R** with distribution:

$$r_{i,j} = \sqrt{n} \times \begin{cases} +1 & \text{with probability } \frac{1}{2\sqrt{n}} \\ 0 & \text{with probability } 1 - \frac{1}{\sqrt{n}} \\ -1 & \text{with probability } \frac{1}{2\sqrt{n}} \end{cases} \tag{5.5}$$

where n is the dimensionality of the original matrix. The use of a sparse projection matrix is computationally attractive, since the complexity of the projection depends on the number of non-zero entries in the projection matrix.

Random Projection is used in several applications, and has become a standard approach for dealing with data of very high dimensionality. In computational linguistics, Random Projection is adopted by Kaski (1998) for text

---

[3] Strictly speaking, what is needed is randomness and **spherical symmetry**, which means the space is invariant under rotations.

$$
\begin{array}{c}
\begin{array}{cccc} c_1 & c_2 & c_3 & c_4 \end{array} \\
\begin{array}{c} t_1 \\ t_2 \\ t_3 \end{array}
\left(\begin{array}{cccc}
2 & 0 & 1 & 0 \\
0 & 0 & 1 & 3 \\
0 & 2 & 0 & 1
\end{array}\right)
\end{array}
\qquad
\begin{array}{l}
c_1 = (\,1 \quad 0 \quad 0 \quad 0\,) \\
c_2 = (\,0 \quad 1 \quad 0 \quad 0\,) \\
c_3 = (\,0 \quad 0 \quad 1 \quad 0\,) \\
c_4 = (\,0 \quad 0 \quad 0 \quad 1\,)
\end{array}
$$

(a)

$$
\begin{array}{l}
r(c_1) = (\,+1 \quad\;\; 0 \quad -1 \quad\;\; 0 \quad\;\; 0\,) \\
r(c_2) = (\;\;\; 0 \quad -1 \quad\;\; 0 \quad +1 \quad\;\; 0\,) \\
r(c_3) = (\;\;\; 0 \quad\;\; 0 \quad +1 \quad\;\; 0 \quad -1\,) \\
r(c_4) = (\;\;\; 0 \quad +1 \quad\;\; 0 \quad -1 \quad\;\; 0\,)
\end{array}
$$

(b)

Figure 5.2 (a) Co-occurrence matrix and one-hot context representation; (b) random index vectors representing contexts

clustering with Self Organizing Maps (cf. Section 5.6), by Papadimitriou et al. (2000) as a preprocessing step before SVD to speed up LSA, by Ravichandran et al. (2005) for large-scale noun clustering. Although Random Projection is a very efficient dimension reduction technique, it suffers from one major drawback: *We still need to collect the initial data matrix* **A**. Since it is this matrix that becomes prohibitively large for large co-occurrence data, it would be beneficial if we could avoid having to explicitly collect the entire matrix. This important novelty is introduced by Random Indexing.

5.3 Random Indexing (RI)

RANDOM
INDEXING

SPARSE
DISTRIBUTED
MEMORY

Random Indexing (RI) is a framework for distributional semantics inspired by **PENTTI KANERVA**'s work on **sparse distributed memory** (Kanerva, 1988). RI is designed to eliminate the need to build the n-dimensional co-occurrence matrix A. Instead, RI accumulates k-dimensional (where $k \ll n$) word embeddings *incrementally* by summation of sparse random vectors.

In the standard co-occurrence matrix (see Figure 5.2a left), the contexts occupy one dimension each and vector dimensionality is thus determined by the number of contexts. The distributional vectors that represent the target lexemes are built by incrementing the frequency counter in the relevant cell when we observe a co-occurrence event with a given context. This amounts to

ONE-HOT
VECTORS

representing contexts as **one-hot vectors** with a single one in a separate dimension for each context (see Figure 5.2a right). The contexts in matrix DSMs are therefore encoded with mutually orthogonal vectors.

RI instead distinguishes two types of vectors: (i) the **random index vec-**
tors representing the contexts, and (ii) the **word embeddings** representing the
target lexemes. A random index vector is not a one-hot vector, but a ternary
(i.e., components are -1, 0 , or +1) sparse vector with *several* – randomly
selected – active dimensions. The dimensionality is thus *fixed*, and contexts
have to share dimensions in the final word embeddings. Differently from
the contexts in co-occurrence matrices, the sparse random index vectors are
approximately orthogonal to each other with very high probability by virtue
of their randomness, as discussed in Section 5.2. Random index vectors thus
share mathematical properties with a random projection matrix (cf. Section
5.3.1). As illustrated in Figure 5.2b, imagine we use a five-dimensional space
and that we have four contexts in our data. For each of these contexts, we randomly select a small predetermined number of dimensions to be active, and for
each of them we assign either a +1 or a −1. In this example, we use two active
dimensions with one +1 and one −1. RI incrementally builds distributional
representations by adding the random index vector of the context to the word
embedding of the target each time the target co-occurs with the context.

Given $T = \{t_1, \ldots, t_m\}$ the set of target lexemes and $C = \{c_1, \ldots, c_n\}$
the set of contexts:

(i) RI assigns a k-dimensional **random index vector** $\mathbf{r}(\mathbf{c_j})$ to each
context c_j, and a k-dimensional **embedding** $\mathbf{t_i}$ to each target t_i;
(ii) for each pair $\langle t_i, c_j \rangle$, representing the co-occurrence of t_i with c_j,
RI sums the random vector $\mathbf{r}(\mathbf{c_j})$ to the embedding $\mathbf{t_i}$.

This means that if we use the entire vocabulary of a corpus both as targets and
as contexts, as is customary in word DSMs, then each lexeme is assigned two
vectors: one word embedding that will be subject to continuous updates during
processing, and one sparse random index vector that remains fixed.

As an example, imagine we observe the sequence *Kim kissed Pat* in the
corpus. To update the embedding **kissed** for the target, we add to it the random
index vectors $\mathbf{r}(\mathbf{Kim})$ and $\mathbf{r}(\mathbf{Pat})$, as illustrated in Figure 5.3. Every time
we observe the target *kissed* in the data, we add the random index vectors of
the neighboring lexemes to its embedding. This means that contexts that are
more common for a specific target will contribute more to its embedding. For
instance, suppose that our data is a love story about Kim and Pat, and that
kissed therefore occurs almost exclusively in the context of *Kim* and *Pat*. The
embedding of *kissed* will in this case become very similar to the random index

$$r(\mathbf{Kim}) = (+1 \quad 0 \quad -1 \quad 0 \quad 0)$$
$$r(\mathbf{Pat}) = (\quad 0 \quad -1 \quad 0 \quad +1 \quad 0)$$

$$\mathbf{kissed} = (+1 \quad -1 \quad -1 \quad +1 \quad 0)$$

Figure 5.3 Given the sentence *Kim kissed Pat*, the embedding of the target *kissed* is updated by summing the random index vectors of *Kim* and *Pat*

vectors of *Kim* and *Pat*. Any other occasional contexts where *kissed* occurs will merely act as random noise in the embedding, without leaving a lasting trace.

The random index vectors can use any distribution that satisfies the Johnson–Lindenstrauss lemma. The early papers on RI use the following variation of the distribution in Equation 5.4 to generate a random index vector $\mathbf{r}$ (Kanerva et al., 2000; Karlgren and Sahlgren, 2001; Sahlgren, 2005, 2006):

$$r_i = \begin{cases} +1 & \text{with probability } \frac{\delta/2}{k} \\ 0 & \text{with probability } \frac{k-\delta}{k} \\ -1 & \text{with probability } \frac{\delta/2}{k} \end{cases}, \tag{5.6}$$

where k is the dimensionality and δ is the number of non-zero components in the random index vectors; k and δ are parameters that depend on the size of the data and typical ranges are $1,000 - 10,000$ for k, and $2 - 10$ for δ (Kanerva et al., 2000). Despite the formulation in Equation 5.6, it is common practice to control for an equal number of positive and negative components ($\delta/2$) in the random index vectors. It would consequently be more correct to express the distribution as defined *per vector* rather than *per component* of the vectors. The important property of RI is that the random index vectors are k-dimensional with δ randomly placed $+1$s and -1s.

RI learns the word embeddings by summing the random index vectors of the contexts co-occurring with the target. Note that this process is applicable to any DOCUMENT RI   type of linguistic context. If we use **documents** as contexts, we assign random index vectors to each document, and add the document's random index vector to the target embedding every time the target occurs in that document. This generates frequency-weighted document-based embeddings that are comparable to the low-dimensional vectors derived from a standard word-by-document matrix. In the first paper on RI, Kanerva et al. (2000) use RI to build a document DSM, replicating the performance of LSA on the TOEFL synonym test.

WINDOW-   If the contexts are **window-based collocates**, RI assigns random index vec-
BASED RI   tors to the lexemes in the vocabulary and, every time a target t is encountered, updates its embedding by adding the random index vectors of the collocates:

$$\mathbf{t} \leftarrow \mathbf{t} + \sum_{c=-n}^{n} h(c_{i+n})\mathbf{r}(\mathbf{c_{i+n}}), \qquad (5.7)$$

where n is the size of the context window, and h a weighting function that quantifies the importance of the context items. Equation 5.7 describes the update rule of RI, and the final embedding of t can be expressed as:

$$\mathbf{t} = \sum_{i=1}^{N} \sum_{c=-n}^{n} h(c_{i+n})\mathbf{r}(\mathbf{c_{i+n}}), \qquad (5.8)$$

where N is the frequency of t in the corpus. As an effect of the RI update rule in Equation 5.7, the embedding of a target lexeme becomes increasingly similar to the embeddings of other lexemes that frequently co-occur with it (e.g., *dog* and *bark*) and to those words that frequently occur in similar contexts (e.g., *dog* and *cat*). Therefore, both first-order and high-order co-occurrences are eventually embedded in RI distributional representations.

Window-based RI is used by Sahlgren and colleagues in a number of experiments that demonstrate significantly improved performance on the TOEFL synonym test compared to Kanerva's original document DSM (Karlgren and Sahlgren, 2001; Sahlgren, 2006). Other types of contexts (e.g., syntactic collocates) can be used in the same way: Assign a random index vector to each context, and add that context's random index vector to the embedding of a target, every time the target occurs with that context.

In the standard setting of RI, $h(c) = 1$ for all context lexemes. In principle, weighting functions like PPMI (cf. Section 2.3.1) can also be used with RI. However, since they need to access the global frequency distribution of targets and contexts, they do not adhere to the incremental character of RI. Sahlgren et al. (2016) introduce the following **dynamic weighting scheme**:

DYNAMIC
WEIGHTING
SCHEME

$$h(c) = \exp(-\lambda \cdot \frac{F(c)}{V}), \qquad (5.9)$$

where $F(c)$ is the cumulative frequency of c, V is the total number of unique context items seen thus far, and λ is an integer that controls the aggressiveness of the frequency weight. Equation 5.9 weights the importance of context items based on the current size of the growing vocabulary, and incrementally changes as new occurrences of c and other contexts are encountered. An alternative weighting scheme is proposed by Norlund et al. (2016).

Table 5.2 shows a sample of nearest neighbors computed with a window-based RI model trained on ukWaC. Note that in RI it is also possible to

Table 5.2 RI nearest neighbors of *bike*, *car*, *dog*, and *lion* ranked by cosine similarity

bike		*car*		*dog*		*lion*	
ride_V	0.67	vehicle	0.62	bark	0.59	tiger	0.79
off-road	0.62	park_V	0.55	kennel	0.55	elephant	0.63
rider	0.57	drive	0.53	cat	0.51	roar	0.46
quad	0.57	driver	0.50	pet	0.48	beast	0.37
ride_N	0.53	van	0.49	puppy	0.47	wild	0.35
motorbike	0.52	park_N	0.48	vet	0.39	spot	0.35
bicycle	0.51	hire_N	0.44	breeder	0.38	safari	0.34
biking	0.48	home	0.43	breed_N	0.38	zoo	0.33
motorcycle	0.48	hire_V	0.42	chase	0.38	den	0.32
cycle_V	0.43	travel	0.42	breed_V	0.37	bear	0.32

The targets and contexts are the 10, 000 most frequent nouns, verbs, and adjectives in ukWaC. Co-occurrences were collected with a [5, 5] context window and weighted with the dynamic scheme in Equation 5.9

retrieve the context items that have contributed the most to the formation of an embedding. This is possible since only frequent contexts leave lasting traces in the RI embeddings, while infrequent contexts act as random noise. In order to retrieve the contexts that have contributed the most to a specific embedding, we simply do a nearest neighbor search comparing the embedding to the random index vectors. The context items whose random index vector is most similar to the embedding are the contexts that have co-occurred most frequently with the target word. Using this operation, it is possible to use RI for the analysis of syntagmatic relations as well as paradigmatic ones.

ONLINE,
INCREMENT-
AL RI
  Another significant advantage of RI is that the assignment of random index vectors and the updating of embeddings can be done in an **online** fashion. The **incremental** formulation of RI makes it attractive to use in settings with streaming or dynamic data, where it is neither possible to define in advance which items will constitute a viable definition of context, nor to allow continuously growing dimensionality. Instead of stopping the processing at some (arbitrary) point and doing dimensionality reduction (e.g., by performing a matrix factorization), RI enables online processing where the embeddings are continuously updated, and where the vector dimensionality never grows.

5.3.1 Random Indexing as Random Projection

The RI process generates implicit distributional representations that are effectively the sum of the random index vectors of the contexts that the target has co-occurred with. These embeddings are equivalent to the vectors produced by

Random Projection, *but without having to first assemble the matrix* **A** *and then projecting it through a random matrix* **R**.

In order to demonstrate the equivalence, we need to revisit the formulation of Random Projection, and express each component of the k-dimensional projected vectors in the $\mathbf{A}'$ matrix as a sum (Kaski, 1998):

$$a'_j = \sum_{i=1}^{n} r_{i,j} a_i, \qquad (5.10)$$

where a_i is the ith component of the original n-dimensional vector that, in the case of DSMs, records the co-occurrence frequency with context i, and $r_{i,j}$ is the ith component of the jth column of the sparse random projection matrix.

If we interpret the random projection matrix as containing one k-dimensional vector for each of n contexts, we may express the sum as follows:

$$a'_j = \sum_{c=1}^{c \in C_t} r(c)_j, \qquad (5.11)$$

where C_t is the set of contexts with which the target lexeme co-occurs. Thus, if we add the jth component of the k-dimensional random vector of the context c to the jth component of the k-dimensional embedding $\mathbf{a}'$ of the target lexeme *each time the target and the context co-occur*, we will produce an exact copy of the $\mathbf{a}'$ vector generated by Random Projection.

The only difference between Equation 5.10 and Equation 5.11 is the use of an explicit frequency factor a_i in the former case, which is replaced by the sum over contexts in the latter formulation. By avoiding the separation of the frequency factor from the context factor, we can arrive at an incremental formulation of a random projection, where the k-dimensional projected embedding $\mathbf{a}'$ is formed by summing the k-dimensional sparse random vectors of the contexts that the target co-occurs with, as in Equation 5.12 below:

$$\mathbf{a}' = \sum_{c=1}^{c \in C_t} \mathbf{r}(\mathbf{c}). \qquad (5.12)$$

This incremental process of performing Random Projection corresponds to RI.

5.4 The BEAGLE Model

Standard window-based RI models use a **bag-of-words** representation of context. Therefore, distributional vectors do not encode any structural information: The sentence *The dog bit the mailman* produces the same distributional representation of *dog* as the sentence *The mailman bit the dog*, because in either case the embedding **dog** is simply the sum of the random vectors of the co-occurring words. Structural information can be captured with RI by encoding contexts extracted from syntactically parsed corpora. Alternatively, RI can be modified to allow encoding of word order (cf. Section 5.3.1).

The first proposal for encoding sequence information with random vectors is the **Bound Encoding of the Aggregate Language Environment** (BEAGLE) model by Jones and Mewhort (2007). BEAGLE is a DSM that aims at explaining how meaning is both stored in and retrieved from semantic memory. BEAGLE reads the training corpus one sentence at a time and collects two kinds of information for each lexical item in the sentence: **context information** (what are the other lexemes it occurs with), and **order information** (in what order they occur). Each target lexeme t is represented by an embedding m_t called **memory vector**, obtained by summing a **context vector** c_t and an **order vector** o_t, extracted from each sentence in which t is observed. These vectors are computed with the aid of k-dimensional **environmental vectors** $r(l)$ (also called **signal vectors** by Recchia et al. 2015), corresponding to RI random vectors and univocally assigned to each lexeme l in the corpus vocabulary. The random vectors used in the BEAGLE model have normally distributed random variables as components with zero mean and $1/k$ variance, where $k = 2,048$.

Similarly to RI, the **context vector** c_t is built by summing the environmental vectors of the words in the same sentence (except for a list of stop words including very frequent function lexemes). The main novelty of BEAGLE is the way the order of the context words is encoded in order vectors. The context is defined as the n-grams (up to a limit on n) that co-occur within the same sentence as the target. Given the sentence *a dog bit the mailman*, and *dog* as the target, then we have the following seven n-grams: *a dog, dog bit, a dog bit, dog bit the, a dog bit the, dog bit the mailman, a dog bit the mailman*. Each of these n-grams is represented with a **binding vector**, obtained by combining the random index vectors of the context lexemes with the operation of **circular convolution** $\circledast$, which is defined in Chapter 9 (cf. Equation 9.10):

BEAGLE

ENVIRON-
MENTAL
VECTOR

CONTEXT
VECTOR

BINDING
VECTOR
CIRCULAR
CONVOLUTION

$$
\begin{aligned}
\text{bind}_{dog,1} &= r(a) \circledast \Phi \\
\text{bind}_{dog,2} &= \Phi \circledast r(bit) \\
\text{bind}_{dog,3} &= r(a) \circledast \Phi \circledast r(bit) \\
\text{bind}_{dog,4} &= \Phi \circledast r(bit) \circledast r(the) \\
\text{bind}_{dog,5} &= r(a) \circledast \Phi \circledast r(bit) \circledast r(the) \\
\text{bind}_{dog,6} &= \Phi \circledast r(bit) \circledast r(the) \circledast r(mailman) \\
\text{bind}_{dog,7} &= r(a) \circledast \Phi \circledast r(bit) \circledast r(the) \circledast r(mailman)
\end{aligned}
$$

$$(5.13)$$

where **bind** are the binding vectors, and Φ is a constant placeholder environmental vector that represents the target position. Models like BEAGLE that combine vectors with convolution are often referred to as **holographic models** because they are based on the same mathematical principles as light holography (Plate, 1994, 1995, 2003). When binding k-dimensional random vectors with circular convolution, the resulting vector will also be k-dimensional, and it will be approximately orthogonal to the included vectors. The effect is that each n-gram gets a unique representation that is nearly orthogonal to both the random index vectors of included words, and to the other n-gram representations. BEAGLE thus assigns a unique random vector to each unique n-gram. However, an important aspect of the model is that the random vectors representing n-grams are built *compositionally*, by combining the vectors of the component lexemes (cf. Section 9.2, where circular convolution is defined as a method to build compositional representations). The binding vectors are then added to form the **order vector** o_t:

HOLOGRAPHIC MODELS

ORDER VECTOR

$$o_t = \sum_{j=1}^{p\lambda-(p^2-p)-1} \text{bind}_{t,j}, \qquad (5.14)$$

where p is the position of the word in the sentence, and λ is a parameter that sets the maximum neighbors the target can be bound with.

Every time the target t is encountered, its **memory vector** is updated by summing the context and order vectors extracted from the sentence:

MEMORY VECTORS

$$m_t \leftarrow m_t + c_t + o_t. \qquad (5.15)$$

When comparing the embeddings produced by BEAGLE, the similarity between lexemes is dependent not only on the overlap of syntagmatic neighbors but also on their *order*. This means that the BEAGLE model is able to distinguish the contexts of the target word *kissed* in the sentences *Kim kissed Pat* and *Pat kissed Kim*, which a bag-of-words DSM would treat as equivalent.

Like in standard RI, it is possible to use the embeddings produced with BEAGLE to retrieve the context items that have contributed most to the formation of a distributional vector. However, the BEAGLE model also enables us to retrieve the context items that have occurred *in a specific position in the context*. This is done by decoding environmental vectors from the memory vector of a probe word with the operation of **circular correlation**, which is an approximate inverse of convolution. The decoded vector y is a noisy version

CIRCULAR CORRELATION

of its original form and needs to be compared to all the environmental vectors. Its nearest neighbors correspond to the lexical items that are most likely to co-occur with the probe word in a given position.

5.5 Encoding Sequences in RI by Random Permutations

Instead of using convolution to bind sequence information in the embeddings, Sahlgren et al. (2008) suggest using a computationally simpler permuted version of RI to achieve similar functionality as in the BEAGLE model. The idea is to use different **random permutations** of the random index vectors to reflect the position of context items in the sequence. A permutation can be any operation that produces a predictable rearrangement of the elements of the vectors. In the original paper, Sahlgren et al. (2008) use rotation as permutation operation, which means that the coordinates of a vector are shifted in some direction. As an example, consider the following random index vector:

RANDOM
PERMUTATIONS

$$r(\mathbf{x}) = \begin{pmatrix} +1 & 0 & 0 & -1 & 0 & +1 & 0 & 0 & 0 & 0 & 0 & -1 & 0 \end{pmatrix} \quad (5.16)$$

Rotating the vector one step to the right produces the following permuted version of the random index vector:

$$\Pi^1 r(\mathbf{x}) = \begin{pmatrix} 0 & +1 & 0 & 0 & -1 & 0 & +1 & 0 & 0 & 0 & 0 & 0 & -1 \end{pmatrix} \quad (5.17)$$

We denote the permutation operation (in this case, rotation) with Π, and use superscripts to indicate the number of steps we rotate: Π^1 means rotating one step to the right, and Π^{-1} means rotating one step to the left, producing the following permuted version of the random index vector:

$$\Pi^{-1} r(\mathbf{x}) = \begin{pmatrix} 0 & 0 & -1 & 0 & +1 & 0 & 0 & 0 & 0 & 0 & -1 & 0 & +1 \end{pmatrix} \quad (5.18)$$

Each permuted version of a random index vector is approximately orthogonal to both the original vector, and to the other permuted random index vectors (i.e., permuting a random index vector is equivalent to producing a new random index vector). The effect of permuting a vector is therefore similar to binding it with another vector by circular convolution. If we permute a random index vector to reflect the position of the context item in a sequence, and add the permuted version of the random index vector to the embeddings, we will achieve the same sequence-sensitive representations as in BEAGLE, but using permutation instead of convolution as the operation.

As an example, if we want to encode the context of the target *dog* in the sequence *a dog bit the mailman*, we can do:

$$\mathbf{dog} = \Pi^{-1} r(\mathbf{a}) + \Pi^1 r(\mathbf{bit}) + \Pi^2 r(\mathbf{the}) + \Pi^3 r(\mathbf{mailman}) \quad (5.19)$$

$$\Pi^{-1}\mathbf{r}(\mathbf{Kim}) = (\quad 0 \quad -1 \quad\; 0 \quad 0 \quad +1\;)$$
$$\Pi^{1}\mathbf{r}(\mathbf{Pat}) = (\,-1 \quad\;\; 0 \quad +1 \quad 0 \quad\;\; 0\;)$$

$$\mathbf{kissed} = (\,-1 \quad -1 \quad +1 \quad 0 \quad +1\;)$$

Figure 5.4 The sequence-sensitive distributional vector of *kissed* consisting of the permuted random index vectors of *Kim* and *Pat* in Figure 5.3

If we use Π^{n} where n is the number of positions away from the target lexeme (and use negative n for preceding items and positive n for succeeding ones), we will generate embeddings that encode the specific order of the context items. Sahlgren et al. (2008) call such vectors **order vectors**. On the other hand, ORDER VECTORS if we only use two permutations – one (e.g., Π^{-1}) for preceding items, and one (e.g., Π^{1}) for succeeding items – we will generate what Sahlgren et al. (2008) call **directional vectors**, which correspond to the direction-sensitive DIRECTIONAL representations used in HAL (cf. Section 4.1.1). VECTORS

As with $\text{bind}_{\text{dog},7}$ in the BEAGLE example (5.13), the embedding **dog** in (5.19) encodes the fact that *dog* is immediately preceded by *a*, is immediately followed by *bit*, which is followed by *the* and then by *mailman*. However, the permutation-based approach produces similar encodings for variations of a specific sequence. For instance, consider the sequences *the dog bit a mailman*, *a dog bit the mailman*, and *a dog bit a mailman*. Building sequence-sensitive distributional vectors for *dog* using random permutations for these sequences leads to embeddings that are similar to each other, due to the nature of vector addition (cf. Section 9.2). A major advantage of this method is that **dog** now represents all seven n-grams at once with very little computation.

As with circular convolution, a random permutation (e.g., in the form of rotation) is invertible, which means that we can query an embedding using a INVERTING reversed permutation to retrieve its most frequent syntagmatic neighbors (i.e., PERMUTATIONS collocates) from a specific context position. Consider again the example of building an embedding for *kissed* from the sequence *Kim kissed Pat*. Whenever we observe this sequence in the data, we add the permuted random index vectors of *Kim* and *Pat* to the embedding for *kissed*, as illustrated in Figure 5.4. In order to retrieve the most frequent syntagmatic neighbors to *kissed*, we cannot simply use its embedding and do a nearest neighbor search over the random index vectors, since they have been permuted before addition. We therefore have to undo the permutation before searching for the nearest random vectors. The most efficient way to do this is to apply the inverse permutation to the embedding before doing nearest neighbor search. As an example, if we want to retrieve the most frequent preceding word (which has been encoded using the permutation Π^{-1}) to *kissed*, we apply the inverse permutation (in

Table 5.3 Top syntagmatic neighbors preceding and
following *car* computed with permuted RI and ranked
by cosine similarity (cf. Table 5.2 for settings)

		car		
preceding contexts			*following contexts*	
saloon	0.16		parking	0.23
sister	0.14		rental_N	0.20
base	0.13		hire_N	0.19
hire_V	0.12		florida	0.17
labourer	0.12		van	0.13
customize	0.11		park_V	0.13
deal	0.11		crash	0.12
rental_A	0.11		chase	0.12
sinister	0.10		insurance	0.11
pedestrian	0.10		dealer	0.10

this case Π^1) to **kissed** before searching for the nearest random index vectors. This will retrieve the random index vector of *Kim* as the most similar vector. Conversely, to retrieve the most frequent succeeding word, we apply the permutation Π^{-1} to **kissed** before doing nearest neighbor search over the random index vectors, returning *Pat* as the most frequent succeeding word. Table 5.3 shows the top collocates preceding and following *car*, according to a RI model with permutations trained on ukWaC.

BEAGLE and RI with random permutations are alternative methods to encode word order information with random vectors. The two models are extensively compared by Recchia et al. (2010, 2015). Their experiments reveal that BEAGLE and permuted RI achieve approximately equal performance on a battery of semantic tasks when trained on a small corpus, but that RI eventually performs better when trained on a larger corpus due to its higher scalability.

5.6 Self-Organizing Maps (SOM)

RI and BEAGLE learn embeddings of target lexemes by summing the random vectors of their linguistic contexts. An alternative use of random encodings is

SOM

provided by **Self-Organizing Maps** (SOM) (Kohonen, 1989, 1995). A SOM uses a specific neural network architecture, in which the neurons are arranged in a lattice, with each node fully connected to the input units, but not to each

WEIGHT AND
INPUT VECTORS

other (see Figure 5.5). The nodes contain **weight vectors w** with the same dimensionality as the **input vector v**. These weight vectors are updated using

COMPETITIVE
LEARNING

competitive learning, which is a form of unsupervised machine learning, in which the nodes of the network compete to respond to a given input.

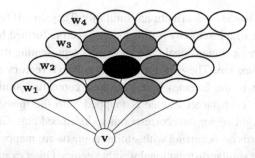

Figure 5.5 Each node in the Self-Organizing Map contains a weight vector **w**. The black node is the best matching unit for the input vector **v**. The gray nodes determined by the neighborhood function h are modified together with the best matching unit

At each learning iteration, an input vector is compared (using Euclidean distance) to the weight vectors (normally initialized with random values) of each node in the network. The node whose weight vector is most similar to the input vector is the **best matching unit** (BMU). The weight vector **w** of the BMU, and the weight vectors of the nodes closest to the BMU in the lattice – determined by a neighborhood function h – are then modified to become more similar to the input vector **v** according to the following update rule:

BEST MATCHING UNIT

$$\mathbf{w} \leftarrow \mathbf{w} + \alpha \cdot h \cdot (\mathbf{v} - \mathbf{w}), \qquad (5.20)$$

where α is the learning rate (cf. Section 6.1), which modulates the weight change and decreases during training. The **neighborhood function** h can be a fixed set of neighboring nodes, or something more sophisticated such as:

NEIGHBORHOOD FUNCTION

$$h_{ij} = \exp\left(-\frac{\text{dist}(\mathbf{w_i}, \mathbf{w_j})^2}{2\sigma^2}\right), \qquad (5.21)$$

where $\text{dist}(\mathbf{w_i}, \mathbf{w_j})$ is the distance between the weight vectors of the ith and jth nodes in the network, and σ is a monotonically decreasing function that shrinks the neighborhood over time. If this learning process is repeated a large number of times for each input vector, the SOM algorithm discovers a cluster structure that preserves the topology of the original space while reducing its dimensionality. This means that there is a similarity between SOMs and approaches based on the Johnson–Lindenstrauss lemma in that they both preserve the local structure of the input data while reducing its dimensionality.

SOMs are a general method for data dimensionality reduction. One example of the use of SOMs to build embeddings is Ritter and Kohonen (1989), who cluster lexemes based on distributional similarity. They do this by representing each occurrence of a lexeme by n-dimensional vectors formed by concatenating two (or more) k-dimensional random vectors representing the surrounding context of the lexeme. These n-dimensional **context vectors** are fed into a SOM that clusters the lexemes based on their contextual similarity. At the end of training, each target lexeme is mapped onto the most similar SOM unit, whose weight vector thus corresponds to its embedding. Given the SOM update rule, words co-occurring with similar contexts are mapped onto nearby units containing similar distributional weight vectors. Other examples of using SOMs to build distributional representations include Honkela (1997), Honkela et al. (1998), and Zhao et al. (2011). SOMs have attracted interest especially in cognitive science, to develop distributional models of dyslexia (Miikkulainen, 1997) and lexical acquisition (Li et al., 2007; Li and Zhao, 2013).

CONTEXT
VECTORS

5.7 Summary

This chapter has presented distributional models based on **random encoding** of the input. We have discussed the underlying mathematics of random projections and its incremental formulation in the form of **Random Indexing**. We have also illustrated methods for binding sequential information in distributed representations (**BEAGLE** and **Random Indexing with permutations**) and the use of random vectors with **Self-Organizing Maps**.

These DSMs belong to the family of count models, because they build distributional vectors by recording the co-occurrence frequency of targets with contexts. However, they do not collect counts into matrices, but directly learn embeddings by accumulating the random vectors encoding the linguistic contexts. Random encoding models emphasize scalability and incrementality, and have a close "family resemblance" with neural models. They are particularly suitable when dealing with large amounts of data and to model the incremental nature of human semantic learning.

5.8 Further Reading

- Random Indexing: Kanerva (1988, 2009); Sandin et al. (2017)
- BEAGLE and holographic models: Plate (2003); Jones and Mewhort (2007)

6

Neural Network Models

The most recent development in distributional semantics is represented by DSMs based on **artificial neural networks**, a family of machine learning algo- ARTIFICIAL NEURAL NETWORKS rithms that are nowadays extensively used in AI and NLP. In this chapter, we focus on the use of neural networks to build static embeddings (for contextual ones, cf. Section 9.6.3). Like random encoding models, neural networks incrementally learn embeddings by reducing the high dimensionality of distributional data without building an explicit co-occurrence matrix. Differing from the first generation of DSMs, also termed **count models**, the distributional representations produced by neural DSMs are the by-product of training COUNT VERSUS PREDICT MODELS the network to predict neighboring words, hence the name of **predict models**. Since semantically similar words tend to co-occur with similar contexts, the network learns to encode similar lexemes with similar distributional vectors.

After introducing the basic concepts of neural computation in Section 6.1, we illustrate **neural language models** and their use to learn distributional representations (Section 6.2). Then we go on to describe the most popular static neural DSMs, **CBOW** and **Skip-Gram** (Section 6.3). We conclude the chapter with a comparison between count and predict models (Section 6.4).

6.1 Neural Networks: A Brief Introduction

Artificial neural networks are computational models inspired by the functional organization of the human brain. The basic processing unit is called **neuron**. It receives input from weighted links with other units, corresponding NEURON to synaptic connections in the brain. The neuron multiplies each input x by its weight w, sums them, and then applies an **activation function** g to produce ACTIVATION FUNCTION the output y, which is passed to other units (see Figure 6.1a). The computation of each neuron is described by the following equation:

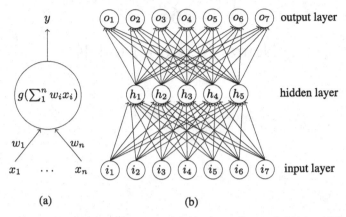

(a)   (b)

Figure 6.1 (a) Artificial neuron; (b) Feed-forward neural network with one hidden layer

$$y = g(\sum_{1}^{n} w_i x_i). \qquad (6.1)$$

LAYERS

Neural networks consist of several **layers** of interconnected neurons. Layers that lie between the input and output layers are called **hidden layers**, and models with many hidden layers are referred to as **deep neural networks**. Figure 6.1b shows a typical **feed-forward network** with one hidden layer, and the arrows reflect the flow of computation from the units. The network has **fully-connected** layers, in which each neuron is connected to all the neurons in the next layer. The weights of the connections between the neurons of the various layers are tuned in a learning phase when the model is trained to produce a certain output based on a certain input. In such scenarios, neural networks are **supervised learning** models.

FEED-FORWARD
NETWORK

SUPERVISED
LEARNING

Mathematically, each layer in a neural network is represented by a **vector** whose dimensionality corresponds to the number of neurons in the layer: for instance, the input layer in Figure 6.1b is the seven-dimensional vector **i**. The connections between two fully-connected layers are represented by a **weight matrix W**, such that $w_{i,j}$ is the weight of the connection from the ith neuron to the jth neuron. A simple feed-forward network with one hidden layer, like the one in Figure 6.1b, consists of two weight matrices: the input-to-hidden matrix $\mathbf{W_1}$, and the hidden-to-output matrix $\mathbf{W_2}$.

WEIGHT
MATRIX

The computation performed by a layer of n units fully connected to a layer of m units consists in **vector-matrix multiplication** (cf. Mathematical notes 3 and 4 in Section 2.5.1):[1]

VECTOR-MATRIX
MULTIPLICATION

$$\mathbf{y} = \mathbf{xW}, \qquad (6.2)$$

where $\mathbf{x}$ is a n-dimensional vector and $\mathbf{W}$ is a $n \times m$ weight matrix. This corresponds to a **linear transformation** of $\mathbf{x}$ into the m-dimensional vector $\mathbf{y}$ such that its jth dimension is $\sum_{i=1}^{n} x_i w_{i,j}$ (i.e., the dot product $\mathbf{x} \cdot \mathbf{w}_{*,j}$). Equation 6.2 generalizes Equation 6.1 to a fully-connected layer of neurons.

The **perceptron** is the simplest neural network and does not contain any PERCEPTRON hidden layer. Mathematically, the output vector $\mathbf{o}$ is a linear transformation of the input vector $\mathbf{i}$, performed by applying Equation 6.2:

$$\text{perceptron}(\mathbf{i}) = \mathbf{iW} + \mathbf{b}, \qquad (6.3)$$

where the vector $\mathbf{b}$ represents a bias term.[2]

In order to deal with tasks that cannot be modeled as linear functions, neu- NONLINEAR ral networks are enriched with hidden layers containing **nonlinear activation** ACTIVATION **functions** that are applied to each vector component. Figure 6.2 shows some FUNCTIONS of the most common activation functions. The **sigmoid** (σ), also called the SIGMOID **logistic** function, and the **hyperbolic tangent** (tanh) are S-shaped functions, TANH respectively transforming each input into the range $[0, 1]$ (i.e., the sigmoid turns the input into a probability estimate) and $[-1, 1]$. The **rectifier** (ReLU) is a RELU simpler function that raises negative values to 0. Although the choice of the activation function is more of an empirical matter, tanh and ReLU have been shown to outperform the sigmoid (Goldberg, 2017).

A feed-forward network with hidden layers is also known as **multi-layer** MULTI-LAYER **perceptron** (MLP). If there is one hidden layer, this produces a vector $\mathbf{h}$ by PERCEPTRON applying a nonlinear function g:

$$\mathbf{h} = g(\mathbf{iW_1} + \mathbf{b_1}). \qquad (6.4)$$

---

[1] The neural networks literature typically represents unit layers as column vectors (i.e., $n \times 1$ matrices) that are left multiplied by weight matrices, $\mathbf{Wx}$. Since in distributional semantics it is customary to use row vectors (i.e., $1 \times n$ matrices), we follow Goldberg (2017) and represent neuron layers with row vectors that are right multiplied by weight matrices.

[2] A bias is an additional unit of a layer that has outgoing connections but does not have any incoming link, and whose value is always one. The bias allows the network to produce output in the next layer that differs from zero when the input is zero. It is analogous to the intercept in a regression model, and it is useful to increase the ability of the network to fit the data.

$$\sigma(x) = \frac{1}{1 + \exp(-x)} \quad \tanh(x) = \frac{\exp(2x) - 1}{\exp(2x) + 1} \quad \text{ReLU}(x) = \max(0, x)$$

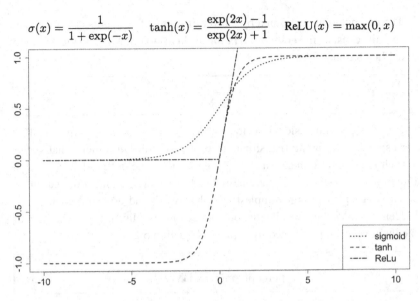

Figure 6.2   Most common nonlinear activation functions

The output vector **o** is generated by multiplying **h** by the next weight matrix **W₂** and adding a new bias term **b₂**. An MLP with one hidden layer is thus defined mathematically as follows (Goldberg, 2017):

$$\text{MLP}_1(\mathbf{i}) = g(\mathbf{i}\mathbf{W_1} + \mathbf{b_1})\mathbf{W_2} + \mathbf{b_2}. \tag{6.5}$$

In the case of multinomial classification scenarios, given n classes $\{c_1, \ldots, c_n\}$, the output vector **o** is then transformed with the **softmax function**:

$$\text{softmax}(o_i) = \frac{\exp(x_i)}{\sum_{j=1}^{n} \exp(x_j)}. \tag{6.6}$$

The softmax is a generalization of the sigmoid function that turns the output vector into a vector of real values in the range $[0, 1]$ that add up to one. This vector represents the probability distribution over the n classes given the network input **i**, that is $\text{softmax}(o_j) = p(c_j|\mathbf{i})$.

PARAMETERS

HYPERPARA
METERS

The **parameters** of the neural network are the weight matrices and the biases. The **hyperparameters** include various factors such as the number of network layers and their dimensionality, the activation function, the training

regime, etc. While these are set up a priori, the parameters are normally trained by **backpropagation** (Rumelhart et al., 1986), a supervised learning algorithm BACKPROPAGATION
that propagates error signals backwards through the network. The error signals
are computed using a **loss** or **cost function**, which maps an output vector $\mathbf{o}$ LOSS FUNCTION
and a true outcome $\mathbf{o^t}$ to a scalar quantifying the loss suffered by predicting $\mathbf{o}$
when the expected output is $\mathbf{o^t}$. The **training objective** of the neural network TRAINING
is to minimize the loss across a set of training examples. OBJECTIVE

When the network output is transformed into probabilities with the softmax,
a common loss function is the **categorical cross-entropy** (also referred to as CATEGORIAL
negative log likelihood): CROSS-ENTROPY

$$L_{\text{cross-entropy}}(\mathbf{o}, \mathbf{o^t}) = -\sum_{i=1}^{n} o_i^t \log o_i. \qquad (6.7)$$

The categorical cross-entropy loss measures the dissimilarity between the true
multinomial distribution $\mathbf{o^t}$ and the predicted probability distribution $\mathbf{o}$. If it is
a hard classification task (i.e., only one class is the correct one), $\mathbf{o^t}$ is a **one-** ONE-HOT
hot vector, with the dimension representing the true class equal to one, and all VECTOR
the other dimensions set to zero. In this case, the categorical cross-entropy is
simply the log probability of the correct class:

$$L_{\text{cross-entropy(hard)}}(\mathbf{o}, \mathbf{o^t}) = -\log o_k^t, \qquad (6.8)$$

where k is the dimension corresponding to the true class. The better the
network classifies the input, the closer to one is o_k^t, and the lower is the loss.

When a network is given pairs of positive and negative input examples, $\mathbf{i_p}$
and $\mathbf{i_n}$, and the task is scoring the positive items above the negative ones, a
suitable function is the **margin (ranking) loss**: MARGIN LOSS

$$L_{\text{margin\_ranking}}(\mathbf{i_p}, \mathbf{i_n}) = \sum_{i=1}^{n} \max(0, 1 - (f(\mathbf{i_p}) - f(\mathbf{i_n})), \qquad (6.9)$$

where $f(\mathbf{i})$ is a scalar score assigned by the network. The training objective is
to rank positive inputs over negative ones with a margin of at least one.

The network weights are iteratively changed with **gradient descent** to GRADIENT
minimize the prediction errors computed by the loss function L: DESCENT

$$w \leftarrow w - \alpha \frac{\partial L}{\partial w}, \tag{6.10}$$

LEARNING RATE

where $\frac{\partial L}{\partial w}$ is the partial derivative of the loss function with respect to the weight w, and α is a constant called **learning rate** determining the size of the weight change. According to Equation 6.10, the larger the partial derivative of the error, the larger the weight change. Given a vector of weights **w**,

GRADIENT

the **gradient** of the loss function is a vector whose components are the partial derivatives of the error with respect to each weight w. The gradient specifies the direction that produces the steepest increase in the error, and gradient descent searches for the optimal parameter configuration by moving the weights in the opposite direction. The gradients are then backpropagated through the network by applying the **chain rule**, which multiplies the gradients, starting from the output layer, and traverses backwards into the hidden layer(s).

STOCHASTIC
GRADIENT
DESCENT

Classical backpropagation updates the weights with Equation 6.10 by computing the gradient over the whole training set at each iteration. A much faster simplification is **stochastic gradient descent** (Bottou, 2012; LeCun et al., 2012), which approximates the gradient by iteratively computing the prediction error on a single randomly sampled item in the training set. Stochastic gradient descent is the most common training algorithm for neural networks.

6.2 Neural Language Models

NEURAL
LANGUAGE
MODELS

The use of neural networks to learn distributional representations stems from the research on **neural language models**.

> Given a sequence of lexemes $c = l_1, \ldots, l_n$ (called the **context**), a **neural language model** is an artificial neural network trained to predict the most likely next lexeme $t = l_{n+1}$ (called the **target**), by computing the conditional probability $p(t|c = l_1, \ldots, l_n)$.

REPRESENTATION
LEARNING

PREDICT DSMS

Neural language models are employed for **representation learning** since the network forms internal representations that encode the distributional properties of lexical items. **Predict DSMs** are neural language models that learn word embeddings as a side-effect of learning to predict the context lexemes of a target word. Though neural networks trained with backpropagation are supervised learning methods, language modeling is typically considered as an unsupervised task (Collobert and Weston, 2008; Turian et al., 2010; Collobert et al., 2011; Goldberg, 2017), because no annotated data are required and the

learning objective of the network is to reproduce the input sequence of lex- self-
emes. This approach is also called **self-supervised learning** (Manning et al., supervised
2020). learning

Various types of networks can be trained via self-supervision and used as predict DSMs. Here, we review Simple Recurrent Networks (Section 6.2.1) and feed-forward ones (Section 6.2.2). More complex neural language models used to learn contextual embeddings are analyzed in Section 9.6.3.

6.2.1 Simple Recurrent Networks (SRN)

Simple Recurrent Networks (SRN), introduced by Elman (1990), are a type Simple
of **recurrent neural network** that augments the standard MLP architecture Recurrent
described in Section 6.1 (input layer, hidden layer, and output layer) with a Networks
context layer linked to the hidden layer with **recurrent connections**, and at context layer
each processing step preserves a copy of the state of the hidden layer at the previous time step (see Figure 6.3). This enables the SRN to keep a short-term memory, which makes it suitable for sequence prediction tasks.

Input lexemes are represented as distinct **one-hot vectors**, with a single one-hot
dimension set to one and all others set to zero. The input and output vector vectors
dimensionality is therefore equal to the number of word types. The network is trained as a neural language model: Each lexeme l_i in a training sequence $l_1, \ldots, l_n$ is fed to the SRN one at a time and the task is to predict the next lexeme l_{i+1}. The hidden state h_i is a function of the current input l_i and the previous hidden state h_{i-1}. The SRN updates the vectors h_i in the hidden layer at step i in the following way:

$$h_i = \sigma(l_i W_1 + h_{i-1} U + b_h), \qquad (6.11)$$

where σ is the sigmoid activation function, W_i is the weight matrix of the hidden layer, l_i is the input vector, U is the context layer weight matrix, h_{i-1} is the vector of the hidden layer at step $i-1$, and b_h is a bias vector. The output prediction of the SRN is computed in the same way as in a standard feed-forward network. The loss function compares the predicted output o_i with the vector of the next word in the sequence, l_{i+1}, and the error is used to modify the network weights with backpropagation.

Elman (1990) shows that SRNs form internal representations that capture semantic properties of target lexemes: If we store the activation in the hidden layer for each occurrence of a lexeme, and take the average of these activation patterns, we arrive at a useful distributional representation. Elman proves that a clustering of the resulting embeddings replicates the original category structure of the lexicon used to produce the input sequences. While Elman (1990)

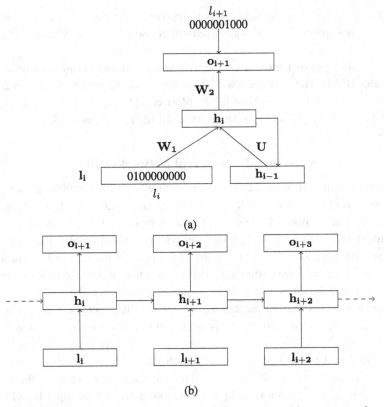

Figure 6.3 (a) Simple recurrent network; (b) the computation of the same network unrolled in time: at each time step i, the hidden layer h_i is a function of the current input vector l_i and of the hidden layer at the previous step

primarily aims at supporting a non-nativist approach to grammar learning by demonstrating that linguistic structures can be viewed as emergent properties of a neural network extracting statistical regularities from the input stream (Elman, 1991, 1993), Borovsky and Elman (2006) specifically apply SRNs to model children's acquisition of semantic categories.[3]

SRNs are an example of predict DSM: By learning to predict the input sequence, the network learns embeddings that represent the co-occurrences of

---

[3] It has been pointed out that the distributional clustering produced by SRNs is a consequence of the averaging of contexts, rather than of the actual learning phase of the neural network (Plate, 1994; Sakurai and Hyodo, 2002). In fact, by summing the representations for each occurrence of a lexeme and then taking the average of these, the SRN is effectively accumulating distributional vectors in a manner similar to Random Indexing (cf. Section 5.3), but with non-linear transformations before summation (Sakurai and Hyodo, 2002).

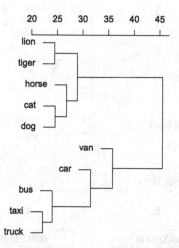

Figure 6.4 Hierarchical clustering of a sample of neural embeddings with 640 dimensions, produced by the SRN in Mikolov et al. (2013d)

the target lexemes, so that distributionally similar words activate similar hidden representations. Elman's experiments with SRNs were carried out with an artificially generated training set of small sentences and a very limited vocabulary of a few tens of words. Mikolov et al. (2013d) are the first to use SRNs to learn distributional representations in a real scale setting, using a training corpus of broadcast news data and a vocabulary of 82,000 lexical items.

Differently from Elman, Mikolov et al. (2013d) use as word embeddings the row vectors in the **weight matrix** $\mathbf{W}_1$ connecting the input to the hidden layer. Since the input words are encoded as one-hot vectors, given n target lexemes and d hidden units, $\mathbf{W}_1$ is a $n \times d$ matrix, whose rows represent d-dimensional embeddings for the target lexemes. Figure 6.4 contains the hierarchical clustering of a sample of embeddings with 640 dimensions, produced by the SRN in Mikolov et al. (2013d). The vehicle and animal clusters are clearly separated in the vector space, showing that the word embeddings capture relevant semantic categories. These embeddings are tested on the analogy task described in Section 7.2.4 and outperform a classic matrix model with SVD.

EMBEDDINGS AS WEIGHT VECTORS

6.2.2 Feed-Forward Language Models

Bengio et al. (2003) pioneered the use of feed-forward networks for language modeling. This sparked a rich line of research aiming at reducing the training costs of neural language models and improving the quality of the word embeddings they learn.

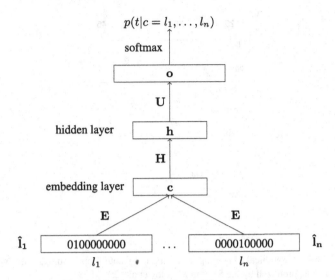

Figure 6.5 Feed-forward neural language model

NNLM

EMBEDDING
LAYER
The architecture of the **Neural Network Language Model** (NNLM) by Bengio et al. (2003) is illustrated in Figure 6.5. A key component of the network is the **embedding layer** (also called **projection layer**), which accumulates word embeddings of the input lexemes. This embedding layer is functionally equivalent to the hidden layer in Elman's original SRN, in the sense that it effectively produces distributional representations in the form of dense, implicit vectors. The main difference is that the embedding layer does not contain a nonlinear activation function. From a theoretical perspective, the point of including an embedding layer in the neural language model is to enable the language model to take advantage of distributional similarities between the input lexemes when predicting the probabilities of different sequences.

EMBEDDING
MATRIX
The **embedding matrix** E contains implicit distributional vectors with latent features, which are normally initialized with random weights. Input lexemes are encoded as one-hot vectors. Given a lexeme l and its one-hot vector $\hat{l}$, the embedding l is a linear transformation of $\hat{l}$ (cf. Equation 6.2):

$$l = \hat{l}E. \tag{6.12}$$

The input is a context sequence $c = l_1, \ldots, l_n$ represented by concatenating the embeddings of its lexemes $c = l_1; \ldots; l_n$, which is then fed to the hidden layer with a tanh activation function, and then to the output layer :

$$o = (\tanh(cH + b))U + d, \tag{6.13}$$

where **b** is the bias vector of the embeddings-to-hidden weight matrix **H**, and **d** is the bias vector of the hidden-to-output weight matrix **U**. The output vector **o** is transformed with the softmax function (cf. Equation 6.6) into a n-dimensional vector whose kth element estimates the probability $p(t = l_k|c)$, and n is the size of the vocabulary. The network parameters, including the embedding matrix **E**, are trained with stochastic gradient descent using negative log likelihood as loss function (cf Equation 6.7).

Since the nonlinear hidden layer makes the NNLM training very expensive, Mnih and Hinton (2007) propose the **Log-BiLinear** (LBL) model that contains only the linear embedding layer. To predict the target word t given the context sequence $c = l_1, \ldots, l_n$, LBL represents the context by summing (instead of concatenating) the embeddings of the lexemes, scaled by a weight matrix $\mathbf{C_i}$ associated with context position i: LOG-BILINEAR MODEL

$$\mathbf{c} = \sum_{i=1}^{n} \mathbf{l_i C_i}. \tag{6.14}$$

The network then computes a **similarity score** between the context and a target word by taking the dot product of the embedding **c** and the embedding of a target lexeme t in the vocabulary: SIMILARITY SCORE

$$s_\theta(\mathbf{t}, \mathbf{c}) = \mathbf{t} \cdot \mathbf{c} + \mathbf{b_t}, \tag{6.15}$$

where θ are the model parameters, including the embeddings, and $\mathbf{b_t}$ is the bias that captures the context-independent frequency of the target lexeme. Finally, the resulting scores are exponentiated and normalized with the softmax function in order to obtain the probability distribution over the next word:

$$p(t|c = l_1, \ldots, l_n) = \frac{\exp(s_\theta(\mathbf{t}, \mathbf{c}))}{\sum_j \exp(s_\theta(\mathbf{l_j}, \mathbf{c}))}. \tag{6.16}$$

Thus, the model assigns a probability to the lexeme t based on its similarity to the context c, as measured by the dot product of their embeddings. The "log-bilinear" name of LBL comes from the fact that the logarithm of the numerator in Equation 6.16 (i.e., the dot product $\mathbf{t} \cdot \mathbf{c}$) is a bilinear map of the two vectors.

Despite the simplification obtained by removing the nonlinear hidden layer, training LBL is extremely expensive for large vocabularies because of the normalization factor in Equation 6.16, which requires computing the dot product between **c** and the embedding of each lexeme. The

Hierarchical Log-BiLinear model (HLBL) (Mnih and Hinton, 2009) accelerates the computations by using **hierarchical softmax** (Morin and Bengio, 2005), which removes the requirement of having to compute probabilities by summing the dot products over the entire vocabulary. Instead, the vocabulary is organized into a binary tree, in which each leaf represents a lexeme and is defined by a sequence of binary decisions to go from the root of the tree to that leaf node. These series of decisions form binary feature vectors that encode the leaves (lexemes) of the tree. Therefore, the standard hidden-to-output weight matrix, whose output layer has a dimensionality equal to the size of the vocabulary, is substituted by a weight matrix whose output layer has a much smaller dimensionality. If the tree is balanced, then the depth of the tree is in order of the logarithm of the size of the vocabulary, which means a model using hierarchical softmax will scale logarithmically in the size of the vocabulary rather than linearly, as with the standard softmax. Mnih and Hinton (2009) use hierarchical clustering on learned embeddings to generate a tree, which not only leads to significant training speed-up, but also to qualitative improvements.

In the models above, training distributional representations in the form of word embeddings is just a way to improve the language model performance. Collobert and Weston (2008), Turian et al. (2010), and Collobert et al. (2011) are among the first to focus on the quality of word representations themselves
and to use the **pretrained embeddings** as features in downstream applications. The goal is to leverage the great availability of unlabeled texts by training neural language models via self-supervision to obtain high-quality word embeddings. These are then fed into supervised networks that can usually count on a much more limited amount of annotated data and can benefit from the semantic knowledge encoded in distributional vectors.

Collobert and Weston (2008) and Collobert et al. (2011) learn word embed-
dings with a **discriminative neural language model**, instead of a probabilistic one. The training objective of the network is to assign a higher score to the n-
grams s observed in the corpus (e.g., *chase the cat*), than to **noise n-grams** $\tilde{s}$ obtained by replacing one of the lexemes with a random word (e.g., *chase the tax*). The model must minimize the following margin loss (cf. Equation 6.9):

$$L = \sum_{s_i}^{T} \max(0, 1 - (f_\theta(s_i) - f_\theta(\tilde{s}_i)), \qquad (6.17)$$

where T is the set of training n-grams, and f_θ is a scoring function corresponding to a feed-forward network with parameters θ, whose input is the concatenation of the embeddings of the words in the n-grams, and the output is a single unit layer producing the score for each n-gram.

Mnih and Kavukcuoglu (2013) present a variation of LBL whose primary goal is to use language modeling to improve semantic representations. One major novelty of their model is that it learns two sets of embeddings, one for the target words (i.e., the words to be predicted) and one for the context lexemes. Thus, each lexeme l is represented with a **target embedding** $l^{(T)}$ and a **context embedding** $l^{(C)}$. According to Mnih and Kavukcuoglu (2013), these embeddings capture complementary aspects of the distributional properties of lexemes. Two versions of this model are proposed. The first one, **vLBL**, is just a variant of LBL and its training objective is to predict the target lexeme t given the context $c = l_1, \ldots, l_n$. The model computes the representation for the target word by averaging the context embeddings of the lexemes in c: TARGET AND CONTEXT EMBEDDINGS VLBL

$$\mathbf{c} = \frac{1}{n} \sum_{i=1}^{n} \mathbf{l}_i^{(C)}. \tag{6.18}$$

This is a simplification of Equation 6.14, which adopts a bag-of-words model of the context, by dropping the position weights. Since words are now represented as continuous vectors, such representation is also called a **continuous bag-of-words** (cf. the CBOW model in Section 6.3 and Section 9.2). The network then measures a similarity score between $\mathbf{c}$ and the target embedding: CONTINUOUS BAG-OF-WORDS

$$s_\theta(t, c) = \mathbf{t}^{(T)} \cdot \mathbf{c} + \mathbf{b_t}. \tag{6.19}$$

The output probability distribution is computed with Equation 6.16.

The second version of the model, **ivLBL**, learns word embeddings by predicting the context based on a target lexeme (hence the "i" for *inverse* vLBL). Context words are treated as independent features, and the context probability is computed as the product of the conditional probability of each lexeme in the context sequence given the target: IVLBL

$$p(c = l_1, \ldots, l_n | t) = \prod_{i=1}^{n} p(l_i | t). \tag{6.20}$$

Each probability $p(l|t)$ is computed with the following scoring function:

$$s_\theta(l, t) = \mathbf{l}^{(T)} \cdot \mathbf{t}^{(C)} + \mathbf{b_{l_i}}, \tag{6.21}$$

which is then turned into a probability with Equation 6.16. Both vLBL and ivLBL are trained with **noise-contrastive estimation**, which is similar to the discriminative method by Collobert and Weston (2008) and includes negative training examples in the scoring function in addition to the normal positive ones. Since the gradients are computed over the set of negative examples NOISE-CONTRASTIVE ESTIMATION

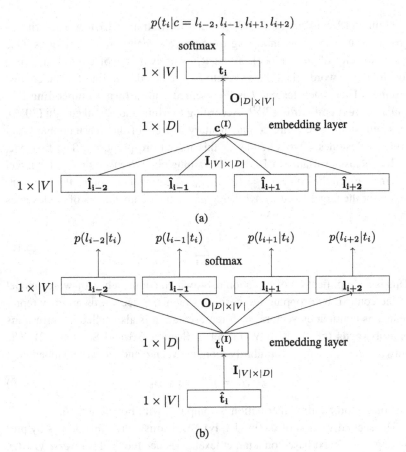

$$p(t_i|c = l_{i-2}, l_{i-1}, l_{i+1}, l_{i+2})$$

(a)

(b)

Figure 6.6 (a) CBOW; (b) Skip-Gram

instead of the entire vocabulary, the model is independent of the vocabulary size.

6.3 Word2vec: Skip-Gram (SG) and CBOW

WORD2VEC The **Skip-Gram** (SG) and **Continuous Bag-Of-Words** (CBOW) DSMs implemented in the **word2vec** library (Mikolov et al., 2013b) are the most famous outcome of the research on neural language models reviewed in the previous section. They are essentially feed-forward networks without a non-linear hidden layer. CBOW (see Figure 6.6a) is similar to vLBL and predicts a target lexeme t based on an input context c, while SG (see Figure 6.6b) is close to ivLBL and predicts the context based on the target. CBOW and SG are window-based DSMs: The context c is represented with a $[n, n]$ window of lexemes surrounding the target t (cf. Section 2.2.1). In word2vec, the set of target lexemes T and the set of context lexemes C coincide with the corpus vocabulary $V = \{l_1, \ldots, l_n\}$. The input layer consists of one-hot vectors with $|V|$ dimensions encoding the lexemes in the vocabulary. The embedding layer is a dense vector with $D = \{d_1, \ldots, d_k\}$ latent dimensions, such that $|D| \ll |V|$. The network learns two embeddings for each lexeme l, the **input** **embedding** $l^{(I)}$ and the **output embedding** $l^{(O)}$, respectively contained in the weight matrices $\mathbf{I}$ and $\mathbf{O}$, called **embedding matrices**. These are the network parameters, which are initialized to uniformly sampled random numbers in the range $[-\frac{1}{2k}, \frac{1}{2k}]$ and then trained with stochastic gradient descent.

INPUT AND OUTPUT EMBEDDINGS

The training objective of **Skip-Gram** is to learn word embeddings that predict the lexemes co-occurring with the targets in the context window. The goal is to set the parameters to maximize the product of probabilities of the context lexemes given the targets in V:

SKIP-GRAM

$$\prod_{i=1}^{|V|} \prod_{i-n \leq j \leq i+n, j \neq i} p(l_j | t_i), \tag{6.22}$$

where $[n, n]$ is the size of the context window surrounding the target. By taking the log probabilities, the SG objective amounts to minimizing the function:

$$J_{SG} = -\sum_{i=1}^{|V|} \sum_{i-n \leq j \leq i+n, j \neq i} \log p(l_j | t_i). \tag{6.23}$$

The better the model predicts a context lexeme l given the target t, the higher $p(l|t)$ and the lower $-\log p(l|t)$ (cf. the negative log likelihood loss function in Equation 6.8). Therefore, minimizing J_{SG} corresponds to maximizing the predictive ability of the network.

The probability $p(l|t)$ is modeled using the softmax function applied to the dot product of the input embedding of the target, $\mathbf{t}^{(I)}$, and the output embedding of the context lexeme, $l^{(O)}$:

$$p(l|t) = \frac{\exp(\mathbf{l}^{(O)} \cdot \mathbf{t}^{(I)})}{\sum_{j=1}^{V} \exp(\mathbf{l_j}^{(O)} \cdot \mathbf{t}^{(I)})}. \tag{6.24}$$

The SG network in Figure 6.6b computes Equation 6.24 in the following way:

1. the input one-hot vector $\hat{t}$ is multiplied by the weight matrix $\mathbf{I}_{|V| \times |D|}$ from the input-to-embedding layer. Since each row vector of $\mathbf{I}$ is an input embedding for a word in V, and $\hat{t}$ is a one-hot vector, the multiplication result is the input embedding of t:

$$t^{(I)} = \hat{t}\mathbf{I}. \qquad (6.25)$$

Given a model with a vocabulary of four words, an embedding matrix $\mathbf{I}$ containing the corresponding input embeddings, and $\hat{dog} = (1\,0\,0\,0)$ the input vector of the target *dog*, the embedding $dog^{(I)}$ is obtained as follows:

$$\hat{dog}\,(1\,0\,0\,0) \begin{array}{c} dog^{(I)} \\ cat^{(I)} \\ eat^{(I)} \\ bark^{(I)} \end{array} \begin{pmatrix} 0.067 & 0.096 & 0.719 \\ 0.157 & 0.380 & 0.424 \\ 0.154 & 0.460 & 0.401 \\ 0.131 & 0.432 & 0.404 \end{pmatrix} = dog^{(I)}(0.067\,0.096\,0.719)$$

$$(6.26)$$

2. the input embedding $t^{(I)}$ is multiplied by the weight matrix $\mathbf{O}_{|D| \times |V|}$ from the embedding-to-output layer, whose column vectors are the output embeddings for the words in V. Importantly, the same matrix $\mathbf{O}$ is shared by all the context lexemes. This produces the vector l:

$$l = t^{(I)}\mathbf{O}. \qquad (6.27)$$

For example, given an output embedding matrix $\mathbf{O}$, and the input embedding $dog^{(I)}$ in Equation 6.26, we obtain the following vector l:

$$dog^{(I)}(0.067\,0.096\,0.719) \begin{array}{cccc} dog^{(O)} & cat^{(O)} & eat^{(O)} & bark^{(O)} \end{array} \begin{pmatrix} 0.236 & 0.220 & 0.424 & 0.064 \\ 0.265 & 0.029 & 0.045 & 0.089 \\ 0.107 & 0.121 & 0.046 & 0.752 \end{pmatrix}$$

$$= l\,(0.118\,0.105\,0.066\,0.554)$$

$$(6.28)$$

The vector l has $|V|$ dimensions, and the kth dimension corresponds to $l_k^{(O)} \cdot t^{(I)}$, that is the dot product between the output embedding of the lexeme $l_k \in V$ and the input embedding of the target.

3. the softmax function turns l into a vector of probabilities, such that the kth dimension corresponds to $p(l = l_k|t)$. The softmax of l in Equation 6.28 is $(0.22\,0.22\,0.21\,0.35)$. This vector represents the network prediction of the context lexeme given the target t. In the example above, the network would predict *bark* as the most likely context given the target *dog*.

CBOW   The training objective of **CBOW** is essentially the mirror image of SG: The network learns word embeddings by predicting the target lexemes given the words in their surrounding context window. This corresponds to setting the parameters that minimize the following function:

$$J_{CBOW} = -\sum_{i=1}^{|V|} \log p(t_i|c = l_{i-n}, \dots, l_{i-1}, l_{i+1}, \dots, l_{i+n}), \quad (6.29)$$

where $[n, n]$ is the size of the symmetric context window surrounding the target. The probability $p(t|c)$ is computed using the softmax function applied to the dot product of the input embedding of the context, $c^{(I)}$, and the output embedding of the target $t^{(O)}$:

$$p(t|c) = \frac{\exp(t^{(O)} \cdot c^{(I)})}{\sum_{j=1}^{V} \exp(l_j^{(O)} \cdot c^{(I)})}. \quad (6.30)$$

Like in vLBL, the context embedding $c^{(I)}$ is obtained by averaging the input embeddings of the context lexemes (cf. Equation 6.18), hence the name of Continuous Bag-Of-Words model. The CBOW network in Figure 6.6a computes Equation 6.30 in the following way:

1. for each lexeme l_j in the context window surrounding t, its input vector $\hat{l}_j$ is multiplied by the weight matrix $I_{|V| \times |D|}$ from the input-to-embedding layer. Like with SG, the same matrix is shared by all the context lexemes. The result of the multiplication is the input embedding of l_j:

$$l_j^{(I)} = \hat{l}_j I. \quad (6.31)$$

2. the input embeddings of the lexemes in the context window are averaged to obtain the input embedding of the context c:

$$c^{(I)} = \frac{1}{2n} \sum_{i-n \le j \le i+n, j \ne i} l_j^{(I)}. \quad (6.32)$$

3. the input embedding $c^{(I)}$ is multiplied by the weight matrix $O_{|D| \times |V|}$ from the embedding-to-output layer, whose column vectors are the output embeddings for the words in V. This produces the vector t:

$$t = c^{(I)} O. \quad (6.33)$$

The vector t has $|V|$ dimensions, and the kth dimension corresponds to $l_k^{(O)} \cdot c^{(I)}$, that is the dot product between the output embedding of the lexeme $l_k \in V$ and the input embedding of the context.

4. the softmax function (cf. Equation 6.30) normalizes t into a vector of probabilities, such that the kth dimension corresponds to $p(t = l_k|c)$. This vector is the network prediction of the target lexeme given the context c.

Table 6.1 SG nearest neighbors of *bike*, *car*, *dog*, and *lion* ranked by cosine similarity. The targets and contexts are the 10,000 most frequent nouns, verbs, and adjectives in ukWaC. Co-occurrences were collected with a [5, 5] context window. SG was trained with negative sampling

bike		car		dog		lion	
motorcycle	0.78	vehicle	0.71	cat	0.78	tiger	0.71
bicycle	0.77	motorbike	0.70	puppy	0.75	elephant	0.69
motorbike	0.77	motorcycle	0.70	rabbit	0.69	eagle	0.69
scooter	0.75	bike	0.69	pet	0.67	dragon	0.65
ride	0.71	van	0.67	kennel	0.67	wolf	0.63
car	0.69	scooter	0.64	kitten	0.65	snake	0.57
off-road	0.67	bicycle	0.62	hound	0.62	bull	0.57
biking	0.48	automobile	0.62	pup	0.60	beast	0.57
rider	0.67	park	0.59	horse	0.59	penguin	0.53
biker	0.62	minibus	0.58	greyhound	0.59	dolphin	0.52

Table 6.1 contains the nearest neighbors of a sample of target lexemes computed with SG. Embeddings have 300 dimensions and were trained with negative sampling (cf. Section 6.3.1) on a portion of ukWaC.

6.3.1 Training Word2vec

Like for the neural language models described in Section 6.2, the bottleneck for training CBOW and SG is represented by the computation of the output probability distribution with the softmax function, which becomes prohibitively expensive for large vocabularies. To speed up training, Mikolov et al. (2013b) use **hierarchical softmax** with the vocabulary represented as a Huffman binary tree, in which the structure of the tree is determined by the frequencies of the lexemes, so that frequent lexemes get short codes.

HIERARCHICAL SOFTMAX

As an alternative to hierarchical softmax, Mikolov et al. (2013a) refine the SG model by introducing **negative sampling**, a simplified variant of the noise-contrastive estimation used in the ivLBL model, which only requires samples from a noise distribution and not their numerical probabilities. The resulting model is called SGNS for **Skip-Gram with Negative Sampling**. SGNS uses a radically different training objective than the original SG one in Equation 6.23. Similarly to Collobert and Weston (2008), for each target-context pair $\langle t, c \rangle$ in the training data (e.g., $\langle dog, bark \rangle$), SGNS generates k pairs $\langle t, \tilde{c} \rangle$ (e.g., $\langle dog, sky \rangle$), such that $\tilde{c}$ is a noise word randomly sampled from the vocabulary V according to the weighted unigram probability distribution. These pairs are

NEGATIVE SAMPLING

SGNS

called **negative examples** because they have been randomly generated, rather negative examples
than being observed in the corpus. The network objective is to discriminate
with logistic regression the positive from the negative examples.

Given a set of target lexemes T and a set of context lexemes C, let D be
the set of co-occurrence pairs $\langle t, c \rangle$ extracted from the corpus and $\tilde{D}$ the set of
randomly generated negative pairs. Following Goldberg and Levy (2014), we
denote with $p(D = 1|t, c)$ the probability that $\langle t, c \rangle$ belongs to the training
corpus. The probability that $\langle t, \tilde{c} \rangle$ does not belong to the training data is
$p(D = 0|t, \tilde{c}) = 1 - p(D = 1|t, \tilde{c})$. The training objective of SGNS consists
in maximizing the following function:

$$J_{SGNS} = \sum_{\langle t,c \rangle \in D} \log p(D = 1|t, c) + \sum_{\langle t,\tilde{c} \rangle \in \tilde{D}} \log(1 - p(D = 1|t, \tilde{c})).$$

$$(6.34)$$

Maximizing J_{SGNS} amounts to set the network parameters that maximize the
probability of the observed pairs (left addend) and minimize the probabilities
of the negative examples (right addend). Like in SG, the probabilities in Equation 6.34 are computed with the dot product between the input embedding of
the target and the output embedding of the context lexeme. However, now we
have a binary classification problem, since we simply need to establish whether
a given pair belongs or not to the training data. Instead of using the softmax,
these probabilities are thus computed with its binary counterpart, the sigmoid
function σ (cf. Section 6.1) applied to the dot product of the embeddings:

$$J_{SGNS} = \sum_{\langle t,c \rangle \in D} \log \sigma(\mathbf{c}^{(O)} \cdot \mathbf{t}^{(I)}) + \sum_{\langle t,\tilde{c} \rangle \in \tilde{D}} \log(1 - \sigma(\tilde{\mathbf{c}}^{(O)} \cdot \mathbf{t}^{(I)})), \quad (6.35)$$

which is equivalent to the following equation (Mikolov et al., 2013a):

$$J_{SGNS} = \sum_{\langle t,c \rangle \in D} \log \sigma(\mathbf{c}^{(O)} \cdot \mathbf{t}^{(I)}) + \sum_{\langle t,\tilde{c} \rangle \in \tilde{D}} \log \sigma(-\tilde{\mathbf{c}}^{(O)} \cdot \mathbf{t}^{(I)}). \quad (6.36)$$

To sum up, in SG the output is a multinomial probability distribution over
the vocabulary, because the network goal is to predict the target word given
the context. SGNS instead produces a binary probability distribution, because
its prediction task is to discriminate between positive and negative examples.
Since the output probabilities are used to generate the error signal and update
the network parameters, the SGNS training time only depends on the number
of the negative examples and is constant with respect to the vocabulary size.[4]

---

[4] Negative sampling was introduced for SG, but it can be used to train CBOW too.

The word2vec library has several hyperparameters (Levy et al., 2015b):

WINDOW SIZE   **Window size** – the n lexemes to the left and to the right of the target forming the context window. Similarly to other types of window-based DSMs (cf. Section 2.2.1), the window size affects the kind of semantic relations captured by the model. Narrow windows (e.g., $[5, 5]$) tend to identify lexemes that are related by paradigmatic relations, such as synonyms and co-hyponyms, while larger windows (e.g., $[10, 10]$) are typically biased toward semantically broader relations (Melamud et al., 2016b). An important implementation detail in word2vec is that the window size is not fixed. The window size parameter n represents the maximum number of left and right context lexemes. The actual window size r is **dynamic** and sampled uniformly between 1 and n during training, for each target token. The effect of the dynamic window is to weight context lexemes according to the their distance from the target (cf. Section 2.2.1). In fact, each context lexeme is weighted with a sampling probability that decreases linearly with its distance from the target. For instance, given $n = 5$, the probability of sampling a context lexeme at distance 5 is $\frac{1}{5}$, because it is only captured if the actual window size r is 5. The probability of sampling a word appearing next to the target is instead $\frac{5}{5}$, because it is selected by any value of r. Therefore, word2vec gives less weight to lexemes more distant from the target by sampling less from these words in the training data (Mikolov et al., 2013b).

DYNAMIC WINDOW

EMBEDDING DIMENSIONAL- ITY   **Embedding dimensionality** – Melamud et al. (2016b) show that the model performance in various semantic similarity tasks increases with the number of dimensions, reaching near-optimal values at around 300 dimensions, which is also the setting used by Mikolov et al. (2013a, 2013b).

NUMBER OF NEGATIVE EXAMPLES   **Number of negative examples** – in word2vec, the default value is 5. A higher number of negative examples means more training data and is expected to produce a better parameter estimation, especially for smaller corpora. As shown by Levy et al. (2015b), numerous negative examples are indeed beneficial to SGNS performance.

WORD PROBABILITY DISTRIBUTION   **Word probability distribution** – this hyperparameter is used to generate the negative examples. Mikolov et al. (2013a) argue that the following smoothed distribution with $\alpha = 0.75$ (cf. Section 2.3.1) performs better than the unsmoothed or the uniform distribution:

$$p_\alpha(l) = \frac{F(l)^\alpha}{\sum_l F(l)^\alpha}, \tag{6.37}$$

where $F(l)$ is the frequency of the lexeme l in the training corpus.

Subsampling – lexical items are discarded from the training set with a   SUBSAMPLING
probability that is proportional to the frequency of the item:

$$p(l) = 1 - \sqrt{\frac{t}{F(l)}}, \qquad (6.38)$$

where t is a threshold that Mikolov et al. (2013a) set at 10^{-5}. The effect
of subsampling is similar to removing stop words (cf. Section 2.2.1).
In the original implementation of word2vec, subsampling is performed
before training the model, so that the context window size is potentially
enlarged.

Minimum frequency threshold – all lexemes whose frequency is lower   MINIMUM
than the threshold are removed from the corpus before training the mod-   FREQUENCY
els. Like with subsampling, this practically widens the context window   THRESHOLD
size.

Levy et al. (2015b) carry out a thorough analysis of the effects of these
hyperparameters on the quality of the word2vec embeddings.

6.3.2 Variations of Word2vec

The success of word2vec has fostered the development of a large number of
variations of the original model. While the word2vec library assumes contexts
to be window-based collocates of the target, **word2vecf** (Levy and Goldberg,   WORD2VECF
2014a) is a syntax-based version of SGNS, in which contexts are dependency-
typed collocates extracted from a parsed corpus: Given a target t, its contexts
are pairs $\langle l, r \rangle$, such that l is a dependent lexeme of t, and r is the type of
syntactic dependency (e.g., subject). Like other syntax-based DSMs, SGNS
trained on syntactic contexts tends to identify taxonomically similar lexemes,
such as co-hyponyms, while in the window-based model neighbors are often
related to the target by broader semantic relations. Such differences are also
confirmed by Bansal et al. (2014) and Melamud et al. (2016b). Similarly to
word2vecf, **GBOW** (Li et al., 2017) is a generalization of CBOW that can   GBOW
learn embeddings either from syntactic or window-based contexts.

The **C-PHRASE** model (Pham et al., 2015b) is a syntax-aware variant of   C-PHRASE
CBOW that takes into account the structure of syntactic constituents. Instead
of predicting a target word from the combination of the previous and following
words, C-PHRASE starts from a parsed corpus and estimates the embeddings
of target lexemes by grouping the context words together according to the

syntactic structure of the sentence. Therefore, words are predicted from the various constituents in the parse tree, each represented with the sum of its vectors. For instance, given the training sentence *A brown dog runs*, the network learns to predict *run* from *dog* and the phrases *brown dog* and *a brown dog*. As the model learns to predict lexemes from syntactic constituents, the resulting embeddings capture generalizations about sentence structure, thereby improving their performance in lexical as well as compositional semantic tasks.

CONTEXT2VEC — Another variation of CBOW is **context2vec** (Melamud et al., 2016a), which employs a more structured representation of contexts. Given a target lexeme, context2vec learns an embedding of the sentence surrounding the target with a Long Short–Term Memory (LSTM) network (cf. Section 9.4). The sentence embedding is then fed into the standard CBOW model. Melamud et al. (2016a) argue that the LSTM is able to provide a better encoding of sentential context information than the standard bag-of-words embeddings.

FASTTEXT — The **FastText** library is one of the most important extensions of word2vec. It learns distributional representations for character n-grams instead of word types, which are represented as the sum of **n-gram embeddings** (Bojanowski

n-GRAM EMBEDDINGS — et al., 2017; Mikolov et al., 2018). Subword vector representations aim at

OUT-OF-VOCABULARY AND RARE WORDS — improving the model ability to cope with **out-of-vocabulary** and **rare** words. The former are lexical items that do not appear in the training corpus vocabulary. The latter are low-frequency lexemes whose distributional vectors are typically of very poor quality because of the limited amount of co-occurrence statistics supporting them. The Zipfian distribution of linguistic data entails that, however big the training corpus is, DSMs can build reliable vectors only for a tiny fraction of the lexicon (cf. Section 2.3.1). This problem is of course even more pronounced for morphologically rich languages, like Italian or Finnish, which have several inflected forms for each lemma. Preprocessing the corpus with a lemmatizer is a very common solution to cope with such issues, but it is itself a costly process that requires lexical resources and is prone to errors. FastText assumes that rare words are often new lexical formations created by productive inflectional and derivational morphological processes. For instance, the verb *disarrange* is derived from *arrange* by adding the negative prefix *dis*. While *arrange* occurs in ukWaC more than $3,000$ times, *disarrange* only occurs twice. FastText does not carry out any morphological decomposition, but approximates the internal structure of lexical

BAGS OF CHARACTER n-GRAMS — items by representing them as **bags of character n-grams**.[5] If $n = 3$, the word *semantics* is represented by the following 3-grams, plus the whole word itself:

---

[5] A very similar solution was originally proposed by Schütze (1993) using a matrix DSM.

⟨*se, sem, ema, man, ant, nti, tic, ics, cs*⟩, ⟨*semantics*⟩

The special boundary symbols ⟨ and ⟩ are added at the beginning and end of lexemes to distinguish prefixes and suffixes from other character sequences. FastText extracts from the training corpus a dictionary of n-grams G and learns an embedding $\mathbf{g}$ for each $g \in G$. Given G_t the set of n-grams in the target lexeme t, its embedding $\mathbf{t}$ is defined in the following way:

$$\mathbf{t} = \sum_{g \in G_t} \mathbf{g}. \qquad (6.39)$$

This way, out-of-vocabulary words can also be represented in the vector space, by summing their n-gram embeddings.

The FastText library contains both CBOW and SGNS models, whose training objective is adapted to the subword representation in Equation 6.39. Bojanowski et al. (2017) show that SGNS with subword embeddings significantly improves the performance of the standard SGNS, especially with morphologically rich languages like German and Czech.

6.4 Count or Predict?

Predict DSMs, in particular word2vec, have fast superseded count models as the preferred methods to build distributional representations. This is at least partially related to the current dominance of neural networks, the learning algorithm of predict models. Predict and count DSMs are prima facie two radically different ways to construct distributional vectors, but a closer inspection actually reveals deeper similarities.

As reviewed in the previous section, word2vec learns two matrices $\mathbf{I}$ and $\mathbf{O}$, respectively containing the input and output embeddings. Following Levy and Goldberg (2014a), we now refer to these matrices as the **target embedding** matrix $\mathbf{T}$ and the **context embedding** matrix $\mathbf{C}$. In SGNS, the prediction of a context c given the target lexeme t is carried out by computing the dot product between the target embedding of t and the context embedding of c. Pennington et al. (2014) show that this is strongly related to the GloVe learning objective (cf. Equation 4.15 in Section 4.5). Moreover, Levy and Goldberg (2014c) prove that there is a direct connection between SGNS and classical matrix models, since SGNS implicitly carries the matrix factorization:

TARGET AND CONTEXT EMBEDDINGS

$$\mathbf{M}_{|T| \times |C|} = \mathbf{T} \times \mathbf{C}^T. \qquad (6.40)$$

In the matrix $\mathbf{M}_{|T| \times |C|}$, each row corresponds to a target lexeme, each column corresponds to a context, and each entry $m_{i,j}$ is the dot product $\mathbf{t_i} \cdot \mathbf{c_j}$. For a given distributional pair $\langle t, c \rangle$, the SGNS training objective is optimized when:

$$m_{t,c} = \mathrm{PMI}_{\langle t,c \rangle} - \log k, \qquad (6.41)$$

where k is the number of negative examples. Therefore, SGNS implicitly factorizes a co-occurrence matrix $\mathbf{M}^{\mathbf{PMI}}$ whose entries contain PMI association scores between targets and contexts, shifted by a global constant $\log k$:

$$\mathbf{T} \times \mathbf{C}^T = \mathbf{M}^{\mathbf{PMI}} - \log k. \qquad (6.42)$$

PMI AND NEGATIVE SAMPLING

Leaving aside the mathematical details of the proof in Levy and Goldberg (2014c), we can see that there is indeed a close link between **PMI and negative sampling.** The latter seeks to maximize the probability that observed distributional pairs belong to the training data and that negative pairs do not belong to the training data, where negative pairs are randomly generated by sampling the contexts according to their unigram probability. PMI also uses a kind of negative information (Johns et al., 2019). In fact, PMI measures the association between a target t and a context c with the log ratio between $p(t, c)$ and $p(t)p(c)$. The former corresponds to the positive information of observing t and c together, while the latter provides the negative information represented by the probability of observing $p(t)$ and $p(c)$ independently from one another.

MARR'S THREE LEVELS

These results highlight a strong relationship between predict models and the classical approach to build embeddings with factorization methods such as SVD (cf. Section 2.5). In order to understand the exact sense of this connection it is useful to refer to **Marr's three levels of analysis** (Marr, 1982), according to which information processing systems, either natural or artificial, must be understood at three distinct levels: (i) the **computational** level, specifying the system behavior as a mapping from one kind of information to another; (ii) the **algorithmic** level, specifying the particular algorithm carrying out this mapping; (iii) the **implementation** level, specifying how this mapping is actually implemented in the system. Levy and Goldberg (2014c) show that predict DSMs like SGNS are equivalent to count models that build embeddings by factorizing a co-occurrence matrix containing PMI association scores between targets and contexts. Therefore these models can be said to be equivalent at the computational level. However, SGNS and count DSMs are also very different at the algorithmic level. For instance, SVD is a least square method and assumes that the reduced dense matrix is the best low-rank approximation to the original co-occurrence matrix according to the Euclidean norm (cf. Section 2.5.1). On the other hand SGNS (like GloVe) uses gradient descent to learn the word embeddings, and does not assume the underlying distributional space to be Euclidean. Other nontrivial differences between SGNS and SVD are reported in Levy and Goldberg (2014c). However, the most important point is that the factorization carried out by SGNS is only *implicit*, because word embeddings are built by learning to predict context lexemes, without explicitly constructing the co-occurrence matrix. This makes SGNS and similar predict DSMs incremental and easily scalable to very large corpora.

Predict DSMs have been argued to be consistent with biologically inspired models of associative learning like the **Rescorla-Wagner model** (Rescorla and Wagner, 1972), which is also based on the deviation between the observed event and the predicted event (Mandera et al., 2017). Claims about the psychological plausibility of computational models must be taken with great caution. For instance, the backpropagation algorithm employed by predict DSMs has often been criticized exactly because of its lack of cognitive plausibility. Moreover, word2vec also relies on a number of hyperparameters whose cognitive realism might be questionable. However, it is undeniable that certain features of predict models make them very attractive from the cognitive point of view. Landauer and Dumais (1997) consider LSA to be just a model to build distributional representations at the computational level in Marr's terminology, without any claim about the actual cognitive import of SVD. Conversely, the incrementality of predict DSMs and the key role that predictive mechanisms have in cognition (Clark, 2013) suggest that these models represent a step forwards toward increasing the cognitive plausibility of DSMs.

Count and predict models are two different but closely related families of methods to learn embeddings from distributional data. Do predict DSMs produce better semantic representations than count ones? Baroni et al. (2014a) report that predict models outperform count models in various semantic tasks, but Levy et al. (2015b) show that this difference actually depends on the lack of proper optimization of count models. Thanks to the equivalence results in Levy and Goldberg (2014c), they adapt the SGNS hyperparameters to classical count DSMs. For instance, they use a smoothed version of PMI for context weighting (Equation 2.12) and the Caron p-transform with SVD (Equation 2.26), downgrading the top latent dimensions ($p = 0.5$) or removing the contribution of singular values altogether ($p = 0$; Equation 2.25). When the hyperparameters of count models are carefully tuned, no significant difference is observed with respect to predict DSMs, with the latter outperforming the former only on one analogy task (Levy et al., 2015b). Lebret and Collobert (2015) also propose alternative methods for the dimensionality reduction of

RESCORLA-
WAGNER MODEL

the co-occurrence matrix that achieve competitive performances with predict models.

Mandera et al. (2017) claim that count and predict DSMs produce very similar results in modeling psycholinguistic data, such as semantic priming. Gamallo (2017) compares syntax-based count and predict DSMs, with the former achieving better performance on synonym identification. Moreover, when trained on smaller corpora some matrix models are better than neural embeddings, which become competitive only when trained on much larger amounts of data (Asr et al., 2016; Sahlgren and Lenci, 2016). As the experiments in Chapter 7 show, count and predict DSMs do not differ for the semantic aspects they can address, and there is no clear superiority of one approach over the other.

6.5 Summary

In this chapter, we have reviewed a family of DSMs that learn word embeddings with **artificial neural networks** trained as **language models** that predict co-occurring lexemes. Therefore, such models are also known as **predict DSMs**. The most important (static) predict DSMs are **CBOW** and **SGNS**.

The recent fortunes of neural networks and deep learning have surely contributed to the great popularity of predict DSMs, though their alleged superiority over traditional count DSMs is disputable. An important finding is that the good performance of predict DSMs is strongly related to the particular setting of their hyperparameters. Thus, the quality of the semantic representations produced by the two families of methods does not depend so much on the count versus predict contrast, but rather on the hyperparameter tuning that improves the smoothing of skewed distributional data and dimensionality reduction. On the other hand, a crucial feature of predict DSMs, which they share with random encoding models, is that they dispense with matrices recording global co-occurrences. This represents an important asset over matrix DSMs with respect to incrementality, efficiency, and scalability to large corpora.

6.6 Further Reading

- Deep learning for AI: Bengio (2009); Goodfellow et al. (2016)
- Neural networks and NLP, neural language models: Goldberg (2016, 2017)
- Count versus predict DSMs: Lenci et al. (2022)

Part III

Practice

Part II

Practice

7

Evaluation of Distributional Semantic Models

In the first two parts of this book, we have dissected the theoretical foundations of distributional semantics, presented the basic methods to build distributional representations, and introduced the main types of DSMs. Now, we focus on their **evaluation**, a question that has enjoyed considerable attention in recent years, with a growing number of publications discussing quality assurance of DSMs, and entire workshops devoted to evaluation procedures in distributional semantics (Levy et al., 2016; Bowman et al., 2017; Rogers et al., 2019).

The typical approach to DSM evaluation consists in measuring *how good* a given model is and which model is *the best* for a particular task. Following Sparck Jones and Galliers (1995), it is customary to distinguish between **intrinsic evaluation**, which evaluates a computational model with respect to intrinsic and the quality of its direct output, and **extrinsic evaluation**, which assesses a extrinsic model outcome in its impact on a task or application external to the model itself evaluation (Resnik and Lin, 2010). Distributional semantics has usually favored intrinsic methods that test DSMs for their ability to model various kinds of semantic similarity and relatedness. Recently, extrinsic evaluation has also become very popular: The distributional vectors are fed into a downstream NLP task and are evaluated with the system's performance.

The goal of this chapter is twofold: (i) to present the most common evaluation methods in distributional semantics, and (ii) to carry out a large-scale comparison between the static DSMs reviewed in Part II. Section 7.1 discusses the notion of semantic similarity, which is central in distributional semantics. Section 7.2 and Section 7.3 present the major tasks for intrinsic and extrinsic evaluation, Section 7.4 analyzes the performance of a representative group of static DSMs on several semantic tasks. In Section 7.5, we explore the differences of the semantic spaces produced by these models with Representational Similarity Analysis, a technique developed in cognitive neuroscience.

7.1 Semantic Similarity and Relatedness

SIMILARITY

According to the philosopher Nelson Goodman, the concept of **similarity** is philosophically "insidious" because it "tends under analysis either to vanish entirely or to require for its explanation just what it purports to explain" (Goodman, 1972, p. 446). However, this does not mean that we need to discard it entirely, because "If statements of similarity [...] cannot be trusted in the philosopher's study, they are still serviceable in the streets" (Goodman, 1972, p. 446). In fact, countless tasks in computational linguistics rely on estimates of the degree of semantic similarity between linguistic units, from single words to full texts. Similarity is the key notion of distributional semantics: The Distributional Hypothesis is stated in terms of semantic similarity (cf. Chapter 1), and DSMs are supposed to provide a quantitative measure thereof. Similarity is often assumed as a primitive concept in distributional semantics, but, at a closer scrutiny, it emerges as a very complex construct with several subtypes.

In psychology, similarity plays a crucial role in theories of cognition and in empirical research on semantic memory and the mental lexicon. It is an essential ingredient of categorization, memory retrieval, reasoning, induction, etc. Words are semantically similar to the extent their meanings share common aspects. As multiple sources of such commonality exist, various types of

ATTRIBUTIONAL AND RELATIONAL SIMILARITY

semantic similarity can be identified. Medin et al. (1993) distinguish between **attributional** and **relational similarity** (cf. Section 4.2). For instance, *dog* and *cat* are similar because they share several attributes or features: They are small, domestic, move, have four legs, and so on (Tversky, 1977). On the other hand, *leg* and *wheel* do not have attributes in common (e.g., legs are typically elongated, while wheels are round, etc.), and yet they serve similar functions as parts of other entities (i.e., enabling ground movement in men and cars, respectively). In the latter case, semantic similarity relies on the comparison between the relational structures involving the two lexemes, rather than a comparison between shared semantic attributes (Medin et al., 1990; Markman and Gentner, 1993; Medin et al., 1993). Attributional similarity is defined between lexemes, while relational similarity is defined between lexeme pairs (Turney, 2006b).

> The **attributional similarity** between two lexemes l_1 and l_2 depends on the degree of correspondence between the features of l_1 and l_2.
>
> Given two lexeme pairs $\langle l_1, l_2 \rangle$ and $\langle l_3, l_4 \rangle$, their **relational similarity** depends on the degree of correspondence between the relation linking l_1 to l_2 and the relation linking l_3 to l_4.

The lexemes *car* and *truck* are attributionally similar because they have several features in common. Attributional similarity is also called **taxonomic** (Wisniewsky and Bassok, 1999; Estes et al., 2011, 2012), as items sharing salient attributes belong to the same taxonomic category (e.g., cars and trucks belong to the category of vehicles). The lexeme pair ⟨*car*, *vehicle*⟩ is relationally similar to ⟨*dog*, *animal*⟩ because the former member of each pair is a hyponym of the latter. Relational similarity is termed **analogical**, since analogical processes depend on the mapping between relational structures (Gentner, 1983, 2010). Thus, we can say that *mind* is analogically similar (or analogous) to *computer* because they both perform computations. Henceforth, we use the term similarity without further qualification to refer to attributional (taxonomic) similarity.

TAXONOMIC SIMILARITY

ANALOGICAL SIMILARITY

The notion of similarity must be distinguished from the much broader and vaguer concept of **semantic relatedness** or **association** (Budanitsky and Hirst, 2006; McRae et al., 2012; Hill et al., 2015).

SEMANTIC RELATEDNESS

> The **semantic relatedness (association)** between lexical items depends on the existence of some semantic relation linking them.

Similarity is a special type of relatedness, but the latter encompasses several other types of relations. In psychology, lexical items are said to be **thematically related** if they have any temporal, spatial, causal, or functional complementary role in the same scenario or event (Wisniewsky and Bassok, 1999; Estes et al., 2011, 2012; Jouravlev and McRae, 2016). Behavioral evidence shows that subjects consider words similar if they are thematically related, despite the lack of taxonomic or relational similarity.

THEMATIC RELATEDNESS

> The **thematic relatedness (similarity)** between lexemes depends on their co-occurring in the same scenarios or events.

For instance, *dog* and *bone* are thematically related (similar), because dogs and bones co-occur in the same eating scenarios (i.e., dogs eat bones).

Semantic relatedness can also depend on the broad concepts of **topic** or **semantic domain** (Gliozzo and Strapparava, 2009). This produces a notion of similarity which is particularly important in information retrieval (cf. Section 2.2.2). Semantic domains or topics are common areas of knowledge and discussion, such as zoology, art, and so on. In distributional semantics, this notion is central in Topic Models (cf. Section 4.4). Words can be considered similar if they come from the same domain (Manning and Schütze, 1999; Turney, 2012).

TOPIC

TOPICAL RELATEDNESS

> The **topical relatedness (similarity)** between lexemes depends on their sharing the same topic or semantic domain.

For instance, *painting* and *poem* are topically related (similar) because they both belong to the art domain.

Rather than the general notions of similarity and relatedness, research in lexical semantics instead investigates the properties of specific types of **semantic relations**. In particular, **paradigmatic relations** are regarded as the cornerstone of the lexicon organization, both at the linguistic and at the cognitive level (Cruse, 1986; Murphy, 2003). They are defined by Murphy (2010) as follows (cf. Section 1.1.1):

> Words in paradigmatic relations belong to the same word class and share some characteristics in common. The words in such relations can be said to form a paradigm – that is, a set of examples that show a pattern. (Murphy, 2010, p. 109)

The most important and widely studied paradigmatic semantic relations are **synonymy** (*sofa – couch*), **antonymy** (*good – bad*), **hypernymy** (*animal – dog*), **co-hyponymy** (*dog – cat*), and **meronymy** (*tail – dog*). These relations have a complex association with semantic similarity and relatedness. Synonymy, hypernymy, and co-hyponymy can all be regarded as instances of taxonomic similarity, because the items they link share many semantic attributes (e.g., *dog* with its hypernym *animal* and with its co-hyponym *cat*). In particular, synonymy corresponds to a high degree of attributional similarity (Turney, 2006b). Antonyms are also characterized by a strong similarity. This is what Cruse (1986) refers to as the **paradox of simultaneous similarity and difference**: Antonyms are identical in every dimension of meaning except for one (cf. Section 8.3.2). For example, *open* and *close* have many features in common, despite denoting opposite events. On the other hand, meronymy is not an instance of similarity, but rather of semantic relatedness: *wheel* and *car* are related by meronymy, but have very different features.

Several other types of semantic relations have been proposed in the literature. For instance, ConceptNet (Speer and Havasi, 2012; Speer et al., 2017) includes the relation *UsedFor*, which links an object-denoting noun (e.g., *bridge*) to the event representing its typical function (e.g., *cross water*), and the relation *HasProperty*, which links an entity (e.g., *ice*) to a typical property (e.g., *cold*). Jouravlev and McRae (2016) distinguish several subtypes of thematic relatedness, such as locative (e.g., *doctor – hospital*) and temporal (e.g., *church – Sunday*) ones. **Semantic roles** (e.g., Agent, Patient, etc.; cf. Section 8.1) are also instances of thematic relatedness.

In summary, *there is no single concept of similarity*, but rather a complex and multifarious family of distinct and yet overlapping notions that differ with respect to their granularity. As illustrated in Figure 7.1, they go from

PARADIGMATIC SEMANTIC RELATIONS

PARADOX OF SIMULTANEOUS DIFFERENCE AND SIMILARITY

SEMANTIC ROLES

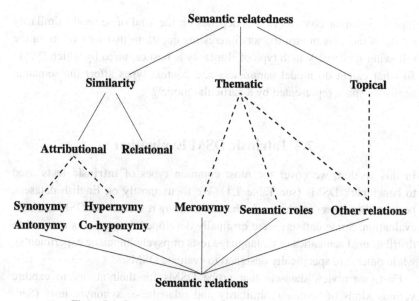

Figure 7.1 Semantic similarity, relatedness, and their subtypes

the broad concept of semantic relatedness, to similarity sensu stricto (i.e., attributional similarity), up to very specific cases of semantic relations. The boundaries between these notions are often difficult to draw. Their defining elements (e.g., attributes, relations, scenarios, topics, etc.) are inherently fuzzy and context-dependent. This entails that similarity (relatedness) judgments can dramatically change depending on which aspects of meanings we focus on. As Goodman (1972) claims, *there is no absolute notion of similarity* (cf. Chapter 3). Many pairs of lexemes can thus be judged similar under more than one perspective at the same time. For example, *cat* and *dog* are not only attributionally similar, but they also share many relations with other entities (e.g, dogs and cats both play with balls), often appear together in the same scenarios or events (e.g., dogs chase cats), and belong to the same topic as well (i.e., zoology). Conversely, there are lexemes that satisfy only some or even just one of the above definitions: *faith* and *baptism* are similar only because they belong to the religious domain. Moreover, different word senses can have diverse semantic relations (e.g., different synonyms).

These properties of similarity raise two important issues for DSM evaluation and for distributional semantics in general. First of all, it is essential to be aware of the particular type of similarity or relatedness represented in the datasets we use to evaluate our models. Secondly, the Distributional Hypothesis itself needs to be relativized: The truth of the statement that similar lexemes tend to appear in similar contexts in fact depends on the kind of semantic similarity we focus on. This in turn triggers interesting questions that we explore in the following sections: Which type of similarity is best captured by which DSM? To what extent do model parameters and context types affect the semantic similarity space represented by a particular model?

7.2 Intrinsic DSM Evaluation

In this section, we cover the most common types of **intrinsic tests** used to benchmark DSMs (see Table 7.1). We focus mostly on English datasets, because they represent the lion's share of existing resources for DSM intrinsic evaluation. Some datasets were originally developed for purposes external to distributional semantics (e.g., language tests or psycholinguistic experiments), while others are specifically designed to evaluate DSMs.

First, we review datasets that probe DSMs for their ability to capture various kinds of semantic similarity and relatedness: synonym tests (Section 7.2.1), similarity and relatedness ratings (Section 7.2.2), categorization tests (Section 7.2.3), analogy tests (Section 7.2.4), and relation tests (Section 7.2.5). In Section 7.2.6, we present some psycholinguistic tasks used for DSM evaluation.

7.2.1 Synonym Tests

Synonymy is a case of strong semantic similarity (cf. Section 7.1) and, in fact,
synonym tests have been among the first benchmarks to evaluate DSMs. They are typically cast as multiple-choice vocabulary tests, where the task is to select the correct synonym to a given target word from a number of alternatives. An example test item is shown in Table 7.2. DSMs are evaluated by measuring the distributional similarity (e.g., the cosine) between the target vector and the vector of each alternative lexeme. The model makes the right decision if the correct word has the highest similarity score among the four alternatives.
The evaluation measure is **accuracy**, computed as the ratio of correct choices returned by the model to the total number of test items.
The most widely used test of this kind is the synonym part of the **TOEFL** (Test Of English as a Foreign Language), introduced by Landauer and Dumais (1997) to evaluate their LSA model (cf. Section 4.1.2). The TOEFL consists of 80 test items, each made of a target word (a noun, verb, adjective, or adverb) and four alternatives. Landauer and Dumais (1997) report a human performance upper bound of 64.5% average accuracy for the TOEFL, obtained by a

Table 7.1 Major English datasets employed for DSM evaluation

Dataset	Semantic task	Size	References
TOEFL	synonym test	80	Landauer and Dumais (1997)
ESL	synonym test	50	Turney (2001)
RG65	similarity ratings	65	Rubenstein and Goodenough (1965)
MC	similarity ratings	30	Miller and Charles (1991)
RW	similarity ratings	2,034	Luong et al. (2013)
SL-999	similarity ratings	999	Hill et al. (2015)
SV-3500	similarity ratings	3,500	Gerz et al. (2016)
WS-353	similarity ratings	353	Finkelstein et al. (2001)
WS-SIM	similarity ratings	203	Agirre et al. (2009)
WS-REL	relatedness ratings	252	Agirre et al. (2009)
MTURK	relatedness ratings	287 (771)	Radinsky et al. (2011)
MEN	relatedness ratings	3,000	Bruni et al. (2014)
TR9856	relatedness ratings	9,856	Levy et al. (2015c)
AP	categorization	402	Almuhareb and Poesio (2005)
BATTIG	categorization	5,231	Battig and Montague (1969)
BATTIG-2010	categorization	82	Baroni et al. (2010)
ESSLLI	categorization	129	Baroni et al. (2008)
SAT	analogy test	374	Turney (2006b)
MSR	analogy test	8,000	Mikolov et al. (2013d)
GOOGLE	analogy test	19,544	Mikolov et al. (2013b)
WORDREP	analogy test	237,409,102	Gao et al. (2014)
BATS	analogy test	98,000	Gladkova et al. (2016)
BLESS	relation test	26,554	Baroni and Lenci (2011)
EVAL	relation test	7,429	Santus et al. (2015)
SEMEVAL-2012	relation test	3,218	Jurgens et al. (2012)
DIFFVEC	relation test	12,458	Vylomova et al. (2016)
HYPERLEX	relation test	2,616	Vulić et al. (2017b)
USF	free association	70,000	Vulić et al. (2017a)

Table 7.2 Test item from the TOEFL
multiple-choice synonym test

target	alternatives	correct
flawed	lustrous imperfect crude tiny	√

large sample of non-native English-speaking applicants to U.S. colleges. Turney (2001) has introduced the **ESL** (English as a Second Language) synonym ESL test, which includes 50 target lexemes belonging to different POSs with four alternatives each. In both TOEFL and ESL, picking alternatives at random would produce on average 25% correct answers.

The DSM performance on the TOEFL has steadily increased, from the original score of 64.38% obtained by Landauer and Dumais (1997). Rapp (2003) reaches 92.5% correct answers using a window-based model trained on the BNC corpus. The co-occurrence counts are weighted with an entropy-based weighting scheme similar to that used in LSA (cf. Equation 2.3.1), and the co-occurrence matrix is reduced with SVD to 300 dimensions. Bullinaria and Levy (2012) achieve a perfect score of 100% correct answers using the 20-times-larger ukWaC corpus, narrow context window sizes, PPMI as weighting function, and inverse SVD (cf. Section 2.5.1).

Despite the fact that the TOEFL has become a kind of standard basic test in distributional semantics, existing synonym datasets have various shortcomings. The first one is their small size. Secondly, they model synonymy as a categorical notion, without considering its gradient nature.

7.2.2 Similarity and Relatedness Tests

The richest family of benchmarks for DSM evaluation consists of sets of word pairs rated by humans, according either to their semantic similarity **SIMILARITY** (**similarity ratings**) or to their semantic relatedness (**relatedness ratings**). **AND** The task of DSMs is to replicate as closely as possible the human ratings. **RELATEDNESS** **RATINGS** The evaluation measure is the **Spearman rank correlation** (ρ) between dis- **SPEARMAN** tributional similarity scores and ratings. The human performance upper bound **CORRELATION** is computed as the average of pairwise correlations between the ratings of all subjects.

RG65 The classic similarity ratings dataset is the **Rubenstein and Goodenough** (RG65), consisting of 65 noun pairs rated by 51 subjects on a 0–4 similarity scale (Rubenstein and Goodenough, 1965). The average rating for each pair is taken as an estimate of the perceived similarity between the two words (e.g., *car – automobile*: 3.9, *cord – smile*: 0.0). The pairwise correlation between the raters is 0.85. Multilingual versions of RG65 have been released by Camacho-**MC** Collados et al. (2015). The **Miller and Charles** (MC) dataset includes 30 pairs from RG65, rated for similarity by 38 subjects (Miller and Charles, 1991). The Pearson correlation between MC and the corresponding RG65 subset is very high ($r = 0.97$), showing the robustness of these similarity ratings.

While RG65 and MC have a small size and were developed for psycholinguistic experiments, more recently much larger similarity ratings benchmarks have been specifically designed for DSM evaluation. The **Rare Words** (RW) **RW** dataset (Luong et al., 2013) consists of 2,034 word pairs of various POSs, rated by ten crowdsourced subjects on a 0–10 similarity scale. The RW words were sampled based on their frequency on a 2010 dump of Wikipedia and on their

Table 7.3 Word pairs with high and low ratings in
SL-999 and WS-353

SL-999		WS-353	
word pair	*rating*	*word pair*	*rating*
large - big	9.55	gem - jewel	8.96
student - pupil	9.35	Maradona - football	8.62
...	...	...	...
ankle - window	0.30	king - cabbage	0.23
new - ancient	0.23	chord - smile	0.54

morphological affixes, in order to capture rare or morphologically complex words. In fact, one peculiar feature of RW is that it contains a large number of low-frequency words (801 items have frequency ≤ 100) and therefore it is quite challenging for DSMs. The complexity of this dataset is also confirmed by the relatively low correlation between the raters ($\rho = 0.41$).

The **SimLex-999** (SL-999) dataset (Hill et al., 2015) contains 999 noun, verb, and adjective pairs (from $1,028$ word types), each rated for semantic similarity on a $0 - 6$ scale by approximately 50 subjects. The ratings were collected with crowdsourcing, averaged, and then converted into the 0–10 interval. Human rating agreement is $\rho = 0.67$. SL-999 has two main novelties. First of all, the dataset is explicitly designed to distinguish semantic similarity from relatedness. The test items include related pairs selected from the University of South Florida Free Association Database (USF) (cf. Section 7.2.6) and unrelated pairs. Subjects were then carefully instructed to assign high scores only to genuinely similar pairs, instead of merely related ones. Raters were also explicitly told not to consider antonyms as similar. As a consequence, in SL-999 highly rated items only include attributionally similar word pairs. Conversely, at the low end of the scale we find pairs of semantically unrelated items, semantically related lexemes that are not attributionally similar, and antonyms (see Table 7.3). Secondly, the items in SL-999 are balanced between concrete and abstract words using the concreteness ratings in USF. Differently from other datasets usually biased toward concrete lexemes, SL-999 thus makes it possible to investigate the behavior of DSMs on these two key lexical domains. Multilingual versions of SL-999 have been realized by Leviant and Reichart (2015) for German, Italian, and Russian, and by Vulić et al. (2017) for Croatian and Hebrew. The English word pairs in SL-999 were first translated into the target languages and then rated by native subjects. Other multilingual datasets have been released by Camacho-Collados et al. (2017) for the SemEval 2017 task on Multilingual and Cross-Lingual Word Similarity task for the evaluation of cross-lingual embeddings (cf. Section 8.4).

SV-3500

The SL-999 methodology has been applied to build **SimVerb-3500** (SV-3500), a dataset of $3,500$ English verb pairs (from 827 verb types), each rated by at least ten subjects for semantic similarity (Gerz et al., 2016). Verbs are sampled from USF, with the further constraint of being representative of verbs classes in VerbNet (Kipper et al., 2008), an online lexicon of English verbs organized according to the classification in Levin (1993). The average pairwise correlation between any two raters is $\rho = 0.84$. SV-3500 is currently the largest similarity rating dataset for verbs, which are instead normally underrepresented in the datasets for DSM evaluation.

WS-353

Other benchmarks target the broader notion of semantic relatedness, rather than similarity. One of the most popular examples is **WordSim-353** (WS-353) (Finkelstein et al., 2001), which contains judgments on a $0-10$ scale by at least 13 subjects for 353 lexical items (nouns, verbs and adjectives). The average inter-rater agreement is $\rho = 0.76$ (Hill et al., 2015). Although the dataset name might suggest it contains similarity ratings, subjects were explicitly instructed to assign high values to words that are very closely related, antonyms included. Therefore, word pairs with high ratings include cases of attributional similarity, like *gem* and *jewel*, as well as instances of related lexemes, such as *Maradona* and *football* (see Table 7.3). In order to sort out similarity from relatedness in

WS-SIM

WS-353, Agirre et al. (2009) partitioned the benchmark into two subsets: **WS-SIM**, including 203 pairs judged by three annotators to be similar or unrelated,

WS-REL

and **WS-REL**, which contains 252 pairs judged to be unrelated, or related but not similar. German, Italian, and Russian translations of WE-353 have been realized by Leviant and Reichart (2015).

MTurk-287

MTurk-287 (WS-353) (Radinsky et al., 2011) contains 287 words evaluated for semantic relatedness on 0–5 scale by Amazon's Mechanical Turk workers, with an average of 23 raters for each word pair. The same methodology

MTurk-771
MEN

was used to build **MTurk-771** (Halawi et al., 2012), consisting of 771 noun pairs. **MEN** (Bruni et al., 2014) contains $3,000$ noun, verb, and adjective pairs from 751 word types. Each pair was randomly matched with a comparison pair and rated by a single subject as either more or less semantically related than the comparison item. The ratings were then normalized between zero and one. Two of the dataset authors who independently rated the data set achieved an agreement of $\rho = 0.68$, and an average correlation with the MEN rating

TR9856

of $\rho = 0.84$. The largest relatedness dataset to date is **TR9856** (Levy et al., 2015c), including $9,856$ lexical pairs rated by ten annotators, answering a binary question (i.e., related $= 1$, unrelated $= 0$). The relatedness score is given as the mean answer of annotators. An interesting peculiarity of TR9856 is that $8,367$ test items are MWEs (e.g., *patent rights – intellectual property rights*).

7.2.3 Categorization Tests

One popular task for DSM evaluation is **categorization**, which consists in CATEGORIZATION grouping lexical items into semantically coherent classes. Categorization plays a prominent role in cognitive research, as a probe into the organization of the lexicon and the ability to arrange concepts in taxonomies (Murphy, 2002). In fact, this type of evaluation tests whether DSMs capture taxonomic similarity. Categorization is typically operationalized as a **clustering** task: Distributional CLUSTERING vectors are fed into a clustering algorithm and the output clusters are compared with the reference semantic classes. A standard clustering quality measure is **purity** (Baroni and Lenci, 2010; Riordan and Jones, 2011): PURITY

$$\text{purity} = \frac{1}{n} \sum_{r=1}^{k} \max_i (n_r^i), \qquad (7.1)$$

where n_r^i is the number of items from the ith true (gold standard) class that are assigned to the rth cluster, n is the total number of items and k the number of clusters. For each cluster, purity counts the number of items that belong to the true class that is most represented in the cluster, and then sums these counts across clusters. The resulting sum is divided by the total number of items so that, in the best case (perfect clusters), purity will be one. As cluster quality deteriorates, purity approaches zero.

Several categorization datasets are available. The **Almuhareb-Poesio** (AP) AP set includes 402 concepts from WordNet grouped into 21 classes, each selected from one of the 21 unique WordNet beginners, and represented by between 13 and 21 nouns (Almuhareb and Poesio, 2005). The **Battig** dataset is derived BATTIG from the Battig and Montague (1969) norms and consists of $5,231$ nouns from 56 fine-grained categories, such as TOY, SCIENCE, TYPE_OF_FOOTGEAR, and so on. The much smaller **Battig-2010** introduced by Baroni et al. (2010) is BATTIG-2010 instead based on the expanded Battig and Montague norms of Van Overschelde et al. (2004). The set comprises 82 nouns from ten common concrete categories (up to ten concepts per class), with the concepts selected so that they are rated as highly prototypical of the class. Class examples include LAND MAMMALS (*dog, elephant*) and TOOLS (*screwdriver, hammer*). The **ESSLLI-** ESSLLI-2008 **2008** (Baroni et al., 2008) dataset is formed by three sections: (a) 44 concrete nouns organized into a hierarchy of classes of increasing abstraction, with six lower-level classes; (b) 40 nouns divided into two classes of high and low

Table 7.4 (a) An example of SAT question; (b) Morphosyntactic and semantic analogies from the GOOGLE dataset

Stem	Alternatives	Solution	
			good : better = heavy : heavier
			walk : walking = code : coding
	teacher : chalk		cow : cows = car : cars
mason : stone	carpenter : wood	√	sit : sits = say : says
	soldier : gun		man : woman = king : queen
	photograph : camera		Madrid : Spain = Rome : Italy
	book : word		Europe : euro = USA : dollar

(a)   (b)

concreteness; (c) 45 verbs organized into nine classes. For verb categorization, VerbNet classes are also commonly employed as reference categories.

7.2.4 Analogy Tests

ANALOGY

DSMs are also evaluated with **analogy tests**. An **analogy** is formed by two word pairs that are relationally similar, that is they have a similar relation to each other (cf. Section 7.1). Analogies are typically written in the form $a : b = c : d$, meaning *a is to b as c is to d* (e.g., $wheel : car = finger : hand$).

ANALOGY
SOLVING TASK

The first type of analogy test is the **analogy solving task**: Given one pair of an analogy (called the *stem*), the model is asked to identify the second pair (called the *solution*). For this task, Turney (2006b) introduced the

SAT

SAT dataset, containing 374 multiple-choice analogy questions from the SAT college entrance exam. Each SAT question includes the stem pair, the solution pair, and four distractor pairs (see Table 7.4). The evaluation measure

ACCURACY

is **accuracy**, computed as the percentage of correct solutions identified by the model. Turney and Littman (2005) report a human performance of 57% achieved by college-bound senior high school students.

ANALOGY
COMPLETION
TASK

The **analogy completion task** instead consists in inferring the missing item in an incomplete analogy $a : b = c : ?$. For instance, given the analogy $Italy : Rome = Sweden : ?$, the correct item in this case is $Stockholm$, since it is the capital of Sweden. The evaluation measure is **accuracy**, as the percentage of correctly inferred items. Two very popular datasets for this task are **MSR**

MSR

GOOGLE

(Mikolov et al., 2013d) and **GOOGLE** (Mikolov et al., 2013b). The former consists of $8,000$ morphosyntactic analogies (e.g., $good : better = heavy : heavier$), while the latter contains nine morphological (e.g., plural) and five semantic relations (e.g., currency) with $20-70$ unique word pairs per category, which are combined in all possible ways to yield $8,869$ semantic and $10,675$ syntactic analogies (see Table 7.4b).

OFFSET
METHOD
VECTOR
DIFFERENCE

The analogy completion task is typically solved with the **offset method**, which is based on the hypothesis that **vector difference** or **vector offset**

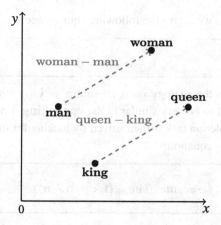

Figure 7.2 The gender relation represented with vector differences

encodes lexical relations. This method was first introduced by Rumelhart and Abrahamson (1973) and has been recently revived and popularized by Mikolov et al. (2013d). It is also called the **parallelogram model** of analogy (Peterson et al., 2020), because the two analogical pairs are assumed to form a parallelogram in vector space (see Figure 7.2). Given the analogy $a : b = c : d$, the difference vector $\mathbf{b} - \mathbf{a}$ is taken to be similar to the difference vector $\mathbf{d} - \mathbf{c}$, as the word pairs $a : b$ and $c : d$ share similar relations:

PARALLELOGRAM MODEL

$$\mathbf{b} - \mathbf{a} \approx \mathbf{d} - \mathbf{c}. \qquad (7.2)$$

Mathematical note 6 – vector addition and the parallelogram rule

In geometric terms, the **parallelogram law of vector addition** states that the sum of two vectors $\mathbf{u}$ and $\mathbf{v}$ corresponds to the diagonal of the parallelogram whose adjacent sides are $\mathbf{u}$ and $\mathbf{v}$. The sum vector therefore points in an intermediate direction with respect to the input vectors. In the figure below, $\mathbf{p}$ is the result of summing $\mathbf{u}$ and $\mathbf{v}$, that is $\mathbf{p} = \mathbf{u} + \mathbf{v}$. Consequently, the two gray vectors correspond to **vector differences**, respectively $\mathbf{p} - \mathbf{u} = \mathbf{v}$ and $\mathbf{p} - \mathbf{v} = \mathbf{u}$.

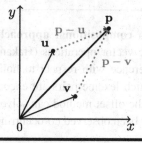

From this equation, we derive the following equivalence:

$$\mathbf{c} + \mathbf{b} - \mathbf{a} \approx \mathbf{d}. \tag{7.3}$$

For instance, given the analogy *man : woman = king : queen*, the vector **queen** is expected to be very similar to the vector **king + woman − man**. The analogy completion task is then solved by looking for the target lexeme *t* that maximizes this equation:

$$\underset{t \in T^*}{\mathrm{argmax}}(\mathrm{sim}_{\cos}(\mathbf{t}, \mathbf{c} + \mathbf{b} - \mathbf{a})), \tag{7.4}$$

where T^* is the set of target lexemes minus a, b, and c. As the cosine normalizes the vectors to unit length, Levy and Goldberg (2014b) prove that Equation 7.4 is mathematically equivalent to:

$$\underset{t \in T^*}{\mathrm{argmax}}(\mathrm{sim}_{\cos}(\mathbf{t}, \mathbf{c}) + \mathrm{sim}_{\cos}(\mathbf{t}, \mathbf{b}) - \mathrm{sim}_{\cos}(\mathbf{t}, \mathbf{a})). \tag{7.5}$$

Completing the analogy *man : woman = king : ?* corresponds to looking for a lexeme which is similar to *king* and *woman*, but is different from *man*. Solving the analogy completion task with the offset method, which Levy and Goldberg (2014b) rename **3CosAdd**, thus amounts to expressing relational similarity as a sum of attributional similarities. This is similar to the method proposed by Turney (2012) to measure relational similarity with a composition of similarities among the lexical items forming the analogy. Levy and Goldberg (2014b) also introduce a multiplicative variant of Equation 7.5, called **3CosMult**, which outperforms 3CosAdd on the MSR and GOOGLE datasets:

3CosAdd

3CosMult

$$\underset{t \in T^*}{\mathrm{argmax}} \frac{\mathrm{sim}_{\cos}(\mathbf{t}, \mathbf{c}) * \mathrm{sim}_{\cos}(\mathbf{t}, \mathbf{b})}{\mathrm{sim}_{\cos}(\mathbf{t}, \mathbf{a})}. \tag{7.6}$$

Compositional and holistic methods

The offset method is a **compositional approach** to analogy resolution, based on simple algebraic vector operations (Hakami and Bollegala, 2017). This is an important difference with respect to **holistic methods** like LRA by Turney (2006b), in which lexeme pairs are encoded with distinct vectors (cf. Section 4.2). In fact, the offset method can solve analogies even between word pairs that have never been observed co-occurring together in the training corpus. The success of this method reported by Mikolov et al. (2013d,a) and others has been taken to indicate that systematic relations between lexical items are encoded in vector differences. This hypothesis has had a great impact on distributional semantics (e.g., the GloVe embeddings are based on this assumption; cf. Section 4.5). However, later research has put in discussion the real generality of such a claim. In fact, the effectiveness of the offset method greatly varies depending on the analogy type. The method is especially successful with analogies representing morphosyntactic relations, but much less so with semantic analogies (Drozd et al., 2016; Linzen, 2016; Vylomova et al., 2016; Finley et al., 2017), in particular those based on paradigmatic relations such as hypernymy or synonymy (Köper et al., 2015).

Church (2017) argues that the good results generally reported on MSR and GOOGLE might be due to some design artifact of such datasets, since every word appears in more than one position in the analogies. Church adapts the SAT dataset to the analogy completion task, and in this case the performance of the offset method drops significantly with respect to MSR and GOOGLE. The limit of the offset method could also depend on the fact that it solves analogies by combining attributional similarities (cf. Equation 7.5). As Turney (2006b) argues, relational similarity cannot always be reduced to attributional one. He distinguishes **near analogies** (e.g., $mason : stone = carpenter : wood$), in which there is a high similarity between a and c and between b and d, from **far analogies** (e.g., $dog : animal = car : vehicle$), in which such similarities do not hold. According to Turney, SAT contains a good number of far analogies, making it a hard case for methods based on attributional similarity only. In fact, the approach proposed by Turney (2012), close to 3CosAdd, performs on SAT significantly worse than the holistic LRA model. NEAR AND FAR ANALOGIES

The debate on the offset method has stimulated the creation of larger datasets for the analogy completion task. **WordRep** (Gao et al., 2014) is a superset of GOOGLE, automatically extended with data extracted from Wikipedia and with 13 new semantic relations derived from WordNet, for a total amount of more than 237 million analogies based on 44,585 lexeme pairs. **BATS** (Bigger Analogy Test Set) is a balanced dataset including 40 categories that cover inflectional and derivational morphology as well as several types of semantic relations (Gladkova et al., 2016). Each category contains 50 unique word pairs, yielding 98,000 analogies (Rogers et al., 2017). WORDREP BATS

7.2.5 Relation Tests

In **relation tests**, the goal is to discriminate between various types of lexical relations. Both supervised and unsupervised approaches are used. A simple SEMANTIC RELATIONS

Table 7.5 A sample of test pairs in BLESS
for the target *cat*

Semantic relation	Example
Coordinate	cat – dog
Hypernymy	cat – animal
Meronymy	cat – fur
Attribute	cat – agile
Event	cat – meow

k-NEAREST NEIGHBOR

PRECISION AND RECALL

RELATION RANKING

AVERAGE PRECISION

BLESS

EVALUTION

SEMEVAL-2012

supervised algorithm is **k-nearest neighbor classification**: A test item is assigned the class of the majority of its k nearest neighbors. Alternatively, more complex classifiers can be applied to the distributional vectors. Supervised methods are typically evaluated with metrics like **precision** and **recall**. Unsupervised approaches model relation discrimination as a **ranking task**: The goal is to rank highest the neighbors that have a certain semantic relation with the target (e.g., its meronyms). In this case, a common performance measure is **average precision** (Manning et al., 2008).

BLESS (Baroni and Lenci Evaluation of Semantic Spaces) contains $26,554$ tuples expressing a relation between a target and a relatum lexeme (Baroni and Lenci, 2011). BLESS includes 200 distinct English concrete nouns as target concepts, equally divided between living and non-living entities, and grouped into 17 broader classes (e.g., BIRD, VEHICLE, etc.). Each target is linked to several relatum words by one of five semantic relations (see Table 7.5). Besides standard paradigmatic relations, the Attribute relation links adjectives expressing a typical attribute of the target (e.g., *cat* - Attribute - *agile*), and the Event relation links verbs expressing typical events in which the target is involved in or which are performed by/with the target (e.g., *cat* - Event - *meow*). The dataset also includes a large number of control tuples with random relata.

EVALution (EVAL) (Santus et al., 2015) complements BLESS with $7,429$ instances of several semantic relations (e.g., synonymy, antonymy, entailment, etc.) extracted from WordNet and ConceptNet, and then rated by five subjects. Both BLESS and EVAL can also be cast as vocabulary tests, where the task is to select a lexeme that has a particular semantic relation with the target, among a number of alternatives. Collections of human-generated paradigmatic semantic relations for DSM evaluation have been created by Scheible and Schulte im Walde (2014) for German, and by Sucameli and Lenci (2017) for Italian.

The **SemEval-2012** (Jurgens et al., 2012) dataset focuses on the fact that word pairs differ for their degree of prototypicality as instances of a given semantic relation (e.g., the pair *dog – bark* is a better prototype of the Entity-Sound relation than *floor – squeak*). SemEval-2012 consists of 79 categories of semantic relations, each associated with a few (usually three) hand-selected example pairs and a set of human-generated pairs relationally similar to them. The dataset contains $3,218$ response pairs with prototypicality scores, derived from judgments of similarity to example pairs of a given relation. The task of DSMs is to rank the pairs according to their relation strength. This ranking is then correlated with the human ratings. SemEval-2012 is also used for the analogy completion task by forming analogies out of the lexeme pairs (Mikolov et al., 2013d; Levy and Goldberg, 2014b; Finley et al., 2017). **DiffVec** DIFFVEC (Vylomova et al., 2016) contains $12,458$ pairs for 15 relations. The dataset combines the items from BLESS, SemEval-2012, and MSR with pairs extracted from WordNet and other web resources. The dataset name derives from the fact that it was originally built to test the offset method for relation classification.

HyperLex (Vulić et al., 2017b) instead represents hypernymy as a contin- HYPERLEX uous notion, to capture the phenomena of typicality and graded membership well attested in the psychological literature (Murphy, 2002). The dataset contains $2,616$ noun and verb pairs $\langle a, b \rangle$ rated on a $0-10$ scale measuring to what degree b is a hypernym of a. The average inter-rater agreement is $\rho = 0.86$.

7.2.6 Psycholinguistic Tasks

DSMs are also evaluated on datasets collected in **psycholinguistic experiments** that involve subconscious computations of semantic similarity (relatedness), rather than explicit judgments. For instance, Ettinger and Linzen (2016) SEMANTIC use data from the Semantic Priming Project (Hutchison et al., 2013). **Seman-** PRIMING **tic priming** is the phenomenon in which, when performing a language task such as deciding whether a target string is a word or a non-word, subjects respond faster if the target is preceded by a semantically related prime word (McNamara, 2005). The **Semantic Priming Project** includes data from 768 SEMANTIC subjects for over $6,000$ word pairs. DSMs are evaluated by using prime-target PRIMING similarity measures as regressors to predict human response times. PROJECT

Vulić et al. (2017a) propose to evaluate DSMs with **word associations,** WORD which represent a traditional source of evidence for the investigation of the ASSOCIATIONS mental lexicon (Deese, 1965). Associations are collected in free association tasks: Subjects are presented with a stimulus word and asked to write the first word that comes into their head that is associated with it. The association task probes into semantic relatedness, because subjects produce responses that are related to the stimulus (McRae et al., 2012). Vulić et al. (2017a) use

USF the **USF** dataset derived from the University of South Florida Free Association Database (Nelson et al., 2004) and containing ca. 70,000 stimulus-response pairs, each associated with an association strength obtained from the number of subjects producing that response. The model evaluation protocol consists in correlating the ranked list of a target's nearest neighbors with the ranked list of

FAST word associations. The **FAST** (Free ASsociation Tasks) benchmark contains 12,329 tuples formed by the stimulus, its most frequently generated response, a hapax response, and a random response (Evert and Lapesa, 2021). Free associations were extracted from the University of South Florida dataset and the Edinburgh Associative Thesaurus (Kiss et al., 1973).

DSM evaluation is also performed on eye-tracking, electroencephalogram (EEG), and functional Magnetic Resonance Imaging (fMRI) data (cf. Section

BRAINBENCH 8.8.3). A large collection of such datasets are available in the **BrainBench**
COGNIVAL (Xu et al., 2016) and the **CogniVal** test suites (Hollenstein et al., 2019).

7.3 Extrinsic DSM Evaluation

EXTRINSIC **Extrinsic methods** use distributional representations as features of supervised
EVALUATION machine learning algorithms to address downstream NLP tasks. Vector quality is then measured with the system's performance. Some of the most common tasks are **POS tagging, chunking, named entity recognition** (NER), **semantic role labeling**, and **sentiment classification**, for which several datasets are available (Nayak et al., 2016; Bakarov, 2018; Rogers et al., 2018).

Extrinsic evaluation has become increasingly popular with the fortune of neural approaches in NLP, because of the key role played by word embeddings in deep learning architectures. Given a supervised target task, neural

EMBEDDING networks represent words with low-dimensional embeddings stored in a so-
LAYER called **lookup** or **embedding layer** (Goldberg, 2017). Embeddings allow the network to capture similarities among lexical items, which are beneficial to learn the target task. The word embeddings can be initialized with random values and trained on the supervised task, together with the other network parameters. The drawback of this approach is that the annotated data for the target supervised task are typically small-sized, thereby resulting in suboptimal lexical representations. The most effective method is instead to train word

PRETRAINED embeddings on a large corpus with an unsupervised DSM, and then learn
EMBEDDINGS the downstream target task by initializing the network with these **pretrained**
TRANSFER **embeddings**. This is an example of **transfer learning**, the process of training
LEARNING a model on large-scale data and then leveraging the acquired knowledge (e.g., the pretrained embeddings) to improve performance on the target task (Ruder, 2019). Collobert and Weston (2008) and Collobert et al. (2011) pioneered the

use of unsupervised pretrained embeddings to boost NLP systems, and Turian et al. (2010) were the first work to systematically evaluate word embeddings on extrinsic tasks like chunking and NER (cf. Section 6.2.2).

Given the widespread use of pretrained embedddings, their performance in NLP tasks has become an important benchmark for DSM evaluation. Extrinsic methods are also claimed to avoid some of the limitations of intrinsic ones. Because of the inherent complexity and vagueness of the notions of similarity and relatedness (cf. Section 7.1), the reliability of intrinsic evaluation has been questioned (Schnabel et al., 2015; Batchkarov et al., 2016; Faruqui et al., 2016; Gladkova and Drozd, 2016). Semantic similarity might be very subjective and highly dependent on the criteria adopted to collect human judgments, possibly resulting in a significant amount of individual variation (though we have seen that in many datasets the average inter-rater correlation is indeed fairly high). Since they do not rely on explicit judgments, extrinsic methods apparently provide a more objective evaluation method. Moreover, the correlation between the intrinsic quality of DSMs and their performances in some NLP tasks has been reported to be quite low (Chiu et al., 2016).

On the other hand, extrinsic evaluation is based on NLP tasks that greatly vary for the lexical knowledge they require. For instance, the semantic information useful for chunking is likely to be very different from the one needed for semantic role labeling or document classification. This is also proved by the high inter-task variability of DSM performance (Schnabel et al., 2015). Extrinsic methods can assess the embedding contribution to a specific NLP task, but provide a very indirect estimate of the overall quality of distributional representations, and are extremely "opaque" with respect to the kind of semantic information they encode. Therefore, extrinsic DSM evaluation should be taken as a complement to rather than a substitute for intrinsic one.

7.4 Quantitative Evaluation of Static DSMs

Intense research has been devoted to the comparative evaluation of DSMs (Curran, 2003; Sahlgren, 2006; Bullinaria and Levy, 2007, 2012; Lapesa and Evert, 2014; Baroni et al., 2014a; Lebret and Collobert, 2014; Levy and Goldberg, 2014a; Levy et al., 2015b; Österlund et al., 2015; Schnabel et al., 2015; Asr et al., 2016; Melamud et al., 2016b; Pereira et al., 2016; Sahlgren and Lenci, 2016; Lapesa and Evert, 2017; Li et al., 2017; Mandera et al., 2017). These studies have mostly aimed at identifying the optimal setting for a certain parameter (e.g., the co-occurrence weighting function, the context window size, the number of vector dimensions, etc.), or have focused only on a subset of DSM types. For instance, Bullinaria and Levy (2007, 2012) and Lapesa and

Table 7.6 Static DSMs and parameter settings

Model	Context	Vector type	Dimensions
Matrix count models			
PPMI	window.{2,10}; syntax.{typed,filtered}	explicit	10,000
SVD	window.{2,10}; syntax.{typed,filtered}	embedding	300; 2,000
LSA	document	embedding	300; 2,000
LDA	document	embedding	300; 2,000
GloVe	window.{2,10}	embedding	300; 2,000
Random encoding count models			
RI	window.{2,10}	embedding	300; 2,000
RI-perm	window.{2,10}	embedding	300; 2,000
Predict models			
SGNS	window.{2,10}; syntax.{typed,filtered}	embedding	300; 2,000
CBOW	window.{2,10}	embedding	300; 2,000
FastText	window.{2,10}	embedding	300; 2,000

Evert (2014, 2017) limit their investigation to matrix models, while Levy et al. (2015b) to window-based ones. In this section, we present a large-scale quantitative evaluation of static DSMs, in which the models reviewed in Part II are tested on a wide range of intrinsic and extrinsic tasks. This is a portion of the larger investigation in Lenci et al. (2022), which also compares static DSMs with contextual ones. It is important to emphasize that the purpose of this analysis is neither to carry out an exhaustive exploration of the parameter space nor to search for the "best model," but rather to identify the key factors affecting the performance of DSMs. Therefore, we have chosen a set of models whose parameter settings exemplify the most important dimensions of variation in the construction of distributional representations.

7.4.1 Model Selection and Training

We have evaluated the distributional vectors of 44 static DSMs defined by the combinations of three main parameters (see Table 7.6):[1]

MODEL A. **Model** – *The type of method used to learn the vectors*. The models are representative of the major algorithms presented in Part II:

  (i) **Matrix count models**

    PPMI – the "standard model" described at the beginning of Section 4.1, with collocate contexts, PPMI weighting (cf. Equation 2.11), and no dimensionality reduction. Therefore, the

---

[1] The DSMs and scripts are available on GitHub: https://github.com/Unipisa/DSMs-evaluation.

distributional representations produced by this DSM are explicit vectors;

SVD – like PPMI, but with embeddings generated with SVD;

LSA – a reimplementation of classical Latent Semantic Analysis (cf. Section 4.1.2) with document contexts, log entropy weighting (cf. Equation 2.18), and SVD. This model was trained with Gensim (Řehůřek and Sojka, 2010);

LDA – a Topic Model with document contexts, based on LDA (cf. Section 4.4.1). This model was trained with Gensim;

GloVe – the model by Pennington et al. (2014) (cf. Section 4.5);

(ii) **Random encoding count models**

RI – Random Indexing with the dynamic weighting scheme in Equation 5.9 (cf. Section 5.3);

RI-perm – Random Indexing with permutations (cf. Section 5.5);

(iii) **Predict models**

SGNS – the Skip-Gram with Negative Sampling model (cf. Section 6.3), trained with word2vecf (Levy and Goldberg, 2014a);

CBOW – the Continuous Bag-Of-Words model (cf. Section 6.3), trained with the word2vec library;

FastText – SGNS with subword information (cf. Section 6.3.2);

B. **Context** – *The type of linguistic contexts.* They are representative of the major kinds reviewed in Section 2.2 (except for constructional contexts): CONTEXT

(i) **Undirected window-based collocates**

window.2 (w2) – narrow context window of size $[2, 2]$;
window.10 (w10) – wide context window of size $[10, 10]$;

(ii) **Syntactic collocates** (only for PPMI, SVD, and SGNS)

syntax.filtered (synf) – dependency-filtered collocates;
syntax.typed (synt) – dependency-typed collocates;

(iii) **Documents** (only for LSA and LDA)

C. **Dimensions** – *the number of vector dimensions.* The settings are 300 and 2, 000 for embeddings, and 10, 000 for explicit PPMI vectors. DIMENSIONS

All 44 models were trained on a concatenation of ukWaC and a 2018 dump of English Wikipedia.[2] The corpus was case-folded, and then POS-tagged and syntactically parsed with CoreNLP (Manning et al., 2014), according to the

---

[2] https://dumps.wikimedia.org

Universal Dependencies (UD) annotation scheme.[3] We removed all words whose frequency was below 100. To reduce the negative effects of high-frequency words, we followed Levy et al. (2015b) and we created a subsampled version of the training corpus with the method by Mikolov et al. (2013a). Every lexical item l whose frequency $F(l)$ was equal to or greater than the threshold t was randomly removed with this probability (cf. Equation 6.38):

$$p(l) = 1 - \sqrt{\frac{t}{F(l)}}, \qquad (7.7)$$

where $t = 10^{-5}$. The vocabulary V of the full training corpus contains $345,232$ unlemmatized word types, corresponding to more than 3.9 billion tokens. The subsampled corpus has the same vocabulary and ca. 2.2 billion tokens (a reduction of 42%). Since word2vec, word2vecf, and FastText perform subsampling natively, predict DSMs were trained on the full corpus, while count DSMs were trained on the subsampled corpus.

The DSM targets T and contexts C were selected as follows:

TARGETS

Targets – $T = V$, for all models. Since targets are unlemmatized lexemes, every DSM assigns a distinct distributional vector to each inflected form. The reason for this choice is that several benchmark datasets (e.g., analogy ones) are not lemmatized;

CONTEXTS

Contexts – the major difference concerns word versus document DSMs:

Word models – $C = V$. For syntax-based models, co-occurrences were identified using the dependency relation (including the UD enhanced dependencies) linking the target and the context lexeme. Both direct and inverse relations were used. For instance, given the sentence *The dog barks*, we considered both $\langle barks, dog \rangle$ and $\langle dog, barks \rangle$ as syntactic co-occurrences. For dependency-typed collocates, we also used direct (e.g., $\langle barks, \langle \text{nsubj}, dog \rangle \rangle$) and inverse (e.g., $\langle dog, \langle \text{nsubj}^{-1}, barks \rangle \rangle$) dependencies, and we applied a context selection heuristic keeping only the typed collocates whose frequency was greater than 500;

Document models – $C = D$, where D includes more than 8.2 million documents, corresponding to the articles in Wikipedia and ukWaC.

Moreover, we applied the following optimization strategies, which the existing literature has shown to improve the model performance:

---

[3] https://stanfordnlp.github.io/CoreNLP/

- we adopted the context probability smoothing by Levy et al. (2015b) to compute the PPMI weights, and we raised the context frequency to the power of $\alpha = 0.75$ (cf. Equation 2.12);
- we applied a context selection heuristics for the explicit PPMI vectors, and we kept only the top $10,000$ most frequent lexemes. In fact, previous studies have proved that further expanding the number of contexts increases the training costs, without substantially improving the quality of distributional representations (Kiela and Clark, 2014; Lapesa and Evert, 2014);
- like Levy et al. (2015b), we discarded the singular value matrix Σ produced by SVD, using the row vectors of $\mathbf{U}$ as embeddings (cf. Equation 2.25);
- we trained predict DSMs with the negative sampling algorithm, using 15 negative examples (instead of the default value of 5), as Levy et al. (2015b) show that increasing their number is beneficial to the model performance.

7.4.2   Tasks and Datasets

We tested the 44 DSMs on the 33 datasets reported in Table 7.7, together with their performance metrics. Vector similarity was measured with the cosine. The correlation index is Spearman ρ, accuracy is the ratio of correct choices returned by a model to the number of test items, purity is the clustering quality metric defined in Equation 7.1, and the F-measure is the harmonic mean between precision (P) and recall (R), computed as $2PR/(P + R)$.

For the **intrinsic evaluation**, we used most of the benchmarks reviewed in Section 7.2, grouped into the following semantic tasks: (i) **synonymy**, INTRINSIC (ii) **similarity**, (iii) **relatedness**, (iv) **categorization**, which was performed TASKS with k-means clustering (BLESS was treated as a categorization test with the 17 semantic classes of the target nouns), (v) and **analogy completion** with the offset method (cf. Equation 7.4).

For the **extrinsic evaluation**, distributional vectors were fed as features into EXTRINSIC supervised classifiers for the following tasks: TASKS

Sequence labeling – the task is to correctly identify the POS tag, chunk tag, or named entity tag of a given token in the English part of the **CoNLL-2003 shared task** dataset (Tjong Kim Sang and Meulder, 2003). The model is a multinomial logistic regression classifier on the concatenated word vectors of a context window of radius two around – and including – the target token;

Semantic relation classification – the task is to correctly identify the semantic relation between two target nominals. The dataset from **SemEval-2 2010, task 8** (Hendrickx et al., 2010) consists of sentences annotated with the semantic relation between selected pairs of nominals. The model is a Convolutional Neural Network (CNN) (cf. Section 9.4.2);

Table 7.7 Datasets used in the experiments with the performance metrics

			Intrinsic evaluation		
Dataset	*Size*	*Metric*	*Dataset*	*Size*	*Metric*
Synonymy			**Categorization**		
TOEFL	80	accuracy	AP	402	purity
ESL	50	accuracy	BATTIG	5,231	purity
Similarity			BATTIG-2010	82	purity
RG65	65	correlation	ESSLLI-2008-1a	44	purity
RW	2,034	correlation	ESSLLI-2008-2b	40	purity
SL-999	999	correlation	ESSLLI-2008-2c	45	purity
SV-3500	3,500	correlation	BLESS	26,554	purity
WS-353	353	correlation	**Analogy**		
WS-SIM	203	correlation	SAT	374	accuracy
Relatedness			MSR	8,000	accuracy
WS-REL	252	correlation	GOOGLE	19,544	accuracy
MTURK	287	correlation	SEMEVAL-2012	3,218	accuracy
MEN	3,000	correlation	WORDREP	237,409,102	accuracy
TR9856	9,856	correlation	BATS	98,000	accuracy

			Extrinsic evaluation	
Dataset	*Training size*	*Test size*	*Task*	*Metric*
CONLL-2003	204,566	46,665	sequence labeling (POS tagging)	F-measure
CONLL-2003	204,566	46,665	sequence labeling (chunking)	F-measure
CONLL-2003	204,566	46,665	sequence labeling (NER)	F-measure
SEMEVAL-2010	8,000	2,717	semantic relation classification	accuracy
MR	5,330	2,668	sentence sentiment classification	accuracy
IMDB	25,000	25,000	document sentiment classification	accuracy
RT	5,000	2,500	subjectivity classification	accuracy
SNLI	550,102	10,000	natural language inference	accuracy

Sentence sentiment classification – the task is to classify snippets of movie reviews labeled as either positive or negative in the **MR** dataset (Pang and Lee, 2005). The binary classification is carried out with the CNN by Kim (2014);

Document sentiment classification – the benchmark for this task is the **Stanford IMDB** dataset of full movie reviews. The documents are labeled as either positive (rating $\geq$ 7 out of 10) or negative ($\leq$ 4), with neutral ratings removed. The classifier is a Long Short–Term Memory (LSTM) network with 100 hidden units (cf. Section 9.4.3);

Subjectivity classification – the task is to identify whether a sentence is subjective or objective. The dataset consists of subjective movie reviews and objective plot summaries (Pang and Lee, 2004). The model is a logistic regression classifier and input sentences are represented as a sum of their constituent word vectors (cf. Section 9.2);

Natural language inference – the dataset for this task is **SNLI** (Bowman et al., 2015) and consists of premise–hypothesis pairs labeled as ENTAIL-MENT, CONTRADICTION, and NEUTRAL, depending on whether the premise entails the hypothesis, contradicts the hypothesis, or neither entails nor contradicts the hypothesis (cf. Section 9.5). The model is based on two LSTMs, one for the premise and one for the hypothesis, whose final representations are concatenated and fed into a multi-layer softmax classifier.

The DSM coverage of the 33 datasets is very high (mean 98%, sd 3.3%). The intrinsic performance measures were obtained with an extended version of the Word Embeddings Benchmarks (Jastrzębski et al., 2017).[4] The eight extrinsic performance measurements were computed with the Linguistic Diagnostic Toolkit (Rogers et al., 2018).[5]

7.4.3 Results and Analyses

Each of the 44 DSMs was tested on the 33 datasets, for a total of $1,452$ experiments. Table 7.8 contains the best score and model for each benchmark. Top performances are generally close to or better than state-of-the-art results for each dataset, and replicate several trends reported in the literature. For instance, the similarity datasets RW and SL-999 are much more challenging than WS-353 and especially MEN. In turn, the verb-only SV-3500 is harder than SL-999, in which nouns represent the lion's share. Coming to the analogy completion task, MSR and GOOGLE prove to be fairly easy. As observed in Section 7.2.4, the performance of the offset method drastically drops with the other datasets, and it strongly depends on the analogy type. The top score by the FastText.w2.300 model is 0.73 on the syntactic subset of GOOGLE analogies, and 0.69 on the semantic one. Differences are much stronger in BATS: The best performance on inflection and derivation analogies is 0.43, against 0.16 on semantic analogies, and just 0.06 on analogies based on paradigmatic relations like hypernymy.

A crucial feature to notice in Table 7.8 is that there is no single "best model." In fact, the performance of DSMs forms a very complex landscape, which we explore here with statistical analyses that focus on the following objectives: (i) determining the role played by the three main factors that define the experiments – model, context, and vector dimensions – and their possible interactions; (ii) identifying which DSMs are significantly different from each other; (iii) check how the task type influences the performance of the DSMs.

---

[4] https://github.com/kudkudak/word-embeddings-benchmarks
[5] http://ldtoolkit.space

Table 7.8 Best score and model for each dataset

			Intrinsic evaluation		
Dataset	Score	Model	Dataset	Score	Model
Synonymy			**Categorization**		
TOEFL	0.92	FastText.w2.2000	AP	0.75	SVD.synt.300
ESL	0.78	SVD.synt.2000	BATTIG	0.48	SGNS.synt.300
Similarity			BATTIG-2010	1.00	SVD.synf.300
RG65	0.87	GloVe.w10.2000	ESSLLI-2008a	0.95	SVD.synf.300
RW	0.48	FastText.w2.300	ESSLLI-2008b	0.92	SGNS.w2.2000
SL-999	0.49	SVD.synt.2000	ESSLLI-2008c	0.75	SGNS.w2.2000
SV-3500	0.41	SVD.synt.2000	BLESS	0.88	SVD.synf.2000
WS-353	0.71	CBOW.w10.300	**Analogy**		
WS-SIM	0.76	SVD.w2.2000	SAT	0.34	SVD.synt.300
Relatedness			MSR	0.68	FastText.w2.300
WS-REL	0.66	CBOW.w10.300	GOOGLE	0.76	FastText.w2.300
MTURK	0.71	FastText.w2.300	SEMEVAL-2012	0.38	SVD.synt.300
MEN	0.79	CBOW.w10.300	WORDREP	0.27	FastText.w2.300
TR9856	0.17	FastText.w2.300	BATS	0.29	FastText.w2.300

	Extrinsic evaluation		
Dataset	Task	Score	Model
CONLL-2003	sequence labeling (POS tagging)	0.88	SGNS.synt.2000
CONLL-2003	sequence labeling (chunking)	0.89	SGNS.synt.300
CONLL-2003	sequence labeling (NER)	0.96	SGNS.w2.2000
SEMEVAL-2010	semantic relation classification	0.78	SGNS.w2.2000
MR	sentence sentiment classification	0.78	SGNS.w2.2000
IMDB	document sentiment classification	0.82	FastText.w2.300
RT	subjectivity classification	0.91	FastText.w2.2000
SNLI	natural language inference	0.70	CBOW.w2.2000

An overall analysis of the role played by the different factors in the experiments poses the problem of having a response (or dependent) variable that is homogeneous across tasks in which performance is evaluated according to different metrics (see Table 7.7). It is evident that an accuracy value of 0.5 has a very different value compared to a correlation coefficient equal to 0.5. In order to address this issue, we defined as response variable the position (**rank**) of a DSM in the performance ranking of each task. If a model A has a higher accuracy than a model B in a task and a higher correlation than B in another task, in both cases we can say that A is "better" than B. Therefore, given a task t, we ordered the performance scores on t in a decreasing way, and each DSM was associated with a value corresponding to its rank in the ordered list (e.g., the top DSM has rank one, the second best scoring DSM has rank two, and so on). The response variable is therefore defined on a scale

PERFORMANCE
RANK

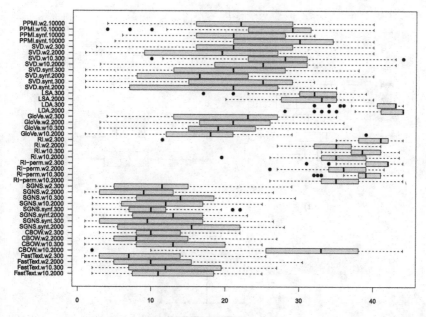

Figure 7.3 Rank distribution of the 44 static DSMs in the 33 datasets

from 1 to 44 (the number of DSMs tested on each task), in which *lower values correspond to better performances*. This conversion determines a loss of information on the distance between the scores, but normalizes the metrics both in terms of meaning and in terms of the statistical characteristics of their distribution.

Figure 7.3 presents the **global rank distribution** of the 44 DSMs. Model is GLOBAL the primary factor in affecting performance, context has a more contained and ANALYSIS nuanced role, while the effect of dimensions is marginal. This is confirmed by the Kruskal-Wallis rank sum non-parametric test: models ($H = 854.27$, df=9, $p < 0.001$**) and contexts ($H = 229.87$, df=4, $p < 0.001$**) differ significantly, while the vector dimension levels do not ($H = 3.14$, df=2, $p = 0.21$), as shown by Figure 7.4c. The only exceptions are the RI models, whose 2,000-dimensional embeddings tend to perform better than the smaller ones.

Looking at Figure 7.4a, we can observe that there are three major groups of models: (i) the best performing ones are the predict models SGNS, CBOW and FastText, (ii) closely followed by the matrix models GloVe, SVD, and PPMI, (iii) while the worst performing models are RI, the document-based LSA, and in particular LDA. Dunn's tests (with Bonferroni correction) were carried out to identify which pairs of models are statistically different. The

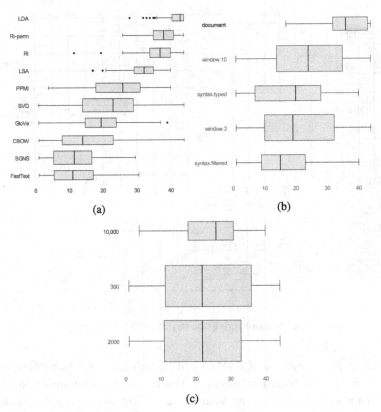

Figure 7.4 Global DSM performance: (a) rank by model type, (b) rank by context type, (c) rank by vector dimensions

p-values of these tests reported in Table 7.9 draw a very elaborate picture that cannot be reduced to the strict contrast between predict and count models: (i) no difference exists between SGNS and FastText; (ii) GloVe does not differ from CBOW and SVD, and the latter two are only marginally different; (iii) interestingly, the PPMI explicit vectors do not differ from their implicit counterparts reduced with SVD and only marginally differ from GloVe; (iv) LSA does not differ from RI and RI-perm, which in turn do not differ from LDA.

With regard to context types, the best scores are for syntax-based ones, either filtered or typed, while document is clearly the worst (see Figure 7.4b). However, we note that syntax.filtered is equivalent to syntax.typed, and the latter does not differ from window.2. On the other hand, window.10 and document are significantly different from all other context types (see Table 7.10).

Table 7.9 P-values of Dunn's tests for multiple comparisons of model types
($* * * = < 0.001$)

	CBOW	FastText	GloVe	LDA	LSA	PPMI	RI	RI-perm	SGNS
FastText	0.03								
GloVe	1	***							
LDA	***	***	***						
LSA	***	***	***	***					
PPMI	***	***	0.036	***	0.008				
RI	***	***	***	**0.508**	**0.379**	***			
RI-perm	***	***	***	**1**	**0.068**	***	1		
SGNS	0.009	1	***	***	***	***	***	***	
SVD	0.037	***	1	***	***	1	***	***	***

Table 7.10 P-values of Dunn's tests for multiple comparisons of context types
($* * * = < 0.001$)

	syntax.filtered	syntax.typed	document	window.10
syntax.typed	1			
document	***	***		
window.10	***	***	***	
window.2	***	**0.356**	***	***

Analyses by Semantic Task

DSM performance greatly varies depending on the benchmark dataset and semantic task. This is already evident from the spread out data distribution in the boxplots in Figure 7.3. In this section, we investigate this issue by analyzing the performance of the different model and context types in the six tasks in which the datasets are grouped: synonymy, similarity, relatedness, categorization, analogy, and extrinsic tasks (see Table 7.7).

Figure 7.5 reports the per-task rank distribution of **model types**. In general, the best performances are obtained by SGNS and FastText for all types of tasks, and the worst ones by LDA, RI, Ri-perm, and LSA. Instead, PPMI, SVD, GloVe, and CBOW produce more intermediate and variable results: They are equivalent or better than the top models in some cases, worse in others. Figure 7.6 shows the model pairs whose performance is statistically different for each task (black dots), according to Dunn's test. We can notice that in several cases the differences between models are actually non-significant: (i) CBOW never differs from SGNS and FastText; (ii) SVD differs from predict models only in the analogy and extrinsic tasks (but for FastText in the relatedness task too), and differs from PPMI for similarity and extrinsic tasks; (iii) GloVe never differs from SGNS and CBOW, and differs from FastText only for relatedness. Interestingly, GloVe differs neither from PPMI explicit vectors, nor

PER TASK PERFORMANCE BY MODEL TYPE

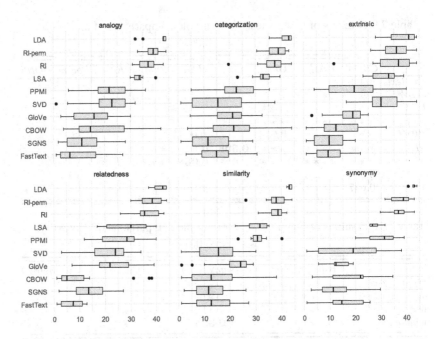

Figure 7.5 DSM performance per semantic task: rank by model type

from SVD (apart from the extrinsic task). If we exclude LDA, LSA, and RI, which are systematically underperforming, models mostly differ in the extrinsic task (40% of the overall cases), with the predict ones having a clear edge over the others. Conversely, the performances in synonymy and categorization tasks are more similar across models, with only the 6% of significant pairwise differences.

Per task performance by context type Figure 7.7 shows the per-task distribution of the various **context types**. Apart from document, which has the worst performance in every task, the other contexts almost never produce significant differences, as confirmed by the results of the Dunn's tests in Figure 7.8. The only exception is the categorization task, in which syntax-based contexts achieve significantly better performances than window-based ones. Moreover, syntax.filtered improves over window.10 in the similarity and the analogy tasks.

Correlations between datasets A further aspect we analyze is the correlation of **DSM performance across datasets**. In the plot in Figure 7.9, dot size is proportional to the Spearman correlation between the 33 datasets with respect to the performance of the 44 DSMs: The higher the correlation between two datasets the more DSMs tend to perform similarly on them. Intrinsic evaluation benchmarks are strongly correlated with each other. The only exceptions are TR9856 and ESSLLI-2008b. The former case probably depends on some idiosyncrasies of the dataset, as

	Task	PPMI	SVD	LSA	LDA	GloVe	RI	RI-perm	SGNS	CBOW
SVD	synonymy	○								
	similarity	●								
	relatedness	○								
	categorization	○								
	analogy	○								
	extrinsic	●	*SVD*							
LSA	synonymy	○	○							
	similarity	○	●							
	relatedness	○	○							
	categorization	○	●							
	analogy	○	○							
	extrinsic	○	○	*LSA*						
LDA	synonymy	○	●	○						
	similarity	○	●	○						
	relatedness	○	●	○						
	categorization	●	●	○						
	analogy	●	●	○						
	extrinsic	●	○	○	*LDA*					
GloVe	synonymy	○	○	○	●					
	similarity	○	○	○	●					
	relatedness	○	○	○	○					
	categorization	○	○	○	●					
	analogy	○	○	●	●					
	extrinsic	○	●	●	●	*GloVe*				
RI	synonymy	○	●	○	○	●				
	similarity	○	●	○	○	●				
	relatedness	○	●	○	○	○				
	categorization	●	●	○	○	●				
	analogy	●	●	○	○	●				
	extrinsic	●	○	○	○	●	*RI*			
RI-perm	synonymy	○	●	○	○	●	○			
	similarity	○	●	○	○	●	○			
	relatedness	○	●	○	○	○	○			
	categorization	●	●	○	○	●	○			
	analogy	●	●	○	○	●	○			
	extrinsic	●	○	○	○	●	○	*RI-perm*		
SGNS	synonymy	●	○	○	●	○	●	●		
	similarity	●	○	●	●	○	●	●		
	relatedness	○	○	○	●	○	●	●		
	categorization	●	○	●	●	○	●	●		
	analogy	○	●	●	●	○	●	●		
	extrinsic	●	●	●	●	○	●	●	*SGNS*	
CBOW	synonymy	○	○	○	○	○	○	○	○	
	similarity	●	○	●	●	○	●	●	○	
	relatedness	●	○	○	●	○	●	●	○	
	categorization	○	○	○	●	○	●	●	○	
	analogy	○	○	○	●	○	●	●	○	
	extrinsic	○	●	●	●	○	●	●	○	*CBOW*
FastText	synonymy	○	○	○	●	○	●	●	○	○
	similarity	●	○	●	●	○	●	●	○	○
	relatedness	●	●	●	●	○	●	●	○	○
	categorization	○	○	●	●	○	●	●	○	○
	analogy	●	●	●	●	○	●	●	○	○
	extrinsic	●	●	●	●	○	●	●	○	○

Figure 7.6 Dunn's tests for multiple comparisons of model types for each semantic task. Black dots mark significantly different models (p< 0.05)

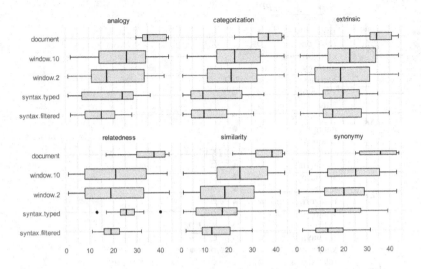

Figure 7.7   DSM performance per semantic task: rank by context type

	Task	window.2			
	synonymy	○			
	similarity	○			
window.10	relatedness	○			
	categorization	○			
	analogy	○			
	extrinsic	○	*window.10*		
	synonymy	○	○		
	similarity	○	●		
syntax.filtered	relatedness	○	○		
	categorization	●	○		
	analogy	○	●		
	extrinsic	○	○	*syntax.filtered*	
	synonymy	○	○	○	
	similarity	○	○	○	
syntax.typed	relatedness	○	○	○	
	categorization	●	●	○	
	analogy	○	○	○	
	extrinsic	○	○	○	*syntax.typed*
	synonymy	●	○	●	●
	similarity	●	●	●	●
document	relatedness	●	●	●	●
	categorization	●	●	●	●
	analogy	●	●	●	●
	extrinsic	●	●	●	●

Figure 7.8 Dunn's tests for multiple comparisons of context types for each semantic task. Black dots mark significantly different contexts ($p < 0.05$)

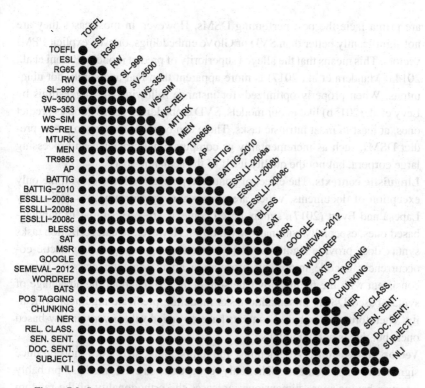

Figure 7.9 Spearman correlation between datasets. The bigger the dot size, the higher the correlation

suggested by the fact that the top performance on TR9856 is significantly lower than the ones scored by the other relatedness benchmarks (see Table 7.8). ESSLLI-2008b instead focuses on concrete-abstract categorization, a task that targets a unique semantic dimension among the tested benchmarks. Intrinsic datasets are strongly correlated with extrinsic ones too, except for POS tagging, chunking, and NER, which, however, have weaker correlations with the other extrinsic datasets as well.

7.4.4 Discussion

The analyses in the previous section confirm the highly complex and multifaceted behaviour of DSMs. We summarize here the most important findings of our evaluation experiments and we draw some general conclusions.

The model is the crucial factor. The method to build distributional vectors is the main factor responsible for global and task-based variability of DSMs. MODEL

Count versus predict. While RI and LDA always lag behind, predict models COUNT VERSUS PREDICT are prima facie the best perfoming DSMs. However, in most cases they are not significantly better than SVD or GloVe embeddings, or even explicit PPMI vectors. This means that the alleged superiority of predict models (Baroni et al., 2014a; Mandera et al., 2017) is more apparent than real and surely not ubiquitous. When properly optimized, for instance following the suggestions by Levy et al. (2015b) like in our models, SVD embeddings are as good as predict ones, at least in most intrinsic tasks. There can be other reasons to prefer predict DSMs, such as incrementality or computational efficiency in processing large corpora, but not the quality itself of the semantic space.

LINGUISTIC CONTEXTS

Linguistic contexts. The effect of context type is more limited, with the only exception of documents, which are always underperforming. As noticed by Lapesa and Evert (2017), syntax-based contexts are very similar to window-based ones, especially with narrow windows. However, in categorization tasks syntax does provide significant improvements, suggesting that syntactic co-occurrences encode important information about semantic classes. This is consistent with the findings by Chersoni et al. (2017) about the advantage of syntax-based DSMs in semantic tasks modeling predicate-argument typicality. Therefore, syntax-based contexts have an added value over window-based ones, but this is not ubiquitous.

DIMENSIONS

Vector dimensions. Augmenting the embedding size does not produce significant improvements. The only exceptions are RI models, probably because having more dimensions increases the orthogonality of the random vectors.

TASK EFFECTS

Tasks do matter. The effect of tasks on DSM performance is extremely high. This means that, for DSM evaluation to be truly reliable, it should always be performed on as large a range as possible of semantic tasks and datasets.

THE LIMITS OF ANALOGY

Analogies must be handled with care. The "linguistic regularities" (Mikolov et al., 2013d) that can be discovered with the offset method are quite limited, except for morphosyntactic analogies. This confirms the doubts raised in several studies (Linzen, 2016; Rogers et al., 2017; Schluter, 2018; Peterson et al., 2020) about the general soundness of such a method to model analogical similarity. While analogy targets an important aspect of semantic similarity, extreme caution should be exercised in using the analogy completion task and its solution with the offset method as a benchmark to evaluate DSMs.

INTRINSIC VERSUS EXTRINSIC EVALUATION

Intrinsic versus extrinsic evaluation. DSM performance on intrinsic tasks correlates with the performance on extrinsic tasks, except for the sequence labeling ones, replicating the findings of Rogers et al. (2018). Differently from what has been sometimes claimed in the literature, this strong correlation indicates that intrinsic evaluation can also be informative about the performance of distributional vectors when embedded in downstream NLP applications. On the other hand, not all extrinsic tasks are equally suitable to evaluate DSMs, as the peculiar behavior of POS, NER, and chunking seems to show.

7.5 Representation Similarity Analysis of Semantic Spaces

One general shortcoming of the standard way to evaluate DSMs is that it is based on testing their performances on benchmark datasets that, despite their increasing size, only cover a limited portion of a model vocabulary (e.g., the large MEN includes just 751 word types). Apart from few exceptions, the selection criteria of test items are not explicit, and do not take into consideration or do not provide information about important factors such as word frequency and POS. As we saw in the previous section, the variance among datasets is often extremely large, even within the same semantic task, and this might be due to differences in sampling and rating criteria.

We present here an alternative approach that explores the shape of the semantic spaces produced by DSMs with **Representational Similarity Analysis** (RSA) (Kriegeskorte et al., 2008; Kriegeskorte and Kievit, 2013), which has been recently adopted in NLP to analyze the representations of neural networks (Abdou et al., 2019; Abnar et al., 2019; Chrupała and Alishahi, 2019). RSA is a method developed in cognitive neuroscience to establish a relationship between a set of stimuli and their brain activations. These are both represented as points in a similarity space (e.g., the stimuli can be represented in terms of their mutual similarity ratings) and are related in terms of the **second-order isomorphism** (Edelman, 1998) determined by *the similarity of the similarity structure* of the two spaces. Therefore, RSA is a methodology to compare two geometrical representations R_1 and R_2 of a set of data: The similarity between R_1 and R_2 depends on how similar the similarity relations among the data according to R_1 are to the similarity relations according to R_2. As DSMs produce geometrical representations of the lexicon, RSA can be applied to investigate the similarity of their semantic spaces by measuring the correlation between the pairwise similarity relations among the lexical items in different spaces.

We performed RSA on 24 DSMs tested in Section 7.4. This set includes the 300-dimensional models, the PPMI explicit vectors, and the RI and RI-perm 2000-dimensional embeddings, which we chose instead of the smaller ones because of their better performance. Given a vocabulary V and a DSM M, the

RSA

SECOND-ORDER
ISOMORPHISM

semantic space representing V corresponds to the matrix $\mathbf{M}$ whose rows are the vectors of the targets $t \in V$. The RSA consisted of the following steps:[6]

REPRESENTATION
SIMILARITY
MATRIX

1. for each DSM M^k generating the semantic space $\mathbf{M}^k$, we built the **representation similarity matrix** $\mathbf{RSM}^k_{|V| \times |V|}$ such that each entry $rsm_{i,j}$ is the cosine similarity between the vectors of the lexical items $t_i, t_j \in V$;[7]
2. for each pair of DSMs M^1 and M^2, we measured their similarity with the Spearman correlation between $\mathbf{RSM}^1$ and $\mathbf{RSM}^2$.

As the size of the DSM vocabulary (more than $345,000$ words) would make the construction of one global similarity matrix computationally too expensive, we randomly sampled 100 disjoint sets of $1,000$ lexemes and we ran separate analyses on each sample. The similarity between the spaces of two DSMs is the average correlation between their respective RSMs of the various samples.

GLOBAL RSA

As we can see from the correlation plot in Figure 7.10, the **global semantic spaces** produced by the various DSMs show significant differences, as only few of them have strong correlations. The mean between-DSM Spearman ρ is 0.17 (median = 0.12), with a high variability (sd = 0.23). The similarity between representations is mainly determined by the model type, once again confirming the far greater importance of this factor than the linguistic context in shaping distributional semantic spaces. The predict DSMs (SGNS, CBOW, and FastText) form a dense cluster of mutually similar spaces. They also have a moderate correlation with window-based SVD. Syntax-based SGNS is particularly close to GloVe and LDA. The latter and especially RI are the real outliers of the overall group, since their lexical spaces have very low similarity with any other DSM. Within the same model type, syntax-based spaces predictably tend to be quite similar to narrow window ones.

Further RSAs were then performed on subsets of the DSM vocabulary sampled according to their **frequency** in the training corpus:

FREQUENCY
RSA

High Frequency (RSA-HF): the $1,000$ most frequent lexemes;

Medium Frequency (RSA-MF): ten disjoint random samples of $1,000$ lexemes, selected among those with frequency greater than 500, except for the $1,000$ most frequent ones;

Low Frequency (RSA-LF): ten disjoint random samples of $1,000$ words, selected among those with frequency from 100 up to 500.

---

[6] We performed RSA with the Python library Neurora: https://neurora.github.io/NeuroRA/

[7] Notice that the original RSA method uses dissimilarity matrices whose entries contain dissimilarity measures between the items.

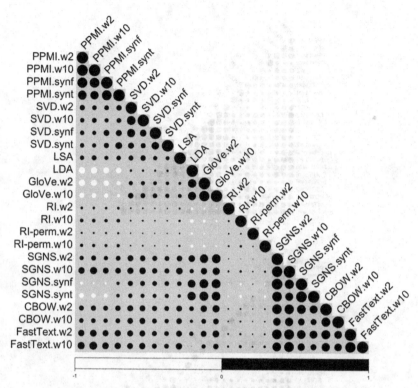

Figure 7.10 Average Spearman correlation between semantic spaces computed with RSA on 100 random samples of 1,000 words. Dot color marks the correlation sign and dot size its magnitude

The results of these analyses are reported in Figure 7.11 (dot color marks the correlation sign – black positive, white negative – and dot size its magnitude). It is interesting to notice the great difference in the similarities among semantic spaces depending on the frequency range of the target lexemes. In RSA-HF, most semantic spaces are strongly correlated to each other, apart from a few exceptions: The average correlation (mean $\rho = 0.48$; median = 0.49; sd = 0.23) is in fact significantly higher than the one of the global spaces. Even those models, like RI and LDA, that behave like outliers in the general RSA represent the high-frequency semantic space very similarly to the other DSMs. The between-model correlations in RSA-MF (mean $\rho = 0.22$; median = 0.18; sd = 0.22) are significantly lower than RSA-HF (Wilcoxon test: $V = 36,081$, p-value < 0.001). A further decrease occurs with low-frequency lexemes (mean $\rho = 0.20$; median = 0.17; sd = 0.20; Wilcoxon test: $V = 25,805$, p-value < 0.001). In this latter case, the effect of model type is particularly strong. The behavior

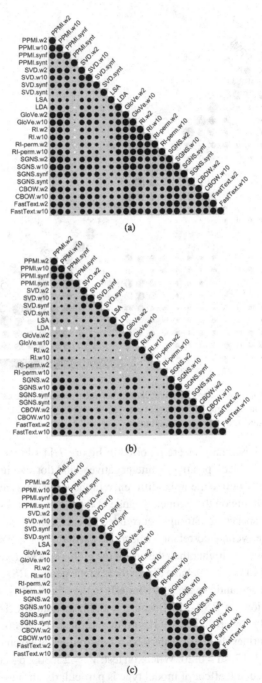

Figure 7.11 Spearman correlation between semantic spaces computed with RSA on (a) high-, (b) medium-, (c) and low-frequency target words

of GloVe is exemplary: Its spaces are very close to the PPMI, SVD, and predict ones for high-frequency words, but in the low-frequency range they have some moderate correlation only with the latter family of models. Interestingly, in RSA-MF and RSA-LF (window-based) SGNS and FastText are more similar to PPMI than to other count models, probably due to the close link between PPMI and negative sampling proved by Levy and Goldberg (2014c).

It is worth mentioning the peculiar behavior of **LDA**, which we had to THE CASE OF exclude from RSA-LF because most low-frequency targets are represented LDA exactly with the same embedding formed by very small values, hence they are not discriminated by the model. We hypothesize that this is due to the way in which word embeddings are defined in Topic Models. As described in Section 4.4.2, given a set of topics $\{z_1, \ldots, z_k\}$, each target is represented with a topic vector $(\phi_1, \ldots, \phi_k)$, such that $\phi_i = p(t|z_i)$. The words that are not relevant to characterize any topic have low probabilities in all of them. Therefore, these lexemes are eventually represented by identical topic vectors. The problem is that the size of this phenomenon is actually huge: The LDA.300 model has $305,050$ targets with the same topic vector, about 88% of its total vocabulary. Low-frequency words are especially affected, probably because they do not appear among the most likely words of any topic, as they occur few times in the documents used as contexts by LDA. This might also explain the systematically low performance of LDA in quantitative evaluation. Moreover, it casts some doubt on its adequacy to build word embeddings in general. Like LSA, Topic Models were originally designed for the semantic analysis of document collections, and were then turned into lexical models on the assumption that, just as documents can be represented with their word distributions, lexical items can be represented with the documents they occur in. However, while this conversion from document to lexical representation works fairly well for LSA, it is eventually problematic for Topic Models.

A third group of RSAs was performed on subsets of the DSM vocabulary sampled according to their **POS** in the training corpus. First, we selected all the POS RSA words with frequency greater than 500, to avoid the idiosyncrasies produced by low-frequency items. Since the DSM targets are not POS-disambiguated, we univocally assigned each selected lexeme to either the noun, verb, or adjective class, if at least 90% of the occurrences of that word in the corpus was tagged with that class. This way, it is likely that the vector of a potentially ambiguous word encodes the distributional properties of its majority POS. At the end of this process we obtained $14,893$ common nouns, $7,780$ verbs, and $5,311$ adjectives. Given the role of target frequency in shaping the semantic spaces,

Table 7.11 Between-DSM correlations with respect to POS and frequency

POS	frequency	mean ρ	median ρ	sd
nouns	high	0.55	0.55	0.18
verbs	high	0.58	0.57	0.17
adjectives	high	0.58	0.58	0.17
nouns	medium	0.31	0.29	0.24
verbs	medium	0.41	0.43	0.26
adjectives	medium	0.41	0.43	0.25

we then split each set in two subsets: High-frequency sets are composed by the first 1,000 most frequent targets of each POS, whereas medium frequency sets include the remaining targets. We randomly selected 4 disjoint samples of 1,000 targets from the medium-frequency set of each POS (notice that almost all adjectives are represented in these selected samples).

This analysis shows the effect of frequency in even a clearer way, since for all POS there is a drastic decrease in the model correlations from the high- to the medium-frequency range, with a symmetric increase in their variability, as shown in Table 7.11. At the same time, important differences among POS emerge. In the high-frequency range, verbs (Wilcoxon test: $V = 9,546$, p-value < 0.001) and adjectives (Wilcoxon test: $V = 12,957$, p-value < 0.001) have a significant higher between-DSM similarity than nouns, and this gap further increases with medium-frequency lexical items (verbs instead do not significantly differ from adjectives). This means that the semantic spaces produced by the various DSMs are more different for nouns than for verbs or adjectives. Future investigations are needed to further explore such differences (e.g., zooming in on particular subclasses, like abstract vs. concrete ones).

In summary, RSAs reveal that frequency and POS strongly affect the shape of distributional semantic spaces and must therefore be carefully considered when comparing DSMs. In particular, we have found that models produce often dramatically different semantic spaces for low-frequency words, while for high-frequency items the correlation among them is extremely high. This suggests that the main locus of variation among the methods to build distributional representations might reside in how they cope with data sparseness and are able to extract information from a limited number of occurrences. In our experiments, we applied to all DSMs the smoothing procedure of predict models, as proposed by Levy et al. (2015b), but count and predict models still behave very differently in the low-frequency range.

Overall, these results highlight the strong **instability** (Antoniak and Mimno, 2018) of distributional vectors. **Stability** is defined as the overlap between the nearest neighbors in different semantic spaces. Pierrejean and Tanguy (2018) and Wendlandt et al. (2018) investigate the effect of hyperparameter settings on the vector (in)stability and its relationship with target POS and frequency. RSA shows that different models produce substantially divergent representations of the lexicon, even when trained on the same corpus data with highly comparable settings, and that this phenomenon is particularly strong for low-frequency items. This instability is especially critical for the application of DSMs in low-resource settings (e.g., digital humanities and studies on language acquisition).

DISTRIBUTIONAL
VECTORS
INSTABILITY

7.6 Summary

Distributional semantics has extensively focused on how to evaluate its representations, a unique feature in semantic studies which contributes to enhance its scientific robustness. In this chapter, we have reviewed the most common approach to DSM evaluation, based on measuring the ability of a model to approximate semantic data collected in benchmark datasets. DSMs are tested on **semantic tasks** designed to probe how distributional vectors capture various kinds of similarity and relatedness (**intrinsic evaluation**) or improve the performance of NLP applications (**extrinsic evaluation**). We have also used **Representation Similarity Analysis** as a magnifying lens to compare the semantic representations produced by DSMs.

All the methods above have been applied in a large-scale experiment in which 44 DSMs have been first tested on 33 datasets and then have been explored with RSA. These analyses have shown the crucial role of the method to build distributional vectors, but have also confirmed the strong dependency of the DSM performance on the type of semantic task and benchmark. At the same time, the differences between several types of DSMs, in particular predict and matrix ones, are often non statistically different, apart from few tasks and models. RSA has also revealed the key effect of target frequency and POS in the correlations among the semantic spaces. Overall, the experiments confirm the multifaceted behaviors of DSMs, as well as the complexity of their evaluation, which will surely continue to attract attention and research.

7.7 Further Reading

- Evaluation methods in distributional semantics: Bakarov (2018)
- The effect of DSM parameters: Bullinaria and Levy (2007, 2012); Baroni et al. (2014a); Lapesa and Evert (2014); Rubin et al. (2014); Levy et al. (2015b); Lapesa and Evert (2017); Pereira et al. (2016); Mandera et al. (2017)
- Large-scale evaluation and RSA of static DSMs: Lenci et al. (2022)

8

Distributional Semantics and the Lexicon

In Chapter 7, we have discussed DSMs mainly as models of semantic similarity and relatedness. However, **lexical semantic competence** (i.e., our knowledge of the meaning of lexical items) is a multifaceted and complex reality which includes the ability of drawing inferences (e.g., *I have a dog* entails *I have an animal*, but does not entail *I have a golden retriever*), distinguishing different word senses (e.g., *bank* can be a financial institution and the land sloping down to a river), referring to the entities in the world, combining words together (e.g., *green* can combine with *grass*, but not with *idea*), and so on. A longstanding tradition of research in linguistics and cognitive science has investigated these issues using **symbolic representations** (Section 8.1). The aim of this chapter is to understand how and to what extent the major aspects of lexical meaning can be addressed with distributional representations.

LEXICAL SEMANTIC COMPETENCE

SYMBOLIC REP-RESENTATIONS

We have selected a group of research topics that have received particular attention in distributional semantics (the combinatorial properties of lexical items are instead treated in Chapter 9): (i) identifying and representing word senses (Section 8.2), (ii) discriminating paradigmatic semantic relations (Section 8.3), (iii) establishing cross-lingual links among lexemes (Section 8.4), (iv) analyzing connotative aspects of meaning (Section 8.5), (v) studying semantic change (Section 8.6), (vi) grounding distributional representations in extralinguistic data (Section 8.7), and (vii) using distributional vectors in cognitive science to model the mental lexicon and semantic memory (Section 8.8).

The work on these topics has been intense and the state of the art is continuously advancing. Therefore, it would be impossible and pointless to provide an exhaustive account of all the different solutions that have been devised. In the following sections, we present the major approaches proposed to tackle these semantic questions with DSMs. Our main goal is to shed light on the potentialities and current limits of distributional representations, and to identify the open challenges that still lie in front of us, in order to evaluate the real descriptive and explanatory adequacy of distributional models of lexical meaning.

8.1 Representing Lexical Meaning

SYMBOLIC
MODELS
In linguistics, word meanings are traditionally couched in symbolic terms.

> **Symbolic models** of the lexicon represent meanings with **symbols** of a formal metalanguage (e.g., predicate logic, feature structures, semantic networks, etc.) and process them through symbol-manipulating rules.

The symbolic approach crosses the divide between conceptualist and referential semantics (Hamm et al., 2006). For instance, symbolic representations are used both by Conceptual Semantics (Jackendoff, 1990) and by Discourse Representation Theory (Kamp and Reyle, 1993), but the former conceives them as mental structures, while the latter assigns them a model-theoretic interpretation (cf. Section 9.1). A major distinction exists between componential and relational models of the semantic lexicon (Vigliocco and Vinson, 2007; Murphy, 2010), both stemming from the structuralist tradition (Geeraerts, 2010).

COMPONENTIAL
MODELS

SEMANTIC
FEATURES
Decompositional or **componential** models conceive lexical meanings as decomposable into structures of basic or primitive components called **semantic features**. In the simplest case, meanings are represented with flat lists of binary features (Katz and Fodor, 1963), like in the examples below:

(1)   a.   *car* [-ANIMATE, +ARTIFACT, +VEHICLE, +FOUR_WHEELS, ...]
      b.   *enter* [+DYNAMIC, +TELIC, -DURATIVE, +MOVEMENT, ...]

CONCEPTUAL
SEMANTICS
As binary features have a limited expressivity, lexical meanings are typically decomposed into more complex formal structures (Dowty, 1979). **Conceptual Semantics** (Jackendoff, 1990, 2002) assumes a repertoire of primitive conceptual categories (e.g., EVENT, OBJECT, PATH, etc.) and functions (e.g., GO, CAUSE, TO, etc.). The latter define conceptual representations that capture compositional aspects of meaning and interface with syntactic structure (cf. Section 9.1). The meaning of *enter* is thus represented as the event of an object moving along a path that terminates inside another object:

(2)   [$_{EVENT}$ GO ([$_{OBJECT}$ x], [$_{PATH}$ TO ([$_{PLACE}$ IN ([$_{OBJECT}$ y])])])]

GENERATIVE
LEXICON
A more elaborated decomposition is proposed in the **Generative Lexicon** (Pustejovsky, 1995), which adopts attribute-value matrices as formal metalanguage. These represent feature structures as sets of attributes whose values can be either atomic symbols or other feature structures:

$$(3) \quad \begin{bmatrix} \textbf{book} \\[4pt] \text{ARGSTR} \quad = \quad \begin{bmatrix} \text{ARG1} = \textbf{x:info} \\ \text{ARG2} = \textbf{y:physobj} \end{bmatrix} \\[12pt] \text{QUALIA} \quad = \quad \begin{bmatrix} \textbf{info·physobj\_lcp} \\ \text{FORMAL} = \textbf{hold(y,x)} \\ \text{CONST} = \textbf{part\_of(z:page,y)} \\ \text{TELIC} = \textbf{read(e,w,x)} \\ \text{AGENT} = \textbf{write(e,v,x)} \end{bmatrix} \end{bmatrix}$$

Lexical items are analyzed into multiple semantic layers, among which the Qualia Structure decomposes word meanings along four major dimensions: the features that distinguish the entities it denotes within a larger domain (FORMAL role), their parts (CONSTITUTIVE role), typical function (TELIC role), and mode of creation (AGENTIVE role). For example, the semantic representation of *book* in (3) specifies that it is a physical object holding information, is created by writing, is used for reading, and contains pages.

In **relational models** of the lexicon, word meanings are not internally decomposed, but are described by their relations with other lexemes. In formal semantics, lexemes are treated as symbols in a logical language (e.g., *bachelor* is represented with the function symbol $\lambda x[\text{bachelor}(x)]$; cf. Section 9.1) and **meaning postulates** (Carnap, 1952; Montague, 1974) capture aspects of lexical meaning by stipulating a relationship between two or more lexical symbols. For example, the postulate $\forall x \Box (\text{bachelor}(x) \rightarrow \neg\text{married}(x))$ describes the meaning of *bachelor* as an individual that must be unmarried. An important class of relational models are **semantic networks** (Collins and Quillian, 1969; Collins and Loftus, 1975): Concepts are nodes in a directed graph whose edges are labeled with semantic relations between conceptual symbols (e.g., CAR − ISA → VEHICLE, CAR − HAS → WHEEL). **WordNet** is a semantic network in which lexical meanings are represented as synsets, groups of synonyms mutually linked by various types of relations, such as hypernymy, meronymy, antonymy, and so on (Miller and Fellbaum, 1991; Fellbaum, 1998). Figure 8.1 reports the WordNet hypernym hierarchy for the synset {*car, auto, automobile, machine, motorcar*}, corresponding to one of the senses of *car*. WordNet was originally developed for English, but then its model has been applied to several languages. Other examples of cross-lingual semantic networks are ConceptNet (Speer et al., 2017) and BabelNet (Navigli and Ponzetto, 2012).

While semantic networks mostly focus on the paradigmatic organization of the lexicon, other relational models characterize the meaning of lexical items in terms of the relations they have with lexemes co-occurring in the same

RELATIONAL MODELS

MEANING POSTULATES

SEMANTIC NETWORKS

WORDNET

{*car, auto, automobile, machine, motorcar*}
⇒ {motor vehicle, automotive vehicle}
⇒ {wheeled vehicle}
⇒ {vehicle}
⇒ {conveyance, transport}
⇒ {instrumentality, instrumentation}
⇒ {artifact, artefact}
⇒ {whole, unit}
⇒ {object, physical object}
⇒ {physical entity}
⇒ {entity}

Figure 8.1 WordNet hypernym hierarchy for one of the synsets of *car*

SEMANTIC ROLES

syntagmatic context. **Semantic (thematic) roles** represent the function played by an argument in the event or situation expressed by the predicate (Levin and Rappaport Hovav, 2005). Roles can be very general, such as the Proto-Agent and Proto-Patient in Dowty (1991), or specific to particular event types, like in FrameNet (Baker et al., 1998; Ruppenhofer et al., 2006), a computational lexicon built according to the principles of **Frame Semantics** (Fillmore, 1982; Croft and Cruse, 2004). In FrameNet, lexical meanings are represented with **semantic frames**, conceptual structures modeling situations in terms of sets of prototypical semantic roles called **frame elements**. For example, the meaning of *eat* is represented with the INGESTION frame formed by an INGESTOR that consumes INGESTIBLES (i.e., food or drink):

FRAME SEMANTICS

SEMANTIC FRAMES

FRAME ELEMENTS

(4)   [INGESTOR The dog] [INGESTION is eating] [INGESTIBLES a bone].

CATEGORICAL REPRESENTA-TIONS

Symbolic lexical representations are **categorical**, hence qualitative and discrete: A lexical item *has* or *does not have* a certain semantic property described by a structure of symbols. This is the reason why symbolic models strive to cope with the gradience of lexical meaning and cannot capture the varying degrees of feature prototypicality in concepts (Murphy, 2002; Boleda and Herbelot, 2016). Secondly, the basic elements of the metalanguage (e.g., the repertoire of primitive components) often lack principled selection criteria, and the lexical representations are typically hand-built on the grounds of experts' intuitions, thereby being possibly affected by a high degree of subjectivity.

AMODALITY

Thirdly, symbolic representations are **amodal**, as they do not natively encode any information in perceptual format (Barsalou, 1999). For instance, the symbolic features describing the meaning of *car* in (1a) are abstract entities that do not contain visual information about the shape and color of cars, auditory information characterizing their sound, and so on (Dove, 2016). Perceptual information can be represented only via its "translation" into other amodal symbols (e.g., the feature RED standing for the color red).

The major advantage of symbolic semantic representations is that they are **interpretable** and **explainable**. These notions are typically used to characterize computational models (Gilpin et al., 2018; Lipton, 2018): A model is interpretable if its structure can be described in such a way to be understandable by a human, and it is explainable if we can explain its behavior and performance. These same concepts also apply to the way meaning is represented.

INTERPRETABILITY
EXPLAINABILITY

> Semantic representations are **interpretable** if a human can inspect and understand the aspects of meaning they encode.
> Semantic representations are **explainable** if they can explain the semantic properties of linguistic expressions.

Both decompositional and relational symbolic models are interpretable because we can directly inspect the meaning properties encoded in their structures. For instance, the semantic component GO in (2) explicitly characterizes *enter* as a movement verb. Moreover, symbolic representations are designed to explain the semantic behavior of lexical items. The WordNet hypernym hierarchy of *car* in Figure 8.1 and the feature analysis in (1a) both account for the inference that *John bought a car* entails *John bought a vehicle*. Analogously, the representation in (3) is used in the Generative Lexicon to explain that the sentence *The man began the book* can mean that the man began reading the book (cf. Section 9.7.1), because the reading event is reconstructed from the noun Qualia Structure. Semantic similarity can also be explained by symbolic structures, in terms of feature overlap (Tversky, 1977) or distance in semantic networks (Budanitsky and Hirst, 2006).

In order to overcome the limits of categorical representations, it is particularly common in cognitive science to model word meanings with **semantic feature vectors** (Smith and Medin, 1981; McRae et al., 1997a).

SEMANTIC
FEATURE VECTORS

> The **semantic feature vector** of a lexical item l is a vector whose dimensions correspond to semantic features, and whose components measure the importance of each feature to characterize the meaning of l.

For instance, Binder et al. (2016) propose 65 cognitively-motivated features for which some specialized neural processor has been identified and described in the neuroscientific literature. These features cover sensory, motor, spatial, temporal, affective, social, and cognitive domains. Word meanings are then represented with 65-dimensional semantic feature vectors containing subjects' ratings of each feature salience (see Figure 8.2). The characterization of lexical meanings as regions in **conceptual spaces** by Gärdenfors (2000, 2014) is

CONCEPTUAL
SPACES

Word	VISION	BRIGHT	...	COGNITION	BENEFIT	HARM	PLEASANT
dog	5.35	1.10	...	0.35	3.58	2.81	3.93
love	0.79	0.48	...	4.52	4.93	1.76	5.48

Figure 8.2 Samples of semantic feature vectors from Binder et al. (2016)

also akin to semantic feature vectors. Conceptual spaces are defined as vector spaces whose dimensions are attributes of objects (e.g., colors are represented in a three-dimensional vector space defined by hue, brightness, and saturation).

Instead of a priori selected features, the dimensions of semantic vectors can correspond to verbal properties generated by native speakers to describe word meanings and collected in **feature (property) norms** (McRae et al., 2005b; Vinson and Vigliocco, 2008; Devereux et al., 2014; Chaigneau et al., 2020). Each feature is associated with a weight corresponding to the number of subjects that listed it for a given concept and is used to estimate its prominence for that concept. The following is a representation of *car* using a subset of its feature distribution from the norms in McRae et al. (2005b):

FEATURE NORMS

(5)

	a_vehicle	*has_four_wheels*	*is_fast*	*is_expensive*
car	9	18	9	11

CONTINUOUS REPRESENTA-TIONS INTERPRETABI-LITY EXPLAINABILITY AMODALITY

Semantic feature vectors are **continuous** representations. Therefore, they are more suited to account for the typicality, vagueness, and graded membership of semantic categories (Croft and Cruse, 2004; Hampton, 2007). On the other hand, like symbolic representations, they are **interpretable, explainable,** and **amodal**: Vector dimensions are explicitly labeled with features that provide explanatory factors of the semantic behavior of lexical items (e.g., *dog* and *cat* are very similar because they share their most salient features), but perceptual information is encoded with amodal symbols (e.g., basic features or linguistic properties), rather than natively in perceptual format.

DISTRIBUTED REPRESENTA-TIONS

A third and radically different approach to characterize lexical meaning adopts **distributed representations**.

> **Distributed representations** are vectors that encode information into distributed patterns of dimensions.

The typical examples of distributed vectors are those used by artificial neural networks, which represent word meanings with patterns of neural activations (Hinton et al., 1986; Jones et al., 2015). For instance, Rogers and McClelland (2004) propose a model of semantic memory in which concepts correspond to

Table 8.1 Major types of semantic representations with their key properties

	continuous	*interpretable*	*amodal*	*learnable*
symbolic representations		√	√	
semantic feature vectors	√	√	√	
distributed representations	√			√

distributed representations learned by a feed-forward neural network trained to learn object properties (e.g., robins can fly). Distributed vectors contrast with **localist** ones, in which each entity is instead represented with a distinct one-hot vector (cf. Chapter 6). Localist representations are de facto symbolic and categorical, since distinct entities are associated with vectors that do not have anything in common (i.e., they are orthogonal; cf. Mathematical note 3 in Section 2.5.1). Conversely, distributed representations are **continuous** vectors that represent similar entities with similar patterns of dimensions.   LOCALIST REP-RESENTATIONS   CONTINUOUS REPRESENTA-TIONS

Distributed vectors have some key properties that distinguish them from semantic feature ones and from symbolic representations. First of all, their dimensions are *not* directly **interpretable**, as argued by Rogers and McClelland: INTERPRETABILITY

> Psychologically meaningful "features" or "dimensions" may be represented in a distributed fashion across many units, with salient or important psychological distinctions leading to robust and widely dispersed differences between patterns of activation. As one simple example [...], the distinction between plant and animal in these networks is not carried by a single unit but is generally widely distributed and redundantly represented across many units. (Rogers and McClelland, 2004, p. 77)

Consequently, distributed representations are also *not* directly **explainable**. The similarity of the distributed vectors of *cat* and *dog* can account for their similar meanings, but the vector dimensions themselves do not explain which semantic properties (e.g., animacy) such similarity depends on. The lack of interpretability makes distributed vectors **"black box" representations** that can be understood only by observing their behavior in some external task, but whose content defies direct inspection. Secondly, distributed vectors can encode information coming from different kinds of sources, such as texts and images, and therefore they are (potentially) **multimodal**. Thirdly, distributed representations are **learnable** from empirical data by computational models.   EXPLAINABILITY   BLACK BOX REP-RESENTATIONS   MULTIMODALITY   LEARNABILITY

Table 8.1 summarizes the main characteristics of the semantic representations we have reviewed so far. What about distributional ones?

Distributional representations are a type of distributed representation.

DISTRIBUTED AND DISTRIBU- TIONAL

Importantly, the terms **distributed** and **distributional** must be kept well distinct: The former concerns the *way* information is encoded (i.e., with distributed patterns of vector dimensions), while the latter refers to the *source* of the information used to build the vectors (i.e., linguistic co-occurrences).

DISTRIBUTIONAL REPRESENTA- TIONS

Distributional representations inherit the properties of distributed vectors:

1. they are **continuous** and **learnable** from text corpora with DSMs;
2. they can integrate distributional data with information coming from other sources (e.g., images) to form **multimodal** representations (cf. Section 8.7);
3. they are *not* directly **interpretable**, since information is distributed across vector dimensions that cannot be labeled with specific semantic values.

The lack of semantic interpretability concerns all kinds of distributional vectors. The dimensions of dense embeddings are latent features extracted from data which do not have a clear and univocal interpretation. In the case of high-dimensional explicit vectors (cf. Section 2.4.1), the labels of their dimensions

HOLISTIC REP- RESENTATIONS

are linguistic contexts, and not semantic features. In fact, several scholars have argued that DSMs generate **holistic** representations, because the content of each word can exclusively be read off from its position relative to other elements in the semantic space, while the coordinates of such space lack any intrinsic semantic value (Landauer et al., 2007; Vigliocco and Vinson, 2007).

Distributional vectors represent a major departure from the way lexical meaning is investigated and characterized in traditional semantic approaches. How are they used to model human lexical competence? Which facets of meaning are they able to tackle? What are their current explanatory limits? These questions, and several others, are the topic of the next sections.

8.2 Word Senses

WORD SENSES

LEXICAL AMBIGUITY

Words can have multiple meanings or **senses**, a phenomenon called **lexical (semantic) ambiguity**.

> A word is **ambiguous** if it has more than one meaning.

Ambiguity is widespread in the lexicon: Over 80% of English words have more than one dictionary definition (Rodd, 2018), with the number of senses increasing along with their frequency. There are two major types of lexical ambiguity,

HOMONYMY AND POLYSEMY

homonymy and **polysemy**:[1]

---

[1] Another pervasive phenomenon is **vagueness**. A word is **vague** if it has an indeterminate meaning. For instance, the adjective *expensive* is vague because it is indeterminate with respect to the exact degree that counts as expensive for any given entity. Several facts support the claim

> A word is **homonymous** if its senses are distinct and unrelated.
> A word is **polysemous** if its senses are related.

An example of homonymy is the English noun *bat*, with its two unrelated animal (6a) and tool (6b) senses:

(6)   a.   There is a bat flying in my room.
        b.   The player hit the ball with the bat.

Actually, homonyms can be regarded as distinct lexemes that happen to share the same form. The noun *oak* is instead polysemous, as its senses – a type of tree (7a) or the material derived from it (7b) – are related:

(7)   a.   There is an oak in my garden.
        b.   This table is made of oak.

Several properties distinguish polysemy from homonymy (Murphy, 2010; Pustejovsky and Batiukova, 2019). The latter is idiosyncratic to specific words in a language (e.g., in Italian the two meanings of *bat* are expressed by different words, *pipistrello* and *mazza*), while polysemy is often preserved across languages (e.g., the Italian *quercia* has the same senses of its English equivalent *oak*) and can apply to whole classes of lexical items (e.g., the same sense pairs of *oak* also appear in other tree names, like *pine*, *chestnut*, etc.). When this occurs we talk about **regular polysemy**. Differently from homonymy, polysemy is therefore a productive and systematic phenomenon in the lexicon. REGULAR POLYSEMY

There are at least two major questions about lexical ambiguity: (i) how to identify and represent word senses? (ii) how to select the sense of a specific word instance in context? In symbolic models, ambiguity is represented *explicitly*. Lexemes are associated with a fixed sense inventory, manually specified by lexicographers, and each sense is encoded with a distinct symbol (e.g., in WordNet words have as many synsets as their meanings). Ambiguous lexemes are then **disambiguated** by selecting the appropriate sense in context. WORD SENSE DISAMBIGUA-TION

> **Word sense disambiguation (WSD)** is the task of determining which of a given number of senses a certain occurrence of a lexeme belongs to.

that vagueness is different from ambiguity (Pustejovsky and Batiukova, 2019). Vagueness is closely related to meaning creation in context (cf. Sections 9.1.1 and 9.6), which specifies vague expressions and generates determinate interpretations.

WSD has enjoyed great attention in NLP and is typically cast as a classification problem, where an occurrence of an ambiguous lexeme is to be labeled with one of a given number of possible senses defined in training data or in some sense inventory. The classification relies on contextual clues in order to determine which sense is appropriate. Most WSD approaches use some kind of machine learning algorithm, while the sense inventory is based on lexical resources like WordNet (Agirre and Edmonds, 2007; Navigli, 2009).

The major shortcoming of representing word senses with discrete symbols, is that their fuzzy and graded nature is not properly accounted for. In fact, "there are no decisive ways of identifying where one sense of a word ends and the next begins" (Kilgarriff, 2007, p. 29). Senses are not all equally distant: The figurative meaning of *cut* in *He cut the expenses* is close to its literal sense in *He cut the grass*, while homonyms like *bat* in (6) have radically different meanings. This fact is hard to capture with categorical representations. Moreover, sense distinctions in lexical resources are based on highly subjective decisions by lexicographers, whether to "lump" different uses of a word in the same sense, or "split" them into distinct meanings.

Distributional representations are a promising alternative to address the continuous nature of word senses. On the other hand, all the DSMs reviewed in

TYPE VECTOR

MEANING
CONFLATION
DEFICIENCY

Part II build a single vector per word type (i.e., a **type vector** cf. Section 2.4), which therefore encodes its various senses attested in the training corpus. The result is what Camacho-Collados and Pilehvar (2018) refer to as the **meaning conflation deficiency**: The inability of distributional vectors to distinguish word senses. This phenomenon is evident by looking at the top ten neighbors of the verb *play* (computed with SGNS trained on the BNC), ordered from left to right by decreasing cosine similarity with the target:

(8)   playing, game, play_N, audition, player, match, sing, star, coach, badminton

The proximal semantic space of *play* contains lexical items that refer to different senses of this verb: the sport/recreation sense (e.g., *game*, *match*, *badminton*) and the musical/performing sense (e.g., *sing*, *audition*, *star*). The frequency of a word sense in the training corpus affects the extent to which it is represented in a distributional vector, which will typically reflect the more dominant usage in the data (Arora et al., 2018).

WORD SENSE
INDUCTION

In this section, we review the main approaches to represent word senses with distributional semantics. Instead of hand-crafting them, word senses are discovered from corpus data in an unsupervised way, a task called **word sense induction** (Navigli, 2009; Camacho-Collados and Pilehvar, 2018).[2]

---

[2] Besides the purely distributional approaches to word sense discovery we review here, there are several "hybrid" solutions that combine corpus data with knowledge coming from lexical resources (Camacho-Collados and Pilehvar, 2018).

> **Word sense induction (WSI)** is the task of inducing the different meanings of a lexeme from its usages in text corpora.

The grounding assumption is that word senses "are to be construed as abstractions over clusters of word usages" (Kilgarriff, 1997, p. 108). This is implemented by aggregating distributional data into **sense clusters** representing word meanings, which now form a continuous rather than categorical space. Methods for word sense discovery have widespread applications in NLP (Navigli, 2009), are used to extend lexical resources, and are an important tool for linguists and lexicographers to study ambiguity in natural languages (Heylen et al., 2015). Polysemy and homonymy are typically treated alike, but interesting experiments to address regular polysemy and to analyze relatedness of word senses are proposed by Boleda et al. (2012b, 2012c), Beekhuizen et al. (2021), and Li and Joanisse (2021).   SENSE CLUSTERS

Models are evaluated for their ability to cluster corpus examples into groups corresponding to hand-annotated gold senses (WSI task), or to identify the correct sense of a specific word token by assigning it to the proper sense cluster (WSD task). The most common WSI and WSD benchmarks are those developed in the **SemEval** campaigns. Model evaluation also uses datasets of human similarity ratings between ambiguous words presented in context. The task of word similarity in context is described in more details in Section 9.6, which also addresses issues closely related to lexical polysemy, but from the perspective of the compositional mechanisms responsible for meaning modulation. On the other hand, distributional models of word senses aim at explicitly representing the repertoire of meanings of lexemes.   SEMEVAL

8.2.1 Senses as Clusters of Contexts

The context in which an ambiguous lexeme occurs is typically conducive to its meaning. For instance, the sense of *bat* in (6b) is made explicit by the co-occurring words *player*, *hit*, and *ball*. Based on this observation, an influential family of distributional models represents word senses as **clusters of similar contexts**. They start from collecting a set of contexts $\{c_1, \ldots, c_n\}$ of a lexeme l, consisting of sentences in which the tokens of l occur or word windows surrounding them. The contexts are represented as vectors $\{\mathbf{c_1}, \ldots \mathbf{c_n}\}$, called **context vectors**, which are then grouped into a predefined number of clusters on the basis of their similarity (see Figure 8.3). Each sense is represented by a **sense vector** or **sense embedding** corresponding to the **centroid** of a cluster.   CLUSTERS OF CONTEXTS   CONTEXT VECTORS   SENSE VECTOR   CENTROID

> The **centroid** of a set of vectors $C = \{\mathbf{u_1}, \ldots, \mathbf{u_n}\}$ is a vector $\mathbf{m}$ such that each component m_i is the average of the values for the ith component of the vectors in C.

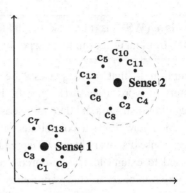

Figure 8.3 The small dots are the context vectors. The large dots are the sense vectors corresponding to the cluster centroids

MULTI-
PROTOTYPE
DSMs
Lexemes are associated with multiple sense vectors, each representing one of its prototypical usages. Therefore, these models are called **multi-prototype DSMs** (Reisinger and Mooney, 2010b), to distinguish them from traditional ones that represent lexical items with a single type vector conflating their different senses. When a new occurrence of an ambiguous lexeme is encountered, WSD is performed by generating a new context vector that is then assigned to the sense whose vector is most similar to it.

Originally introduced by Schütze (1997, 1998), multi-prototype DSMs have been developed by Purandare and Pedersen (2004), Pedersen (2010), Reisinger and Mooney (2010a, 2010b, 2011), and Huang et al. (2012), among several others. Models mainly differ for the method to construct the context vectors and the clustering algorithm. Schütze (1998) first generates type embeddings with a window-based count DSM and SVD, and then builds the context vectors by averaging the type embeddings of their items (cf. Section 9.2). These context vectors are clustered with the Buckshot algorithm (Cutting et al., 1992). Jurgens and Stevens (2010) adopt a similar method but with Random Indexing (cf. Section 5.3) type vectors to represent the context items and k-means clustering. Huang et al. (2012) cluster context vectors represented as averages of predict embeddings trained with a neural network. As an element of novelty, sense vectors are generated by training the same network on the corpus labeled with the cluster associated to each word occurrence.

TOKEN VECTOR
Instead of representing contexts as averages of type embeddings, Reisinger and Mooney (2010b) encode each word occurrence with a distinct **token vector**. These are window-based explicit vectors weighted with tf-idf, which are then grouped into sense clusters with the mixture of von Mises-Fisher

distributions algorithm. Chronis and Erk (2020) adopt a similar approach, but word tokens are represented with the **contextual embeddings** generated by the BERT neural language model (cf. Section 9.6.3), clustered with k-means.

CONTEXTUAL EMBEDDINGS

The above multi-prototype DSMs build sense embeddings in two steps (i.e., context vector generation and clustering), and the number of clusters is a pre-defined hyperparameter that is fixed for all lexical items. This assumption is problematic, as words differ for the number of senses. Neelakantan et al. (2014) instead introduce a multi-prototype variation of Skip-Gram (SGNS) that jointly learns the embeddings and the clusters (cf. Section 6.3). Moreover, the system is non-parametric, since the number of senses of each word is learned by the network. Other non-parametric joint models of sense vectors with SGNS are proposed by Li and Jurafsky (2015) and Bartunov et al. (2016).

Besides WSI and WSD, multi-prototype DSMs are also used to compute the semantic similarity of lexical items as a function of the similarity of their sense embeddings. Reisinger and Mooney (2010b) introduce the following two **multi-prototype similarity measures**:

MULTI-PROTOTYPE SIMILARITY MEASURES

$$\text{AvgSim}(l_1, l_2) = \frac{1}{N^2} \sum_{i=1}^{n} \sum_{j=1}^{n} \text{sim}(\mathbf{s_i}(\mathbf{l_1}), \mathbf{s_j}(\mathbf{l_2})) \qquad (8.1)$$

$$\text{MaxSim}(l_1, l_2) = \max_{1 \le i \le n, 1 \le j \le n} \text{sim}(\mathbf{s_i}(\mathbf{l_1}), \mathbf{s_j}(\mathbf{l_2})) \qquad (8.2)$$

where $\{\mathbf{s_1}(\mathbf{l_1}), \ldots, \mathbf{s_n}(\mathbf{l_1})\}$ and $\{\mathbf{s_1}(\mathbf{l_2}), \ldots, \mathbf{s_n}(\mathbf{l_2})\}$ are the sets of sense embeddings representing the lexemes l_1 and l_2. AvgSim computes word similarity as the average similarity of all pairs of sense vectors (i.e., l_1 and l_2 are similar if many of their senses are similar). Instead, MaxSim measures similarity as the maximum overall pairwise sense similarities (i.e., it only requires a single pair of senses to be close for the words to be judged similar). Multi-prototype models have been shown to be competitive with traditional DSMs on similarity and relatedness tasks (Reisinger and Mooney, 2010a; Neelakantan et al., 2014; Chronis and Erk, 2020), but Li and Jurafsky (2015) report much more variable performances on extrinsic tasks.

There have also been several attempts to discover word senses with **Topic Models** (cf. Section 4.4). Brody and Lapata (2009) use LDA with pseudo-documents defined as the context window surrounding each occurrence of ambiguous lexemes, and senses corresponding to induced topics. They assume that each lexeme l in a context c is generated by the following distribution:

TOPIC MODELS

$$p(l|c) = \sum_{z=1}^{k} p(l|z)p(z|c), \tag{8.3}$$

where $Z = \{z_1, \dots, z_k\}$ is a set of k senses (i.e., topics) of the ambiguous target. LDA infers a latent topic structure for each word, starting from a set of its contexts. This consists of a sense distribution for each context c, $\theta^{(c)} = p(z|c)$, and a representation of each sense z of the target as a probability distribution over words $\phi^{(z)} = p(l|z)$. Yao and Van Durme (2011) and Lau et al. (2012) replace LDA with a non-parametric Hierarchical Dirichlet Process, which avoids the problem of fixing the number of senses in advance. Arora et al. (2018) represent lexical items as linear combinations of sense vectors encoding latent "discourse atoms." These are reminiscent of topics, but they are learned from word embeddings with k-SVD sparse coding (Aharon et al., 2006).

8.2.2 Senses as Clusters of Neighbors

As (8) shows, the semantic space surrounding ambiguous words tends to be populated by lexemes related to their different senses. Another group of distributional methods exploits this fact to represent word senses as **clusters of similar neighbors**. This is illustrated in Figure 8.4, in which the embeddings of the 30 most similar words to the verb *play* have been analyzed with t-SNE (Van Der Maaten and Hinton, 2008), a statistical method for visualizing high-dimensional data in a two-dimensional map. The plot shows three main groups of highly similar neighbors, respectively related to the sport sense (left), the musical sense (right), and the acting sense (center-right) of *play*.

CLUSTERS OF
NEIGHBORS

First, a standard DSM is used to generate the k most similar words of a target lexical item l. The vectors of the neighbors of l are then fed into a clustering algorithm, and the resulting clusters are taken as a representation of the senses of l. An advantage of this solution is that the cluster elements are useful to identify the content of word senses (e.g., the musical sense of *play* in Figure 8.4 is made explicit by the neighbors *sing*, *piano*, etc.).

CBC

An influential implementation of this approach is the **Clustering by Committee (CBC)** model by Pantel and Lin (2002a), which can be described as a multi-step clustering procedure. The method is non-parametric, as the number of sense clusters is not defined a priori. In the first step, the top-k nearest neighbors of each lexeme are computed. The second phase recursively finds tight clusters called **committees**, and identifies items that are not covered by any committee (i.e., the elements whose similarity to the centroid of the committee

COMMITTEE

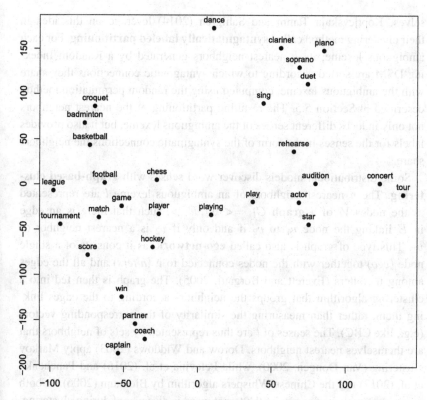

Figure 8.4 Two-dimensional t-SNE plot of the 30 nearest neighbors of the verb
play. The neighbors were computed with SGNS trained on the BNC

exceeds some predefined threshold). The algorithm then recursively attempts
to find more committees among the residue elements. For each new committee, its features are also removed from the distributional representation of the
lexeme. This last step ensures that the clusters do not become too similar, and
that clusters representing less frequent senses can be discovered. The output
of the CBC algorithm is the union of all committees found in each recursive step. Chatterjee and Mohan (2008) also use CBC with Random Indexing
distributional vectors as input to the algorithm.

Tomuro et al. (2007) argue that CBC may produce clusters that are themselves polysemous, which is not a desirable property of a WSI algorithm.
As a solution to this problem, they propose to cluster lexemes according to feature domain similarity, which refers to the similarity between the
contextual features of the lexical items, rather than between the items them-

selves. Koptjevskaja Tamm and Sahlgren (2014) leverage on this idea in their clustering method called **syntagmatically labeled partitioning**. For each ambiguous lexeme, its k nearest neighbors generated by a Random Indexing DSM are sorted according to which syntagmatic connections they share with the ambiguous lexeme, computed using the random permutation method described in Section 5.5. The resulting partitioning of the nearest neighbors not only induces different senses of the ambiguous lexeme, but it also provides labels for the senses in the form of the syntagmatic connections the neighbors share.

Some distributional models discover word senses with **graph-based clustering**. The n nearest neighbors of an ambiguous lexeme l are represented as the nodes V_l of a **graph** $G_l = < V_l, E >$, such that there is an edge in E linking the node v_1 to v_2 if and only if v_2 is a nearest neighbor of v_1. This type of graph is also called **ego-network**, as it consists of a single node (*ego*) together with the nodes connected to it (*alters*) and all the edges among the alters (Everett and Borgatti, 2005). The graph is then fed into a clustering algorithm that groups the neighbors according to the edges linking them, rather than measuring the similarity of the corresponding vectors (e.g., like CBC). The senses of l are thus represented by sets of neighbors that are themselves nearest neighbors. Dorow and Widdows (2003) apply Markov clustering (Van Dongen, 2000), while Pelevina et al. (2016) and Panchenko et al. (2017) use the Chinese Whispers algorithm by Biemann (2006). In both cases, the number of senses of the target word is discovered during clustering, and the only parameter is the number of neighbors selected as graph nodes

and to establish the edges. Instead of clustering **paradigmatic neighbors** (i.e., words whose distributional vectors are similar), other models start from a graph of **syntagmatic neighbors** (Véronis, 2004; Klapaftis and Manandhar, 2008; Reddy et al., 2011b; Di Marco and Navigli, 2013): The nodes are collocates of the target, and the edges link two nodes v_1 and v_2 if and only if they are also collocate. Senses are clusters of words co-occurring with the target, which themselves co-occur.

8.3 Paradigmatic Semantic Relations

A key aspect of the lexicon is that words are linked by different types of **semantic relations** (Murphy, 2003). Semantic networks like WordNet explicitly address this feature by modeling concepts with symbols connected by qualitative and discrete relations (cf. Section 8.1). On the other hand, DSMs represent the lexicon as a continuous space whose elements differ for the

Table 8.2 Nearest neighbors of the noun *car*, the adjective *good*, and the verb *buy*. The neighbors were generated with SGNS trained on the BNC

car	good	buy
van	excellent	sell
vehicle	bad	purchase
Mercedes	well	borrow
BMW	nice	secondhand
scooter	marvellous	lease
Escort	wonderful	own
truck	lousy	resell
Fiesta	terrific	rent
garage	jolly	invest
park	fine	auction

degree of their distributional similarity (e.g., measured with the cosine), but they do not distinguish the *type* of semantic relation between them. As illustrated in Table 8.2, the nearest neighbors produced by DSMs have multifarious relations with the target: *van* is a co-hyponym of *car*, but it is followed by an hypernym (*vehicle*), hyponyms (e.g., *Mercedes*), and other kinds of related lexemes (e.g., *garage*). The proximal space of the adjective *good* is populated with synonyms, intermingled with antonyms like *bad* and *lousy*. Similarly, the neighbors of the verb *buy* include both its antonym *sell* and the synonym *purchase*.

Their inability to discriminate between specific semantic relations is an important limit of DSMs and is often taken as evidence that they provide a coarse-grained representation of meaning, thereby lacking cognitive plausibility as models of the lexicon (Murphy, 2002). Knowing the meaning of *dog* entails recognizing not only that *animal* and *tail* are related to it, but also that the former is a broader term, while the latter is a meronym. Moreover, semantic relations have very different inferential properties (e.g., *Mary has a dog* entails *Mary has an animal*, but does not entail *Mary has a cat*), and confounding them has critical drawbacks both from a theoretical and an application perspective (e.g., in tasks like natural language inference or question-answering).

Intense research has been devoted to address these limits and develop distributional methods for **semantic relation detection**.

SEMANTIC RELATION DETECTION

> **Semantic relation detection** is the task of identifying the semantic relation between two lexemes on the basis of their distributional properties.

This task is closely related to the wider topic of semantic relation classification (cf. Section 7.2.5). Here, we focus on distributional methods specifically geared to detect hypernymy (Section 8.3.1) and antonymy (Section 8.3.2), which are two of the most important paradigmatic relations (cf. Section 7.1).

8.3.1 Hypernymy

HYPERNYMY

Hypernymy (also called **IS_A**) is a semantic relation between a general lexical item and a more specific one (Pustejovsky and Batiukova, 2019).[3]

> The lexeme l_1 is a **hypernym** of l_2 if and only if the meaning of l_2 is a subtype of the meaning of l_1. Symmetrically, l_2 is a **hyponym** of l_1.

A lexeme (e.g., *dog*) has a narrower meaning than its hypernym (e.g., *animal*) in two respects: (i) the category of entities denoted by the hypernym includes the one denoted by the hyponym (e.g., every dog is an animal); (ii) the concept expressed by the hyponym includes the properties of the broader hypernym, but has more specific properties than the latter (e.g., "being able to move" is a property of animals and therefore of dogs, but dogs have also the property of "barking" that distinguishes them from other types of animals). Therefore,

INCLUSION

hypernymy is an **inclusion** relation (Murphy, 2010) that is (i) **asymmetrical** (if l_1 is a hypernym of l_2, then l_2 is not a hypernym of l_1), differently from co-hyponymy (e.g., since they share the common hypernym *animal*, *dog* is a co-hyponym of *cat* and *cat* is a co-hyponym of *dog*); and (ii) **transitive** (if l_1 is a hypernym of l_2, and l_2 is a hypernym of l_3, then l_1 is a hypernym of l_3),

TAXONOMIC
HIERARCHIES

thus arranging lexical meanings into **taxonomic hierarchies**.

Given its properties, hypernymy licenses the following entailment relation: If l_1 is a hypernym of l_2, then the truth of *A is l_2* entails the truth of *A is l_1* (e.g., *Ferrari is a car* entails *Ferrari is a vehicle*). However, hypernymy is dis-

LEXICAL
ENTAILMENT

tinct from the more loosely defined notion of **lexical entailment** introduced by Zhitomirsky-Geffet and Dagan (2005, 2009) and Turney and Mohammad (2015) within the NLP task of recognizing textual entailments (cf. Section 9.5). Although hypernymy is one of the most important types of lexical entailment, the latter overlaps with several other relations (e.g., synonymy, meronymy, etc.). For example, Zhitomirsky-Geffet and Dagan (2009) claim that *government* lexically entails *minister*, because *The government voted for the new law* entails *A minister in the government voted for the new law*.

---

[3] Strictly speaking, hypernymy is a relation between word senses: *mammal* is a hypernym only of the animal sense of the ambiguous word *bat*.

Hypernymy is a key organizing principle of semantic memory, especially for nouns (Murphy, 2002). It is also the backbone of semantic networks like WordNet, and the entailments it licenses are central for several NLP and AI tasks. However, its identification is particularly difficult for distributional models. In fact, hypernyms are semantically broader than hyponyms, but they also share many attributes and, consequently, linguistic contexts, like co-hyponyms. Therefore, models are challenged to capture the attributional similarity of hypernymy pairs, and at the same to account for their asymmetrical character.

Several distributional methods have been proposed to address one or both of the following issues (Vulić et al., 2017b): (i) discriminating hypernymy from other paradigmatic semantic relations (**hypernymy detection**), and (ii) identifying the directionality (i.e., what is the hypernym and the hyponym) in a given hypernymy pair (**hypernymy prediction**). Models are typically evaluated on the relation datasets reviewed in Section 7.2.5 (e.g., BLESS, EVALution, etc.), or on benchmarks specifically targeting hypernymy, such as **LEDS** (Baroni et al., 2012), the Lexical Entailment Data Set consisting of 2, 770 noun pairs balanced between positive hypernymy examples and randomly shuffled negative pairs, and the very large dataset by Shwartz et al. (2016), formed by 70, 679 pairs collected from a mixture of WordNet, DBPedia, and other resources. The evaluation metrics are **average precision**, which measures a model's ability to rank highest hypernymy pairs, or **accuracy**, **precision**, and **recall** of relation and directionality classifiers. Vulić et al. (2017b) introduce the harder task of **graded entailment** on the HyperLex dataset: Models are evaluated with the **Spearman correlation** with human ratings quantifying the degree of the hypernymy relation between a pair of lexemes.

HYPERNYMY DETECTION

HYPERNYMY PREDICTION

LEDS

EVALUATION METRICS

GRADED ENTAILMENT

Pattern-based Models

These methods exploit the lexico-syntactic patterns linking candidate pairs and represent the first generation of distributional models of hypernymy:

PATTERN-BASED APPROACHES

> **Pattern-based approaches** use the **lexico-syntactic patterns** connecting l_1 and l_2 in the corpus to detect whether $\langle l_1, l_2 \rangle$ is a hypernymy pair.

The method was introduced by Hearst (1992), who identifies a small set of lexico-syntactic patterns (commonly referred to as **Hearst patterns**; cf. Section 4.2) that indicate hypernymy/hyponymy relations (e.g., *such* NP_1 *as* NP_2). Instead of using hand-selected patterns, Snow et al. (2004) start with a set of seed hypernymy pairs $\langle l_i, l_j \rangle$ from WordNet, which are used to automatically

HEARST PATTERNS

identify all the dependency paths linking l_i and l_j in a parsed corpus. Similarly to LRA (Turney, 2006b), candidate lexical pairs are represented with vectors whose components contain their co-occurrence frequency with the selected patterns. A logistic regression classifier is then trained on these vectors to predict whether a given pair is an instance of hypernymy. Pattern-based approaches are typically hampered by data sparseness, since the patterns that are strongly indicative of hypernymy are rare in corpora or occur in several variants, thus negatively affecting the recall of these methods. A way to mitigate this problem is to generalize the patterns harvested from corpora by replacing lexical items with wild cards and POS tags (Shwartz et al., 2016).

Several refinements have been proposed to improve pattern-based methods, which remain a very popular and effective approach. For instance, Roller et al. (2018) use PPMI to estimate the pattern salience and apply SVD to smooth the problems produced by data sparseness, thereby obtaining a significant performance increase. Similarly, Schulte im Walde (2020) shows that supervised models using vectors of lexico-syntactic patterns are able to outperform simple combinations of window-based vectors.

Vector-based Models

A second family of methods identifies hypernymy from the distributional vector of lexemes, rather than from the patterns linking them:[4]

VECTOR-BASED
APPROACHES

> **Vector-based approaches** use the distributional vectors of l_1 and l_2 to detect whether $\langle l_1, l_2 \rangle$ is a hypernymy pair.

UNSUPERVISED
MODELS

Unsupervised models compute a hypernymy score between distributional vectors, which is expected to be higher for hypernymy pairs than for negative instances. The general assumption is that the standard vector similarity measures used by DSMs are not suitable for hypernymy detection, because they are symmetrical (cf. Section 2.6). In fact, Schulte im Walde (2020) shows that the various paradigmatic relations of a target word tend to have very similar cosine values, as also illustrated by the examples in Table 8.2.

DIRECTIONAL
SIMILARITY
MEASURES

One approach consists in defining **directional similarity measures** that are asymmetrical and are optimized for hypernymy detection. They are based on variations of the **Distributional Inclusion Hypothesis** (DIH), originally proposed by Zhitomirsky-Geffet and Dagan (2005) for lexical entailment, but

DISTRIBUTIONAL
INCLUSION
HYPOTHESIS

applied to hypernymy as well:

---

4 Shwartz et al. (2016) call these methods "distributional." However, the name "vector-based" is more appropriate to characterize their specific character, as strictly speaking lexico-syntactic patterns are also distributional information.

$$\text{WeedsPrec}(\mathbf{u}, \mathbf{v}) = \frac{\sum_{i \in C_u^+ \cap C_v^+} w_{u,c_i}}{\sum_{i \in C_u^+} w_{u,c_i}} \qquad \text{Weeds et al. (2004)}$$

$$\text{CL}(\mathbf{u}, \mathbf{v}) = \frac{\sum_{f \in C_u^+ \cap C_v^+} min(w_{u,c_i}, w_{v,c_i})}{\sum_{i \in C_u^+} w_{u,c_i}} \qquad \text{Clarke (2009)}$$

$$\text{APinc}(\mathbf{u}, \mathbf{v}) = \frac{\sum_{r=1}^{|C_u^+|} P(r) rel'(u_r)}{|C_u^+|} \qquad \text{Kotlerman et al. (2010)}$$

$$\text{invCL}(\mathbf{u}, \mathbf{v}) = \sqrt{\text{CL}(\mathbf{u}, \mathbf{v})(1 - \text{CL}(\mathbf{v}, \mathbf{u}))} \qquad \text{Lenci and Benotto (2012)}$$

Figure 8.5 Directional similarity measures based on the DIH

> If the lexeme l_1 is semantically narrower than l_2, then a significant number of salient contexts of l_1 is included in the vector of l_2.

The DIH is an attempt to recast in distributional terms the *extensional* definition of the asymmetric character of hypernymy: Since the class of entities denoted by a hyponym (i.e., its extension; cf. Section 9.1) is included in the class denoted by the hypernym, hyponyms are expected to occur in a subset of the contexts of their hypernyms.

Figure 8.5 reports some of the most common directional similarity measures based on the DIH: $\mathbf{u} = (w_{u,c_1}, \ldots, w_{u,c_n})$ and $\mathbf{v} = (w_{v,c_1}, \ldots, w_{v,c_n})$ are respectively the explicit vectors of a narrow and broader lexeme, whose components are weighted distributional features (i.e., linguistic contexts, typically window-based or syntactic collocates); C_u^+ and C_v^+ are the sets of the "active contexts" of the two terms, corresponding to those with a weight greater than zero (according to any of the weighting functions in Section 2.3.1). These measures are asymmetrical and range between zero and one: The higher the value, the more $\mathbf{v}$ is semantically broader than $\mathbf{u}$. **WeedsPrec** (Weeds et al., 2004) WEEDSPREC and its close relative **CL** (Clarke, 2009) measure the weighted inclusion of the CL contexts of the narrow term $\mathbf{u}$ within the contexts of the broader term $\mathbf{v}$. This is akin to the precision measure in information retrieval, which estimates the amount of retrieved documents (i.e., the features of $\mathbf{u}$) that are relevant (i.e., included in the features of $\mathbf{v}$). Similarly, **APinc** (Kotlerman et al., 2010) is a APINC modification of the average precision measure (cf. Section 7.2.5) and considers the rank r of the features sorted in descending order according to their weight. APinc computes precision $P(r)$ at every rank r among the feature of $\mathbf{u}$ (u_r is the feature of $\mathbf{u}$ of rank r), weighting it by the rank of the same feature in the broader term, $rel'(u_r)$. Therefore, APinc measures to what extent the top-ranked contexts of $\mathbf{u}$ appear among the top-ranked contexts of $\mathbf{v}$. The **invCL** INVCL measure (Lenci and Benotto, 2012) uses CL to compute both the distributional inclusion of **u** in **v** and distributional *non-inclusion* of **v** in **u**, given the hypothesis that, if *animal* is semantically broader than *dog*, then it is also expected to be found in contexts of other animals besides *dog*.

SEMANTIC
GENERALITY
Other unsupervised distributional models depart from the DIH and pursue an *intensional* approach to hypernymy that targets the notion of **semantic generality** (Herbelot and Ganesalingam, 2013; Rimell, 2014; Santus et al., 2014a). The starting observation is that the DIH is not fully correct, as the typical contexts of a hyponym are not necessarily salient contexts of its hypernym: for instance, *gallop* is a very frequent context for *horse* in ukWaC, but its co-occurrence frequency with *animal* is extremely low, since galloping is not a typical attribute of all animals (Pannitto et al., 2018). A key feature of hypernymy is rather that the properties of the concept (i.e., its intension) expressed by the broader term are semantically more *general* (e.g., *move* for *animal*) than the ones of the concept expressed by its narrower terms (e.g., *gallop* or *has a mane* for *horse*). This corresponds to the idea that the properties of superordinate terms like *animal* are less informative than those of their hyponyms, like *dog* or *horse* (Murphy, 2002).

INFORMA
TIVENESS
Santus et al. (2014a) propose the following distributional interpretation of the notion of semantic generality:

> If the lexeme l_1 is semantically narrower than l_2, then the most typical contexts of l_2 are less **informative** than the most typical contexts of l_1.

SLQS
Using entropy as an estimate of context informativeness (cf. Section 2.3.1), Santus et al. (2014a) introduce **SLQS** to measure the semantic generality of a word with the entropy of its statistically most prominent contexts. Given a DSM that generates explicit vectors for a set of target lexemes T, Santus et al. (2014a) select the k most salient contexts of a lexeme l from the vector features with the highest association weight (e.g., LMI; cf. Section 2.3.1). Then, the entropy of a selected context c, $H(c)$, is defined as:

$$H(c) = -\sum_{i=1}^{n} p(l_i|c) \log_2 p(l_i|c), \qquad (8.4)$$

where $p(l|c)$ is the probability of l given the context c, computed as the ratio between the co-occurrence frequency $F(l, c)$ and the total frequency of c. For each lexeme l, E_l is the median entropy of its k top contexts. This is assumed as a semantic generality index for l: The higher E_l, the more semantically general l is, because its most typical contexts tend to have a higher entropy (i.e., to co-occur with several lexemes). Finally, SLQS is defined as the reciprocal difference between the semantic generality of two lexemes l_1 and l_2:

$$\text{SLQS}(l_1, l_2) = 1 - \frac{E_{l_1}}{E_{l_2}}. \tag{8.5}$$

SLQS is asymmetrical by design and Santus et al. (2014a) apply it to hypernym prediction and detection, under the assumption that $\text{SLQS}(l_1, l_2) > 0$ implies that l_1 is semantically narrower than l_2. In a related vein, Kiela et al. (2015a) introduce an index for hypernymy based on the notion of **visual semantic generality** and computed with multimodal vectors (cf. Section 8.7). The intuition is that the images of entities denoted by the broader term *animal* represent different kinds of animals, and are therefore expected to exhibit greater visual variability than the images of subordinate lexemes such as *dog*. VISUAL SEMANTIC GENERALITY

A common attribute of the above unsupervised measures is that they presuppose explicit count vectors, because they use linguistics contexts as features to identify hypernymy pairs. The advent of predict DSMs and the fortune of word embeddings have boosted vector-based approaches based on **supervised methods** relying on a training set of hypernymy pairs. Each pair $\langle l_1, l_2 \rangle$ is represented as a **combination of the vectors** of the hyponym l_1 and the hypernym l_2, which is then fed into the classifier: concatenation $\mathbf{l_1}; \mathbf{l_2}$ (Baroni et al., 2012), difference $\mathbf{l_2} - \mathbf{l_1}$ (Roller et al., 2014; Weeds et al., 2014), element wise multiplication $\mathbf{l_1} \odot \mathbf{l_2}$ (Weeds et al., 2014; cf. Section 9.2), or more complex combinations thereof (Vu and Shwartz, 2018). Interestingly, Roller et al. (2014) observe that the vector difference is analogous to a supervised version of the DIH: The difference between two vectors on a particular dimension captures the degree of distributional inclusion on that dimension. On the other hand, Levy et al. (2015a) notice that classifiers trained on vector concatenation tend to learn features that correspond to the most common Hearst patterns. Roller and Erk (2016) rely on this fact and propose a method similar to PCA to automatically detect Hearst-like features in the hyperplane vector learned by a Linear SVM classifier.[5] These meta-features are in turn used for supervised hypernymy detection. Shwartz et al. (2016) explicitly integrate lexico-syntactic patterns into a vector-based supervised setting. The syntactic paths linking l_1 and l_2 are collected with the method by Snow et al. (2004) and are encoded as vectors with a LSTM (cf. Section 9.4.3). Each $\langle l_1, l_2 \rangle$ pair is then represented as the weighted-average of its path vectors, $\mathbf{v_{\text{paths}(l_1, l_2)}}$. The classifier uses as features the concatenated vector $\mathbf{l_1}; \mathbf{v_{\text{paths}(l_1, l_2)}}; \mathbf{l_2}$. SUPERVISED METHODS VECTOR COMBINATION

Supervised models of hypernymy are generally reported to achieve better performances than unsupervised ones (Shwartz et al., 2017; Vulić et al., 2017b). However, Levy et al. (2015a) show that supervised methods tend to

---

[5] Linear classifiers like Logistic Regression or Linear SVM learn a decision hyperplane represented by a vector **p**. Data points are then classfied by comparing their vectors to **p** with the dot product.

carry out a sort of **lexical memorization**: Given a pair $\langle l_1, l_2 \rangle$, they mostly learn whether l_2 is a prototypical hypernym or not, rather than learning the relation between the two lexemes. For instance, if the training set contains pairs such as $\langle dog, animal \rangle$ and $\langle horse, animal \rangle$, the algorithm may learn that *animal* is a prototypical hypernym, classifying any new $\langle l, animal \rangle$ pair as positive, regardless of the relation between the lexeme l and *animal*. Therefore, Levy et al. (2015a) propose a **lexical split** of the train and test sets, such that each will contain a distinct vocabulary, in order to prevent the model from overfitting by lexical memorization. When supervised models are evaluated with a lexical split setting, their performance indeed drastically drops. This suggests that word embeddings do contain some signal relevant to hypernym detection, but this is not enough to capture the truly relational properties of a given pair. The addition of Hearst patterns by Shwartz et al. (2016) is a way to smooth this problem. Among unsupervised methods, generality measures like SLQS tend to outperform the inclusion ones, which according to Bott et al. (2021) have a frequency bias, as they strongly correlate with a simple baseline measure that assumes hypernyms to be more frequent than their hyponyms.

Shwartz et al. (2017) observe that there is no single measure or vector combination that is able to discriminate hypernymy from all other semantic relations and Vulić et al. (2017b) claim that graded entailment adds a further level of difficulty for all models, whose performance is very distant from human ones. Even the latest contextual DSMs like BERT (cf. Section 9.6.3) have a very brittle and limited capability of identifying hypernyms, and they do not possess a truly general and systematic knowledge of such semantic relation (Ravichander et al., 2020; Hanna and Mareček, 2021). Overall, this shows that capturing hypernymy is still a challenging issue for distributional semantics.

Hypernymy-Specific Embeddings

Some distributional models of hypernymy leverage information coming from lexical resources like WordNet. This approach is called **semantic specializa-
tion**, since the goal is to obtain embeddings that are specialized to represent a certain semantic relation, such as hypernymy. There are two major kinds of specialization: (i) refining pretrained vectors with lexical knowledge, and (ii) training embeddings by combining corpus data and lexical constraints.

The most common example of the former type is **retrofitting** (Faruqui et al., 2015), which moves closer in the semantic space the pretrained embeddings of lexemes that are connected via a specific relation in a given semantic network. Kiela et al. (2015c) apply this method to specialize distributional vectors for either attributional similarity or semantic relatedness. Vulić and Mrkšić (2018)
and Kamath et al. (2019) propose **LEAR** to specialize word embeddings

for hypernymy, by extending the ATTRACT-REPEL retrofitting algorithm by Mrkšić et al. (2017) (cf. Section 8.3.2). LEAR fine-tunes embeddings with a network that is trained to minimize the loss functions in Equations 8.6–8.8, corresponding to the following three objectives: (i) bringing closer the vectors of the set B_A of synonyms and hyponym–hypernym pairs (*Att*); (ii) pushing apart vectors of the set B_R of antonymy pairs (*Rep*); (iii) making the hypernym vector $\mathbf{l_2}$ longer (i.e., with a larger norm; cf. Mathematical note 2 in Section 2.4) than the hyponym vector $\mathbf{l_1}$ in the set of hyponym-hypernym pairs B_L (*LE*):

$$Att(B_A, T_A) = \sum_{i=1}^{k} [\max(0, \delta_{Att} + \mathrm{sim}_{\cos}(\mathbf{l_1^i}, \mathbf{t_1^i}) - \mathrm{sim}_{\cos}(\mathbf{l_1^i}, \mathbf{l_2^i})) \qquad (8.6)$$
$$+ \max(0, \delta_{Att} + \mathrm{sim}_{\cos}(\mathbf{l_2^i}, \mathbf{t_2^i}) - \mathrm{sim}_{\cos}(\mathbf{l_1^i}, \mathbf{l_2^i}))]$$

$$Rep(B_R, T_R) = \sum_{i=1}^{k} [\max(0, \delta_{Rep} + \mathrm{sim}_{\cos}(\mathbf{l_1^i}, \mathbf{l_2^i}) - \mathrm{sim}_{\cos}(\mathbf{l_1^i}, \mathbf{t_1^i})) \qquad (8.7)$$
$$+ \max(0, \delta_{Rep} + \mathrm{sim}_{\cos}(\mathbf{l_1^i}, \mathbf{l_2^i}) - \mathrm{sim}_{\cos}(\mathbf{l_2^i}, \mathbf{t_2^i}))]$$

$$LE(B_L, T_L) = \sum_{i=1}^{k} \frac{||\mathbf{l_1^i}|| - ||\mathbf{l_2^i}||}{||\mathbf{l_1^i}|| + ||\mathbf{l_2^i}||} \qquad (8.8)$$

where the set B_A, B_R, and B_L contain k pairs $\langle l_1, l_2 \rangle$ that are positive instances of the semantic relations extracted from WordNet, and T_A, T_R, and T_L contain lexical pairs $\langle t_1, t_2 \rangle$ that are negative instances. Equations 8.6 and 8.7 are **margin loss** functions (cf. Section 6.1), and δ is the cosine similarity ᴍᴀʀɢɪɴ ʟᴏss margin required between the negative and positive vector pairs. In summary, the LEAR network generates hypernymy-specific embeddings by changing pretrained vectors to increase the similarity between the hypernym and the hyponym, like with synonyms, and the length of the hypernym vector, to capture the asymmetric character of the relation. The specialized embeddings of a candidate lexeme pair $\langle l_1, l_2 \rangle$ are then used in the following hypernymy measure:

$$I_{LE}(l_1, l_2) = \mathrm{sim}_{\cos}(\mathbf{l_1}, \mathbf{l_2}) + \frac{||\mathbf{l_1}|| - ||\mathbf{l_2}||}{||\mathbf{l_1}|| + ||\mathbf{l_2}||}, \qquad (8.9)$$

where the second term corresponds to the *LE* loss function in Equation 8.8. This unsupervised measure assumes hypernyms to be highly similar to their hyponyms, like synonyms, but also semantically broader. Arora et al. (2020) adopt an approach related to LEAR, which carves the vector space into several relation-specific subspaces.

Other models directly inject lexical constraints into the training objective of networks that generate hypernymy-specific vectors from scratch. Tuan et al. (2016) propose a network that works like Skip-Gram, but with the objective function of predicting the hypernym from an input hyponym and its context:

$$O = \frac{1}{T} \sum_{i=1}^{T} \log p(hype_i | hypo_i, l_i^1, \ldots, l_i^n), \quad (8.10)$$

where T is the set of training tuples consisting of a hypernym ($hype$), a hyponym ($hypo$), and a set of context lexemes $\{l^1, \ldots, l^n\}$ of the latter, which are expected to provide pattern-like information to identify the hypernym. Nguyen et al. (2017) extend the training objective of SGNS in a way inspired by the DIH, to increase the similarity of hyponyms and hypernyms sharing a certain

HYPERSCORE   context. The resulting embeddings are then used in the **HyperScore** measure:

$$\text{HyperScore}(l_1, l_2) = \text{sim}_{\cos}(\mathbf{l_1}, \mathbf{l_2}) \frac{||\mathbf{l_2}||}{||\mathbf{l_1}||}. \quad (8.11)$$

Like LEAR, HyperScore assumes that the broader nature of hypernyms is reflected in their larger vector norm.

The knowledge coming from lexical resources allows specialized embeddings, in particular retrofitted ones, to outperform standard distributional vectors, when they are used for hypernymy detection and prediction, as well as for graded entailment (Vulić and Mrkšić, 2018).

8.3.2 Antonymy

ANTONYMY   **Antonymy** is a relation of oppositeness (Pustejovsky and Batiukova, 2019).

> The lexeme l_1 is an **antonym** of l_2 if and only if the meaning of l_1 is the opposite of the meaning of l_2.

If hypernymy is the core relation for nouns, antonymy is crucial to characterize the meaning of adjectives (e.g., *big – small*). According to Deese (1965), antonymous adjectives are strongly associated in the mental lexicon. However, antonymy also applies to nouns (e.g., *life – death*) and verbs (e.g., *buy – sell*).

CONTRARY AND   The philosophical and linguistic literature has identified various subtypes of
CONTRADIC-   antonymy (Murphy, 2003, 2010). One major distinction is between **contrary**
TORY   and **contradictory** (or **complementary**) antonyms. The former are pairs like
ANTONYMS   *tall* and *small*, such that the assertion of one entails the negation of the other,

but the negation of one does not entail the assertion of the other (e.g., *Mary is tall* → *Mary is not small*, but *Mary is not tall* ↛ *Mary is small*). These are also called **scalar** or **gradable** antonyms, because they correspond to the extremes of a continuous scale (e.g., height) that has also intermediate values (e.g., somebody can be neither tall nor small).[6] Contradictory antonyms like *dead* and *alive* instead express a binary opposition, and thus the assertion of one entails the negation of the other and vice versa (e.g., *John is alive* → *John is not dead* and *John is not alive* → *John is dead*). Another widely studied notion, especially in cognitive linguistics, is the one of **canonicity** (Paradis et al., 2009; Paradis and Willners, 2011; Van de Weijer et al., 2014), which refers to the extent to which an antonymy pair is highly conventionalized to express opposition along a certain dimension. For instance, in the speed domain, the canonical pair *slow* and *fast* is perceived by speakers to be a more prototypical instance of antonymy than *slow* and *rapid*.

SCALAR ANTONYMS

CANONICITY

Cruse (1986) claims that antonyms are characterized by the **paradox of simultaneous difference and similarity**: They are identical in every dimension of meaning except for one, along which they occupy the opposing poles. As a consequence of this property, antonyms are expected to occur in similar contexts: For example, cars can be *fast* or *slow*, and temperature can *increase* and *decrease*. As noted by Miller and Charles (1991), this makes antonymy a potential conundrum for distributional semantics. Since the Distributional Hypothesis assumes that semantic similarity correlates with context similarity, it predicts that antonyms are very close in the semantic space, without capturing the opposition they express. In fact, Mohammad et al. (2013) show that synonyms and antonyms are indistinguishable in terms of their average degree of distributional similarity, as also illustrated by the nearest neighbors of *buy* and *good* in Table 8.2. This is theoretically unsatisfactory and hampers the effectiveness of word vectors in applications (e.g., sentiment analysis, where it is essential not to conflate positive and negative lexemes; cf. Section 8.5.1).

PARADOX OF SIMULTANEOUS DIFFERENCE AND SIMILARITY

Differently from hypernymy, purely distributional methods for **antonymy detection** (i.e., the task of discriminating antonyms from synonyms and semantically similar lexemes) are scarce. Several models adopt a **pattern-based approach**. Charles and Miller (1989) argue that the strong association in the mental lexicon between antonymous adjectives depends on their frequently occurring together, and propose the **Co-occurrence Hypothesis**:

ANTONYMY DETECTION

PATTERN-BASED APPROACH

---

[6] Cruse (1986) reserves the term antonymy for gradable adjectives only. Mohammad et al. (2013) employ the terms **opposites** and **contrastive word pairs** to refer to lexemes that are *strongly* opposing, versus lexemes that are opposing *to some degree*. Here we use antonymy to refer to *any* pair of lexemes that have opposing meanings.

> Two adjectives are learned as antonyms because they occur together in the same sentences more frequently than chance would allow.

CO-OCCURRENCE HYPOTHESIS

This hypothesis finds empirical confirmation in the corpus analyses by Justeson and Katz (1991), Fellbaum (1995), who extends it to nouns and verbs too, and Paradis et al. (2009), who find the Co-occurrence Hypothesis to hold particularly for canonical adjectives. Moreover, Justeson and Katz (1991) and Fellbaum (1995) show that antonyms not only have a strong syntagmatic association, but they also tend to co-occur in specific patterns, like *from X to Y* or *either X or Y*. These two patterns are used by Lin et al. (2003) for the automatic

PAIRCLASS

discrimination of antonyms from synonyms, while the **PairClass** method by Turney (2008b) extends the LRA framework (cf. Section 4.2) to automatically generate patterns that are fed into a supervised antonymy classifier.

VECTOR-BASED METHODS

The fact that standard DSMs systematically confound lexemes with similar and opposite meanings is prima facie an argument against **vector-based methods** for antonymy detection. However, Scheible et al. (2013) report that a simple window-based DSM can successfully discriminate antonymous from synonymous adjectives with a decision tree classifier, *if the proper linguistic contexts* are selected to generate the distributional vectors. The best results are obtained with vectors of verbal collocates, while poor discrimination is achieved with nouns. In fact, although both synonymous and antonymous adjectives can co-occur with similar nouns, more differences exist with respect to the verbs associated with them. For instance, *happy* is likely to be found with verbs like *laugh* or *smile*, while *sad* with verbs like *moan* or *cry*. This is consistent with the behavioral findings by Charles and Miller (1989) that subjects tend to associate antonymous adjectives with different sentential contexts. The large array of experiments in Schulte im Walde (2020) confirms the possibility of discriminating adjectival, nominal, and verbal antonyms with a supervised classifier applied to distributional vectors, and that performance greatly varies depending on the type of contexts and on the POS of the target lexemes (e.g., vectors with lexico-syntactic patterns are particularly effective to discriminate verbal antonyms). One of the few unsupervised measures for antonymy

APANT

detection is **APAnt** by Santus et al. (2014b), which uses average precision to estimate the extent and salience of the intersection among the most important contexts of two target words, under the assumption that antonyms should share a smaller number of contexts than synonyms. This measure is quite effective with nominal antonyms, but much less so with adjectival ones. Overall, these results show that the prediction that vector-based models based on the Distributional Hypothesis are not able to distinguish antonyms because of their alleged context similarity is not totally borne out. The linguistic contexts of antonyms can provide useful signals for their detection, although the picture is highly complex and variable. Much research is still needed to identify the most important distributional clues for this semantic relation.

Several methods for antonymy detection combine corpus data with information extracted from lexical resources. In Mohammad et al. (2013), lexical pairs that occur in the same thesaurus category are assumed to be synonyms, while those occurring in contrasting categories are marked as opposites. Following the Co-occurrence Hypothesis, the PMI of a given pair is then used to estimate its degree of contrast. A much more common way to leverage lexical knowledge is to **specialize** embeddings for antonymy. Yih et al. (2012) introduce a variant of LSA called **Polarity Inducing LSA**, in which the documents in the co-occurrence matrix correspond to entries in a thesaurus (e.g., Word-Net synsets). The matrix entries are weighted with tf-idf, and the antonyms in the thesaurus receive a negative tf-idf weight. Therefore, after applying SVD, synonyms and antonyms tend to occur in opposite regions of the semantic space.

SEMANTIC SPECIALIZATION

POLARITY INDUCING LSA

Both Ono et al. (2015) and Pham et al. (2015a) propose variations of SGNS to train antonymy-specific embeddings. The latter work adds to the standard training objective of SGNS the following **lexical contrast objective**:

LEXICAL CONTRAST OBJECTIVE

$$J_{LC}(t) = - \sum_{s \in S, a \in A} [\max(0, \delta - \text{sim}_{\cos}(\mathbf{t}, \mathbf{s}) + \text{sim}_{\cos}(\mathbf{t}, \mathbf{a}))], \qquad (8.12)$$

where S and A are respectively a set of synonyms and antonyms of the target lexeme t extracted from WordNet. This training objective is based on the margin loss (cf. Section 6.1) and tries to maximize the constraint that contrasting pairs should have lower similarity than synonymous ones by a margin δ. Pham et al. (2015a) show that the specialized embeddings outperform standard SGNS ones both in antonymy detection and in semantic similarity tasks, because they better separate similar and contrasting lexemes.

Antonymy-specific embeddings are also created with retrofitting methods. **ATTRACT-REPEL** (Mrkšić et al., 2017) and its close relative **counterfitting** (Mrkšić et al., 2016) refine pretrained embeddings with a network trained with the *Att* and *Rep* loss functions in Equation 8.6 and Equation 8.7, which try to increase the similarity between synonyms and decrease the one between antonyms (*Rep* is in fact very similar to the J_{LC} objective). The model by Arora et al. (2020) is also applied to specialize embeddings for antonymy.

ATTRACT-REPEL

The research in distributional semantics on antonymy has mostly focused on distinguishing it from synonymy. However, there are several aspects of antonymy that remain little explored and understood. One is the characterization of the different properties on gradable and complementary antonyms

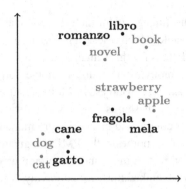

Figure 8.6 A bilingual semantic space containing the distributional vectors of Italian (black) and English (gray) lexemes

NEGATION

(Kim and de Marneffe, 2013), another is the crucial link between antonymy and **negation**. It is not enough to separate *dead* and *alive* in the vector space, it is also necessary to explain that being *dead* entails *not* being *alive*. To what extent distributional models are able to provide a satisfactory account of such phenomena is still largely an open issue.

8.4 Cross-Lingual DSMs

CROSS-LINGUAL
DSMs

Understanding and representing how the meaning of a word is expressed across languages is a central question in linguistics and NLP. **Cross-lingual DSMs** pursue such a goal by generating semantic spaces containing the distributional vectors of lexical items of multiple languages. These representations are called **cross-lingual embeddings** (Ruder et al., 2019).

CROSS-LINGUAL
EMBEDDINGS

> **Cross-lingual embeddings** are distributional representations of words from several languages in the same vector space.

MONOLINGUAL
AND
CROSS-LINGUAL
OBJECTIVES

Figure 8.6 shows an example of an Italian-English semantic space. Cross-lingual DSMs have a twofold learning objective: (i) representing the similarity relations in each language (**monolingual objective**), and (ii) placing each word in a language near its translation in the other language (**cross-lingual objective**). Given $l^{(S)}$ a lexeme in a source language S, its translation in the target language T, $tr(l^{(S)})$, is its nearest neighbor lexeme in T:

$$tr(l^{(S)}) = \underset{l^{(T)} \in V^{(T)}}{\mathrm{argmax}} \left(\mathrm{sim}(\mathbf{l^{(S)}}, \mathbf{l^{(T)}}) \right), \qquad (8.13)$$

where $V^{(T)}$ is the set of lexemes of T in the cross-lingual DSM. Cross-lingual embeddings can be used to compare the organization of semantic spaces across languages (e.g., to study how the same concepts are expressed in different languages, and vice versa the differences in the polysemy patterns). They also have several applications in NLP for **cross-lingual transfer learning**, which aims at applying models developed for a language with ample training resources, to solve tasks (e.g., parsing) in another low-resourced language.

CROSS-LINGUAL TRANSFER LEARNING

Cross-lingual DSMs differ in the method to generate the embeddings and in the type of data they use to align the semantic representations across languages. Two major approaches can be identified: (i) **mapping models** that map onto a common space pretrained monolingual embeddings (Section 8.4.1), and (ii) **joint models** that learn monolingual and cross-lingual vectors together (Section 8.4.2). They rely on one or more among the following kinds of cross-lingual data: (i) **bilingual dictionaries** containing translation pairs of lexemes; (ii) **parallel corpora** with texts that are exact translations of each other (e.g., OPUS; Tiedemann, 2012); (iii) **comparable corpora** with texts in one language paired with texts in another language discussing the same themes or subjects (e.g., Wikipedia). Most research has focused on generating bilingual semantic spaces, but some approaches have been extended to the multilingual setting as well (Ammar et al., 2016; Duong et al., 2017; Dufter et al., 2018).

MAPPING AND JOINT MODELS

BILINGUAL DICTIONARIES

PARALLEL AND COMPARABLE CORPORA

Cross-lingual DSMs are evaluated in intrinsic and extrinsic tasks (Glavaš et al., 2019). The most common intrinsic task is **bilingual lexicon induction**: Given a set of correct translation pairs $\langle l^{(S)}, l^{(T)} \rangle$, the performance of a DSM is evaluated on its ability to retrieve $\mathbf{l^{(T)}}$ as the nearest neighbor of $\mathbf{l^{(S)}}$ in the common semantic space, and is measured with **precision**. Alternatively, performance is computed by retrieving the ranked list of the k nearest neighbors and then measuring **precision-at-k** (P@k) (i.e., $\mathbf{l^{(T)}}$ must be found among the k neighbors, typically with $k \in \{5, 10\}$) or with **mean average precision**. Another intrinsic method is **cross-lingual semantic similarity** (Camacho-Collados et al., 2017), to replicate the similarity ratings between words in two languages (e.g., the English *cat* and the Italian *cane* "dog"). Extrinsic evaluation instead consists in using the embeddings for cross-lingual transfer learning in downstream NLP tasks, such as document classification, natural language inference, or information retrieval. A model is first trained on the data in the source language S using as features the cross-lingual embeddings for S, and then tested on the data in the target language T.

BILINGUAL LEXICON INDUCTION

CROSS-LINGUAL SEMANTIC SIMILARITY

8.4.1 Mapping Models

Based on the observation that distributional semantic spaces tend to be shaped similarly across languages (Mikolov et al., 2013c), **mapping** (or **offline**) **models** learn cross-lingual embeddings by aligning pretrained monolingual ones.

MAPPING CROSS-LINGUAL DSMs

> **Mapping cross-lingual DSMs** learn a mapping from monolingual vector spaces to a common cross-lingual space.

This approach consists of the following steps:

1. the monolingual distributional vectors spaces $\mathbf{S}$ and $\mathbf{T}$ are independently trained respectively for the vocabulary $V^{(S)}$ of the source language S and the vocabulary $V^{(T)}$ of the target language T;

LINEAR TRANS-
FORMATION
MATRIX
2. given a set of seed translation pairs $\langle l^{(S)}, l^{(T)} \rangle$, with $l^{(S)} \in V^{(S)}$ and $l^{(T)} \in V^{(T)}$, the cross-lingual DSM learns a **linear transformation matrix** $\mathbf{W}^{\mathbf{S} \rightarrow \mathbf{T}}$ that maps the $\mathbf{S}$ vectors onto $\mathbf{T}$ (cf. Mathematical note 4 in Section 2.5.2). Thus, $\mathbf{W}^{\mathbf{S} \rightarrow \mathbf{T}}$ turns $\mathbf{T}$ into a joint vector space for S and T;

3. for any new word $l^{(S)} \in V^{(S)}$ that is not part of the training set, its vector $\mathbf{1}^{(\mathbf{S})}$ in $\mathbf{S}$ is mapped onto a vector $\hat{\mathbf{1}}^{(\mathbf{S})}$ in $\mathbf{T}$, such that $\hat{\mathbf{1}}^{(\mathbf{S})} = \mathbf{1}^{(\mathbf{S})} \mathbf{W}^{\mathbf{S} \rightarrow \mathbf{T}}$;

4. $tr(l^{(S)})$ is the lexeme $l^{(T)} \in V^{(T)}$ whose vector $\mathbf{1}^{(\mathbf{T})}$ in $\mathbf{T}$ is the nearest neighbor of $\hat{\mathbf{1}}^{(\mathbf{S})}$ (see Equation 8.13).

ZERO-SHOT
LEARNING
The mapping approach is actually a case of the **zero-shot learning** paradigm (Palatucci et al., 2009), because the resulting cross-lingual DSM is evaluated on lexical pairs not used to learn the transformation matrix. This paradigm was originally introduced for neural decoding in cognitive science (cf. Section 8.7), but is now applied in several other settings, including the cross-lingual one. The main advantage of mapping models is their simplicity, as they only require a seed bilingual dictionary, which can also be fairly small. On the other hand, the assumption that there is a linear mapping between semantic spaces across languages oversimplifies the complexity of the cross-lingual meaning relations and polysemy patterns.

LINEAR
REGRESSION
Variations of the mapping approach mainly concern the method to generate the transformation matrix. Mikolov et al. (2013c) learn $\mathbf{W}^{\mathbf{S} \rightarrow \mathbf{T}}$ with **linear regression**, as the linear transformation that minimizes the squared Frobenius norm (cf. Section 2.5.1) between the mapped S embeddings and the T vectors:

$$\mathbf{W}^{\mathbf{S} \rightarrow \mathbf{T}} = \underset{W}{\operatorname{argmin}} ||\mathbf{XW} - \mathbf{Y}||_F^2, \qquad (8.14)$$

where $\mathbf{X}$ and $\mathbf{Y}$ are the embedding matrices of the seed words in S and T.

RIDGE
REGRESSION
Lazaridou et al. (2015c) revise the method by Mikolov et al. (2013c) using **ridge regression**, which adds to Equation 8.14 the regularization term $\lambda||\mathbf{W}||_F^2$, but they also propose a new method to learn the transformation matrix by minimizing the following margin loss (cf. Section 6.1):

$$\sum_{i=1}^{n} \sum_{j \neq i}^{k} \max(0, \delta + \text{dist}(\hat{l}_i^{(S)}, l_i^{(T)}) - \text{dist}(\hat{l}_i^{(S)}, l_j^{(T)})), \qquad (8.15)$$

where $\hat{l}^{(S)} = l^{(S)} \mathbf{W}$ is the predicted mapping of $l^{(S)}$ in the target space $\mathbf{T}$, the distance measure is the inverse cosine, and δ and k are two hyperparameters respectively corresponding to the margin and the number of negative examples for each training pair. The negative examples are pairs $\langle l_i^{(S)}, l_j^{(T)} \rangle$, with $1 \leq j \leq k$, such that each $l_j^{(T)}$ is a wrong translation for $l_i^{(S)}$. Therefore, the transformation matrix is learned with the objective of ranking the correct translations higher than the wrong ones. Like in Mikolov et al. (2013c), the matrix parameters are estimated with stochastic gradient descent.

Lazaridou et al. (2015c) argue that the margin loss in Equation 8.15 is able to reduce the **hubness problem** in cross-lingual embeddings. As discussed in HUBNESS Section 2.4.1, hubness is a phenomenon observed in high-dimensional spaces PROBLEM where some words (known as **hubs**) are the nearest neighbors of many other HUBS items (Radovanović et al. 2010a, 2010b). Dinu et al. (2015) and Lazaridou et al. (2015c) show that the distributional vectors mapped onto the target language space present an even higher degree of hubness. Since the translation of a source language lexeme is assumed to be the nearest neighbor of its mapped vector, hubness negatively affects cross-lingual retrieval. Besides refining the mapping function, an alternative approach to mitigate the hubness problem is to correct the nearest neighbor method to retrieve the translations (Dinu et al., 2015). For instance, Conneau et al. (2018b) propose the following **Cross-domain Similarity Local Scaling** (CSLS) measure: CSLS

$$\text{CSLS}(\hat{l}^{(S)}, l^{(T)}) = 2\text{sim}_{\cos}(\hat{l}^{(S)}, l^{(T)}) - r^{(T)}(\hat{l}^{(S)}) - r^{(S)}(l^{(T)}), \quad (8.16)$$

where $\hat{l}^{(S)} = l^{(S)} \mathbf{W}^{S \to T}$ is the mapped embedding of the source language lexeme $l^{(S)}$, $r^{(T)}(\hat{l}^{(S)})$ and $r^{(S)}(l^{(T)})$ are respectively the mean cosine between $\hat{l}^{(S)}$ and $l^{(T)}$ and their top k neighbors in $\mathbf{T}$. The effect of CSLS is to decrease the similarity between vectors lying in dense areas of the target language space $\mathbf{T}$, thereby increasing the quality of translation retrieval by smoothing the negative effects of hubness. Joulin et al. (2018) incorporate this criterion in learning the transformation matrix itself, using a margin loss, similarly to Lazaridou et al. (2015c), in which cosine similarity is replaced by CSLS.

Another method to learn a linear transformation matrix $\mathbf{W}^{S \to T}$ is to constrain it to be orthogonal (Xing et al., 2015; Artetxe et al., 2016). An **orthogonal matrix** $\mathbf{M}$ is a square matrix whose rows and columns are ortho- ORTHOGONAL normal vectors (cf. Section 2.5.1). In this case, $\mathbf{M}^T \mathbf{M} = \mathbf{I}$, where $\mathbf{I}$ is the MATRIX

IDENTITY
MATRIX
identity matrix, a square matrix with ones on the main diagonal and zeros elsewhere. An important property of an orthogonal transformation matrix $\mathbf{W}^{S \to T}$ is that the mapped elements in $\mathbf{T}$ maintain the same distances they have in $\mathbf{S}$. This allows the mapped embeddings in the target space to keep their similarity relations in the source one. Finding the orthogonal transformation matrix $\mathbf{W}^{S \to T}$ that maps a set of points closest to another given set of points (where the correspondence is the set of seed pairs in our case) is called the

PROCRUSTES
PROBLEM
Procrustes problem and can be solved in the following way:

$$\mathbf{W}^{S \to T} = \mathbf{U}\mathbf{V}^T, \tag{8.17}$$

where $\mathbf{U}\Sigma\mathbf{V}^T$ is the SVD of the matrix $\mathbf{T}^T\mathbf{S}$. Artetxe et al. (2016) show that this method is able to significantly improve the quality of the cross-lingual embeddings. Orthogonal mapping models are indeed among the best performing and most common type of cross-lingual DSMs (Ruder, 2019).

Faruqui and Dyer (2014) take a prima facie different route to generate cross-lingual embeddings: Instead of mapping the source embeddings onto the target language semantic space, they learn two transformation matrices $\mathbf{W}^{S \to B}$ and $\mathbf{W}^{T \to B}$ that respectively map the source and target language embeddings to

CANONICAL
CORRELATION
ANALYSIS
a new joint bilingual space $\mathbf{B}$. The transformation matrices are learned with **canonical correlation analysis** (CCA), which aims at maximizing the correlation between the mapped vectors $\hat{\mathbf{l}}^{(S)} = \mathbf{l}^{(S)}\mathbf{W}^{S \to B}$ and $\hat{\mathbf{l}}^{(T)} = \mathbf{l}^{(T)}\mathbf{W}^{T \to B}$ for a set of seed translation pairs. Faruqui and Dyer (2014) originally propose CCA as a method to improve monolingual embeddings with bilingual correlations, but then Ammar et al. (2016) apply it to a multilingual scenario. Interestingly, Artetxe et al. (2018) prove that, despite surface differences, CCA has strong similarities with the regression and orthogonal methods, and they all can be regarded as instances of the same framework.

SEED
BILINGUAL
LEXICON
The **seed bilingual lexicon** plays a key role in mapping models. Mikolov et al. (2013c) create the training pairs by automatically translating the $5,000$ most frequent words in the source language corpus, while Lazaridou et al. (2015c) derive the same number of seed pairs from the Europarl aligned corpus. The effect of the seed lexicon size is investigated in Vulić and Korhonen (2016), who show that a careful choice of the translation pairs is more important than their sheer number. For instance, Artetxe et al. (2017) report that it is possible to learn cross-lingual embeddings even with 25 seed pairs. Other models use as seeds lists of cognates (i.e., words that have similar meanings and spelling in two languages because of their common etymological origin, such as the English *family* and the Italian *famiglia*), shared numerals, and identically spelled strings, obtaining very competitive results (Artetxe et al., 2017; Søgaard et al., 2018). A more extreme case is represented by fully

unsupervised models that learn the mapping between semantic spaces without any seed lexicon (Conneau et al., 2018b). Despite their strong appeal especially for low-resource languages, they assume a strong isomorphism between the source and target semantics space. In fact, Søgaard et al. (2018) show that these cross-lingual DSMs fail with distant languages and Glavaš et al. (2019) report that seed-based models typically outperform unsupervised ones.

8.4.2 Joint Models

Joint models directly learn a common cross-lingual semantic space from distributional data, without relying on pretrained embeddings.

JOINT CROSS-LINGUAL DSMs

> **Joint cross-lingual DSMs** simultaneously learn the embeddings for different languages in the same vector space.

They are based on a cross-lingual extension of the Distributional Hypothesis:

> If two lexemes are mutual translations, they tend to co-occur with contexts that are likely to be mutual translations as well.

Classical count DSMs typically formalize this assumption with a **cross-lingual co-occurrence matrix**, in which the contexts correspond to translation pairs of lexical collocates (Rapp, 1999; Laroche and Langlais, 2010; Peirsman and Padó, 2010, among many others). The co-occurrence matrix defines a joint vector space, such that a pair $\langle l^{(S)}, l^{(T)} \rangle$ of source and target language lexemes is assigned similar distributional vectors if the collocates of $l^{(S)}$ are translations of the collocates of $l^{(T)}$. The matrix contains the co-occurrences of lexemes from the source and target language with the context words derived from monolingual or comparable corpora for the respective language. The main bottleneck of this approach is the selection of the context translation pairs, which are usually identified with a bilingual lexicon. Peirsman and Padó (2010) address this issue by adopting a bootstrapping approach: First, a cross-lingual space is built using cognates as contexts, then the nearest bilingual neighbors of this space are identified and added to the contexts.

CROSS-LINGUAL CO-OCCURRENCE MATRIX

A second group of joint cross-lingual DSMs is based on Topic Models (Mimno et al., 2009; Vulić et al., 2011, 2015). Given a comparable corpus with texts in a set of languages $\{L_1, \ldots, L_n\}$ and a set of k topics $Z = \{z_1, \ldots, z_k\}$, a **multilingual Topic Model** learns with LDA the distribution $p^{(L)}(l^{(L)}|z)$, for each language L, each lexeme $l^{(L)} \in V^{(L)}$, and each topic z (cf. Section 4.4). Extending the monolingual setting, topics are latent dimensions shared across multiple languages, and a topic is defined by

MULTILINGUAL TOPIC MODEL

the probability distributions of words in each language of the training corpus. Cross-lingual embeddings are then generated from the topic vectors described in Section 4.4.2. A source language lexeme $l^{(S)}$ is represented with the topic vector $\mathbf{l^{(S)}} = (p^{(S)}(z_1|l^{(S)}),\ldots,p^{(S)}(z_k|l^{(S)}))$, and its translation in T is the lexeme l_T whose topic vector $\mathbf{l^{(T)}} = (p^{(T)}(z_1|l^{(T)}),\ldots,p^{(T)}(z_k|l^{(T)}))$ is the nearest neighbor of $\mathbf{l^{(S)}}$.

CROSS-LINGUAL NEURAL DSMs

Nowadays, most joint models are **cross-lingual neural DSMs** trained on sentence-aligned parallel corpora (i.e., each sentence in one language is linked to its corresponding sentence in the other language). While in some cases (e.g., Klementiev et al., 2012) the corpus is required to be previously word-aligned (i.e., each word is linked to its translation with unsupervised tools, such as FastAlign by Dyer et al., 2013), other models learn the cross-lingual embeddings directly from the aligned sentences. Hermann and Blunsom (2014) encode each source and target sentence $s^{(S)}$ and $s^{(T)}$ in the parallel corpus C respectively with the vectors $\mathbf{s^{(S)}}$ and $\mathbf{s^{(T)}}$ obtained by summing their word embeddings (cf. Section 9.2), learned with this multilingual objective:

$$J = \sum_{\langle s^{(S)},s^{(T)}\rangle \in C} \sum_{i=1}^{k} \max(0, 1 + \mathrm{dist}(\mathbf{s^{(S)}}, \mathbf{s^{(T)}}) - \mathrm{dist}(\mathbf{s^{(S)}}, \mathbf{s_i^{(T)}})). \quad (8.18)$$

This is the margin loss function (cf. Section 6.1) and aims at making the squared Euclidean distance between aligned sentences smaller than the ones between k negative examples formed by randomly paired sentences. By exploiting the associations between translated sentences in the parallel corpus, the source and target language lexemes are represented in a joint vector space that captures both monolingual and cross-lingual similarity relations.

CROSS-LINGUAL SGNS

While Hermann and Blunsom (2014) use only a multilingual objective, **cross-lingual SGNS** models (Coulmance et al., 2015; Gouws et al., 2015; Luong et al., 2015) combine monolingual and cross-lingual loss functions:

$$L = J_{SGNS}^{S} + J_{SGNS}^{T} + \Omega, \quad (8.19)$$

where J_{SGNS}^{S} and J_{SGNS}^{T} are the standard SGNS objectives (see Equation 6.36), which capture the similarity relations in the source and target languages, and Ω is the cross-lingual objective that is used to align the two semantic spaces. Thus, the cross-lingual embeddings are learned by exploiting both the monolingual co-occurrences and their correspondences across languages.

BILBOWA

In **BilBOWA** (Bilingual Bag-of-Words without Word Alignments) by Gouws et al. (2015), Ω minimizes the squared Euclidean distance between the embeddings of the aligned sentences, like in Equation 8.18. On the other hand, in

Trans-gram by Coulmance et al. (2015) and in **BiSkip** (Bilingual Skip-Gram)   TRANS-GRAM
model by Luong et al. (2015), Ω extends the SGNS prediction objective: Each   BISKIP
source language lexeme $l^{(S)}$ is used to predict the words in the context of the
target language lexeme $l^{(T)}$ is aligned to, and vice versa. Given the aligned
sentences $s^{(S)}$ and $s^{(T)}$, the prediction objective from S to T is defined as:

$$\Omega^{S \to T} = - \sum_{\langle s^{(S)}, s^{(T)} \rangle \in C} \frac{1}{|s^{(S)}|} \sum_{l^{(S)} \in s^{(S)}} \sum_{c_{l^{(T)}} \in s^{(T)}} \log p(c_{l^{(T)}} | l^{(S)}), \quad (8.20)$$

where $l^{(S)}$ and $l^{(T)}$ are aligned lexemes and $c_{l^{(T)}}$ is a context lexeme of $l^{(T)}$
in $s^{(T)}$. This objective is optimized in both directions, $S \to T$ and $T \to S$.
Although Equation 8.20 requires aligned words, Trans-gram and BiSkip use
only sentence-aligned data and adopt word alignment approximations: The
former assumes a uniform alignment (i.e., each word in $s^{(S)}$ is aligned to every
word in $s^{(T)}$), while the latter assumes a monotonic alignment, such that each
$l_i^{(S)}$ is aligned to the target lexeme $l_j^{(T)}$, where $j = i * (|s^{(S)}|/|s^{(T)}|)$ and $|s|$
is the sentence length. Luong et al. (2015) show that this alignment is able to
rival the performance obtained by preprocessing the parallel corpus with an
unsupervised word aligner. Instead of changing the training objective of predict models, other joint models learn cross-lingual embeddings by training the   PSEUDO-
standard monolingual CBOW (cf. Section 6.3) on a **pseudo-bilingual corpus**   BILINGUAL
obtained by randomly replacing words in a source language corpus with their   CORPUS
translations in a seed bilingual dictionary (Gouws and Søgaard, 2015; Duong
et al., 2016). The advantage of this method is that it dispenses with parallel
corpora and leverages the information from bilingual lexicons.

The growing availability of parallel data is expected to boost joint cross-
lingual DSMs, which seem to have some advantages over mapping ones. For
instance, Ormazabal et al. (2019) show that the vectors learned by BiSkip are
less affected by hubness than the ones generated by mapping models. However, both approaches still suffer of serious limitations. In fact, they all assume
translation to be a one-to-one relation between words. This assumption is too
simplistic for two reasons. First, translation is actually *a relation between word
senses*. This is clearly shown by homonyms, whose meanings are translated by
different lexemes (e.g., the animal sense of *bat* corresponds in Italian to *pipistrello*, and its tool sense to *mazza*). In fact, current cross-lingual DSMs inherit
the meaning conflation deficiency of monolingual ones (cf. Section 8.2). Second, translation is not always a one-to-one relation either, because it frequently
happens that a word in a language corresponds to a multiword expression in
another (e.g., the verb *dispense* in the sentence *We will dispense with the for-
malities* is translated in Italian with the complex expression *fare a meno di*).

Further research in this area is needed to develop cross-lingual DSMs that might overcome such limitations.

8.5 Connotative Meaning

DENOTATIVE
MEANING

CONNOTATIVE
MEANING

Knowing that *dog* is semantically similar to *cat* or that it is a hyponym of *animal* is part of our knowledge of what linguists call the **denotative** or **conceptual meaning** of *dog*, since it concerns the concept this word expresses and the entities it denotes. Lexical items also have a **connotative meaning** or **connotation** (Murphy, 2010; Pustejovsky and Batiukova, 2019).

> The **connotative meaning** of a word is the set of emotional and evaluative associations beyond its denotative meaning.

For instance, *cat* and *kitty* denote the same type of animal, but the latter adds a dimension of affection. Besides referring to a set of people, *gang* has also a negative connotation with respect to the neutral *group* (e.g., the sentence *This paper was written by a gang of linguists* expresses the idea that the authors somehow behaved like criminals). Similarly, *wop* is an offensive term for a person of Italian origins. As these examples show, connotative meaning encompasses a wide range of phenomena, such as affective content, social stereotypes, and register (e.g., *kitty* is a suitable term to refer to a cat in an informal context, but not in a scientific paper). The connotations of a lexeme are strongly related to the way it is used: The fact that *gang* often co-occurs with words like *violence*, *criminal*, *rape*, and so on surely influences its negative associations. This suggests that the distributional properties of lexical items are important factors in determining their connotations.

8.5.1 Distributional Models of Affect

AFFECTIVE
CONTENT
VALENCE
EMOTION

One aspect of connotative meaning that has attracted great attention in distributional semantics is the **affective content** of lexemes, in particular their **valence** (i.e., where they are positive or negative) and **emotion** (e.g., joy, fear, etc.). Having information about the affect expressed by words is extremely important in NLP tasks like sentiment analysis, but also for cognitive studies on the relationship between language and emotions (Vigliocco et al., 2009). Available affective resources include extensions of WordNet such as SentiWordNet (Baccianella et al., 2010) or WordNet Affect (Strapparava and Valitutti, 2004), crowdsourced emotion lexicons like EmoLex (Turney and Mohammad, 2013), or human ratings collected by psycholinguists in affective norms, like ANEW

(Bradley and Lang, 2017). Despite their importance, these resources have a limited coverage, are available for few languages, and are extremely expensive and difficult to develop. This has motivated research to estimate the affect of words on the basis of the following assumption, which Lenci et al. (2018) call **Affective Distributional Hypothesis**:

A lexeme is associated with a given affective value if it co-occurs in similar contexts of other lexemes associated with the same value.

AFFECTIVE DIS-
TRIBUTIONAL
HYPOTHESIS

Therefore, DSMs can be used to bootstrap the affective ratings of new words by computing their similarity with a set of previously rated seed lexemes.

Turney and Littman (2003) assume that the valence of a lexeme depends on its syntagmatic associations with positive or negative words. Given a set P of positive lexemes (e.g., *good*, *nice*, etc.) and a set N of negative lexemes (e.g., *bad*, *nasty*, etc.), they compute this **semantic orientation score**:

SEMANTIC
ORIENTATION
SCORE

$$SO(l) = \sum_{l_j \in P} PMI(l, l_j) - \sum_{l_k \in N} PMI(l, l_k). \tag{8.21}$$

If $SO(l)$ is positive, l is classified as having a positive valence, otherwise a negative one. Bestgen and Vincze (2012) and Recchia and Louwerse (2015) instead determine the valence ratings for l by using a standard DSM to select its k nearest neighbors and then computing the average ratings of the neighbors attested in the ANEW affective norms. Passaro and Lenci (2016) and Lenci et al. (2018) use the Affective Distributional Hypothesis to bootstrap emotion ratings for Italian words. They first collect with crowdsourcing a small set of seed words highly associated with one of the eight basic emotions identified by Plutchik (1994): joy, anger, surprise, disgust, fear, sadness, anticipation, and trust. Emotions are represented with the **centroid vectors** (cf. Section 8.2.1) built from the pretrained embeddings of the seed nouns. The rating of a lexeme l for a given emotion corresponds to the cosine similarity of the vector for l with that emotion vector. Table 8.3 shows the nouns with the highest score for disgust and fear computed by the DSM in Lenci et al. (2018).

CENTROID
VECTOR MODEL

One limit of standard DSMs in capturing the affective content of lexemes derives from their tendency to conflate words with opposite meanings (cf. Section 8.3.2). Since antonyms are often associated with contrasting affective values, lexical items with opposite valence (e.g., *happy* and *sad*) are eventually represented with similar distributional vectors. This has particularly negative consequences when using word embeddings as features in NLP models for opinion mining and sentiment analysis (Pang and Lee, 2008). In order to reduce this problem, two solutions are typically adopted, like with semantic relations (cf. Section 8.3). The first consists in post-processing pretrained

Table 8.3 Italian nouns with the highest rating for disgust and
fear according to the DSM in Lenci et al. (2018)

disgust		*fear*	
fetore	"stink"	disorientamento	"disorientation"
escremento	"excrement"	angoscia	"anguish"
putrefazione	"rot"	turbamento	"disruption"
carogna	"carcass"	prostrazione	"prostration"
miasma	"miasma"	inquietudine	"inquietude"

embeddings with methods like retrofitting (Faruqui et al., 2015). For instance,
Ye et al. (2018) uses a Convolutional Neural Network (cf. Section 9.4.2) to
refine vectors with knowledge coming from SentiWordNet. Alternatively, new
DSMs are directly optimized to encode affective information. These **sentiment**
embeddings are typically learned by predicting the sentiment of training texts.
Maas et al. (2011) propose a Topic Model extended with the objective to maximize the probability of the sentiment value for each word in a corpus of rated
movie reviews. In order to overcome the difficulty of creating corpora manually annotated with affective labels, a common approach consists in using
distant supervision, in which noisy training data are automatically created
with some heuristics, such as the presence of emoticons indicative of the text
valence. Tang et al. (2014) learn sentiment embeddings from distantly annotated tweets with a modified version of the language model by Collobert et al.
(2011). The network is trained with a twofold margin loss that maximizes the
probability of a true n-gram over a corrupted one (cf. Section 6.2) and the prediction of the valence of a tweet given the true n-gram. Agrawal et al. (2018)
use a LSTM (cf. Section 9.4.3) to learn sentiment embeddings from a corpus
distantly annotated with emotion scores from WordNet Affect and Emolex.
Sentiment embeddings show an improved ability to separate words that have
different affective contents, while preserving other similarity relations.

SENTIMENT
EMBEDDINGS

DISTANT
SUPERVISION

8.5.2 Cultural Biases and Stereotypes in DSMs

STEREOTYPES

The idea that Swedes are blond is an example of **cultural stereotype**.

> A **cultural stereotype** is a preconceived belief that attributes certain
> characteristics to all the members of a group of people or things.

Stereotypes are not necessarily negatives, but they can create potentially dangerous and discriminatory **biases** in our behaviors and decisions. The idea

BIASES

Table 8.4 Top occupations and adjectives by gender in
Garg et al. (2018)

occupations		adjectives	
man	*woman*	*man*	*woman*
carpenter	nurse	honorable	maternal
mechanic	midwife	ascetic	romantic
mason	librarian	amiable	submissive
blacksmith	housekeeper	dissolute	hysterical

that surgeons are male while nurses are female is a **gender stereotype**, which GENDER STEREOTYPE
determines a **gender bias** if we use it as a criterion to hire someone for a job.

Language both reflects and perpetuates cultural stereotypes (Maas, 1999; Burgers and Beukeboom, 2020). These can be transmitted intentionally by speakers who explicitly state them, but for the most part they are conveyed implicitly through distributional associations in language use. For instance, observing that the name for a certain ethnic group frequently co-occurs with negative terms can reinforce negative bias toward it. This is a manifestation of the Strong Distributional Hypothesis (cf. Section 1.2), according to which the distributional properties of lexical items contribute to shape conceptual representations. Research has shown that several cultural stereotypes are indeed captured by DSMs, thereby producing biases in their representations (Bolukbasi et al., 2016; Caliskan et al., 2017). As illustrated in Table 8.4, the vector for *mechanic* is closer to the vector for *man*, while the vector for *librarian* is closer to the vector of *woman*, revealing a gender bias in the embeddings.

The fact that distributional vectors encode cultural stereotypes is by itself not surprising. Like any other data-driven method, DSMs simply learn what is in the training corpus (cf. Section 2.1.2). Therefore, if co-occurrence statistics reflect biased associations and stereotypes, these will eventually pass to distributional vectors as well. DSMs can be used as a lens to discover the stereotypes and biases hidden in language. In fact, distributional semantics offers interesting potentialities for social studies to explore the interaction between language and culture. Caliskan et al. (2017) propose a measure called **Word-Embedding Association Test** (WEAT) to quantify the **embedding** WEAT
bias: EMBEDDING BIAS

> Given two groups (e.g., men and women) each represented by a set of words, the **embedding bias** of a lexeme *l* is the strength of the association of its vector **l** with the embeddings of the words in either group.

In WEAT, the association strength is computed with the cosine. Two groups A and B are represented with a set of attribute lexemes L_A and L_B (e.g., men are represented with the set of terms $L_M = \{man, male, boy, \dots\}$, while women are described with the set of terms $L_F = \{woman, female, girl, \dots\}$). The embedding bias of l with repect to A and B is then computed as follows:

$$\text{bias}(l, A, B) = \frac{1}{|A|} \sum_{l_i \in A} \text{sim}_{\cos}(l, l_i) - \frac{1}{|B|} \sum_{l_j \in B} \text{sim}_{\cos}(l, l_j). \quad (8.22)$$

This score is very similar to Equation 8.21. The bias of an embedding depends on its average similarity with the vectors of the words in A or B: If the value is positive, then l is biased toward (i.e., has a stronger association with) group A, otherwise it is biased toward B. The closer to zero is $\text{bias}(l, A, B)$, the less biased is l. A variant of Equation 8.22 is used by Garg et al. (2018) for their diachronic study of the changes in cultural stereotypes in the twentieth and twenty-first centuries in the United States. Interestingly, both Caliskan et al. (2017) and Garg et al. (2018) show a strong correlation between distributional and social data (e.g., the gender embedding bias of names for occupations correlates with the percentage of women in each of these occupations).

The stereotypes learned by DSMs could be problematic if their representations are used in sensitive NLP and AI applications (e.g., curriculum vitae evaluation, legal decisions, etc.), since they might inherit the same biases. This has sparked a line of research to develop methods for **word embedding debiasing**, with the goal of removing unintended biases from distributional vectors (Sun et al., 2019b). This is part of the growing field that aims at fostering the **fairness** of NLP and AI models, to ensure that their decisions are consistent with ethical values.

Bolukbasi et al. (2016) propose a **post-processing approach** that focuses on gender bias. Following the offset method for analogies (cf. Section 7.2.4), they assume that gender is encoded in the difference vectors between male and female lexemes (e.g., **woman** − **man**). They identify a "gender direction" in the semantic space by selecting the top principal component vector **g** with the SVD of the matrix formed by the difference vectors of ten seed gender pairs. Then, for each lexeme l to be debiased, they take its normalized projection orthogonal to the bias direction **g** (cf. Mathematical note 5 in Section 2.6.1):

$$l' = \frac{1 - l_g}{||1 - l_g||}, \quad (8.23)$$

where l_g is the projection of l onto the gender direction, and $l_g = (l \cdot g)g$, if the vectors are normalized. The gender component of l is zeroed, because l' is

EMBEDDING DEBIASING

FAIRNESS

POST-PROCESSING

orthogonal to the gender direction in the vector space. The dot product $l \cdot g$ is the magnitude of the projection of l along g, and quantifies the embedding bias of l. Finally, Bolukbasi et al. (2016) make sure that all gender-neutral lexemes are equidistant to both words in a set of gendered pairs.

Instead of refining pretrained vectors, Zhao et al. (2018) learn **debiased embeddings** from scratch. They train vectors where gender information is encoded in a single vector component, which corresponds to the bias direction in the semantic space and is then removed to obtain debiased embeddings. Lexemes are represented with vectors consisting of two parts $l = (l^a; l^g)$, where l^g is the last component of l and is reserved to encode gender, while l^a contains gender-neutral information. Zhao et al. (2018) learn these embeddings by extending the training objective of GloVe (cf. Section 4.5), so that, given two groups of male/female seed lexemes, gender information is pushed into l^g. Gender-neutral words are encouraged to be orthogonal to this component.

DEBIASED EMBEDDINGS

Gonen and Goldberg (2019) show that these debiasing methods fall short of providing really neutral representations. In fact, a classifier trained to predict the gender of words represented with debiased vectors can achieve very high accuracy, meaning that such embeddings still contain a lot of gender information. Gonen and Goldberg (2019) argue that identifying a gender direction in semantic space is useful to quantify the bias of words, but its neutralization is not enough to eliminate the bias itself. This also suggests that sterotyped biases are deeply encoded in distributional vectors, and more sophisticated methods are required to improve the fairness of word embeddings.

8.6 Semantic Change

Languages change over time, and so do the meanings of words (Traugott, 2017). For instance, *epic* originally refers to a literary genre (*Odissey is an epic poem*), but now it also means impressive (*You have an epic car*).

DIACHRONIC SEMANTICS

> **Semantic changes** are meaning shifts in time. **Diachronic semantics** is the study of semantic change.

Linguistic research has identified several types of semantic changes (Bréal, 1897; Bloomfield, 1933; Traugott, 2017), such as metaphorization (meaning shifts induced by metaphorical associations; e.g., *tissue*: woven cloth > aggregation of cells), broadening (extensions of meaning; e.g., *cupboard*: in Middle English sideboard to display cups > small storage cabinet), and so on. Semantic changes can be due to regular linguistic and cognitive processes (Traugott and Dasher, 2001; Deo, 2015), such as metaphor, as well as to cultural factors,

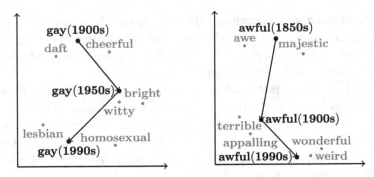

Figure 8.7 The semantic change of *gay* (left plot) and *awful* (right plot) as displacement in vector space, adapted from Hamilton et al. (2016b)

like technological innovations (e.g., *virtual*: almost a particular thing or quality > created by computer technology but not existing in the physical world). Meaning shifts are also one of the main sources of lexical ambiguity (cf. Section 8.2), when a new sense evolves from a former one without replacing it.

Semantic changes occur because a word starts being used in a new way. Therefore, meaning shifts are correlated with changes in the distributional properties of a word, as its new uses entail different co-occurrences with linguistic contexts, like in the above example of *epic*. In fact, corpus-based methods have become important tools to investigate semantic change (Tang, 2018). In particular, **diachronic distributional semantics** uses DSMs to detect lexical meaning shifts (Kutuzov et al., 2018).

DIACHRONIC
DISTRIBU-
TIONAL
SEMANTICS

> **Diachronic distributional semantics** studies the meaning changes of lexical items by analyzing their shifts in distributional vector spaces.

Since the position of a lexeme in a semantic space is a function of its distributional properties, its displacement is expected to reflect a meaning shift (see Figure 8.7). Diachronic distributional models typically consist of three major components: (i) a diachronic corpus, (ii) a DSM trained on different time slices of the corpus, (iii) a method to compare the resulting spaces and measure their changes. In general, models aim at tracking the shift of a particular word through the semantic spaces, or to identify the lexical items that change the most. Evaluation is often performed on a small number of handpicked cases of semantic change taken from the linguistic literature, as benchmarks for model evaluation are still rare. An interesting example are the datasets for English, Latin, German, and Swedish released by the SemEval 2020 task on Unsupervised Lexical Semantic Change Detection (Schlechtweg et al., 2020b).

A **diachronic corpus** is a collection of texts belonging to different periods of diachronic corpus time (Davidse and De Smet, 2020). Important training resources for DSMs are the Corpus of Historical American (COHA), which contains English texts from 1820 to 2019, and the Google Books Ngrams corpus, the largest diachronic corpus with texts in different languages spanning several centuries. Studies that focus on semantic changes on a small temporal scale (e.g., to explore shifts induced by cultural drifts and events) also use time-stamped data from social media like Twitter or newspaper articles.

Given a diachronic corpus C and $t_1, \ldots, t_n$ time periods, a DSM is trained on each separate sub-corpus C_{t_i} containing texts belonging to the time t_i. This produces a series of vector spaces $\mathbf{T_1}, \ldots, \mathbf{T_n}$ in which a target lexeme l is associated with the series of vectors $l^{(\mathbf{T_1})} \in \mathbf{T_1}, \ldots, l^{(\mathbf{T_n})} \in \mathbf{T_n}$, such that $l^{(\mathbf{T_i})}$ represents the meaning of l at time t_i. We refer to these representations as **diachronic vectors (embeddings)**. diachronic vectors

> The **diachronic vector (embedding)** $l^{(\mathbf{T})}$ of a target lexeme l is the distributional representation of l at time t.

Two measures of semantic change have been proposed. The first measures the meaning shift of l from t_i and t_{i+1} with the cosine distance between its corresponding diachronic vectors (Hamilton et al., 2016b):

$$\text{dist}_{\cos}(l^{(\mathbf{T_i})}, l^{(\mathbf{T_{i+1}})}) = 1 - \text{sim}_{\cos}(l^{(\mathbf{T_i})}, l^{(\mathbf{T_{i+1}})}). \tag{8.24}$$

Hamilton et al. (2016a) refers to Equation 8.24 as a **global measure of seman-** global measure **tic change**, because it measures how far a lexeme moved in semantic space between two time periods. The second measure is the **local neighborhood** lnd **distance** (LND) and detects semantic change by quantifying the variation in the neighborhood of a target lexeme (Hamilton et al., 2016a). First, the k nearest neighbors of $l^{(\mathbf{T_i})}$ and $l^{(\mathbf{T_{i+1}})}$, $N_k(l^{(T_i)})$ and $N_k(l^{(T_{i+1})})$, are selected and similarity used to build the **similarity vectors** $s(l^{(\mathbf{T_i})})$ and $s(l^{(\mathbf{T_{i+1}})})$. These are second- vectors order vectors containing the cosine similarities of $l^{(\mathbf{T_i})}$ and $l^{(\mathbf{T_{i+1}})}$ with the vectors of $N_k(l^{(T_i)}) \cup N_k(l^{(T_{i+1})})$ in $\mathbf{T_i}$ and $\mathbf{T_{i+1}}$ respectively. Then, LND is computed as the cosine distance between the two similarity vectors:

$$\text{LND}(l_{t_i}, l_{t_{i+1}}) = \text{dist}_{\cos}(s(l^{(\mathbf{T_i})}), s(l^{(\mathbf{T_{i+1}})})). \tag{8.25}$$

Hamilton et al. (2016a) argue that the cosine distance and LCD identify different types of semantic change, respectively corresponding to regular linguistic changes and irregular cultural drifts.

The cosine distance measure in Equation 8.24 compares diachronic vectors from different semantic spaces. This presupposes that the vectors are **aligned** vector in one common coordinate system. On the other hand, LND does not require alignment vector alignment, because it compares vectors whose components are similarities computed in each space separately. If the vectors are explicit, alignment is trivially guaranteed by fixing the same contexts for all the spaces, since each vector component corresponds to a distinct context (cf. Section 2.4.1). For instance, Gulordava and Baroni (2011) use an explicit count DSM in which the diachronic vectors of a target lexeme are different rows in a word-by-word co-occurrence matrix sharing the same context lexemes for all the periods. The case of embeddings is instead more complex. The matrix factorization produced by SVD is not unique (i.e., the same matrix can be factorized in different, non-equivalent ways). Moreover, both RI and predict DSMs are based on random initializations, respectively of the index vectors and of the network parameters. Therefore, distinct runs of these DSMs on the same data produce rotated spaces whose embeddings have different coordinates, even when they have the same nearest neighbors. Schlechtweg et al. (2020a) show that alignment is a crucial step before comparing diachronic embeddings, and that unaligned vectors produce a significant decrease in the quality of the analyses.

ONLINE METHODS

Online methods learn natively aligned diachronic embeddings, by exploiting the incremental nature of non-matrix DSMs. Jurgens and Stevens (2009)

TEMPORAL RI

introduce **Temporal Random Indexing** (TRI), a variation of RI that accumulates a distinct embedding for each time period from the linguistic co-occurrences recorded in that period (cf. Section 5.3). The alignment is guaranteed by using the same random index vectors for all the periods. Kim et al.

DIACHRONIC SGNS

(2014) propose a **diachronic SGNS**, in which the embeddings trained at time t_i initialize the network to train the embeddings at t_{i+1}, so that all the diachronic embeddings eventually share the same coordinates. If a lexical item does not change in meaning, its vector will be updated only slightly, because the word is used in similar contexts in t_i and t_{i+1}, while more different contexts lead to a stronger update, and therefore a stronger change in space.

OFFLINE METHODS

Offline (mapping) methods instead align pretrained diachronic embeddings by projecting them onto a common vector space. The approach is exactly the same adopted for cross-lingual embeddings (cf. Section 8.4.1), the only difference being that now it is applied to vector spaces representing different temporal phases of the same language. Given the pretrained spaces T_i and

LINEAR TRANS-FORMATION MATRIX

T_{i+1}, a **linear transformation matrix** $W^{T_i \rightarrow T_{i+1}}$ is learned to project the T_i embeddings onto T_{i+1}. Kulkarni et al. (2015) learn this matrix with linear regression (cf. Equation 8.14), while Hamilton et al. (2016b) use orthogonal Procrustes analysis (cf. Equation 8.17). The comparative experiments by Shoemark et al. (2019) and Schlechtweg et al. (2020a) suggest that the latter is the best performing alignment method for diachronic embeddings. On the other hand, Gonen et al. (2020) argue that the mapping approach has an inherent limitation due to its projecting the entire vocabulary of a DSM onto itself, because this also includes words that have changed meaning and therefore should not appear near each other in the semantic space.

Other models dispense with vector alignment by measuring semantic change with the variation in the similarity relations within the spaces, rather than directly comparing the diachronic vectors themselves. Sagi et al. (2009, 2012) train a single window-based matrix DSM with SVD, whose embeddings are used to build context vectors representing the distinct occurrences of a target lexeme (cf. Section 8.2.1). Then, they compute the **semantic density** of the SEMANTIC target as the average similarity between its context vectors: A word with a DENSITY very restricted meaning is expected to have a higher semantic density than a semantically broader lexeme, because the former tends to occur in more similar contexts. Finally, they use semantic density variation in time as a distributional correlate of semantic shifts like broadening and narrowing. Eger and Mehler (2016) and Rodda et al. (2017) detect changes with similarity vectors built from the full model vocabulary, instead of the k nearest neighbors used in LND. As observed by Rodda et al. (2017) in their study on Ancient Greek, this method actually corresponds to performing Representation Similarity Analysis (cf. Section 7.5) to compare differences between diachronic spaces. Gonen et al. (2020) introduce a simple score for semantic change detection based on the intersection of the k nearest neighbors of a target lexeme in two spaces:

$$\text{score}^k(l) = -|N_k(l^{(t_i)}) \cap N_k(l^{(t_{i+1})})|. \qquad (8.26)$$

A smaller intersection is expected to correspond to a stronger semantic shift.

Distributional models for WSI are also applied to track **word sense changes**. WORD SENSE Mitra et al. (2014) measure the variation of senses represented as clusters of CHANGES neighbors (cf. Section 8.2.2). Analyzing the intersection of clusters of two different time periods, they detect cases of sense splitting, merging, emergence, and disappearance. Montariol et al. (2021) study the temporal dynamics of senses as clusters of BERT contextual token vectors (cf. Sections 8.2.1 and 9.6.3). Extending the Dynamic Topic Models approach proposed by Blei and Lafferty (2006), and the Bayesian models for WSI in Brody and Lapata (2009) and Lau et al. (2012), Frermann and Lapata (2016) infer a **topic structure** TOPIC MODELS from the contexts of a target word at each period. Given $Z = \{z_1, \ldots, z_k\}$ a set of k senses (i.e., topics) of the target, the topic structure at time t_i consists of a k-dimensional multinomial distribution over senses θ_{t_i} and a multinomial distribution over the vocabulary $\phi_i^{(z)}$ for each sense z. Semantic changes are detected by looking at the variation in time of the topic distribution for the target lexeme. Since the $\phi_i^{(z)}$ distribution also varies in time, it is possible to identify changes in a single sense from the differences in its word distribution. In the topic corresponding to the energy sense of *power*, *water* has a very high probability in the 1700s, while in the 2000s the most probable word is *nuclear*.

Most studies in diachronic distributional semantics focus on developing methods to detect the lexical items that undergo meaning shifts. However, there are also attempt at identifying general patterns of change. For instance,

LAWS OF
SEMANTIC
CHANGE

Hamilton et al. (2016b) carry out a regression analysis with differences in cosine distance as a dependent variable, which leads them to propose two **laws of semantic change** (the "law of conformity": frequent words change more slowly; the "law of innovation": polysemous words change more quickly), though these results are questioned by Dubossarsky et al. (2017). Dubossarsky et al. (2016) show that verbs change faster than nouns, and Perek (2016) uses DSMs to study the change in productivity of argument constructions. This suggests that distributional semantics has a strong potential to become an important tool for linguistic studies on language change, especially given the increasing availability of diachronic corpora. Moreover, the same methods can be applied to investigate other types of meaning variation, such as geographical (Hovy and Purschke, 2018) and social ones (Del Tredici and Fernández, 2017).

8.7 Grounded Distributional Representations

REFERENTIAL
COMPETENCE

Words are used to refer to entities in the world. Marconi (1997) calls this aspect of the knowledge of meaning **referential competence**.

> **Referential competence** is the ability to relate lexemes to the world.

For instance, it is our referential competence of *dog* that allows us to correctly use this word to identify a dog in a picture. On the other hand, knowing that *dog* is semantically similar to *puppy*, is a hyponym of *mammal*, and

INFERENTIAL
COMPETENCE

is related to *kennel* are elements of what Marconi (1997) terms **inferential competence**. Differently from the referential one, inferential competence is knowledge about the relationships among words.

> **Inferential competence** is the ability to relate lexemes to other lexemes.

These two kinds of abilities are interrelated, but also distinct, even at the neurocognitive level (Marconi et al., 2013; Calzavarini, 2017). For example, we may know several things about the meaning of *aardvark* (e.g., that it is a nocturnal mammal native to Africa), without being able to refer to one.

Conversely, someone could name with *kangaroo* the proper type of animal, without knowing that it is related to *Australia* or is semantically narrower than *marsupial*.

Inferential competence is clearly the main target of distributional semantics. In fact, the most important aspects of lexical meaning addressed by DSMs concern semantic similarity and relatedness, in their various kinds (cf. Section 7.1). Can distributional semantics model referential competence too? Prima facie, the answer is "no," because it requires *some access to the extralinguistic world*, which DSMs do not have. The referential competence about *cherry* is based on the direct experience of this type of fruit. If we lacked such experience and we simply read the sentence *Cherries are small, round, red fruits*, we could probably tell a cherry apart from a banana, but only provided we had referential abilities about colors, sizes, and shapes. On the other hand, DSMs have only access to statistical co-occurrences derived from texts. They can correctly learn that *cherry* and *red* are related, but they are not able to map *red* onto the proper color. In other terms, DSMs produce **ungrounded representations**.

UNGROUNDED REPRESENTA-TIONS

This lack of grounding has raised several criticisms against distributional semantics as a plausible model of meaning (cf. Sections 1.2.2 and 8.8). Glenberg and Robertson (2000) argue that DSMs suffer from the same **symbol grounding problem** (Harnad, 1990) that affects any AI system based on purely symbol manipulation. Distributional vectors encode associations between symbols (i.e., the orthographic words observed in corpora), but meaning cannot spring from symbol–symbol relations only. This is in turn related to the **Chinese room argument** by Searle (1980). If a system, either human or artificial, learned to manipulate Chinese symbols so well as to be able to produce perfect Chinese utterances, still it could not be said to "understand" Chinese expressions, unless it was also able to ground them onto something else than associations with other symbols. However, these arguments apply to distributional semantics only partially: *It is true that the distributional vectors produced by DSMs are ungrounded, but this does not entail that they cannot be grounded.*

SYMBOL GROUNDING PROBLEM

CHINESE ROOM ARGUMENT

The theoretical foundations of distributional semantics lie in the structuralist assumption that the meaning of a lexical item stems from its syntagmatic and paradigmatic relations with other lexemes (cf. Section 1.1). Within such a view, reference has a secondary role and is beyond the scope of semantic analysis, which focuses on reconstructing the inferential properties of words from the way they are used in language. This epistemological background and the progress in statistical methods for text processing have favored the development of computational models that learn representations *only* from linguistic data, but this is a contingent fact, rather than an inherent limit of DSMs. In fact,

distributional representations are real-valued vectors that can be grounded by
adding information coming from our perceptual experience of the world.

GROUNDED
DISTRIBU-
TIONAL
REPRESENTA-
TIONS

> **Grounded distributional representations** are real-valued vectors that combine information extracted from distributional and experiential data.

EXPERIENTIAL
DATA

While **distributional data** are intralinguistic, because they are based on word
co-occurrences in language, **experiential data** are derived from "human perception and interaction with the physical world" (Andrews et al., 2009, p. 463).
Methods to learn grounded representations differ for the type of experiential
data and for the level of their integration with distributional information.

FEATURE
NORMS

A first approach uses human-generated semantic properties (e.g., *is_green*
and *has_seeds* for *apple*) collected in **feature (property) norms** (cf. Section
8.1) as a proxy for experiential data. Johns and Jones (2012) represent word
meaning with the concatenation of two explicit vectors, a document-based dis-

PERCEPTUAL
VECTOR

tributional vector and a **perceptual vector**, whose dimensions correspond to
the properties in feature norms. In this case, distributional and experiential
information do not undergo any type of fusion. Silberer and Lapata (2012)
also learn distributional and perceptual vectors independently, but then combine their information by mapping the two original vectors with canonical
correlation analysis in a shared low-dimensional space that maximizes the
correlation between the projected representation (cf. Section 8.4). The final
grounded representation is obtained by concatenating the mapped embeddings.

TOPIC MODELS

Andrews et al. (2009) and Steyvers (2010) extend **Topic Models** (cf. Section 4.4) to learn a grounded vector jointly from corpus data and properties
in feature norms. Andrews et al. (2009) treat words in documents and semantic features as observed variables that are explained by a generative process.
The training data is a corpus of documents, in which the lexemes included
in the feature norms are paired with a randomly sampled property (e.g., *The
dog:has_fur is eating an apple:is_round*). Lexical items are represented with
vectors of latent dimensions learned with LDA and corresponding to probability distributions over words and features. Andrews et al. (2009) and Silberer
and Lapata (2012) show that joint models produce better representations than
those treating experiential and distributional data independently.

IMAGE TAGS
AND CAPTIONS

Feature norms usually cover a relatively small number of concepts, since
they are very time-consuming to collect. Therefore, other approaches approximate experiential features with **tags and captions** describing the content of
images. Baroni and Lenci (2008), Hill and Korhonen (2014), and Hill et al.

ESPGAME

(2014b) extract tag co-occurrences from the **ESPGame** dataset (Von Ahn and
Dabbish, 2004) of photographs annotated with a list of entities depicted in

that image. Young et al. (2014) instead introduce a notion of **denotational** DENOTATIONAL
similarity computed from the crowdsourced descriptions of a large dataset of SIMILARITY
pictures, which they compare with standard corpus-based distributional similarity. Hill and Korhonen (2014) learn grounded embeddings by training SGNS
to jointly predict linguistic contexts and experiential data, with the latter corresponding to ESPGame image tags and/or properties from feature norms. The
training corpus is augmented in such a way that, each time a sentence s contains a lexical item l attested in the experiential sources, s is followed by a
pseudo-sentence $\hat{s}(l)$ constructed by alternating the token l with a randomly
extracted semantic feature (e.g., $\hat{s}(crocodile) = Crocodile\ legs\ crocodile\ teeth$
$scales\ crocodile$). Gupta et al. (2019) learn grounded GloVe (cf. Section 4.5)
embeddings using co-occurrences extracted from the annotations of the **Vis-**
ual Genome dataset (Krishna et al., 2017), which contains pictures of scenes VISUAL
labeled with objects, attributes, and relations. GENOME

Grounded distributed representations are typically tested in semantic tasks
that target semantic similarity and relatedness, categorization, and human
associations (cf. Section 7.2). All studies report a significant improvement produced by grounded representations over vectors that encode only distributional
or experiential information (Andrews et al., 2009; Hill and Korhonen, 2014).
However, one major limit of using feature norms or image tags is that, although
they reflect human sensory-motor experience with the world, they are amodal
linguistic data (cf. Section 8.1), which at most provide a sort of "proxy grounding": A DSM whose vector of *apple* is augmented with the property *is_green* is
still unable to link this representation to green apples. A solution is to extract
experiential knowledge directly from extralinguistic data.

8.7.1 Multimodal Distributional Semantics

To obtain a truly multimodal grounding of semantic representations, it is possible to encode images of objects with vectors recording their low-level features, MULTIMODAL
which are then combined with distributional data to obtain **multimodal vec-** VECTORS
tors (embeddings) (Baroni, 2016). Computational models that learn semantic
representations from texts and images are called **multimodal DSMs**. MULTIMODAL
DSMS

> Given a lexeme l, its **multimodal vector (embedding)** $l^{(M)}$ is a combi-
> nation of the **distributional vector** $l^{(D)}$ extracted from textual data, and
> the **image vector** $l^{(I)}$ extracted from images of entities l refers to.

As illustrated in Figure 8.8, the grounded multimodal representation of *dog*,
$\mathbf{dog}^{(M)}$, is the result of combining the **image vector** $\mathbf{dog}^{(I)}$ derived from a
dog picture, with a vector $\mathbf{dog}^{(D)}$ recording linguistic co-occurrences.

The image vector of a lexical item is extracted with computer vision techniques from images associated with the lexeme in question. A common dataset
is **ImageNet** (Deng et al., 2009), a large-scale collection of images organized
according to the WordNet hierarchy. One of the first methods to learn image
vectors is the **Bag-of-Visual-Words** (BoVW) approach (Sivic and Zisserman,
2003), which is the visual equivalent of the Vector Space Model for information retrieval (cf. Section 1.2.1). First, an image is divided into areas of pixels,
each represented by a local descriptor, a vector of low-level features such as
SIFT or SURF, which encode geometric or other information about the area.
These descriptors are then clustered into a discrete set of **visual words** using a
standard algorithm like k-means. Visual words typically capture simple visual
properties, such as oriented edges, textures, or colors. Each area is then mapped
to a visual word by comparing its local descriptors with the cluster centroids.
Finally, the image is represented with a vector such that each dimension corresponds to a visual word and its value counts how many areas from the image
map to it. The visual vector of a word is the average of the BoVW vectors
extracted from the images labeled with that word.

The advances of deep learning methods in computer vision have favored
the use of **Convolutional Neural Networks** (CNNs) (LeCun et al., 1998;
Krizhevsky et al., 2012). As described in Section 9.4.2, CNNs consist of weight
vectors called **filters** and organized in a sequence of **convolution** and **pooling**
layers: the former extract features that are then combined into a new vector
by the latter. CNNs induce a hierarchy of increasingly more abstract properties
from the image (e.g., edges, colors, etc.), and generally learn better vectors than
BoVW. CNNs are first trained to classify images into a set of categories. Then,
the network parameters are frozen, the classifier layer is removed, and the last
remaining layer is used to compute the vector of an input image. The visual
representation of a word is generated either by averaging or by computing the
component-wise maximum of the vectors of its images.

Multimodal DSMs differ both for the method to learn image vectors and for
the way they are combined with linguistic data. Bruni et al. (2012) and Kiela
and Bottou (2014) concatenate independently trained vectors:

$$\mathbf{l}^{(M)} = \alpha \mathbf{l}^{(D)}; (1 - \alpha)\mathbf{l}^{(I)}, \tag{8.27}$$

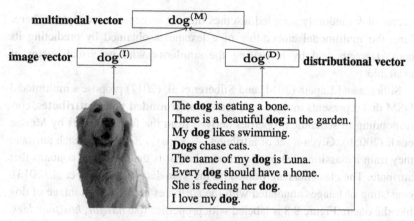

Figure 8.8 Multimodal vector (embedding)

where α is a parameter that weights the contribution of linguistic and visual information in the grounded representation. In Bruni et al. (2014), the multimodal vector is generated by applying SVD to a matrix of concatenated image and distributional vectors, to obtain a deeper fusion of their information.

A different solution consists in learning multimodal vectors directly from a mixture of text and image data. This simulates the idea that word learning occurs in a situated context, in which we are exposed to linguistic information and extralinguitic input about the word referents. Feng and Lapata (2010) and Roller and Schulte im Walde (2013) extend the approach by Andrews et al. (2009) and learn multimodal topic vectors with LDA trained on a text corpus augmented with the visual words extracted with BoVW. Lazaridou et al. (2015a, 2017) also learn the grounded representation from a corpus in which some lexems are associated with pretrained image vectors generated with a CNN. They propose a **Multimodal Skip-Gram** (MMSG) with this objective: MMSG

$$J_{MMSG} = J_{ling} + J_{vision}, \qquad (8.28)$$

where J_{ling} is the Skip-Gram objective in Equation 6.23 (cf. Section 6.3), and J_{vision}, which is active only for the lexemes associated with image data, aims at minimizing the following margin loss, derived from Frome et al. (2013):

$$J_{vision} = \sum_{i=1}^{|V|} \sum_{j=1}^{k} [\max(0, \delta - \text{sim}_{\cos}(l_i^{(D)}, l_i^{(I)}) + \text{sim}_{\cos}(l_i^{(D)}, \tilde{l}_j^{(I)}))], \quad (8.29)$$

where δ is the margin, V is the vocabulary, $l^{(D)}$ is the target multimodally-enhanced distributional embedding, $l^{(I)}$ its image vector, and $\tilde{l}^{(I)}$ is the image vector of k randomly sampled lexemes that act as negative examples. Therefore, the multimodal embedding of a lexeme is obtained by predicting its context words and by increasing the similarity with its visual vector, if available.

GROUNDED
VISUAL
ATTRIBUTES

Silberer and Lapata (2014) and Silberer et al. (2017) propose a multimodal DSM that represents images with vectors of **grounded visual attributes**, corresponding to semantic properties derived from the feature norms by McRae et al. (2005b). Given a set of attributes $A = \{a_1, \ldots, a_n\}$, for each attribute they train a classifier that predicts how likely it is that an image contains that attribute. The classifiers are trained on the **Visa** dataset (Silberer et al., 2013),

VISA

consisting of images annotated with the attributes in A (e.g., an image of dog like the one in Figure 8.8 is labeled with properties like *has_fur*, *has_four_legs*, etc.). An image is then represented with a vector whose ith dimension corresponds to the attribute $a_i \in A$, and its component is the prediction score generated for that image by the a_i classifier. The visual representation of a lexical item is the average of the attribute vectors extracted from its images. This method is particularly appealing because the vectors of grounded attributes are interpretable in terms of explicit semantic properties, differently from those produced by BoVW or CNNs. Silberer and Lapata (2014) combine the image and the distributional vector of a lexical item by feeding them to a

DENOISING
AUTOENCODER

denoising autoencoder, a deep neural network that is trained to reconstruct the correct input from a corrupted version (cf. Section 9.6.3). The fused multimodal representation is the vector produced by the hidden layer of the trained network.

All studies show that multimodal representations perform better than vectors that encode only distributional or experiential information in several semantic tasks (Roller and Schulte im Walde, 2013; Bruni et al., 2014; Kiela and Bottou, 2014; Lazaridou et al., 2015a; Silberer et al., 2017), and even sim-

REFERENCE
PROBLEM

ple vector concatenation is highly competitive with respect to more complex fusion methods. Moreover, multimodal DSMs address the **reference problem** of linking words to perceptual representations of entities in the world. Jackendoff argues that "the connection from vision to language must be mediated by one or more interface modules that establish a partial relation between visual and conceptual formats" (Jackendoff, 1997, p. 43). If we assume that both visual and linguistic information is represented as vectors, this interface can

CROSS-MODAL
MAPPING

be modeled as a **cross-modal mapping** between vectors encoding visual features extracted from images and distributional vectors that represent aspects of conceptual content. This approach is equivalent to the one adopted for cross-lingual embeddings (cf. Section 8.4.1). Instead of mapping monolingual vectors to translate lexical items from one language to another, the cross-modal mapping "translates" visual representations into linguistic ones.

The cross-modal mapping is typically formalized as a **linear transformation matrix** that generates distributional vectors from image ones.

LINEAR TRANS-
FORMATION
MATRIX

> Given a semantic space $\mathbf{D}$ of distributional vectors and a semantic space $\mathbf{I}$ of image vectors, a **cross-modal mapping** is a **linear transformation matrix** $\mathbf{W}^{\mathbf{I} \rightarrow \mathbf{D}}$ that maps the vectors in $\mathbf{I}$ onto $\mathbf{D}$.

Given a set of seed lexical items, such that for each lexeme l there is a distributional vector $\mathbf{l}^{(\mathbf{D})} \in \mathbf{D}$ and an image vector $\mathbf{l}^{(\mathbf{I})} \in \mathbf{I}$, the matrix $\mathbf{W}^{\mathbf{I} \rightarrow \mathbf{D}}$ is learned with linear regression, canonical correlation analysis, or neural networks, by attempting to minimize the difference between the distributional vectors mapped from the visual space and the original ones (Socher et al., 2013b; Lazaridou et al., 2014). Frome et al. (2013) map the vectors with a neural model and the margin loss in Equation 8.29 applied at pretrained image and distributional embeddings. Lazaridou et al. (2015a) instead learn a mapping matrix $\mathbf{W}^{\mathbf{D} \rightarrow \mathbf{I}}$ from distributional vectors to image ones with an extension of MMSG such that the objective function is a variation of Equation 8.29 in which $\mathbf{l}_i^{(\mathbf{D})}$ is replaced by the projected image vector $\hat{\mathbf{l}}_i^{(\mathbf{I})} = \mathbf{l}_i^{(\mathbf{D})} \mathbf{W}^{\mathbf{D} \rightarrow \mathbf{I}}$.

Cross-modal mapping can be regarded as a model of referential competence, since it links words and images of their referents, and the reference problem as a case of the **zero-shot learning** scenario (Palatucci et al., 2009). A small set of training data is used to learn a general mapping function from vectors in the domain of interest (e.g., pictures of objects) to distributional vectors, and then the induced function is applied to map vectors representing new entities (e.g., images that were not seen in training) onto the distributional space, retrieving the nearest neighbor words as their labels (cf. Sections 8.4.1 and 8.8). This setting is used to label images with nouns (Frome et al., 2013; Socher et al., 2013b; Lazaridou et al., 2015a) or attribute-denoting adjectives (Lazaridou et al., 2015b), and to model word meaning learning in a multimodal scenario. Lazaridou et al. (2014, 2017) investigate the **fast mapping** problem of a learner that is exposed to a new word in context and has to search for its referent. They show that cross-modal mapping can solve the task even when distributional vectors are trained on a very limited amount of linguistic input.

ZERO-SHOT
LEARNING

FAST MAPPING

Differently from models that represent meaning with amodal symbols and must explain how these are grounded in perceptual information (cf. Section 8.1), distributional semantics encodes both linguistic and experiential data in the same vector-based format and can integrate them into multimodal representations including visual but also auditory (Kiela and Clark, 2015; Lopopolo and Van Mieltenburg, 2015) and even olfactory (Kiela et al., 2015b) data.

Therefore, distributional semantics can not only address referential aspects of meaning, but also model how language is grounded in the world. The progress in computer vision and the increasing availability of richly annotated image and video datasets will surely contribute to further advances in this area, with important consequences for NLP and AI applications (e.g., visual question-answering), as well as for cognitive research on word meaning.

8.8 Distributional Semantics in Cognitive Science

Distributional semantics plays a key role in cognitive science to investigate how word meaning is represented, acquired, and processed, and to explain human performance in psycholinguistic tasks. Moreover, distributional vectors are used as proxies for semantic representations in computational models of the mental lexicon and semantic memory (Jones et al., 2015; Yee et al., 2018). In fact, the strong connection with psychological research dates back to the very beginnings of distributional semantics (cf. Section 1.1.4).

ESTIMATING SEMANTIC SIMILARITY

The most straightforward application of DSMs in cognitive science is to **estimate semantic similarity,** as an alternative to the direct elicitation of human ratings or to lexical resources like WordNet. For several years, LSA has been the preferred model, though now it has been superseded by better-performing DSMs, such as GloVe or word2vec (Mandera et al., 2017). Extensive experimental results show that distributional similarity can predict human behavior in a wide range of semantic tasks (Pereira et al., 2016; Günther et al., 2019), including categorization (Louwerse, 2011; Riordan and Jones, 2011), priming (Lund et al., 1995; Jones et al., 2006; Mandera et al., 2017), and word associations (Griffiths et al., 2007; Mandera et al., 2017). Some of these tasks have also become important testbeds to evaluate DSMs (cf. Section 7.2). Since collecting human ratings about psycholinguistic variables (e.g., concreteness) for a large amount of lexical items is a daunting task, DSM are also used

EXTRAPOLATING NORMED DATA

to **extrapolate normed data** to new lexemes (Keuleers and Balota, 2015; Mandera et al., 2015). Bestgen and Vincze (2012) and Recchia and Louwerse (2015) apply the nearest neighbors method illustrated in Section 8.5.1 to extrapolate affect (valence, arousal, and dominance) ratings, and the former study concreteness and imagery judgments too. Hollis et al. (2017) extrapolate affective ratings with regression and SGNS embeddings.

The idea that distributional semantics is a useful tool to investigate meaning is uncontroversial in cognitive science. As words with similar meanings tend to appear in similar contexts, their distribution in texts can be used as a

proxy for their meaning. This is consistent with what we have called **Weak** WEAK AND STRONG DISTRI-BUTIONAL HYPOTHESIS
Distributional Hypothesis in Section 1.2. On the other hand, several psy-
chologists have defended a **Strong Distributional Hypothesis**, according to
which word meaning is not merely *reflected* in language use, but *determined*
by it. Jenkins (1954) argues that distributional statistics are responsible for
the formation of word associations in the mental lexicon. Miller and Charles
(1991) define the contextual representation formed by subjects after repeated
encounters with a word as a cognitive structure (cf. Section 1.1.4). Moreover,
Landauer and Dumais (1997) propose LSA as a psychologically plausible theory of word meaning acquisition, and HAL (cf. Section 4.1.1) is claimed to be
a general model for semantic memory (Burgess, 1998). In Section 8.8.1, we
review the debate about the cognitive plausibility of distributional representations. Then, we present methods to interpret the semantic information encoded
in word embeddings (Section 8.8.2) and the use of distributional vectors to
decode meaning in the brain (cf. Section 8.8.3).

8.8.1 The Cognitive Plausibility of Distributional Representations

Differently from its weak version, the cognitive validity of the Strong Distributional Hypothesis has been intensively debated (Günther et al., 2019).
The major attacks have come from **embodied (grounded) cognition**, which EMBODIED COGNITION
departs from traditional theories in cognitive science and AI according to
which "the meaning of a concept consists of the links between the abstract
symbol for that concept and the abstract symbols for other concepts· or
for semantic features" (Pecher and Zwaan, 2005, p. 1). Embodied cognition
instead assumes that concepts are inherently grounded in our bodily experience
with the environment, and therefore in perception and action (Barsalou, 1999,
2020). This view has led some of its proponents to express deep skepticism
toward the cognitive plausibility of distributional semantics, because it learns
semantic representations without any extralinguistic grounding (Perfetti, 1998;
Glenberg and Robertson, 2000). The success of DSMs in predicting human
semantic behavior should be explained as a mere correlation between grounded
concepts and language use: *Grounded meanings would determine linguistic
co-occurrences, but not vice versa* (Glenberg and Mehta 2008a, 2008b).

Research in distributional semantics and cognitive science has contributed to MULTIMODAL DSMS
dispel these critical arguments. On the one hand, **multimodal DSMs** show that
it is possible to generate grounded distributional representations (cf. Section
8.7.1). Thus, distributional semantics differs from classic symbolic theories
that represent concepts and meanings with amodal symbols, since its vectors
can accommodate linguistic and extralinguistic data. On the other hand, there

STRONG
EMBODIMENT

REPRESENTA
TIONAL
PLURALISM

is growing evidence from cognitive neuroscience against **strong embodiment** theories of semantic memory (Meteyard et al., 2012), which claim that *all* concepts are analogical simulations of sensory-motor experience, and instead in favor of a form of **representational pluralism** (Dove, 2009; Binder, 2016).

> The **multiple representation view** assumes that all concepts consist of sensory-motor and linguistic representations.

This perspective opens the way to the possibility of reconciling embodied and distributional models of meaning (Andrews et al., 2014), under the assumption that language is also part of the environment that we experience and that determines our conceptual representations (Clark, 2006). According to Zwaan and Madden (2005), interactions with the world leave traces of experience in the brain. Word meaning results from the combination of two types of experiential traces: **referent traces**, which derive from perception of and action with the world, and **linguistic traces**, which are left by the words we produce and receive. The role of distributional information in constructing conceptual knowledge is also defended by Dove (2020, 2023), who argues for a **linguistic embodiment hypothesis**, according to which language is a source of embodiment and concepts in part rely on simulations of linguistic experiences. This view is compatible with the Strong Distributional Hypothesis: *Linguistic co-occurrences shape our meanings, alongside other types of multimodal experiences.*

REFERENT AND
LINGUISTIC
TRACES

LINGUISTIC
EMBODIMENT
HYPOTHESIS

ABSTRACT
WORDS

The multiple representation view of semantic memory is particularly effective to explain the meaning of **abstract words** (e.g., *idea*), which challenge strong embodiment for their lack of perceptual referents (Andrews et al., 2014; Borghi et al., 2017; Dove, 2022). Abstract and concrete lexemes are organized, represented, and processed differently (Crutch and Warrington, 2005; Kousta et al., 2011; Hill et al., 2014a), and have also distinct distributional properties (Recchia and Jones, 2012; Frassinelli et al., 2017). Given the hypothesis that all concepts are represented both in the language and in the sensory-motor domains, the difference between concrete and abstract words can be explained with the relative salience of embodied and linguistic information, the latter being more preponderant for the abstract items. Various versions of this view have been proposed, such as the **Language and Situated Simulation** (LASS) theory by Barsalou et al. (2008) and the **Word as Social Tools** (WAT) theory by Borghi and Binkofski (2014). Therefore, statistical distributions extracted from linguistic contexts are expected to play a major role in the acquisition of abstract words (Vigliocco et al., 2009; Lupyan, 2019). For instance, Andrews et al. (2009) show that the neighbors identified by a standard DSM tend to

LASS

WAT

contain more abstract terms than the ones produced by a model enhanced with experiential information extracted from feature norms (cf. Section 8.7).

Distributional and sensory-motor information have a complex interplay in conceptual representations. Riordan and Jones (2011) compare distributional vectors and experiential representations obtained from feature norms in a categorization task, and conclude that the two types of information are "both correlated and complementary data streams" (Riordan and Jones, 2011, p. 339). The **complementarity** of linguistic and experiential knowledge is supported by various kinds of evidence. First of all, their integration in grounded representations achieve better performance than vectors that encode only one type of data (cf. Section 8.7). Expectedly, this improvement is higher for concrete words (Bruni et al., 2014), given the prominence of sensory-motor information in their meaning. Secondly, distributional and experiential vectors identify different types of properties of lexical items: The former tend to provide more abstract or encyclopedic information, while the latter are biased toward information related to sensory-motor dimensions (Baroni and Lenci, 2008; Andrews et al., 2009; Bruni et al., 2014). COMPLEMENTARY INFORMATION

The fact that certain physical properties are not captured by DSMs can be an effect of the so-called **reporting bias** (Gordon and Van Durme, 2013), according to which people tend to omit information that is obvious. The reporting bias is a consequence of the **maxim of quantity** postulated by Grice (1975), which states that communication should be as informative as necessary, but no more, leaving unstated information that can be expected to be known. For example, the corpus analysis in Paik et al. (2021) shows that color information about concepts associated with a single color (e.g., strawberry) is worst represented. Various experiments also reveal that even the most advanced neural language models like BERT (cf. Section 9.6.3) are affected by the reporting bias and struggle to capture highly implied information, probably because their training corpora provide weak distributional signals about it (Shwartz and Choi, 2020; Apidianaki and Garí Soler, 2021; Paik et al., 2021). REPORTING BIAS
MAXIM OF QUANTITY

On the other hand, evidence indicates that there is also a strong **correlation** between distributional and extralinguistic information. Language has evolved as a tool to communicate our experience of the world, and therefore several aspects of this experience have become encoded in linguistic structures. This redundancy between distributional and experiential data is explicitly stated in the **Symbol Interdependency Hypothesis** (Louwerse, 2008, 2011): CORRELATED INFORMATION

SYMBOL INTER-DEPENDENCY HYPOTHESIS

> Language encodes relations in the world, including embodied ones.

Distributional semantics provides empirical support to the Symbol Interdependency Hypothesis. Louwerse and Zwaan (2009) and Louwerse and Benesh (2012) report that LSA embeddings encode spatial and geographical relations, while Louwerse and Connell (2011) predict with distributional vectors the category of perceptual modality (auditory, olfactory–gustatory, visual–haptic) a word belongs to. Lenci et al. (2018) estimate the affective content of lexemes with a DSM (cf. Section 8.5.1) and find that abstract words have higher emotive values than concrete lexemes, consistently with the evidence in Kousta et al. (2011) about the key role of affective grounding in the abstract domain. Abdou et al. (2021) show that the color space of word embeddings has significant correspondences with the human one, and that the similarities are even stronger with contextual DSMs (cf. Section 9.6.3).

An important effect of the interdependency between linguistic and embodied knowledge is that it is possible to infer perceptual representations even for lexical items with whose referents we have no direct experience. Consider the verse *Beware the Jabberwock, my son! The jaws that bite, the claws that catch!* from the poem written by Lewis Carroll about the killing of a creature named "Jabberwock," and included in his novel *Through the Looking-Glass*. The words it co-occurs with allow us to infer some physical aspects of the referent of *Jabberwock*, which is probably a kind of a wild predator like a tiger or a lion. Therefore, even though we lack any direct experience, this name has some grounded content for us, brought by the linguistic contexts it is observed in. Howell et al. (2005) call this phenomenon **propagation of grounding** and argue that it plays a fundamental role in meaning acquisition. Their hypothesis is that children acquire their first concrete concepts via direct sensory-motor experiences. As learning progresses, children are exposed to novel words in speech or text that are not directly grounded in immediate sensory data. These words are acquired and grounded only indirectly thanks to their paradigmatic and syntagmatic distributional associations with more imageable lexical items. Therefore, given a set of concepts for which we have a **direct grounding** in sensory-motor experiences, linguistic co-occurrences determine the **indirect grounding** of a much larger number of concepts (Vincent-Lamarre et al., 2016; Günther et al., 2020). This projection is responsible for the grounding of novel concepts acquired via language only: concrete concepts like the *Jabberwock*, but abstract ones too. In fact, the latter are also grounded in sensory-motor information (Barsalou and Wiemer-Hastings, 2005), though in a more complex and indirect way than concrete ones, since they are related to diverse situations and their grounding is mediated by linguistic associations (e.g., *religion* can be grounded in images of a church, people praying in a mosque, and so on).

The meaning-projecting role of language is reminiscent of the **Syntactic Bootstrapping Hypothesis** (Landau and Gleitman, 1985; Gleitman, 1990), which assumes that the observation of a verb syntactic environments (e.g., its syntactic constructions or the arguments it co-occurs with) is a crucial component of the relevant input needed by learners to acquire its meaning.

PROPAGATION
OF GROUNDING

DIRECT AND
INDIRECT
GROUNDING

SYNTACTIC
BOOTSTRAP-
PING
HYPOTHESIS

While first verbs are learned through the direct sensory-motor experience of concrete actions, it is distributional information that allows learners to rapidly expand the verb lexicon by acquiring progressively more abstract predicates. The projection effect of distributional learning remains active in adults too, allowing them to infer the meaning of new verbs occurring in familiar syntactic frames.

The fact that language users can exploit linguistic cues to learn semantic properties referring to embodied experiences is also supported by neurocognitive evidence coming from **congenital blind subjects**. Bedny et al. (2019) CONGENITAL BLIND SUBJECTS show that the semantic spaces of verbs of visual perception and light emission in blind people are extremely similar to the ones in sighted subjects. A possible explanation is that the meaning of these verbs can be reconstructed from language even without direct first-person experience (Lewis et al., 2019). Wang et al. (2020) compare the neural representations of object color knowledge in blind and sighted individuals and find two independent, linked forms of encodings: one derived from language/conceptual reasoning, shared between the two experimental groups, and one derived from sensory experience, unique to the sighted population.

Strong similarities exist in the color domain between sighted and blind subjects, but with important differences. Although blind adults' similarity judgments produce a color wheel qualitatively similar to that of sighted adults (e.g., blue is more similar to green than red), there is a higher variability across blind individuals (Saysani et al., 2018). Moreover, the latter are less likely than sighted subjects to use color during semantic similarity judgments (Connolly et al., 2007) and to produce color-related features to describe concrete concepts (Lenci et al., 2013). This contrast might be related to the reporting bias phenomenon affecting the color domain, while syntactic frames and arguments would provide stronger distributional cues to infer verb meaning. Kim et al. (2021) argue that blind subjects do derive colors from language, but using more complex inferential processes than co-occurrence statistics. Therefore, unsurprisingly, the effectiveness of distributional learning depends on the extent to which semantic properties are encoded in the linguistic input.

Distributional semantics offers interesting opportunities to model the process of grounding propagation. Johns and Jones (2012) represent lexical meaning as the concatenation of a distributional and of a perceptual vector (cf. Section 8.7), and infer the perceptual component $t^{(P)}$ for an ungrounded target lexeme t as the centroid perceptual representations of other lexical items l, weighted by the similarity between the distributional vector $l^{(D)}$ and $t^{(D)}$:

$$t^{(P)} = \sum_{l \in G} l^{(P)} \text{sim}_{\cos}(l^{(D)}, t^{(D)}) \qquad (8.30)$$

where G is a set of grounded lexemes. Therefore, a word inherits grounding from the lexemes that occur in similar linguistic contexts. Lazaridou et al. (2017) apply MMSG to propagate grounding to newly acquired words, finding correlations with human distributional learning. Hill et al. (2014b) and Lazaridou et al. (2015a) use the cross-modal mapping to propagate perceptual information to abstract concepts. Kiela et al. (2014) introduce a measure IMAGE of **image dispersion**, which is defined as the average pairwise cosine distance between a set of vectors extracted from images associated with a lexical item. They show that concrete words have smaller image dispersion than abstract lexemes, consistently with the hypothesis that the latter are grounded in more varied situations (Barsalou and Wiemer-Hastings, 2005). Lazaridou et al. (2015a) also report that the multimodal vectors generated by MMSG for abstract lexemes have a higher degree of variability.

In summary, nowadays there is a growing consensus about the cognitive plausibility of the Strong Distributional Hypothesis.

> Distributional representations participate in a **pluralistic** semantic memory, in which they work **synergistically** with embodied information derived from sensory-motor and affective experiences of the world.

This is consistent with the hypothesis of an interplay between referential and inferential aspects of meaning (Marconi, 1997). Co-occurrence statistics complement and project conceptual grounding beyond our first-hand experiences. CLINE OF A **cline of embodiment** (Lenci et al., 2018) is likely to exist, with *strongly* EMBODIMENT *embodied* concepts, acquired with direct sensory-motor experiences, *weakly or indirectly embodied* concepts, whose grounding is mostly due to linguistic projection, up to purely *linguistic concepts*, almost exclusively composed of associations obtained via distributional learning (Lupyan and Lewis, 2019).

8.8.2 From Word Embeddings to Semantic Features

INTERPRETA A frequent objection advanced against distributional semantics is the lack of BILITY **interpretability** of its representations (Günther et al., 2019). In particular, the distributed character of word embeddings prevents us from directly labeling each dimension with a specific semantic value (cf. Section 8.1). This contrasts with one of the most influential and longstanding approach to semantic representation, which assumes that the conceptual content of lexical items is decom- SEMANTIC posable into explicit **semantic features (properties)** that identify meaning
FEATURES

components (Vigliocco and Vinson, 2007). In fact, the relationship between distributional representations and semantic features is a widely debated topic (Baroni and Lenci, 2008; Boleda and Erk, 2015). Moreover, the poor interpretability of embeddings raises the issue of understanding which aspects of meaning they encode. DSMs are mostly used to estimate semantic similarity or relatedness, but this still leaves open the problem of determining which dimensions are shared by similar lexemes.

A widely used method to investigate the linguistic properties captured by embeddings is the design of **probing tasks** (Ettinger et al., 2016) based on PROBING TASKS the assumption that, if a given attribute (e.g., animacy) can be predicted using some embeddings as input (e.g., by means of a classifier or a regressor), then the embeddings encode information about this attribute (cf. Section 9.5). Rubinstein et al. (2015) train both binary classifiers and linear regressors to predict the properties in the feature norms by McRae et al. (2005a) using count and predict embeddings. Their analysis shows that embeddings generally predict taxonomic properties (e.g., *is_an_animal*) better than attributive ones (e.g., *is_yellow*), confirming the fact that not all types of features are equally recoverable from distributional data. Collell and Moens (2016) adopt a similar approach and show that distributional and image vectors encode complementary information: The former are better at predicting encyclopedic and taxonomic features, and the latter features referring to color, motion, or physical form.

Instead of "probing" embeddings for single properties, an alternative approach consists in using a set of training lexemes to learn a **feature map-** FEATURE **ping** from embeddings to continuous vectors of semantic properties, similarly MAPPING to the cross-lingual and multimodal settings (cf. Sections 8.4.1 and 8.7).

> Given a semantic space D of word embeddings and a semantic space F of feature vectors, a **feature mapping** is a **linear transformation matrix** $W^{D \to F}$ that maps the embeddings in D onto the vectors in F.

The advantage of this approach lies in the general nature of the mapping function, which can be applied to generate semantic features vectors from word embeddings that were not seen during training. Făgărăsan et al. (2015) use partial least squares regression to learn a mapping from word embeddings onto semantic vectors derived from McRae's norms. Bulat et al. (2016) and Derby et al. (2020) extend this model to image and multimodal vectors. Derby et al. (2019) instead learn a mapping from feature norms onto the GloVe embedding space with a variation of SGNS that takes in input the embedding of a target lexeme and is trained to predict its properties. Instead of using linguistic features from property norms, Utsumi (2020) and Chersoni et al. (2021a) map embeddings onto the 65 features introduced by Binder et al. (2016), which correspond to semantic primitives covering a wide variety of sensory-motor, affective and cognitive dimensions (cf. Section 8.1).

ZERO-SHOT
LEARNING

The feature mapping is typically evaluated in a **zero-shot learning** task: Given a test lexeme l with gold-standard feature vector $\mathbf{l}^{(\mathbf{F})}$, the embedding $\mathbf{l}^{(\mathbf{D})}$ is mapped onto a feature vector $\hat{\mathbf{l}}^{(\mathbf{F})}$, and the model is evaluated with its accuracy in retrieving $\mathbf{l}^{(\mathbf{F})}$ within the k nearest neighbors of $\hat{\mathbf{l}}^{(\mathbf{F})}$. Moreover, the mapping can be used to identify which semantic dimensions are better encoded by embeddings. Chersoni et al. (2021a) compute the average of the Spearman correlation between human ratings in the Binder's dataset and mapping predictions across words and features obtained with partial least squares regression. In the heatmap in Figure 8.9a, it is possible to observe the average correlations per each of the 14 domains in which the Binder's feature are grouped (the DSMs are the same used in the experiments in Section 7.4 and a subset of those tested by Chersoni et al., 2021a). It is striking that the features belonging to the Cognition, Causal, and Social domains are among the best-predicted ones. The Emotion domain also shows good correlation, confirming the role of distributional information in shaping the affective content of lexical items (Lenci et al., 2018). On the other hand, somatosensorial features are predicted with lower accuracy, except for Gustation and Olfation. This can be explained by the fact that DSMs learn word meaning only from textual data and encode abstract semantic dimensions better. On the other hand, although they clearly miss several aspects of perceptual information, this is to some extent "redundantly" encoded in linguistic expressions, consistently with the Symbol Interdependency Hypothesis (cf. Section 8.8.1). A similar picture emerges in Figure 8.9b: Abstract lexical items are generally better modeled by embeddings, while the worst ones are those referring to physical properties.

Word embeddings and featural symbolic representations are often regarded as antithetic and possibly incompatible ways of representing semantic information which pertain to very different approaches to the study of language and cognition. However, current research on feature mapping shows that new bridges between distributed and symbolic lexical representations can indeed be laid, to exploit their complementary strengths: The gradience and robustness of the former and the interpretability of the latter.

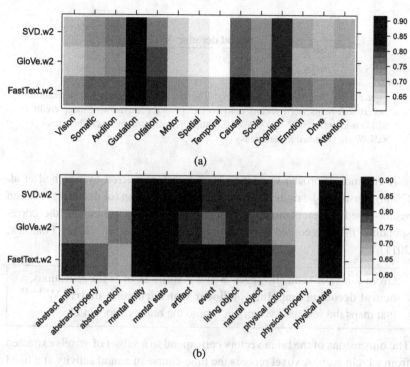

Figure 8.9 Spearman correlations (a) per feature domain and (b) per word class between the predicted and the original data in Binder et al. (2016)

8.8.3 Neurosemantic Decoding

Neuroscientific evidence supports the view that the brain represents concepts in terms of patterns of neural activations, encoded as distributed vectors in a neural semantic space, similar to word embeddings (Huth et al., 2012). Since brain activations defy direct interpretation, several methods have been developed in computational neuroscience to "read off meaning" from distributed brain activity patterns. This task is called **neurosemantic decoding**.

NEUROSEMANTIC
DECODING

> **Neurosemantic decoding** aims at identifying the mental state represented by brain activity recorded with neuroimaging techniques such as fMRI (functional Magnetic Resonance Imaging).

For instance, the activation pattern produced by the stimulus *dog* is correctly decoded if the pattern can be labeled with that word.

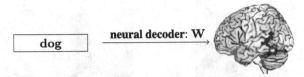

Figure 8.10 Neurosemantic decoding: The decoder is a linear transformation matrix that maps word vectors onto vectors of brain activations (image credit: Mikkelwallentin, CC BY-SA 4.0, https://creativecommons.org/licenses/by-sa/4.0/, via Wikimedia Commons)

A common approach to address such a task pioneered by Mitchell et al. (2008) consists in learning a **neural decoding mapping** (or **decoder**) between vector-based representations of concepts and vectors containing the corresponding fMRI recorded brain activity (Naselaris et al., 2011; Poldrack, 2011).

NEURAL
DECODING
MAPPING

> Given a lexical semantic space $\mathbf{S}$ and a space $\mathbf{B}$ of brain activations, a **neural decoding mapping** is a **linear transformation matrix** $\mathbf{W}^{\mathbf{S} \rightarrow \mathbf{B}}$ that maps the semantic vectors in $\mathbf{S}$ onto the brain vectors in $\mathbf{B}$.

VOXEL

The dimensions of the brain vectors correspond to a subset of voxels extracted from a brain scan. A **voxel** records the time-course of neural activity at a fixed location in the brain. Semantic vectors can be any kind of continuous representation of word meaning. Chang et al. (2011) represent lexemes with vectors of properties derived from feature norms, and Anderson et al. (2016) with vectors of Binder's features. However, the use of distributional representations for neurosemantic decoding has become the most popular choice.

Mitchell et al. (2008) learn the mapping with a linear regression model trained on 60 words with their fMRI scans. Lexemes are represented with explicit distributional vectors containing co-occurrences with 25 verbs capturing basic semantic dimensions (e.g., *hear*, *eat*, etc.). Given a lexeme l and its n-dimensional vector $\mathbf{l}$, the predicted activation y_v of a voxel v is given by:

$$y_v = \sum_{i=1}^{n} w_{i,v} l_i, \tag{8.31}$$

where $w_{i,v}$ is a weight of the mapping matrix $\mathbf{W}$ specifying the degree to which the ith distributional dimension activates the voxel v. Decoding performance is evaluated in a **zero-shot learning** task (Palatucci et al., 2009), aiming at predicting the correct fMRI scan of unseen words. Mitchell et al. (2008) introduce a **leave-two-out** (or **two-vs-two**) crossvalidation test. The model is repeatedly trained with 58 word-scan pairs. Each trained model is

ZERO-SHOT
LEARNING

LEAVE-TWO-
OUT

used to predict the fMRI images for the two held-out words l_i and l_j: The predicted scans $\hat{1}_i^{(B)}$ and $\hat{1}_j^{(B)}$ are compared with cosine similarity to their corresponding gold-standard brain vectors $1_i^{(B)}$ and $1_j^{(B)}$, and the classification is correct if $\hat{1}_i^{(B)}$ is closer to $1_i^{(B)}$ than to $1_j^{(B)}$, and vice versa. Another common evaluation measure for neural decoding is the accuracy in retrieving the correct scan $1_i^{(B)}$ within the k nearest neighbors of the brain image $\hat{1}_i^{(B)}$ predicted from l_i.

Later studies have refined the method by Mitchell et al. (2008), which has also been applied to decode other types of brain data obtained with electroencephalography (EEG) and magnetoencephalography (MEG). Huth et al. (2016) use explicit vectors of co-occurrences with 985 English words to decode more than 10, 000 lexical items belonging to 12 categories and create a "semantic atlas" of the brain. Different kinds of word embeddings have been tested in neurosemantic decoding experiments: classical count DSMs (Devereux et al., 2010; Murphy et al., 2012), Topic Models (Pereira et al., 2011, 2013), predict DSMs with different types of linguistic contexts (Bulat et al., 2017; Abnar et al., 2018), up to the more recent contextual embeddings and fine-tuning techniques (Beinborn et al., 2019; Gauthier and Levy, 2019; cf. Section 9.6.3). The decoding task itself has been proposed as a benchmark for DSMs, as an alternative to the traditional use of behavioral datasets (Murphy et al., 2012; Xu et al., 2016; Hollenstein et al., 2019). Neurosemantic decoding has been extended beyond words to interpret the meaning of entire sentences (Gauthier and Ivanova, 2018; Pereira et al., 2018; Sun et al., 2019a), which are represented with compositional embeddings (cf. Chapter 9). Athanasiou et al. (2018) show that neural activation semantic models built out of these mappings can also be used to successfully carry out NLP tasks like textual entailment.

Anderson et al. (2015, 2017) decode brain images by comparing DSMs and neural semantic spaces with **Representation Similarity Analysis** (cf. Section 7.5). Anderson et al. (2015) report greater correlations between image vectors and visual brain areas (i.e., ventral-temporal and lateral-occipital regions), and between distributional embeddings and linguistically dominant areas (i.e., posterior-parietal, lateral-temporal and inferior-frontal regions). They also record overall higher decoding accuracies with multimodal embeddings. Anderson et al. (2017) observe that image and distributional vectors decode concrete nouns, but in the case of abstract nouns distributional vectors achieve a significantly greater accuracy, supporting the stronger prominence of linguistic information in the abstract domain (cf. Section 8.8.1).

Research on neurosemantic decoding represents an important aspect of the synergies between cognitive science and distributional semantics. On the one hand, the strong correlation between corpus-based and brain-derived semantic representations means that the former can be used as a reliable model to decode neural data and to project brain data even to unseen lexical items. On the other hand, if the mapping between distributional and brain vectors is successful, we can infer that linguistic co-occurrences are encoded in the brain and successfully capture some aspects of our representation of meaning, thereby bringing further support to the cognitive plausibility of distributional representations.

8.9 Summary

Distributional semantics represents lexical meaning with **distributed vectors** automatically learned from text corpora. The continuous and usage-based nature of its representations is a major departure from **symbolic models** of the lexicon and makes distributional semantics particularly effective to tackle the **gradient** nature of meaning. For instance, the **senses** of a word are modeled as a continuous space obtained by clustering their distribution in corpora, **semantic change** is investigated by tracking shifts in vector space, and **connotative aspects** of meaning are addressed by studying how usage determines the affective content of words or propagates cultural stereotypes.

A further advantage of vectors is that they provide a shared format to encode information about lexemes, images, brain activity, and so forth. This allows distributional semantics to offer a general and common framework to model the relations between languages with **cross-lingual DSMs**, between language and the world with **multimodal DSMs**, and between language and the brain with **neurosemantic decoding**. Prima facie distinct phenomena are now subsumed under the same paradigm: *Learning a mapping between vector spaces representing different types of information.*

Lexical semantic knowledge can be distinguished into **inferential competence** of the relationships between words, and **referential competence** of the relationships between words and the their referents in the world (Marconi, 1997). Concerning the former, DSMs satisfactorily model semantic similarity and especially relatedness, but still strive to account for **paradigmatic semantic relations** like hypernymy or antonymy, despite the intense research on this topic. This might suggest an uneven ability of distributional semantics to address the various aspects of inferential competence, with a bias toward associative relations rather than logical ones. On the other hand, the alleged impossibility for DSMs to account for referential competence is disproved by multimodal DSMs that integrate linguistic and extralinguistic information. Distributional semantics is consistent with a pluralistic view of semantic representations in which linguistic, sensory-motor, and affective knowledge work together synergistically. This supports the cognitive plausibility of distributional representations and the active role of linguistic co-occurrences in shaping our semantic memory.

8.10 Further Reading

- Types of semantic representations: Markman (1999); Vigliocco and Vinson (2007); Pustejovsky and Batiukova (2019); Acquaviva et al. (2020); Erk (2022)
- Word senses: Navigli (2009); Camacho-Collados and Pilehvar (2018); Pilehvar and Camacho-Collados (2020)
- Paradigmatic semantic relations: Murphy (2003); Pustejovsky and Batiukova (2019); Schulte im Walde (2020)
- Cross-lingual embeddings: Ruder et al. (2019)
- Connotative meaning: Pang and Lee (2008); Murphy (2010); Sun et al. (2019b)
- Semantic change: Traugott and Dasher (2001); Deo (2015); Traugott (2017); Kutuzov et al. (2018); Shoemark et al. (2019)
- Grounded distributional semantics: Baroni (2016); Kiela (2016)
- Distributional semantics in cognitive science: Vigliocco et al. (2009); Louwerse (2011); Meteyard et al. (2012); Jones et al. (2015); Pereira et al. (2016); Mandera et al. (2017); Yee et al. (2018); Günther et al. (2019); Cao et al. (2021); Kumar (2021)

9

Distributional Semantics beyond the Lexicon

The Distributional Hypothesis is mainly a conjecture about the representation and learning of lexical meaning from co-occurrence statistics (cf. Chapter 1.1). However, distributional semantics cannot be claimed to contribute to a general theory of meaning, unless it provides a satisfactory model of the content of complex expressions such as phrases and sentences. The simplest solution might consist in the **holistic approach** (Turney, 2012): Representing complex expressions as single units to which standard DSMs assign a distributional vector, just like with any other lexical item. This way, phrases such as *red car* or *The dog chases the cat* would be treated as kinds of "words with spaces" and added to the set of DSM targets. However, the holistic solution is not satisfactory (with the possible exception of some idiomatic expressions),[1] because it does not account for a key property of natural language: **productivity**.

HOLISTIC REP-
RESENTATIONS

PRODUCTIVITY

> **Productivity** is the ability to produce and interpret a potentially infinite number of novel linguistic expressions.

Natural language contains grammatical and lexical processes that are productive because they can be applied to open-ended classes of expressions that satisfy certain properties. For instance, morphological affixes allow us to create an endless number of new lexical items: If we know that *gorp* is a verb, we can infer that *gorper* refers to the agent of gorping, whatever the meaning of *gorp*. Similarly, it is the productivity of natural language that allows us to use its expressions to communicate novel situations, like in the following sentence:

(1)   A dog wearing sun glasses is surfing in the ocean.

---

[1] Actually, even idioms cannot always be treated holistically from the semantic point of view (Nunberg et al., 1994). Idioms are a very heterogeneous class of linguistic expressions that differ in their degree of structural variability. Despite their idiosyncratic meaning, they cannot be regarded as just "words with spaces" (Cacciari, 2014).

Productivity is constitutive of the "magic of language" (Pelletier, 2006) and is usually considered one of the main arguments that semantic competence includes some general and systematic procedure to build the interpretation of an expression by combining the meaning of its components. Such central feature of natural language semantics is called **compositionality**.

COMPOSITIONALITY

> The meaning of a linguistic expression is **compositional** if it can be obtained by combining the meaning of its parts.

The notion of compositionality has been the subject of an intense debate in philosophy and cognitive science (Werning et al., 2012). Though not all aspects of natural language are compositional (e.g., idiomatic expressions), it is a fact that the meanings of complex expressions can be derived from the meanings of their parts (Dowty, 2007; Martin and Baggio, 2019). This explains our ability to understand (1), even if we have never seen it before. The key question is to identify and model the mechanisms that are used to compose meanings. Here, we focus on a more specific aspect of this general issue: *the computational processes to compose distributional representations.*

In this chapter, we present current research in **compositional distributional semantics**, which aims at designing methods to construct the interpretation of complex linguistic expressions from the distributional representations of the lexical items they contain. This theme includes two major questions that we are going to explore in the following sections: (i) *what is the distributional representation of a phrase or sentence and to what extent it is able to encode key aspects of its meaning?* (ii) *how can we build such representations compositionally?* Addressing these issues is crucial to prove the ability of distributional semantics to provide a general model of natural language interpretation, but also for NLP and AI applications that need distributional representations for phrases and sentences, to be used in tasks such as textual semantic similarity, paraphrase detection, machine translation, natural language inference, question answering, among many others.

COMPOSITIONAL DISTRIBUTIONAL SEMANTICS

The mainstream approach in compositional distributional semantics consists in representing phrase and sentence meanings with vectors:

PHRASE AND SENTENCE VECTORS

> The meaning of a phrase (sentence) is a **phrase (sentence) vector**.

After introducing the classical symbolic paradigm of compositionality based on function-argument structures and function application (Section 9.1), we review different methods to create phrase and sentence vectors – simple vector operations (Section 9.2), linear-algebraic models of function application

(Section 9.3), neural networks trained to learn sentence embeddings (Section 9.4) – and the main tasks and datasets to evaluate compositional DSMs (Section 9.5). Then, we investigate how distributional semantics addresses two issues that are strictly related to compositionality: the context-sensitive nature of semantic representations, with a particular focus on the last generation of CONTEXTUAL EMBEDDINGS **contextual embeddings** (Section 9.6), and the semantic constraints governing the combination of lexical items, also known as selectional preferences (Section 9.7). We end with some general considerations about compositionality, semantic structures, and vector models of meaning (Section 9.8).

9.1 Semantic Representations and Compositionality

The philosopher and logician **GOTTLOB FREGE** (1848–1925) claims that the productivity of natural language would be impossible

were we not able to distinguish parts in the thought corresponding to the parts of a sentence, so that the structure of the sentence serves as an image of the structure of the thought. [...] If, then, we look upon thoughts as composed of simple parts, and take these, in turn, to correspond to the simple parts of sentences, we can understand how a few parts of sentences can go to make up a great multitude of sentences, to which, in turn, there correspond a great multitude of thoughts. (Frege, 1923, p. 1)

PRINCIPLE OF COMPOSITIONALITY In logic and linguistics, this idea has been expressed as the **Principle of Compositionality**, usually stated in the following way (Partee, 1984):

> The meaning of a linguistic expression is a function of the meaning of its lexical items and of the way they are syntactically combined.

This is also named **Frege's Principle** or **Fregean Compositionality**.[2] According to the Principle of Compositionality, the interpretation of linguistic expressions is built with a recursive process that combines the meaning of lexical items through semantic operations associated with syntactic structures.

FUNCTIONS AND ARGUMENTS

PREDICATES In symbolic semantic models, compositional meaning construction is formalized with **function-argument structures**, which represent the fact that it is possible to analyze meaning into parts that can then be recombined one independently of the other to produce new meanings. Linguistic expressions are divided into **predicates** and **arguments**. Predicates express properties, events, and relations involving one or more arguments. The number of arguments

---

[2] Whether this principle was explicitly endorsed by Frege is still a matter of dispute (Werning et al., 2012; Pelletier, 2016), but it undoubtedly resonates with his words quoted above.

required by a predicate is also called its **valence** or **arity**. In (2), *run* is the VALENCE
predicate and *Tom* is the argument:

(2)   Tom runs.

The operation of applying a predicate to an argument is called **predication**. PREDICATION
The meaning of a predicate is treated as an "unsaturated" entity (Frege, 1891)
and is formalized as a **function** with **variables**, each representing an open FUNCTIONS
slot to be filled by an argument. In fact, "every theory of semantics back to WITH
Frege acknowledges that word meanings may contain variables that are sat- VARIABLES
isfied by arguments expressed elsewhere in the sentence" (Jackendoff, 2002,
p. 360). Using the **lambda notation**, the meaning of the unary predicate *run* is LAMBDA
represented by the following function symbol: NOTATION

(3) $\lambda x[run(x)]$

The "λ" marks the variable "x" as the unsaturated element of the function
"run." A function is a **mapping** between two sets, the **domain** and the **range** FUNCTION
of the function. The function $\lambda x[f(x)] : A \rightarrow B$ has domain A and range B: DOMAIN AND
RANGE

> The **function** $\lambda x[f(x)] : A \rightarrow B$ maps an argument $a \in A$ to one and
> only one element $b \in B$ called the **value** for the function given a.

Predication is formally modeled as **function application**, the process of
saturating (i.e., filling) the variable of a function with an argument: PREDICATION AS
FUNCTION

> The **application** of the function $\lambda x[f(x)]$ to an argument a, $\lambda x[f(x)](a)$, APPLICATION
> turns the function into the saturated expression $f(a)$, obtained by replacing
> the variable with a; $f(a)$ is the value of the function $\lambda x[f(x)]$ applied to a.

The semantic representation of (2) is built by applying (3) to "Tom":

(4) $\lambda x[run(x)](Tom) \Rightarrow run(Tom)$

Function application is the general operation to combine the meaning of lexical
items into the interpretation of complex linguistic expressions.

In **formal semantics**, the meaning of a sentence is its **truth conditions**, TRUTH
"something that determines the conditions under which the sentence is true or CONDITIONS
false" (Lewis, 1970, p. 22). In this framework, predicates correspond to functions that are true or false of their arguments, and function application is the
operation to build the truth conditions of sentences. One of the most influential

MONTAGUE
SEMANTICS

formal models of meaning based on Fregean Compositionality is **Montague Semantics** (Montague, 1974). **RICHARD MONTAGUE** (1930–1971) aims at describing natural language interpretation with a fully compositional truth-conditional semantics (Lenci and Sandu, 2009). Natural language items are translated into expressions of an unambiguous logical language called **logical forms**, which are then interpreted on a **model** $\langle D, I \rangle$ (hence the name of **model-theoretic semantics**). A model consists of a **domain** D, the set of all individuals in the world, and the **interpretation function** I, which assigns to each logical form its **extension** (i.e., its reference in the world), formally expressed with $[\![\ ]\!]$.[3] Lexical items are mapped onto expressions of the formal language, which are then combined with function application to derive the logical forms that represent the truth conditions of sentences.

LOGICAL
FORMS
MODEL
DOMAIN
INTERPRETATION
FUNCTION
EXTENSION

In Montague Semantics, the expressions of the logical language are assigned a **semantic type** τ that individuates the domain of their interpretation, D_τ. Types are recursively defined in the following way:

SEMANTIC TYPE

> (i) e is the type of **individual entities**: $D_e = D$;
> (ii) t is the type of **truth values**: $D_t = \{0, 1\}$;
> (iii) if a and b are types, then the type $\langle a, b \rangle$ is the type of **functions** whose arguments are of type a and whose values are of type b: $D_{\langle a,b \rangle}$ is the set of functions $f : D_a \to D_b$.

Individual entities and truth values are saturated basic types, while functions are unsaturated types. Each syntactic category is mapped onto a logical form of suitable semantic type. As illustrated in Table 9.1, a proper noun like *Tom* is associated with the logical expression "Tom : e" (i.e., a constant; the column introduces the type) that denotes the individual Tom. Common nouns and intransitive verbs are translated into one-place predicates of type $\langle e, t \rangle$ that denote functions from individuals to truth values. For instance, the extension of the logical form of the verb *run*, "$\lambda x[run(x)]$," is the function that for each individual produces the value 1 if it runs and 0 otherwise. A function f of type $\langle e, t \rangle$ is equivalent to the set A of individuals for which f gives the value 1, and is called the **characteristic function** of A. Therefore, formal expressions of type $\langle e, t \rangle$ denote sets of individuals (e.g., $[\![\lambda x[run(x)]]\!]$ is the set of individuals that run). Transitive verbs are mapped into two-place predicates of type $\langle e, \langle e, t \rangle \rangle$ that denote functions from individuals to functions from individuals to truth values. These are characteristic functions of sets of pairs of individuals,

CHARACTERISTIC
FUNCTION

---

[3] Actually, Montague Semantics uses an intensional logic: I assigns to logical expressions their **intensions**, defined as functions from possible worlds to extensions (Lewis, 1970; Montague, 1974). For the sake of simplicity, here we ignore intensional aspects.

Table 9.1 Categories of linguistic expressions associated with their logical form, semantic type, and extensional interpretation in Montague Semantics

Syntactic category	Example	Type	Logical form	Interpretation
proper noun	*Tom*	e	Tom	individual
sentence	*Tom runs*	t	run(Tom)	truth value
common noun	*dog*	$\langle e, t \rangle$	$\lambda x[\text{dog}(x)]$	set
intransitive verb	*run*	$\langle e, t \rangle$	$\lambda x[\text{run}(x)]$	set
transitive verb	*chase*	$\langle e, \langle e, t \rangle \rangle$	$\lambda y \lambda x[\text{chase}(x, y)]$	binary relation

which are equivalent to binary relations (e.g., $[\![\lambda y \lambda x[\text{chase}(x, y)]]\!]$ is the relation defined by the set of pairs of individuals a and b such that a chases b). More in general, predicates with n arguments denote n-place relations.

The operation of meaning composition is **typed function application**, which combines functions and arguments of suitable type:

> If α is of type a and β is of type $\langle a, b \rangle$, then $\beta(\alpha)$ is of type b.

Typed function application and syntactic rules work *in parallel* to derive the logical form of sentences compositionally. This strict syntax-semantics correspondence is called **rule-by-rule interpretation**:

> Let $[_X Y \ Z]$ be a syntactic node, α and β the logical forms of Y and Z.
>
> The logical form of X is $\begin{cases} \beta(\alpha) : b & \text{if } \alpha : a \text{ and } \beta : \langle a, b \rangle \\ \alpha(\beta) : b & \text{if } \alpha : \langle a, b \rangle \text{ and } \beta : a \end{cases}$

Figure 9.1 shows the compositional derivation of the interpretation of *Tom chases Jerry*. Lexical items are mapped onto typed logical forms. The meaning of the VP is obtained by applying the function of type $\langle e, \langle e, t \rangle \rangle$ expressed by the verb to the representation of the object NP of type e. The result of function application is the logical form "$\lambda x[\text{chase}(x, \text{Jerry})] : \langle e, t \rangle$" that denotes the set of individuals that chase Jerry. This function is then applied to the interpretation of the subject NP to obtain the logical form "chase(Tom, Jerry) : t" that is true if and only if Tom chases Jerry.

Typed functions also represent the constraints that determine the appropriate arguments of a predicate. Traditionally, these constraints are called **selectional restrictions** (Katz and Fodor, 1963; Chomsky, 1965; Asher, 2011, 2015; Pustejovsky and Batiukova, 2019). The sentences in (5) are well-formed from the syntactic point of view, but (5b) is semantically anomalous, because the combinations of lexemes do not satisfy their selectional constraints:

TYPED
FUNCTION
APPLICATION

RULE-BY-RULE
INTERPRETATION

SELECTIONAL
RESTRICTIONS

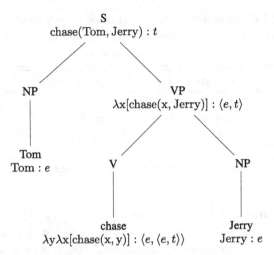

S
chase(Tom, Jerry) : t

NP

VP
$\lambda x[\text{chase}(x, \text{Jerry})] : \langle e, t \rangle$

Tom
Tom : e

V

NP

chase
$\lambda y \lambda x[\text{chase}(x, y)] : \langle e, \langle e, t \rangle \rangle$

Jerry
Jerry : e

Figure 9.1 The compositional derivation of the meaning of the sentence *Tom chases Jerry* in Montague Semantics

(5) a. The tall man drinks beer.

  b. * The red idea drinks beer.

The predicate *drink* requires the subject argument to be animate, and the adjective *red* must modify concrete entities, while *idea* is an abstract noun. Another famous example of selectional restriction violation is the sentence *Colorless green ideas sleep furiously* in Chomsky (1957).

Selectional restrictions are modeled by typing the variables of predicates with symbols that identify semantic categories or features, such as ANIMATE, LOCATION, LIQUID, and so on. These can be regarded as subtypes of the Montagovian type e of individual entities (Asher, 2011). For example, the selectional restrictions of the verb *drink* are represented in the following way:

(6) $\lambda y{:}\text{LIQUID} \ \lambda x{:}\text{ANIMATE} \ [\text{drink}(x, y)]$

The verb *drink* must combine with direct objects denoting individual entities of type LIQUID and with subjects denoting individual entities of type ANIMATE.

FRAME
SEMANTICS

SEMANTIC
FRAMES

CONCEPTUAL
SEMANTICS

The function-argument distinction is the cornerstone to build phrasal meaning also outside formal semantics. In **Frame Semantics** (Fillmore, 1982), the meaning of a sentence is not its truth conditions, but the conceptual representation of a situation or event. The **semantic frames** representing predicates (cf. Section 8.1) can be regarded as functions to be saturated by the event participants. In **Conceptual Semantics** (Jackendoff, 1990, 2002), the grammatically relevant aspects of meaning are encoded in a symbolic level of mental representation called **Conceptual Structure** (CS). As illustrated in Section 8.1, Conceptual Semantics adopts a decompositional approach to lexical meaning. The ingredients of CS are a small set of conceptual categories that define a universal repertoire of semantic types (e.g., EVENT, PATH, PLACE, OBJECT, etc.) and a set of primitive conceptual functions (e.g., GO, TO, IN, etc.) that are used to describe the interpretation of predicates. Lexical items are represented with fragments of CS that are combined mainly through typed function application proceeding parallel to syntactic structure:

CONCEPTUAL
STRUCTURE

(7) a. [s [NP The dog]1 [VP entered2 [NP the room]3]]
     b. [EVENT GO ([OBJECT DOG]1, [PATH TO ([PLACE IN ([OBJECT ROOM]3)])])]2

The indexes in (7) mark the links between syntactic and semantic constituents. The verb *enter* is associated with the following typed function in CS, which maps two arguments x and y of type OBJECT into an event of x going into y:

(8) [EVENT GO ([OBJECT x], [PATH TO ([PLACE IN ([OBJECT y])])])]

The interpretation of the subject is the CS [OBJECT DOG] that saturates the first argument of the function, while the second argument is saturated by the CS [OBJECT ROOM] representing the meaning of the direct object.

9.1.1 The Problems of Fregean Compositionality

Fregean Compositionality claims that the meaning of complex expressions is a function of the meaning of its lexical items. Adopting this principle and its formalization with typed function-argument structures entails assuming that semantic composition in natural language obeys to the following properties:

1. lexical items are assigned their interpretation and fully disambiguated before being composed;
2. the meaning of lexemes is not affected by their composition, as the operation of application does not modify functions and arguments;
3. the semantic interpretation of linguistic expressions is strictly separated from pragmatic and contextual information;
4. if a type mismatch occurs between a predicate and its argument, their combination is semantically anomalous;
5. all elements of phrasal meaning are to be found in the meanings of their component lexical items.

Semantic research has shown that these assumptions raise several problems and are seriously challenged by empirical evidence (Pustejovsky, 1995; Jackendoff, 1997; Asher, 2011; Pustejovsky and Batiukova, 2019).

Traditionally, lexical meaning has been regarded as context-free and autonomous from the compositional process. Fodor and Pylyshyn (1988) claim that the principle of compositionality requires that a lexical item must "make approximately the same contribution to each expression in which it occurs" (p. 42). Representing a predicate as a function with unsaturated variables indeed entails assuming that its meaning is virtually independent from the arguments it can apply to (Martin and Baggio, 2019). However, this alleged context-independence of predicates from their arguments is often proved wrong. For instance, **vagueness** is a pervasive phenomenon in language (cf. Section 8.2): Lexemes have often vague meanings that are "modulated" and specified by their syntagmatic combinations. The adjective *red* corresponds to distinct chromatic varieties in the phrases *red hair*, *red wine*, *red face*, and *red brick*. Analogously, the subjects in (9) and the direct objects in (10) produce different, albeit related, events of running and opening (Kintsch, 2001):

VAGUENESS

(9)   a.   The man runs.
        b.   The ship runs before the wind.

(10)   a.   Mary opened the letter from her mother.
        b.   The rangers opened the trail for the season.
        c.   John opened the door for the guests.

CONTEXT-
SENSITIVE
MEANING

These examples support the hypothesis that lexical meaning is highly **context-sensitive** (Yee and Thompson-Schill, 2016) and that predication should not be modeled just with the standard function application, since the predicate itself can be modified by the argument, a phenomenon called **co-compositionality** (Pustejovsky, 1995, 2012).

CO-
COMPOSITION-
ALITY
METAPHOR
METONYMY

Fregean Compositionality is also directly challenged by the widespread processes of **metaphor** and **metonymy**:

(11)   a.   My car drinks gasoline.
        b.   Plato is on the second shelf.
        c.   The student finished the book.
        d.   The student finished the cigarette.
        e.   fast car; fast guitarist; fast lane

As Wilks (1978) points out, the selectional restrictions that the subjects of *drink* must be animate are not satisfied in (11a), but the sentence is acceptable because the verb has a metaphoric interpretation. In (11b), *Plato* is used metonymically to refer to the philosopher's books. The sentences (11c) and (11d) exemplify a phenomenon known as **logical metonymy**, in which a type LOGICAL clash between an event-selecting verb and an entity-denoting object triggers METONYMY the recovery of an implicit event depending on the argument noun: (11c) means that the student finished *reading* the book and (11d) that the student finished *smoking* the cigarette. Similarly, the interpretation of the phrases in (11e) includes an implicit event related to the noun head: *fast plane* means a plane that flies quickly, *fast guitarist* a guitarist that plays the guitar fast, and *fast lane* a lane in which one can drive at high speed. These examples suggest that semantic constraints should be regarded as **selectional preferences** (Wilks, SELECTIONAL 1978) rather than as hard type restrictions, since their failure does not always PREFERENCES lead to semantic anomaly. Moreover, the process of semantic composition must include mechanisms of **coercion** to adjust the meaning of predicates or argu- COERCION ments and overcome selectional preference violations, and to add information that is not overtly expressed in the linguistic input and depends on contextual knowledge (Pustejovsky, 1995; Asher, 2011; Lauwers and Willems, 2011).

It is of course possible to argue that the alleged problems of Fregean Compositionality are instead just cases of lexical ambiguity. According to this view, which Pustejovsky (1995) refers to as the **sense-enumerative** explana- SENSE-tion, the different interpretations in (9) and (10) would correspond to distinct ENUMERATIVE verb senses. Once the proper word meaning is selected in a given context, EXPLANATION composition would proceed according to standard function application. However, such an explanation does not account for the close relationship between the word interpretations and the productive nature of the phenomenon. The examples above are rather instances of what Pustejovsky and Batiukova (2019) SELECTIONAL call **selectional polysemy**: They result from systematic and general processes POLYSEMY that lead lexemes to acquire new meanings or modulate their interpretation in context. Jackendoff (1997, 2002) argues that Fregean Compositionality must be complemented with mechanisms of **enriched composition** that integrate ENRICHED lexical meaning with pragmatic information about the extralinguistic context, COMPOSITION which is therefore an integral component of the process of constructing complex semantic representations. Similarly, the **Generative Lexicon** theory by GENERATIVE Pustejovsky (1995) does not regard compositionality as the mere combination LEXICON of lexical meanings, but rather as a generative process that allows words to acquire new senses in context. This is obtained by representing lexical items with complex structures that contain elements of contextual knowledge (cf. the lexical entry of *book* in Section 8.1). Classical function application is then extended to access the rich information inside lexical representations and model phenomena like co-compositionality and logical metonymy.

After this brief overview of the characters and problems of compositionality, we can conclude that, in order to account for natural language creativity and productivity, we need to explain (i) *how lexical items can be combined to construct the interpretation of complex linguistic expressions*, as well as (ii) *how word meaning is affected by the compositional processes and change in context*. In fact, as Rabovsky and McClelland (2019) claim, natural language

understanding should be better described as **quasi-compositional**. Symbolic semantic theories provide a general formal model of meaning composition in terms of function-argument structures and function application as the operation to carry out predication. On the other hand, the assignment of the proper interpretation to lexical items is typically presupposed rather than explained by symbolic models. These also struggle to provide a general and satisfactory explanation of the dynamic processes leading to the formation of new senses in context, which is often achieved at the cost of complicating lexical representations or introducing ad hoc compositional mechanisms. The gradient and continuous nature of distributional representations is particularly appealing as a computational model of the context sensitivity of word meaning. However, we first need to understand how to build vectors representing complex linguistic expressions and to what extent distributional semantics can offer an empirically adequate account of phrase and sentence meaning.

9.2 Vector Composition Functions

The most common approach in distributional semantics assumes the representation of phrase and sentence meaning to be a **vector**, exactly like lexical items. An influential method to build **phrase and sentence vectors** consists in applying **vector composition functions** (see Table 9.2) to the distributional vectors of lexical items (Mitchell and Lapata, 2010).

> Let $[_X Y\ Z]$ be a syntactic node, $\mathbf{u}$ the distributional vector of Y, $\mathbf{v}$ the distributional vector of Z, and f a **vector composition function**. The distributional representation of X is the vector $\mathbf{p} = f(\mathbf{u}, \mathbf{v})$.

We henceforth refer to $\mathbf{u}$ and $\mathbf{v}$ as the input vectors and to $\mathbf{p}$ as the output vector of the composition function.

The **(simple) additive model**, which was first introduced by Landauer and Dumais (1997), uses the **vector addition** to compose the input vectors:

$$\mathbf{p} = \mathbf{u} + \mathbf{v} \tag{9.1}$$

Table 9.2 Main types of vector composition
functions

Model	Vector composition function
simple additive	$\mathbf{u} + \mathbf{v}$
weighted additive	$\alpha\mathbf{u} + \beta\mathbf{v}$
full additive	$\mathbf{A}\mathbf{u} + \mathbf{B}\mathbf{v}$
multiplicative	$\mathbf{u} \odot \mathbf{v}$
tensor product	$\mathbf{u} \otimes \mathbf{v}$
circular convolution	$\mathbf{u} \circledast \mathbf{v}$

$\mathbf{u}$	(2	0	3	1	0)
$\mathbf{v}$	(1	2	2	0	0)
$\mathbf{u}+\mathbf{v}$	(3	2	5	1	0)

Figure 9.2 Additive vector composition

Given a linguistic sequence $s = l_1, \ldots, l_n$, such as a phrase, a sentence, or a whole text, the distributional representation of s is defined as follows:

$$\mathbf{s} = \sum_{i=1}^{n} \mathbf{l_i}. \tag{9.2}$$

The vector addition is arguably the most common composition method in distributional semantics. It generates output vectors that retain *all* elements of the input vectors. As illustrated in Figure 9.2, shared elements get higher weight in the composed vector. In set theoretic terms, the meaning of the composed expression is the *union* of the distributions of the components. This implies that all the features of **red** and **car** are also features of the combined vector **red car**. In neural network models, vector addition is traditionally considered equivalent to **logical conjunction** (Smolensky, 1990). Therefore, **red** + **car** LOGICAL CONJUNCTION corresponds to saying that *red car* means something that is a car *and* is red (i.e., $\lambda x[\text{red}(x) \wedge \text{car}(x)]$).

The sum vector points in an intermediate direction with respect to the input vectors (cf. Mathematical note 6 in Section 7.2.4). In fact, the additive model VECTOR AVERAGE can be formulated as the **arithmetic average** of the lexical vectors:

$$\mathbf{s} = \frac{1}{n} \sum_{i=1}^{n} \mathbf{l_i}. \tag{9.3}$$

Since averaging only rescales the sum vector by n, Equations 9.2 and 9.3 produce vectors that point in the same direction. This entails that vector addition and average are equivalent under cosine similarity, because the cosine is only sensitive to vector direction and not to vector length (cf. Section 2.6.1). Lexical vectors can also be weighted to emphasize the most informative words in the sequence s (Hill et al., 2016; Arora et al., 2017):

$$\mathbf{s} = \frac{1}{n} \sum_{i=1}^{n} w_i \mathbf{l_i}, \qquad (9.4)$$

where w is typically tf-idf (cf. Section 2.3.1) or a similar kind of weight.

Despite its simplicity, the additive model is extremely competitive even with respect to more sophisticated approaches (cf. Sections 9.3 and 9.4). On the other hand, it has several shortcomings that undermine its plausibility as a general model for composing distributional representations. First of all, the additive model simply "mixes" word meanings, thereby leading to the rather counterintuitive consequence that the semantic representation of a complex expression is something in-between the interpretation of its lexical components. However, the meaning of *red car* is not the average of the meanings of *red* and *car*. Secondly, since vector addition is commutative (i.e., $\mathbf{u} + \mathbf{v} = \mathbf{v} + \mathbf{u}$), the additive model ignores syntactic structure completely. This is the reason why it is also called **continuous bag-of-words** (CBOW) model.[4] Thus, the sentences *Dogs bite men* and *Men bite dogs* are assigned identical semantic representations. Moreover, lexical vectors are not affected by the additive process: The distributional representation of *red car* and *red wine* contains the very same *red* vector. Therefore, the additive model is not able to address the meaning modulations determined by the composition process (cf. Section 9.1.1). Finally, the additive model makes linguistic expressions more ambiguous as their length increases, because the distributional vector will eventually include all the information brought by their lexical items. This contrasts with the fact that linguistic context typically reduces lexical ambiguities. For example, the verb *play* is ambiguous between a music and a game sense, and the noun *bass* can mean either a type of fish or a kind of musical instrument, but the phrase *play bass* has just the musical interpretation. In fact, vector composition should select those aspects of lexical meanings that are mutually relevant, rather than simply adding all their possible interpretations.

Various improvements of the simple additive model have been proposed to overcome some of its problematic aspects. Mitchell and Lapata (2008) add weights to encode the order of the sequence:

CBOW

---

[4] Not to be confused with the homonymous DSM in the `word2vec` library (cf. Section 6.3).

$$
\begin{array}{lccccc}
\mathbf{u} & (2 & 0 & 3 & 1 & 0) \\
\mathbf{v} & (1 & 2 & 2 & 0 & 0) \\
\hline
\mathbf{u} \odot \mathbf{v} & (2 & 0 & 6 & 0 & 0)
\end{array}
$$

Figure 9.3 Multiplicative vector composition

$$\mathbf{p} = \alpha \mathbf{u} + \beta \mathbf{v}, \tag{9.5}$$

where α and β are weight factors. Assuming as an example $\alpha = 0.4$ and $\beta = 0.6$, we would multiply $\mathbf{u}$ with 0.4 and $\mathbf{v}$ with 0.6 before summation. This way, different distributional representations can be assigned to the sentences *Dogs bite men* and *Men bite dogs*, respectively the vector $\alpha\mathbf{dogs} + \beta\mathbf{bite} + \gamma\mathbf{men}$ and the vector $\alpha\mathbf{men} + \beta\mathbf{bite} + \gamma\mathbf{dogs}$.

The simple additive model in Equation 9.1 and its variant in Equation 9.5 are then generalized as follows (Mitchell and Lapata, 2008, 2010):

$$\mathbf{p} = \mathbf{A}\mathbf{u} + \mathbf{B}\mathbf{v}, \tag{9.6}$$

where $\mathbf{A}$ and $\mathbf{B}$ are $n \times n$ weight matrices that determine the different contributions made by $\mathbf{u}$ and $\mathbf{v}$, thereby breaking the symmetry of vector sum.[5] This is called the **full additive model** (Zanzotto et al., 2010; Dinu et al., 2013). As the word vectors are multiplied by weight matrices before being summed, the full additive model can capture the effects of word order and contextual meaning shifts occurring in the composition. Guevara (2010, 2011) and Zanzotto et al. (2010) estimate the weight matrices in Equation 9.6 with multivariate linear regression trained to predict the output vector $\mathbf{p}$ from the input vectors $\mathbf{u}$ and $\mathbf{v}$. Guevara (2010) focuses on adjective-noun combinations such as *red car*: Partial least squares regression learns to predict the holistic vectors for the training adjective-noun phrases from the vectors of the component words (cf. Section 9.3). In Zanzotto et al. (2010), the regression model is trained to map the distributional vector of an input pair (e.g., *close contact*) onto the vector of a single-word paraphrase (e.g., *interaction*). FULL ADDITIVE MODEL

Compositional models can also be defined in terms of vector multiplication instead of addition (Mitchell and Lapata, 2008, 2010). The **multiplicative model** composes vectors by multiplying them elementwise (Figure 9.3): MULTIPLICATIVE MODEL

$$\mathbf{p} = \mathbf{u} \odot \mathbf{v}. \tag{9.7}$$

---

[5] Equation 9.6 corresponds to the original formulation of the model in Mitchell and Lapata (2010), which assumes distributional vectors to be column vectors (i.e., $n \times 1$ matrices). With row vectors (i.e., $1 \times n$ matrices), $\mathbf{p} = \mathbf{u}\mathbf{A} + \mathbf{v}\mathbf{B}$ (cf. Mathematical note 4 in Section 2.5.2).

The output vector retains the elements the input vectors have in common. In set theoretic terms, the meaning of a phrase is the *intersection* of the distributions of its lexemes. This implies that the features of *red car* are *only* the features shared by *red* and *car*. Interestingly, the multiplicative model also averages the lexical vectors. In fact, each p_i is the square of the **geometric average** $\sqrt{u_i v_i}$ between the corresponding components in the input vectors.

GEOMETRIC
AVERAGE

Like addition, vector multiplication is commutative (i.e., $\mathbf{u} \odot \mathbf{v} = \mathbf{v} \odot \mathbf{u}$), but it avoids the problem of increasing the ambiguity of the composed expression. Since it selects only those dimensions that are mutually relevant for the component words, it performs an implicit form of disambiguation and captures meaning modulation in context. Mitchell and Lapata (2008) show that the multiplicative model outperforms the additive one in measuring how an intransitive verb's meaning is modified by its subject, and Mitchell and Lapata (2010) prove its superiority in a phrase similarity task with adjective–noun, noun–noun, and verb–noun pairs (cf. Section 9.5). On the other hand, the multiplicative model does not easily scale up to longer sequences, because it incrementally reduces the information brought by the resulting vector. For instance, if we multiply sparse vectors, the number of zero components increases with sentence length (Grefenstette and Sadrzadeh, 2015). More generally, by filtering out dimensions that are not shared by all the lexical items, the vector product determines the counterintuitive result that the longer a linguistic expression, the less information is encoded in its semantic representation. As a matter of fact, Hill et al. (2016) report a very poor performance of the multiplicative model for building sentence vectors of arbitrary length.

A variant of the multiplicative model is the **tensor product** (Smolensky, 1990; Clark and Pulman, 2007; Mitchell and Lapata, 2008; Widdows, 2008):

TENSOR
PRODUCT

$$\mathbf{p} = \mathbf{u} \otimes \mathbf{v}. \qquad (9.8)$$

Tensors are multidimensional arrays of numbers, and can be thought of as a generalization of vectors and matrices, where a vector is a first-order tensor and a matrix is a second-order tensor (cf. Section 4.3.1). Given two n-dimensional vectors $\mathbf{u}$ and $\mathbf{v}$, the tensor product $\mathbf{u} \otimes \mathbf{v}$ is a matrix $M_{n \times n}$ such that $m_{i,j} = u_i v_j$ (Figure 9.4a). The tensor product is asymmetric and can therefore account for word order. On the other hand, its major drawback is the increase in dimensionality of the output representation as more items are composed. For instance, **dogs** $\otimes$ **chase** is a second-order tensor,

$$
\begin{array}{cc}
\mathbf{u} & (2 \quad 0 \quad 3 \quad 1 \quad 0) \\
\mathbf{v} & (1 \quad 2 \quad 2 \quad 0 \quad 0) \\
\hline
\end{array}
$$

$$
\mathbf{u} \otimes \mathbf{v} \quad
\begin{pmatrix}
2 & 4 & 4 & 0 & 0 \\
0 & 0 & 0 & 0 & 0 \\
3 & 6 & 6 & 0 & 0 \\
1 & 2 & 2 & 0 & 0 \\
0 & 0 & 0 & 0 & 0
\end{pmatrix}
$$

(a)

$$
\mathbf{u} \circledast \mathbf{v}
\begin{pmatrix} 4 \\ 4 \\ 7 \\ 7 \\ 8 \end{pmatrix}
=
\begin{pmatrix}
m_{5,2} + m_{4,3} + m_{3,4} + m_{2,5} + m_{1,1} \\
m_{5,3} + m_{4,4} + m_{3,5} + m_{1,2} + m_{2,1} \\
m_{5,4} + m_{4,5} + m_{1,3} + m_{2,2} + m_{3,1} \\
m_{5,5} + m_{1,4} + m_{2,3} + m_{3,2} + m_{4,1} \\
m_{5,1} + m_{4,2} + m_{3,3} + m_{2,4} + m_{1,5}
\end{pmatrix}
\Leftarrow
\begin{pmatrix}
2 & 4 & 4 & 0 & 0 \\
0 & 0 & 0 & 0 & 0 \\
3 & 6 & 6 & 0 & 0 \\
1 & 2 & 2 & 0 & 0 \\
0 & 0 & 0 & 0 & 0
\end{pmatrix}
$$

(b)

Figure 9.4 (a) Tensor product vector composition and (b) its compression with circular convolution

dogs $\otimes$ chase $\otimes$ cats is a third-order tensor, dogs $\otimes$ chase $\otimes$ black $\otimes$ cats is a fourth-order tensor, and so forth. Tensors can be unfolded into matrices (cf. Section 4.3.2) that can then be vectorized by concatenating their columns or rows. If $\mathbf{u}$ and $\mathbf{v}$ have n dimensions, $\mathbf{u} \otimes \mathbf{v}$ corresponds to a vector with n^2 dimensions. Since the number of dimensions of the resulting vector grows exponentially with the tensor order (e.g., given word vectors of 300 dimensions, a ten-word sentence would be represented by a vector of 5.9×10^{24} dimensions), tensor product quickly becomes computationally intractable. Moreover, linguistic expressions of different length cannot be compared because they correspond to vectors with a different number of dimensions.

One way to deal with this exploding dimensionality is to use **circular convolution** (Plate, 2003; Jones and Mewhort, 2007) to compress the tensor product into a vector of the same number of dimensions of the original input vectors:

CIRCULAR CONVOLUTION

$$
\mathbf{p} = \mathbf{u} \circledast \mathbf{v}, \tag{9.9}
$$

where $\circledast$ denotes circular convolution, defined as follows (cf. Section 5.4):

$$
\mathbf{p}_i = \sum_{j=0}^{n-1} \mathbf{u}_{j \bmod n} \cdot \mathbf{v}_{i-j \bmod n}. \tag{9.10}
$$

The subscripts are modular over n (e.g., $j \bmod n$ is the remainder of j/n), and the operation sums along the transdiagonal elements of the tensor product, which is what gives the operation its circular nature (see the black and gray boldfaced entries in the matrix in Figure 9.4b). Importantly, circular convolution is specifically designed for random encoding vectors (Grefenstette and Sadrzadeh, 2015). In fact, Mitchell and Lapata (2010) show that it greatly underperforms when applied to other kinds of distributional representations (e.g., explicit vectors and topic vectors).

FILLER-ROLLER
BINDINGS

The tensor product is proposed by Smolensky (1990) as a model of the variable-argument binding operations (e.g., function saturation) typical of compositional symbolic structures. A sequence s of n elements is decomposed into the sum of n **filler-roller bindings**, each corresponding to the tensor product of a filler vector $\mathbf{f}$ representing an element in the sequence, and a vector $\mathbf{r}$ representing its role in the sequence:

$$\mathbf{s} = \sum_{i=1}^{n} \mathbf{f_i} \otimes \mathbf{r_i}. \tag{9.11}$$

Roles can correspond to positions in a sentence, syntactic relations, semantic roles, and so on. For instance, given $\mathbf{p_1}, \ldots, \mathbf{p_n}$ role vectors, such that $\mathbf{p_i}$ encodes the ith position of a lexeme in a sentence, *Dogs bite men* is represented with the vector $(\mathbf{dogs} \otimes \mathbf{p_1}) + (\mathbf{bite} \otimes \mathbf{p_2}) + (\mathbf{men} \otimes \mathbf{p_3})$. The additive nature of Equation 9.11 makes the dimensionality of the vector independent of the sequence length. On the other hand, the filler-role binding carried out by the tensor product allows sentence vectors to encode differences in word order or argument structure saturation (e.g., *Dogs bite men* and *Men bite dogs* are associated with different vectors). McCoy et al. (2019b) implement this model with a seq2seq recurrent neural network (cf. Sections 6.2.1 and 9.4.3) that learns role vectors and combines them with pretrained filler embeddings.

9.2.1 Predicting the Compositionality of Multiword Expressions

Besides expressions whose interpretation is obtained compositionally, natural languages contain a wide array of (semi-)preconstructed phrases. These are commonly referred to as **multiword expressions** (MWEs) and include several types of constructions such as idioms, compounds, light verb constructions, and phrasal verbs (cf. Section 2.1.3). An interesting application of vector composition functions is to predict the compositionality of MWEs.

MULTIWORD
EXPRESSIONS

Sag et al. (2002) define MWEs as "idiosyncratic interpretations that cross word boundaries" (p. 2), since their meaning is not simply a function of the content of their constituent words. MWEs display a continuum of compositionality. For instance, the light verb construction *give confidence* is more compositional than the idiomatic expressions *give a whirl*, whose interpretation of giving a try cannot be derived from the meaning of its parts (Fazly and Stevenson, 2008). In fact, different shades of (non)compositionality exist among idiomatic expressions too: Nunberg et al. (1994) distinguish between **idiomatically combining expressions** like *pop the question*, where each idiom component directly contributes its literal meaning to the figurative meaning of the whole string, and **idiomatic phrases** like *kick the bucket*, whose figurative meaning is distributed over the phrase as a whole and cannot be traced back to any of its parts. Therefore, the compositionality of linguistic expressions is more a gradient property than a dichotomous phenomenon.

IDIOMATICALLY COMBINING EXPRESSIONS

IDIOMATIC PHRASES

A simple but effective approach to **compositionality prediction** is to measure the similarity between the vector of the MWE and the vector obtained by composing the vector of its lexical parts:

COMPOSITIONALITY PREDICTION

Given a MWE $m = l_1, l_2$, the **compositionality** of m, comp(m), is:

$$\text{comp}(m) = \text{sim}(\mathbf{m}, \alpha \mathbf{l_1} + \beta \mathbf{l_2}), \qquad (9.12)$$

where **m** is the **holistic vector** of m (i.e., the vector of the MWE treated as a single target lexeme), and sim is a vector similarity measure (e.g, the cosine). For example, the compositionality of *give confidence* is estimated with the similarity between the holistic vector **give_confidence** and the sum of **give** and **confidence**. Though various vector composition functions can be used, experimental results show that addition is the best-performing one (Reddy et al., 2011a; Salehi et al., 2015). The α and β weights in Equation 9.12 determine the asymmetric contribution of each of the components to the meaning of the whole MWE. In *give confidence*, it is the noun rather than the verb that transparently occurs in the overall meaning of the construction, while in *break the ice* the reverse situation applies. Some methods compare the holistic vector of the MWE only with the vector of either of its lexical parts (Fazly and Stevenson, 2008; Salehi et al., 2015). This can be considered as a special case of Equation 9.12 with α or β equal to zero.

HOLISTIC VECTOR

Most research has focused on noun compounds, but other types of MWEs, such as light verb constructions and particle verbs, have been targeted too. DSMs are tested on predicting compositionality ratings. Reddy et al. (2011a) introduce a dataset of judgments for 90 English noun–noun and adjective–noun compounds, in terms of three numerical scores corresponding to the compositionality of the compound and the literal contribution of each of its parts. Similar ratings have been collected for German by Schulte im Walde et al. (2013) and by Cordeiro et al. (2019) for several languages. The latter study shows that DSMs are able to achieve a strong correlation with human ratings, supporting the potentialities of distributional semantics for compositionality prediction.

9.3 The Distributional Functional Model (DFM)

The compositional DSMs we have seen so far share the assumption that every lexical item is represented with the *same type* of entity, namely a distributional vector. The interpretation of a complex linguistic expression is a new vector resulting from averaging (with addition or multiplication) the features of the input lexical vectors, hence the name of "vector-mixture models" suggested by Baroni et al. (2014b). This is a major difference with respect to symbolic models of Fregean Compositionality, which assume that semantic representations result from the application of functions to arguments, as distinct types of formal entities (cf. Section 9.1).

DISTRIBUTIONAL FUNCTIONAL MODEL   We use the term **Distributional Functional Model** (DFM) to refer to a group of related proposals (Clark et al., 2008; Baroni and Zamparelli, 2010; Coecke et al., 2010; Grefenstette et al., 2011; Baroni et al., 2014b; Clark, 2015; Grefenstette and Sadrzadeh, 2015; Maillard et al., 2015) that are directly inspired by Montague's type-driven theory and aim at providing a distributional interpretation of function application as the core operation to carry out predication. A key aspect of DFM is that the meaning of predicates is represented with higher-order linear-algebraic objects (e.g., matrices and tensors). Like Montague Semantics, DFM specifies a mapping between syntactic categories and semantic types. While Montagovian types define

DISTRIBUTIONAL TYPES   denotation domains, DFM includes **distributional types** that specify the kinds of linear-algebraic objects representing categories of linguistic expressions.

DFM takes Montague's distinction between basic saturated types, which are assigned to nouns and sentences, and unsaturated functional types. The basic distributional types are vectors:[6]

> The distributional representation of **nouns** and **sentences** are **vectors**.

DISTRIBUTIONAL FUNCTIONS

ONE-PLACE PREDICATES AS MATRICES   Predicates are represented with **distributional functions** that transform linear-algebraic objects into other objects. Intransitive verbs and adjectives express one-place distributional functions and are represented as **linear transformations** (or **linear maps**), in turn corresponding to **matrices** (cf. Mathematical

---

[6] An important difference from Montague Semantics is that DFM treats proper and common nouns alike (Baroni et al., 2014a).

$$\begin{pmatrix} 0.5 & 1 \\ 0.8 & 0 \end{pmatrix} \begin{pmatrix} 3 \\ 6 \end{pmatrix} = \begin{pmatrix} (0.5 * 3) + (1 * 6) \\ (0.8 * 3) + (0 * 6) \end{pmatrix} = \begin{pmatrix} 7.5 \\ 2.4 \end{pmatrix}$$

FAST   dog   **fast_dog**

(a)

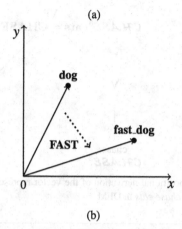

(b)

Figure 9.5 (a) In DFM, the compositional interpretation of *fast dog* is obtained with the matrix-vector product; (b) the distributional representation of the adjective *fast* is a linear map from the vector **dog** onto the vector representing the noun phrase *fast dog*

note 4 in Section 2.5.2). Their application to an argument noun is modeled with matrix-vector multiplication:[7]

> The distributional representation of a one-place predicate $\lambda x[P(x)]$ is a **matrix $P_{m \times n}$**. Given an argument a represented by the n-dimensional vector **a**, the distributional representation of $\lambda x[P(x)](a) = P(a)$ is the m-dimensional vector $\mathbf{b} = \mathbf{Pa}$.

Figure 9.5 shows the compositional interpretation of the phrase *fast dog*, which takes from Montague Semantics the idea that attributive adjectives are functions that map the meaning of the noun head onto the meaning of the modified noun (Montague, 1974; Baroni and Zamparelli, 2010; Coecke et al., 2010). The adjective *fast* is represented with the matrix **FAST**, which is multiplied by **dog** to produce the vector of the noun phrase *fast dog*.

The representation of one-place predicates as matrices is generalized to n-place predicates with **tensors**, which also correspond to linear transformations:

N-PLACE PREDICATES AS TENSORS

---

[7] We follow the original notation of DFM, in which distributional vectors are column vectors.

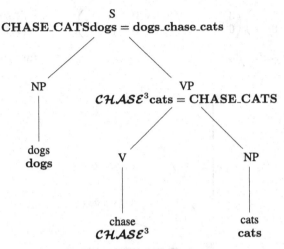

Figure 9.6 The compositional derivation of the vector representing the meaning of the sentence *Dogs chase cats* in DFM

The distributional representation of a n-place predicate $\lambda x_1, \ldots, \lambda x_n [P(x_1, \ldots, x_n)]$ is an **$n+1^{th}$-order tensor** $\mathcal{P}^{n+1}$.

For instance, the two-place transitive verb *chase* is represented with a third-order tensor $\mathcal{CHASE}^3$ viewed as a linear map of a noun vector onto a matrix encoding the verb phrase meaning. This explicitly resembles Montague's analysis of transitive verbs as expressions of type $\langle e, \langle e, t \rangle \rangle$ that denote functions from one argument into one-place functions. Matrix-vector product is also extended to tensors as a general linear-algebraic model of function application. Since matrices and vectors are respectively second- and first-order tensors, semantic composition in DFM can be expressed in the following generalized form, adopting the rule-by-rule interpretation typical of Montague Semantics:

Let $[_X Y\ Z]$ be a syntactic node. The distributional representation of X is the tensor $\mathcal{X}^{n-1}$ such that:

$$\mathcal{X}^{n-1} = \begin{cases} \mathcal{Y}^n \mathbf{z} & \text{if } \mathcal{Y}^n \text{ represents Y and the vector } \mathbf{z} \text{ represents Z} \\ \mathcal{Z}^n \mathbf{y} & \text{if } \mathcal{Z}^n \text{ represents Z and the vector } \mathbf{y} \text{ represents Y} \end{cases}$$

As illustrated in Figure 9.6, the tensor $\mathcal{CHASE}^3$ is multiplied by the object NP vector **cats** to produce the matrix **CHASE_CATS** that represents the VP. The sentence vector is then obtained by multiplying the VP matrix by the subject NP vector **dogs**.

While noun vectors are generated with standard DSMs, DFM learns the tensors that represent the distributional functions with **linear regression**, adapting the method introduced by Guevara (2010). For instance, Baroni and Zamparelli (2010) learn the matrix of the adjective *fast* by training a regression model to predict output holistic vectors of *fast*-noun pairs (e.g., *fast car*) from the input vector of the noun head. The regression weights form the entries of the adjective matrix **FAST**. Differently from Guevara (2010) and Zanzotto et al. (2010), Baroni and Zamparelli (2010) train a distinct regression model for each adjective. Similarly, the matrix representing the intransitive verb *run* consists of the regression weights learned by predicting the holistic vector of subject-*run* pairs (e.g., *horse runs*) from the subject vector. This method is generalized to train higher-order tensors by Grefenstette et al. (2013) with multi-step regression. To learn the tensor $\mathcal{CHASE}^3$, matrices for VPs (e.g., *chase car*, *chase ball*, etc.) are estimated with linear regression on input subject and output holistic subject–verb–object vector pairs. The final tensor is then obtained by applying linear regression to predict the matrices estimated in the previous step from the vectors for the corresponding objects. The weights in the tensor entries thus capture possible dependencies between subject and object arguments (e.g., *cats* is the typical subject of the VP *chase mice*, while *cops* is the preferred subject of the VP *chase thieves*).

DFM is an elegant attempt to provide a distributional model of Fregean Compositionality and function application, and it has been applied to address various semantic phenomena, with a particular focus on adjectival modification (Baroni and Zamparelli, 2010; Asher et al., 2016; Vecchi et al., 2016). For instance, treating adjectives as matrices that map noun vectors onto adjective-noun vectors captures phenomena of co-composition and contextual meaning shift (e.g., the interpretation of *heavy* is different in *heavy rain* and *heavy book*), and Boleda et al. (2012a, 2013) adopt this approach to study the difference between intersective, subsective, and intensional adjectives.[8] Gutiérrez et al. (2016) apply the DFM to model metaphorical uses of adjectives (e.g., *cold* has a figurative interpretation in *cold reception*). Marelli and Baroni (2015) use DFM to provide a compositional representation of morphologically complex words: Affixes are represented with matrices and the vector of a derived word like *nameless* is built by multiplying the matrix of the affix

---

[8] An adjective is **intersective** if the denotation of the adjective–noun pair AN is the intersection of the denotations of A and N, and therefore AN entails both A and N: a *red car* is both *red* and a *car*. An adjective is **subsective** if the denotation of AN is a subset of the denotation of N, and AN entails N: a *skillful violinist* is a *violinist*, but not necessarily *skillful* in general. An adjective is **intensional** if AN does not entail N: an *alleged terrorist* is not necessarily a *terrorist* (Pustejovsky and Batiukova, 2019).

-less by the vector of the base *name* (e.g., **nameless** = **LESSname**). This solution is extended by Marelli et al. (2017) to compounds such as *boathouse*.

Despite these interesting applications, the definition of distributional types as a strict association between n-place functions and $n + 1^{th}$-order tensors is problematic for several reasons. First of all, the complexity of the model grows exponentially with the number of predicate arguments. Given vectors of 300 dimensions, two-place predicates are represented with tensors formed by $300^3 = 27$ million entries. A three-place predicate like *give* is instead represented with a fourth-order tensor of $300^4 = 81$ billion entries. This means that estimating the distributional functions becomes unwieldy and runs against huge data sparseness problems, especially for less frequent lexical items. Secondly, it is not clear how DFM can account for unexpressed arguments. For instance, the verb *eat* is transitive, but it can also be used intransitively in a sentence like *Dogs eat*. If *eat* is represented with a third-order tensor, than it is not possible to derive the representation of *Dogs eat*, unless we postulate two distinct representations for transitive and intransitive *eat*. Moreover, since in DFM nouns and verbs correspond to tensors of different orders, they cannot be directly compared. Thus, the model cannot account for the strong similarity between deverbal nouns like *destruction* and their base verb (*destroy*). In general, DFM inherits from Montague Semantics most of the limits stemming from a one-to-one mapping between semantic types and syntactic categories. In fact, phenomena like coercion and logical metonymy can hardly be addressed in DFM, unless by introducing type-shifting mechanisms similar to those often adopted in formal semantics (Pustejovsky and Batiukova, 2019). Therefore, while DFM offers a promising approach to explain local compositional phenomena, such as adjectival modification, it has great difficulties to tackle more complex linguistic constructions.

In order to overcome some of these limits, Paperno et al. (2014) propose a simplification of the DFM called **Practical Lexical Function** model (PLF), which represents every lexical item l in the following way:

$$\langle l, \mathbf{L_1}, \ldots, \mathbf{L_n} \rangle, \tag{9.13}$$

where l is a standard distributional vector and $\mathbf{L_i}$ is a matrix corresponding to the ith argument slot of l. The number of matrices associated with a lexical item depends on its arity. A word without arguments like *dog* is represented just with its vector (i.e., $\langle \mathbf{dog} \rangle$). The one-place predicate *run* is associated with a vector and a matrix for the subject slot (i.e., $\langle \mathbf{run}, \mathbf{RUN_S} \rangle$), and the two-place predicate *chase* with a vector and two matrices for the subject and the object slots (i.e., $\langle$chase, **CHASE$_S$**, **CHASE$_O$**$\rangle$). Matrices are estimated with linear regression from corpus-extracted holistic vectors of predicate-argument pairs and predication is modeled with matrix-vector product: Each matrix slot is multiplied by the vector argument, and the result is summed to the predicate vector. The interpretation of the sentence *Dogs chase cats* is constructed as follows, like in the filler-role bindings model (cf. Section 9.2):

$$\text{chase} + \textbf{CHASE}_S\text{dogs} + \textbf{CHASE}_O\text{cats} \qquad (9.14)$$

Gupta et al. (2015) slightly amend PLF by not adding the verb vector, in order to solve a problem in the original formulation of the model. By representing every lexical item only with vectors and matrices, PLF avoids the problems deriving from higher-order tensors, though this way it gives up capturing dependencies between different arguments. Moreover, since predication is carried out with matrix-vector product, PLF can assign different vectors to *Dogs chase cats* and *Cats chase dogs*, thereby bypassing the problem of simple additive model (cf. Section 9.2). On the other hand, Rimell et al. (2016) show that even the much more versatile PLF is not able to outperform the simple additive model when tested on the RELPRON dataset (cf. Section 9.5).

9.3.1 Matrix-Vector Recursive Neural Networks (MV-RNN)

The **Matrix-Vector Recursive Neural Network** (MV-RNN) by Socher et al. MV-RNN (2012) shares with DFM the idea of representing the meaning of lexical items with higher-order linear-algebraic objects. While DFM follows Montague Semantics in assigning functional semantic types only to certain categories of lexemes (e.g., adjectives, verbs, etc.), MV-RNN assumes that any word can both have a content and act as an operator (i.e., a function) that modifies the meaning of the expressions it combines with. Therefore, every lexical item l is represented with the pair $\langle 1, \mathbf{L} \rangle$, such that 1 is a n-dimensional vector and $\mathbf{L}$ is a $n \times n$ item-specific matrix. The vector is expected to encode the meaning of l, and the matrix to capture its operator semantics. Words may differ for the relative salience of either component: If a word has mainly a functional nature (e.g., the negation *not*), its vector will be close to zero, while if a word lacks operator semantics (e.g., the noun *dog*), its matrix will be the identity matrix $\mathbf{I}$ (cf. Section 8.4.1), corresponding to the identity function (i.e., $\mathbf{uI} = \mathbf{u}$).

Like PLF, MV-RNN dispenses with higher-order tensors, but instead of combining lexemes with matrix-vector product the composition function is now a feed-forward neural network (cf. Section 6.1) that recursively projects the vector-matrix pairs of two child nodes in the syntactic tree onto the vector-matrix pair representing their parent node:

> Let $[_X Y\ Z]$ be a syntactic node, $\langle \mathbf{y}, \mathbf{Y} \rangle$ and $\langle \mathbf{z}, \mathbf{Z} \rangle$ the representations of Y and Z. The representation of X is the pair $\langle \mathbf{x}, \mathbf{X} \rangle$ such that:
>
> $$\mathbf{x} = g([\mathbf{yZ}; \mathbf{zY}]\mathbf{W}) \quad \mathbf{X} = g([\mathbf{Y}; \mathbf{Z}]\mathbf{W_M}), \qquad (9.15)$$

where $g = \tanh$, ";" denotes concatenation, and $\mathbf{W}$ and $\mathbf{W_M}$ are $2n \times n$ network weight matrices. First, the vector of either child node is multiplied by the matrix of the other, to capture co-composition effects. The resulting vectors are then concatenated and mapped onto the vector of the parent node by the weight matrix $\mathbf{W}$, followed by the nonlinear function g. The concatenation of the component matrices is mapped onto the parent node matrix in a similar way, but using the weight matrix $\mathbf{W_M}$. The composition network is **recursive** (hence the model name), because it is applied to its own previous output until it reaches the tree top node. The lexical vector-matrix pairs and the weights of the composition function are model parameters that are learned with backpropagation by adding a softmax classifier to each parent node and using a supervised task (e.g., sentiment classification). Variations of MV-RNN are proposed by Socher et al. (2011, 2013a).

RECURSIVE COMPOSITION

DFM and its closest relatives like MV-RNN provide a linguistically motivated treatment of phrasal meaning and a theoretically well-grounded distributional interpretation of Fregean Compositionality (Potts, 2019). On the other hand, these compositional DSMs have a high number of parameters to be estimated. Such increased complexity often hampers the model scalability to a large range of linguistic constructions and, at the same time, does not produce substantial improvements in the quality of semantic representations. Though Dinu et al. (2013) report positive empirical results of DFM in various phrase similarity tasks, these are not always significantly better than those achieved by vector addition. Similarly, Blacoe and Lapata (2012) show that a simple additive model is able to match the neural network in Socher et al. (2011).

9.4 Sentence Embeddings

The advent of deep learning has also stormed compositional distributional semantics, introducing a new generation of DSMs that build **sentence embeddings** with artificial neural networks.

SENTENCE EMBEDDINGS

> Given a sentence $s = l_1, \ldots, l_n$, the **sentence embedding** $\mathbf{s}$ is a vector such that $\mathbf{s} = N(\mathbf{l_1}, \ldots, \mathbf{l_n})$, where N is a neural network and $\mathbf{l_1}, \ldots, \mathbf{l_n}$ are the embeddings of the words in s.

The network N is trained on some self-supervised or supervised task to build a vector s that encodes relevant aspects of the sentence meaning. The model can learn both word and sentence embeddings from the same training data, but it is also customary to represent words with pretrained vectors built with DSMs such as word2vec or FastText. This way, the network can leverage the semantic information encoded in the pretrained word embeddings.

9.4.1 Paragraph Vector (doc2vec)

Le and Mikolov (2014) propose **Paragraph Vector** (aka **doc2vec**), a gener- DOC2VEC alization of word2vec that learns embeddings for paragraphs, defined as any variable-length piece of texts, ranging from phrases up to sentences and whole documents. In word2vec, words are represented with vectors in an embedding matrix whose parameters are optimized by predicting context words. Similarly, in Paragraph Vector, each paragraph in the training corpus is treated as a kind of new "token" and represented with a distributional vector in a separate embedding matrix whose weights are learned by predicting the words in the paragraph itself. Therefore, Paragraph Vector rests on the assumption that the distributional representation of a linguistic sequence (e.g., a sentence) contains the information relevant to predict its component lexemes.

Paragraph Vector comes in two variants. Given a paragraph corresponding to a sentence $s = l_1, \ldots, l_n$, the **Distributed Memory Model of Paragraph Vectors** (PV-DM) combines (by average or concatenation) the sentence PV-DM embedding s with the embeddings of k consecutive words $l_i, \ldots, l_{i+k}$ sampled from the sentence. This combined vector is then used to predict l_{i+k+1}. For instance, if $s = $ *The dog chases the cat* and $k = 2$, the vector s is combined with the embeddings of the and dog to predict *chases*. While PV-DM is a close relative of CBOW, the **Distributed Bag of Words Paragraph Vector** PV-DBOW (PV-DBOW) is similar to SG in word2vec. In this case, the sentence embedding s is directly used to predict lexemes randomly sampled from s, without including the embeddings of the context words.

Le and Mikolov (2014) finally represent each paragraph with the concatenation of the embeddings produced by PV-DM and PV-DBOW, which are then tested on sentiment analysis and information retrieval tasks. During training, Paragraph Vector stores representations for every sentence (and word) in the training corpus. One limit of this approach is that the model needs to be partially retrained to obtain embeddings for unobserved sentences. For instance, to build the embedding for a new sentence s', a new vector is added to the sentence embedding matrix, which is again trained with backpropagation, after freezing the weights of the word embeddings.

SENT2VEC
Another model based on word2vec is **Sent2Vec** (Pagliardini et al., 2018). The CBOW algorithm is extended to learn word and n-gram embeddings. Sentences are then represented as the average of their unigram and n-gram vectors.

9.4.2 Convolutional Neural Networks (CNNs)

After being first designed for object recognition in computer vision by LeCun et al. (1998), **Convolutional Neural Networks** (CNNs) have also been applied to NLP tasks (Collobert and Weston, 2008; Collobert et al., 2011) and to build sentence embeddings (Kalchbrenner et al., 2014; Kim, 2014). CNNs consist of a set of **filters** trained to identify features of the input, which are then combined to form a single embedding encoding key aspects of its structure. In computer vision, the filters learn to identify important features of an object like edges, shape, and colors (cf. Section 8.7.1), while in computational linguistics the filters learn features of the most informative n-grams of a sentence.

CONVOLUTIONAL
NEURAL
NETWORKS

FILTERS

Given an input sentence s, each lexeme l_i in s is represented with the embedding $\mathbf{l_i}$. A sliding window of size n (often called **receptive field**) is then applied to s to identify k n-grams $c_1, \ldots, c_k$. Each n-gram c_i is represented with a vector $\mathbf{c_i} = [\mathbf{l_i}; \ldots; \mathbf{l_n}]$ obtained by concatenating the embeddings of its lexemes. The CNN includes q filters corresponding to weight vectors $\mathbf{w_1} \ldots \mathbf{w_q}$ arranged into a matrix $\mathbf{W}$, which are trainable parameters. The filters extract features from the n-grams with a sequence of convolution and pooling layers:

RECEPTIVE
FIELD

CONVOLUTION

convolution – given the n-gram c_i, the convolution layer produces a new vector $\mathbf{f_i}$ in the following way:

$$\mathbf{f_i} = g(\mathbf{c_i}\mathbf{W} + \mathbf{b}), \tag{9.16}$$

where g is a nonlinear activation function and $\mathbf{b}$ a bias term. The convolution layers output $\mathbf{f_1}, \ldots, \mathbf{f_k}$ q-dimensional vectors representing the n-grams of the input sentences. The jth component of $\mathbf{f_i}$ encodes the feature extracted by the filter $\mathbf{w_j}$ from the n-gram c_i;

POOLING

pooling – this layer combines the vectors produced by convolution into a single q-dimensional embedding $\mathbf{s}$. The most common pooling operation is the **max pooling**, such that the component s_i is the maximum value for that dimension across the various $\mathbf{f_1}, \ldots, \mathbf{f_k}$ vectors. Alternatively, the **average pooling** is applied to take the average value.

Therefore, the CNN represents a sentence with an embedding whose dimensions correspond to features identified by the filters from its various n-grams.

CNN can have more complex architectures with multiple stacks of convolution and pooling layers, or with several convolutions working in parallel on different types of n-grams. An important aspect of the embeddings produced by CNNs is that they are trained with supervised tasks, rather than the self-supervised prediction task used by Paragraph Vector. The output of the pooling layer is passed to a fully connected layer with a softmax classifier. This is used to optimize the network parameters, with backpropagation using annotated sentences (e.g., with sentiment or other semantic labels).

9.4.3 Encoder–Decoder Models (seq2seq)

The most common approach to build neural sentence embeddings is based on the **encoder-decoder** architecture, also known as **sequence-to-sequence** SEQ2SEQ (seq2seq) model (Cho et al., 2014; Sutskever et al., 2014).

> In the **seq2seq** architecture, a network (the **encoder**) is used to produce a vector representation of a sentence s_i, which is then fed into another network (the **decoder**) that uses it to generate a sentence s_j.

From a probabilistic point of view, seq2seq models learn the conditional probability $p(s_j|s_i)$, where s_i and s_j may have different length. These models have been first introduced for machine translation: in this setting, s_j is the translation of s_i in a target language. However, the same approach can be applied to any type of sequence pairs (e.g., s_i can be a question and s_j its answer). The encoder-decoder architecture is successfully used to develop end-to-end NLP applications. However, since the vector produced by the encoder captures several aspects of the input sentence that are useful for the decoder to carry out its task, seq2seq models can also be regarded as general purpose mechanisms to learn sentence vectors (Adi et al., 2017). The encoder and the decoder networks are trained together with backpropagation. Then, the decoder is discarded and the encoder is used to produce embeddings for new sentences.

Encoders and decoders are typically **Long Short-Term Memory** (LSTM) LSTM networks (Hochreiter and Schmidhuber, 1997). LSTMs are a type of recurrent network designed to solve some limitations of the Simple Recurrent Networks (SRNs) we have presented in Section 6.2.1, in particular the so-called **van-** VANISHING **ishing gradient** problem. The gradient is the derivative of the error signal GRADIENT used by backpropagation to update the network weights (cf. Section 6.1). In SRNs, gradients tend to become exponentially smaller during training, making

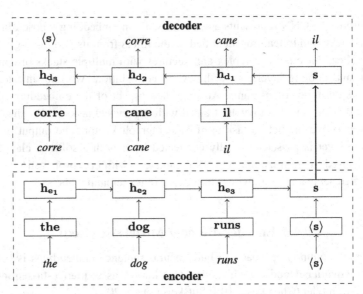

Figure 9.7 Seq-2-seq model that reads the sentence *The dog runs* and generates its Italian translation *Il cane corre*. The encoder and decoder are LSTMs

it difficult for the network to keep track of long-distance dependencies (Goodfellow et al., 2016). Each SRN hidden state h_i is a function of the current input l_i and the previous hidden state h_{i-1}. LSTMs have a similar recurrent structure, but the hidden states consist of **memory cells** with a set of **gates** to decide the amount of the input to be written to the memory cell, and the amount of the previous hidden state to be forgotten. A gate is a vector **g** of real-valued weights that filter the content of another vector **x** by elementwise multiplication **g** $\odot$ **x** (e.g., the components of **g** that are close to zero tend to block the corresponding components of **x**). The gates are parameters trained to regulate the information flow across the recurrent steps, thereby reducing the vanishing of gradients and improving the ability of the network to encode long-distance dependencies. A similar solution is adopted by **Gated Recurrent Unit** (GRU) networks, introduced for seq2seq modeling by Cho et al. (2014). Other types of encoder-decoder architectures are based on CNNs enriched with attention mechanisms (Gehring et al., 2017) and on Transformers (cf. Section 9.6.3).

Figure 9.7 shows a seq2seq model in which the encoder and the decoder are LSTMs. Each input word is represented with an embedding, which is either randomly initialized or a pretrained distributional vector. Word embeddings may be left fixed during the network training, or may be further fine-tuned (i.e., treated as model parameters) and therefore affected by sentence-level

MEMORY CELLS
GATES

GRU

information. The embedding s of the input sentence *The dog runs* corresponds to the last hidden state of the encoder network ($\langle$s$\rangle$ is a special symbol that marks sentence boundaries). The sentence embedding is then used by the decoder to generate the Italian translation of the input, *Il cane corre*. In this example, the sentence embedding initializes the first hidden state of the decoder, like in Sutskever et al. (2014). Alternatively, the sentence embedding can be concatenated to the word embeddings used by the decoder in each step of the output sentence generation (Goldberg, 2017).

The major difference among seq2seq models of sentence meaning concerns the training task. Dai and Le (2015) and Li et al. (2015) train the model as an **autoencoder** in which the decoder learns to reconstruct the input sentence. **SkipThought** (Kiros et al., 2015) extends the Distributional Hypothesis and assumes that the meaning of a sentence depends on the sentences it co-occurs with. Given a tuple $\langle s_{i-1}, s_i, s_{i+1} \rangle$ of contiguous sentences, the encoder (a recurrent network with GRUs) represents s_i with an embedding that is then used by the decoder to reconstruct the previous and the next sentences. As recurrent networks are slow to train, Hill et al. (2016) propose **FastSent**, a simplification and much faster version of SkipThought in which the encoder and decoder networks are replaced by an additive model. Given a representation of a sentence as the sum of its word embeddings, the network is trained to predict adjacent sentences that are also represented with vector addition. In **DisSent** (Nie et al., 2019), the sentence embeddings are learnt with a discourse prediction task. Given a pair of sentences in the training corpus, an LSTM encodes them with vectors that are used to predict the word (e.g., *but*, *because*, etc.) expressing the discourse relation between them.

The models above are trained with variations of a self-supervised language modeling task (cf. Section 6.2). Other seq2seq networks use supervised tasks. Wieting et al. (2016b) extend the **Paragram** model by Wieting et al. (2015) to learn word embeddings and create sentence vectors with an encoder trained on paraphrase pairs from the annotated Paraphrase Database (Ganitkevitch et al., 2013). In **InferSent** (Conneau et al., 2017), the model is trained on a natural language inference task, and consists in classifying pairs of sentences from the SNLI annotated dataset (cf. Section 9.5) into *entailment*, *contradiction*, or *neutral*. The encoder produces a vector representation of the premise and the hypothesis sentences of each inference pairs. The vectors are combined with different methods and fed into a feed-forward layer with a softmax classifier. The **Universal Sentence Encoder** (Cer et al., 2018) learns sentence embeddings with Transformers trained using multi-task learning, which includes the SkipThought prediction objective and the InferSent supervised task.

AUTOENCODER

SKIPTHOUGHT

FASTSENT

DISSENT

PARAGRAM

INFERSENT

UNIVERSAL
SENTENCE
ENCODER

Neural models like seq2seq architectures can encode any type of sequence with vectors. Therefore, they clearly improve on other types of compositional DSMs, like for instance the DFM (cf. Section 9.3), which instead focus on specific phrasal types, but strive to scale up to more complex linguistic constructions. This explains the popularity enjoyed by neural sentence embeddings in NLP and AI, which need general methods to represent text structures with vectors to be used in downstream deep learning applications, such as dialogue understanding, question-answering, etc. On the other hand, neural networks often require a lot of time and text to be trained. The question is therefore whether this complexity is worth the effort, and whether neural architectures do provide better representations of sentence meaning.

THE LIMITS OF SENTENCE EMBEDDINGS

Research has shown that this is not always the case and that the much simpler – but theoretically unsatisfactory – additive model (cf. Section 9.2) is highly competitive with respect to neural models in intrinsic and extrinsic tasks (cf. Section 9.5). For instance, Wieting et al. (2016a) represent sentences with the average of embeddings encoding character n-grams, and obtain better results than LSTMs and CNNs. More generally, additive models, possibly improved with more sophisticated vector weighting methods, are able to outperform neural sentence embeddings (Hill et al., 2016; Wieting et al., 2016b; Arora et al., 2017; Shen et al., 2018). This means that the contribution of the neural network combining the word embeddings is actually quite limited. Such a conclusion is consistent with the findings by Conneau et al. (2017, 2018a) that untrained LSTMs encoders using pretrained embeddings behave as well as trained encoders. This fact has been systematically investigated by Wieting and Kiela (2019), who compare the performance of trained seq2seq models with LSTMs with random weights. Surprisingly, the trained models do not significantly outperform the random ones. Wieting and Kiela (2019) conclude that the added value brought by neural sentence embeddings to NLP systems depends more on the quality of the component word vectors rather than on the composition process carried out by the encoder network.

9.5 Evaluation of Compositional DSMs

A crucial question for compositional distributional semantics is how to evaluate its representation of phrase and sentence meaning. In symbolic models, the semantic properties of complex linguistic expressions can be directly "read off" from the formal structures representing them. In fact, the very purpose of semantic analysis is to associate sentences with structures of symbols that make explicit their logical form. Compositional distributional representations are instead radically different. The models we have seen in the previous sections encode complex expressions with vectors whose content is not immediately interpretable. Therefore, evaluation should not only aim at comparing the performances of compositional DSMs, but also understanding the aspects of meaning captured by distributional representations of phrases and sentences.

Like with lexical models, we can distinguish intrinsic and extrinsic evaluation methods (cf. Chapter 7). **Intrisic evaluation** uses tasks and datasets that are specifically designed to test the model's ability to perform semantic composition. One of the most common approaches consists in testing compositional DSMs to predict human ratings of **phrase and sentence similarity**, as the compositional analogue of the task used to evaluate lexical DSMs (cf. Section 7.2.2). The evaluation measure is the **Spearman rank correlation** (ρ) between distributional similarity scores and ratings.

INTRISIC EVALUATION

PHRASE AND SENTENCE SIMILARITY

SPEARMAN CORRELATION

The first generation of benchmarks mainly focuses on fixed and small linguistic constructions. The dataset in Mitchell and Lapata (2008), **ML2008**, is formed by 120 pairs of subject–verb sentences. A reference subject–verb sentence (e.g., *horse ran*) is paired with two "landmark" intransitive verbs (cf. Section 9.6.1), whose meaning is compatible (e.g., *horse galloped*) or incompatible (e.g., *horse dissolved*) to the reference one. The resulting sentence pairs are then rated for similarity. Mitchell and Lapata (2010) introduce a dataset (**ML2010**) consisting of similarity judgments for 324 adjective–noun, noun–noun, and verb–object combinations rated on a $1 - 7$ scale. For example, *vast amount – large quantity*, *marketing director – assistant manager*, and *produce effect – achieve result* have high similarity, while *general level – federal assembly*, *bedroom window – education office*, and *encourage child – leave house* have low similarity. The **GS2011** (Grefenstette and Sadrzadeh, 2011) and **KS2014** (Kartsaklis and Sadrzadeh, 2014) datasets extend the same approach to transitive sentences. The former is inspired by ML2008 and contains similarity ratings for 200 pairs of subject–verb–object sentences differing only for their verb (e.g., *government provide cash – government supply cash*), while KS2014 includes 108 sentence pairs without lexical overlap (e.g., *project present problem – programme face difficulty*).

ML2008

ML2010

GS2011

KS2014

Other benchmarks evaluate compositional DSMs on **cross-level semantic similarity** (Jurgens et al., 2014), which involves comparing linguistic expressions of different lengths, like a single word with a synonym phrase, whose vector is generated by the model. Turney (2012) introduces a dataset (**T2012**) of 2,180 noun–noun compounds and adjective–noun phrases and frames the task as a multiple-choice synonym test (cf. Section 7.2.1): Given a target phrase called the *stem* (e.g., *dog house*), the task is to select the *solution* synonym word (e.g., *kennel*) out of seven alternatives. **RELPRON** (Rimell et al., 2016) consists of 1,087 term-property pairs, where the *term* is a noun (e.g., *army*) and the *property* is a noun phrase providing the definition of the term

CROSS-LEVEL SEMANTIC SIMILARITY

T2012

RELPRON

Table 9.3 An example of sentences from the SICK dataset

Sentence A	Sentence B	Relatedness score
A man is talking	A man is speaking	4.9
A baby is crying	A man is exercising	1

Sentence A	Sentence B	Entailment label
A sad man is crying	A man is crying	ENTAILMENT
A jet is not flying	A jet is flying	CONTRADICTION
A man is sitting in a field	A man is running in a field	NEUTRAL

(e.g., *organization that general commands*). Each term has between four and ten different properties. All properties have the same structure: a noun head, which is a hypernym of the term (e.g., *organization*), and a transitive restrictive relative clause, whose subject or direct object is the term. RELPRON is primarily conceived for a property ranking task. Composed vectors are produced for all properties in the dataset. Given a term, a model must rank properties by their similarity to the term. The ideal system will rank all properties corresponding to that term above the other properties.

SICK
The **SICK** (Sentences Involving Compositional Knowledge) dataset (Marelli et al., 2014; Bentivogli et al., 2016) has two important elements of novelty with respect to the first-generation benchmarks. Firstly, while those contain small "skeleton" sentences with fixed structure and no function words, SICK consists of real sentences of various complexity and inclusive of all their components (e.g., determiners, prepositions, conjunctions, etc.). Secondly, besides predicting sentence similarity, SICK tests compositional DSMs ENTAILMENT RELATIONS to recognize **entailment relations** between sentences. In fact, knowing the meaning of a sentence entails understanding which other sentences follow from its truth (e.g., the truth of *John met a dog* entails the truth of *An animal was met by John*). Therefore, assessing a model ability to identify entailments is an important vantage point to evaluate the semantic representations generated by compositional DSMs. SICK contains 9,840 sentence pairs including different kinds of linguistic phenomena relevant to determine its meaning and inferential potential, such as negation, active/passive alternations, quantifiers, lexical entailments, and so on. As illustrated in Table 9.3, each sentence pair is rated for semantic relatedness on a 1 − 5 scale (SICK-R) and labeled with an entailment relation (SICK-E). The labels in SICK-E are those used in the **rec-** NATURAL LANGUAGE INFERENCE **ognizing textual entailment** task, also known as **natural language inference** (NLI). Given a pair of sentences A (the *premise*) and B (the *hypothesis*), the pair is classified as ENTAILMENT if the hypothesis is true given the premise,

CONTRADICTION if the hypothesis is false given the premise, and NEUTRAL if the hypothesis is underdetermined by the premise (cf. Section 7.4.2).

NLI is also one of the most important tasks for the extrinsic evaluation of compositional DSMs. **Extrinsic evaluation** assesses models by using their sentence vectors in downstream applications. Besides NLI, common tasks include paraphrase identification (i.e., given a pair of sentences, classify them as paraphrases or not), question-answering, and sentiment analysis. Since carrying out these tasks presupposes the ability to represent sentence meaning, the improvement achieved by a certain model is then taken as a measure of the quality of its representations. Extrinsic evaluation tasks are also available in general platforms to benchmark sentence vectors, such as **SentEval** (Conneau and Kiela, 2018) and **GLUE** (Wang et al., 2019a).

Extrinsic methods have become the leading evaluation paradigm for sentence embeddings, as they measure their contribution to NLP systems in application scenarios. On the other hand, the datasets are not designed to investigate compositionality, but rather to test the system's ability to solve natural language understanding problems. The model's mastery of meaning composition is inferred indirectly from its performance in downstream tasks. Unfortunately, sheer extrinsic performance is often unreliable evidence. In fact, existing evaluation datasets contain biases that enable models to achieve high scores based on superficial cues rather than on truly compositional construction of sentence meaning (Ettinger et al., 2018). An interesting example is provided by NLI itself: Gururangan et al. (2018) and Poliak et al. (2018) show that some of the most widely used datasets, such as **SNLI** (Stanford NLI; Bowman et al., 2015) and **MultiNLI** (Multi-Genre NLI Corpus; Williams et al., 2018), contain annotation artifacts that allow models to perform surprisingly well using only the hypothesis, without actually learning the entailment relation. In SICK, 86.4% of CONTRADICTION sentence pairs can be identified only by the presence of negation (Bentivogli et al., 2016). This has prompted the development of challenging benchmarks that include more complex tasks, like **SuperGLUE** (Wang et al., 2019b), or are specifically designed to reduce artifacts in the data, like **SWAG**, a dataset of commonsense inferences (Zellers et al., 2018), and **WinoGrande** (Sakaguchi et al., 2020). The latter extends the Winograd Schema Challenge (Levesque, 2011) and consists of pronoun resolution problems requiring advanced compositional and commonsense reasoning abilities.

An alternative approach to sentence vector evaluation is provided by **probing tasks** (Ettinger et al., 2016; Belinkov and Glass, 2019), which have become extremely popular to interpret the information encoded by deep neural networks (cf. Section 8.8.2).

EXTRINSIC EVALUATION

SENTEVAL
GLUE

SNLI
MULTINLI

SUPERGLUE
SWAG
WINOGRANDE

PROBING TASKS

> Given a representation generated by a model (e.g., a sentence embedding), a **probing task** is a classifier trained to predict a specific property based on this representation.

The successful performance of the classifier is then used to deduce that the representations of the model encode that property. Compared with extrinsic evaluation in downstream tasks, probing tasks aim at providing more nuanced analyses with respect to specific linguistic dimensions.

Several tasks are designed to target syntactic phenomena, such as word order and constituency structure (Adi et al., 2017; Conneau et al., 2018a; Gulordava et al., 2018). Others instead specifically address compositional semantics.

SEMROLE The **SemRole** task in Ettinger et al. (2016, 2018) aims at identifying whether sentence embeddings encode information about semantic roles. The classifier receives in input the embedding **n** of a probe noun n, the embedding **v** of a probe verb v, and the embedding **s** of sentence s containing n and v, and must decide whether n has the AGENT role in s or not (e.g., in the sentence *The dog chases the cat*, the classifier should identify the probe *dog* as a positive instance, and the probe *cat* as a negative instance). The classifier accuracy then measures whether the sentence embedding discriminates the semantic roles. Zhu et al. (2018) propose a battery of probing tasks to test argument structure and negation, while Shwartz and Dagan (2019) target phenomena related to figurative meaning and multiword expressions. The **edge probing** suite of

EDGE PROBING tasks introduced by Tenney et al. (2019b) test various syntactic and semantic aspects of sentence structure (e.g., semantic roles, anaphora, etc.).

Probing tasks are a form of "black box" testing, as they provide indirect evidence about the embedding content. Moreover, they crucially depend on the careful and balanced design of training and test sets, which must single out the phenomenon of interest and avoid any confounding factor (Belinkov, 2022). However, probing classifiers represent important tools to explore the semantic properties captured by compositional DSMs.

9.6 Context-Sensitive Distributional Representations

In the previous sections, we have presented the main methods to create and evaluate distributional representations of phrases and sentences. Now, we move to the related question of how DSMs capture the context-sensitive behaviour of lexical meaning. As illustrated in Section 9.1.1, Fregean Compositionality presupposes that word meaning is essentially context-independent, but this

Table 9.4 Top: Two items from the WiC dataset. Bottom: lexical substitutes (in parenthesis the number of annotators that selected them) for two occurrences of the adjective *bright* from the SemEval 2007 dataset

Sentence 1	Sentence 2	Same meaning
The expanded **window** will give us time to catch the thieves.	You have a two-hour **window** of clear weather to finish working on the lawn.	TRUE
There's a lot of trash on the **bed** of the river.	I keep a glass of water next to my **bed** when I sleep	FALSE

Sentence	Lexical substitutes
He was **bright** and independent and proud. She turns eyes **bright** with excitement.	intelligent (3); clever (3) shining (4); alight (1)

assumption is challenged by the wealth of cases in which lexemes undergo meaning modulation in context, as the verb *run* in the following examples:

(12) a. The horse runs.
      b. The water runs.
      c. The virus runs.

Symbolic semantic models strive to represent contextual meaning shifts and co-compositonality phenomena, which are reduced to cases of lexical ambiguity (Fodor and Pylyshyn, 1988; Pustejovsky, 1995). The continuous nature of distributional vectors instead promises to provide more satisfactory and explanatory ways to address this phenomenon. In this section, we illustrate current approaches to build **context-sensitive distributional representations** that capture contextualization effects. Meaning modulation is a source of lexical polysemy, which is discussed in Section 8.2, but from a different, albeit related, perspective. There we target the problem of how DSMs represent word senses, while here we focus on the compositional mechanisms that change the meaning of a lexeme depending on its contexts. CONTEXT-SENSITIVE DISTRIBUTIONAL REPRESENTATIONS

One of the most common tasks to evaluate context-sensitive representations is **word similarity in context**, which consists in modeling human similarity ratings for words presented *in linguistic contexts*, rather than in isolation, as in the standard similarity task (cf. Section 7.2.2). It is thus possible to estimate the effect of context in modulating semantic similarity judgments. The **Stanford Contextual Word Similarity** (SCWS) dataset (Huang et al., 2012) and the **USim** dataset (Erk et al., 2013) respectively contain 2,003 and 1,142 pairs of WORD SIMILARITY IN CONTEXT SWCS USIM

WiC

words in distinct sentences annotated with graded similarity judgments. The **Words-in-Context** (WiC) dataset (Pilehvar and Camacho-Collados, 2019) includes 7, 466 words, each presented in two different contexts and labeled as to whether it has the same meaning in the two examples or not (see Table 9.4). **CoSimLex** (Armendariz et al., 2020) consists of similarity ratings of 333 word pairs derived from SimLex 999, appearing together in two shared contexts. The dataset is multilingual, as it also contains Croatian, Finnish, and Slovene data.

Another setting to evaluate contextualized vectors is **lexical substitution**, which is the task of finding a suitable meaning-preserving substitute for a target word in the context of a sentence. The **SemEval 2007** dataset (McCarthy and Navigli, 2009) contains 200 target nouns, verbs, adjectives, and adverbs, each occurring in ten distinct sentential contexts for a total of 2, 000 test items. Five human annotators were asked to provide substitutes for these target words (see Table 9.4). The evaluation of vector contextualization models is framed as a ranking task: The list of substitute words must be ranked so that for each item the suitable paraphrases are ranked higher than the inappropriate ones. For instance, given the context *She turns eyes bright with excitement*, the model should rank *shining* and *alight* higher than *clever* and *intelligent*, as replacements for *bright*. Much larger lexical substitution benchmarks for English are the **Turk Bootstrap Word Sense Inventory** (TWSI) by Biemann (2013), and **CoInCo** (Concepts in Context) by Kremer et al. (2014), which is also proposed as an evaluation dataset for semantic composition in Buljan et al. (2018).

9.6.1 Vector Contextualization

Standard DSMs represent the meaning of lexical items with type vectors (cf. Section 2.4). These vectors are context-independent, because they "summarize" the whole distributional history of lexical items. A first strategy to obtain context-sensitive semantic representations consists in **contextualizing** the type vector of a target lexeme to create **word-in-context vectors**.

> Given a lexeme l, its type distributional vector l, and a context c, the **word-in-context vector** l^c represents the meaning of l in c and is obtained by modifying l with information about c.

In order to capture the meaning shifts resulting from predication, Kintsch (2001) modifies the vector sum of a one-place predicate p and its argument a by adding their mutual **nearest neighbors**:

$$p(a) = p + a + \sum_i n_i, \tag{9.17}$$

where n is a lexeme selected among the top nearest neighbors of the predicate that are also closest to the argument. For instance, the meaning of *The horse runs* is represented by summing the vector of *run*, the vector of *horse*, and the vectors of some of the nearest neighbors of *run* that are also closest to *horse* (e.g., *jump*, *race*, etc.). The result is to strengthen the features of the predicate that are more appropriate for the argument (e.g., the horse-like aspects of running). Kintsch (2001) evaluates vector contextualization with the **landmark method**: Given a target lexeme l_1 (e.g., *run*) and a context lexeme l_2 (e.g., *horse*), the model must predict the similarity of the word-in-context vector $l_1^{l_2}$ to the vector of another lexeme l_3 (e.g., *gallop*) called *landmark*.   LANDMARK METHOD

Instead of using nearest neighbors, Erk and Padó (2008) contextualize type vectors by combining them with vectors representing **selectional preferences** (cf. Section 9.7), which they assume to correspond to the "expectations" that words trigger about associated events and their participants (McRae et al., 2005b). The selectional preferences of predicates are determined by their expected arguments (e.g., *horse* for *gallop*). In turn, arguments have **inverse preferences** about their expected predicates (e.g., *gallop* for *horse*). When words are composed together, the mutual selectional preferences affect their meaning. Given a tuple $\langle l_1, r, l_2 \rangle$ formed by a lexeme l_1 occurring in the context of l_2 with the syntactic relation r (e.g., $\langle run, \text{nsubj}, horse \rangle$ derived from *The horse runs*), Erk and Padó (2008) assign to l_1 a type vector $\mathbf{l_1}$ and a word-in-context vector $\mathbf{l_1}^{\langle r, l_2 \rangle}$ obtained by combining $\mathbf{l_1}$ via componentwise multiplication with the vector $\mathbf{sp}^{\langle r, l_2 \rangle}$ representing the (inverse) selectional preferences of l_2 with respect to the syntactic relation r:[9]   SELECTIONAL PREFERENCES   INVERSE PREFERENCES

$$\mathbf{l_1}^{\langle r, l_2 \rangle} = \mathbf{l_1} \odot \mathbf{sp}^{\langle r, l_2 \rangle}. \tag{9.18}$$

The vector $\mathbf{sp}^{\langle r, l_2 \rangle}$ is the weighted centroid vector of the words l_j co-occurring with l_2 with the relation r, whose co-occurrence frequency $F(\langle l_j, r, l_2 \rangle)$ is above the empirically determined threshold θ:

$$\mathbf{sp}^{\langle r, l_2 \rangle} = \sum_{j : F(\langle l_j, r, l_2 \rangle) > \theta} F(\langle l_j, r, l_2 \rangle) \mathbf{l_j}. \tag{9.19}$$

---

[9] The symmetric procedure is used to assign to l_2 the word-in-context vector $\mathbf{l_2}^{\langle l_1, r \rangle}$, in which the type vector of l_2 is modified according to the (inverse) selectional preferences of l_1.

For instance, *run* in the tuple $\langle run, \text{nsubj}, horse \rangle$ is represented with the word-in-context vector $\mathbf{run}^{\langle \text{nsubj,horse} \rangle}$, which is obtained by multiplying the type vector $\mathbf{run}$ with $\mathbf{sp}^{\langle \text{nsubj,horse} \rangle}$, in turn computed as the weighted sum of the vectors of the most frequent verbs having *horse* as subject (e.g., *gallop, trot,* etc.). Erk and Padó (2008) evaluate their model with the landmark method applied to the ML2008 dataset (cf. Section 9.5). For each test pair, they create the word-in-context vector of the verb in the reference sentence (e.g., *shoulder slumped*) and compare it with the vector of the verb (e.g., *slouched*) in the other sentence, treated as landmark. The model predictions are then correlated with the human similarity ratings in the dataset.

COMPONENT
RE-WEIGHTING

A similar approach is used by Thater et al. (2010), while Thater et al. (2011) contextualize distributional vectors by **re-weighting** their components, based on the similarity with the context. Lexemes are represented with explicit type vectors produced by a syntax-based matrix DSM. The jth component of a target vector $\mathbf{t}$ contains the weight w_{t,c_j} corresponding to the PPMI association score between t and a dependency-typed collocate $c_j = \langle r, l_j \rangle$, such that the lexeme l_j is linked to t by the syntactic relation r (cf. Section 2.2.1). A lexeme l_1 in the tuple $\langle l_1, r', l_2 \rangle$ is represented with the word-in-context vector $\mathbf{l_1}^{\langle r', \mathbf{l_2} \rangle}$ whose components are computed as follows:

$$ l_{1_i}^{\langle r', l_2 \rangle} = \begin{cases} w_{l_1, c_i} \cos_{\text{sim}}(\mathbf{l_j}, \mathbf{l_2}) & \text{if } c_i = \langle r, l_j \rangle \text{ and } r = r' \\ 0 & \text{otherwise} \end{cases} . \quad (9.20) $$

Contextualization reinforces the components of the vector $\mathbf{l_1}$ that have the same syntactic relation as r' and whose collocate l_j has a high cosine similarity with l_2. For example, in the case of $\langle run, \text{nsubj}, horse \rangle$, the result of contextualizing $\mathbf{run}$ is to increase the salience of those features of running that are more relevant for animals like horses (e.g., promoting the component $\langle \text{nsubj}, stallion \rangle$ while demoting $\langle \text{nsubj}, car \rangle$). These methods are all close variations of the same approach (Dinu et al., 2012), and comparative analyses demonstrate fairly similar performances.

TOPIC MODELS

Other approaches to vector contextualization are based on **Topic Models** (cf. Section 4.4). Given a set $Z = \{z_1, \ldots, z_k\}$ of topics corresponding to latent word senses, Dinu and Lapata (2010) describe each lexeme l_1 with a type vector $\mathbf{l_1} = (p(z_1|l_1), \ldots, p(z_k|l_1))$ containing the probability distribution of l_1 over these senses. Similarly, they represent a lexeme l_1 in the context of a lexeme l_2 with the following word-in-context topic vector:

$$ \mathbf{l_1^{l_2}} = (p(z_1|l_1, l_2), \ldots, p(z_k|l_1, l_2)). \quad (9.21) $$

The effect of contextualization is thus to modulate the sense distribution of l_1 with respect to the context l_2. Adopting the simplifying assumption that l_1 and l_2 are conditionally independent given the sense z_i, each component $p(z_i|l_1, l_2)$ is computed as follows:

$$p(z_i|l_1, l_2) \approx \frac{p(z_i|l_1)p(l_2|z_i)}{\sum_{j=1}^{k} p(z_j|l_1)p(l_2|z_j)}. \tag{9.22}$$

The parameters of the probabilistic model (i.e., the topics and the distributions $p(z|l_1)$ and $p(l_2|z)$) are learned with LDA from a word-by-word co-occurrence matrix with window-based contexts. Ó Séaghdha and Korhonen (2011, 2014) generalize this model to account for the contextualization effects produced by complex syntactic contexts formed by multiple dependency relations (e.g., in *The dog chases the cat*, the meaning of *chase* is affected both by the subject *dog* and the object *cat*). While Dinu and Lapata (2010) contextualize the latent senses themselves, Van de Cruys et al. (2011) represent lexemes with type vectors containing the probability distribution with respect to syntactic collocates, and use the topics to promote the features in the original vector that are most salient given a particular context. Latent topics are learnt with NMF, which has a probabilistic interpretation similar to LDA (cf. Section 4.4.1).

Multi-prototype DSMs, which represent lexemes with sense vectors (cf. Section 8.2.1), predict word similarity in a context c (Reisinger and Mooney, 2010b; Huang et al., 2012) with the following generalization of Equation 8.1. MULTI-PROTOTYPE DSMs

$$\text{AvgSimC}(l_1, l_2, c) = \frac{1}{N^2} \sum_{i=1}^{n} \sum_{j=1}^{n} p(\mathbf{c}, \mathbf{s_i}(\mathbf{l_1}))p(\mathbf{c}, \mathbf{s_j}(\mathbf{l_2}))\text{sim}(\mathbf{s_i}(\mathbf{l_1}), \mathbf{s_j}(\mathbf{l_2})),$$

$$\tag{9.23}$$

where $p(\mathbf{c}, \mathbf{s}(\mathbf{l_1}))$ and $p(\mathbf{c}, \mathbf{s}(\mathbf{l_2}))$ are the probabilities of the context vector $\mathbf{c}$ to belong to the sense cluster $\mathbf{s}(\mathbf{l_1})$ and $\mathbf{s}(\mathbf{l_2})$ (Equation 8.2 can be similarly modified). As word senses are inherently represented as clusters of contexts, contextual meaning modulation is modeled by making the similarity measure context-sensitive, without modifying the representation of the lexemes. The similarity between *run* and *gallop* in the context of *horse* depends on the likelihood of *horse* being one of the contexts defining the senses of *run* and *gallop*.

9.6.2 Exemplar DSMs

Instead of modifying a context-independent type vector to create word-in-context representations, an alternative strategy to account for contextual meaning shifts is to use **exemplar DSMs**. EXEMPLAR DSMs

> **Exemplar DSMs** represent each instance of a word with a distinct **token vector** that encodes aspects of its context.

Although Westera and Boleda (2019) limit the scope of distributional semantics to DSMs that generate type vectors representing context-invariant aspects of meaning, exemplar models are DSMs in every respect: They learn inherently context-sensitive representations that encode the distributional properties of each word token. Their name refers to **exemplar models of concepts** (Murphy, 2002; Bybee, 2010), according to which a concept is a collection of instances of a category (e.g., the different exemplars of dogs we have experienced) stored in the semantic memory, and categorization is similarity computation between a new stimulus and each remembered exemplar. Standard DSMs instead learn from the various occurrences of a lexical item in the training corpus one or more vectors that encode its most prototypical distributional features. Therefore, they share characteristics with **prototype models of concepts**, which assume that humans abstract features across the exemplars of a category and represent a concept with a prototypical representation of the category that is the central tendency of its instances. Categorisation of a new exemplar depends on its similarity to category prototypes.

In the exemplar DSM by Erk and Padó (2010), a type lexeme l is represented with the set E_l of its **token vectors**, each built from the content words appearing in the sentence in which the token occurs. For example, the instance of *run* in *The horse runs in the field* is associated with a token vector $\mathbf{run^i}$ containing its co-occurrences with the collocates *horse* and *field*, while the instance of *run* in *The car runs in the freeway* is represented with the token vector $\mathbf{run^j}$ containing its co-occurrences with *car* and *freeway*. The meaning shift of a lexeme l produced by the context c is modeled by assuming that c activates the subset of E_l containing the most similar token vectors to c. The **activation** of the **exemplar set** $\mathrm{act}(E_l, c)$ is defined as follows:

$$\mathrm{act}(E_l, c) = \{\mathbf{l^i} \in E_l \mid \cos_{\mathrm{sim}}(\mathbf{l^i}, \mathbf{c}) > \theta\}, \qquad (9.24)$$

where $\mathbf{l^i}$ is the vector of the ith token of l, $\mathbf{c}$ is the token vector of c, and θ is an empirically determined similarity threshold. The similarity in context between the exemplar sets of two lexemes l_1 and l_2 is measured with the cosine similarity between the centroid vectors of $\mathrm{act}(E_{l_1}, c)$ and $\mathrm{act}(E_{l_2}, c)$. Erk and Padó (2010) test their model on a lexical substitution task.

A similar approach is proposed by Melamud et al. (2015), who represent lexemes with sets of **substitute vectors**, each representing a specific context of

(margin notes)
EXEMPLAR MODELS OF CONCEPTS

PROTOTYPE MODELS OF CONCEPTS

TOKEN VECTORS

ESEMPLAR SET ACTIVATION

SUBSTITUTE VECTORS

a lexeme. Substitute vectors are second-order token vectors whose components correspond to a weight estimating how fit a lexical item is to substitute a target word in a certain context. For instance, the substitute vector of *run* in *The horse runs in the field* contains the conditional probability of each word in the model vocabulary given the context *The horse ___ in the field*. Melamud et al. (2015) define the **out-of-context type vector** $\mathbf{l}$ of a lexeme l as the average of the substitute vectors of its contexts:

OUT-OF-CONTEXT TYPE VECTOR

$$\mathbf{l} = \frac{1}{|C_l|} \sum_{i \in C_l} \mathbf{c_i}, \qquad (9.25)$$

where C_l is a collection of the observed contexts for l in the training corpus, and $\mathbf{c}$ are their substitute vectors. The meaning shift of l produced by a context c is then modeled by selecting only the substitute vectors of l that are most similar to the substitute vector of c.

Johns and Jones (2015), Jamieson et al. (2018), and Jones (2019) propose an exemplar DSM based on the **BEAGLE** random encoding model (cf. Section 5.4) and inspired by the **MINERVA 2** multiple-trace model of episodic memory (Hintzman, 1986). Each context c of a lexeme l is represented as the sum of the random vectors of its n words and stored as a distinct **memory trace**:

BEAGLE EXEMPLAR DSM

MINERVA 2

MEMORY TRACE

$$\mathbf{c_l} = \sum_{j=1}^{n} \mathbf{r}(l_j). \qquad (9.26)$$

When the random vector of l is presented to the memory as a probe, it activates a set of traces with a strength proportional to their similarity with the probe vector, like in Erk and Padó (2010). The sum of the activated memory traces, weighted by their activation strength, is called an **echo vector** and corresponds to the out-of-context meaning of l. If l is presented together with another contextual probe c, the echo vector will be formed by the memory traces similar to both l and c, and will correspond to the word-in-context representation of l.

ECHO VECTOR

9.6.3 Contextual DSMs

The most recent and popular kind of context-sensitive distributional representation are **contextual embeddings** learned with deep neural networks (Liu et al., 2020). By contrast, standard type vectors are now referred to as **static embeddings**. **Contextual DSMs** represent each word token in a linguistic sequence with a contextual embedding that is a function of the whole input sequence.

CONTEXTUAL EMBEDDINGS

STATIC EMBEDDINGS

CONTEXTUAL DSMs

> Given a sequence of lexemes $s = l_1, \ldots, l_n$, a **contextual DSM** assigns to each token l_i the **contextual embedding** $\mathbf{h}_{l_i}$, such that $\mathbf{h}_{l_i} = f(\mathbf{l_n}, \ldots, \mathbf{l_1})$, where $\mathbf{l_i}$ is a non-contextual (static) embedding of l_i.

NEURAL
LANGUAGE
MODEL

The function f is typically a deep **neural language model** trained with self-supervised learning (cf. Section 6.2), and the contextual embeddings $\mathbf{h}_l$ correspond to its **hidden vectors**. The idea that the hidden states of networks trained to predict linguistic sequences encode context-sensitive lexical representations is already present in Elman (2011). He shows that the hidden vector generated by an SRN for *cut* in *The butcher cuts the meat* is different from the vector generated for the same verb in *The lumberjack cuts the meat*. In fact, the internal states of recurrent networks depend on previous states and therefore capture relevant aspects of a word context. Current contextual DSMs are based on the same assumption, but learn context-sensitive embeddings with much more complex neural architectures.

Recurrent Models: ELMo

CoVe

A first group of contextual DSMs is based on recurrent networks. The **Contextual Vector** (CoVe) model (McCann et al., 2017) is an encoder-decoder architecture (cf. Section 9.4.3) with two layers of bidirectional LSTMs (biL-

BiLSTM

STMs). A **biLSTM** (Graves and Schmidhuber, 2005) is formed by two networks: (i) a forward LSTM that reads the input sequence from left to right and for each lexeme l_i in the input sequence $s = l_1, \ldots, l_n$ produces the hidden representation $\overrightarrow{\mathbf{h}_i}$; (ii) a backward LSTM that reads s from right to left and produces the hidden vector $\overleftarrow{\mathbf{h}_i}$. The hidden state of the biLSTM $\mathbf{h}_i$ for the lexeme l_i is the concatenated vector $[\overrightarrow{\mathbf{h}_i}; \overleftarrow{\mathbf{h}_i}]$. In CoVe, the hidden vector generated by the first LSTM layer is then fed into the second LSTM, whose hidden layer is the contextual embedding of l_i. The biLSTM is trained with a machine translation task and the input embeddings are GloVe vectors. McCann et al. (2017) apply the CoVe embeddings to various NLP downstream tasks. Generally, CoVe outperforms context-independent pretrained vectors, thereby showing the positive effects of contextualization.

ELMo

A more effective model is **ELMo** (Embeddings from Language Models; Peters et al., 2018), which learns contextual embeddings with a two-layer biL-STM architecture very similar to CoVe, except for three major differences: (i) the encoder-decoder model is trained with the self-supervised language modeling task (Peters et al., 2017); (ii) the LSTMs are fed with word embeddings generated by a CNN input layer operating on character embeddings (Kim et al., 2016), to encode sub-word information and to represent out-of-vocabulary words unseen during training; (iii) the contextual embedding of l_i is the weighted average of its representations in the network layers:

$$\mathbf{ELMo_i} = \gamma \sum_{j=0}^{k} w_j \mathbf{h_i^j}, \qquad (9.27)$$

where k is the number of ELMo layers, $\mathbf{h_i^j}$ is the vector representation of l_i produced by the jth layer, and γ and w_j are parameters optimized in the tasks in which the ELMo vectors are employed as pretrained representations.

Since $j = 0$ is the input layer, $\mathbf{h_i^0}$ is a static embedding for l_i. Each $\mathbf{h_i^j}$, with $j > 0$, is a contextual embedding, because it encodes information coming from the word context. Peters et al. (2018) show that the different layers of the biLSTM encode distinct aspects of the context. Lower layers tend to capture morphosyntactic information, while semantic information is better represented at higher layers. Pooling the various hidden vectors with Equation 9.27 is reported to produce better representations, when used as pretrained features in downstream tasks. In general, ELMo is able to achieve significant improvements over CoVe, a result that supports the beneficial effect of language modeling as training task.

Transformer Models: BERT and GPT

Further advancements in learning contextual embeddings have been obtained by using Transformers instead of recurrent networks. The **Transformer** is an TRANSFORMER encoder-decoder architecture proposed by Vaswani et al. (2017) for machine translation and based on the mechanism of **attention** (Bahdanau et al., 2015). ATTENTION

In the standard seq2seq model, the input sequence is represented by a single sentence embedding corresponding to the last hidden state of the encoder, which is then employed by the decoder to generate the output sequence (cf. Section 9.4.3). In attention-based architectures, the input is encoded as a sequence of hidden vectors $\mathbf{h_1}, \ldots, \mathbf{h_n}$, and the decoder has an attention mechanism that allows it to focus on specific parts of the input sequence to generate the output. Attention consists of weight vectors associated with each decoding ATTENTION step. At step j, the input embeddings are multiplied by the **attention vector** VECTOR $\mathbf{a_j}$ (whose components are all positive and sum to one) and added to obtain a context vector $\mathbf{c_j}$, which is then fed into the decoder:

$$\mathbf{c_j} = \sum_{i=1}^{n} a_{j_i} \mathbf{h_i}. \qquad (9.28)$$

CONTEXT
VECTOR
The **context vector** c_j thus modulates the contribution of the input embeddings to produce the jth output word. The attention vectors vary from step to step, making the network shift its focus as well. The attention weights are trained with the rest of the network parameters, so that the decoder learns to "attend" to those aspects of the input that are most important for each generation step.

The main novelty of the Transformer consists in dispensing with recurrent networks and using attention as the only mechanism to carry out the seq2seq mapping. While recurrent networks process the input sequentially (i.e., each word internal representation depends on the hidden states of the previous words), the key property of the Transformer is that the input words are processed *in parallel*. This allows the network to achieve a better encoding of long-distance dependencies. As the Transformer does not have any recurrent structure, it needs to have information about the position of each word in

POSITIONAL
EMBEDDINGS
the input sequence. This is achieved by using **positional embeddings** that encode the absolute position of input elements (Gehring et al., 2017). Let $s_i = l_1, \ldots, l_n$ be the input sequence and l_i the m-dimensional embedding of the ith lexeme ($m = 512$ in Vaswani et al., 2017) contained in an input embedding matrix (cf. Section 6.2.2). The Transformer input vector of l_i is the embedding e_i, such that:

$$e_i = l_i + p_i, \tag{9.29}$$

where p_i is the m-dimensional embedding for the ith position. Thus, the two tokens of *dog* in *The brown dog chases the white dog* are represented by different input vectors that give to the network information about their positions. Position embeddings can be either learned (Gehring et al., 2017) or created with a function that maps positions to distinct vectors (Vaswani et al., 2017).

TRANSFORMER
BLOCKS
The Transformer encoder and decoder are formed by a stack of n layers L called **blocks**, in turn composed of sublayers. The input of the block L_i is the output of the block L_{i-1}. The structure of an encoder block is illustrated

MULTI-HEAD
SELF-
ATTENTION
in Figure 9.8. Its heart is represented by the **multi-head self-attention** layer, which allows every word to differentially "attend" to all the words in the same sentence, including itself. Self-attention is the method the Transformer uses to encode information about other relevant words into the one that it is currently processing, which is then represented as a weighted sum of its context word vectors. Let $x_1, \ldots, x_n$ be the sequence of m-dimensional vectors received in input by the block L_j, and corresponding to the sentence $s_i = l_1, \ldots, l_n$. The multi-head self-attention layer of L_j produces a new sequence $y_1, \ldots, y_n$ of m-dimensional vectors. Each y_i is generated in the following way:[10]

---

[10] Like in Chapter 6, we assume that $x_1, \ldots, x_n$ are row vectors.

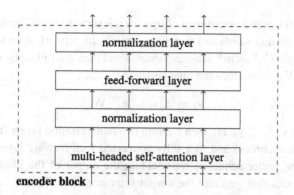

Figure 9.8 Transformer encoder block

1. every input vector $\mathbf{x_j}$, with $1 \leq j \leq n$, is turned into three vectors: a query, key, and value vectors k-dimensional **query** vector ($\mathbf{q_j}$), a k-dimensional **key** vector ($\mathbf{k_j}$), and a v-dimensional **value** vector ($\mathbf{v_j}$), possibly with $k = v$. This is obtained by multiplying $\mathbf{x_j}$ by three distinct weight matrices, $\mathbf{W_Q}$, $\mathbf{W_K}$, and $\mathbf{W_V}$:

$$\mathbf{q_j} = \mathbf{x_j}\mathbf{W_Q} \quad \mathbf{k_j} = \mathbf{x_j}\mathbf{W_K} \quad \mathbf{v_j} = \mathbf{x_j}\mathbf{W_V} \quad (9.30)$$

2. the weight $w_{i,j}$ is computed for each word pair $\langle l_i, l_j \rangle$:

$$w_{i,j} = \text{softmax}\left(\frac{\mathbf{q_i} \cdot \mathbf{k_j}}{\sqrt{k}}\right), \quad (9.31)$$

where $\sqrt{k}$ is a scaling value, and the softmax function normalizes the scores. The weight $w_{i,j}$ measures the attention level of the word l_i for l_j as a function of the dot product of their query and key vectors;

3. the **self-attention vector** $\mathbf{a_i}$ is computed as follows: self-attention vector

$$\mathbf{a_i} = \sum_{j=1}^{n} w_{i,j}\mathbf{v_j} \quad (9.32)$$

The self-attention vector is the weighted sum of the value vectors of the other words in the sequence s. This is very similar to the attention mechanism in Equation 9.28;

4. self-attention is multi-headed and consists of h **heads** each corresponding attention heads to a function that carries out the three steps above with separate parameter matrices. The result is the sequence $\mathbf{a_i^1}, \ldots, \mathbf{a_i^h}$ of self-attention vectors.

The multi-headed mechanism allows each lexeme to focus simultaneously to more context words and therefore expands the network attention ability;

5. the vectors $a_i^1, \ldots, a_i^h$ are concatenated and then multiplied by the weight matrix $\mathbf{W_O}$ to produce the final vector y_i:

$$y_i = [a_i^1; \ldots; a_i^h]\mathbf{W_O}. \qquad (9.33)$$

The vectors $y_1, \ldots, y_n$ are then fed into two regularization layers (to improve the network accuracy) and to a fully connected feed-forward layer that produces a new vector sequence representing the output of the block L_j. The decoder blocks that generate the output sequence $s_j = l_{n+1}, \ldots, l_z$ have a similar structure, except for two aspects: (i) they have an extra layer that operates multi-head attention over the vectors produced by the encoder blocks; (ii) the self-attention sub-layer is unidirectional and operates left-to-right. This is achieved by "masking" the positions following any output lexeme that is being processed, so that only the positions to its left can be attended to.

The cornerstone of the Transformer architecture is the self-attention mechanism whose weights are computed with the dot product that expresses how related two vectors in the input sequence are. The training task allows the network to learn which words are most related to the one that is being processed and to encode in the output vectors relevant aspects of the context structure. The output vectors generated by each layer are weighted sums over the whole input sequence, and therefore are inherently context-sensitive.

TRANSFORMER
CONTEXTUAL
EMBEDDINGS

> Given a Transformer with n layers, $L_1, \ldots, L_n$, the vectors $h_1^i, \ldots, h_n^i$ generated by each layer L_i are **contextual embeddings** of the input words.

In fact, the Transformer has become the "engine" of several contextual DSMs.

GPT

UNIDIRECTIONAL
LANGUAGE MODEL

AUTOREGRESSIVE
LANGUAGE MODEL

The various versions of **GPT** (Generative Pre-trained Transformer; Radford et al., 2018, 2019; Brown et al., 2020) use the decoder stack of the Transformer trained on a standard **unidirectional language modeling** task, whose input units are subwords generated through Byte Pair Encoding (Sennrich et al., 2016). Unidirectional language models are also called **autoregressive** or **causal**.

> Given a sequence $s = l_1, \ldots, l_n$, an **autoregressive (unidirectional, causal) language model** is trained to predict the probability of a target word $t = l_i$ by computing its probability either given the preceding context, $p(t|c = l_1, \ldots, l_{i-1})$, or given the following context, $p(t|c = l_{i+1}, \ldots, l_n)$.

GPT is an autoregressive model with left-to-right self-attention. Therefore, its embeddings are contextualized only with respect to the preceding context.

Differently from GPT, **BERT** (Bidirectional Encoder Representations from Transformers; Devlin et al., 2019) employs the Transformer encoder stack and is fully **bidirectional**. The autoregressive language modeling task cannot be used to train a bidirectional self-attention model, since each word would be allowed to indirectly "see itself," and the model could eventually predict the target word trivially. The solution adopted with BERT consists in training it with a **masked language modeling** task, inspired to the Cloze test in psychology: Some of the tokens from the input are randomly masked, and the training objective is to predict the original masked words based on their context. This training task is an example of **denoising autoencoding**.[11]

BERT

BIDIRECTIONAL
LANGUAGE MODEL

MASKED
LANGUAGE MODEL

DENOISING
AUTOENCODERS

> **Denoising autoencoders** are neural networks trained to reconstruct an input text where a random subset of the words has been masked out.

BERT is also trained with an additional task of **next-sentence prediction**: Given a sentence pair, the network must predict whether the latter is the next sentence that actually follows the former. This allows BERT to learn relations between sentences, which are useful in applications like question-answering and natural language inference.

NEXT-SENTENCE
PREDICTION

The BERT input is a sequence formed by a single sentence or by a pair of sentences A and B, separated by the special token [SEP] (see Figure 9.9). The first token of the input sequence is the special [CLS] token. The BERT input units are a combination of word, subword and character embeddings, to deal with out-of-vocabulary lexemes. If a whole word is not in the vocabulary, BERT tries to tokenize it into the largest possible subwords contained in the vocabulary, and as a last resort will decompose the word into individual characters. The subword units are learned from the training corpus with Word-Piece (Wu et al., 2016). Each ith input token is represented with the embedding e_i, obtained by summing a token embedding, a positional embedding (like in Equation 9.29), and a segment embedding specifying whether the unit belongs to sentence A or B. These embeddings are learned together with the other Transformer parameters. During training, 15% of all the tokens are chosen for the random masking procedure: 80% of the selected units are replaced by the special [MASK] token, 10% are replaced with a random word, and 10% are left unchanged. The vectors corresponding to these tokens produced by the final layer are converted into probabilities by first applying a non-linear

---

[11] Denoising autoencoders do not explicitly estimate the probability distribution of a target given its context, so they are not language models in the strictest sense of this term.

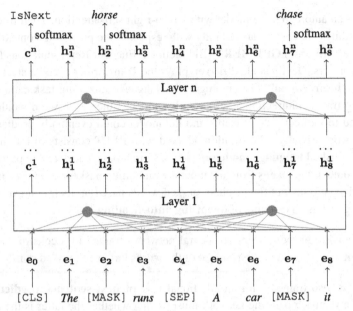

Figure 9.9 The structure of BERT. During training, some random items in the input sequence are masked, and the objective is to predict the corresponding words. The gray dots represent the bidirectional self-attention heads

transformation, then a linear one whose weight matrix is the transpose of the input embedding matrix of the Transformer. The result is fed into a softmax function over the vocabulary, to predict the correct lexeme. Like in Vaswani et al. (2017), the weights of the BERT input and output matrices are shared, a solution called **weight-tying trick** (Press and Wolf, 2017), which improves the performance of neural language models and reduces the number of their parameters. The hidden state c^i produced by the layer L_i for the token [CLS] is the aggregate embedding of the whole input sequence and is used for the next-sentence prediction. This is a binary classification task, in which the vector c^n of the last layer is assigned the label IsNext, if the sentence B actually follows A, and the label NotNext, otherwise.

WEIGHT-TYING
TRICK

Thanks to the self-attention mechanism of the Transformer encoder, BERT is "deeply bidirectional" (Devlin et al., 2019). This is a major difference with respect to ELMo too, which instead just concatenates two unidirectional representations. The original BERT model comes into two variants: (i) **BERT**$_{base}$, with 12 layers and vectors of 768 dimensions; (ii) **BERT**$_{large}$, with 24 layers and vectors of $1,024$ dimensions. Table 9.5 shows how the vectors generated by the last layer of BERT$_{base}$ capture co-compositionality effects

Table 9.5 Cosine similarity between the contextual embeddings of the target lexemes in boldface, generated by the layer 12 of BERT$_{base}$

	The professor **opened** the conference.
The professor **began** the conference.	**0.81**
The professor **unlocked** the door.	0.57

	The professor **opened** the door.
The professor **began** the conference.	0.53
The professor **unlocked** the door.	**0.77**

	The horse **runs** fast.
The horse **gallops** fast.	**0.73**
The water **flows** fast.	0.70

	The water **runs** fast.
The horse **gallops** fast.	0.54
The water **flows** fast.	**0.85**

(cf. Section 9.1.1). For instance, the vector **run** in *The horse runs* is closer to **gallops** than to **flows**, and vice versa for **run** in *The water runs*.

The Success of Contextual Embeddings

Contextual DSMs represent a very different approach to generate distributional representations with respect to static ones.

STATIC AND CONTEXTUAL DSMs

> **Static DSMs** produce a single distributional vector for each word type in the model vocabulary. **Contextual DSMs** take in input a whole sentence and generate embeddings for each of its word tokens.

Since they generate inherently context-sensitive token vectors through a language modeling training objective, contextual DSMs are **exemplar predict models**. However, generating contextual embeddings is not the end goal of systems like GPT or BERT, which are designed chiefly as general, multi-task architectures to develop NLP applications based on **fine-tuning** (Dai and Le, 2015; Radford et al., 2018; Devlin et al., 2019). This is a method of **transfer learning** that represents a different way of using word embeddings in downstream tasks. The classical approach based on **pretrained features** (cf. Section 7.3) consists in having two separate models: the first one (e.g., word2vec) learns the embeddings that are then fed as features into a distinct task-specific model. In fine-tuning, it is instead the same architecture that deals with the whole process in two steps:

EXEMPLAR PREDICT DSMs

FINE-TUNING

TRANSFER LEARNING

PRETRAINED FEATURES

pretraining – the model is first trained with a general unsupervised or self-supervised task (i.e., language modeling) on large amounts of texts; **fine-tuning** – the pretrained model is then re-trained on a specific supervised task (e.g., question-answering), by replacing the softmax layer employed in the former phase with another task-specific softmax classifier.

During fine-tuning, the model leverages the linguistic knowledge encoded in the pretrained distributional representations, and requires a smaller amount of annotated data to learn the final task. Devlin et al. (2019) show that BERT can achieve state-of-art results in several NLP tasks using either the feature-based or the fine-tuning method. The success of BERT has sparked the development of several improved models, such as **RoBERTa** (Liu et al., 2019), **XLNet** (Yang et al., 2019), **ELECTRA** (Clark et al., 2020), **DeBERTa** (He et al., 2021), among many others (Han et al., 2021).

BERT is trained on monolingual textual data, but the same approach has been extended to the multilingual and multimodal settings as well. **mBERT** (Devlin et al., 2019) and **XLM** (Conneau and Lample, 2019) are multilingual versions of BERT that learn **cross-lingual contextual embeddings** (cf. Section 8.4) using concatenated monolingual data from 100 languages. The models have a shared vocabulary across languages and are trained with **multilingual masked language modeling**: The model must reconstruct masked words that belong to multiple languages. Both mBERT and XLM obtain strong performances on zero-shot cross-lingual transfer in downstream NLP tasks, proving that they can learn regularities among languages even without parallel data. This is also confirmed by Conneau et al. (2020), who show that similar embedding spaces emerge from monolingual BERT models, whose contextual representations in different languages can be aligned in a joint space by using a linear mapping (cf. Section 8.4.1).

Other language models learn **multimodal contextual embeddings** from texts and images (cf. Section 8.7.1). **ViLBERT** (Lu et al., 2019) consists of two parallel Transformer streams for visual and linguistic processing that are then fused through co-attentional layers attending in each stream to information in the other one. ViLBERT is trained on a corpus of image-caption pairs with two tasks. In **masked multimodal learning**, the model must reconstruct masked regions (i.e., whose features are zeroed) from images and masked words from their caption. In **multimodal alignment prediction**, the model must predict whether the text is a correct description of the image. ViLBERT learns multimodal representations that achieve state-of-the art performances in tasks such as visual question answering or grounding referring expressions. **CLIP**

CROSS-LINGUAL
CONTEXTUAL
EMBEDDINGS

MULTILINGUAL
MASKED
LANGUAGE
MODELING

MULTIMODAL
CONTEXTUAL
EMBEDDINGS

MASKED
MULTIMODAL
LEARNING

MULTIMODAL
ALIGNMENT
PREDICTION

CLIP

(Contrastive Language-Image Pre-training; Radford et al., 2021) is a multi-modal extension of GPT which jointly trains an image and a text encoder to predict the correct pairings of a set of image-text training examples.

The improvements achieved by deep neural language models in several tasks have granted huge popularity to contextual embeddings, which have fast replaced static ones, especially in downstream applications. In fact, contextual embeddings are often preferred to sentence embeddings too (cf. Section 9.4), and it has become customary to represent sentences with the sequence or the average of the contextualized vectors of their component words.[12] The reason for this success is ascribed to the ability of deep neural language models to generate lexical representations that capture context-dependent aspects of word meaning, thereby overcoming the meaning conflation deficiency of static embeddings (cf. Section 8.2). Several studies aiming at exploring the "geometry" of contextual semantic spaces show that they encode a fine-grained representation of polysemy and word senses (Coenen et al., 2019; Wiedemann et al., 2019; Garí Soler and Apidianaki, 2021). Ethayarajh (2019) introduces the following **self-similarity** measure to estimate the degree of contextualization of the n token embeddings $l_1^L, \ldots, l_n^L$ of a lexeme type l produced by the layer L: SELF-SIMILARITY

$$\mathrm{SelfSim}_L(l) = \frac{1}{n^2 - n} \sum_{i=1}^{n} \sum_{j \neq i}^{n} \mathrm{cos}_{\mathrm{sim}}(l_i^L, l_j^L). \qquad (9.34)$$

The self-similarity of l is the average cosine similarity between its contextualized token vectors, and measures the uniformity of the semantic space of l in the different contexts: The higher the self-similarity of l, the less contextualized are its token embeddings. Ethayarajh (2019) reports that in ELMo, BERT, and GPT the higher layers produce more context-specific embeddings than lower ones, though with important differences depending on the model. Garí Soler and Apidianaki (2021) use the same measure to show that BERT discriminates between monosemous and polysemous lexemes.

Contextual DSMs only generate embeddings of word tokens, as a function of the sequences in which they occur. This is consistent with exemplar semantic models, which assume there is no such thing as a context-independent lexical meaning (Bybee, 2010; Jones, 2019). The latter is simply viewed as a

---

[12] In BERT, the final hidden state for the [CLS] is a sentence embedding that is close to the weighted average of its word embeddings. Reimers and Gurevych (2019) introduce **Sentence-BERT**, which learns sentence embeddings by fine-tuning BERT on natural language inference data.

second-order entity corresponding to a set of exemplar meanings (cf. Section 9.6.2). On the other hand, several semantic tasks concern out-of-context words and it is therefore important to evaluate to what extent contextual DSMs are also able to capture **type-level** aspects of lexical knowledge. Although context modulates word meaning, several properties also remain constant across contexts: The fact that *dog* is more similar to *cat* than to *strawberry* is a type-level semantic property which is essentially context-independent. Contextual DSMs should be able to learn embeddings that preserve these type-level properties, beyond the contextual modulation encoded in each token vector. Mickus et al. (2020) show that BERT token embeddings indeed form coherent clusters when grouped by lexical types. Other studies compare the type embeddings produced by static DSMs with those obtained by pooling token contextual vectors. The simplest approach consists in defining the **type contextual embedding** l as the average of the token embeddings obtained from a set S of n randomly selected sentences in which l occurs (Bommasani et al., 2020):

TYPE-LEVEL LEXICAL MEANING

TYPE CONTEXTUAL EMBEDDING

$$\mathbf{l}^{\mathbf{L}} = \frac{1}{|S|} \sum_{i \in S} \mathbf{l}_i^{\mathbf{L}}, \tag{9.35}$$

where $\mathbf{l}_i^{\mathbf{L}}$ is the embedding of the ith token of the lexeme l generated by the layer L of the model (it is also customary to average embeddings across multiple layers, as this can improve the representations). When tested on some of the tasks and datasets used for the intrinsic evaluation of standard DSMs (cf. Section 7.2), Bommasani et al. (2020) and Vulić et al. (2020) report that type contextual embeddings are competitive with static ones, even if they are generated with a small number of contexts (e.g., $|S| = 10$). On the other hand, Lenci et al. (2022) compare BERT type embeddings with those produced by the DSMs in Section 7.4.1, and show that static embeddings significantly outperform the type vectors derived from BERT in almost all tasks. Therefore, they argue that, when properly optimized, static DSMs still have an edge in out-of-context semantic tasks, though the performance of contextual DSMs might be improved by adopting more complex methods to build type embeddings. For instance, Chronis and Erk (2020) propose a multi-prototype model to generate sense vectors by clustering BERT token vectors (cf. Section 8.2.1).

The ability of contextual DSMs to capture semantic knowledge is also affected by the strong **anisotropy** of their embedding space (Ethayarajh, 2019).

(AN)ISOTROPY

> A vector space is **isotropic** if the vectors are distributed uniformly.

Perfect isotropy entails that the average cosine similarity between randomly sampled words would be zero (Arora et al., 2016). The more anisotropic the space is, the more its vectors are instead distributed in a narrow cone, in which even unrelated words have high cosine similarities. A high degree of isotropy is a desirable property, because it means a better ability of word embeddings to capture similarity relations. Mimno and Thompson (2017) and Mu and Viswanath (2018) notice the anisotropy of the word2vec and GloVe semantic spaces, but Ethayarajh (2019) shows that this phenomenon is particularly strong in BERT and GPT, thereby producing unwanted anomalies in the semantic space. For instance, Rajaee and Pilehvar (2021) report that the representations for different senses of a verb tend to be closer than the embeddings for the same sense that correspond to different verb tenses. Gao et al. (2019) relate the high degree of anisotropy of contextual DSMs – which they call **representation degeneration problem** – to the fact that they are neural language models trained to optimize the likelihood of the words to be predicted using the weight-tying trick. This would make some dimensions highly dominant in the embeddings, thereby grouping them in a narrow area. Both Cai et al. (2021) and Rajaee and Pilehvar (2021) show that the phenomenon of anisotropy is less pronounced in local clusters of lexical items, which would explain the good performance of contextual embeddings anyway. Some common solutions to smooth anisotropy is to standardize the embeddings by turning their components into z-scores, or to remove the top principal components of the embeddings identified with PCA (Mu and Viswanath, 2018; Timkey and Van Schijndel, 2021). This latter solution is similar to the case of inverse truncated SVD in count models (cf. Section 2.5.1), in which discarding the top singular values results into better distributional representations. REPRESENTATION DEGENERATION PROBLEM

A major drawback of Transformer contextual DSMs resides in their huge **complexity**. BERT$_{large}$ has 340 million parameters, some of the later models have hundreds of billions of parameters and are trained on huge amounts of text. Such complexity causes excessive costs to learn the embeddings and greatly limits their sustainability (Strubell et al., 2019). This has prompted several attempts to develop lighter models that aim at preserving the original quality of the representations while reducing the parameters or the training data, such as **DistilBERT** (Sanh et al., 2019) and **BabyBERTa** (Huebner et al., 2021). The latter is trained with just five million words of child-directed speech, to match the quantity and quality of the input children are exposed to. Zhang et al. (2021) instead explore the relationship between the amount of training data and the type of linguistic knowledge that BERT is able to learn, and show that the model performance in syntactic and semantic tasks peaks after only ten to one hundred million words. COMPLEXITY DISTILBERT BABYBERTA

The complexity of contextual DSMs also decreases the **interpretability** of their representations, thereby exacerbating a problem that affects all neural INTERPRETABILITY architectures. Some works attempt to explore the attention mechanism to identify the contextual elements the model attends to (Clark et al., 2019; Kovaleva et al., 2019). However, the overall picture is still fairly unclear, proving the difficulty to get at a full understanding of the actual model behavior. While static DSMs aim at representing type-level aspects of lexical meaning (e.g., similarity relations), the goal of contextual models like BERT is to produce representations that encode large amounts of linguistic information, including but not limited to semantic ones, which can be leveraged in downstream tasks.

BERTOLOGY A new research trend, which Rogers et al. (2020) call **BERTology**, aims at investigating the nature and extent of this linguistic knowledge, mostly using probing tasks. For example, Tenney et al. (2019a) show that BERT lower layers tend to capture morphosyntactic information, while higher layers focus on semantic dimensions, similarly to what happens in ELMo. At the same time, Tenney et al. (2019b) report that, though contextual embeddings improve over static ones, this mainly concerns syntactic tasks (e.g., constituent labeling) rather than semantic ones (e.g., coreference), suggesting that these embeddings encode more syntactic than semantic information.

PROMPTING Another method to explore the knowledge encoded by contextual DSMs is **prompting** (Liu et al., 2021). Instead of fine-tuning the models and using auxiliary supervised classifiers, propting is based on an unsupervised zero-shot setting. A *prompt* is fed to the language model, which either predicts the continuation of the prompt (with autoregressive models like GPT) or the identity of one or more masked words (with bidirectional ones like BERT). The output of the language model is then used as the response to the task at hand. Ettinger (2020) introduces a suite of tasks derived from psycholinguistic research to test BERT semantic knowledge by looking at its word predictions. Prompts are formed by a context plus a [MASK] token (e.g., *A robin is a* [MASK].) in the position of interest, and evaluation measures the prediction accuracy for this [MASK] token. The results of her experiments show that BERT is sensible to certain aspects of semantic roles (e.g., *The waiter served the customer* vs. *The customer served the waiter*), but in general it has limited knowledge of event inference and negation, as also confirmed by Staliūnaitė and Iacobacci (2020).

OLMPICS The **oLMpics** test suite by Talmor et al. (2020) is structured in the same fashion and reveals the models have in many cases poor reasoning abilities. Ravichander et al. (2020) and Hanna and Mareček (2021) show with prompting the difficulty of contextual DSMs to capture hypernymy (cf. Section 8.3.1).

In summary, the huge popularity gained by contextual DSMs is surely justified by the fact that they provide distributional representations of lexical items in their sentential contexts, thereby capturing context-sensitive dimensions of meaning, alongside other linguistic information that is crucial to improve the performances of NLP and AI systems. On the other hand, such benefits should not make us underestimate the limits of these models, whose real semantic competence is still an open research question.

9.7 Distributional Models of Selectional Preferences

Selectional preferences are the constraints that govern semantic composition (cf. Section 9.1). In symbolic models, they are represented with symbols drawn from a stipulated ontology of semantic types that should characterize the necessary and sufficient conditions for a lexeme to be the argument of a predicate. However, predicates greatly differ for the granularity of argument types they admit, and in several cases it is impossible to find an independently motivated ontological class that capture their semantic constraints (Zeldes, 2013). For instance, the verb *achieve* admits as direct objects nouns like *result, aim, goal, success,* and so on. In this case, the only possible way to group the selected entities into a categorical type is by referring to the predicate itself (e.g., *achieve* selects for ENTITIES_THAT_CAN_BE_ACHIEVED), thereby making the identification of semantic types dangerously circular.

SELECTIONAL PREFERENCES

Asher (2011) correctly points out that semantic types are "mind-dependent representations" that are part of the "conceptual apparatus necessary for linguistic understanding" (p. 37). Like other kinds of conceptual representations, semantic constraints show typicality effects (Murphy, 2002): The possible arguments of a predicate are not all equally favored. For instance, the verb *arrest* prefers animate direct objects. However, though *arrest a policeman* and *arrest a thief* are both well-formed, *thief* is a more prototypical patient of *arrest* than *policeman*. In psycholinguistics, the typicality of an argument with respect to a predicate is called **thematic fit** (McRae et al., 1997b, 1998).

THEMATIC FIT

> The **thematic fit** is a word plausibility as the argument of a predicate.

Thematic fit derives from our linguistic and first-hand experience of events and their typical participants. McRae and Matsuki (2009) call this information **generalized event knowledge**. Typicality effects in argument selection pose an important challenge to symbolic models of selectional preferences and call for a different kind of representation to address their gradient nature.

GENERALIZED EVENT KNOWLEDGE

Distributional models of selectional preferences share this assumption:

> The semantic constraints of predicates derive from the **co-occurrences with their arguments**.

However, selectional constraints do not simply consist in the set of observed arguments in a corpus, because they are by definition general knowledge about the semantic classes of the *possible* arguments of a predicate. For instance, if we know that *ponche* is a kind of liquor, we can understand the sentence *I drank a ponche*, even if we have never heard it before. Therefore, the process of inducing selectional preferences from corpus data must include a

GENERALIZATION **generalization step** to infer the degree of preference for new, unseen lexemes
STEP
USAGE-BASED as fillers of a given predicate slot. This is consistent with a **usage-based** view
VIEW of selectional preferences, according to which they are abstractions from the lexemes that are observed as arguments of a particular predicate.

Though the notion of selectional constraint applies to every category of predicate, research has mostly focused on verbs. Early computational mod-

LEXICAL els of selectional preferences, such as Resnik (1996), rely on existing **lexical**
RESOURCES **resources** like WordNet to identify the semantic types selected by predicates. In Resnik's model, the generalization from observed predicate–argument pairs is performed with an information-theoretic similarity measure defined over the class hierarchy of WordNet. This has been an influential model, which has spawned a number of similar approaches, including Clark and Weir (2002), Brockmann and Lapata (2003) for German, Schulte im Walde et al. (2008), Ó Séaghdha and Korhonen (2012), which combine WordNet with Topic Models, and Judea et al. (2012), who use Wikipedia as lexical resource. DSMs are attractive alternatives to lexical resources for generalization in selectional preference models, since by design they are not limited to a particular data set, domain, or language. Moreover, they do not depend on the a priori stipulated structure of semantic classes that we find in manually constructed resources.

CLUSTERING A first group of DSMs generalize observed co-occurrences by **clustering** the distributional vectors of arguments extracted from the training corpus. The resulting clusters represent the semantic classes selected by the predicates and are used to estimate the plausibility of unseen arguments. Pereira et al. (1993) model the probability of a noun n as the argument of a predicate v in the following way, with C a set of distributionally induced clusters:

$$p(n, v) = \sum_{c \in C} p(c)p(c|n)p(c|v). \qquad (9.36)$$

Pereira et al. (1993) group nouns that occur as heads of direct objects of verbs with hierarchical clustering. Rooth et al. (1999) and Prescher et al. (2000) formulate the distributional clustering method as an Expectation-Maximization algorithm. Other approaches include Pantel et al. (2007), Basili et al. (2007), who employ a variant of k-means clustering of LSA vectors, and the discriminative model of Bergsma et al. (2008) with CBC clustering (cf. Section 8.2.2).

The most influential family of distributional approaches to selectional preferences dispenses with clustering and is based on the following assumption:

> The thematic fit of a new lexeme as argument of a predicate depends on its distributional similarity with previously observed arguments.

Erk (2007), Padó et al. (2007), and Erk et al. (2010) propose **EPP**, an **exemplar model** of selectional preferences in which the thematic fit of a noun n as the argument of a verb v in a syntactic role r is measured with the similarity between the distributional vector of n and the vectors of a set of noun exemplars occurring in the same argument role of the predicate. Erk et al. (2010) compute the following selectional preference score:

$$\text{SelPref}_{\text{EPP}}(n, r, v) = \sum_{n_i \in \text{SeenArg}(r,v)} \frac{w_{r,v}(n_i)}{Z_{r,v}} \text{sim}(\mathbf{n}, \mathbf{n_i}), \quad (9.37)$$

where sim is a vector similarity measure, $\text{SeenArg}(r, v)$ is a set of nouns occurring as arguments of v in the role r in the corpus, $w_{r,v}(n)$ is a weight (e.g., the co-occurrence frequency) estimating the salience of the observed argument n for v, and $Z_{r,v}$ is a normalization factor to make the score independent of the number of selected exemplars ($Z_{r,v} = \sum_{n_i \in \text{SeenArg}(r,v)} w_{r,v}(n_i)$). Selpref$_{\text{EPP}}$ is essentially the weighted average over similarities between the noun n and the previously observed arguments of v. Erk et al. (2010) experiment with different similarity measures and weights, showing that EPP is generally able to outperform WordNet-based and EM-based models.

Selectional preferences are typically defined as semantic constraints that predicates place on their arguments. Erk et al. (2010) also apply the EPP model to **inverse preferences**, namely the preferences that arguments have for their predicates. For instance, the noun *book* prefers to appear as direct object of verbs like *read* and *write*, while *violinist* prefers to occur as subjects of verbs like *play* and *perform*. In fact, psycholinguistic studies have shown with different experimental paradigms (e.g., semantic priming, self-paced reading, etc.) that nouns trigger expectations about the most typical verbs they co-occur with (McRae et al., 2005a). Inverse preferences are related to the Generative Lexicon model of lexical entries (Pustejovsky, 1995), in which a noun like *book* is represented as containing event information that refers to its typical function (e.g., *read*) and its typical mode of creation (e.g., *write*) (cf. Section 8.1).

Baroni and Lenci (2010) propose a variation of EPP inspired by prototype representations of concepts (Murphy, 2002). The thematic fit of a noun n as an argument of a verb v in a syntactic role r is measured with the similarity between the distributional vector of n and a **prototype vector $\mathbf{r_v}$**:

$$\text{SelPref}_{\text{Prot}}(n, r, v) = \text{sim}(\mathbf{n}, \mathbf{r_v}). \qquad (9.38)$$

The prototype vector is the centroid vector (cf. Section 8.2.1) of the most typical arguments of r observed in the training corpus:

$$\mathbf{r_v} = \frac{1}{|\text{SeenArg}(\mathbf{r}, \mathbf{v})|} \sum_{n_i \in \text{SeenArg}(\mathbf{r}, \mathbf{v})} \mathbf{n_i}. \qquad (9.39)$$

Baroni and Lenci (2010) define the set $\text{SeenArg}(r, v)$ as the k arguments in the training corpus ($k = 20$ in their original setting) with the highest association score (e.g., PLMI; cf. Section 2.3.1) with v in the role r. Other variations of the exemplar and prototype models of selectional preferences and thematic fit have been explored by Schulte im Walde (2010), Greenberg et al. (2015), Sayeed et al. (2015), and Santus et al. (2017). Peirsman and Padó (2010) introduce a cross-lingual version of EPP that employs a bilingual DSM (cf. Section 8.4).

Selectional preferences are usually modeled as two-way relations between a predicate and an argument. However, this representation does not take into account the fact that the semantic constraints of a particular syntactic role depend on how other roles in the same sentence are filled (Elman, 2009, 2011, 2014). For instance, the expected patient of the verb *cut* is likely to be *meat* if
the agent is *butcher*, and to be *hair* if the agent is *coiffeur*. Lenci (2011) extends the prototype model to account for **multi-way selectional preferences** with a dynamic process of compositional update of semantic constraints. The distributional information coming from the agent and the predicate are composed with either an additive or a multiplicative model (cf. Section 9.2), to generate a prototype vector that represents the expectations on the likely fillers of the patient role, given the agent filler. This makes it possible to model the dynamic aspect of thematic fit, since the expectations on an argument are progressively updated as the other roles in the sentence are filled (cf. Chersoni et al., 2017 for a variant of the same approach). Van de Cruys (2010a) uses Non-negative Tensor Factorization (NTF), which is a generalization of Non-negative Matrix Factorization (cf. Section 2.5.3), to capture the multi-way selectional preferences of transitive predicates with a third-order tensor representing subject-verb-object co-occurrence data.

Other distributional approaches to selectional preferences use **Topic Models** (cf. Section 4.4). In particular, the EM-based approach of Rooth et al. (1999) has inspired more recent works that use LDA. The idea is to model selectional preferences with a probability distribution over topics representing latent semantic classes selected by predicates. Ó Séaghdha (2010) proposes a probabilistic model of thematic fit, by computing the probability of a noun n as the argument of v in the role r as follows:

$$p(n|v,r) = \sum_{z \in Z} p(n|z)p(z|v,r), \qquad (9.40)$$

where Z is a set of latent topics induced with LDA. Ritter et al. (2010) use a very similar solution to model multi-way selectional preferences of binary predicates (e.g., companies and organizations are likely to fill the first argument of *x is headquartered in y*, and locations the second argument). LDA approaches to selectional preferences are competitive with the EM-based model of Rooth et al. (1999), the similarity-based approach of Erk (2007), and the clustering-based approach of Pantel et al. (2007).

Selectional preferences are also modeled with **neural networks**. Van de Cruys (2014) use a feed-forward network that takes in input the concatenation of the embeddings of the verb and one or two arguments (the latter case for multi-way preferences) and computes their plausibility score. Similarly to Collobert and Weston (2008), the network is trained to discriminate attested verb-argument tuples from noisy ones obtained by replacing the verb with a random one. Tilk et al. (2016) model two-way and multi-way selectional preferences with a recurrent neural network trained to predict the filler of the semantic role of a given verb. However, their network needs to be trained on a corpus previously annotated with semantic roles. Other approaches model the preferred arguments of a predicate directly with the predictions of **neural language models**. Elman and McRae (2019) use an SRN (cf. Section 6.2.1) to represent generalized event knowledge, while Metheniti et al. (2020) study to what extent selectional preferences are reflected in the word predictions by BERT. Given an example sentence containing a target predicate with its argument masked using a [MASK] token (e.g., *The journalist writes the* [MASK].), the probability that BERT assigns to the masked position is retrieved and correlated with the predicate-argument plausibility. Generally, the correlations are not very strong, suggesting a limited mastery of selectional preferences. Similarly, the experiments by Pedinotti et al. (2021a) reveal that the thematic fit predictions of contextual DSMs often depend on surface linguistic features, such as frequent words, collocations, and syntactic patterns, thereby showing sub-optimal generalization abilities.

Distributional models of selectional preferences are typically evaluated in two tasks: pseudo-disambiguation and the prediction of human thematic fit

NEURAL NETWORKS

NEURAL LANGUAGE MODELS

Table 9.6 An example of thematic fit ratings
from the McRae dataset

verb	role	noun	thematic fit
arrest	agent	cop	6.7
arrest	patient	cop	1.6
fire	agent	employer	6.1
fire	patient	employer	2.4

PSEUDO-
DISAMBIGUATION

ratings. In the **pseudo-disambiguation** task (Dagan et al., 1999; Rooth et al., 1999), the model decides which of two words is a better argument for a syntactic role r in a predicate p. Given an observed set of tuples $\langle p, r, l \rangle$ (e.g., $\langle drink,$ dobj, $beer \rangle$), each lexeme l is paired with a randomly selected word l' (e.g., *computer*). The tuples $\langle p, r, l \rangle$ and $\langle p, r, l' \rangle$ are removed from the training corpus to make sure that we measure a model's ability to generalize from observed items and predict the plausibility of unseen arguments of a predicate.

ACCURACY

Models are then evaluated for their **accuracy** in choosing for each pair $\langle l, l' \rangle$ (e.g., $\langle beer, computer \rangle$) the most plausible filler for p in the role r. Pseudo-disambiguation can be viewed as a kind of WSD task in which the two lexemes l and l' together form a "pseudo-word" that models disambiguate by choosing the lexical item that fits better in the given predicate.

THEMATIC FIT

Thematic fit evaluation (Padó et al., 2007; Baroni and Lenci, 2010; Sayeed et al., 2016) is instead based on datasets of human ratings about the plausibility of nouns as arguments of verbs (cf. Table 9.6). The evaluation measure is

SPEARMAN
CORRELATION

the **Spearman rank correlation** (ρ) between distributional similarity scores and thematic fit ratings. The **McRae** (McRae et al., 1998) and **Padó** datasets

MCRAE – PADÓ

(Padó, 2007) respectively consist of $1,444$ and 414 typicality scores for verb–agent (e.g., *doctor-advise*) and verb–patient pairs (e.g., *hit-ball*), whereas the

FERRETTI

Ferretti dataset (Ferretti et al., 2001) includes ratings for 374 verb–instrument (e.g., *cut-mower*) and 248 verb–location pairs (e.g., *teach-classroom*). The scores range from 1 (atypical) to 7 (very typical). The largest dataset avail-

SP-10K

able to date is **SP-10K** (Zhang et al., 2019), which contains over ten thousand predicate argument pairs rated for their plausibility.

DTFIT

Differently from the previous datasets, **DTFit** (Vassallo et al., 2018) contains tuples of different lengths, so that crowdsourced typicality ratings of an argument depend on its interaction with the other arguments in the tuple. The dataset consists of triples and quadruples that differ for typical (e.g., *sergeant-assign-mission*) vs. atypical (e.g., *sergeant-assign-homework*) patients,

BICKNELL

locations, or instruments. The much smaller **Bicknell** dataset (Bicknell et al., 2010) includes 100 typical and atypical agent–verb–patient triples. Rather

than focusing on typicality, the **Wang2018** dataset (Wang et al., 2018) con- WANG2018
tains 3,080 agent–verb–patient triples distinguishing an atypical but physically
plausible event (e.g., *The student climbed the ship*) from an atypical and
physically implausible one (e.g., *The student climbed the water*).

9.7.1 Modeling Coercion: The Case of Logical Metonymy

The term **(complement) coercion** refers to a wide range of phenomena in COERCION
which an argument is reinterpreted to overcome the violation of the selectional
preferences of its predicate (Lauwers and Willems, 2011; Pustejovsky and LOGICAL
Batiukova, 2019). One well-known case of coercion is **logical metonymy**: METONYMY

(13)   a.   The author began the book.
       b.   The dog finished the bone.

The verb *begin* in (13a) normally selects for an event and the noun *book*
denotes an object, but it is reinterpreted as the participant of an implicit event
that is recovered, like *write* or *read* (cf. Section 9.1.1). This reinterpretation
also produces extra processing costs during online sentence comprehension
(McElree et al., 2001; Traxler et al., 2002; Zarcone et al., 2014).

Formal semantics models logical metonymy with type-shifting mechanisms
(Asher, 2011, 2015) or with complex lexical entries, like in the Generative
Lexicon. Pustejovsky (1995) argues that the implicit event is retrieved from
the information encoded in the Qualia Structure (cf. Section 8.1). According to this hypothesis, the TELIC role of *book* in (13a) includes the event
of reading as its typical purpose, and the AGENTIVE role specifies the event
of writing as its mode of creation. These events are retrieved to solve the
predicate-argument type mismatch, thereby producing a semantic representation equivalent to *begin to write (read) the book*. However, several cases cannot
be accounted by Qualia roles equally well. The most straightforward interpretation of (13b) is that the dog finished eating the bone, but being eaten can
hardly be regarded as the typical purpose of bones (cf. also Lascarides and
Copestake, 1998).

An alternative explanation of logical metonymy is that it relies on our generalized event knowledge (Zarcone et al., 2014). Reading and writing are part
of the interpretation of (13a), because they are likely events associated with
book and *author*. Similarly, eating is recovered from (13b), because it is the
most typical action performed by a dog on a bone. Distributional semantics
has pursued this argument by representing knowledge about events and their
participants with co-occurrence data extracted from corpora. Lapata and Lascarides (2003) propose a **probabilistic model** of logical metonymy in which PROBABILISTIC
the recovered event $\hat{e}$ is the one that maximizes the following joint probability: MODEL

$$\hat{e} = \operatorname*{argmax}_{e} p(e, n_1, v, n_2), \qquad (9.41)$$

where v is the metonymic verb, n_1 its subject, and n_2 its direct object. Assuming that n_2 is conditionally independent of v and n_1 and that n_1 is conditionally independent of v, they obtain:

$$p(e, n_1, v, n_2) \approx p(e)p(n_2|e)p(v|e)p(n_1|e). \qquad (9.42)$$

The probabilities in Equation 9.42 are estimated with simple co-occurrence frequencies. Therefore, (13b) is interpreted as *The dog finished eating the bone* because *eat* is the most probable event given *finished*, *dog*, and *bone*.

Other distributional analyses of logical metonymy are based on the notion of **thematic fit** (Zarcone et al., 2012, 2013; Chersoni et al., 2017, 2021b). Differently from Lapata and Lascarides (2003), these models predict both the implicit event and the higher cognitive cost of logical metonymy. Chersoni et al. (2017, 2021b) analyze logical metonymy within a general model of processing complexity, which is based on the hypothesis that the cognitive load of a sentence is inversely proportional to the mutual typicality of its components, estimated with a distributional measure of thematic fit. Given a transitive sentence $s = \langle n_1, v, n_2 \rangle$, its **typicality score** θ_s is defined as follows:

THEMATIC FIT MODEL

TYPICALITY SCORE

$$\theta_s = \theta(n_1|v)\theta(n_2|v)\theta(n_2|n_1), \qquad (9.43)$$

where $\theta(n_1|v)$ is the thematic fit of the subject noun with the verb, $\theta(n_2|v)$ the thematic fit of the object noun with the verb, and $\theta(n_2|n_1)$ the thematic fit of the object with the subject. For instance, the typicality score of (13a) is the product of the typicality of *author* as the subject of *began*, the typicality of *book* as the object of *began*, and the typicality of *book* as an object of events involving *author* as subject. The θ scores are computed with a prototype model of thematic fit, adapting Equation 9.38. Chersoni et al. (2017) use the typicality scores to account for the experimental results in McElree et al. (2001) and Traxler et al. (2002), which show that metonymic sentences produce higher processing costs than control sentences with no coercion (e.g., *The author wrote the book*). In fact, metonymic sentences have significantly lower values of θ_s than control sentences, supporting the hypothesis that the low thematic fit between the metonymic verb and the object-denoting noun triggers complement coercion and, at the same time, causes the extra processing load.

Chersoni et al. (2017, 2021b) adopt the same model to predict the **implicit event** $\hat{e}$ recovered in interpreting logical metonymy. Extending Equation 9.43, this is the event that maximizes the following product of thematic fit scores:

IMPLICIT EVENT

$$\hat{e} = \underset{e}{\operatorname{argmax}} \, \theta(n_1|v)\theta(e|v)\theta(n_1|e)\theta(n_2|e)\theta(n_2|n_1). \qquad (9.44)$$

Assuming that the choice of the implicit event does not depend on $\theta(n_1|v)$ and on $\theta(n_2|n_1)$, this equation can be further simplified as:

$$\hat{e} = \underset{e}{\operatorname{argmax}} \, \theta(e|v)\theta(n_1|e)\theta(n_2|e). \qquad (9.45)$$

For instance, *eat* is the preferred implicit event in (13b), because it is the event with the highest thematic fit with the various sentence components: the subject, the metonymic verb, and the direct object. Like in Lapata and Lascarides (2003), this model is able to account for the fact that the event recovered when interpreting logical metonymy also depends on the choice of verb subject (e.g., the preferred implicit event in *The student began the book* is *read*, while in *The author began the book* is *write*). Rambelli et al. (2020) also test the ability of Transformer language models to predict the implicit event, comparing them with probabilistic and thematic fit approaches.

9.8 Compositional Distributional Semantics: Limits and Prospects

In order to explain the **productivity** of natural language, a semantic theory must contain some general process to assign an interpretation to a potentially infinite number of complex expressions. The classical approach to address productivity is assuming that the construction of semantic representations is governed by the **Principle of Compositionality**: The meaning of a whole expression is determined by the meaning of its syntactic parts and their combination (cf. Section 9.1). This entails that there is a computational procedure to combine the interpretation of lexical items to obtain the interpretation of the expressions they are part of, according to syntactic structure. In symbolic models, this procedure is function application, which in turn relies on a basic distinction between lexemes acting as functions with variables, and lexemes acting as arguments that saturate them. In this chapter, we have reviewed several ways to tackle productivity with compositional distributional semantics. Now, it is time to make a general appraisal of the state of the art in this area, to highlight its current limits and possible future research lines.

PRODUCTIVITY

PRINCIPLE OF COMPOSITIONALITY

A first group of methods to construct the distributional representation of complex linguistic expressions substantially adheres to the Principle of Compositionality (Liang and Potts, 2015; Potts, 2019).

> Given the syntactic node $[_C AB]$ and the distributional representations of A and B, $\mathbf{DR}(A)$ and $\mathbf{DR}(B)$, there is a composition function f such that $\mathbf{DR}(C) = f(\mathbf{DR}(A), \mathbf{DR}(B))$.

Proposals vary for the type of distributional representation and for the choice of f. For instance, $\mathbf{DR}(A)$ and $\mathbf{DR}(B)$ can be vectors and f an operation like sum or tensor product (cf. Section 9.2). DFM assumes that $\mathbf{DR}(A)$ and $\mathbf{DR}(B)$ are tensors of different order (e.g., a matrix and a vector), and f is tensor-vector multiplication (cf. Section 9.3). The composition function can also be a feed-forward neural network, like in MV-RNN (cf. Section 9.3.1). Despite its being theoretically unsatisfactory, vector sum remains extremely competitive with approaches directly inspired by formal models of compositionality, such as DFM, which also suffer from great problems of scalability.

The limits of the methods above have prompted the popularity of a different paradigm based on the idea that the distributional representation of an input sentence (**sentence embedding**) is the hidden state of a neural network trained on some linguistic task, such as prediction or inference (cf. Section 9.4). The attractiveness of this approach lies in its simplicity and scalability. The networks are able to generalize beyond their training data and to assign a vector to any new input sentence, thereby showing some sort of productivity. Moreover, their sensitivity to word order allows sentence embeddings to avoid the problems of commutative vector operations, like addition or multiplication.

Neural sentence embeddings depart from the main assumptions grounding the Principle of Compositionality. This is based on a neat separation between syntax and semantics: The former identifies the structure of linguistic expressions, following which the semantic operations combine the meaning of their parts. As Nefdt (2020) argues, while the Principle of Compositionality presupposes the notion of "**meaningful part**," that is some correspondence between the parts of a sentence and the parts of its meaning, no such notion is clearly identifiable in neural networks, whose embeddings are not constructed by combining the meaning of independently identified syntactic components. In fact, the sentence embeddings are just internal network states that come to encode a mixture of linguistic information, including several syntactic dimensions alongside semantic ones (Adi et al., 2017; Conneau et al., 2018a), as a by-product of learning a certain sentence-related task.

The lack of compositionality in neural networks has been a topic of intense discussion at least since when Fodor and Pylyshyn (1988) proposed it as a key argument against connectionist models of cognition. This debate has been

SENTENCE EMBEDDING

MEANINGFUL PART

raging throughout these last decades and is still alive today, when new generations of neural models are available (Elman et al., 1996; Marcus, 2001; Calvo
and Symons, 2014; Baroni, 2019; Berent and Marcus, 2019; Rabovsky and
McClelland, 2019). Fodor and Pylyshyn (1988) argue that human cognition
and linguistic competence in particular are characterized by the properties of
systematicity and **compositionality**, which they define in the following way:

SYSTEMATICITY
COMPOSITIONALITY

> **Systematicity**: The ability to produce/understand some sentences is
> intrinsically connected to the ability to produce/understand certain others.
> **Compositionality**: A lexical item must make approximately the same
> contribution to each expression in which it occurs.

For instance, (14a) and (14b) are systematically related, because whoever
understands the former must also understand the latter:

(14)   a.   The black cat chases the brown dog.
       b.   The black dog chases the brown cat.

This systematic relation depends on the fact that the sentences are instances
of the same general structures licensed by English syntax. According to Fodor
and Pylyshyn (1988), systematicity presupposes compositionality: The relation
between (14a) and (14b) is possible only provided that the words have the same
meaning in the two sentences. Therefore, while systematicity is a property
about the nature of syntactic structures, compositionality is a property about
the contribution of the lexicon to the interpretation of complex expressions.
Taken together the two principles essentially correspond to Fregean Compositionality: The meaning of a complex expression is a structured entity, and the
syntactic parts of the expression correspond to the parts of its meaning.

Fodor and Pylyshyn (1988) use systematicity and compositionality as arguments against neural models and distributed representations (cf. Section 8.1).
According to them, these properties can be explained only by systems, like
symbolic ones, that combine internally structured representations. Since neural
networks generate unstructured representations, they cannot tackle systematicity and compositionality, and therefore they would lack explanatory value. For
instance, a neural network that produces two distinct sentence embeddings for
(14a) and (14b), might capture some aspects of their content, but nevertheless
would not account for their systematic relations and the fact that the two sentences are instances of the same general structure that could generate other –
potentially unlimited – systematically related sentences.

The same argument is adopted by Marcus (2001) and Berent and Marcus
(2019) to defend their **algebraic hypothesis** of human mind.

ALGEBRAIC
HYPOTHESIS

> Learning mechanisms operate **algebraically** over abstract rules and include the capacity to form abstract categories that treat all of their members alike and to operate over such classes using variables.

Berent and Marcus (2019) argue that algebraic rules with open variables explain a further property of human cognition, consisting in the ability of carrying out **across-the-board generalizations**:

ACROSS-THE-
BOARD
GENERALIZA-
TIONS

The hallmark of algebraic rules is not simply the capacity to generalize. Rules generalize across the board. They can extend generalizations to any member of a category, irrespective of its similarity to training items, and they obey systematicity and compositionality. (Berent and Marcus, 2019, p. e80)

This property corresponds to the way symbolic models construct the interpretation of complex expressions by combining functional symbols with open variables and arguments saturating them (cf. Section 9.1). For instance, representing *run* with the function $\lambda x[\text{run}(x)]$ explains the productivity of this predicate that can be applied to any argument satisfying the type constraints of the variable. According to Berent and Marcus (2019), since neural networks do not operate on symbolic rules with variables, they are not able to generalize across the board. They *do* generalize to new items, but only as long as they are **similar** to training data. Therefore, their productivity would be limited to **analogical generalizations**, while across-the-board ones are not similarity-driven, since algebraic rules can be applied to any new item that can fill their variables. This argument is supported by experiments that show that seq2seq models – similar to those used to generate sentence embeddings (cf. Section 9.4.3) and trained on simplified or artificial language data – show generalization abilities, but fail to generalize in a systematic and compositional way (Lake and Baroni, 2018; Loula et al., 2018; Goodwin et al., 2020; Hupkes et al., 2020).

SIMILARITY

ANALOGICAL
GENERALIZA-
TIONS

The debate sparked by Fodor and Pylyshyn (1988) and Marcus (2001) concerns distributional semantics too, since its representations are distributed and neural networks are the mainstream approach to learn them. Their critical arguments rest on the assumption that compositionality, systematicity, and across-the-board generalizations are the hallmarks of natural language. However, these assumptions are quite disputable. As discussed in Section 9.1.1, several linguistic phenomena are not compatible with Fregean Compositionality and suggest that natural language is actually **quasi-compositional** (Rabovsky and McClelland, 2019). The hypothesis about the contextually invariant nature of lexical meaning contrasts with the sense modulation

QUASI-COMPOSI-
TIONALITY

that lexical items constantly undergo when they are composed. In fact, the productivity that a semantic theory is called to explain concerns not only the ability of generating and understanding a potentially unlimited number of complex expressions, but also the ability of generating and understanding a potentially unlimited number of new word senses in context (Pustejovsky, 1995). The systematicity assumption has also been questioned in light of the pervasiveness of nonsystematic and semiregular processes in language, which apply to categories of entities governed by overlapping and complex constraints (Johnson, 2004). Rather than being the realm of across-the-board generalizations, natural language is characterized by the **partial productiv-** PARTIAL
ity (Goldberg, 2019) of analogical generalizations based on the similarity to PRODUCTIVITY
previously witnessed exemplars. Therefore, the fact that sentence embeddings learnt by neural models do not comply with the Principle of Compositionality and strive to generalize systematically does not entail that they could not have explanatory value for natural language semantics, since this also departs from those same properties (Baroni, 2019).

However, sentence embeddings suffer from several empirical limitations concerning their ability to encode significant aspects of meaning. For instance, Zhu et al. (2018) show that current models are not able to discriminate between different syntactic realizations of semantic roles and fail to recognize that *Lilly loves Imogen* is more similar to its passive counterpart than to *Imogen loves Lilly*. Sentence embeddings apparently perform very well in inference tasks, but this is mostly due to statistical artifacts in the training and test datasets (cf. Section 9.5). When the biases are removed, the performance of the models drops significantly (McCoy et al., 2019a). Glockner et al. (2018) test various sentence embeddings on a dataset of inferences carefully designed to avoid annotation artifacts and confirm their scarce generalization abilities. Simple additive models remain a very strong baseline (cf. Section 9.4), revealing that neural networks are really not successful in constructing sentence meaning, independently of their lack of systematicity or compositionality. These problems have surely contributed to shift the focus from methods to learn sentence embeddings to **contextual DSMs**. The expectation is that the deeply CONTEXTUAL
contextualized embeddings of word tokens might encode several aspects of DSMS
sentence meaning. Although this happens to a certain extent (Klafka and Ettinger, 2020), several analyses show that, their increasing complexity notwithstanding, contextual DSMs too have strong limits in capturing key aspects of compositional meaning such as semantic roles and negation (Ettinger, 2020; Staliūnaitė and Iacobacci, 2020), as well as partially productive structures like metaphorical and multiword expressions (Shwartz and Dagan, 2019; Pedinotti et al., 2021b).

Despite the improvements of the last generation of models, we cannot but conclude that distributional semantics still lacks a theoretically and empirically satisfactory account of the processes to construct the meaning of complex expressions. Berent and Marcus (2019) depict a strong contrast between symbolic models that explain natural language productivity in terms of rules with open variables operating on structured representations, and models – like neural ones and DSMs – that use distributed, unstructured representations. The problem is that neither paradigm alone seems to be able to provide an adequate explanation of meaning construction. Formal models represent sentences with logical forms that are suitable to capture their inferential properties, but do not capture the graded aspects of meaning or its context-sensitiveness. Continuous vectors are instead particularly apt to deal with similarity-driven generalizations, meaning shifts in contexts, and other phenomena that are challenging for classical compositionality, but they strive to capture several core aspects of sentence meaning and lack sufficient generalization strength. These con-

HYBRID DSMs
siderations have prompted the development of **hybrid DSMs** that integrate the complementary features of symbolic and distributional representations (Boleda and Herbelot, 2016). Thus, hybrid models can exploit their mutual elements of strength, in particular the flexibility of the latter and the structured nature of the former. This line of research is pursued by Beltagy et al. (2016), McNally and Boleda (2016), McNally (2017), and Chersoni et al. (2019). They hypothesize a "division of labor" between formal and distributional semantics and depart from the assumption shared by all the models reviewed in this chapter that the distributional representation of a sentence is a vector, exactly like lexical items. They instead represent sentences with logical forms enriched with distribu-

SDM
tional vectors of their lexemes. For instance, in the **Structured Distributional Model** (SDM) by Chersoni et al. (2019), the semantic representation of a sentence is a formal structure inspired by Discourse Representation Theory (Kamp and Reyle, 1993) and containing vectors that replace the logical constants associated with lexical items. This structure is dynamically and incrementally built by integrating knowledge about events and their typical participants, as they are activated by lexical items. Other models that combine formal and distributional semantics are proposed by Emerson and Copestake (2017) and Herbelot and Copestake (2021). The results of this line of research are promising, and Chersoni et al. (2019) and Pedinotti et al. (2021b) obtain performances that are competitive with neural language models. However, they are still applied to a limited number of phenomena, and much research is needed to improve their scalability and performance in downstream tasks.

Berent and Marcus (2019) argue that the ability to operate on structured representations with open variables is an essential precondition to explain natural language productivity. It is indeed possible that further improvements might come from developing more explicit mechanisms in distributional semantics to represent abstract schemas with open slots that are filled to produce new instances of linguistic expressions. On the other hand, the continuous nature of distributional representations is an equally crucial aspect to capture the flexibility and quasi-regularity of natural language, whose constructions have slots with a prototype rather than categorical structure, and similarity and analogy are key mechanisms driving their composition with new arguments.

9.9 Summary

The representation of phrases and sentences has become an intense research area that has definitely pushed the boundary of distributional semantics beyond its original territory, the lexicon. **Compositional distributional semantics** typically represents complex linguistic expressions with vectors that are constructed with different types of methods. A first group of models combine the vectors or higher-order linear-algebraic objects associated with the component lexemes and are consistent with the **Fregean Principle of Compositionality**, traditionally adopted by formal semantics to explain natural language productivity. A second approach consists in learning **sentence embeddings** with deep neural networks that instead radically depart from such a principle. Distributional semantics is also actively engaged in modeling **selectional preferences** and coercion phenomena in predicate-argument composition.

An important outcome of this research has been the development of context-sensitive representations that can account for the meaning changes that words undergo when they are combined with other expressions. This has sparked a new generation of **contextual DSMs**, which are a significant novelty in the distributional semantic landscape, especially for their increased performances in AI and NLP downstream applications.

Still, how distributional representations can be effectively projected from the lexical to the sentence or even discourse level remains largely an open issue, because even the most advanced models fall short of capturing important meaning dimensions. The future challenges for compositional distributional semantics concern both the methods to construct the representation of complex expressions, and their evaluation. In fact, better methodologies and more reliable benchmarks are needed to understand the aspects of compositional meaning encoded by distributional representations.

9.10 Further Reading

- The Principle of Compositionality: Heim and Kratzer (1998); Marcus (2001); Werning et al. (2012); Baggio (2018); Martin and Baggio (2019)
- Compositional DSMs: Mitchell and Lapata (2010); Erk (2012); Baroni (2013); Baroni et al. (2014b); Liang and Potts (2015); Potts (2019)
- Neural networks and sentence embeddings: Goldberg (2017); Pavlick (2022)
- Neural language models: Han et al. (2021)
- Contextual DSMs: Liu et al. (2020); Erk and Chronis (2022); Lenci et al. (2022)
- Analysis of contextual DSMs and neural language models: Belinkov and Glass (2019); Rogers et al. (2020); Belinkov (2022)
- Selectional preferences and coercion: Light and Greiff (2002); Erk et al. (2010); Lauwers and Willems (2011); Pustejovsky and Batiukova (2019)

10

Conclusions and Outlook

This book has attempted to give a comprehensive and detailed account of both theoretical and practical aspects of distributional semantics. We have covered its underlying theoretical assumptions, as well as the practical implementations, developments, applications, and considerations of DSMs. We have also linked the traditional models to the more recent contextual DSMs based on deep neural language models. It is now time to conclude this journey by highlighting the changes that distributional semantics has undergone throughout its brief and yet intense life, and by pointing out its future challenges.

10.1 The Golden Age of Distributional Semantics

Looking at the body of work covered in this book, we can distinguish a clear timeline with a number of well-delineated eras (cf. Chapter 3, Figure 3.3):

1950s: the basic theoretical foundation for distributional semantics is formulated, in particular in the works of Harris, Firth, and Wittgenstein;
1990s: the earliest count DSMs: matrix models such as HAL, LSA, and random encoding models like RI;
2010s: the inception of predict DSMs, in the form of word embeddings learned with neural networks;
2020s: the era of contextual DSMs begins.

We can trace the popularity of distributional semantic models in the field of computational linguistics and NLP by counting the occurrence of the keyword *distributional* in titles of publications in this field. This crude statistic will obviously not give a very precise measure, but if there is an observable trend, it should be able to detect it. Fortunately, most of the academic

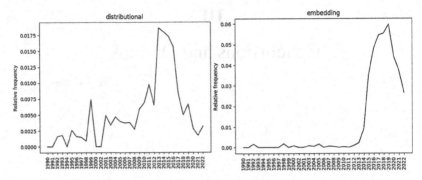

Figure 10.1 Relative frequencies of the terms *distributional* and *embedding* in titles of publications in the ACL Anthology 1990–2022

ACL
ANTHOLOGY

publications in computational linguistics are collected in the **ACL Anthology**, which lists all the major conferences and workshops in the field.[1] Figure 10.1 shows the relative frequency of the terms *distributional* (left) and *embedding* (right) in titles of publications in the ACL Anthology 1990–2022. The use of the term *distributional* peaked around 2013, with a steady, and rapid, decline in usage after that. This is also the year when the word2vec library was published (Mikolov et al. 2013a, 2013b), and soon after became one of the most widespread libraries in NLP, popularizing the term *embedding* to refer to distributional vectors. In fact, we can see a swift increase in usage of this term after 2013, with a peak around 2019, and an almost equally swift decline after that.

Interestingly, the decline in usage of the term *embedding* coincides with an increase in the usage of the term *language model* (see Figure 10.2, left), which has exploded during the last couple of years, no doubt due to the success and popularity of contextual DSMs. These plots show three consecutive trends, progressing from using the term *distributional* over the term *embedding* to the currently dominating term *language model*. Note also that the relative frequency increases with each of these trends. While the peak for *distributional* in 2013 contained only approximately 2% of all papers, almost 8% of all paper titles in 2022 contain the term *language model*.

We make two observations from this simple keyword analysis. Firstly, distributional approaches take different shapes at different times: from count models to contextual DSMs. It is not far-fetched to assume that there will be other distributional approaches in the future that will take over after language models eventually decline in popularity. But even if the particular terminology

---

[1] https://aclanthology.org.

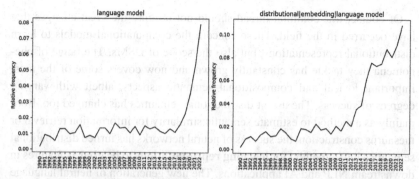

Figure 10.2 Relative frequencies of the terms *language model* and the union of the terms *distributional, embedding,* and *language model* in titles of publications in the ACL Anthology 1990–2022

and computational machinery changes over time, the distributional foundation remains more or less constant throughout this development. The right part of Figure 10.2 shows the relative frequency of use of any of the terms *distributional, embedding,* and *language model* in titles of publications in the ACL Anthology between 1990 and 2022. We observe an increasing usage of terms related to distributional methods, in particular during the last couple of years. One conclusion we might draw from this picture is that the interest in distributional methods is not decreasing – quite the opposite, actually – despite the fact that the term *distributional* is no longer in fashion.

The era of contextual DSMs has just begun and it is under constant and rapid development at the time of writing this book. Therefore, it has been practically impossible to include all of the recent developments in this field. Section 9.6.3 covers both encoders such as BERT and decoders such as GPT, but it does not mention Transformer-based encoder-decoders such as **T5** (Raffel et al., 2020) and **BART** (Lewis et al., 2020), and it does not cover the most recent development with *very large* language models such as **GPT-3** (Brown et al., 2020), GPT-3 **Megatron-Turing NLG** (Smith et al., 2022), or **PaLM** (Chowdhery et al., 2022). We are aware that this may be seen as a significant omission – especially if we continue to see further breakthroughs from contextualized models in the near future – but, from our perspective, these models are all DSMs, despite their reliance on slightly different learning objectives, and despite their slightly different semantic capabilities. As a matter of fact, even the latest and more sophisticated models rest on the very same distributional foundations that grounded the first DSMs: *Lexical items are represented with vectors encoding their co-occurrences with linguistic contexts extracted from corpora, as samples of language usage.*

Of course, this common thread should not obscure the great changes that have occurred in the field. These concern the computational models to learn distributional representations, but also the scope of DSMs. The range of phenomena they tackle has constantly grown and now covers some of the most important lexical and compositional semantic aspects, albeit with varying degrees of success. The use of distributional semantics has changed too. Born mainly as a method to estimate semantic similarity for information retrieval or thesaurus construction, the success of neural networks has turned distributional semantics into a method for **learning representations** to be used as features in downstream NLP and AI applications. The new generation of neural language models has favored a further change: Instead of feeding the pretrained vectors into a different module, the same DSM is **fine-tuned** to tackle specific tasks.

REPRESENTATION
LEARNING

FINE-TUNING

One aspect of the more recent developments that is worth mentioning as an outlook to the future is the **zero-shot learning** capacity of very large generative language models such as GPT-3. This consists in being able to solve tasks that the model has not been trained for, by taking advantage of the generative ability of the model, and simply giving it a carefully constructed instruction (called **prompt**) as input sequence. As an example, if we want to do sentiment analysis, we can feed the text as input to the model together with the instruction "the sentiment of this text is:" We would then expect the model to generate a suitable sentiment for the input text. Similarly, if we want to do machine translation from Swedish to Italian, we would simply tell the model "translate from Swedish to Italian:" and input the text we want the model to translate. The task of designing suitable instructions for such models is called **prompt engineering**, and is a matter of trial and error. Another interesting possibility is **p-tuning** (Liu et al., 2021), which replaces the textual instructions with a set of input embeddings that can be trained by an external, and much smaller, prompt model. Such input embeddings act as a continuous prompt for the generative model, and can be trained for each specific task we want the model to solve. Thus, we are moving away from using the distributional model as primarily being a representation learning mechanism. In prompt-based usage, we are instead relying directly on the generative capacity of the decoder model, which marks a shift of focus away from the quality of the *distributional representations* learned by the DSM to the quality of its *predictions*.

ZERO-SHOT
LEARNING

PROMPT
ENGINEERING

P-TUNING

10.2 Are We Climbing the Right Hill?

Distributional semantics has become the mainstream paradigm in the computational analysis of meaning, with a growing popularity in NLP, AI, cognitive science, and linguistics. This recent success, in particular of contextual DSMs, has not only generated cheer and celebration. There are also critical voices that question the domination of language models in the field at the moment (the right part of Figure 10.2 indicates that some 10% of all current papers contain a term in the title that refers to a distributional method). The gist of this critique concerns the question whether the distributional paradigm, of which contextual DSMs are only the last development, is sufficient for building computational models of meaning, or if we need something *more* or something *else* to arrive at meaning. Bender and Koller (2020) aptly formulate this doubt in the question *are we climbing the right hill?*

Their own answer to this question is a resounding *no, we are not climbing the right hill.* The main argument for this position in Bender and Koller (2020) is that it is not possible to learn meaning by only observing linguistic co-occurrences, since meaning is something external to language. It is the *intent* of the (human) language user, which is encoded in, and decoded from, the linguistic expression. The reasoning is then that a purely distributional method that only observes the interplay of linguistic expressions will never be able to connect these expressions to the intents, since it has no access to stimuli outside of the linguist signal itself. What emerges is a classic dualistic view on meaning that evokes the **symbol grounding problem** (Harnad, 1990) as a central concern for modeling meaning (cf. Section 8.7). A similar view is expressed by Lake and Murphy (2021), who regard even the latest and most sophisticated DSMs as quite far from being psychologically plausible models of meaning, because they are not connected with perception, action, and reasoning.

SYMBOL GROUNDING PROBLEM

Merrill et al. (2021) expand on one specific argument in Bender and Koller (2020), and provide what they claim is a formal proof that it is not possible to learn meaning from a purely distributional approach. The specific argument they focus on is the task of learning to execute a program by only reading examples of code in that programming language, something that is assumed to be impossible by both Bender and Koller (2020) and Merrill et al. (2021). A possible counterargument considered by the latter work is the existence of assertions in the code that represent examples of input and output, and it is argued that such assertions occur also in natural language, providing a connection to the outside world (i.e., grounding). Merrill et al. (2021) then proceed to demonstrate formally that the presence of such assertions is not sufficient to fully emulate a denotational semantic system.

One takeaway from the discussion in Bender and Koller (2020) and Merrill et al. (2021) is that if we posit meaning to be something outside of language, then it does seem problematic for a semantic model to only look inside of language. Sahlgren and Carlsson (2021) reply to these critiques against language models by claiming that they rest on an argumentation error they call **singleton fallacy**, which consists in assuming that a concept refers to a single well-defined phenomenon, when in reality it is used for many different and vaguely interrelated phenomena. The concepts under discussion in this case are "meaning" and "understanding," and Sahlgren and Carlsson (2021) argue that the dualistic and mentalistic position adopted by Bender and Koller (2020) inevitably brings us back to the original motivation for developing distributional methods in computational linguistics that we discuss in Section 1.1.1: If we posit meaning as something unobtainable from the bare linguistic signal then all we can do (*from a linguistic perspective*) is to describe the distributional correlates of meaning. A similar argument against the critiques in Bender and Koller (2020) is formulated by Piantadosi and Hill (2022).

Sahlgren and Carlsson (2021) also point out that distributional approaches are not necessarily constrained to a textual input signal. Multimodal DSMs (cf. Sections 8.7.1 and 9.6.3) build representations by combining information from different types of signals, like texts and images. Such combinations have also been the locus of recent developments in generative multimodal models that can produce text from images, such as **CLIP** (Radford et al., 2021), and models that can produce images from text, like **DALL·E** and its successor **DALL·E 2** (Ramesh et al., 2021). Distributional models that are built by multimodal learning are grounded at least in the sense of combining different modalities, and as such, they do reach "outside of language."

Even if the ontological argument for the insufficiency of distributional semantics remains controversial, there is also another side to the critique against distributional approaches that concerns ethical and economic factors. Bender et al. (2021) provide a summary of potential issues and impacts of building and using very large language models, such as the environmental impact and economic cost of training deep neural networks, and the possible misuse of generative models. Though their primary targets are large language models such as GPT-3, Megatron-Turing NLG, and PaLM, some of their points apply more broadly to distributional models in general. In particular, problems related to training data apply to all types of DSMs. Bender et al. (2021) point to issues such as insufficient diversity and demographic representativity, and the occurrence of various types of biases (cf. Section 8.5.2). As training corpora grow larger, it becomes more difficult to fully document their composition. This may be problematic, not only because it risks obfuscating issues with representativeness and biases, but also because it may have legal repercussions, in particular in the European Union where there are strong data protection laws such as the General Data Protection Regulation

SINGLETON
FALLACY

CLIP

DALL·E

(**GDPR**).[2] Somewhat simplified, this regulation protects against unsolicited use of personally identifiable information, which means that data needs to be properly documented and any use of such information needs to be motivated and deliberate. There is a growing awareness of these potential problems and challenges, and we will likely see more focus on data issues and data documentation in the near future.

GDPR

A last point raised by Bender et al. (2021) is the propensity of human interlocutors to assign **intentionality** to artificial systems they interact with. In the case of generative language models like GPT-3, Bender et al. (2021) warn that coherent textual behavior on the model's part may lead human interlocutors to assign human qualities to the model. Such assignments are erroneous, because language models are only "stochastic parrots." As a stroke of good (or bad, depending on your perspective) luck, what Bender et al. (2021) warn against actually happened in a very public and sensational way, not more than a year after their paper was published. In July of 2022, press reported that Google fired one of their engineers for having claimed in an interview with the *Washington Post* a couple of weeks earlier that the **LaMDA** language model (Thoppilan et al., 2022) had become sentient (Tiku, 2022). What happened was that an engineer tasked with quality control of the LaMDA chatbot had conducted a large number of conversations with the system (primarily in order to investigate the model's propensity for discriminatory language and hate speech), during which he increasingly felt that the model's replies indicated sentience. He then proceeded to document his findings and present them to his superiors at Google, who apparently dismissed his claims, after which the engineer decided to go public with his findings instead.

INTENTIONALITY

LAMDA

The LaMDA incident demonstrates that the quality of generative language models have reached a level where they can undeniably pass the **Turing test** (Elkins and Chun, 2020). Even if the LaMDA incident is not an exact instantiation of the original test based on the "imitation game,"[3] it does describe an equally challenging task: convincing a human expert interlocutor that the system is sentient. The significance of the Turing test has been debated ever since the early days of **ELIZA** (Weizenbaum, 1966), in particular considering the human propensity for anthropomorphization (i.e., the tendency to attribute human traits to non-human entities), but the fact remains that current language models repeatedly reach – and surpass – human-level performance on test sets that are designed to measure language understanding.

TURING TEST

ELIZA

---

[2] https://gdpr.eu/.
[3] In the original Turing test, the task is described as convincing the human counterpart that the system is human. Being sentient is not necessarily the same thing as being human.

Works like Bender and Koller (2020) and Bender et al. (2021) have the merit of warning us against the enthusiastic and uncritical celebration of alleged "intelligent" technologies. As Floridi and Chiriatti (2020) argue, "the real point about AI is that we are increasingly decoupling the ability to solve a problem effectively – as regards the final goal – from any need to be intelligent to do so" (p. 683). In fact, the good performance of many NLP models often depends on just exploiting shallow statistics (McCoy et al., 2019a; Niven and Kao, 2019), rather than deriving from real language understanding. Solid scientific advancement will only be achieved through fine-grained tests on carefully designed datasets that can give us reliable evidence of models' ability to account for specific semantic aspects. As we have seen in this book, evaluation has always played a central role in distributional semantics, which is constantly engaged in developing improved resources and methods to ana-
BIG-BENCH   lyse DSMs. One recent example is **BIG-bench** (Beyond the Imitation Game benchmark; Srivastava et al., 2022), resulting from a large collective effort to assemble 204 tasks that cover a wide range of linguistic phenomena.

However, the radical and generalized downsizing of the potentialities of distributional approaches is equally dangerous (Bowman, 2022) and does not benefit truly scientific progress in this area. Interestingly, the argument by Bender and Koller (2020) that it is not possible to learn meaning by only observing linguistic co-occurrences, which is also explicitly adopted by Bisk et al. (2020), is reminiscent of the objection raised by embodied cognition against the first generation of DSMs in the early 2000s (cf. Section 8.8.1). In those years, the cognitive plausibility of models like HAL and LSA was dismissed because of the ungrounded nature of their representations, under the assumption that concepts are inherently embodied in sensory-motor experience. Nowadays, there is almost unanimous consensus in cognitive science about the role of distributional information as a source of human knowledge, sometimes the only one that is available to learn a concept. On the other hand, no serious scholar would claim that meaning can be reduced totally to distributional co-occurrences unless the term "meaning" is again used to refer to a specific aspect, rather than to the full range of its phenomenology, which again leads us back to the singleton fallacy described by Sahlgren and Carlsson (2021).

10.3 Climbing Meaning with Distributional Semantics

PLATO'S   At the outset of distributional semantics, Landauer and Dumais (1997) entitled
PROBLEM   their groundbreaking paper *A solution to Plato's problem*. **Plato's problem**

has been variously formulated in the history of philosophy and linguistics, and can be expressed in the following terms:

> People have much more knowledge than appears to be present in the information to which they have been exposed.

Though Plato's problem has often been taken as an argument for the existence of an innate language acquisition device (Chomsky, 1986), Landauer and Dumais (1997) claim the solution can (at least partly) come from LSA, as a general model of inducing and abstracting knowledge from texts. In fact, distributional learning plays a key role in language acquisition (cf. Section 8.8.1). The ability to infer knowledge from observing linguistic co-occurrences is a powerful tool that allows children and adults to accelerate the learning of new concepts and to project sensory-motor and affective experiences.

However, when we look at the evolution of distributional semantics, we are faced with a different sort of problem. On the one hand, the amount of data DSMs extract their knowledge from has grown exponentially. This is illustrated in Figure 10.3, which reports the size (in log million tokens) of the training corpora of various DSMs. The trend has further accelerated with the last generation of contextual neural language models (e.g., the PaLM corpus contains 780 billion tokens). In fact, DSMs are trained on quantities of linguistic data that vastly exceed the linguistic input that an educated learner

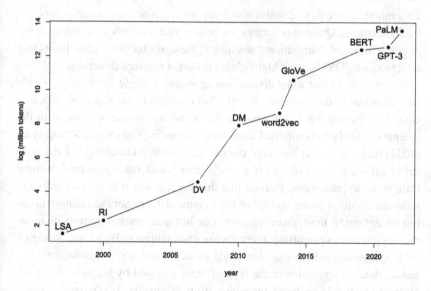

Figure 10.3 The size of training corpora in distributional semantics

is exposed to in their overall life. On the other hand, the data growth is not matched by an equally strong increase in the semantic abilities of the models. If the improvement of their performances is undeniable, it is also true that the semantic competence of even the most complex models is still severely limited in many respects. The large training corpora allow models to learn huge arrays of "factoids" (e.g., that two plus two equals four, or that Napoleon won the battle of Austerlitz in 1805). However, semantic knowledge is not merely a collection of facts, but consists of general and abstract structures. DSMs are often biased toward surface linguistic patterns rather than human-like generalizations. As we have repeatedly observed in Part III, the quality of the semantic representations of the last models is often not significantly better than the one of older DSMs, despite the increase in training data. Several semantic areas are addressed only partially or in a largely unsatisfactory way. These include crucial phenomena like inference, semantic relations, function words like discourse connectives and quantifiers, negation, argument structure, compositional construction of sentence meaning, and so on. In general, the semantic abilities of DSMs are still far from human ones, although they are exposed to a much larger amount of data. Therefore, instead of contributing to solve Plato's problem, DSMs seem to be affected by the opposite problem:

> DSMs still lack aspects of human semantic competence despite being trained on very large amounts of text data.

This might induce us to dismiss distributional semantics and its epistemological foundations. Quite the contrary, we believe that it allows us to envisage the possible future of distributional semantics. Here, we focus on three limits that affect existing DSMs, each highlighting different research directions.

A first limit is that *some dimensions of meaning might be missing or only weakly occur in the linguistic signal*. One example is the reporting bias discussed in Section 8.8.1: Information that speakers assume to share with the listeners is likely to be omitted from their linguistic productions. Zhang et al. (2022) find that neural language models have limited knowledge of the typical visual attributes of objects (e.g., their shape), and that bigger models show little or no improvement. Results like this suggest that it is necessary to pay renewed attention to the *quality* of the training data, rather than simply keeping on enlarging their sheer quantity. For instance, natural conversations or movies might be a promising alternative or complement to Web texts. Research on language acquisition can also guide us to collect more "echological" linguistic data, to approximate the type of input received by learners. After all, children do not learn word meanings from Wikipedia. Likewise, linguistic information should be complemented with multimodal data extracted from images and videos. Multimodality will certainly play an important role in the future development of distributional models, and we have likely only seen the very first steps in this direction.

A second limit is that *existing models are not yet able to fully exploit the signals in the linguistic input.* Distributional semantics has evolved toward models that are more and more data greedy. On the other hand, humans can learn semantic information even from very few occurrences of a new word, because they exploit their rich knowledge of the contexts it is observed in. In fact, human learning is always an *incremental* process. New words are learned from co-occurrences with other lexical items for which we have already acquired information. Most standard DSMs learn all the embeddings of their vocabulary *simultaneously*. Conversely, acquiring word meaning is a piecemeal process in which the learner's vocabulary is progressively expanded and the first lexical items provide the scaffolding for learning following words. Looking more closely at the patterns of lexical acquisition and at the cognitive mechanisms driving distributional learning is likely to provide important insights to develop new generations of DSMs that will focus on incrementality and data parsimony, paired with greater abilities to exploit distributional information.

A third limit is that *current models ignore the interactive and inferential nature of human communication.* In Chapter 1, we have emphasized the connection between distributional semantics and the later philosophy of Wittgenstein. When he says that "the meaning of a word is its use in the language" (Wittgenstein, 1953, §43), the term "use" presupposes the existence of language games providing the horizon of meaning. In fact, meaning grows and lives in communication games, in which a speaker produces linguistic expressions (the *observables*) with the intention of communicating a certain content, relying on the abilities of the listener to decode that content, because it knows how to play the same game. Existing DSMs still exploit only a tiny part of these communication games, that is the textual observables, without considering the rest of the game and its participants, in particular the inferential and interactive mechanisms that are responsible for semantic acquisition and processing. These current limitations will be overcome by fostering the integration of DSMs with semantic and pragmatic inferences, inserting distributional semantics within more general computational models of linguistic communication.

These observations indicate that we have not reached the boundaries of distributional semantics. Several opportunities and challenges lie in front us. These pages are yet to be written, but the future of distributional semantics surely depends on its dialogue with other approaches to meaning and on a closer attention to the cognitive mechanisms underlying natural language understanding. Meaning is not just a hill, but a huge mountain range, with several different peaks. Distributional semantics might not be able to lead us onto all of them, but it will remain an essential tool for our climb.

References

Abbreviated names of major conferences and journals in the references:

CL Computational Linguistics
JAIR Journal of Artificial Intelligence Research
LRE Language Resources and Evaluation
TACL Transactions of the Association for Computational Linguistics
TopiCS Topics in Cognitive Science
Proc. AAAI Proceedings of AAAI Conference on Artificial Intelligence
Proc. ACL Proceedings of the Annual Meeting of the Association for Computational
    Linguistics
Proc. COGSCI Proceedings of the Annual Meeting of the Cognitive Science Society
Proc. COLING Proceedings of the International Conference on Computational Lin-
    guistics
Proc. CoNLL Proceedings of the Conference on Computational Natural Language
    Learning
Proc. EACL Proceedings of the Conference of the European Chapter of the Associa-
    tion for Computational Linguistics
Proc. EMNLP Proceedings of the Conference on Empirical Methods in Natural
    Language Processing
Proc. ICLR Proceedings of the International Conference on Learning Representations
Proc. ICML Proceedings of the International Conference on Machine Learning
Proc. IJCAI Proceedings of the International Joint Conference on Artificial Intelli-
    gence
Proc. IWCS Proceedings of the International Workshop on Computational Semantics
Proc. LREC Proceedings of the Language Resources and Evaluation Conference
Proc. NAACL-HLT Proceedings of the Annual Conference of the North American
    Chapter of the Association for Computational Linguistics: Human Language
    Technologies
Proc. NIPS Proceedings of the Conference on Neural Information Processing Systems
Proc. *SEM Proceedings of the Joint Conference on Lexical and Computational
    Semantics
Proc. SemEval Proceedings of the International Workshop on Semantic Evaluation

Abdou, Mostafa, Kulmizev, Artur, Hill, Felix, Low, Daniel M., and Søgaard, Anders.
    2019. Higher-order comparisons of sentence encoder representations. Pages 5838–
    5845 of: *Proc. EMNLP*.

Abdou, Mostafa, Kulmizev, Artur, Hershcovich, Daniel et al. 2021. Can language models encode perceptual structure without grounding? A case study in color. Pages 109–132 of: *Proc. CoNLL*.

Abnar, Samira, Ahmed, Rasyan, Mijnheer, Max, and Zuidema, Willem. 2018. Experiential, distributional and dependency-based word embeddings have complementary roles in decoding brain activity. Pages 57–66 of: *8th Workshop on Cognitive Modeling and Computational Linguistics*.

Abnar, Samira, Beinborn, Lisa, Choenni, Rochelle, and Zuidema, Willem. 2019. Blackbox meets blackbox: Representational similarity and stability analysis of neural language models and brains. Pages 191–203 of: *2nd BlackboxNLP Workshop on Analyzing and Interpreting Neural Networks for NLP*.

Achlioptas, Dimitris. 2003. Database-friendly random projections: Johnson-Lindenstrauss with binary coins. *Journal of Computer and Systems Sciences*, **66**(4), 671–687.

Acquaviva, Paolo, Lenci, Alessandro, Paradis, Carita, and Raffaelli, Ida. 2020. Models of lexical meaning. Pages 353–404 of: Pirrelli, Vito, Plag, Ingo, and Dressler, Wolfgang U. (eds.), *Word Knowledge and Word Usage*. Berlin: Mouton de Gruyter.

Adi, Yossi, Kermany, Einat, Belinkov, Yonatan, Lavi, Ofer, and Goldberg, Yoav. 2017. Fine-grained analysis of sentence embeddings using auxiliary prediction tasks. In: *Proc. ICLR*.

Aggarwal, Charu C., and Reddy, Chandan K. (eds.). 2013. *Data Clustering: Algorithms and Applications*. Boca Raton: CRC Press.

Agirre, Eneko, and Edmonds, Philip. 2007. *Word Sense Disambiguation: Algorithms and Applications*. Berlin: Springer.

Agirre, Eneko, Alfonseca, Enrique, Hall, Keith et al. 2009. A study on similarity and relatedness using distributional and WordNet-based approaches. Pages 19–27 of: *Proc. NAACL-HLT*.

Agrawal, Ameeta, An, Aijun, and Papagelis, Manos. 2018. Learning emotion-enriched word representations. Pages 950–961 of: *Proc. COLING*.

Aharon, Michal, Elad, Michael, and Bruckstein, Alfred. 2006. K-SVD: An algorithm for designing overcomplete dictionaries for sparse representation. *IEEE Transactions on Signal Processing*, **54**(11), 4311–4322.

Almuhareb, Abdulrahman, and Poesio, Massimo. 2004. Attribute-based and value-based clustering: An evaluation. Pages 158–165 of: *Proc. EMNLP*.

Almuhareb, Abdulrahman, and Poesio, Massimo. 2005. Concept learning and categorization from the Web. Pages 103–108 of: *Proc. COGSCI*.

Ammar, Waleed, Mulcaire, George, Tsvetkov, Yulia et al. 2016. Massively multilingual word embeddings. *arXiv*, 1602.01925.

Anderson, Andrew J., Bruni, Elia, Lopopolo, Alessandro, Poesio, Massimo, and Baroni, Marco. 2015. Reading visually embodied meaning from the brain: Visually grounded computational models decode visual-object mental imagery induced by written text.*NeuroImage*, **120**, 309–322.

Anderson, Andrew J., Binder, Jeffrey R., Fernandino, Leonardo et al. 2016. Predicting neural activity patterns associated with sentences using a neurobiologically motivated model of semantic representation. *Cerebral Cortex*, **27**(9), 4379–4395.

Anderson, Andrew J., Kiela, Douwe, Clark, Stephen, and Poesio, Massimo. 2017. Visually grounded and textual semantic models differentially decode brain activity associated with concrete and abstract nouns. *TACL*, **5**, 17–30.

Andrews, Mark, and Vigliocco, Gabriella. 2010. The Hidden Markov Topic Model: A probabilistic model of semantic representation. *TopiCS*, **2**(1), 101–113.

Andrews, Mark, Vigliocco, Gabriella, and Vinson, David P. 2009. Integrating experiential and distributional data to learn semantic representations. *Psychological Review*, **116**(3), 463–498.

Andrews, Mark, Frank, Stefan L., and Vigliocco, Gabriella. 2014. Reconciling embodied and distributional accounts of meaning in language. *TopiCS*, **6**(3), 359–370.

Antoniak, Maria, and Mimno, David. 2018. Evaluating the stability of embedding-based word similarities. *TACL*, **6**, 107–119.

Apidianaki, Marianna, and Garí Soler, Aina. 2021. ALL dolphins are intelligent and SOME are friendly: Probing BERT for nouns' semantic properties and their prototypicality. Pages 79–94 of: *4th BlackboxNLP Workshop on Analyzing and Interpreting Neural Networks for NLP*.

Apresjan, Jurij D. 1966. Analyse distributionnelle des significations et champs sémantiques structurés. *Langages*, **1**(1), 44–74.

Armendariz, Carlos S., Purver, Matthew, Ulcar, Matej et al. 2020. CoSimLex: A resource for evaluating graded word similarity in context. Pages 5878–5886 of: *Proc. LREC*.

Arora, Kushal, Chakraborty, Aishik, and Cheung, Jackie Chi Kit. 2020. Learning lexical subspaces in a distributional vector space. *TACL*, **8**, 311–329.

Arora, Sanjeev, Li, Yuanzhi, Liang, Yingyu, Ma, Tengyu, and Risteski, Andrej. 2016. A latent variable model approach to PMI-based word embeddings. *TACL*, **4**, 385–399.

Arora, Sanjeev, Liang, Yingyu, and Ma, Tengyu. 2017. A simple but tough-to-beat baseline for sentence embeddings. In: *Proc. ICLR*.

Arora, Sanjeev, Li, Yuanzhi, Liang, Yingyu, Ma, Tengyu, and Risteski, Andrej. 2018. Linear algebraic structure of word senses, with applications to polysemy. *TACL*, **6**(1), 483–495.

Artetxe, Mikel, Labaka, Gorka, and Agirre, Eneko. 2016. Learning principled bilingual mappings of word embeddings while preserving monolingual invariance. Pages 2289–2294 of: *Proc. EMNLP*.

Artetxe, Mikel, Labaka, Gorka, and Agirre, Eneko. 2017. Learning bilingual word embeddings with (almost) no bilingual data. Pages 451–462 of: *Proc. ACL*.

Artetxe, Mikel, Labaka, Gorka, and Agirre, Eneko. 2018. Generalizing and improving bilingual word embedding mappings with a multi-step framework of linear transformations. Pages 5012–5019 of: *Proc. AAAI*.

Asher, Nicholas. 2011. *Lexical Meaning in Context*. Cambridge: Cambridge University Press.

Asher, Nicholas. 2015. Types, meanings and coercions in lexical semantics. *Lingua*, **157**, 66–82.

Asher, Nicholas, Van de Cruys, Tim, Bride, Antoine, and Abrusán, Márta. 2016. Integrating type theory and distributional semantics: A case study on adjective–noun compositions. *CL*, **42**(4), 703–725.

Asr, Fatemeh Torabi, Willits, Jon A., and Jones, Michael N. 2016. Comparing predictive and co-occurrence based models of lexical semantics trained on child-directed speech. Pages 1092–1097 of: *Proc. COGSCI*.

Assent, Ira. 2012. Clustering high dimensional data. *WIRESs Data Mining and Knowledge Discovery*, **2**(4), 340–350.

Athanasiou, Nikos, Iosif, Elias, and Potamianos, Alexandros. 2018. Neural activation semantic models: Computational lexical semantic models of localized neural activations. Pages 2867–2878 of: *Proc. COLING*.

Baayen, Harald. 2001. *Word Frequency Distributions*. Dordrecht: Kluwer.

Baccianella, Stefano, Esuli, Andrea, and Sebastiani, Fabrizio. 2010. SentiWordNet 3.0: An enhanced lexical resource for sentiment analysis and opinion mining. Pages 2200–2204 of: *Proc. LREC*.

Baggio, Giosuè. 2018. *Meaning in the Brain*. Cambridge, MA: The MIT Press.

Bahdanau, Dzmitry, Cho, Kyung Hyun, and Bengio, Yoshua. 2015. Neural machine translation by jointly learning to align and translate. In: *Proc. ICLR*.

Bakarov, Amir. 2018. A survey of word embeddings evaluation methods. *arXiv*, 1801.09536.

Baker, Collin F., Fillmore, Charles J., and Lowe, John B. 1998. The Berkeley FrameNet project. Pages 86–90 of: *Proc. COLING-ACL*.

Bansal, Mohit, Gimpel, Kevin, and Livescu, Karen. 2014. Tailoring continuous word representations for dependency parsing. Pages 809–815 of: *Proc. ACL*.

Baroni, Marco. 2008. Distributions in text. Pages 803–821 of: Lüdeling, Anke, and Kytö, Merja (eds.), *Corpus Linguistics: An International Handbook*. Berlin: Mouton de Gruyter.

Baroni, Marco. 2013. Composition in distributional semantics. *Linguistics and Language Compass*, **7**(10), 511–522.

Baroni, Marco. 2016. Grounding distributional semantics in the visual world. *Linguistics and Language Compass*, **10**(1), 3–13.

Baroni, Marco. 2019. Linguistic generalization and compositionality in modern artificial neural networks. *Philosophical Transactions of the Royal Society B*, **375**, 20190307.

Baroni, Marco, and Lenci, Alessandro. 2008. Concepts and properties in word spaces. *Italian Journal of Linguistics*, **20**(1), 53–86.

Baroni, Marco, and Lenci, Alessandro. 2009. One distributional memory, many semantic spaces. Pages 1–8 of: *GEMS 2009 Workshop on GEometrical Models of Natural Language Semantics*.

Baroni, Marco, and Lenci, Alessandro. 2010. Distributional Memory: A general framework for corpus-based semantics. *CL*, **36**(4), 673–721.

Baroni, Marco, and Lenci, Alessandro. 2011. How we BLESSed distributional semantic evaluation. Pages 1–10 of: *GEMS 2011 Workshop on GEometrical Models of Natural Language Semantics*.

Baroni, Marco, and Zamparelli, Roberto. 2010. Nouns are vectors, adjectives are matrices: Representing adjective-noun constructions in semantic space. Pages 1183–1193 of: *Proc. EMNLP*.

Baroni, Marco, Evert, Stefan, and Lenci, Alessandro (eds.). 2008. *Bridging the Gap between Semantic Theory and Computational Simulations: Proceedings of the ESSLLI Workshop on Distributional Lexical Semantics*. Hamburg: FOLLI.

Baroni, Marco, Bernardini, Sara, Ferraresi, Adriano, and Zanchetta, Eros. 2009. The WaCky Wide Web: A collection of very large linguistically processed web-crawled corpora. *LRE*, **43**, 209–226.

Baroni, Marco, Barbu, Eduard, Murphy, Brian, and Poesio, Massimo. 2010. Strudel: A distributional semantic model based on properties and types. *Cognitive Science*, **34**(2), 222–254.

Baroni, Marco, Bernardi, Raffaella, Do, Ngoc-Quynh, and Chieh Shan, Chung. 2012. Entailment above the word level in distributional semantics. Pages 23–32 of: *Proc. EACL*.

Baroni, Marco, Dinu, Georgiana, and Kruszewski, Germán. 2014a. Don't count, predict! A systematic comparison of context-counting vs. context-predicting semantic vectors. Pages 238–247 of: *Proc. ACL*.

Baroni, Marco, Bernardi, Raffaella, and Zamparelli, Roberto. 2014b. Frege in space: A program of compositional distributional semantics. *Linguistic Issues in Language Technology*, **9**(6), 5–110.

Barsalou, Lawrence W. 1999. Perceptual symbol systems. *Behavioral and Brain Sciences*, **22**, 577–660.

Barsalou, Lawrence W. 2020. Challenges and opportunities for grounding cognition. *Journal of Cognition*, **3**(1), 1–24.

Barsalou, Lawrence W., and Wiemer-Hastings, Katja. 2005. Situating abstract concepts. Pages 224–245 of: Pecher, Diane, and Zwaan, Rolf A. (eds.), *Grounding Cognition: The Role of Perception and Action in Memory, Language, and Thinking*. Cambridge: Cambridge University Press.

Barsalou, Lawrence W., Santos, Ava, Simmons, W. Kyle, and Wilson, Christine D. 2008. Language and simulation in conceptual processing. Pages 245–283 of: de Vega, Manuel, Glenberg, Arthur, and Graesser, Arthur (eds.), *Symbols, Embodiment, and Meaning*. Oxford: Oxford University Press.

Bartunov, Sergey, Kondrashkin, Dmitry, Osokin, Anton, and Vetrov, Dmitry P. 2016. Breaking sticks and ambiguities with adaptive Skip-Gram. Pages 130–138 of: *19th International Conference on Artificial Intelligence and Statistics*.

Basili, Roberto, Cao, Diego De, Marocco, Paolo, and Pennacchiotti, Marco. 2007. Learning selectional preferences for entailment or paraphrasing rules. Pages 452–457 of: *Recent Advances in NLP*.

Batchkarov, Miroslav, Kober, Thomas, Reffin, Jeremy, Weeds, Julie, and Weir, David. 2016. A critique of word similarity as a method for evaluating distributional semantic models. Pages 7–12 of: *1st Workshop on Evaluating Vector Space Representations for NLP*.

Battig, William F., and Montague, William E. 1969. Category norms for verbal items in 56 categories: A replication and extension of the Connecticut norms. *Journal of Experimental Psychology*, **80**, 1–46.

Beckner, Clay, Blythe, Richard, Bybee, Joan et al. 2009. Language is a complex adaptive system: Position paper. *Language Learning*, **59**(S1), 1–26.

Bedny, Marina, Koster-Hale, Jorie, Elli, Giulia V., Yazzolino, Lindsay, and Saxe, Rebecca. 2019. There's more to "sparkle" than meets the eye: Knowledge of vision and light verbs among congenitally blind and sighted individuals. *Cognition*, **189**, 105–115.

Beekhuizen, Barend, Armstrong, Blair C., and Stevenson, Suzanne. 2021. Probing lexical ambiguity: Word vectors encode number and relatedness of senses. *Cognitive Science*, **45**(5), e12943.

Beinborn, Lisa, Abnar, Samira, and Choenni, Rochelle. 2019. Robust evaluation of language-brain encoding experiments. *arXiv*, 1904.02547.

Belinkov, Yonatan. 2022. Probing classifiers: Promises, shortcomings, and advances. *CL*, **48**(1), 1–13.

Belinkov, Yonatan, and Glass, James. 2019. Analysis methods in neural language processing: A survey. *TACL*, **7**, 49–72.

Beltagy, Islam, Roller, Stephen, Cheng, Pengxiang, Erk, Katrin, and Mooney, Raymond J. 2016. Representing meaning with a combination of logical and distributional models. *CL*, **42**(4), 763–808.

Bender, Emily M., and Koller, Alexander. 2020. Climbing towards NLU: On meaning, form, and understanding in the age of data. Pages 5185–5198 of: *Proc. ACL*.

Bender, Emily M., Gebru, Timnit, McMillan-Major, Angelina, and Shmitchell, Shmargaret. 2021. On the dangers of stochastic parrots: Can language models be too big? Pages 610—623 of: *ACM Conference on Fairness, Accountability, and Transparency*.

Bengio, Yoshua. 2009. Learning deep architectures for AI. *Foundations and Trends in Machine Learning*, **2**(1), 1–127.

Bengio, Yoshua, Ducharme, Réjean, Vincent, Pascal, and Janvin, Christian. 2003. A neural probabilistic language model. *Journal of Machine Learning Research*, **3**, 1137–1155.

Bentivogli, Luisa, Bernardi, Raffaella, Marelli, Marco et al. 2016. SICK through the SemEval glasses: Lesson learned from the evaluation of compositional distributional semantic models on full sentences through semantic relatedness and textual entailment. *LRE*, **50**(1), 95–124.

Berent, Iris, and Marcus, Gary F. 2019. No integration without structured representations: Response to Pater. *Language*, **95**(1), e75–e86.

Bergsma, Shane, Lin, Dekang, and Goebel, Randy. 2008. Discriminative learning of selectional preference from unlabeled text. Pages 59–68 of: *Proc. EMNLP*.

Berland, Matthew, and Charniak, Eugene. 1999. Finding parts in very large corpora. Pages 57–64 of: *Proc. COLING*.

Bestgen, Yves, and Vincze, Nadja. 2012. Checking and bootstrapping lexical norms by means of word similarity indexes. *Behavior Research Methods*, **44**(4), 998–1006.

Beyer, Kevin, Goldstein, Jonathan, Ramakrishnan, Raghu, and Shaft, Uri. 1999. When is the "nearest neighbor" meaningful? Pages 217–235 of: *7th Conference on Database Theory ICDT99*.

Bicknell, Klinton, Elman, Jeffrey L., Hare, Mary, McRae, Ken, and Kutas, Marta. 2010. Effects of event knowledge in processing verbal arguments. *Journal of Memory and Language*, **63**(4), 489–505.

Biemann, Chris. 2006. Chinese Whispers: An efficient graph clustering algorithm and its application to natural language processing problems. Pages 73–80 of: *1st Workshop on Graph Based Methods for NLP*.

Biemann, Chris. 2013. Creating a system for lexical substitutions from scratch using crowdsourcing. *LRE*, **47**(1), 97–122.

Biemann, Chris. 2016. Vectors or graphs? On differences of representations for distributional semantic models. Pages 1–7 of: *5th Workshop on Cognitive Aspects of the Lexicon*.

Biemann, Chris, and Riedl, Martin. 2013. Text: Now in 2D! A framework for lexical expansion with contextual similarity. *Journal of Language Modelling*, 1(1), 55–95.

Binder, Jeffrey R. 2016. In defense of abstract conceptual representations. *Psychonomic Bulletin & Review*, **23**, 1096–1108.

Binder, Jeffrey R., Conant, Lisa L., Humphries, Colin J. et al. 2016. Toward a brain-based componential semantic representation. *Cognitive Neuropsychology*, **33**(3–4), 130–174.

Bingham, Ella, and Mannila, Heikki. 2001. Random projection in dimensionality reduction: Applications to image and text data. Pages 245–250 of: *7th International Conference on Knowledge Discovery and Data Mining*.

Bisk, Yonatan, Holtzman, Ari, Thomason, Jesse et al. 2020. Experience grounds language. Pages 8718–8735 of: *Proc. EMNLP*.

Blacoe, William, and Lapata, Mirella. 2012. A comparison of vector-based representations for semantic composition. Pages 546–556 of: *Proc. EMNLP*.

Blei, David M. 2012. Probabilistic topic models. *Communications of the ACM*, **55**(4), 77–84.

Blei, David M., and Lafferty, John D. 2006. Dynamic topic models. Pages 113–120 of: *Proc. ICML*.

Blei, David M., Ng, Andrew, and Jordan, Michael. 2003. Latent Dirichlet Allocation. *Journal of Machine Learning Research*, **3**, 993–1022.

Bloomfield, Leonard. 1933. *Language*. New York: Holt.

Bloomfield, Leonard. 1943. Meaning. *Monatschefte für Deutschen Unterricht*, **35**, 101–106. Reprinted in *A Leonard Bloomfield Anthology*, Charles F. Hockett (ed.), Bloomington, IN: Indiana University Press, 1970, 400–405.

Bojanowski, Piotr, Grave, Edouard, Joulin, Armand, and Mikolov, Tomas. 2017. Enriching word vectors with subword information. *TACL*, **5**, 135–146.

Boleda, Gemma. 2020. Distributional semantics and linguistic theory. *Annual Review of Linguistics*, **6**, 213–234.

Boleda, Gemma, and Erk, Katrin. 2015. Distributional semantic features as semantic primitives – or not. Pages 2–5 of: *Knowledge Representation and Reasoning: Integrating Symbolic and Neural Approaches: 2015 AAAI Spring Symposium*.

Boleda, Gemma, and Herbelot, Aurélie. 2016. Formal distributional semantics: Introduction to the special issue. *CL*, **42**(4), 619–635.

Boleda, Gemma, Vecchi, Eva Maria, Cornudella, Miquel, and McNally, Louise. 2012a. First-order vs. higher-order modification in distributional semantics. Pages 1223–1233 of: *Proc. EMNLP*.

Boleda, Gemma, Schulte im Walde, Sabine, and Badia, Toni. 2012b. Modeling regular polysemy: A study on the semantic classification of Catalan adjectives. *CL*, **38**(3), 575–616.

Boleda, Gemma, Padó, Sebastian, and Utt, Jason. 2012c. Regular polysemy: A distributional model. Pages 151–160 of: *Proc. *SEM*.

Boleda, Gemma, Baroni, Marco, Pham, Nghia The, and McNally, Louise. 2013. Intensionality was only alleged: On adjective-noun composition in distributional semantics. Pages 35–46 of: *Proc. IWCS*.

Bolukbasi, Tolga, Chang, Kai-Wei, Zou, James, Saligrama, Venkatesh, and Kalai, Adam. 2016. Man is to computer programmer as woman is to homemaker? Debiasing word embeddings. In: *Proc. NIPS*.

Bommasani, Rishi, Davis, Kelly, and Cardie, Claire. 2020. Interpreting pretrained contextualized representations via reductions to static embeddings. Pages 4758–4781 of: *Proc. ACL*.

Borghi, Anna Maria, and Binkofski, Ferdinand. 2014. *Words as Social Tools: An Embodied View on Abstract Concepts*. New York: Springer.

Borghi, Anna Maria, Binkofski, Ferdinand, Castelfranchi, Cristiano et al. 2017. The challenge of abstract concepts. *Psychological Bulletin*, **143**(3), 263–292.

Borovsky, Arielle, and Elman, Jeffrey L. 2006. Language input and semantic categories: A relation between cognition and early word learning. *Journal of Child Language*, **33**(4), 759–790.

Bott, Thomas, Schlechtweg, Dominik, and Schulte im Walde, Sabine. 2021. More than just frequency? Demasking unsupervised hypernymy prediction methods. Pages 186–192 of: *Findings of ACL: ACL-IJCNLP 2021*.

Bottou, Léon. 2012. Stochastic gradient descent tricks. Pages 421–436 of: Montavon, Grégoire, Orr, Geneviève B., and Müller, Klaus-Robert (eds.), *Neural Networks: Tricks of the Trade*. Berlin: Springer.

Bowman, Samuel. 2022. The dangers of underclaiming: Reasons for caution when reporting how NLP systems fail. Pages 7484–7499 of: *Proc. ACL*.

Bowman, Samuel, Goldberg, Yoav, Hill, Felix et al. (eds.). 2017. *2nd Workshop on Evaluating Vector Space Representations for NLP*. Copenhagen: ACL.

Bowman, Samuel R., Angeli, Gabor, Potts, Christopher, and Manning, Christopher D. 2015. A large annotated corpus for learning natural language inference. Pages 632–642 of: *Proc. EMNLP*.

Boyd-Graber, Jordan L., and Blei, David M. 2009. Syntactic topic models. Pages 185–192 of: *Proc. NIPS*.

Bradford, Roger B. 2008. An empirical study of required dimensionality for large-scale latent semantic indexing applications. Pages 153–162 of: *17th ACM Conference on Information and Knowledge Management*.

Bradley, Margaret M., and Lang, Peter J. 2017. Affective norms for English words (ANEW). In: *Technical Report C-3*. Gainesville, FL: UF Center for the Study of Emotion and Attention.

Bréal, Michelle. 1897. *Essai de sémantique: Science des significations*. Paris: Hachette.

Brockmann, Carsten, and Lapata, Mirella. 2003. Evaluating and combining approaches to selectional preference acquisition. Pages 27–34 of: *Proc. EACL*.

Brody, Samuel, and Lapata, Mirella. 2009. Bayesian word sense induction. Pages 103–111 of: *Proc. EACL*.

Brown, Tom B., Mann, Benjamin, Ryder, Nick et al. 2020. Language models are few-shot learners. *arXiv*, 2005.14165.

Bruni, Elia, Boleda, Gemma, Baroni, Marco, and Tran, Nam-Khanh. 2012. Distributional semantics in technicolor. Pages 136–145 of: *Proc. ACL*.

Bruni, Elia, Tran, Nam-Khanh, and Baroni, Marco. 2014. Multimodal distributional semantics. *JAIR*, **49**, 1–47.

Budanitsky, Alexander, and Hirst, Graeme. 2006. Evaluating WordNet-based measures of lexical semantic relatedness. *CL*, **32**, 13–47.

Bulat, Luana, Kiela, Douwe, and Clark, Stephen. 2016. Vision and feature norms: Improving automatic feature norm learning through cross-modal maps. Pages 579–588 of: *Proc. NAACL-HLT*.

Bulat, Luana, Clark, Stephen, and Shutova, Ekaterina. 2017. Speaking, seeing, understanding: Correlating semantic models with conceptual representation in the brain. Pages 1081–1091 of: *Proc. EMNLP*.

Buljan, Maja, Padó, Sebastian, and Šnajder, Jan. 2018. Lexical substitution for evaluating compositional distributional models. Pages 206–211 of: *Proc. NAACL-HLT*.

Bullinaria, John, and Levy, Joseph P. 2007. Extracting semantic representations from word co-occurrence statistics: A computational study. *Behavior Research Methods*, **39**, 510–526.

Bullinaria, John, and Levy, Joseph P. 2012. Extracting semantic representations from word co-occurrence statistics: Stop-lists, stemming, and SVD. *Behavior Research Methods*, **44**, 890–907.

Burgers, Christian, and Beukeboom, Camiel J. 2020. How language contributes to stereotype formation: Combined effects of label types and negation use in behavior descriptions. *Journal of Language and Social Psychology*, **39**(4), 438–456.

Burgess, Curt. 1998. From simple associations to the building blocks of language: Modeling meaning in memory with the HAL model. *Behavior Research Methods, Instruments, & Computers*, **30**, 188–198.

Burgess, Curt, and Lund, Kevin. 2000. The dynamics of meaning in memory. Pages 117–156 of: Dietrich, Erich, and Markman, Arthur B. (eds.), *Cognitive Dynamics: Conceptual Change in Humans and Machines*. New York: Psychology Press.

Burnard, Lou. 1995. *The BNC Reference Manual*. Oxford: Oxford University Computing Service.

Bybee, Joan L. 2010. *Language, Usage and Cognition*. Cambridge: Cambridge University Press.

Bybee, Joan L. 2013. Usage-based theory and exemplar representations of constructions. Pages 49–68 of: Hoffman, Thomas, and Trousdale, Graeme (eds.), *The Oxford Handbook of Construction Grammar*. Oxford: Oxford University Press.

Bybee, Joan L., and McClelland, James L. 2005. Alternatives to the combinatorial paradigm of linguistic theory based on domain general principles of human cognition. *The Linguistic Review*, **22**(2–4), 381–410.

Cacciari, Cristina. 2014. Processing multiword idiomatic strings: Many words in one? *The Mental Lexicon*, **9**(2), 267–293.

Cai, Xingyu, Huang, Jiaji, Bian, Yuchen, and Church, Kenneth. 2021. Isotropy in the contextual embedding space: Clusters and manifolds. In: *Proc. ICLR*.

Caliskan, Aylin, Bryson, Joanna J., and Narayanan, Arvind. 2017. Semantics derived automatically from language corpora necessarily contain human biases. *Science*, **356**, 183–186.

Calvo, Paco, and Symons, John. 2014. *The Architecture of Cognition: Rethinking Fodor and Pylyshyn's Systematicity Challenge*. Cambridge, MA: The MIT Press.

Calzavarini, Fabrizio. 2017. Inferential and referential lexical semantic competence: A critical review of the supporting evidence. *Journal of Neurolinguistics*, **44**, 163–189.

Camacho-Collados, José, and Pilehvar, Mohammad Taher. 2018. From word to sense embeddings: A survey on vector representations of meaning. *JAIR*, **63**, 743–788.

Camacho-Collados, José, Pilehvar, Mohammad Taher, and Navigli, Roberto. 2015. A framework for the construction of monolingual and cross-lingual word similarity datasets. Pages 1–7 of: *Proc. ACL.*

Camacho-Collados, José, Pilehvar, Mohammad Taher, Collier, Nigel, and Navigli, Roberto. 2017. SemEval-2017 Task 2: Multilingual and cross-lingual semantic word similarity. Pages 15–26 of: *Proc. SemEval.*

Cao, Lu, Huang, Dandan, and Zhang, Yue. 2021. When computational representation meets neuroscience: A survey on brain encoding and decoding. Pages 4339–4347 of: *Proc. IJCAI.*

Carlson, Andrew, Betteridge, Justin, Kisiel, Bryan et al. 2010. Toward an architecture for never-ending language learning. Pages 1306–1313 of: *Proc. AAAI.*

Carnap, Rudolf. 1952. Meaning postulates. *Philosophical Studies*, 3(5), 65–73.

Caron, John. 2001. Experiments with LSA scoring: Optimal rank and basis. Pages 157–169 of: Berry, Michael W. (ed.), *Computational Information Retrieval.* Philadelphia: SIAM.

Cer, Daniel, Yang, Yinfei, Kong, Sheng-yi et al. 2018. Universal sentence encoder. Pages 169–174 of: *Proc. EMNLP.*

Chaigneau, Sergio E., Canessa, Enrique, Lenci, Alessandro, and Devereux, Barry J. 2020. Eliciting semantic properties: Methods and applications. *Cognitive Processing*, 21, 583–586.

Chang, Kai-min Kevin, Mitchell, Tom M., and Just, Marcel Adam. 2011. Quantitative modeling of the neural representation of objects: How semantic feature norms can account for fMRI activation. *NeuroImage*, 56(2), 716–727.

Charles, Walter G., and Miller, George A. 1989. Contexts of antonymous adjectives. *Applied Psycholinguistics*, 10, 357–375.

Chatterjee, Niladri, and Mohan, Shiwali. 2008. Discovering word senses from text using random indexing. Pages 299–310 of: *International Conference on Intelligent Text Processing and Computational Linguistics.*

Chersoni, Emmanuele, Lenci, Alessandro, Santus, Enrico, Blache, Philippe, and Huang, Chu-Ren. 2016. Representing verbs with rich contexts: An evaluation on verb similarity. Pages 1967–1972 of: *Proc. EMNLP.*

Chersoni, Emmanuele, Santus, Enrico, Blache, Philippe, and Lenci, Alessandro. 2017. Is structure necessary for modeling argument expectations in distributional semantics? In: *Proc. IWCS.*

Chersoni, Emmanuele, Santus, Enrico, Pannitto, Ludovica et al. 2019. A structured distributional model of sentence meaning and processing. *Natural Language Engineering*, 25(4), 483–502.

Chersoni, Emmanuele, Santus, Enrico, Huang, Chu-Ren, and Lenci, Alessandro. 2021a. Decoding word embeddings with brain-based semantic features. *CL*, 47(3), 663–698.

Chersoni, Emmanuele, Santus, Enrico, Lenci, Alessandro, Blache, Philippe, and Huang, Chu Ren. 2021b. Not all arguments are processed equally: A distributional model of argument complexity. *LRE*, 55(4), 873–900.

Chiu, Billy, Korhonen, Anna, and Pyysalo, Sampo. 2016. Intrinsic evaluation of word vectors fails to predict extrinsic performance. Pages 1–6 of: *1st Workshop on Evaluating Vector Space Representations for NLP.*

Chklovski, Timothy, and Pantel, Patrick. 2004. VerbOcean: Mining the web for fine-grained semantic verb relations. Pages 33–40 of: *Proc. EMNLP*.

Cho, Kyunghyun, van Merriënboer, Bart, Gulcehre, Caglar et al. 2014. Learning phrase representations using RNN encoder–decoder for statistical machine translation. Pages 1724–1734 of: *Proc. EMNLP*.

Chomsky, Noam. 1957. *Syntactic Structures*. The Hague: Mouton.

Chomsky, Noam. 1965. *Aspects of the Theory of Syntax*. Cambridge, MA: The MIT Press.

Chomsky, Noam. 1986. *Knowledge of Language: Its Nature, Origin and Use*. New York: Praeger.

Chowdhery, Aakanksha, Narang, Sharan, Devlin, Jacob et al. 2022. PaLM: Scaling language modeling with pathways. *arXiv*, 2204.02311.

Chronis, Gabriella, and Erk, Katrin. 2020. When is a bishop not like a rook? When it's like a rabbi! Multi-prototype BERT embeddings for estimating semantic relationships. Pages 227–244 of: *Proc. CoNLL*.

Chrupała, Grzegorz, and Alishahi, Afra. 2019. Correlating neural and symbolic representations of language. Pages 2952–2962 of: *Proc. ACL*.

Church, Kenneth W. 2017. Emerging trends: Word2vec. *Natural Language Engineering*, **23**(1), 155–162.

Church, Kenneth W., and Hanks, Patrick. 1989. Word association norms, mutual information and lexicography. Pages 76–83 of: *Proc. ACL*.

Church, Kenneth W., and Hanks, Patrick. 1990. Word association norms, mutual information and lexicography. *CL*, **16**(1), 22–29.

Cimiano, Philipp, and Wenderoth, Johanna. 2007. Automatic acquisition of ranked qualia structures from the web. Pages 888–895 of: *Proc. ACL*.

Ciobanu, Alina Maria, and Dinu, Anca. 2013. Alternative measures of word relatedness in distributional semantics. Pages 80–84 of: *Joint Symposium on Semantic Processing*.

Clark, Andy. 2006. Language, embodiment, and the cognitive niche. *Trends in Cognitive Sciences*, **10**(8), 370–374.

Clark, Andy. 2013. Whatever next? Predictive brains, situated agents, and the future of cognitive science. *Behavioral and Brain Sciences*, **36**(3), 1–73.

Clark, Kevin, Khandelwal, Urvashi, Levy, Omer, and Manning, Christopher D. 2019. What does BERT look at? An analysis of BERT's attention. Pages 276–286 of: *2nd BlackboxNLP Workshop on Analyzing and Interpreting Neural Networks for NLP*.

Clark, Kevin, Luong, Minh-Thang, Le, Quoc V., and Manning, Christopher D. 2020. ELECTRA: Pre-training text encoders as discriminators rather than generators. In: *Proc. ICLR*.

Clark, Stephen. 2015. Vector space models of lexical meaning. Pages 493–522 of: Lappin, Shalom, and Fox, Chris (eds.), *Handbook of Contemporary Semantics, 2nd ed*. Oxford: Wiley-Blackwell.

Clark, Stephen, and Pulman, Stephen. 2007. Combining symbolic and distributional models of meaning. Pages 52–55 of: *AAAI Spring Symposium on Quantum Interaction*.

Clark, Stephen, and Weir, David. 2002. Class-based probability estimation using a semantic hierarchy. *CL*, **28**(2), 187–206.

Clark, Stephen, Coecke, Bob, and Sadrzadeh, Mehrnoosh. 2008. A compositional distributional model of meaning. Pages 133–140 of: *2nd Symposium on Quantum Interaction*.

Clarke, Daoud. 2009. Context-theoretic semantics for natural language: An overview. Pages 112–119 of: *GEMS 2009 Workshop on GEometrical Models of Natural Language Semantics*.

Coecke, Bob, Sadrzadeh, Mehrnoosh, and Clark, Stephen. 2010. Mathematical foundations for a compositional distributional model of meaning. *Linguistic Analysis*, **36**(1–4), 345–384.

Coenen, Andy, Reif, Emily, Yuan, Ann et al. 2019. Visualizing and measuring the geometry of BERT. In: *Proc. NIPS*.

Collell, Guillem, and Moens, Marie-Francine. 2016. Is an image worth more than a thousand words? On the fine-grain semantic differences between visual and linguistic representations. Pages 2807–2817 of: *Proc. COLING*.

Collins, Allan M., and Loftus, Elizabeth F. 1975. A spreading-activation theory of semantic memory. *Psychological Review*, **82**(6), 407–428.

Collins, Allan M., and Quillian, M. Ross. 1969. Retrieval time from semantic memory. *Journal of Verbal Learning and Behavior*, **8**(2), 240–247.

Collobert, Ronan, and Weston, Jason. 2008. A unified architecture for natural language processing: Deep neural networks with multitask learning. Pages 160–167 of: *Proc. ICML*.

Collobert, Ronan, Weston, Jason, Bottou, Léon et al. 2011. Natural language processing (almost) from scratch. *Journal of Machine Learning Research*, **12**, 2493–2537.

Conneau, Alexis, and Kiela, Douwe. 2018. SentEval: An evaluation toolkit for universal sentence representations. Pages 1699–1704 of: *Proc. LREC*.

Conneau, Alexis, and Lample, Guillaume. 2019. Cross-lingual language model pretraining. In: *Proc. NIPS*.

Conneau, Alexis, Kiela, Douwe, Schwenk, Holger, Barrault, Loïc, and Bordes, Antoine. 2017. Supervised learning of universal sentence representations from natural language inference data. Pages 670–680 of: *Proc. EMNLP*.

Conneau, Alexis, Kruszewski, German, Lample, Guillaume, Barrault, Loïc, and Baroni, Marco. 2018a. What you can cram into a single $&!#* vector: Probing sentence embeddings for linguistic properties. Pages 2126–2136 of: *Proc. ACL*.

Conneau, Alexis, Lample, Guillaume, Ranzato, Marc'Aurelio, Denoyer, Ludovic, and Jégou, Hervé. 2018b. Word translation without parallel data. In: *Proc. ICLR*.

Conneau, Alexis, Wu, Shijie, Li, Haoran, Zettlemoyer, Luke, and Stoyanov, Veselin. 2020. Emerging cross-lingual structure in pretrained language models. Pages 6022–6034 of: *Proc. ACL*.

Connolly, Andrew C., Gleitman, Lila R., and Thompson-Schill, Sharon L. 2007. Effect of congenital blindness on the semantic representation of some everyday concepts. *Proceedings of the National Academy of Sciences*, **104**(20), 8241–8246.

Cordeiro, Silvio, Villavicencio, Aline, Idiart, Marco, and Ramisch, Carlos. 2019. Unsupervised compositionality prediction of nominal compounds. *CL*, **45**(1), 1–57.

Coulmance, Jocelyn, Marty, Jean-Marc, Wenzek, Guillaume, and Benhalloum, Amine. 2015. Trans-gram, fast cross-lingual word-embeddings. Pages 1109–1113 of: *Proc. EMNLP*.

Cover, Thomas M., and Thomas, Joy A. 2006. *Elements of Information Theory*, 2nd ed New York: John Wiley.

Cristia, Alejandrina, Dupoux, Emmanuel, Gurven, Michael, and Stieglitz, Jonathan. 2019. Child-directed speech is infrequent in a forager-farmer population: A time allocation study. *Child Development*, **90**(3), 759–773.

Croft, William, and Cruse, Alan D. 2004. *Cognitive Linguistics*. Cambridge: Cambridge University Press.

Cruse, D. Alan. 1986. *Lexical Semantics*. Cambridge: Cambridge University Press.

Crutch, Sebastian J., and Warrington, Elizabeth K. 2005. Abstract and concrete concepts have structurally different representational frameworks. *Brain*, **128**(3), 615–627.

Curran, James R. 2003. *From Distributional to Semantic Similarity*. PhD thesis, University of Edinburgh.

Curran, James R., and Moens, Marc. 2002. Improvements in automatic thesaurus extraction. Pages 59–66 of: *ACL Workshop on Unsupervised Lexical Acquisition*.

Cutting, Douglass R., Karger, David R., Pedersen, Jan O., and Tukey, John W. 1992. Scatter/Gather: A cluster-based approach to browsing large document collections. Pages 318–329 of: *15th International ACM SIGIR Conference*.

Dagan, Ido. 2003. Contextual word similarity. Pages 459–476 of: Dale, Robert, Moisl, Hermann, and Somers, Harold (eds.), *A Handbook of Natural Language Processing*. New York: Marcel Dekker.

Dagan, Ido, Marcus, Shaul, and Markovitch, Shaul. 1993. Contextual word similarity and estimation from sparse data. Pages 164–171 of: *Proc. ACL*.

Dagan, Ido, Lee, Lillian, and Pereira, Fernando C. N. 1997. Similarity-based methods for word sense disambiguation. Pages 56–63 of: *Proc. ACL*.

Dagan, Ido, Lee, Lillian, and Pereira, Fernando C. N. 1999. Similarity-based models of word cooccurrence probabilities. *Machine Learning*, **34**(1–3), 43–69.

Dai, Andrew M., and Le, Quoc V. 2015. Semi-supervised sequence learning. Pages 3079–3087 of: *Proc. NIPS*.

Dasgupta, Sanjoy, and Gupta, Anupam. 2003. An elementary proof of the Johnson-Lindenstrauss lemma. *Random Structures and Algorithms*, **22**(1), 60–65.

Dattola, Robert T., and Murray, Daniel M. 1967. An experiment in automatic thesaurus construction. Pages 1–26 of: *Information Storage and Retrieval, Report No. ISR-13*.

Davidse, Kristin, and De Smet, Hendrik. 2020. Diachronic corpora. Pages 211–233 of: Paquot, Magali, and Gries, Stefan Th. (eds.), *A Practical Handbook of Corpus Linguistics*. Cham: Springer.

Davies, Mark. 2009. The 385+ million word Corpus of Contemporary American English (1990–2008+): Design, architecture, and linguistic insights. *International Journal of Corpus Linguistics*, **14**(2), 159–190.

de Marneffe, Marie-Catherine, Dozat, Timothy, Silveira, Natalia et al. 2014. Universal Stanford dependencies: A cross-linguistic typology. Pages 4585–4592 of: *Proc. LREC*.

Deerwester, Scott, Dumais, Susan T., Furnas, George W., Landauer, Thomas K., and Harshman, Richard. 1990. Indexing by Latent Semantic Analysis. *Journal of the American Society for Information Science*, **41**(6), 391–407.

Deese, James. 1965. *The Structure of Associations in Language and Thought*. Baltimore: Johns Hopkins University Press.

Del Tredici, Marco, and Fernández, Raquel. 2017. Semantic variation in online communities of practice. In: *Proc. IWCS*.

Deng, Jia, Dong, Wei, Socher, Richard et al. 2009. ImageNet: A large-scale hierarchical image database. Pages 248–255 of: *IEEE Conference on Computer Vision and Pattern Recognition*.

Deo, Ashwini. 2015. Diachronic semantics. *Annual Review of Linguistics*, **1**(1), 179–197.

Derby, Steven, Miller, Paul, and Devereux, Barry J. 2019. Feature2vec: Distributional semantic modelling of human property knowledge. Pages 5853–5859 of: *Proc. EMNLP*.

Derby, Steven, Miller, Paul, and Devereux, Barry J. 2020. Encoding lexico-semantic knowledge using ensembles of feature maps from deep convolutional neural networks. Pages 1906–1921 of: *Proc. COLING*.

Devereux, Barry J., Kelly, Colin, and Korhonen, Anna. 2010. Using fMRI activation to conceptual stimuli to evaluate methods for extracting conceptual representations from corpora. Pages 70–78 of: *1st Workshop on Computational Neurolinguistics*.

Devereux, Barry J., Tyler, Lorraine K., Geertzen, Jeroen, and Randall, Billi. 2014. The Centre for Speech, Language and the Brain (CSLB) concept property norms. *Behavior Research Methods*, **46**(4), 1119–1127.

Devlin, Jacob, Chang, Ming-Wei, Lee, Kenton, and Toutanova, Kristina. 2019. BERT: Pre-training of deep bidirectional transformers for language understanding. Pages 4171–4186 of: *Proc. NAACL-HLT*.

Di Marco, Antonio, and Navigli, Roberto. 2013. Clustering and diversifying web search results with graph-based word sense induction. *CL*, **39**(3), 709–754.

Dickey, James. 1983. Multiple hypergeometric functions: Probabilistic interpretations and statistical uses. *Journal of the American Statistical Association*, **78**(383), 628–637.

Ding, Chris, Li, Tao, and Peng, Wei. 2008. On the equivalence between Non-negative Matrix Factorization and Probabilistic Latent Semantic Indexing. *Computational Statistics and Data Analysis*, **52**(8), 3913–3927.

Dinu, Georgiana, and Lapata, Mirella. 2010. Measuring distributional similarity in context. Pages 1162–1172 of: *Proc. EMNLP*.

Dinu, Georgiana, Thater, Stefan, and Laue, Sören. 2012. A comparison of models of word meaning in context. Pages 611–615 of: *Proc. NAACL-HLT*.

Dinu, Georgiana, Pham, Nghia The, and Baroni, Marco. 2013. General estimation and evaluation of compositional distributional semantic models. Pages 50–58 of: *Workshop on Continuous Vector Space Models and their Compositionality*.

Dinu, Georgiana, Lazaridou, Angeliki, and Baroni, Marco. 2015. Improving zero-shot learning by mitigating the hubness problem. In: *Proc. ICLR*.

Dorow, Beate, and Widdows, Dominic. 2003. Discovering corpus-specific word senses. Pages 79–82 of: *Proc. EACL*.

Dove, Guy. 2009. Beyond perceptual symbols: A call for representational pluralism. *Cognition*, **110**(3), 412–431.

Dove, Guy. 2014. Thinking in words: Language as an embodied medium of thought. *TopiCS*, **6**(3), 371–389.

Dove, Guy. 2016. Three symbol ungrounding problems: Abstract concepts and the future of embodied cognition. *Psychonomic Bulletin & Review*, **23**(4), 1109–1121.

Dove, Guy. 2020. More than a scaffold: Language is a neuroenhancement. *Cognitive Neuropsychology*, **37**, 288–311.

Dove, Guy. 2022. *Abstract Concepts and the Embodied Mind*. Oxford: Oxford University Press.

Dove, Guy. 2023. Rethinking the role of language in embodied cognition. *Philosophical Transactions of the Royal Society B*, **378**, 20210375.

Dowty, David. 1979. *Word Meaning and Montague Grammar*. Dordrecht: Reidel.

Dowty, David. 1991. Thematic proto-roles and argument selection. *Language*, **67**(3), 547–619.

Dowty, David. 2007. Compositionality as an empirical problem. Pages 23–101 of: Barker, Chris, and Jacobson, Pauline (eds.), *Direct Compositionality*. Oxford: Oxford University Press.

Drozd, Aleksandr, Gladkova, Anna, and Matsuoka, Satoshi. 2016. Word embeddings, analogies, and machine learning: Beyond king - man + woman = queen. Pages 3519–3530 of: *Proc. COLING*.

Dubossarsky, Haim, Weinshall, Daphna, and Grossman, Eitan. 2016. Verbs change more than nouns: A bottom-up computational approach to semantic change. *Lingue e Linguaggio*, **15**(1), 7–27.

Dubossarsky, Haim, Grossman, Eitan, and Weinshall, Daphna. 2017. Outta control: Laws of semantic change and inherent biases in word representation models. Pages 1147–1156 of: *Proc. EMNLP*.

Dufter, Philipp, Zhao, Mengjie, Schmitt, Martin, Fraser, Alexander, and Schütze, Hinrich. 2018. Embedding learning through multilingual concept induction. Pages 1520–1530 of: *Proc. ACL*.

Dumais, Susan T. 1991. Improving the retrieval of information from external sources. *Behavior Research Methods, Instruments, & Computers*, **23**(2), 229–236.

Dumais, Susan T. 1993. LSI meets TREC: A status report. Pages 137–152 of: *Text REtrieval Conference*.

Dunning, Ted. 1993. Accurate methods for the statistics of surprise and coincidence. *CL*, **19**(1), 61–74.

Duong, Long, Kanayama, Hiroshi, Ma, Tengfei, Bird, Steven, and Cohn, Trevor. 2016. Learning crosslingual word embeddings without bilingual corpora. Pages 1285–1295 of: *Proc. EMNLP*.

Duong, Long, Kanayama, Hiroshi, Ma, Tengfei, Bird, Steven, and Cohn, Trevor. 2017. Multilingual training of crosslingual word embeddings. Pages 894–904 of: *Proc. EACL*.

Dyer, Chris, Chahuneau, Victor, and Smith, Noah A. 2013. A simple, fast, and effective reparameterization of IBM model 2. Pages 644–648 of: *Proc. NAACL-HLT*.

Edelman, Shimon. 1998. Representation is representation of similarities. *Behavioral and Brain Sciences*, **21**, 449–498.

Eger, Steffen, and Mehler, Alexander. 2016. On the linearity of semantic change: Investigating meaning variation via dynamic graph models. Pages 52–58 of: *Proc. ACL*.

Elkins, Katherine, and Chun, Jon. 2020. Can GPT-3 pass a writer's Turing test? *Journal of Cultural Analytics*, **5**(2).

Ellis, Nick C. 1998. Emergentism, connectionism and language learning. *Language Learning*, **48**(4), 631–664.

Ellis, Nick C., and O'Donnell, Matthew Brook. 2012. Statistical construction learning: Does a Zipfian problem space ensure robust language learning? Pages 265–304 of: Rebuschat, Patrick, and Williams, John (eds.), *Statistical Learning and Language Acquisition*. Berlin: Mouton de Gruyter.

Ellis, Nick C., O'Donnell, Matthew Brook, and Römer, Ute. 2014. Does language Zipf right along? Investigating robustness in the latent structure of usage and acquisition. Pages 33–50 of: Connor-Linton, Jeffrey, and Amoroso, Luke Wander (eds.), *Measured Language: Quantitative Studies of Acquisition, Assessment, Processing and Variation*. Washington, DC: Georgetown University Press.

Ellis, Nick C., Römer, Ute, and O'Donnell, Matthew Brook. 2016. *Usage-based Approaches to Language Acquisition and Processing: Cognitive and Corpus Investigations of Construction Grammar*. Hoboken: Wiley-Blackwell.

Elman, Jeffrey L. 1990. Finding structure in time. *Cognitive Science*, **14**, 179–211.

Elman, Jeffrey L. 1991. Distributed representations, simple recurrent networks, and grammatical structure. *Machine Learning*, **7**, 195–225.

Elman, Jeffrey L. 1993. Learning and development in neural networks: The importance of starting small. *Cognition*, **48**, 71–99.

Elman, Jeffrey L. 1998. Language as a dynamical system. Pages 195–225 of: Port, Robert, and van Gelder, Timothy (eds.), *Mind as Motion: Explorations in the Dynamics of Cognition*. Cambridge, MA: The MIT Press.

Elman, Jeffrey L. 2009. On the meaning of words and dinosaur bones: Lexical knowledge without a lexicon. *Cognitive Science*, **33**(4), 547–582.

Elman, Jeffrey L. 2011. Lexical knowledge without a lexicon? *The Mental Lexicon*, **6**(1), 1–34.

Elman, Jeffrey L. 2014. Systematicity in the lexicon: On having your cake and eating it too. Pages 1–33 of: Calvo, Paco, and Symons, John (eds.), *The Architecture of Cognition: Rethinking Fodor and Pylyshyn's Systematicity Challenge*. Cambridge, MA: The MIT Press.

Elman, Jeffrey L., and McRae, Ken. 2019. A model of event knowledge. *Psychological Review*, **126**(2), 252–291.

Elman, Jeffrey L., Bates, Elizabeth A., Johnson, Mark H. et al. 1996. *Rethinking Innateness: A Connectionist Perspective on Development*. Cambridge, MA: The MIT Press.

Emerson, Guy, and Copestake, Ann. 2017. Semantic composition via probabilistic model theory. In: *Proc. IWCS*.

Erk, Katrin. 2007. A simple, similarity-based model for selectional preferences. Pages 216–223 of: *Proc. ACL*.

Erk, Katrin. 2012. Vector space models of word meaning and phrase meaning: A survey. *Linguistics and Language Compass*, **6**(10), 635–653.

Erk, Katrin. 2013. Towards a semantics for distributional representations. Pages 95–106 of: *Proc. IWCS*.

Erk, Katrin. 2022. The probabilistic turn in semantics and pragmatics. *Annual Review of Linguistics*, **8**, 101–122.

Erk, Katrin, and Chronis, Gabriella. 2022. Word embeddings are word story embeddings (and that's fine). Pages 189–218 of: Lappin, Shalom, and Bernardy, Jean-Philippe (eds.), *Algebraic Structures in Natural Language*. Boca Raton: Taylor & Francis.

Erk, Katrin, and Padó, Sebastian. 2008. A structured vector space model for word meaning in context. Pages 897–906 of: *Proc. EMNLP*.

Erk, Katrin, and Padó, Sebastian. 2010. Exemplar-based models for word meaning in context. Pages 92–97 of: *Proc. ACL*.

Erk, Katrin, Padó, Sebastian, and Padó, Ulrike. 2010. A flexible, corpus-driven model of regular and inverse selectional preferences. *CL*, **36**(4), 723–763.

Erk, Katrin, McCarthy, Diana, and Gaylord, Nicholas. 2013. Measuring word meaning in context. *CL*, **39**(3), 511–554.

Estes, Zachary, Golonka, Sabrina, and Jones, Lara L. 2011. Thematic thinking: The apprehension and consequences of thematic relations. Pages 249–294 of: Ross, Brian (ed.), *Psychology of Learning and Motivation*, Vol. 54. San Diego: Academic Press.

Estes, Zachary, Gibbert, Michael, Guest, Duncan, and Mazursky, David. 2012. A dual-process model of brand extension: Taxonomic feature-based and thematic relation-based similarity independently drive brand extension evaluation. *Journal of Consumer Psychology*, **22**(1), 86–101.

Ethayarajh, Kawin. 2019. How contextual are contextualized word representations? Comparing the geometry of BERT, ELMo, and GPT-2 embeddings. Pages 55–65 of: *Proc. EMNLP*.

Ettinger, Allyson. 2020. What BERT is not: Lessons from a new suite of psycholinguistic diagnostics for language models. *TACL*, **8**, 34–48.

Ettinger, Allyson, and Linzen, Tal. 2016. Evaluating vector space models using human semantic priming results. Pages 72–77 of: *1st Workshop on Evaluating Vector Space Representations for NLP*.

Ettinger, Allyson, Elgohary, Ahmed, and Resnik, Philip. 2016. Probing for semantic evidence of composition by means of simple classification tasks. Pages 134–139 of: *1st Workshop on Evaluating Vector Space Representations for NLP*.

Ettinger, Allyson, Elgohary, Ahmed, Phillips, Colin, and Resnik, Philip. 2018. Assessing composition in sentence vector representations. Pages 1790–1801 of: *Proc. COLING*.

Everett, Martin, and Borgatti, Stephen P. 2005. Ego network betweenness. *Social Networks*, **27**(1), 31–38.

Evert, Stefan. 2008. Corpora and collocations. Pages 1212–1248 of: Lüdeling, Anke, and Kytö, Merja (eds.), *Corpus Linguistics: An International Handbook*. Berlin: Mouton de Gruyter.

Evert, Stefan, and Lapesa, Gabriella. 2021. FAST: A carefully sampled and cognitively motivated dataset for distributional semantic evaluation. Pages 588–595 of: *Proc. CoNLL*.

Făgărăşan, Luana, Vecchi, Eva Maria, and Clark, Stephen. 2015. From distributional semantics to feature norms: Grounding semantic models in human perceptual data. Pages 52–57 of: *Proc. IWCS*.

Faruqui, Manaal, and Dyer, Chris. 2014. Improving vector space word representations using multilingual correlation. Pages 462–471 of: *Proc. EACL*.

Faruqui, Manaal, Dodge, Jesse, Jauhar, Sujay K. et al. 2015. Retrofitting word vectors to semantic lexicons. Pages 1606–1615 of: *Proc. NAACL-HLT*.

Faruqui, Manaal, Tsvetkov, Yulia, Rastogi, Pushpendre, and Dyer, Chris. 2016. Problems with evaluation of word embeddings using word similarity tasks. Pages 30–35 of: *1st Workshop on Evaluating Vector Space Representations for NLP*.

Fazly, Afsaneh, and Stevenson, Suzanne. 2008. A distributional account of the semantics of multiword expressions. *Italian Journal of Linguistics*, **20**(1), 153–175.

Fellbaum, Christiane. 1995. Co-occurrence and antonymy. *International Journal of Lexicography*, **8**(4), 281–303.

Fellbaum, Christiane (ed.). 1998. *WordNet: An Electronic Lexical Database*. Cambridge, MA: The MIT Press.

Feng, Yansong, and Lapata, Mirella. 2010. Visual information in semantic representation. Pages 91–99 of: *Proc. NAACL-HLT*.

Ferretti, Todd R., McRae, Ken, and Hatherell, Andrea. 2001. Integrating verbs, situation schemas, and thematic role concepts. *Journal of Memory and Language*, **44**(4), 516–547.

Fillmore, Charles J. 1982. Frame semantics. Pages 111–137 of: *Linguistics in the Morning Calm*. Seoul: Hanshin.

Finkelstein, Lev, Gabrilovich, Evgeniy, Matias, Yossi et al. 2001. Placing search in context: The concept revisited. *ACM Transactions on Information Systems*, **20**(1), 116–131.

Finley, Gregory P., Farmer, Stephanie, and Pakhomov, Serguei V. S. 2017. What analogies reveal about word vectors and their compositionality. Pages 1–11 of: *Proc. *SEM*.

Firth, John R. 1951. Modes of meaning. Pages 118–149 of: *Essays and Studies*. Oxford: The English Association. Reprinted in *Papers in Linguistics 1934–1951*, John R. Firth (ed.), London: Oxford University Press, 1957, 190–215.

Firth, John R. 1955. Structural linguistics. *Transactions of the Philological Society*, **54**(1), 83–103.

Firth, John R. 1957. A synopsis of linguistic theory 1930–1955. Pages 1–32 of: *Studies in Linguistic Analysis*. Oxford: Blackwell.

Floridi, Luciano, and Chiriatti, Massimo. 2020. GPT-3: Its nature, scope, limits, and consequences. *Minds and Machines*, **30**, 681–694.

Fodor, Jerry A., and Pylyshyn, Zenon A. 1988. Connectionism and cognitive architecture: A critical analysis. *Cognition*, **28**, 3–71.

Francis, W. Nelson, and Kučera, Henry. 1964. *Manual of Information to Accompany a Standard Corpus of Present-day Edited American English, for Use with Digital Computers*. Providence: Brown University.

Frankl, Peter, and Maehara, Hiroshi. 1987. The Johnson-Lindenstrauss lemma and the sphericity of some graphs. *Journal of Combinatorial Theory Series A*, **44**(3), 355–362.

Frassinelli, Diego, Naumann, Daniela, Utt, Jason, and Schulte im Walde, Sabine. 2017. Contextual characteristics of concrete and abstract words. In: *Proc. IWCS*.

Frege, Gottlob. 1891. *Funktion und Begriff – Vortrag gehalten in der Sitzung vom 9. Januar 1891 der Jenaischen Gesellschaft für Medicin und Naturwissenschaft*. Jena: Verlag von Hermann Pohle.

Frege, Gottlob. 1923. Logische Untersuchungen. Dritter Teil: Gedankengefüge. *Beitrǧe zur Philosophie des deutschen Idealismus*, **3**, 36–51. [English translation: Compound thoughts, *Mind*, 1963, **32**, 1–17].

Frermann, Lea, and Lapata, Mirella. 2016. A Bayesian model of diachronic meaning change. *TACL*, **4**, 31–45.

Frome, Andrea, Corrado, Greg S., Shlens, Jonathon et al. 2013. DeViSE: A deep visual-semantic embedding model. In: *Proc. NIPS*.

Furnas, George W., Deerwester, Scott, Dumais, Susan T. et al. 1988. Information retrieval using a singular value decomposition model of latent semantic structure. Pages 465–480 of: *11th International ACM SIGIR Conference*.

Furnas, George W., Landauer, Thomas K., Gomez, Louis M., and Dumais, Susan T. 1983. Statistical semantics: Analysis of the potential performance of key-word information systems. *Bell System Technical Journal*, **62**(6), 1753–1806.

Gabrilovich, Evgeniy, and Markovitch, Shaul. 2007. Computing semantic relatedness using Wikipedia-based Explicit Semantic Analysis. Pages 1606–1611 of: *Proc. IJCAI*.

Gallant, Stephen I. 1991. A practical approach for representing context and for performing word sense disambiguation using neural networks. *Neural Computation*, **3**, 293–309.

Gamallo, Pablo. 2017. Comparing explicit and predictive distributional semantic models endowed with syntactic contexts. *LRE*, **51**(3), 727–743.

Gamallo, Pablo, and Bordag, Stefan. 2011. Is singular value decomposition useful for word similarity extraction? *LRE*, **45**(2), 95–119.

Ganitkevitch, Juri, Van Durme, Benjamin, and Callison-Burch, Chris. 2013. PPDB: The paraphrase database. Pages 758–764 of: *Proc. NAACL-HLT*.

Gao, Bin, Jiang, Bian, and Liu, Tie-Yan. 2014. WordRep: A benchmark for research on learning word representations. Pages 1–6 of: *Proceedings of ICML 2014 Workshop on Knowledge-Powered Deep Learning for Text Mining*.

Gao, Jun, He, Di, Tan, Xu et al. 2019. Representation degeneration problem in training natural language generation models. In: *Proc. ICLR*.

Gärdenfors, Peter. 2000. *Conceptual Spaces: On the Geometry of Thought*. Cambridge, MA: The MIT Press.

Gärdenfors, Peter. 2014. *The Geometry of Meaning: Semantics Based on Conceptual Spaces*. Cambridge, MA: The MIT Press.

Garg, Nikhil, Schiebinger, Nikhil, Jurafsky, Dan, and Zou, James. 2018. Word embeddings quantify 100 years of gender and ethnic stereotypes. *Proceedings of the National Academy of Sciences*, **115**(16), E3635–E3644.

Garí Soler, Aina, and Apidianaki, Marianna. 2021. Let's play Mono - Poly : BERT can reveal words' polysemy level and partitionability into senses. *TACL*, **9**, 825–844.

Garvin, Paul L. 1962. Computer participation in linguistic research. *Language*, **38**(4), 385–389.

Gastaldi, Juan Luis. 2021. Why can computers understand natural language? *Philosophy & Technology*, **34**, 149–214.

Gauthier, Jon, and Ivanova, Anna A. 2018. Does the brain represent words? An evaluation of brain decoding studies of language understanding. *arXiv*, 1806.00591.

Gauthier, Jon, and Levy, Roger P. 2019. Linking artificial and human neural representations of language. Pages 529–539 of: *Proc. EMNLP*.

Geeraerts, Dirk. 2010. *Theories of Lexical Semantics*. Oxford: Oxford University Press.

Gehring, Jonas, Auli, Michael, Grangier, David, Yarats, Denis, and Dauphin, Yann N. 2017. Convolutional sequence to sequence learning. Pages 2029–2042 of: *Proc. ICML*.

Gentner, Dedre. 1983. Structure-mapping: A theoretical framework for analogy. *Cognitive Science*, **7**, 155–170.

Gentner, Dedre. 2010. Bootstrapping the mind: Analogical processes and symbol systems. *Cognitive Science*, **34**(5), 752–775.

Gerz, Daniela, Vulić, Ivan, Hill, Felix, Reichart, Roi, and Korhonen, Anna. 2016. SimVerb-3500: A large-scale evaluation set of verb similarity. Pages 2173–2182. In: *Proc. EMNLP*.

Gilpin, Leilani H., Bau, David, Yuan, Ben Z. et al. 2018. Explaining explanations: An overview of interpretability of machine learning. Pages 80–89 of: *5th International Conference on Data Science and Advanced Analytics*.

Giuliano, Vincent E., and Jones, Paul E. 1962. Linear associative information retrieval. Pages 1–42 of: *Studies for the Design of an English Command and Control Language System, ESD-TR-62-294*. Cambridge, MA: Arthur D. Little.

Gladkova, Anna, and Drozd, Aleksandr. 2016. Intrinsic evaluations of word embeddings: What can we do better? Pages 36–42 of: *1st Workshop on Evaluating Vector Space Representations for NLP*.

Gladkova, Anna, Drozd, Aleksandr, and Matsuoka, Satoshi. 2016. Analogy-based detection of morphological and semantic relations with word embeddings: What works and what doesn't. Pages 8–15 of: *Proc. NAACL-HLT*.

Glavaš, Goran, Litschko, Robert, Ruder, Sebastian, and Vulić, Ivan. 2019. How to (properly) evaluate cross-lingual word embeddings: On strong baselines, comparative analyses, and some misconceptions. Pages 710–721 of: *Proc. ACL*.

Gleitman, Lila. 1990. The structural sources of verb meanings. *Language Acquisition*, **1**, 3–55.

Glenberg, Arthur M., and Mehta, Sarita. 2008a. Constraint on covariation: It's not meaning. *Italian Journal of Linguistics*, **20**(1), 237–262.

Glenberg, Arthur M., and Mehta, Sarita. 2008b. The limits of covariation. Pages 11–32 of: de Vega, Manuel, Glenberg, Arthur M., and Graesser, Arthur (eds.), *Symbols and Embodiment: Debates on Meaning and Cognition*. Oxford: Oxford University Press.

Glenberg, Arthur M., and Robertson, David A. 2000. Symbol grounding and meaning: A comparison of high-dimensional and embodied theories of meaning. *Journal of Memory and Language*, **43**(3), 379–401.

Gliozzo, Alfio, and Strapparava, Carlo. 2009. *Semantic Domains in Computational Linguistics*. Berlin: Springer.

Glockner, Max, Shwartz, Vered, and Goldberg, Yoav. 2018. Breaking NLI systems with sentences that require simple lexical inferences. Pages 650–655 of: *Proc. ACL*.

Goldberg, Adele E. 1995. *Constructions: A Construction Grammar Approach to Argument Structure*. Chicago: University of Chicago Press.

Goldberg, Adele E. 2006. *Constructions at Work: The Nature of Generalization in Language*. Oxford: Oxford University Press.

Goldberg, Adele E. 2019. *Explain Me This. Creativity, Competition, and the Partial Productivity of Constructions*. Princeton: Princeton University Press.

Goldberg, Yoav. 2016. A primer on neural network models for natural language processing. *JAIR*, **57**, 345–420.

Goldberg, Yoav. 2017. *Neural Network Methods for Natural Language Processing*. San Rafael: Morgan & Claypool.

Goldberg, Yoav, and Levy, Omer. 2014. Word2vec explained: Deriving Mikolov et al.'s negative-sampling word-embedding method. *arXiv*, 1402.3722.

Goldsmith, John. 2005. Review to Nevin, B. (ed.) The legacy of Zellig Harris. *Language*, **81**, 719–736.

Goldsmith, John, and Huck, Geoffrey. 1991. Distribution et médiation dans la théorie linguistique. *Communications*, **53**, 51–67.

Gonen, Hila, and Goldberg, Yoav. 2019. Lipstick on a pig: Debiasing methods cover up systematic gender biases in word embeddings but do not remove them. Pages 609–614 of: *Proc. NAACL-HLT*.

Gonen, Hila, Jawahar, Ganesh, Seddah, Djamé, and Goldberg, Yoav. 2020. Simple, interpretable and stable method for detecting words with usage change across corpora. Pages 538–555 of: *Proc. ACL*.

Goodfellow, Ian, Bengio, Yoshua, and Courville, Aaron. 2016. *Deep Learning*. Cambridge, MA: The MIT Press.

Goodman, Nelson. 1972. Seven strictures on similarity. Pages 437–447 of: *Problems and Projects*. Indianapolis: Bobbs-Merrill.

Goodwin, Emily, Sinha, Koustuv, and O'Donnell, Timothy J. 2020. Probing linguistic systematicity. Pages 1958–1969 of: *Proc. ACL*.

Gordon, Jonathan, and Van Durme, Benjamin. 2013. Reporting bias and knowledge acquisition. Pages 25–29 of: *Workshop on Automated Knowledge Base Construction*.

Gouws, Stephan, and Søgaard, Anders. 2015. Simple task-specific bilingual word embeddings. Pages 1386–1390 of: *Proc. NAACL-HLT*.

Gouws, Stephan, Bengio, Yoshua, and Corrado, Greg. 2015. BilBOWA: Fast bilingual distributed representations without word alignments. Pages 748–756 of: *Proc. ICML*, Vol. 1.

Graves, Alex, and Schmidhuber, Jürgen. 2005. Framewise phoneme classification with bidirectional LSTM and other neural network architectures. *Neural Networks*, **18**, 602–610.

Greenberg, Clayton, Sayeed, Asad, and Demberg, Vera. 2015. Improving unsupervised vector-space thematic fit evaluation via role-filler prototype clustering. Pages 21–31 of: *Proc. NAACL-HLT*.

Grefenstette, Edward, and Sadrzadeh, Mehrnoosh. 2011. Experimental support for a categorical compositional distributional model of meaning. Pages 1394–1404 of: *Proc. EMNLP*.

Grefenstette, Edward, and Sadrzadeh, Mehrnoosh. 2015. Concrete models and empirical evaluations for the categorical compositional distributional model of meaning. *CL*, **41**(1), 71–118.

Grefenstette, Edward, Sadrzadeh, Mehrnoosh, Clark, Stephen, Coecke, Stephen, and Pulman, Stephen. 2011. Concrete sentence spaces for compositional distributional models of meaning. Pages 125–134 of: *Proc. IWCS*.

Grefenstette, Edward, Dinu, Georgiana, Sadrzadeh, Mehrnoosh, and Baroni, Marco. 2013. Multi-step regression learning for compositional distributional semantics. Pages 131–142 of: *Proc. IWCS*.

Grefenstette, Gregory. 1994. *Explorations in Automatic Thesaurus Discovery*. Dordrecht: Kluwer.

Grice, H. Paul. 1975. Logic and conversation. Pages 41–58 of: Cole, Peter, and Morgan, Jerry L. (eds.), *Syntax and Semantics, Vol. 3: Speech Acts*. New York: Academic Press.

Gries, Stefan Th, and Ellis, Nick C. 2015. Statistical measures for usage-based linguistics. *Language Learning*, **65**(s1), 1–28.

Griffiths, Thomas L., Steyvers, Mark, Blei, David M., and Tenenbaum, Joshua. 2005. Integrating topics and syntax. Pages 537–544 of: *Proc. NIPS*.

Griffiths, Thomas L., Tenenbaum, Joshua, and Steyvers, Mark. 2007. Topics in semantic representation. *Psychological Review*, **114**(2), 211–244.

Gruber, Amit, Weiss, Yair, and Rosen-Zvi, Michal. 2007. Hidden topic Markov models. Pages 163–170 of: *11th International Conference on Artificial Intelligence and Statistics*.

Guevara, Emiliano. 2010. A regression model of adjective-noun compositionality in distributional semantics. Pages 33–37 of: *GEMS 2010 Workshop on GEometrical Models of Natural Language Semantics*.

Guevara, Emiliano. 2011. Computing semantic compositionality in distributional semantics. Pages 135–144 of: *Proc. IWCS*.

Gulordava, Kristina, and Baroni, Marco. 2011. A distributional similarity approach to the detection of semantic change in the Google Books Ngram corpus. Pages 67–71 of: *GEMS 2011 Workshop on GEometrical Models of Natural Language Semantics*.

Gulordava, Kristina, Bojanowski, Piotr, Grave, Edouard, Linzen, Tal, and Baroni, Marco. 2018. Colorless green recurrent networks dream hierarchically. Pages 1195–1205 of: *Proc. NAACL-HLT*.

Günther, Fritz, Rinaldi, Luca, and Marelli, Marco. 2019. Vector-space models of semantic representation from a cognitive perspective: A discussion of common misconceptions. *Perspectives on Psychological Science*, **14**(6), 1006–1033.

Günther, Fritz, Nguyen, Tri, Chen, Lu et al. 2020. Immediate sensorimotor grounding of novel concepts learned from language alone. *Journal of Memory and Language*, **115**, 104172.

Gupta, Abhijeet, Utt, Jason, and Padó, Sebastian. 2015. Dissecting the practical Lexical Function Model for compositional distributional semantics. Pages 153–158 of: *Proc. *SEM*.

Gupta, Tanmay, Schwing, Alexander, and Hoiem, Derek. 2019. ViCo: Word embeddings from visual co-occurrences. Pages 7424–7433 of: *IEEE International Conference on Computer Vision*.

Gururangan, Suchin, Swayamdipta, Swabha, Levy, Omer et al. 2018. Annotation artifacts in natural language inference data. Pages 107–112 of: *Proc. NAACL-HLT*.

Gutiérrez, E. Darío, Shutova, Ekaterina, Marghetis, Tyler, and Bergen, Benjamin K. 2016. Literal and metaphorical senses in compositional distributional semantic models. Pages 183–193 of: *Proc. ACL*.

Hakami, Huda, and Bollegala, Danushka. 2017. Compositional approaches for representing relations between words: A comparative study. *Knowledge-Based Systems*, **136**, 172–182.

Halawi, Guy, Dror, Gideon, Gabrilovich, Evgeniy, and Koren, Yehuda. 2012. Large-scale learning of word relatedness with constraints. Pages 1406–1414 of: *18th International Conference on Knowledge Discovery and Data Mining*.

Hamilton, William L., Leskovec, Jure, and Jurafsky, Dan. 2016a. Cultural shift or linguistic drift? Comparing two computational measures of semantic change. Pages 2116–2121 of: *Proc. EMNLP*.

Hamilton, William L., Leskovec, Jure, and Jurafsky, Dan. 2016b. Diachronic word embeddings reveal statistical laws of semantic change. Pages 1489–1501 of: *Proc. ACL*.

Hamm, Fritz, Kamp, Hans, and Van Lambalgen, Michiel. 2006. There is no opposition between formal and cognitive semantics. *Theoretical Linguistics*, **32**(1), 1–40.

Hampton, James A. 2007. Typicality, graded membership, and vagueness. *Cognitive Science*, **31**, 355–383.

Han, Xu, Zhang, Zhengyan, Ding, Ning et al. 2021. Pre-trained models: Past, present and future. *arXiv*, 2106.07139.

Hanna, Michael, and Mareček, David. 2021. Analyzing BERT's knowledge of hypernymy via prompting. Pages 275–282 of: *4th BlackboxNLP Workshop on Analyzing and Interpreting Neural Networks for NLP*.

Harnad, Stevan. 1990. The symbol grounding problem. *Physica D*, **42**, 335–346.

Harper, Kenneth E. 1961. Procedures for the determination of distributional classes. Pages 688–698 of: *International Conference on Machine Translation of Languages and Applied Language Analysis*.

Harper, Kenneth E. 1965. Measures of similarity between nouns. Pages 688–698 of: *Proc. COLING*.

Harris, Roy. 1988. *Language, Saussure and Wittgenstein: How to Play Games with Words*. London: Routledge.

Harris, Zellig S. 1951. *Methods in Structural Linguistics*. Chicago: University of Chicago Press.

Harris, Zellig S. 1954. Distributional structure. *Word*, **10**(2–3), 146–162.

Harris, Zellig S. 1968. *Mathematical Structures of Language*. New York: Interscience Publishers.

Harris, Zellig S. 1991. *A Theory of Language and Information: A Mathematical Approach*. Oxford: Clarendon Press.

Hays, David G. 1960. Linguistic research at the RAND Corporation. Pages 13–25 of: *National Symposium on Machine Translation*.

He, Pengcheng, Liu, Xiaodong, Gao, Jianfeng, and Chen, Weizhu. 2021. DeBERTa: Decoding-enhanced BERT with disentangled attention. *arXiv*, 2006.03654.

Hearst, Marti A. 1992. Automatic acquisition of hyponyms from large text corpora. Pages 539–545 of: *Proc. COLING*.

Heim, Irene, and Kratzer, Angelika. 1998. *Semantics in Generative Grammar*. Oxford: Blackwell.

Hendrickx, Iris, Kim, Su Nam, Kozareva, Zornitsa et al. 2010. SemEval-2010 task 8: Multi-way classification of semantic relations between pairs of nominals. Pages 33–38 of: *Proc. SemEval*.

Herbelot, Aurélie, and Copestake, Ann. 2021. Ideal words: A vector-based formalisation of semantic competence. *Kunstliche Intelligenz*, **35**, 271–290.

Herbelot, Aurélie, and Ganesalingam, Mohan. 2013. Measuring semantic content in distributional vectors. Pages 440–445 of: *Proc. ACL*.

Hermann, Karl Moritz, and Blunsom, Phil. 2014. Multilingual models for compositional distributed semantics. Pages 58–68 of: *Proc. ACL*.

Heylen, Kris, Wielfaert, Thomas, Speelman, Dirk, and Geeraerts, Dirk. 2015. Monitoring polysemy: Word space models as a tool for large-scale lexical semantic analysis. *Lingua*, **157**, 153–172.

Hill, Felix, and Korhonen, Anna. 2014. Learning abstract concept embeddings from multi-modal data: Since you probably can't see what I mean. Pages 255–265 of: *Proc. EMNLP*.

Hill, Felix, Korhonen, Anna, and Bentz, Christian. 2014a. A quantitative empirical analysis of the abstract/concrete distinction. *Cognitive Science*, **38**(1), 162–177.

Hill, Felix, Reichart, Roi, and Korhonen, Anna. 2014b. Multi-modal models for concrete and abstract concept meaning. *TACL*, **2**, 285–296.

Hill, Felix, Reichart, Roi, and Korhonen, Anna. 2015. SimLex-999: Evaluating semantic models with (genuine) similarity estimation. *CL*, **41**(4), 665–695.

Hill, Felix, Cho, Kyunghyun, and Korhonen, Anna. 2016. Learning distributed representations of sentences from unlabelled data. Pages 1367–1377 of: *Proc. NAACL-HLT*.

Hindle, Donald. 1990. Noun classification from predicate-argument structures. Pages 268–275 of: *Proc. ACL*.

Hinton, Geoffrey E., McClelland, James L., and Rumelhart, David E. 1986. Distributed representations. Pages 77–109 of: Rumelhart, David E., and McClelland, James L. (eds.), *Parallel Distributed Processing*. Cambridge, MA: The MIT Press.

Hintzman, Douglas L. 1986. "Schema abstraction" in a multiple-trace memory model. *Psychological Review*, **93**(4), 411–428.

Hirschman, Lynette, Grishman, Ralph, and Sager, Naomi. 1975. Grammatically-based automatic word class formation. *Information Processing and Management*, **11**, 39–57.

Hochreiter, Sepp, and Schmidhuber, Jürgen. 1997. Long short-term memory. *Neural Computation*, **9**(8), 1735–1780.

Hoffman, Matthew, Blei, David M., and Bach, Francis. 2010. Online learning for Latent Dirichlet Allocation. Pages 856–864 of: *Proc. NIPS*.

Hoffman, Thomas, and Trousdale, Graeme (eds.). 2013. *The Oxford Handbook of Construction Grammar*. Oxford: Oxford University Press.

Hofmann, Thomas. 1999. Probabilistic Latent Semantic Indexing. Pages 50–57 of: *22nd International ACM SIGIR Conference*.

Hollenstein, Nora, de la Torre, Antonio, Langer, Nicolas, and Zhang, Ce. 2019. CogniVal: A framework for cognitive word embedding evaluation. Pages 538–549 of: *Proc. CONLL*.

Hollis, Geoff, Westbury, Chris F., and Lefsrud, Lianne. 2017. Extrapolating human judgments from Skip-Gram vector representations of word meaning. *Quarterly Journal of Experimental Psychology*, **70**(8), 1603–1619.

Honkela, Timo. 1997. *Self-Organizing Maps in Natural Language Processing*. PhD thesis, Helsinki University of Technology.

Honkela, Timo, Kaski, Samuel, Lagus, Krista, and Kohonen, Teuvo. 1998. WEBSOM: Self-Organizing Maps of document collections. *Neurocomputing*, **21**(1), 101–117.

Hovy, Dirk, and Purschke, Christoph. 2018. Capturing regional variation with distributed place representations and geographic retrofitting. Pages 4383–4394 of: *Proc. EMNLP*.

Howell, Steve R., Jankowicz, Damian, and Becker, Suzanna. 2005. A model of grounded language acquisition: Sensorimotor features improve lexical and grammatical learning. *Journal of Memory and Language*, **53**, 258–276.

Huang, Eric H., Socher, Richard, Manning, Christopher D., and Ng, Andrew Y. 2012. Improving word representations via global context and multiple word prototypes. Pages 873–882 of: *Proc. ACL*.

Huebner, Philip A., Sulem, Elior, Fisher, Cynthia, and Roth, Dan. 2021. BabyBERTa: Learning more grammar with small-scale child-directed language. Pages 624–646 of: *Proc. CoNLL*.

Hupkes, Dieuwke, Dankers, Verna, Mul, Mathijs, and Bruni, Elia. 2020. Compositionality decomposed: How do neural networks generalise? *JAIR*, **67**, 757–795.

Hutchison, Keith A., Balota, David A., Neely, James H. et al. 2013. The semantic priming project. *Behavior Research Methods*, **45**(4), 1099–1114.

Huth, Alexander G., Nishimoto, Shinji, Vu, An T., and Gallant, Jack L. 2012. A continuous semantic space describes the representation of thousands of object and action categories across the human brain. *Neuron*, **76**(6), 1210–1224.

Huth, Alexander G., De Heer, Wendy A., Griffiths, Thomas L., Theunissen, Frédéric E., and Gallant, Jack L. 2016. Natural speech reveals the semantic maps that tile human cerebral cortex. *Nature*, **532**(7600), 453–458.

Indyk, Piotr, and Motwani, Rajeev. 1998. Approximate nearest neighbors: Towards removing the curse of dimensionality. Pages 604–613 of: *30th Annual ACM Symposium on Theory of Computing*.

Jackendoff, Ray. 1990. *Semantic Structures*. Cambridge, MA: The MIT Press.

Jackendoff, Ray. 1997. *The Architecture of the Language Faculty*. Cambridge, MA: The MIT Press.

Jackendoff, Ray. 2002. *Foundations of Language: Brain, Meaning. Grammar, Evolution*. Cambridge, MA: The MIT Press.

Jakobson, Roman. 1959. On linguistic aspects of translation. Pages 232–239 of: Brower, Reuben A. (ed.), *On Translation*. Cambridge, MA: Harvard University Press.

Jamieson, Randall K., Avery, Johnathan E., Johns, Brendan T., and Jones, Michael N. 2018. An instance theory of semantic memory. *Computational Brain & Behavior*, **1**(2), 119–136.

Jastrzębski, Stanisław, Leśniak, Damian, and Czarnecki, Wojciech Marian. 2017. How to evaluate word embeddings? On importance of data efficiency and simple supervised tasks. *arXiv*, 1702.02170.

Jenkins, James J. 1954. Transitional organization: Association techniques. Pages 112–118 of: Osgood, Charles E., and Sebeok, Thomas A. (eds.), *Psycholinguistics: A Survey of Theory and Research Problems. Journal of Abnormal and Social Psychology*. Baltimore: Waverly Press.

Johns, Brendan T., and Jones, Michael N. 2012. Perceptual inference through global lexical similarity. *TopiCS*, **4**(1), 103–120.

Johns, Brendan T., and Jones, Michael N. 2015. Generating structure from experience: A retrieval-based model of language processing. *Canadian Journal of Experimental Psychology*, **69**(2), 233–251.

Johns, Brendan T., Mewhort, Douglas J. K., and Jones, Michael N. 2019. The role of negative information in distributional semantic learning. *Cognitive Science*, **43**, e12730.

Johnson, Kent. 2004. On the systematicity of language and thought. *The Journal of Philosophy*, **101**(3), 111–139.

Johnson, William, and Lindenstrauss, Joram. 1984. Extensions of Lipschitz mappings into a Hilbert space. Pages 189–206 of: *Conference in Modern Analysis and Probability*, Vol. 26.

Jones, Michael N. 2019. When does abstraction occur in semantic memory: Insights from distributional models. *Language, Cognition and Neuroscience*, **34**(10), 1338–1346.

Jones, Michael N., and Mewhort, Douglas J. K. 2007. Representing word meaning and order information in a composite holographic lexicon. *Psychological Review*, **22**(6), 701–708.

Jones, Michael N., Kintsch, Walter, and Mewhort, Douglas J. K. 2006. High-dimensional semantic space accounts of priming. *Journal of Memory and Language*, **55**(4), 534–552.

Jones, Michael N., Willits, Jon A., and Dennis, Simon. 2015. Models of semantic memory. Pages 232–254 of: Busemeyer, Jerome R., Wang, Zheng, Townsend, James T., and Eidels, Ami (eds.), *Oxford Handbook of Mathematical and Computational Psychology*. Oxford: Oxford University Press.

Jones, Paul E. 1964. Historical foundations of research on statistical association techniques for mechanized documentation. Pages 3–8 of: *Symposium on Statistical Association Methods for Mechanized Documentation*.

Jones, Susan, and Sinclair, John M. 1974. English lexical collocations: A study in computational linguistics. *Cahiers de Lexicologie*, **24**, 15–61.

Joos, Martin. 1950. Description of language design. *Journal of the Acoustical Society of America*, **114**(1), 1–37.

Joulin, Armand, Bojanowski, Piotr, Mikolov, Tomas, Jégou, Hervé, and Grave, Edouard. 2018. Loss in translation: Learning bilingual word mapping with a retrieval criterion. Pages 2979–2984 of: *Proc. EMNLP*.

Jouravlev, Olessia, and McRae, Ken. 2016. Thematic relatedness production norms for 100 object concepts. *Behavior Research Methods*, **48**, 1349–1357.

Judea, Alex, Nastase, Vivi, and Strube, Michael. 2012. Concept-based selectional preferences and distributional representations from Wikipedia articles. Pages 2985–2990 of: *Proc. LREC*.

Jurafsky, Daniel, and Martin, James A. 2008. *Speech and Language Processing: An Introduction to Natural Language Processing, Computational Linguistics, and Speech Recognition*, 2nd ed. Upper Saddle River: Prentice Hall.

Jurgens, David A., and Stevens, Keith. 2009. Event detection in blogs using temporal Random Indexing. Pages 9–16 of: *Workshop on Events in Emerging Text Types*.

Jurgens, David A., and Stevens, Keith. 2010. HERMIT: Flexible clustering for the SemEval-2 WSI task. Pages 359–362 of: *Proc. SemEval*.

Jurgens, David A., Mohammad, Saif M., Turney, Peter D., and Holyoak, Keith J. 2012. SemEval-2012 task 2: Measuring degrees of relational similarity. Pages 356–364 of: *Proc. *SEM*.

Jurgens, David A., Pilehvar, Mohammad Taher, and Navigli, Roberto. 2014. SemEval-2014 task 3: Cross-level semantic similarity. Pages 17–26 of: *Proc. *SEM*.

Justeson, John S., and Katz, Slava M. 1991. Co-occurrences of antonymous adjectives and their contexts. *CL*, **17**(1), 1–19.

Kalchbrenner, Nal, Grefenstette, Edward, and Blunsom, Phil. 2014. A convolutional neural network for modelling sentences. Pages 655–665 of: *Proc. ACL*.

Kamath, Aishwarya, Pfeiffer, Jonas, Ponti, Edoardo Maria, Glavaš, Goran, and Vulić, Ivan. 2019. Specializing distributional vectors of all words for lexical entailment. Pages 72–83 of: *4th Workshop on Representation Learning for NLP*.

Kamp, Hans, and Reyle, Uwe. 1993. *From Discourse to Logic: Introduction to Modeltheoretic Semantics of Natural Language, Formal Logic and Discourse Representation Theory*. Dordrecht: Kluwer.

Kanerva, Pantti. 1988. *Sparse Distributed Memory*. Cambridge, MA: The MIT Press.

Kanerva, Pentti. 2009. Hyperdimensional computing: An introduction to computing in distributed representation with high-dimensional random vectors. *Cognitive Computation*, **1**(2), 139–159.

Kanerva, Pentti, Kristofersson, Jan, and Holst, Anders. 2000. Random indexing of text samples for Latent Semantic Analysis. Page 1036 of: *Proc. COGSCI*.

Karlgren, Jussi, and Sahlgren, Magnus. 2001. From words to understanding. Pages 294–308 of: Uesaka, Yoshinori, Kanerva, Pentti, and Asoh, Hideki (eds.), *Foundations of Real-World Intelligence*. Stanford: CSLI Publications.

Kartsaklis, Dimitri, and Sadrzadeh, Mehrnoosh. 2014. A study of entanglement in a categorical framework of natural language. Pages 249–261 of: *Quantum Physics and Logic Conference*.

Kaski, Samuel. 1998. Dimensionality reduction by random mapping: Fast similarity computation for clustering. Pages 413–418 of: *International Joint Conference on Neural Networks*.

Katz, Jerrold J., and Fodor, Jerry A. 1963. The structure of a semantic theory. *Language*, **39**(2), 170–210.

Keenan, Edward L., and Comrie, Bernard. 1977. Noun phrase accessibility hierarchy and universal grammar. *Linguistic Inquiry*, **8**(1), 63–99.

Keuleers, Emmanuel, and Balota, David A. 2015. Megastudies, crowdsourcing, and large datasets in psycholinguistics: An overview of recent developments. *The Quarterly Journal of Experimental Psychology*, **68**(8), 1457–1468.

Kiela, Douwe. 2016. MMFEAT: A toolkit for extracting multi-modal features. Pages 55–60 of: *Proc. ACL*.

Kiela, Douwe, and Bottou, Léon. 2014. Learning image embeddings using convolutional neural networks for improved multi-modal semantics. Pages 36–45 of: *Proc. EMNLP*.

Kiela, Douwe, and Clark, Stephen. 2014. A systematic study of semantic vector space model parameters. Pages 21–30 of: *2nd Workshop on Continuous Vector Space Models and their Compositionality*.

Kiela, Douwe, and Clark, Stephen. 2015. Multi- and cross-modal semantics beyond vision: Grounding in auditory perception. Pages 2461–2470 of: *Proc. EMNLP*.

Kiela, Douwe, Hill, Felix, Korhonen, Anna, and Clark, Stephen. 2014. Improving multi-modal representations using image dispersion: Why less is sometimes more. Pages 835–841 of: *Proc. ACL*.

Kiela, Douwe, Rimell, Laura, Vulić, Ivan, and Clark, Stephen. 2015a. Exploiting image generality for lexical entailment detection. Pages 119–124 of: *Proc. ACL*.

Kiela, Douwe, Bulat, Luana, and Clark, Stephen. 2015b. Grounding semantics in olfactory perception. Pages 231–236 of: *Proc. ACL*.

Kiela, Douwe, Hill, Felix, and Clark, Stephen. 2015c. Specializing word embeddings for similarity or relatedness. Pages 2044–2048 of: *Proc. EMNLP*.

Kilgarriff, Adam. 1997. I don't believe in word senses. *Computers and the Humanities*, **31**, 91–113.

Kilgarriff, Adam. 2007. Word senses. Pages 29–46 of: Agirre, Eneko, and Edmonds, Philip (eds.), *Word Sense Disambiguation: Algorithms and Applications*. Berlin: Springer.

Kim, Joo-Kyung, and de Marneffe, Marie-Catherine. 2013. Deriving adjectival scales from continuous space word representations. Pages 1625–1630 of: *Proc. EMNLP*.

Kim, Judy Sein, Aheimer, Brianna, Manrara, Verónica Montané, and Bedny, Marina. 2021. Shared understanding of color among sighted and blind adults. *Proceedings of the National Academy of Sciences*, **118**(33), e2020192118.

Kim, Yoon. 2014. Convolutional neural networks for sentence classification. Pages 1746–1751 of: *Proc. EMNLP*.

Kim, Yoon, Chiu, Yi-I, Hanaki, Kentaro, Hegde, Darshan, and Petrov, Slav. 2014. Temporal analysis of language through neural language models. Pages 61–65 of: *Workshop on Language Technologies and Computational Social Science*.

Kim, Yoon, Jernite, Yacine, Sontag, David, and Rush, Alexander M. 2016. Character-aware neural language models. Pages 2741–2749 of: *Proc. AAAI*.

Kintsch, Walter. 2001. Predication. *Cognitive Science*, **25**(2), 173–202.

Kipper, Karin, Korhonen, Anna, Ryant, Neville, and Palmer, Martha. 2008. A large-scale classification of English verbs. *LRE*, **42**(1), 21–40.

Kiros, Ryan, Zhu, Yukun, Salakhutdinov, Ruslan et al. 2015. Skip-Thought vectors. Pages 3294–3302 of: *Proc. NIPS*.

Kiss, George R., Armstrong, Christine, Milroy, Robert, and Piper, James. 1973. An associative thesaurus of English and its computer analysis. Pages 153–165 of: Aitken, Adam J., Bailey, Richard W., and Hamilton-Smith, Neil (eds.), *The Computer and Literary Studies*. Edinburgh: Edinburgh University Press.

Klafka, Josef, and Ettinger, Allyson. 2020. Spying on your neighbors: Fine-grained probing of contextual embeddings for information about surrounding words. Pages 4801–4811 of: *Proc. ACL*.

Klapaftis, Ioannis P., and Manandhar, Suresh. 2008. Word sense induction using graphs of collocations. Pages 298–302 of: *18th European Conference on Artificial Intelligence*.

Klementiev, Alexander, Titov, Ivan, and Bhattarai, Binod. 2012. Inducing crosslingual distributed representations of words. Pages 1459–1474 of: *Proc. COLING*.

Kohonen, Teuvo. 1989. *Self-Organization and Associative Memory*. New York, Springer-Verlag.

Kohonen, Teuvo. 1995. *Self-Organizing Maps*. New York: Springer-Verlag.

Kolda, Tamara. 2006. *Multilinear Operators for Higher-Order Decompositions.* Technical Report 2081, SANDIA.

Kolda, Tamara, and Bader, Brett. 2009. Tensor decompositions and applications. *SIAM Review,* **51**(3), 455–500.

Köper, Maximilian, Scheible, Christian, and Schulte im Walde, Sabine. 2015. Multilingual reliability and "semantic" structure of continuous word spaces. Pages 40–45 of: *Proc. IWCS.*

Koptjevskaja Tamm, Maria, and Sahlgren, Magnus. 2014. Temperature in word space: Sense exploration of temperature expressions using word-space modelling. Pages 231–267 of: Szmrecsanyi, Benedikt, and Wälchli, Bernhard (eds.), *Aggregating Dialectology, Typology, and Register Analysis.* Berlin: De Gruyter.

Korhonen, Anna. 2002. *Subcategorization Acquisition.* PhD thesis, University of Cambridge.

Kotlerman, Lili, Dagan, Ido, Szpektor, Idan, and Zhitomirsky-Geffet, Maayan. 2010. Directional distributional similarity for lexical inference. *Natural Language Engineering,* **16**(4), 359–389.

Kousta, Stavroula T., Vigliocco, Gabriella, Vinson, David P., Andrews, Mark, and Del Campo, Elena. 2011. The representation of abstract words: Why emotion matters. *Journal of Experimental Psychology: General,* **140**(1), 14–34.

Kovaleva, Olga, Romanov, Alexey, Rogers, Anna, and Rumshisky, Anna. 2019. Revealing the dark secrets of BERT. Pages 4364–4373 of: *Proc. EMNLP.*

Kremer, Gerhard, Erk, Katrin, Padó, Sebastian, and Thater, Stefan. 2014. What substitutes tell us: Analysis of an "all-words" lexical substitution corpus. Pages 540–549 of: *Proc. EACL.*

Kriegeskorte, Nikolaus, and Kievit, Rogier A. 2013. Representational geometry: Integrating cognition, computation, and the brain. *Trends in Cognitive Sciences,* **17**(8), 401–412.

Kriegeskorte, Nikolaus, Mur, Marieke, and Bandettini, Peter. 2008. Representational similarity analysis: Connecting the branches of systems neuroscience. *Frontiers in Systems Neuroscience,* **2**(4).

Krishna, Ranjay, Zhu, Yuke, Groth, Oliver et al. 2017. Visual Genome: Connecting language and vision using crowdsourced dense image annotations. *International Journal of Computer Vision,* **123**(1), 32–73.

Krizhevsky, Alex, Sutskever, Ilya, and Hinton, Geoffrey E. 2012. ImageNet classification with deep convolutional neural networks. In: *Proc. NIPS.*

Kulkarni, Vivek, Al-Rfou, Rami, Perozzi, Bryan, and Skiena, Steven. 2015. Statistically significant detection of linguistic change. Pages 625–635 of: *24th International Conference on World Wide Web.*

Kumar, Abhilasha A. 2021. Semantic memory: A review of methods, models, and current challenges. *Psychonomic Bulletin and Review,* **28**, 40–80.

Kutuzov, Andrey, Øvrelid, Lilja, Szymanski, Terrence, and Velldal, Erik. 2018. Diachronic word embeddings and semantic shifts: A survey. Pages 1384–1397 of: *Proc. COLING.*

Lake, Brenden M., and Baroni, Marco. 2018. Generalization without systematicity: On the compositional skills of sequence-to-sequence recurrent networks. Pages 4487–4499 of: *Proc. ICML.*

Lake, Brenden M., and Murphy, Gregory L. 2021. Word meaning in minds and machines. *Psychological Review*, **130**(2), 401–431.

Landau, Barbara, and Gleitman, Lila. 1985. *Language and Experience: Evidence from the Blind Child*. Cambridge, MA: The MIT Press.

Landauer, Thomas K., and Dumais, Susan. 1997. A solution to Plato's problem: The Latent Semantic Analysis theory of acquisition, induction, and representation of knowledge. *Psychological Review*, **104**(2), 211–240.

Landauer, Thomas K., McNamara, Danielle S., Dennis, Simon, and Kintsch, Walter (eds.). 2007. *Handbook of Latent Semantic Analysis*. Mahwah: Lawrence Erlbaum.

Lapata, Mirella, and Lascarides, Alex. 2003. A probabilistic account of logical metonymy. *CL*, **29**(2), 261–315.

Lapesa, Gabriella, and Evert, Stefan. 2014. A large scale evaluation of distributional semantic models: Parameters, interactions and model selection. *TACL*, **2**, 531–545.

Lapesa, Gabriella, and Evert, Stefan. 2017. Large-scale evaluation of dependency-based DSMs: Are they worth the effort? Pages 394–400 of: *Proc. EACL*.

Laroche, Audrey, and Langlais, Philippe. 2010. Revisiting context-based projection methods for term-translation spotting in comparable corpora. Pages 617–625 of: *Proc. COLING*.

Lascarides, Alex, and Copestake, Ann. 1998. Pragmatics and word meaning. *Journal of Linguistics*, **34**, 378–414.

Lau, Jey Han, Cook, Paul, McCarthy, Diana, Newman, David, and Baldwin, Timothy. 2012. Word sense induction for novel sense detection. Pages 591–601 of: *Proc. EACL*.

Lauwers, Peter, and Willems, Dominique. 2011. Coercion: Definition and challenges, current approaches, and new trends. *Linguistics*, **49**(6), 1219–1235.

Lazaridou, Angeliki, Bruni, Elia, and Baroni, Marco. 2014. Is this a wampimuk? Cross-modal mapping between distributional semantics and the visual world. Pages 1403–1414 of: *Proc. ACL*.

Lazaridou, Angeliki, Pham, Nghia The, and Baroni, Marco. 2015a. Combining language and vision with a multimodal Skip-Gram model. Pages 153–163 of: *Proc. NAACL-HLT*.

Lazaridou, Angeliki, Dinu, Georgiana, Liska, Adam, and Baroni, Marco. 2015b. From visual attributes to adjectives through decompositional distributional semantics. *TACL*, **3**, 183–196.

Lazaridou, Angeliki, Dinu, Georgiana, and Baroni, Marco. 2015c. Hubness and pollution: Delving into cross-space mapping for zero-shot learning. Pages 270–280 of: *Proc. ACL*.

Lazaridou, Angeliki, Marelli, Marco, and Baroni, Marco. 2017. Multimodal word meaning induction from minimal exposure to natural text. *Cognitive Science*, **41**, 677–705.

Le, Quoc V., and Mikolov, Tomas. 2014. Distributed representations of sentences and documents. Pages 1188–1196 of: *Proc. ICML*.

Lebret, Rémi, and Collobert, Ronan. 2014. Word embeddings through Hellinger PCA. Pages 482–490 of: *Proc. EACL*.

Lebret, Rémi, and Collobert, Ronan. 2015. Rehabilitation of count-based models for word vector representations. Pages 417–429 of: *International Conference on Intelligent Text Processing and Computational Linguistics*.

LeCun, Yann, Bottou, Léon, Bengio, Yoshua, and Haffner, Patrick. 1998. Gradient-based learning applied to document recognition. *Proceedings of the IEEE*, **86**(11), 2278–2323.

LeCun, Yann A., Bottou, Léon, Orr, Genevieve B., and Müller, Klaus-Robert. 2012. Efficient backprop. Pages 9–48 of: Montavon, Grégoire, Orr, Geneviève B., and Müller, Klaus-Robert (eds.), *Neural Networks: Tricks of the Trade*. Berlin: Springer.

Lee, Daniel D., and Seung, H. Sebastian. 2001. Algorithms for Non-negative Matrix Factorization. Pages 556–562 of: *Proc. NIPS*.

Lee, Lillian. 1999. Measures of distributional similarity. Pages 25–32 of: *Proc. ACL*.

Lemaire, Benoît, and Denhière, Guy. 2006. Effects of high-order co-occurrences on word semantic similarity. *Current Psychology Letters*, **18**(1), 2–12.

Lenci, Alessandro. 2008. Distributional approaches in linguistic and cognitive research. *Italian Journal of Linguistics*, **20**(1), 1–31.

Lenci, Alessandro. 2011. Composing and updating verb argument expectations: A distributional semantic model. Pages 58–66 of: *2nd Workshop on Cognitive Modeling and Computational Linguistics*.

Lenci, Alessandro. 2018. Distributional models of word meaning. *Annual Review of Linguistics*, **4**, 151–171.

Lenci, Alessandro, and Benotto, Giulia. 2012. Identifying hypernyms in distributional semantic spaces. Pages 75–79 of: *Proc. *SEM*.

Lenci, Alessandro, and Sandu, Gabriel. 2009. Logic and linguistics in the twentieth century. Pages 775–847 of: Haaparanta, Leila (ed.), *The Development of Modern Logic*. Oxford: Oxford University Press.

Lenci, Alessandro, Baroni, Marco, Cazzolli, Giulia, and Marotta, Giovanna. 2013. BLIND: A set of semantic feature norms from the congenitally blind. *Behavior Research Methods*, **45**(4), 1218–1233.

Lenci, Alessandro, Lebani, Gianluca E., and Passaro, Lucia C. 2018. The emotions of abstract words: A distributional semantic analysis. *TopiCS*, **10**(3), 550–572.

Lenci, Alessandro, Sahlgren, Magnus, Jeunieaux, Patrick, Cuba Gyllensten, Amaru, and Miliani, Martina. 2022. A comparative evaluation of three generations of Distributional Semantic Models. *Language Resources and Evaluation*, **56**, 1269–1313.

Levesque, Hector J. 2011. The Winograd schema challenge. Pages 63–68 of: *CommonSense-11 Symposium*.

Leviant, Ira, and Reichart, Roi. 2015. Separated by an un-common language: Towards judgment language informed vector space modeling. *arXiv*, 1508.00106.

Levin, Beth. 1993. *English Verb Classes and Alternations: A Preliminary Investigation*. Chicago: University of Chicago Press.

Levin, Beth, and Rappaport Hovav, Malka. 2005. *Argument Realization*. Cambridge: Cambridge University Press.

Levy, Omer, and Goldberg, Yoav. 2014a. Dependency-based word embeddings. Pages 302–308 of: *Proc. ACL*.

Levy, Omer, and Goldberg, Yoav. 2014b. Linguistic regularities in sparse and explicit word representations. Pages 171–180 of: *Proc. CoNLL*.

Levy, Omer, and Goldberg, Yoav. 2014c. Neural word embedding as implicit matrix factorization. In: *Proc. NIPS*.

Levy, Omer, Remus, Steffen, Biemann, Chris, and Dagan, Ido. 2015a. Do supervised distributional methods really learn lexical inference relations? Pages 970–976 of: *Proc. NAACL-HLT.*

Levy, Omer, Goldberg, Yoav, and Dagan, Ido. 2015b. Improving distributional similarity with lessons learned from word embeddings. *TACL*, **3**, 211–225.

Levy, Omer, Hill, Felix, Korhonen, Anna et al. (eds.). 2016. *1st Workshop on Evaluating Vector Space Representations for NLP.* Berlin: ACL.

Levy, Ran, Ein-Dor, Liat, Hummel, Shay, Rinott, Ruty, and Slonim, Noam. 2015c. TR9856: A multi-word term relatedness benchmark. Pages 419–424 of: *Proc. ACL.*

Lewis, David. 1970. General semantics. *Synthese*, **22**(1/2), 18–67.

Lewis, David D., Yang, Yiming, Rose, Tony G., and Li, Fan. 2004. RCV1: A new benchmark collection for text categorization research. *Journal of Machine Learning Research*, **5**, 361–397.

Lewis, Mike, Liu, Yinhan, Goyal, Naman et al. 2020. BART: Denoising sequence-to-sequence pre-training for natural language generation, translation, and comprehension. Pages 7871–7880 of: *Proc. ACL.*

Lewis, Molly, Zettersten, Martin, and Lupyan, Gary. 2019. Distributional semantics as a source of visual knowledge. *Proceedings of the National Academy of Sciences*, **116**(39), 19237–19238.

Lewis, Peter A. W., Baxendale, Phyllis B., and Bennett, John L. 1967. Statistical discrimination of the synonymy/antonymy relationship between words. *Journal of the Association for Computing Machinery*, **14**(1), 20–44.

Li, Bofang, Tao, Liu, Zhao, Zhe et al. 2017. Investigating different context types and representations for learning word embeddings. Pages 2411–2421 of: *Proc. EMNLP.*

Li, Jiangtian, and Joanisse, Marc F. 2021. Word senses as clusters of meaning modulations: A computational model of polysemy. *Cognitive Science*, **45**(4), e12955.

Li, Jiwei, and Jurafsky, Dan. 2015. Do multi-sense embeddings improve natural language understanding? Pages 1722–1732 of: *Proc. EMNLP.*

Li, Jiwei, Luong, Thang, and Jurafsky, Dan. 2015. A hierarchical neural autoencoder for paragraphs and documents. Pages 1106–1115 of: *Proc. ACL.*

Li, Ping, and Zhao, Xiaowei. 2013. Self-organizing map models of language acquisition. *Frontiers in Psychology*, **4**, 1–15.

Li, Ping, Hastie, Trevor, and Church, Kenneth. 2006. Very sparse random projections. Pages 287–296 of: *12th International Conference on Knowledge Discovery and Data Mining.*

Li, Ping, Zhao, Xiaowei, and Mac Whinney, Brian. 2007. Dynamic self-organization and early lexical development in children. *Cognitive Science*, **31**, 581–612.

Liang, Percy, and Potts, Christopher. 2015. Bringing machine learning and compositional semantics together. *Annual Review of Linguistics*, **1**, 355–376.

Light, Marc, and Greiff, Warren. 2002. Statistical models for the induction and use of selectional preferences. *Cognitive Science*, **26**, 269–281.

Lin, Dekang. 1998a. Automatic retrieval and clustering of similar words. Pages 768–774 of: *Proc. COLING-ACL.*

Lin, Dekang. 1998b. An information-theoretic definition of similarity. Pages 296–304 of: *Proc. ICML.*

Lin, Dekang, and Pantel, Patrick. 2001. Discovery of inference rules for question answering. *Natural Language Engineering*, **7**, 343–360.

Lin, Dekang, Zhao, Shaojun, Qin, Lijuan, and Zhou, Ming. 2003. Identifying synonyms among distributionally similar words. Pages 1492–1493 of: *Proc. IJCAI.*

Linzen, Tal. 2016. Issues in evaluating semantic spaces using word analogies. Pages 13–18 of: *1st Workshop on Evaluating Vector Space Representations for NLP.*

Lipton, Zachary C. 2018. The mythos of model interpretability. *Communications of the ACM*, **61**(10), 35–43.

Liu, Pengfei, Yuan, Weizhe, Fu, Jinlan et al. 2021. Pre-train, prompt, and predict: A systematic survey of prompting methods in natural language processing. *arXiv*, 2107.13586.

Liu, Qi, Kusner, Matt J., and Blunsom, Phil. 2020. A survey on contextual embeddings. *arXiv*, 2003.07278.

Liu, Yinhan, Ott, Myle, Goyal, Naman et al. 2019. RoBERTa: A robustly optimized BERT pretraining approach. *arXiv*, 1907.11692.

Lopopolo, Alessandro, and Van Mieltenburg, Emiel. 2015. Sound-based distributional models. Pages 70–75 of: *Proc. IWCS.*

Loula, João, Baroni, Marco, and Lake, Brenden M. 2018. Rearranging the familiar: Testing compositional generalization in recurrent networks. Pages 108–114 of: *1st BlackboxNLP Workshop on Analyzing and Interpreting Neural Networks for NLP.*

Louwerse, Max M. 2008. Embodied relations are encoded in language. *Psychonomic Bulletin & Review*, **15**(4), 838–844.

Louwerse, Max M. 2011. Symbol interdependency in symbolic and embodied cognition. *TopiCS*, **3**(2), 273–302.

Louwerse, Max M., and Benesh, Nick. 2012. Representing spatial structure through maps and language: Lord of the Rings encodes the spatial structure of Middle Earth. *Cognitive Science*, **36**(8), 1556–1569.

Louwerse, Max M., and Connell, Louise. 2011. A taste of words: Linguistic context and perceptual simulation predict the modality of words. *Cognitive Science*, **35**(2), 381–398.

Louwerse, Max M., and Zwaan, Rolf A. 2009. Language encodes geographical information. *Cognitive Science*, **33**(1), 51–73.

Lowe, Will. 2000. *Topographic Maps of Semantic Space.* PhD thesis, University of Edinburgh.

Lowe, Will. 2001. Towards a theory of semantic space. Pages 576–581 of: *Proc. COGSCI.*

Lu, Jiasen, Batra, Dhruv, Parikh, Devi, and Lee, Stefan. 2019. ViLBERT: Pretraining task-agnostic visiolinguistic representations for vision-and-language tasks. In: *Proc. NIPS.*

Luhn, Hans P. 1957. A statistical approach to mechanized encoding and searching of literary information. *IBM Journal of Research and Development*, **1**(4), 309–317.

Luhn, Hans P. 1958. Automatic creation of literature abstracts. *IBM Journal of Research and Development*, **2**(2), 159–165.

Lund, Kevin, and Burgess, Curt. 1996. Producing high-dimensional semantic spaces from lexical co-occurrence. *Behavior Research Methods, Instruments, & Computers*, **28**, 203–208.

Lund, Kevin, Burgess, Curt, and Atchley, Ruth A. 1995. Semantic and associative priming in high-dimensional semantic space. Pages 660–665 of: *Proc. COGSCI*.

Luong, Minh-Thang, Socher, Richard, and Manning, Christopher D. 2013. Better word representations with recursive neural networks for morphology. Pages 104–113 of: *Proc. CoNLL*.

Luong, Minh-Thang, Pham, Hieu, and Manning, Christopher D. 2015. Bilingual word representations with monolingual quality in mind. Pages 151–159 of: *Proc. NAACL-HLT*.

Lupyan, Gary. 2019. Language as a source of abstract concepts. *Physics of Life Reviews*, **29**, 154–156.

Lupyan, Gary, and Lewis, Molly. 2019. From words-as-mappings to words-as-cues: The role of language in semantic knowledge. *Language, Cognition and Neuroscience*, **34**, 1319–1337.

Maas, Andrew L., Delay, Raymond E., Pham, Peter T. et al. 2011. Learning word vectors for sentiment analysis. Pages 142–150 of: *Proc. ACL*.

Maas, Anne. 1999. Linguistic intergroup bias: Stereotype perpetuation through language. *Advances in Experimental Social Psychology*, **31**, 79–121.

MacWhinney, Brian (ed.). 1999. *The Emergence of Language*. Mahwah: Lawrence Erlbaum.

MacWhinney, Brian. 2000. *The CHILDES Project: Tools for Analyzing Talk*, 3rd ed. Mahwah: Lawrence Erlbaum.

MacWhinney, Brian, and O'Grady, William (eds.). 2015. *The Handbook of Language Emergence*. Mahwah: Wiley-Blackwell.

Maillard, Jean, Clark, Stephen, and Grefenstette, Edward. 2015. A type-driven tensor-based semantics for CCG. Pages 46–54 of: *EACL 2014 Workshop on Type Theory and Natural Language Semantics*.

Mandera, Paweł, Keuleers, Emmanuel, and Brysbaert, Marc. 2015. How useful are corpus-based methods for extrapolating psycholinguistic variables? *The Quarterly Journal of Experimental Psychology*, **68**(8), 1623–1642.

Mandera, Paweł, Keuleers, Emmanuel, and Brysbaert, Marc. 2017. Explaining human performance in psycholinguistic tasks with models of semantic similarity based on prediction and counting: A review and empirical validation. *Journal of Memory and Language*, **92**, 57–78.

Manning, Christopher D., and Schütze, Hinrich. 1999. *Foundations of Statistical Natural Language Processing*. Cambridge, MA: The MIT Press.

Manning, Christopher D., Raghavan, Prabhakar, and Schütze, Hinrich. 2008. *Introduction to Information Retrieval*. Cambridge: Cambridge University Press.

Manning, Christopher D., Surdeanu, Mihai, Bauer, John et al. 2014. The Stanford CoreNLP natural language processing toolkit. Pages 55–60 of: *Proc. ACL*.

Manning, Christopher D., Clark, Kevin, Hewitt, John, Khandelwal, Urvashi, and Levy, Omer. 2020. Emergent linguistic structure in artificial neural networks trained by self-supervision. *Proceedings of the National Academy of Sciences*, **117**(48), 30046–30054.

Marconi, Diego. 1997. *Lexical Competence*. Cambridge, MA: The MIT Press.

Marconi, Diego, Manenti, Rosa, Catricalà, Eleonora et al. 2013. The neural substrates of inferential and referential semantic processing. *Cortex*, **49**(8), 2055–2066.

Marcus, Gary F. 2001. *The Algebraic Mind: Integrating Connectionism and Cognitive Science*. Cambridge, MA: The MIT Press.

Marelli, Marco, and Baroni, Marco. 2015. Affixation in semantic space: Modeling morpheme meanings with compositional distributional semantics. *Psychological Review*, **122**(3), 485–515.

Marelli, Marco, Menini, Stefano, Baroni, Marco et al. 2014. A SICK cure for the evaluation of compositional distributional semantic models. Pages 216–223 of: *Proc. LREC*.

Marelli, Marco, Gagné, Christina L., and Spalding, Thomas L. 2017. Compounding as abstract operation in semantic space: Investigating relational effects through a large-scale, data-driven computational model. *Cognition*, **166**, 207–224.

Markman, Arthur B. 1999. *Knowledge Representation*. Mahwah: Lawrence Erlbaum.

Markman, Arthur B., and Gentner, Dedre. 1993. Structural alignment during similarity comparisons. *Cognitive Psychology*, **25**, 431–467.

Marr, David. 1982. *Vision: A Computational Investigation into the Human Representation and Processing of Visual Information*. New York: Freeman.

Martin, Andrea E., and Baggio, Giosuè. 2019. Modelling meaning composition from formalism to mechanism. *Philosophical Transactions of the Royal Society B*, **375**, 20190298.

Martin, Dian I., and Berry, Michael W. 2007. Mathematical foundations behind Latent Semantic Analysis. Pages 35–55 of: Landauer, Thomas K., McNamara, Danielle S., Dennis, Simon, and Kintsch, Walter (eds.), *Handbook of Latent Semantic Analysis*. Mahwah: Lawrence Erlbaum.

McCann, Bryan, Bradbury, James, Xiong, Caiming, and Socher, Richard. 2017. Learned in translation: Contextualized word vectors. In: *Proc. NIPS*.

McCarthy, Diana, and Navigli, Roberto. 2009. The English lexical substitution task. *LRE*, **43**(2), 139–159.

McClelland, James L., Botvinick, Matthew M., Noelle, David C. et al. 2010. Letting structure emerge: Connectionist and dynamical systems approaches to cognition. *Trends in Cognitive Sciences*, **14**(8), 348–356.

McCoy, R. Thomas, Pavlick, Ellie, and Linzen, Tal. 2019a. Right for the wrong reasons: Diagnosing syntactic heuristics in natural language inference. Pages 3428–3448 of: *Proc. ACL*.

McCoy, R. Thomas, Linzen, Tal, Dunbar, Ewan, and Smolensky, Paul. 2019b. RNNs implicitly implement tensor-product representations. In: *Proc. ICLR*.

McElree, Brian, Traxler, Matthew J., Pickering, Martin J., Seely, Rachel E., and Jackendoff, Ray. 2001. Reading time evidence for enriched composition. *Cognition*, **78**, B17–B25.

McNally, Louise. 2017. Kinds, descriptions of kinds, concepts, and distributions. Pages 39–61 of: Balogh, Kata, and Petersen, Wiebke (eds.), *Bridging Formal and Conceptual Semantics*. Düsseldorf: Düsseldorf University Press.

McNally, Louise, and Boleda, Gemma. 2016. Conceptual vs. referential affordance in concept. Pages 1–20 of: Hampton, James A., and Winter, Yoad (eds.), *Compositionality and Concepts in Linguistics and Psychology*. Berlin: Springer Verlag.

McNamara, Timothy P. 2005. *Semantic Priming: Perspectives from Memory and Word Recognition*. New York: Psychology Press.

McRae, Ken, and Jones, Michael N. 2013. Semantic memory. Pages 206–219 of: Reisberg, Daniel (ed.), *The Oxford Handbook of Cognitive Psychology*. Oxford: Oxford University Press.

McRae, Ken, and Matsuki, Kazunaga. 2009. People use their knowledge of common events to understand language, and do so as quickly as possible. *Language and Linguistics Compass*, **3**(6), 1417–1429.

McRae, Ken, de Sa, Virginia R., and Seidenberg, Mark S. 1997a. On the nature and scope of featural representations of word meaning. *Journal of Experimental Psychology: General*, **126**(2), 99–130.

McRae, Ken, Ferretti, Todd R., and Amyote, Liane. 1997b. Thematic roles as verb-specific concepts. *Language and Cognitive Processes*, **12**(2/3), 137–176.

McRae, Ken, Spivey-Knowlton, Michael J., and Tanenhaus, Michael K. 1998. Modeling the influence of thematic fit (and other constraints) in on-line sentence comprehension. *Journal of Memory and Language*, **38**, 283–312.

McRae, Ken, Hare, Mary, Elman, Jeffrey L., and Ferretti, Todd R. 2005a. A basis for generating expectancies for verbs from nouns. *Memory & Cognition*, **33**(7), 1174–1184.

McRae, Ken, Cree, George S., Seidenberg, Mark S., and McNorgan, Chris. 2005b. Semantic feature production norms for a large set of living and nonliving things. *Behavior Research Methods*, **37**(4), 547–559.

McRae, Ken, Khalkhali, Saman, and Hare, Mary. 2012. Semantic and associative relations: Examining a tenuous dichotomy. Pages 39–66 of: Reyna, Valerie F., Chapman, Sandra B., Dougherty, Michael R., and Confrey, Jere (eds.), *The Adolescent Brain: Learning, Reasoning, and Decision Making*. Washington, DC: APA.

Medin, Douglas L., Goldstone, Robert L., and Gentner, Dedre. 1990. Similarity involving attributes and relations: Judgments of similarity and difference are not inverses. *Psychological Science*, **1**(1), 64–69.

Medin, Douglas L., Goldstone, Robert L., and Gentner, Dedre. 1993. Respects for similarity. *Psychological Review*, **100**(2), 254–278.

Melamud, Oren, Dagan, Ido, Goldberger, Jacob, Szpektor, Idan, and Yuret, Deniz. 2014. Probabilistic modeling of joint-context in distributional similarity. Pages 181–190 of: *Proc. ACL*.

Melamud, Oren, Dagan, Ido, and Goldberger, Jacob. 2015. Modeling word meaning in context with substitute vectors. Pages 472–482 of: *Proc. NAACL-HLT*.

Melamud, Oren, Goldberger, Jacob, and Dagan, Ido. 2016a. Context2vec: Learning generic context embedding with bidirectional LSTM. Pages 51–61 of: *Proc. CoNLL*.

Melamud, Oren, McClosky, David, Patwardhan, Siddharth, and Bansal, Mohit. 2016b. The role of context types and dimensionality in learning word embeddings. Pages 1030–1040 of: *Proc. NAACL-HLT*.

Merrill, William, Goldberg, Yoav, Schwartz, Roy, and Smith, Noah A. 2021. Provable limitations of acquiring meaning from ungrounded form: What will future language models understand? *TACL*, **9**, 1047–1060.

Meteyard, Lotte, Rodriguez Cuadrado, Sara, Bahrami, Bahador, and Vigliocco, Gabriella. 2012. Coming of age: A review of embodiment and the neuroscience of semantics. *Cortex*, **48**, 788–804.

Metheniti, Eleni, Van de Cruys, Tim, and Hathout, Nabil. 2020. How relevant are selectional preferences for transformer-based language models? Pages 1266–1278 of: *Proc. COLING.*

Mickus, Timothee, Paperno, Denis, Constant, Mathieu, and van Deemter, Kees. 2020. What do you mean, BERT? Assessing BERT as a distributional semantics model. Pages 235–245 of: *Society for Computation in Linguistics.*

Miikkulainen, Risto. 1997. Dyslexic and category-specific aphasic impairments in a self-organizing feature map model of the lexicon. *Brain and Language*, **59**(2), 334–366.

Mikolov, Tomas, Sutskever, Ilya, Chen, Kai, Corrado, Greg S., and Dean, Jeffrey. 2013a. Distributed representations of words and phrases and their compositionality. Pages 3111–3119 of: *Proc. NIPS.*

Mikolov, Tomas, Chen, Kai, Corrado, Greg S., and Dean, Jeffrey. 2013b. Efficient estimation of word representations in vector space. In: *Proc. ICLR.*

Mikolov, Tomas, Le, Quoc V., and Sutskever, Ilya. 2013c. Exploiting similarities among languages for machine translation. *arXiv*, 1309.4168.

Mikolov, Tomas, Yih, Wen-tau, and Zweig, Geoffrey. 2013d. Linguistic regularities in continuous space word representations. Pages 746–751 of: *Proc. NAACL-HLT.*

Mikolov, Tomas, Grave, Edouard, Bojanowski, Piotr, Puhrsch, Christian, and Joulin, Armand. 2018. Advances in pre-training distributed word representations. Pages 52–55. In: *Proc. LREC.*

Miller, George, and Charles, Walter. 1991. Contextual correlates of semantic similarity. *Language and Cognitive Processes*, **6**(1), 1–28.

Miller, George A. 1954. Communication. *Annual Review of Psychology*, **5**, 401–420.

Miller, George A. 1967. Empirical methods in the study of semantics. Pages 51–73 of: *Journeys in Science: Small Steps – Great Strides*. Albuquerque, NM: University of New Mexico Press. Reprinted in Steinberg , Danny D., and Jakobovitz, Leon A. (eds.), *Semantics: An Interdisciplinary Reader in Philosophy, Linguistics and Psychology*. Cambridge: Cambridge University Press, 1971, 569–585.

Miller, George A., and Fellbaum, Christiane. 1991. Semantic networks of English. *Cognition*, **41**, 197–229.

Mimno, David, and Thompson, Laure. 2017. The strange geometry of Skip-Gram with negative sampling. Pages 2873–2878 of: *Proc. EMNLP.*

Mimno, David, Wallach, Hanna M., Naradowsky, Jason, Smith, David A., and McCallum, Andrew. 2009. Polylingual topic models. Pages 880–889 of: *Proc. EMNLP.*

Mitchell, Jeff, and Lapata, Mirella. 2008. Vector-based models of semantic composition. Pages 236–244 of: *Proc. ACL.*

Mitchell, Jeff, and Lapata, Mirella. 2010. Composition in distributional models of semantics. *Cognitive Science*, **34**(8), 1388–1439.

Mitchell, Tom M., Shinkareva, Svetlana V., Carlson, Andrew et al. 2008. Predicting human brain activity associated with the meanings of nouns. *Science*, **320**(5880), 1191–1195.

Mitra, Sunny, Mitra, Ritwik, Riedl, Martin et al. 2014. That's sick dude! Automatic identification of word sense change across different timescales. Pages 1020–1029 of: *Proc. ACL.*

Mnih, Andriy, and Hinton, Geoffrey. 2007. Three new graphical models for statistical language modelling. Pages 641–648 of: *Proc. ICML.*

Mnih, Andriy, and Hinton, Geoffrey. 2009. A scalable hierarchical distributed language model. Pages 1081–1088 of: *Proc. NIPS.*

Mnih, Andriy, and Kavukcuoglu, Koray. 2013. Learning word embeddings efficiently with noise-contrastive estimation. Pages 2265–2273 of: *Proc. NIPS.*

Mohammad, Saif M., Dorr, Bonnie J., Hirst, Graeme, and Turney, Peter D. 2013. Computing lexical contrast. *CL*, **39**(3), 555–590.

Montague, Richard. 1974. *Formal Philosophy: Selected Papers by Richard Montague* (edited by Richmond H. Thomason). New Haven: Yale University Press.

Montariol, Syrielle, Martinc, Matej, and Pivovarova, Lidia. 2021. Scalable and interpretable semantic change detection. Pages 4642–4652 of: *Proc. NAACL-HLT.*

Morin, Frederic, and Bengio, Yoshua. 2005. Hierarchical probabilistic neural network language model. Pages 246–252 of: *10th International Workshop on Artificial Intelligence and Statistics.*

Mrkšić, Nikola, Ó Séaghdha, Diarmuid, Thomson, Blaise et al. 2016. Counter-fitting word vectors to linguistic constraints. Pages 142–148 of: *Proc. NAACL-HLT.*

Mrkšić, Nikola, Vulić, Ivan, Ó Séaghdha, Diarmuid et al. 2017. Semantic specialisation of distributional word vector spaces using monolingual and cross-lingual constraints. *TACL*, **5**, 309–324.

Mu, Jiaqui, and Viswanath, Pramod. 2018. All-but-the-top: Simple and effective post-processing for word representations. In: *Proc. ICLR.*

Murphy, Brian, Talukdar, Partha P., and Mitchell, Tom M. 2012. Selecting corpus-semantic models for neurolinguistic decoding. Pages 114–123 of: *Proc. *SEM.*

Murphy, Gregory. 2002. *The Big Book of Concepts.* Cambridge, MA: The MIT Press.

Murphy, M. Lynne. 2003. *Semantic Relations and the Lexicon: Antonymy, Synonymy, and the Other Paradigms.* Cambridge: Cambridge University Press.

Murphy, M. Lynne. 2010. *Lexical Meaning.* Cambridge: Cambridge University Press.

Nakov, Preslav, Popova, Antonia, and Mateev, Plamen. 2001. Weight functions impact on LSA performance. Pages 187–193 of: *Recent Advances in NLP.*

Naselaris, Thomas, Kayand, Kendrick N., Nishimoto, Shinji, and Gallant, Jack L. 2011. Encoding and decoding in fMRI. *Neuroimage*, **56**(2), 400–410.

Nastase, Vivi, and Szpakowicz, Stan. 2003. Exploring noun-modifier semantic relations. Pages 285–301 of: *Proc. IWCS.*

Navigli, Roberto. 2009. Word sense disambiguation: A survey. *ACM Computing Surveys*, **41**(2), 10:1–10:69.

Navigli, Roberto, and Ponzetto, Simone Paolo. 2012. BabelNet: The automatic construction, evaluation and application of a wide-coverage multilingual semantic network. *Artificial Intelligence*, **193**, 217–250.

Nayak, Neha, Angeli, Gabor, and Manning, Christopher D. 2016. Evaluating word embeddings using a representative suite of practical tasks. Pages 19–23 of: *1st Workshop on Evaluating Vector Space Representations for NLP.*

Neelakantan, Arvind, Shankar, Jeevan, Passos, Alexandre, and McCallum, Andrew. 2014. Efficient non-parametric estimation of multiple embeddings per word in vector space. Pages 1059–1069 of: *Proc. EMNLP*.

Nefdt, Ryan M. 2020. A puzzle concerning compositionality in machines. *Minds and Machines*, **30**(1), 47–75.

Nelson, Douglas L., McEvoy, Cathy L., and Schreiber, Thomas A. 2004. The University of South Florida free association, rhyme, and word fragment norms. *Behavior Research Methods, Instruments, & Computers*, **36**(3), 402–407.

Nevin, Bruce E. 1993. A minimalist program for linguistics: The work of Zellig Harris on meaning and information. *Historiographia Linguistica*, **20**, 355–398.

Nguyen, Kim Anh, Köper, Maximilian, Schulte im Walde, Sabine, and Vu, Ngoc Thang. 2017. Hierarchical embeddings for hypernymy detection and directionality. Pages 233–243 of: *Proc. EMNLP*.

Nie, Allen, Bennett, Erin, and Goodman, Noah. 2019. DisSent: Learning sentence representations from explicit discourse relations. Pages 4497–4510 of: *Proc. ACL*.

Niven, Timothy, and Kao, Hung-Yu. 2019. Probing neural network comprehension of natural language arguments. Pages 4658–4664 of: *Proc. ACL*.

Niwa, Yoshiki, and Nitta, Yoshihiko. 1994. Co-occurrence vectors from corpora vs. distance from dictionaries. Pages 304–309 of: *Proc. COLING*.

Norlund, Tobias, Nilsson, David, and Sahlgren, Magnus. 2016. Parameterized context windows in Random Indexing. Pages 166–173 of: *1st Workshop on Representation Learning for NLP*.

Nunberg, Geoffrey, Sag, Ivan A., and Wasow, Thomas. 1994. Idioms. *Language*, **70**(3), 491–538.

Ono, Masataka, Miwa, Makoto, and Sasaki, Yutaka. 2015. Word embedding-based antonym detection using thesauri and distributional information. Pages 984–989 of: *Proc. NAACL-HLT*.

Ormazabal, Aitor, Artetxe, Mikel, Labaka, Gorka, Soroa, Aitor, and Agirre, Eneko. 2019. Analyzing the limitations of cross-lingual word embedding mappings. Pages 4990–4995 of: *Proc. ACL*.

Ó Séaghdha, Diarmuid. 2010. Latent variable models of selectional preference. Pages 435–444 of: *Proc. ACL*.

Ó Séaghdha, Diarmuid, and Korhonen, Anna. 2011. Probabilistic models of similarity in syntactic context. Pages 1047–1057 of: *Proc. EMNLP*.

Ó Séaghdha, Diarmuid, and Korhonen, Anna. 2012. Modelling selectional preferences in a lexical hierarchy. Pages 170–179 of: *Proc. *SEM*.

Ó Séaghdha, Diarmuid, and Korhonen, Anna. 2014. Probabilistic distributional semantics with latent variable models. *CL*, **40**(3), 587–631.

Osgood, Charles E. 1952. The nature and measurement of meaning. *Psychological Bulletin*, **49**, 197–237.

Osgood, Charles E., Suci, George J., and Tannenbaum, Percy H. 1957. *The Measurement of Meaning*. Urbana: University of Illinois Press.

Österlund, Arvid, Ödling, David, and Sahlgren, Magnus. 2015. Factorization of latent variables in distributional semantic models. Pages 227–231 of: *Proc. EMNLP*.

Padó, Sebastian, and Lapata, Mirella. 2007. Dependency-based construction of semantic space models. *CL*, **33**(2), 161–199.

Padó, Sebastian, Padó, Ulrike, and Erk, Katrin. 2007. Flexible, corpus-based modelling of human plausibility judgements. Pages 400–409 of: *Proc. EMNLP*.

Padó, Ulrike. 2007. *The Integration of Syntax and Semantic Plausibility in a Wide-coverage Model of Human Sentence Processing*. PhD thesis, Saarland University.

Pagliardini, Matteo, Gupta, Prakhar, and Jaggi, Martin. 2018. Unsupervised learning of sentence embeddings using compositional n-gram features. Pages 528–540 of: *Proc. NAACL-HLT*.

Paik, Cory, Aroca-Ouellette, Stéphane, Roncone, Alessandro, and Kann, Katharina. 2021. The world of an octopus: How reporting bias influences a language model's perception of color. Pages 823–835 of: *Proc. EMNLP*.

Palatucci, Mark M., Hinton, Geoffrey E., Pomerleau, Dean, and Mitchell, Tom M. 2009. Zero-shot learning with semantic output codes. In: *Proc. NIPS*.

Panchenko, Alexander, Ruppert, Eugen, Faralli, Stefano, Ponzetto, Simone Paolo, and Biemann, Chris. 2017. Unsupervised does not mean uninterpretable: The case for word sense induction and disambiguation. Pages 86–98 of: *Proc. EACL*.

Pang, Bo, and Lee, Lillian. 2004. A sentimental education: Sentiment analysis using subjectivity summarization based on minimum cuts. Pages 271–278 of: *Proc. ACL*.

Pang, Bo, and Lee, Lillian. 2005. Seeing stars: Exploiting class relationships for sentiment categorization with respect to rating scales. Pages 115–124 of: *Proc. ACL*.

Pang, Bo, and Lee, Lillian. 2008. Opinion mining and sentiment analysis. *Foundations and Trends in Information Retrieval*, **2**(1–2), 1–135.

Pannitto, Ludovica, Salicchi, Lavinia, and Lenci, Alessandro. 2018. Refining the distributional inclusion hypothesis for unsupervised hypernym identification. *Italian Journal of Computational Linguistics*, **4**(2), 45–56.

Pantel, Patrick, and Lin, Dekang. 2002a. Discovering word senses from text. Pages 613–619 of: *8th International Conference on Knowledge Discovery and Data Mining*.

Pantel, Patrick, and Lin, Dekang. 2002b. Document clustering with committees. Pages 199–206 of: *25th International ACM SIGIR Conference*.

Pantel, Patrick, and Pennacchiotti, Marco. 2006. Espresso: Leveraging generic patterns for automatically harvesting semantic relations. Pages 113–120 of: *Proc. NAACL-HLT*.

Pantel, Patrick, Bhagat, Rahul, Coppola, Bonaventura, Chklovski, Timothy, and Hovy, Eduard H. 2007. ISP: Learning inferential selectional preferences. Pages 564–571 of: *Proc. NAACL-HLT*.

Papadimitriou, Christos, Raghavan, Prabhakar, Tamaki, Hisao, and Vempala, Santosh. 2000. Latent Semantic Indexing: A probabilistic analysis. *Journal of Computer and System Sciences*, **61**(2), 217–235.

Paperno, Denis, Pham, Nghia The, and Baroni, Marco. 2014. A practical and linguistically-motivated approach to compositional distributional semantics. Pages 90–99 of: *Proc. ACL*.

Paradis, Carita, and Willners, Caroline. 2011. Antonymy: From conventionalization to meaning-making. *Review of Cognitive Linguistics*, **9**(2), 367–391.

Paradis, Carita, Willners, Caroline, and Jones, Steven. 2009. Good and bad opposites: Using textual and experimental techniques to measure antonym canonicity. *The Mental Lexicon*, **4**(3), 380–429.

Partee, Barbara H. 1984. Compositionality. Pages 281–311 of: Landman, Fred, and Veltman, Frank (eds.), *Varieties of Formal Semantics*. Dordrecht: Foris.

Passaro, Lucia C., and Lenci, Alessandro. 2016. Evaluating context selection strategies to build emotive vector space models. Pages 2185–2191 of: *Proc. LREC*.

Pavlick, Ellie. 2022. Semantic structure in deep learning. *Annual Review of Linguistics*, **8**, 447–471.

Pecher, Diane, and Zwaan, Rolf A. (eds.). 2005. *Grounding Cognition: The Role of Perception and Action in Memory, Language, and Thinking*. Cambridge: Cambridge University Press.

Pedersen, Ted. 2010. Duluth-WSI: SenseClusters applied to the sense induction task of SemEval-2. Pages 363–366 of: *Proc. SemEval*.

Pedinotti, Paolo, Rambelli, Giulia, Chersoni, Emmanuele et al. 2021a. Did the cat drink the coffee? Challenging transformers with generalized event knowledge. Pages 1–11 of: *Proc. *SEM*.

Pedinotti, Paolo, Di Palma, Eliana, Cerini, Ludovica, and Lenci, Alessandro. 2021b. A howling success or a working sea? Testing what BERT knows about metaphors. Pages 192–204 of: *4th BlackboxNLP Workshop on Analyzing and Interpreting Neural Networks for NLP*.

Peirsman, Yves, and Padó, Sebastian. 2010. Cross-lingual induction of selectional preferences with bilingual vector spaces. Pages 921–929 of: *Proc. NAACL-HLT*.

Peirsman, Yves, Heylen, Kris, and Speelman, Dirk. 2007. Finding semantically related words in Dutch: Cooccurrences versus syntactic contexts. Pages 9–16 of: *CoSMO workshop, CONTEXT-07*.

Pelevina, Maria, Arefiev, Nikolay, Biemann, Chris, and Panchenko, Alexander. 2016. Making sense of word embeddings. Pages 174–183 of: *1st Workshop on Representation Learning for NLP*.

Pelletier, Francis J. 2006. Compositionality: Philosophical aspects. Pages 712–716 of: Brown, Keith (ed.), *Encyclopedia of Language & Linguistics*, 2nd ed., Vol, 2. Oxford: Elsevier.

Pelletier, Francis J. 2016. Semantic compositionality. In: Aronoff, Mark (ed.), *The Oxford Research Encyclopedia of Linguistics*. Oxford: Oxford University Press.

Pennington, Jeffrey, Socher, Richard, and Manning, Christopher D. 2014. GloVe: Global vectors for word representation. Pages 1532–1543 of: *Proc. EMNLP*.

Pereira, Fernando, Tishby, Naftali, and Lee, Lillian. 1993. Distributional clustering of English words. Pages 183–190 of: *Proc. ACL*.

Pereira, Francisco, Detre, Greg, and Botvinick, Matthew. 2011. Generating text from functional brain images. *Frontiers in Human Neuroscience*, **5**, 72.

Pereira, Francisco, Botvinick, Matthew, and Detre, Greg. 2013. Using Wikipedia to learn semantic feature representations of concrete concepts in neuroimaging experiments. *Artificial Intelligence*, **194**, 240–252.

Pereira, Francisco, Gershman, Samuel J., Ritter, Samuel, and Botvinick, Matthew. 2016. A comparative evaluation of off-the-shelf distributed semantic representations for modelling behavioural data. *Cognitive Neuropsychology*, **33**(3–4), 175–190.

Pereira, Francisco, Lou, Bin, Pritchett, Brianna et al. 2018. Toward a universal decoder of linguistic meaning from brain activation. *Nature Communications*, **9**(963).

Perek, Florent. 2016. Using distributional semantics to study syntactic productivity in diachrony: A case study. *Linguistics*, **54**(1), 149–188.

Perfetti, Charles A. 1998. The limits of co-occurrence: Tools and theories in language research. *Discourse Processes*, **25**(2–3), 363–377.

Peters, Matthew E., Ammar, Waleed, Bhagavatula, Chandra, and Power, Russell. 2017. Semi-supervised sequence tagging with bidirectional language models. Pages 1756–1765 of: *Proc. ACL*.

Peters, Matthew E., Neumann, Mark, Iyyer, Mohit et al. 2018. Deep contextualized word representations. Pages 2227–2237 of: *Proc. NAACL-HLT*.

Peterson, Joshua C., Chen, Dawn, and Griffiths, Thomas L. 2020. Parallelograms revisited: Exploring the limitations of vector space models for simple analogies. *Cognition*, **205**, 104440.

Pham, Nghia The, Lazaridou, Angeliki, and Baroni, Marco. 2015a. A multitask objective to inject lexical contrast into distributional semantics. Pages 21–26 of: *Proc. ACL*.

Pham, Nghia The, Kruszewski, Germán, Lazaridou, Angeliki, and Baroni, Marco. 2015b. Jointly optimizing word representations for lexical and sentential tasks with the C-PHRASE model. Pages 971–981 of: *Proc. ACL*.

Piantadosi, Steven T., and Hill, Felix. 2022. Meaning without reference in large language models. In: *Workshop on Neuro Causal and Symbolic AI (nCSI)@NeurIPS*.

Pierrejean, Benedicte, and Tanguy, Ludovic. 2018. Towards qualitative word embeddings evaluation: Measuring neighbors variation. Pages 32–39 of: *Proc. NAACL-HLT*.

Pilehvar, Mohammad Taher, and Camacho-Collados, José. 2019. WIC: The word-in-context dataset for evaluating context-sensitive meaning representations. Pages 1267–1273 of: *Proc. NAACL-HLT*.

Pilehvar, Mohammad Taher, and Camacho-Collados, José. 2020. *Embeddings in Natural Language Processing: Theory and Advances in Vector Representations of Meaning*. San Rafael: Morgan & Claypool.

Plate, Tony A. 1994. *Distributed Representations and Nested Compositional Structure*. PhD thesis, University of Toronto.

Plate, Tony A. 1995. Holographic reduced representations. *IEEE Transactions on Neural Networks*, **6**(3), 623–641.

Plate, Tony A. 2003. *Holographic Reduced Representation: Distributed Representation for Cognitive Structures*. Stanford: CSLI Publications.

Plutchik, Robert. 1994. *The Psychology and Biology of Emotion*. New York: Harper Collins.

Polajnar, Tamara, and Clark, Stephen. 2014. Improving distributional semantic vectors through context selection and normalisation. Pages 230–238 of: *Proc. EACL*.

Poldrack, Russell A. 2011. Inferring mental states from neuroimaging data: From reverse inference to large-scale decoding. *Neuron*, **72**(5), 692–697.

Poliak, Adam, Naradowsky, Jason, Haldar, Aparajita, Rudinger, Rachel, and Van Durme, Benjamin. 2018. Hypothesis only baselines in natural language inference. Pages 180–191 of: *Proc. *SEM*.

Potts, Christopher. 2019. A case for deep learning in semantics: Response to Pater. *Language*, **95**(1), e115–e124.

Prescher, Detlef, Riezler, Stefan, and Rooth, Mats. 2000. Using a probabilistic class-based lexicon for lexical ambiguity resolution. Pages 649–655 of: *Proc. COLING*.

Press, Ofir, and Wolf, Lior. 2017. Using the output embedding to improve language models. Pages 157–163 of: *Proc. EACL*.

Purandare, Amruta, and Pedersen, Ted. 2004. Word sense discrimination by clustering contexts in vector and similarity spaces. Pages 41–48 of: *Proc. CoNLL*.

Pustejovsky, James. 1995. *The Generative Lexicon*. Cambridge, MA: The MIT Press.

Pustejovsky, James. 2012. Co-compositionality in grammar. Pages 371–382 of: Werning, Markus, Hinzen, Wolfram, and Machery, Edouard (eds.), *The Oxford Handbook of Compositionality*. Oxford: Oxford University Press.

Pustejovsky, James, and Batiukova, Olga. 2019. *The Lexicon*. Cambridge: Cambridge University Press.

Qi, Peng, Zhang, Yuhao, Zhang, Yuhui, Bolton, Jason, and Manning, Christopher D. 2020. Stanza: A Python natural language processing toolkit for many human languages. Pages 101–108 of: *Proc. ACL*.

Rabovsky, Milena, and McClelland, James L. 2019. Quasi-compositional mapping from form to meaning: A neural network-based approach to capturing neural responses during human language comprehension. *Philosophical Transactions of the Royal Society B*, **375**, 20190313.

Radford, Alec, Narasimhan, Karthik, Salimans, Tim, and Sutskever, Ilya. 2018. *Improving Language Understanding by Generative Pre-training*. Technical Report, OpenAI.

Radford, Alec, Wu, Jeff, Child, Rewon et al. 2019. *Language Models are Unsupervised Multitask Learners*. Technical Report, OpenAI.

Radford, Alec, Kim, Jong Wook, Hallacy, Chris et al. 2021. Learning transferable visual models from natural language supervision. *arXiv*, 2103.00020.

Radinsky, Kira, Agichtein, Eugene, Gabrilovich, Evgeniy, and Markovitch, Shaul. 2011. A word at a time. Pages 337–346 of: *20th International Conference on World Wide Web*.

Radovanović, Miloš, Nanopoulos, Alexandros, and Ivanović, Mirjana. 2010a. Hubs in space: Popular nearest neighbors in high-dimensional data. *Journal of Machine Learning Research*, **11**, 2487–2531.

Radovanović, Miloš, Nanopoulos, Alexandros, and Ivanović, Mirjana. 2010b. On the existence of obstinate results in vector space models. Pages 186–193. In: *33rd International ACM SIGIR Conference*.

Raffel, Colin, Shazeer, Noam, Roberts, Adam et al. 2020. Exploring the limits of transfer learning with a unified text-to-text transformer. *Journal of Machine Learning Research*, **21**(140), 1–67.

Rajaee, Sara, and Pilehvar, Mohammad Taher. 2021. A cluster-based approach for improving isotropy in contextual embedding space. Pages 575–584 of: *Proc. ACL*, Vol. 2.

Rambelli, Giulia, Chersoni, Emmanuele, Lenci, Alessandro, Blache, Philippe, and Huang, Chu-Ren. 2020. Comparing probabilistic, distributional and transformer-based models on logical metonymy interpretation. Pages 224–234 of: *1st Conference of the Asia-Pacific Chapter of the ACL*.

Ramesh, Aditya, Pavlov, Mikhail, Goh, Gabriel et al. 2021. Zero-shot text-to-image generation. *arXiv*, 2102.12092.

Rapp, Reinhard. 1999. Automatic identification of word translations from unrelated English and German corpora. Pages 519–526 of: *Proc. ACL.*

Rapp, Reinhard. 2003. Word sense discovery based on sense descriptor dissimilarity. Pages 315–322 of: *9th Machine Translation Summit.*

Ravichander, Abhilasha, Hovy, Eduard, Suleman, Kaheer, Trischler, Adam, and Cheung, Jackie Chi Kit. 2020. On the systematicity of probing contextualized word representations: The case of hypernymy in BERT. Pages 88–102 of: *Proc. *SEM.*

Ravichandran, Deepak, Pantel, Patrick, and Hovy, Eduard. 2005. Randomized algorithms and NLP: Using locality sensitive hash function for high speed noun clustering. Pages 622–629 of: *Proc. ACL.*

Recchia, Gabriel, and Jones, Michael N. 2009. More data trumps smarter algorithms: Comparing pointwise mutual information with latent semantic analysis. *Behavior Research Methods*, **41**, 657–663.

Recchia, Gabriel, and Jones, Michael N. 2012. The semantic richness of abstract concepts. *Frontiers in Human Neuroscience*, **6**, 1–16.

Recchia, Gabriel, and Louwerse, Max M. 2015. Reproducing affective norms with lexical co-occurrence statistics: Predicting valence, arousal, and dominance. *The Quarterly Journal of Experimental Psychology*, **68**(8), 1584–1598.

Recchia, Gabriel, Jones, Michael, Sahlgren, Magnus, and Kanerva, Pentti. 2010. Encoding sequential information in vector space models of semantics: Comparing holographic reduced representation and random permutation. Pages 865–870. In: *Proc. COGSCI.*

Recchia, Gabriel, Jones, Michael N., Sahlgren, Magnus, and Kanerva, Pentti. 2015. Encoding sequential information in vector space models of semantics: Comparing holographic reduced representation and random permutation. *Computational Intelligence and Neuroscience*, **2015**, 86574.

Reddy, Siva, McCarthy, Diana, and Manandhar, Suresh. 2011a. An empirical study on compositionality in compound nouns. Pages 210–218 of: *5th International Joint Conference on Natural Language Processing.*

Reddy, Siva, Klapaftis, Ioannis, McCarthy, Diana, and Manandhar, Suresh. 2011b. Dynamic and static prototype vectors for semantic composition. Pages 705–713 of: *5th International Joint Conference on Natural Language Processing.*

Řehůřek, Radim, and Sojka, Petr. 2010. Software framework for topic modelling with large corpora. Pages 45–50 of: *Proc. LREC.*

Reimers, Nils, and Gurevych, Iryna. 2019. Sentence-BERT: Sentence embeddings using siamese BERT-networks. Pages 3980–3990 of: *Proc. EMNLP.*

Reisinger, Joseph, and Mooney, Raymond J. 2010a. A mixture model with sharing for lexical semantics. Pages 1173–1182 of: *Proc. EMNLP.*

Reisinger, Joseph, and Mooney, Raymond J. 2010b. Multi-prototype vector-space models of word meaning. Pages 109–117 of: *Proc. NAACL-HLT.*

Reisinger, Joseph, and Mooney, Raymond J. 2011. Cross-cutting models of lexical semantics. Pages 1405–1415 of: *Proc. EMNLP.*

Rescorla, Robert A., and Wagner, Allan R. 1972. A theory of Pavlovian conditioning: Variations in the effectiveness of reinforcement and nonreinforcement. Pages 64–99 of: Black, Abraham H., and Prokasy, William F. (eds.), *Classical Conditioning II Current Research and Theory.* New York: Appleton-Century-Crofts.

Resnik, Philip. 1996. Selectional constraints: An information-theoretic model and its computational realization. *Cognition*, **61**(1–2), 127–159.

Resnik, Philip, and Lin, Jimmy. 2010. Evaluation of NLP systems. Pages 271–295 of: Clark, Alexander, Fox, Chris, and Lappin, Shalom (eds.), *The Handbook of Computational Linguistics and Natural Language Processing*. Oxford: Wiley-Blackwell.

Riedel, Sebastian, Yao, Limin, McCallum, Andrew, and Marlin, Benjamin M. 2013. Relation extraction with matrix factorization and universal schemas. Pages 74–84 of: *Proc. NAACL-HLT*.

Rimell, Laura. 2014. Distributional lexical entailment by topic coherence. Pages 511–519 of: *Proc. EACL*.

Rimell, Laura, Maillard, Jean, Polajnar, Tamara, and Clark, Stephen. 2016. RELPRON: A relative clause evaluation data set for compositional distributional semantics. *CL*, **42**(4), 661–701.

Riordan, Brian, and Jones, Michael N. 2011. Redundancy in perceptual and linguistic experience: Comparing feature-based and distributional models of semantic representation. *TopiCS*, **3**(2), 303–345.

Ritter, Alan, Mausam, and Etzioni, Oren. 2010. A Latent Dirichlet Allocation method for selectional preferences. Pages 424–434 of: *Proc. ACL*.

Ritter, Helge, and Kohonen, Teuvo. 1989. Self-organizing semantic maps. *Biological Cybernetics*, **61**(4), 241–254.

Rodd, Jennifer. 2018. Lexical ambiguity. Pages 96–116 of: Rueschemeyer, Shirley-Ann, and Gaskell, M. Gareth (eds.), *Oxford Handbook of Psycholinguistics*, 2nd ed. Oxford: Oxford University Press.

Rodda, Martina A., Senaldi, Marco S. G., and Lenci, Alessandro. 2017. Panta rei: Tracking semantic change with distributional semantics in ancient Greek. *Italian Journal of Computational Linguistics*, **3**(1), 11–24.

Rogers, Anna, Drozd, Aleksandr, and Li, Bofang. 2017. The (too many) problems of analogical reasoning with word vectors. Pages 135–148 of: *Proc. *SEM*.

Rogers, Anna, Ananthakrishna, Shashwath Hosur, and Rumshisky, Anna. 2018. What's in your embedding, and how it predicts task performance. Pages 2690–2703 of: *Proc. COLING*.

Rogers, Anna, Drozd, Aleksandr, Rumshisky, Anna, and Goldberg, Yoav (eds.). 2019. *3rd Workshop on Evaluating Vector Space Representations for NLP*. Minneapolis: ACL.

Rogers, Anna, Kovaleva, Olga, and Rumshisky, Anna. 2020. A primer in BERTology: What we know about how BERT works. *TACL*, **8**, 842–866.

Rogers, Timothy, and McClelland, James. 2004. *Semantic Cognition: A Parallel Distributed Processing Approach*. Cambridge, MA: The MIT Press.

Rohde, Douglas L. T., Gonnerman, Laura M., and Plaut, David C. 2006. An improved model of semantic similarity based on lexical co-occurrence. *Communications of the ACM*, **8**, 627–633.

Roller, Stephen, and Erk, Katrin. 2016. Relations such as hypernymy: Identifying and exploiting Hearst patterns in distributional vectors for lexical entailment. Pages 2163–2172 of: *Proc. EMNLP*.

Roller, Stephen, and Schulte im Walde, Sabine. 2013. A multimodal LDA model integrating textual, cognitive and visual modalities. Pages 1146–1157 of: *Proc. EMNLP*.

Roller, Stephen, Erk, Katrin, and Boleda, Gemma. 2014. Inclusive yet selective: Supervised distributional hypernymy detection. Pages 1025–1036 of: *Proc. COLING*.

Roller, Stephen, Kiela, Douwe, and Nickel, Maximilian. 2018. Hearst patterns revisited: Automatic hypernym detection from large text corpora. Pages 358–363 of: *Proc. ACL*.

Rooth, Mats, Riezler, Stefan, Prescher, Detlef, Carroll, Glenn, and Beil, Franz. 1999. Inducing a semantically annotated lexicon via EM-based clustering. Pages 104–111 of: *Proc. ACL*.

Rubenstein, Herbert, and Goodenough, John B. 1965. Contextual correlates of synonymy. *Communications of the ACM*, **8**(10), 627–633.

Rubin, Timothy N., Kievit-Kylar, Brent, Willits, Jon A., and Jones, Michael N. 2014. Organizing the space and behavior of semantic models. Pages 1329–1334 of: *Proc. COGSCI*.

Rubinstein, Dana, Levi, Effi, Schwartz, Roy, and Rappoport, Ari. 2015. How well do distributional models capture different types of semantic knowledge? Pages 726–730 of: *Proc. ACL*.

Ruder, Sebastian. 2019. *Neural Transfer Learning for Natural Language Processing*. PhD thesis, National University of Ireland.

Ruder, Sebastian, Vulić, Ivan, and Søgaard, Anders. 2019. A survey of cross-lingual word embedding models. *JAIR*, **65**, 569–631.

Ruge, Gerda. 1992. Experiments on linguistically-based term associations. *Information Processing & Management*, **28**(3), 317–332.

Rumelhart, David E., and Abrahamson, Adele A. 1973. A model for analogical reasoning. *Cognitive Psychology*, **5**, 1–28.

Rumelhart, David E., and McClelland, James L. (eds.). 1986. *Parallel Distributed Processing: Explorations in the Microstructure of Cognition, Vol. 1: Foundations*. Cambridge, MA: The MIT Press.

Rumelhart, David E., Hinton, Geoffrey E., and Williams, Ronald J. 1986. Learning representations by back-propagating errors. *Nature*, **323**(6088), 533–536.

Ruppenhofer, Josef, Ellsworth, Michael, Petruck, Miriam R. L., Johnson, Christopher R., and Scheffczyk, Jan. 2006. *FrameNet II: Extended Theory and Practice*. Berkeley: ICSI.

Sag, Ivan A., Baldwin, Timothy, Bond, Francis, Copestake, Ann, and Flickinger, Dan. 2002. Multiword expressions: A pain in the neck for NLP. Pages 1–15 of: *International Conference on Intelligent Text Processing and Computational Linguistics*.

Sagi, Eyal, Kaufmann, Stefan, and Clark, Brady. 2009. Semantic density analysis: Comparing word meaning across time and phonetic space. Pages 104–111 of: *GEMS 2009 Workshop on GEometrical Models of Natural Language Semantics*.

Sagi, Eyal, Kaufmann, Stefan, and Clark, Brady. 2012. Tracing semantic change with Latent Semantic Analysis. Pages 161–183 of: Allen, Kathryn, and Justyna, Robinson (eds.), *Current Methods in Historical Semantics*. Berlin: Mouton de Gruyter.

Sahlgren, Magnus. 2005. An introduction to Random Indexing. Pages 1–9 of: *Methods and Applications of Semantic Indexing Workshop, TKE 2005.*

Sahlgren, Magnus. 2006. *The Word-Space Model: Using Distributional Analysis to Represent Syntagmatic and Paradigmatic Relations between Words in High-Dimensional Vector Spaces.* PhD thesis, Stockholm University.

Sahlgren, Magnus. 2008. The distributional hypothesis. *Italian Journal of Linguistics,* **20**(1), 31–51.

Sahlgren, Magnus, and Carlsson, Fredrik. 2021. The singleton fallacy: Why current critiques of language models miss the point. *Frontiers in Artificial Intelligence,* **4**, 682578.

Sahlgren, Magnus, and Lenci, Alessandro. 2016. The effects of data size and frequency range on distributional semantic models. Pages 975–980 of: *Proc. EMNLP.*

Sahlgren, Magnus, Holst, Anders, and Kanerva, Pentti. 2008. Permutations as a means to encode order in word space. Pages 1300–1305 of: *Proc. COGSCI.*

Sahlgren, Magnus, Cuba Gyllensten, Amaru, Espinoza, Fredrik et al. 2016. The Gavagai living lexicon. Pages 344–350 of: *Proc. LREC.*

Sakaguchi, Keisuke, Bras, Ronan Le, Bhagavatula, Chandra, and Choi, Yejin. 2020. WINOGRANDE: An adversarial Winograd schema challenge at scale. Pages 8732–8734 of: *Proc. AAAI.*

Sakurai, Akito and Hyodo, Daisuke 2002. Simple recurrent networks and random indexing. Pages 35–39 of: *9th International Conference on Neural Information Processing.*

Salehi, Bahar, Cook, Paul, and Baldwin, Timothy. 2015. A word embedding approach to predicting the compositionality of multiword expressions. Pages 977–983 of: *Proc. NAACL-HLT.*

Salton, Gerald (ed.). 1971a. *The SMART Retrieval System: Experiments in Automatic Document Processing.* Englewood Cliff: Prentice Hall.

Salton, Gerard. 1964. *A Flexible Automatic System for the Organization, Storage, and Retrieval of Language Data (SMART).* Technical Report ISR-5 to NSF, Harvard Computation Laboratory.

Salton, Gerard. 1971b. Experiments in automatic thesaurus construction for information retrieval. Pages 43–49 of: *IFIP Congress.*

Salton, Gerard, and Buckley, Christopher. 1988. A term-weighting approaches in automatic text retrieval. *Information Processing and Management,* **24**(5), 513–523.

Salton, Gerard, and Lesk, Michael E. 1966. *Information Analysis and Dictionary Construction.* Technical Report ISR-11 to NSF, Cornell University.

Salton, Gerard, Wong, Andrew, and Yang, Chung-Shu. 1975. A vector space model for automatic indexing. *Communications of the ACM,* **18**(11), 613–620.

Sandin, Fredrik, Emruli, Blerim, and Sahlgren, Magnus. 2017. Random Indexing of multidimensional data. *Knowledge and Information Systems,* **52**(1), 267–290.

Sanh, Victor, Debut, Lysandre, Chaumond, Julien, and Wolf, Thomas. 2019. Distil-BERT, a distilled version of BERT: Smaller, faster, cheaper and lighter. *arXiv,* 1910.01108.

Santus, Enrico, Lenci, Alessandro, Lu, Qin, and Schulte im Walde, Sabine. 2014a. Chasing hypernyms in vector spaces with entropy. Pages 38–42 of: *Proc. EACL.*

Santus, Enrico, Lu, Qin, Lenci, Alessandro, and Huang, Chu-Ren. 2014b. Taking antonymy mask off in vector space. Pages 135–144 of: *28th Pacific Asia Conference on Language, Information and Computation.*

Santus, Enrico, Young, Francis, Lenci, Alessandro, and Huang, Chu-Ren. 2015. EVALution 1.0: An evolving semantic dataset for training and evaluation of distributional semantic models. Pages 64–69 of: *4th Workshop on Linked Data in Linguistics.*

Santus, Enrico, Chersoni, Emmanuele, Lenci, Alessandro, and Blache, Philippe. 2017. Measuring thematic fit with distributional feature overlap. Pages 659–669 of: *Proc. EMNLP.*

Saussure, Ferdinand de. 1916. *Cours de linguistique générale.* Paris: Payot.

Sayeed, Asad, Demberg, Vera, and Shkadzko, Pavel. 2015. An exploration of semantic features in an unsupervised thematic fit evaluation framework. *Italian Journal of Computational Linguistics*, **1**(1), 25–40.

Sayeed, Asad, Greenberg, Clayton, and Demberg, Vera. 2016. Thematic fit evaluation: An aspect of selectional preferences. Pages 99–105. In: *1st Workshop on Evaluating Vector Space Representations for NLP.*

Saysani, Armin, Corballis, Michael C., and Corballis, Paul M. 2018. Colour envisioned: Concepts of colour in the blind and sighted. *Visual Cognition*, **26**(5), 382–392.

Scheible, Silke, and Schulte im Walde, Sabine. 2014. A database of paradigmatic semantic relation pairs for German nouns, verbs, and adjectives. Pages 111–119 of: *Workshop on Lexical and Grammatical Resources for Language Processing.*

Scheible, Silke, Schulte im Walde, Sabine, and Springorum, Sylvia. 2013. Uncovering distributional differences between synonyms and antonyms in a word space model. Pages 489–497 of: *6th International Joint Conference on Natural Language Processing.*

Schlechtweg, Dominik, Hätty, Anna, del Tredici, Marco, and Schulte im Walde, Sabine. 2020a. A wind of change: Detecting and evaluating lexical semantic change across times and domains. Pages 732–746 of: *Proc. ACL.*

Schlechtweg, Dominik, McGillivray, Barbara, Hengchen, Simon, Dubossarsky, Haim, and Tahmasebi, Nina. 2020b. SemEval-2020 task 1: Unsupervised lexical semantic change detection. Pages 1–23 of: *Proc. SemEval.*

Schluter, Natalie. 2018. The word analogy testing caveat. Pages 242–246 of: *Proc. NAACL-HLT.*

Schnabel, Tobias, Labutov, Igor, Mimno, David, and Joachims, Thorsten. 2015. Evaluation methods for unsupervised word embeddings. Pages 298–307 of: *Proc. EMNLP.*

Schulte im Walde, Sabine. 2006. Experiments on the automatic induction of German semantic verb classes. *CL*, **32**(2), 159–194.

Schulte im Walde, Sabine. 2009. The induction of verb frames and verb classes from corpora. Pages 952–972 of: Lüdeling, Anke, and Kytö, Merja (eds.), *Corpus Linguistics. An International Handbook*, Vol. 2. Berlin: Walter de Gruyter.

Schulte im Walde, Sabine. 2010. Comparing computational models of selectional preferences: Second-order co-occurrence vs. latent semantic clusters. Pages 1381–1388 of: *Proc. LREC.*

Schulte im Walde, Sabine. 2020. Distinguishing between paradigmatic semantic relations across word classes: Human ratings and distributional similarity. *Journal of Language Modelling*, **8**(1), 53–101.

Schulte im Walde, Sabine, Hying, Christian, Scheible, Christian, and Schmid, Helmut. 2008. Combining EM training and the MDL principle for an automatic verb classification incorporating selectional preferences. Pages 496–504 of: *Proc. ACL*.

Schulte im Walde, Sabine, Müller, Stefan, and Roller, Stephen. 2013. Exploring vector space models to predict the compositionality of German noun-noun compounds. Pages 255–265 of: *Proc. *SEM*.

Schütze, Hinrich. 1992. Dimensions of meaning. Pages 787–796 of: *Supercomputing*.

Schütze, Hinrich. 1993. Word space. Pages 895–902 of: *Proc. NIPS*.

Schütze, Hinrich. 1997. *Ambiguity Resolution in Language Learning*. Stanford: CSLI Publications.

Schütze, Hinrich. 1998. Automatic word sense discrimination. *CL*, **24**(1), 97–123.

Schütze, Hinrich, and Pedersen, Jan. 1993. A vector model for syntagmatic and paradigmatic relatedness. Pages 104–113 of: *9th Annual Conference of the UW Centre for the New OED and Text Researches*.

Searle, John R. 1980. Minds, brains, and programs. *The Behavioral and Brain Sciences*, **3**, 417–424.

Sennrich, Rico, Haddow, Barry, and Birch, Alexandra. 2016. Neural machine translation of rare words with subword units. Pages 1715–1725 of: *Proc. ACL*.

Shannon, Claude E. 1948. A mathematical theory of communication. *The Bell System Technical Journal*, **27**(3), 379–423.

Shaoul, Cyrus, and Westbury, Chris F. 2006. Word frequency effects in high-dimensional co-occurrence models: A new approach. *Behavior Research Methods*, **38**, 190–195.

Shaoul, Cyrus, and Westbury, Chris F. 2010. Exploring lexical co-occurrence space using HiDEx. *Behavior Research Methods*, **42**(2), 393–413.

Shen, Dinghan, Wang, Guoyin, Wang, Wenlin et al. 2018. Baseline needs more love: On simple word-embedding-based models and associated pooling mechanisms. Pages 440–450 of: *Proc. ACL*.

Shoemark, Philippa, Liza, Farhana Ferdousi, Nguyen, Dong, Hale, Scott A., and McGillivray, Barbara. 2019. Room to Glo: A systematic comparison of semantic change detection approaches with word embeddings. Pages 66–76 of: *Proc. EMNLP*.

Shwartz, Vered, and Choi, Yejin. 2020. Do neural language models overcome reporting bias? Pages 6863–6870 of: *Proc. COLING*.

Shwartz, Vered, and Dagan, Ido. 2019. Still a pain in the neck: Evaluating text representations on lexical composition. *TACL*, **7**, 403–419.

Shwartz, Vered, Goldberg, Yoav, and Dagan, Ido. 2016. Improving hypernymy detection with an integrated pattern-based and distributional method. Pages 2389–2398 of: *Proc. ACL*.

Shwartz, Vered, Santus, Enrico, and Schlechtweg, Dominik. 2017. Hypernyms under Siege: Linguistically-motivated artillery for hypernymy detection. Pages 65–75 of: *Proc. EACL*.

Silberer, Carina, and Lapata, Carina. 2012. Grounded models of semantic representation. Pages 1423–1433 of: *Proc. EMNLP*.

Silberer, Carina, and Lapata, Mirella. 2014. Learning grounded meaning representations with autoencoders. Pages 721–732 of: *Proc. ACL*.

Silberer, Carina, Ferrari, Vittorio, and Lapata, Mirella. 2013. Models of semantic representation with visual attributes. Pages 572–582 of: *Proc. ACL*.

Silberer, Carina, Ferrari, Vittorio, and Lapata, Mirella. 2017. Visually grounded meaning representations. *IEEE Transactions on Pattern Analysis and Machine Intelligence*, **39**(11), 2284–2297.

Sinclair, John M. 1966. Beginning the study of lexis. Pages 410–430 of: Bazell, Charles E., Catford, John C., Halliday, Michael A. K., and Robins, Robert H. (eds.), *In Memory of J. R. Firth*. London: Longmans.

Sinclair, John M. 1991. *Corpus, Concordance, Collocation*. Oxford: Oxford University Press.

Sivic, Josef, and Zisserman, Andrew. 2003. Video google: A text retrieval approach to object matching in videos. Pages 1470–1477 of: *IEEE International Conference on Computer Vision*.

Smith, Edward E., and Medin, Douglas L. 1981. *Categories and Concepts*. Cambridge, MA: Harvard University Press.

Smith, Shaden, Patwary, Mostofa, Norick, Brandon et al. 2022. Using DeepSpeed and Megatron to train Megatron-Turing NLG 530B, a large-scale generative language model. *arXiv*, 2201.11990.

Smolensky, Paul. 1990. Tensor product variable binding and the representation of symbolic structures in connectionist systems. *Artificial Intelligence*, **46**(1–2), 159–216.

Snow, Rion, Jurafsky, Daniel, and Ng, Andrew Y. 2004. Learning syntactic patterns for automatic hypernym discovery. Pages 1297–1304 of: *Proc. NIPS*.

Socher, Richard, Pennington, Jeffrey, Huang, Eric, Ng, Andrew Y., and Manning, Christopher D. 2011. Semi-supervised recursive autoencoders for predicting sentiment distributions. Pages 151–161 of: *Proc. EMNLP*.

Socher, Richard, Huval, Brody, Manning, Christopher D., and Ng, Andrew Y. 2012. Semantic compositionality through recursive matrix-vector spaces. Pages 1201–1211 of: *Proc. EMNLP*.

Socher, Richard, Perelygin, Alex, Wu, Jean Y. et al. 2013a. Recursive deep models for semantic compositionality over a sentiment treebank. Pages 1631–1642 of: *Proc. EMNLP*.

Socher, Richard, Ganjoo, Milind, Manning, Christopher D., and Ng, Andrew Y. 2013b. Zero-shot learning through cross-modal transfer. In: *Proc. NIPS*.

Søgaard, Anders, Ruder, Sebastian, and Vulić, Ivan. 2018. On the limitations of unsupervised bilingual dictionary induction. Pages 778–788 of: *Proc. ACL*.

Sparck Jones, Karen. 1961. Mechanised semantic classification. Pages 418–433 of: *Machine Translation of Languages and Applied Language Analysis*.

Sparck Jones, Karen. 1964. *Synonymy and Semantic Classification*. PhD thesis, University of Cambridge.

Sparck Jones, Karen. 1971. *Automatic Keyword Classification for Information Retrieval*. London: Butterworths.

Sparck Jones, Karen. 1972. A statistical interpretation of term specificity and its application in retrieval. *Journal of Documentation*, **28**(1), 11–21.

Sparck Jones, Karen. 2005. Some points in a time. *CL*, **31**(1), 1–14.

Sparck Jones, Karen, and Galliers, Julia R. 1995. *Evaluating Natural Language Processing Systems: An Analysis and Review*. Berlin: Springer Verlag.

Speer, Robert, and Havasi, Catherine. 2012. Representing general relational knowledge in ConceptNet 5. Pages 3679–3686 of: *Proc. LREC*.

Speer, Robert, Chin, Joshua, and Havasi, Catherine. 2017. ConceptNet 5.5: An open multilingual graph of general knowledge. Pages 4444–4451 of: *Proc. AAAI*.

Sridharan, Seshadri, and Murphy, Brian. 2012. Modeling word meaning: Distributional semantics and the corpus quality-quantity trade-off. Pages 53–68 of: *3rd Workshop on Cognitive Aspects of the Lexicon*.

Srivastava, Aarohi, Rastogi, Abhinav, Rao, Abhishek et al. 2022. Beyond the imitation game: Quantifying and extrapolating the capabilities of language models. *arXiv*, 2206.04615.

Staliūnaité, Ieva, and Iacobacci, Ignacio. 2020. Compositional and lexical semantics in RoBERTa, BERT and DistilBERT: A case study on CoQA. Pages 7046–7056 of: *Proc. EMNLP*.

Stefanowitsch, Anatol, and Gries, Stefan Th. 2003. Collostructions: Investigating the interaction of words and constructions. *International Journal of Corpus Linguistics*, **8**(2), 209–243.

Stevens, Mary Elizabeth, Giuliano, Vincent E., and Heilprin, Laurence B. 1964. *Proceedings of the Symposium on Statistical Association Methods for Mechanized Documentation*. Washington, DC: National Bureau of Standards.

Steyvers, Mark. 2010. Combining feature norms and text data with topic models. *Acta Psychologica*, **133**(3), 234–243.

Steyvers, Mark, and Griffiths, Thomas L. 2007. Probabilistic topic models. Pages 427–448 of: Landauer, Thomas, Mcnamara, Danielle, Dennis, Simon, and Kintsch, Walter (eds.), *Handbook of Latent Semantic Analysis*. Mahwah: Laurence Erlbaum.

Steyvers, Mark, Griffiths, Thomas L., and Dennis, Simon. 2006. Probabilistic inference in human semantic memory. *Trends in Cognitive Sciences*, **10**(7), 327–334.

Stiles, H. Edmund. 1961. The association factor in information retrieval. *Journal of the Association for Computing Machinery*, **8**, 271–279.

Strang, Gilbert. 2016. *Introduction to Linear Algebra*, 5th ed. Wellesley: Wellesley - Cambridge Press.

Strapparava, Carlo, and Valitutti, Alessandro. 2004. WordNet-Affect: An affective extension of WordNet. Pages 1083–1086 of: *Proc. LREC*.

Strubell, Emma, Ganesh, Ananya, and McCallum, Andrew. 2019. Energy and policy considerations for deep learning in NLP. Pages 3645–3650 of: *Proc. ACL*.

Sucameli, Irene, and Lenci, Alessandro. 2017. PARAD-it: Eliciting Italian paradigmatic relations with crowdsourcing. Pages 310–315 of: *4th Italian Conference on Computational Linguistics*.

Sun, Jingyuan, Wang, Shaonan, Zhang, Jiajun, and Zong, Chengqing. 2019a. Towards sentence-level brain decoding with distributed representations. Pages 7047–7054 of: *Proc. AAAI*.

Sun, Lin, and Korhonen, Anna. 2009. Improving verb clustering with automatically acquired selectional preferences. Pages 638–647 of: *Proc. EMNLP*.

Sun, Tony, Gaut, Andrew, Tang, Shirlyn et al. 2019b. Mitigating gender bias in natural language processing: Literature review. Pages 1630–1640 of: *Proc. ACL*.

Sutskever, Ilya, Vinyals, Oriol and Le, Quoc V. 2014. Sequence to sequence learning with neural networks. Pages 3104–3112 of: *Proc. NIPS*.

Talmor, Alon, Elazar, Yanai, Goldberg, Yoav, and Berant, Jonathan. 2020. oLMpics: On what language model pre-training captures. *TACL*, **8**, 743–758.

Tang, Duyu, Wei, Furu, Yang, Nan et al. 2014. Learning sentiment-specific word embedding. Pages 1555–1565 of: *Proc. ACL*.

Tang, Xuri. 2018. A state-of-the-art of semantic change computation. *Natural Language Engineering*, **24**(5), 649–676.

Taylor, John R. 1995. *Prototypes in Linguistic Theory*. Oxford: Oxford University Press.

Tenney, Ian, Das, Dipanjan, and Pavlick, Ellie. 2019a. BERT rediscovers the classical NLP pipeline. Pages 4593–4601 of: *Proc. ACL*.

Tenney, Ian, Xia, Patrick, Chen, Berlin et al. 2019b. What do you learn from context? Probing for sentence structure in contextualized word representations. Pages 235–249 of: *Proc. ICLR*.

Tesnière, Lucien. 1959. *Elements de syntaxe structurale*. Paris: Klincksieck.

Thater, Stefan, Fürstenau, Hagen, and Pinkal, Manfred. 2010. Contextualizing semantic representations using syntactically enriched vector models. Pages 948–957 of: *Proc. ACL*.

Thater, Stefan, Fürstenau, Hagen, and Pinkal, Manfred. 2011. Word meaning in context: A simple and effective vector model. Pages 1134–1143 of: *5th International Joint Conference on Natural Language Processing*.

Thoppilan, Romal, Freitas, Daniel De, Hall, Jamie et al. 2022. LaMDA: Language models for dialog applications. *arXiv*, 2201.08239.

Tiedemann, Jörg. 2012. Parallel data, tools and interfaces in OPUS. Pages 2214–2218 of: *Proc. LREC*.

Tiku, Natasha. 2022. The Google engineer who thinks the company's AI has come to life. *The Washington Post*.

Tilk, Ottokar, Demberg, Vera, Sayeed, Asad B., Klakow, Dietrich, and Thater, Stefan. 2016. Event participant modelling with neural networks. Pages 171–182 of: *Proc. EMNLP*.

Timkey, William, and Van Schijndel, Marten. 2021. All bark and no bite: Rogue dimensions in transformer language models obscure representational quality. Pages 4527–4546 of: *Proc. EMNLP*.

Tjong Kim Sang, Erik F., and Meulder, Fien De. 2003. Introduction to the CoNLL-2003 shared task: Language-independent named entity recognition. Pages 142–147 of: *Proc. NAACL-HLT*.

Tomasello, Michael. 2003. *Constructing a Language: A Usage-Based Theory of Language Acquisition*. Cambridge, MA: Harvard University Press.

Tomuro, Noriko, Kanzaki, Kyoko, and Isahara, Hitoshi. 2007. Discovering word senses for polysemous words using feature domain similarity. Page 298–307 of: *10th Conference of the Pacific Association for Computational Linguistics*.

Traugott, Elizabeth. 2017. Semantic change. *Oxford Research Encyclopedias: Linguistics*.

Traugott, Elizabeth, and Dasher, Richard B. 2001. *Regularity in Semantic Change*. Cambridge: Cambridge University Press.

Traxler, Matthew J., Pickering, Martin J., and McElree, Brian. 2002. Coercion in sentence processing: Evidence from eye-movements and self-paced reading. *Journal of Memory and Language*, **47**(4), 530–547.

Tuan, Luu Anh, Tay, Yi, Hui, Siu Cheung, and Ng, See Kiong. 2016. Learning term embeddings for taxonomic relation identification using dynamic weighting neural network. Pages 403–413 of: *Proc. EMNLP*.

Turian, Joseph, Ratinov, Lev, and Bengio, Yoshua. 2010. Word representations: A simple and general method for semi-supervised learning. Pages 384–394 of: *Proc. ACL*.

Turney, Peter D. 2001. Mining the web for synonyms: PMI-IR versus LSA on TOEFL. Pages 491–502 of: *12th European Conference on Machine Learning*.

Turney, Peter D. 2005. Measuring semantic similarity by latent relational analysis. Pages 1136–1141 of: *Proc. IJCAI*.

Turney, Peter D. 2006a. Expressing implicit semantic relations without supervision. Pages 313–320 of: *Proc. COLING-ACL*.

Turney, Peter D. 2006b. Similarity of semantic relations. *CL*, **32**(3), 379–416.

Turney, Peter D. 2007. *Empirical Evaluation of Four Tensor Decomposition Algorithms*. Technical Report ERB-1152, NRC.

Turney, Peter D. 2008a. The latent relation mapping engine: Algorithm and experiments. *JAIR*, **33**, 615–655.

Turney, Peter D. 2008b. A uniform approach to analogies, synonyms, antonyms, and associations. Pages 905–912 of: *Proc. COLING*.

Turney, Peter D. 2012. Domain and function: A dual-space model of semantic relations and compositions. *JAIR*, **44**, 533–585.

Turney, Peter D., and Littman, Michael L. 2003. Measuring praise and criticism: Inference of semantic orientation from association. *ACM Transactions on Information Systems*, **21**(4), 315–346.

Turney, Peter D., and Littman, Michael L. 2005. Corpus-based learning of analogies and semantic relations. *Machine Learning*, **60**(1–3), 251–278.

Turney, Peter D., and Mohammad, Saif M. 2013. Crowdsourcing a word-emotion association lexicon. *Computational Intelligence*, **59**(3), 436–465.

Turney, Peter D., and Mohammad, Saif M. 2015. Experiments with three approaches to recognizing lexical entailment. *Natural Language Engineering*, **21**(3), 437–476.

Turney, Peter D., and Pantel, Patrick. 2010. From frequency to meaning: Vector space models of semantics. *JAIR*, **37**, 141–188.

Tversky, Amos. 1977. Features of similarity. *Psychological Review*, **84**(4), 327–352.

Utsumi, Akira. 2020. Exploring what is encoded in distributional word vectors: A neurobiologically motivated analysis. *Cognitive Science*, **44**(6), e12844.

Van de Cruys, Tim. 2008. A comparison of bag of words and syntax-based approaches for word categorization. Pages 47–54 of: *Bridging the Gap between Semantic Theory and Computational Simulations: Proceedings of the ESSLLI Workshop on Distributional Lexical Semantic*.

Van de Cruys, Tim. 2010a. A non-negative tensor factorization model for selectional preference induction. *Natural Language Engineering*, **16**(4), 417–437.

Van de Cruys, Tim. 2010b. *Mining for Meaning: The Extraction of Lexico-Semantic Knowledge from Text*. PhD thesis, University of Groningen.

Van de Cruys, Tim. 2014. A neural network approach to selectional preference acquisition. Pages 26–35 of: *Proc. EMNLP*.

Van de Cruys, Tim, Poibeau, Thierry, and Korhonen, Anna. 2011. Latent vector weighting for word meaning in context. Pages 1012–1022 of: *Proc. EMNLP*.

Van de Weijer, Joost, Paradis, Carita, Willners, Caroline, and Lindgren, Magnus. 2014. Antonym canonicity: Temporal and contextual manipulations. *Brain and Language*, **128**(1), 1–8.

Van Der Maaten, Laurens, and Hinton, Geoffrey E. 2008. Visualizing high-dimensional data using t-SNE. *Journal of Machine Learning Research*, **9**, 2579–2605.

Van Dongen, Stijn. 2000. *Graph Clustering by Flow Simulation*. PhD thesis, University of Utrecht.

Van Overschelde, James, Rawson, Katherine, and Dunlosky, John. 2004. Category norms: An updated and expanded version of the Battig and Montague (1969) norms. *Journal of Memory and Language*, **50**, 289–335.

Vassallo, Paolo, Chersoni, Emmanuele, Santus, Enrico, Lenci, Alessandro, and Blache, Philippe. 2018. Event knowledge in sentence processing: A new dataset for the evaluation of argument typicality. Pages 1–7. In: *LREC Workshop on Linguistic and Neurocognitive Resources*.

Vaswani, Ashish, Shazeer, Noam, Parmar, Niki et al. 2017. Attention is all you need. In: *Proc. NIPS*.

Vecchi, Eva Maria, Marelli, Marco, Zamparelli, Roberto, and Baroni, Marco. 2016. Spicy adjectives and nominal donkeys: Capturing semantic deviance using compositionality in distributional spaces. *Cognitive Science*, **41**(1), 102–136.

Véronis, Jean. 2004. HyperLex: Lexical cartography for information retrieval. *Computer Speech & Language*, **18**(3), 223–252.

Vigliocco, Gabriella, and Vinson, David P. 2007. Semantic representation. Pages 195–215 of: Gaskell, Gareth (ed.), *The Oxford Handbook of Psycholinguistics*. Oxford: Oxford University Press.

Vigliocco, Gabriella, Meteyard, Lotte, Andrews, Mark, and Kousta, Stavroula Thaleia. 2009. Toward a theory of semantic representation. *Language and Cognition*, **1**(2), 219–247.

Vincent-Lamarre, Philippe, Massé, Alexandre Blondin, Lopes, Marcos et al. 2016. The latent structure of dictionaries. *TopiCS*, **8**(3), 625–659.

Vinson, David P., and Vigliocco, Gabriella. 2008. Semantic feature production norms for a large set of objects and events. *Behavior Research Methods*, **40**(1), 183–190.

Von Ahn, Luis, and Dabbish, Laura. 2004. Labeling images with a computer game. Pages 319–326 of: *Conference on Human Factors in Computing Systems*.

Vu, Tu, and Shwartz, Vered. 2018. Integrating multiplicative features into supervised distributional methods for lexical entailment. Pages 160–166 of: *Proc. *SEM*.

Vulíc, Ivan, and Korhonen, Anna. 2016. On the role of seed lexicons in learning bilingual word embeddings. Pages 247–257 of: *Proc. ACL*.

Vulić, Ivan, and Mrkšić, Nikola. 2018. Specialising word vectors for lexical entailment. Pages 1134–1145 of: *Proc. NAACL-HLT*.

Vulić, Ivan, De Smet, Wim, and Moens, Marie-Francine. 2011. Identifying word translations from comparable corpora using latent topic models. Pages 479–484 of: *Proc. ACL*.

Vulić, Ivan, De Smet, Wim, Tang, Jie, and Moens, Marie-Francine. 2015. Probabilistic topic modeling in multilingual settings: An overview of its methodology and applications. *Information Processing and Management*, **51**(1), 111–147.

Vulić, Ivan, Kiela, Douwe, and Korhonen, Anna. 2017a. Evaluation by association: A systematic study of quantitative word association evaluation. Pages 163–175 of: *Proc. EACL*.

Vulić, Ivan, Gerz, Daniela, Kiela, Douwe, Hill, Felix, and Korhonen, Anna. 2017b. HyperLex: A large-scale evaluation of graded lexical entailment. *CL*, **43**(4), 781–835.

Vulić, Ivan, Mrkšić, Nikola, Reichart, Roi et al. 2017c. Morph-fitting: Fine-tuning word vector spaces with simple language-specific rules. Pages 56–68 of: *Proc. ACL*.

Vulić, Ivan, Ponti, Edoardo M., Litschko, Robert, Glavaš, Goran, and Korhonen, Anna. 2020. Probing pretrained language models for lexical semantics. Pages 7222–7240 of: *Proc. EMNLP*.

Vylomova, Ekaterina, Rimell, Laura, Cohn, Trevor, and Baldwin, Timothy. 2016. Take and took, gaggle and goose, book and read: Evaluating the utility of vector differences for lexical relation learning. Pages 1671–1682 of: *Proc. ACL*.

Wang, Alex, Singh, Amanpreet, Michael, Julian et al. 2019a. GLUE: A multi-task benchmark and analysis platform for natural language understanding. In: *Proc. ICLR*.

Wang, Alex, Pruksachatkun, Yada, Nangia, Nikita et al. 2019b. SuperGLUE: A stickier benchmark for general-purpose language understanding systems. Pages 3266–3280 of: *Proc. NIPS*.

Wang, Su, Durrett, Greg, and Erk, Katrin. 2018. Modeling semantic plausibility by injecting world knowledge. Pages 303–308 of: *Proc. NAACL-HLT*.

Wang, Xiaoying, Men, Weiwei, Gao, Jiahong, Caramazza, Alfonso, and Bi, Yanchao. 2020. Two forms of knowledge representations in the human brain. *Neuron*, **107**, 383–393.e5.

Weeds, Julie, Weir, David, and McCarthy, Diana. 2004. Characterising measures of lexical distributional similarity. Pages 1015–1021 of: *Proc. COLING*.

Weeds, Julie, Clarke, Daoud, Reffin, Jeremy, Weir, David, and Keller, Bill. 2014. Learning to distinguish hypernyms and co-hyponyms. Pages 2249–2259 of: *Proc. COLING*.

Weizenbaum, Joseph. 1966. ELIZA: A computer program for the study of natural language communication between man and machine. *Communications of the ACM*, **9**(1), 36–45.

Wendlandt, Laura, Kummerfeld, Jonathan K., and Mihalcea, Rada. 2018. Factors influencing the surprising instability of word embeddings. Pages 2092–2102 of: *Proc. NAACL-HLT*.

Werning, Markus, Hinzen, Wolfram, and Machery, Edouard (eds.). 2012. *The Oxford Handbook of Compositionality*. Oxford: Oxford University Press.

Westera, Matthijs, and Boleda, Gemma. 2019. Don't blame distributional semantics if it can't do entailment. Pages 120–133 of: *Proc. IWCS*.

Widdows, Dominic. 2004. *Geometry and Meaning*. Stanford: CSLI Publications.

Widdows, Dominic. 2008. Semantic vector products: Some initial investigations. In: *2nd AAAI Symposium on Quantum Interaction*.

Wiedemann, Gregor, Remus, Steffen, Chawla, Awi, and Biemann, Chris. 2019. Does BERT make any sense? Interpretable word sense disambiguation with contextualized embeddings. Pages 161–170 of: *Conference on Natural Language Processing (KONVENS)*.

Wieting, John, and Kiela, Douwe. 2019. No training required: Explored random encoders for sentence classification. In: *Proc. ICLR*.

Wieting, John, Bansal, Mohit, Gimpel, Kevin, and Livescu, Karen. 2015. From paraphrase database to compositional paraphrase model and back. *TACL*, **3**, 345–358.

Wieting, John, Bansal, Mohit, Gimpel, Kevin, and Livescu, Karen. 2016a. Charagram: Embedding words and sentences via character n-grams. Pages 1504–1515 of: *Proc. EMNLP*.

Wieting, John, Bansal, Mohit, Gimpel, Kevin, and Livescu, Karen. 2016b. Towards universal paraphrastic sentence embeddings. In: *Proc. ICLR*.

Wilks, Yorick. 1978. Making preferences more active. *Artificial Intelligence*, **11**(3), 197–223.

Wilks, Yorick, Fass, Dan, Cheng, Cheng-ming, et al. 1990. Providing machine tractable dictionary tools. *Machine Translation*, **5**(2), 99–151.

Williams, Adina, Nangia, Nikita, and Bowman, Samuel R. 2018. A broad-coverage challenge corpus for sentence understanding through inference. Pages 1112–1122 of: *Proc. NAACL-HLT*.

Wisniewsky, Edward J., and Bassok, Miriam. 1999. What makes a man similar to a tie? Stimulus compatibility with comparison and integration. *Cognitive Psychology*, **39**, 208–238.

Witten, Ian H., Moffat, Alistair, and Bell, Timothy C. 1999. *Managing Gigabytes: Compressing and Indexing Documents and Images*. San Diego: Academic Press.

Wittgenstein, Ludwig. 1922. *Tractatus Logico-Philosophicus*. London: Routledge & Kegan Paul.

Wittgenstein, Ludwig. 1953. *Philosophical Investigations*. Oxford: Blackwell.

Wittgenstein, Ludwig. 1958. *The Blue and Brown Books*. Oxford: Blackwell.

Wu, Yonghui, Schuster, Mike, Zhifeng, Chen et al. 2016. Google's neural machine translation system: Bridging the gap between human and machine translation. *arXiv*, 1609.08144.

Xing, Chao, Wang, Dong, Liu, Chao, and Lin, Yiye. 2015. Normalized word embedding and orthogonal transform for bilingual word translation. Pages 1006–1011 of: *Proc. NAACL-HLT*.

Xu, Haoyan, Murphy, Brian, and Fyshe, Alona. 2016. BrainBench: A brain-image test suite for distributional semantic models. Pages 2017–2021 of: *Proc. EMNLP*.

Yang, Zhilin, Dai, Zihang, Yang, Yiming et al. 2019. XLNet: Generalized autoregressive pretraining for language understanding. Pages 5753–5763 of: *Proc. NIPS*.

Yao, Xuchen, and Van Durme, Benjamin. 2011. Nonparametric Bayesian word sense induction. Pages 10–14 of: *TextGraphs-6: Graph-based Methods for Natural Language Processing*.

Ye, Zhe, Li, Fang, and Baldwin, Timothy. 2018. Encoding sentiment information into word vectors for sentiment analysis. Pages 997–1007 of: *Proc. COLING*.

Yee, Eiling, and Thompson-Schill, Sharon L. 2016. Putting concepts into context. *Psychonomic Bulletin & Review*, **23**(4), 1015–1027.

Yee, Eiling, Jones, Michael N., and McRae, Ken. 2018. Semantic memory. Pages 319–356 of: Wixted, John T., and Thompson-Schill, Sharon L. (eds.), *The Stevens' Handbook of Experimental Psychology and Cognitive Neuroscience, 4th ed., Vol. 3: Language and Thought*. New York: Wiley Blackwell.

Yih, Wen-tau, Zweig, Geoffrey, and Platt, John C. 2012. Polarity inducing latent semantic analysis. Pages 1212–1222 of: *Proc. EMNLP*.

Young, Peter, Lai, Alice, Hodosh, Micah, and Hockenmaier, Julia. 2014. From image descriptions to visual denotations: New similarity metrics for semantic inference over event descriptions. *TACL*, **2**, 67–78.

Zanzotto, Fabio Massimo, Korkontzelos, Ioannis, Fallucchi, Francesca, and Manandhar, Suresh. 2010. Estimating linear models for compositional distributional semantics. Pages 1263–1271 of: *Proc. COLING*.

Zarcone, Alessandra, Utt, Jason, and Padó, Sebastian. 2012. Modeling covert event retrieval in logical metonymy: Probabilistic and distributional accounts. Pages 70–79 of: *3rd Workshop on Cognitive Modeling and Computational Linguistics*.

Zarcone, Alessandra, Lenci, Alessandro, Padó, Sebastian, and Utt, Jason. 2013. Fitting, not clashing! A distributional semantic model of logical metonymy. Pages 404–410 of: *Proc. IWCS*.

Zarcone, Alessandra, Padó, Sebastian, and Lenci, Alessandro. 2014. Logical metonymy resolution in a words-as-cues framework: Evidence from self-paced reading and probe recognition. *Cognitive Science*, **38**(5), 973–996.

Zeldes, Amir. 2013. Productive argument selection: Is lexical semantics enough? *Corpus Linguistics and Linguistic Theory*, **9**(2), 263–291.

Zellers, Rowan, Bisk, Yonatan, Schwartz, Roy, and Choi, Yejin. 2018. SWAG: A large-scale adversarial dataset for grounded commonsense inference. Pages 93–104 of: *Proc. EMNLP*.

Zhang, Chenyu, Durme, Benjamin Van, Li, Zhuowan, and Stengel-Eskin, Elias. 2022. Visual commonsense in pretrained unimodal and multimodal models. Pages 5321–5335 of: *Proc. NAACL-HLT*.

Zhang, Hongming, Ding, Hantian, and Song, Yangqiu. 2019. SP-10K: A large-scale evaluation set for selectional preference acquisition. Pages 722–731 of: *Proc. ACL*.

Zhang, Yian, Warstadt, Alex, Li, Haau Sing, and Bowman, Samuel R. 2021. When do you need billions of words of pretraining data? Pages 1112–1125 of: *Proc. ACL*.

Zhao, Jieyu, Zhou, Yichao, Li, Zeyu, Wang, Wei, and Chang, Kai-Wei. 2018. Learning gender-neutral word embeddings. Pages 4847–4853 of: *Proc. EMNLP*.

Zhao, Xiaowei, Li, Ping, and Kohonen, Teuvo. 2011. Contextual self-organizing map: Software for constructing semantic representations. *Behavior Research Methods*, **43**(1), 77–88.

Zhitomirsky-Geffet, Maayan, and Dagan, Ido. 2005. The distributional inclusion hypotheses and lexical entailment. Pages 107–114 of: *Proc. ACL*.

Zhitomirsky-Geffet, Maayan, and Dagan, Ido. 2009. Bootstrapping distributional feature vector quality. *CL*, **35**(3), 4351–4461.

Zhu, Xunjie, Li, Tingfeng, and De Melo, Gerard. 2018. Exploring semantic properties of sentence embeddings. Pages 632–637 of: *Proc. ACL*.

Zimek, Arthur. 2014. Clustering high-dimensional data. Pages 201–229 of: Aggarwal, Charu C., and Reddy, Chandan K. (eds.), *Data Clustering: Algorithms and Applications*. Boca Raton: Chapman & Hall.

Zipf, George K. 1935. *The Psycho-Biology of Language*. Boston: Houghton Mifflin.

Zipf, George K. 1949. *Human Behavior and the Principle of the Least Effort: An Introduction to Human Ecology*. New York: Hafner.

Zwaan, Rolf A., and Madden, Carol J. 2005. Embodied sentence comprehension. Pages 224–245 of: Pecher, Diane, and Zwaan, Rolf A. (eds.), *Grounding Cognition: The Role of Perception and Action in Memory, Language, and Thinking*. Cambridge: Cambridge University Press.

Index

Printed in the United States
by Baker & Taylor Publisher Services

Printed in the United States
by Baker & Taylor Publisher Services